The CCC Chronicles

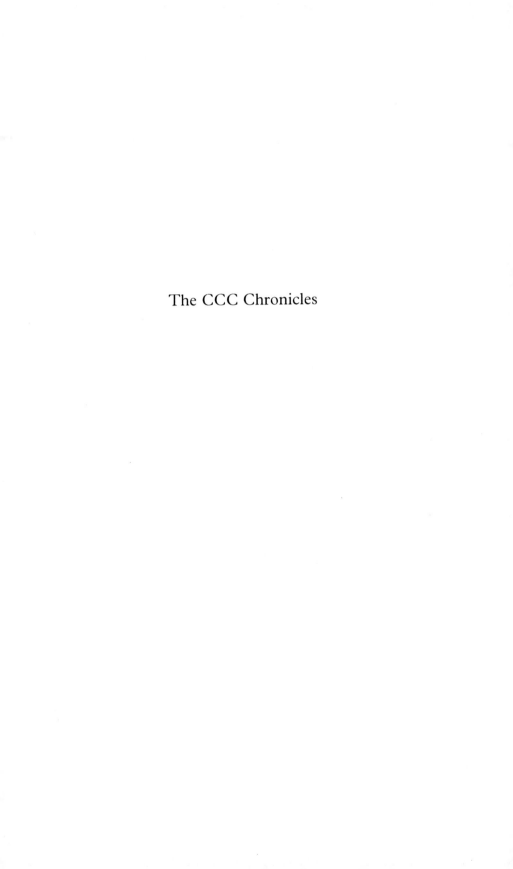

The CCC Chronicles

Camp Newspapers of the Civilian Conservation Corps, 1933–1942

ALFRED EMILE CORNEBISE

McFarland & Company, Inc., Publishers
Jefferson, North Carolina, and London

333.720973
C 8/c

LIBRARY OF CONGRESS CATALOGUING-IN-PUBLICATION DATA

Cornebise, Alfred E.
  The CCC chronicles : camp newspapers of the Civilian
Conservation Corps, 1933–1942 / Alfred Emile Cornebise.
    p.   cm.
  Includes bibliographical references and index.

  ISBN 0-7864-1831-1 (softcover : 50# alkaline paper)

  1. Civilian Conservation Corps (U.S.)—Newspapers—
History—20th century. 2. Civilian Conservation Corps
(U.S.)—Officials and employees—History—20th century.
I. Title.
S930.C677   2004
333.72'0973—dc22   2004004059

British Library cataloguing data are available

Manufactured in the United States of America

Cover photograph ©2004 Photospin

McFarland & Company, Inc., Publishers
  Box 611, Jefferson, North Carolina 28640
  www.mcfarlandpub.com

For Rachel and Nicholas O'Connor

Acknowledgments

This study would not have been possible without the assistance of numerous people who have given unstintingly of their time and efforts. These include Jane Smith and the staff—especially Lois Leffler—at the interlibrary loan office at the University of Northern Colorado, Greeley. In addition, I am especially indebted to Marlys Rudeen, the Microform Projects and Preservation Coordinator at the Center for Research Libraries in Chicago, for much ongoing assistance during the course of my research. Thanks are also due to those unknown librarians at the University of Illinois, Champaign, who painstakingly collected issues of CCC papers, amassing a huge, wonderful collection, a treasure trove indeed. Hearty thanks go to Ann E. Billesbach, Head of Reference Services, Library/Archives Division, Nebraska State Historical Society in Lincoln, for helping me obtain additional microfilm from that institution. Nadine Cohen, Reference Librarian, Main Library of University of Georgia, Athens, greatly aided me in locating copies of *Happy Days*. As always, Linda Wheeler, Reference Librarian at the Hoover Institution, Stanford, California, answered my requests promptly and with her usual efficiency, providing me with many of the files of *Happy Days*. James P. Danky and Jim Buckett at the State Historical Society of Wisconsin helped in locating additional runs of that paper. Karl J. Crosby, Serial Reference Specialist, and Travis Westly, also a Reference Specialist, both at the Library of Congress, went out of their way to run to earth important sources for me. Rob Rucker, of the General Research Division at the New York Public Library, similarly gave my requests much time and attention. At the University of Southern California, Ed Cray provided me with much useful information, and Larry Bland at the George C. Marshall Library in Lexington, Virginia, was of considerable assistance.

Recognition and appreciation goes out to dozens of CCC alumni for their patience over the years in answering my queries and allowing interviews about "their" CCC, especially Francis J. Derwin, President, Chapter Sixty, and Albert S. Coven, President, Chapter Seven, National Association of CCC Alumni. The members of Chapter Seven, Morrison, Colorado, invited me to a scheduled meeting of their chapter, permitting me to interview many of the members. Especially helpful were Donald C. Bess, who possesses a wealth of data about the history of the CCC in Colorado, and Mervin Chester Nolte. Many other people provided me with information about, or copies of, camp papers. Among these are James England, *The Camp Buzzer*, Company 1711; Fred A. Fretheim, the *Spruce Lake Splash*, Company 3707; Donald Halverson, *Prairie Dog of Camp Roy* and the *Green Guard*, Company 2941; Warren O. McGuire, *The Easterner*, Company 192; Robert L. Robeson, *The Shoshonean*, Company 1852; William W. Robinson, the *Harold Parker Review*, Company 110; Harry W. Smith, *The Lighthouse*, Company 5428; Kathy Mays Smith, *Police-Up Gazette*, paper of Company 1538; Donald Sorensen, the *Belknap News*, Company 927; Homer J. Tennant, *The Littlefork Ripple*, Company 2587; John A. Theodore, the *Salmon River Hi-Lights*, Company 1274; Alderic O. Violette, *The Kearsarge Kettle* and the *Tory Hill Sentinel*, Company 1147, and other papers; Matthew Walczak, *The Woodtick*, Company 1696; and Harold M. Winnen, the *Sylvan Echo*, Company 4707.

Vernon E. "Bud" Schertel, the executive director of the National Association of Civilian Conservation Corps Alumni and the editor of that organization's *Journal*, has also encouraged me in the development of this study.

Last, but not least, I wish to thank my wife, Jan Miller Cornebise, for her untiring assistance in helping me to edit the manuscript at various stages in its writing, as well as for her unfailing love and support throughout.

Table of Contents

ix

Preface

In an April 1940 issue of a Civilian Conservation Corps camp news-paper, *The Alaskan*, published by the Admiralty CCC Division in Juneau, Alaska, one of the paper's reporters, Abraham F. Cohen, cleverly parodied Lincoln's Gettysburg Address to describe the organization's creation and its importance: "Four days and seven years ago, our Congress, gathered in general assembly at Washington, D.C., brought forth [the Civilian Con-servation Corps] conceived in liberty, and dedicated to the proposition that all unemployed young men are entitled to work on the vast depleted nat-ural resources of this great country." Indeed, "in the past few years of industrial development, we have largely forgotten our prime duty to nature. [But] now we are engaged in a great war, testing whether fire, flood or soil erosion, so destructive and so depreciatory, can long endure. With shovel in hand and determination in heart, we are met on the battlefield of that war. Our grounds range from Maine to California, and from Alaska to Florida. We have eliminated to a great extent the threat that forced idle-ness brings to spiritual and moral stability." Routinely, he went on, "in the short period of six months, we [can take] a baffled, furtive, tough city youngster, and transform him into a bronzed, clear-eyed, well-muscled lad," turning his life around, and while "little will the world remember what we say here, ... the present and future generations can never forget what they are doing here." But there were dangers associated with the enterprise, and some CCCers died in active service, especially fighting forest fires, lead-ing Cohen to reflect that "it is for us, the present members of the CCC to keep up the spirit which our past comrades have so nobly advanced, that from these honored dead we bind ourselves to the one humane cause for which they gave their last full measure of devotion, and that the CCC shall remain a public service of the people, by the people, and for the people."[1]

Cohen's journalistic effort calls attention to one manifestation of the Civilian Conservation Corps largely neglected by scholars and students of the era, but worthy of serious study and evaluation—the CCC press. When FDR founded the organization in 1933, almost immediately news sheets were launched relating to the new organization. In Washington, D.C., a remarkable national weekly publication, the professional semi-official *Happy Days*, was founded by Melvin Ryder and others. Ryder, a regimental sergeant major in the American Expeditionary Forces in France during World War I, had been on the staff of the famous dough-boy newspaper, *The Stars and Stripes*. He knew from that experience the interests of men in camps and he launched a paper which clearly told the CCC story. Acting as a sounding board for opinion among CCC enrollees, his paper also encouraged and instructed the men in assuming their new roles. In addition, the paper in general supported the aims of the Administration's New Deal programs. It also provided a detailed running account of all aspects of the organization's operations. Launched on May 20, 1933, it lasted for the entire career of the CCC, ending only in August 1942.

Happy Days also played an active role in the establishment and nurturing of the camp papers which immediately sprang up. It is impossible to determine which CCC newspaper was the first to appear, but eventually there would be well over five thousand camp papers published by almost three thousand of the CCC companies, some of whose publications appeared under more than one title. Subsequently, many of these were systematically accumulated by the library at the University of Illinois, the Library of Congress, and other institutions. These collections were eventually taken over by the Center for Research Libraries in Chicago, and, supported in part by grants from the National Endowment for the Humanities, were preserved in microform, either microfilm or microfiche.

The first camp papers were mimeographed, and the use of this form of reproduction was the norm throughout the career of the CCC. However, there were some printed papers, while others were produced by the presses of local newspapers or commercial print shops. The most frequent publisher was a journalism class usually created in the company by the educational adviser who at times edited the paper. Some of the papers were magazines, usually monthlies, and could reach as high as fifty pages of mimeographed material. Others were published as semi-monthlies or weeklies, and a few editors attempted to bring out dailies. Sheets appearing irregularly were also common, reflecting the difficulties of maintaining a staff, or of obtaining supplies or the means of publication, and the further handicaps of pressing work demands, blizzards, forest fires, or floods. Papers often had runs of several months or years, sometimes with name changes; others appeared for a much shorter time.

The typical paper focused on camp life and activities, rather than on national or international news. It might include advertising, and would have sections or columns devoted to wit and humor, coverage of sports and entertainment, and some emphasis on the educational program and safety matters.

While much literature is now available for assessing key aspects as well as details of what was accomplished by the now popularly-called "rendezvous generation"—the foundation of the CCC and the later war years—the maw of history demands ever more substance to add to the repository enabling a more accurate and precise analysis of what transpired in the twentieth century. While lacking the skills and experience of an Ernie Pyle, camp reporters, some aided by professionals, produced in the pages of the CCC press a collective "Here Is Your War" detailing the CCC's efforts in defense of the nation's endangered natural resources and in rescuing and buttressing thousands of its needy citizens. While not possessing the incisive sketching pen of a Bill Mauldin, nonetheless CCC cartoonists portrayed, at an early stage of their existence, those who would later emerge as "Willie" and "Joe."

Orchestrated by *Happy Days*, the CCC's sometimes crude newspapers provide students and interested observers—and participants—with a means of assessing something of the CCC's life and significance. Additionally, they provide windows—though not the whole panorama—for viewing aspects of America's life—socially, politically, culturally and militarily—in the momentous years of the Great Depression.[2]

Nonetheless, this account is not a recapitulation of the history of either the CCC or the New Deal. It was not written with an eye to support or refute any point of view in terms of traditional academic debate and discussion of these topics. A narrative account, its subjects are rather the camp newspapers of the CCC and its semi-official organ, *Happy Days*: how they were created and distributed, who wrote for them and what they contained. In addition, gleaned from the thousands of papers available, this work is essentially a collective memoir of men in the CCC camps from which the reader can learn much—but not everything—about the CCCers and their thoughts and way of life. The conclusions drawn are necessarily tentative; much more work will have to be done before the treasure trove of the camp newspapers is exhausted and analyzed from the many dimensions that a consideration of the New Deal and CCC in the nation's history entails. This study is therefore a beginning—a sampler—rather than an end, and while providing considerable insight, it suggests what can be gleaned by further mining expeditions in these endlessly fascinating sources.

Introduction:
Something Was
Dreadfully Wrong

"This generation of Americans has a rendezvous with destiny."
—Franklin Delano Roosevelt, June 27, 1936

We're here to tell you fellows,
    When we're standing here in line,
It's great to have a messkit,
    When you haven't got a dime.
                                —Anonymous poem from
                        Company 1633, Fairfax, Washington,
                            Happy Days, September 30, 1933

"They've Made the Good Earth Better."
                        —*The New York Daily News* as quoted
                            in *Happy Days*, July 22, 1939

"They Came, They Saw(ed), They Conquered."
                            —*Happy Days*, September 28, 1935

Suggested slogan for the CCC: "Farewell to Alms."

Few people have heard of such pieces of "literature" as the brief, continuing story "Anthony Obtuse," or the extremely short one-act play of three scenes titled, "Morning Becomes Electrified." But these were among the reading fare of members of two companies of the Civilian Conservation Corps (CCC) in 1930s America. They were printed in the

organizations' respective camp newspapers produced for the enlighten-
ment, edification and entertainment of the 200 or so men who made up
each company. The first installment of "Anthony Obtuse"—(author
unknown) an obvious reference to the popular novel *Anthony Adverse*,
published in 1933 by Hervey Allen—appeared in the August 1936 issue
of CCC Company 297's mimeographed paper, the *Kanona Daze*.[1]
"Morning Becomes Electrified," a parody of Eugene O'Neill's 1931 play,
Mourning Becomes Electra, was written by "George Bernard" Egarian and
"William Shakespear" Gilliam, two members of Company 909, then
based at Highland, California. It was printed in the February 1, 1938,
issue of the *Tabloid Owl*, that unit's colorful, provocative, and often
humorous sheet. A nonsensical piece, "Anthony Obtuse" was billed as
"a short story of haze and blue daze," while "Morning" was concerned
with the chaos in a typical camp barracks resulting from the sounding
of reveille.

The events preceding the creation of these pieces, and the establishment of the papers in which they appeared, were complex. A hint
as to what it all meant was suggested by one Civilian Conservation
Corps enrollee, Paul A. Coleman, who wrote, "We're living a wonderful story." Further reflecting on his experiences in FDR's innovative
conservation program, he enthused, "This is our Forest of Arden! Here,
we too, are nobles in the retinue of a duke—only our chief is a Prince!
And he knows just as well as Mr. Shakespeare did that there are 'Books
in running brooks, sermons in stones and good in everything!'" "But
Shakespeare," he concluded, "with all his wisdom, never stole a play
so wonderful as the very romantic drama in which we're playing our
part!"[2]

If living in a remote spartan camp in some national forest with about
two hundred men under the control of a handful of military officers,
being supervised by personnel from the U.S. Forest Service or Agricultural Department or some other state or federal agency, and being dressed
in cast-off army uniforms was a "romantic drama," then certainly young
men living at another time—earlier or later—might be excused if they
might disagree. Yet, given the circumstances surrounding the launching
of the CCC and its subsequent operations, to the young men—and some
not so young—the experience was indeed a life saver if not "a wonderful story."[3]

In the dark, desperate days of the early 1930s, the nation was reel-
ing under the blows of a seemingly unstoppable economic depression
compounded by what was soon to be nature on a rampage: widespread
flooding, an intense drought resulting in a dustbowl in mid–America,
and a profusion of forest fires. Indeed, to Americans living through
these days, it must have seemed that humanity had been placed in

double jeopardy. The devastating Great War of 1914–18 had destroyed much of the foundation upon which civilized existence had rested until then. After a decade or so of improving conditions, a world-wide economic depression had descended, further eroding civilization's underpinnings, as well as much that had been recreated or plastered over in the interim between 1919 and 1929. Throughout Europe, extremist political parties and governments grappled with the unsettled times. Though remaining short of outright totalitarian solutions, nonetheless Franklin Roosevelt's New Deal was a far-reaching revolution touching the life of every living American.

Among the plethora of new endeavors and innovations was a remarkable undertaking: the Civilian Conservation Corps. Its creation was one of the first of the strong measures that Washington launched after FDR's inauguration on March 4, 1933. It was intended to attack two major problems of the era simultaneously. Paul V. McNutt, of the Federal Security Agency, later described it as follows: "In build-ing the health and character and skills of young men, and in preserving and restoring the land and the forests upon which men depend for existence, the Civilian Conservation Corps creates strength with which to resist and withstand the batterings of economic and political forces."[4]

Certainly, by 1933 the United States faced the problem of vast unemployment, one consequence of "the worst business depression in history."[5] Perhaps as many as fourteen million out-of-work Americans simply stayed at home. With few prospects of employment, they were victims of unremitting despair and grinding poverty. Of this number, as many as two million (including about 250,000 youths with no future hopes to encourage and sustain them) took to the highways and byways of the country, seeking employment and the bare necessities of life. They were often in trouble with authorities and were charged with vagrancy, theft and other crimes. Ray D. Smith of CCC Company 991, Feather Falls, California, had seen them, those young men, with "the mark of shattered ambitions and blasted hopes written in their faces ... the result of fruitless tramping of the city streets showing in every stride." This "discouraged horde" would subsequently appear in the CCC camps, and were promptly inserted "into the life-giving, wine-laden air of the mountains for a fresh start." This defeated army would be rejuvenated physically and morally, and were thereafter profoundly thankful to a generous government for the opportunity it had given them.[6]

Equally pressing was the deteriorating state of the nation's forests and farms; the trees had been ruthlessly cut down, leaving the land unprotected. The soil had been heedlessly depleted and neglected, and widespread erosion marred over fifty million acres of land that had earlier produced abundant crops. When a severe drought ensued and the wind arose, huge dust storms, especially in the mid–American farm belt, created a "dust bowl" of vast proportions. Unable to hold the land, millions of people became dispossessed migrants, usually moving toward the West, especially California, further endangering the nation's welfare and stability.

Both the land and its citizens were alike blighted then, and the Depression forced a thorough examination and analysis of all the country's ills. Perhaps a detailed and sustained relief program, taking into account the short-term and long-range aspects of the problem, might be implemented to mitigate the weaknesses that had emerged. One solution, at once simple in its essentials, seemed to hold out the key: put young men to work in the forests and on the land, thereby saving them all.

The new president, Franklin Delano Roosevelt, was well equipped to initiate such a plan. He was aware that in the states of California and Washington, the Forest Service cooperated in setting up subsistence camps to assist the unemployed. Foreign governments, such as Norway, Sweden, Austria and Germany among others, had established conservation camps for unemployed young people. Roosevelt himself had long been engaged in conservation practices on his Hyde Park estate in New York. He had also been aware of the conservation policies of President Theodore Roosevelt before him. When FDR became governor of New York, he applied similar solutions to problems of trees, soil and water in that state. He persuaded the state legislature to amend the New York constitution to provide an appropriation of twenty million dollars over an eleven-year period for the purchase and reforestation of more than a million acres of submarginal agricultural land. In Roosevelt's last year as governor, over ten thousand unemployed men were put to work transplanting and growing young trees.[7]

During his speech accepting the Democratic presidential nomination on July 2, 1932, Roosevelt promised to fight for soil and timber conservation, coupling it with the substantial employment of those out of work. True to his word, after his inauguration he asked the secretaries of War, Interior, Agriculture and Labor to prepare a program to be introduced in the Congress. This they did on March 15, 1933.[8]

The president then sent his proposals to Congress in his message of March 21, only seventeen days after his inauguration, asking for legislation creating the Civilian Conservation Corps. Instead of establishing one huge new agency to undertake the conservation scheme, FDR planned to utilize ten bureaus already in existence in the departments of Labor, Agriculture, War and Interior to carry out the program. Careful not to alienate labor leaders or rank-and-file workers, the president proposed that the new creation would "be used in simple work, not interfering with normal employment, and confining itself to forestry, the prevention of soil erosion, flood control and similar projects." In this way, the program would "conserve our precious natural resources," thereby paying dividends "to the present and future generations."[9]

Congress responded with alacrity, and identical bills for "The Relief of Unemployment through the Performance of Useful Public Work and for other Purposes" were introduced in both houses. After spirited debate, on March 31, 1933, Congress gave the president the authority to proceed, at the same time empowering him to use any and all government departments that might be required.[10] Initially involving about 250,000 men located in 1,330 camps, the Emergency Conservation Work Act (ECW), implemented by Presidential Executive Order No. 6101 on April 5, 1933, created the Civilian Conservation Corps.[11] Especially aimed at the nation's forest lands, specific goals included "the prevention of forest fires, floods and soil erosion, plant pest and disease control," and the construction, maintenance or repair of "paths, trails and fire-lanes in the national parks and national forests," as well as similar work in state forest lands.[12] Of course, with almost fourteen million unemployed in the United States by March 1933, the numbers enrolled were relatively small, but for those involved, the program provided a physical and spiritual lift of immeasurable value.[13]

While straightforward in concept and initiation, the implementation and administration of the CCC became an intricate matter requiring much coordination. In order to placate the powerful labor unions, which worried that the government was moving into their bailiwicks, Roosevelt appointed Bostonian Robert Fechner, a member of the General Executive Board of the International Association of Machinists, as head of the CCC. The assistant director was James J. McEntee, also an executive of the IAM. These two men ran the CCC from its inception to its dissolution.[14] Fechner was sworn in as Director of Emergency Conservation Work on April 5, 1933, the date thereafter celebrated as the birthday of the CCC. The term "Emergency Conservation Work" was the official name of the new organization, though it was soon popularly known as the "CCC," and much later, on June 28, 1937, Congress made that designation official. The Office of the Director was charged with the overall direction and coordination of the program. However, the departments of War, Agriculture, Interior and Labor were also to be directly involved, and one man from each of the four departments comprised an "Advisory Council to the Director."[15]

The Department of Labor supervised the selecting of the men to be enrolled in the Corps. Working with the CCC Office of the Director's Division of Selection, the Department appointed more than 4,500 selecting agents to enlist enrollees in the local communities. Some of these functionaries were accused of choosing community trouble makers, using the CCC as a dumping ground for their local problems. However, this procedure was roundly condemned by headquarters, and agents were instructed to accept only those boys who seemed eager to work and learn, and willing to accept discipline. In addition, enrollees should have sufficient mental capacity to master one or more of the camp jobs to a reasonable level of competency. As McEntee observed, "it obviously avails nothing and wastes Government money to send troublesome youths to camp to rid the local community of them, if a few days later the boys are right back home again after an enjoyable train ride." In fact, he insisted, "the CCC is no kindergarten; it is a work organization." Accordingly, "the boys must be willing to work hard without being coddled."[16]

The War Department was responsible for building the camps—there would eventually be over 4,500—as well as for transporting the men to them, and for feeding, clothing and caring for the enrollees. The camps were grouped within the nine Army Corps administrative areas within the United States, and in certain American possessions abroad.[17] The department also administered the camp routine, was in charge of discipline, and was responsible for the administration of the educational program under advice from the U.S. Office of Education. It appointed the camp commanders, doctors, dentists and chaplains. The Office of the Chief of Finance, United States Army, was the fiscal officer for the CCC. It kept the accounts, paid the bills, and took charge of the money deposited by CCC members. The Office of Education advised the War Department on camp education.[18]

The departments of the Interior and Agriculture were charged with designating the sites of the camps along with the planning, supervision and carrying out of all work programs. They cooperated with state agencies in work done on non-federal lands. The supervision of large flood control projects was carried out under the direction of the Army Corps of Engineers.

The Department of the Interior, the National Park Service, the General Land Office, the Bureau of Reclamation, the Grazing Service, the Office of Indian Affairs, the Fish and Wildlife Service, and the Tennessee Valley Authority, as well as the War and Navy departments, all supervised work projects undertaken by the CCC. Agencies of the Department of Agriculture that were involved included the U.S. Forest Service, the Soil Conservation Service, the Beltsville Research Center, the Bureau of Plant Industry, the Bureau of Animal Industry, and the Bureau of Entomology and Plant Quarantine. Numerous state and local entities were also included in this work.[19]

The men who entered the program were called "junior enrollees." They were to be unemployed, unmarried citizens of the United States between the ages of 18 and 25 (later 17 to 23), in good health, and with no criminal record. Usually, but not exclusively, the men were also selected from families that were on the public relief rolls. The first of these men were enrolled on April 7 in Pennsylvania. On April 17, 1933, the first 200-man unit in the nation—Company 322 (its number was drawn from a hat)—was established at Camp Roosevelt in the George Washington National Forest near Luray, Virginia.[20]

The press of men eager to enroll was considerable, so the rate of selection was speeded up, and by June almost 9,000 men were being sent to the camps each day. Within two months, 255,237 enrollees had been assigned. By July 22, the Corps had reached 301,230 members lodged in more than 1,500 camps across the nation with more on the way. The Army's share in running the CCC was expanded almost immediately, when it was discovered that the other departments lacked the manpower, machinery, facilities, and the knowledge to mobilize such a large force virtually overnight. The Army's role was exceptional, and it was widely recognized that it had "successfully undertaken the largest peacetime mobilization of men the United States had ever seen."[21] But by August, it was decided that the CCC would have to dispense with some 1,450 officers of the armed forces, as well as 2,500 enlisted men. There were then 2,945 Regular Army officers with the CCC. Of these, 1,130 were to be relieved, together with 320 Navy and Marine Corps officers. Each camp would for a time have two commissioned officers and two enlisted men. The gaps would be filled by reserve officers called to active service. Some of the reserve officers attended a newly created reserve Officers CCC Preparatory School at Governors Island, New York, with Regular Army officers as instructors. Enlisted men slated for CCC duty as cooks and bakers attended a course at the Army Cooks and Bakers School at Fort Slocum in New Rochelle, New York. Eventually, only reserve officers and men would be involved, and even the positions of the enlisted men would be filled by civilian enrollees.[22]

In addition to the junior enrollees, "locally enrolled men," or "LEM'S" were also utilized in the camps. These were "experienced, unemployed, and physically fit woodsmen (and other professionals), residing in the vicinity of the work projects." By using them, the CCC camps better fitted into the local scene, and headed off widespread local discontent and no doubt confrontations that might otherwise have occurred. Often skilled in the use of heavy machinery as well as work in the forests and on the land in general, the LEM's numbers were eventually set at 35,250, though initially 24,375 were provided for. These men were hired at standard Civil Service rates of pay, and greatly assisted in making the CCC a success.

The problem of unemployed World War I veterans was also addressed at least partially, providing initially for the enrollment of 28,225 men. This was stipulated by Executive Order No. 6129 of May 11, 1933, which authorized the Veterans Administration to select qualified veterans on the basis of a state quota system. Eventually, 225,000 veterans were involved, and by 1941 there were about 150 camps made up of these men who had often thought heretofore that their sacrifices in the Great War had been largely forgotten. Blacks were accommodated as well, both in their own segregated companies and sometimes in racially mixed units.

The Department of the Interior's Office of Indian Affairs on April 14, 1933, was authorized to enlist 14,861 American Indians, the first enrollments coming on June 23.[23] These enrollees, often married men with families, normally worked on projects on Indian reservations and lived at home, there being few camps established for them. The Indians, usually working through their traditional tribal councils, were given wide latitude in selecting projects and choosing their supervisors. The CCC work on the reservations was one of the most successful programs that the organization undertook. By the end of the CCC's career, 88,349 Indians had participated.

In addition to the work in the continental United States, there were about 4,000 enrollees in Hawaii, the Virgin Islands, Alaska and Puerto Rico at any given time.[24]

The typical junior enrollees were inducted into the CCC for a six-month stint, usually having the option of additional terms up to a maximum of two years, while being paid thirty dollars per month. In addition, their food, clothing and medical care were provided (calculated to be worth about 67 dollars per man per month). It was normally expected that the men would send 25 dollars of their pay home to assist their families. In the event the men had no dependents, they were required to deposit the 25 dollars to the CCC's general Chief Finance Office, the money being returned at the time of discharge. Out of their spending money enrollees bought cigarettes, candy, and toilet articles, paid for their personal laundry, sometimes purchased a suit of clothes ("civies," as they called them), and financed their recreation in nearby towns and villages.[25] Some of the enrollees were promoted to leaders or assistant leaders. Called "rated" men, they received 45 and 36 dollars per month respectively. There were about 10 to 12 leaders and 15 to 20 assistant leaders in each camp. Among the leaders would be the company clerk, the canteen steward, enrollee cooks, and also section leaders or foremen. The assistant leaders included the group or squad bosses. Company commanders or overseers made the appointments with the advice of the forestry superintendents.[26] Because each term of service was six months, there was a rapid turnover in personnel, and the opportunities for promotion were considerable. Anyone with ambition usually had an opportunity to progress during his term of service.

The enrollees were initially given a two-week orientation program run by the U.S. Army, consisting of standard military drill and discipline programs. They were issued Army uniforms and, following their initial training, were sent to a camp, usually deep in the forest.

In the first months some of the men were housed under canvas, but barracks were soon constructed as were other buildings familiar to Army cantonments. The average camp had five barracks, each accommodating about forty men. A mess hall; a recreation hall; a canteen; educational buildings, often including a library; headquarters and supply buildings; a camp hospital, infirmary or dispensary; and shops and technical service buildings were common.[27] At first, commanding officers of the camps were Regular Army officers, usually a first lieutenant or captain, or on occasion Marine Corps, Navy or Coast Guard officers.[28] The CO served as the mayor, the director of public safety, and the common pleas court judge, all in one. He was assisted by a second-in-command—a subaltern—usually a second lieutenant. However, the Regular officers were soon returned to their usual duty posts and the CCC officers were appointed from the Army's list of reserve officers.

In 1939, FDR issued an order that all camp commanding officers would henceforth be civilians. Their Army uniforms were replaced by a distinctive green CCC uniform, and they were henceforth called "mister," rather than addressed by their Army rank. In practice, though, reserve officers often continued to serve in these capacities, and were customarily referred to by military title.[29] Under the CO's command, in addition, was the camp doctor (an Army or sometimes a Naval officer), who frequently served more than one camp, as did the Army Dental Corps dentist, who rotated his services. Army chaplains, also "riding a circuit," served the spiritual needs of the enrollees.[30] The civilian educational advisers, usually college graduates appointed by the U.S. Office of Education in Washington, were likewise part of the "overhead," i.e., the administration.

Despite the presence of military leadership, however, the CCC was not a military organization and much resistance developed within the government and among the public to oppose its being cast along those lines.[31] Yet, while there were no rifles in the CCC camps, the enrollees did learn rudimentary aspects of the military life: their barracks were regularly inspected as though they were in the Army; they stood evening retreat formations with the lowering of the flag; there was some close-order drill, especially late in the CCC's career; and their day's round of activities followed a quasi-military schedule.[32]

The CCC shared another military attribute: the uniform. In the beginning, the men were outfitted from Army supplies of "OD's" and khakis, and dressed in blue denims while working. Eventually a new, distinctive CCC winter uniform was brought out in "spruce green."[33]

Clearly, their service in the organization had helped prepare many men to live together in encampments, to drill, to dress in uniform, to care for themselves, and work together as a unit, all useful preparation for more intensive military service with the coming of war to America after Pearl Harbor. There is little question, then, that the expanding American military complex, coming in the early 1940s, benefited from the establishment and operations of the CCC camps, operating on a quasi-military basis. The CCC provided a training ground for the officers, whether Regular or reserve, in an era when military expenditures were severely curtailed and command opportunities limited.

Other professional assistance at the camps included the all-important camp superintendents and foremen, who were in charge of the work projects. They worked under the general supervision of the U.S. departments of the Interior or Agriculture. If a forestry camp, the superintendent might be a forest ranger able to manage forestry projects. Agricultural experts served as superintendents and foremen in camps engaged in soil erosion relief.

Engineers directed road and bridge construction. Skilled carpenters directed building programs. Explosives experts were also widely used. Most camps utilized trucks and heavy machinery which required skilled personnel such as drivers, operators, mechanics and machinists. These were frequently the LEMs, though enrollees often developed the skills necessary to operate such equipment. In the beginning, the cooks were drawn from the ranks of Army personnel who served as sergeants or civilians. Their numerous assistants were enrollees, many of whom became cooks themselves. An enrollee operated the camp canteen which sold candy, soft drinks, tobacco and personal items. The profits supported a company fund which made possible the purchase of athletic equipment and uniforms, as well as providing for the publication of camp newspapers.

Typically, at six o'clock in the morning, the men were awakened by a bugle call or the whistle of the senior leader. Calisthenics took up 15 minutes before breakfast at 6:45 A.M. The work call came at 7:45 A.M. By the time the men left for work, they had cleaned their rooms and policed the grounds in military fashion. They proceeded to their day's work, working for eight hours with a half-hour lunch, their food being brought to them in the field if they worked some distance from the camp. If they lost work time because of the weather, they normally made it up on Saturday. The workday ended at four o'clock, and the men returned to camp. They then shed their blue denim work clothes, cleaned up, and donned their dress uniforms. They stood retreat at about five, in observance of the lowering of the flag. They then had the evening meal. Following this, until lights out at 10 P.M., the men had several options: they might attend classes provided by various educational programs, drop in at the recreation hall to play games or sports, or attend a movie screened at the camp.

On one night a week, there was usually a company meeting at which the commanding officer presided. At this time, the medical officer might lecture them on personal hygiene, or they would be instructed about courtesy, etiquette, or safety. Attendance at these presentations was normally compulsory. On other nights, a camp truck made a run into a local town or village, the men being required to return to camp at 9:30 P.M. Not all of the enrollees were free to select their entertainment, however. Those who were classified as "illiterates" had to attend classes in the basics of elementary education. The men spent Saturday mornings working around their camps doing fix-up, paint-up or scrubbing chores, planting plants and other projects of upkeep and maintenance, prior to the afternoon's trips to a nearby town for recreation. On some Saturday nights, the camp might stage a dance, the company providing buses or trucks to bring in girls and their chaperones from local areas. Bands or orchestras might also be hired for the entertainment. Sundays were days of leisure with opportunities to attend religious services at the camp or in nearby towns.

The Army, from the outset, recognized that recreation was of primary importance. Accordingly, Brigadier General James F. McKinley, the Adjutant General of the Army, was put in charge of recreational work in the camps. With Major Joseph J. Teter designated to take the matter in hand, soon traveling libraries of 150 to 200 volumes and magazines and daily papers were provided. Sports equipment was also issued to each camp, and camp exchanges were set up.[34]

The educational programs undertaken by the CCC were controversial as to what was done and, perhaps more importantly, what was not done.[35] Very few of the boys had finished high school, and less than one percent had any college training. The average CCC boy had completed nine grades of public school. He had quit school because his family needed his labor, could not afford to send him on, or simply because he did not like school. In some respects, the educational endeavors, at least in the traditional sense, were among the least effective of the programs undertaken by the organization. This and other relevant topics will be discussed in separate chapters below. But the CCC's reputation rested not on its recreational and educational programs, but on its work projects, many of which, at least initially, consisted of setting out trees in the nation's forests. By 1940, it was estimated that more than two billion trees had been planted in the cut-over or burned-over land, and in marginal areas that needed new vegetation. More than half of the men in the CCC were employed in this program. In addition, about 300 of the camps worked under the supervision of the Soil Conservation Service helping farmers save their soil. This involved something over fifty thousand men at any given time. The Conservation Service identified the areas needing assistance and the farmers themselves decided which individual farms would be most suitable for aid. The farmers involved were required to provide the necessary materials, and they signed agreements to continue conservation practices for at least five years. The CCC then furnished the necessary labor. The farmers also agreed to permit their neighbors to observe the work being done so that some of them might take similar action on their farms. CCCers surveyed and mapped the farms upon which they worked; they leveled gullies; built check dams; and established contour farming operations, using terracing, strip cropping techniques, as well as mulching and contour cultivation methods. By the autumn of 1940, they had built more than five million small dams to check floods; had set out 200 million trees on over 200 million acres of the nation's farmland; and planted grass, vines and shrubs on 700,000 additional acres.

The national and state park services were also assisted by the CCC. Under the general supervision of the National Park Service, the men built thousands of miles of trails in park lands as well as many miles of roads, numerous bridges, and cabins. They constructed fences and guard rails, water and sewage systems, lookout towers, shelters, fish rearing ponds, and stocked streams and lakes. In some states, CCC projects created the first parks in existence.

Another considerable activity involved the prevention and fighting of forest fires. A large number of CCC enrollees emerged as trained firefighters with sufficient skills to participate in this ongoing activity in the nation's woodlands. But this was always dangerous work, and a number of CCC men lost their lives on the fire lines.

These operations not only brought attention and popular support for the CCC, but the president took a strong personal interest in his new creation. On August 15, 1933, he made the first of many tours of inspection, visiting five CCC camps in Virginia. Receiving "a grand reception," he obviously greatly enjoyed his contact with the personnel. Taking along one of the chief critics of the Corps, AF of L president William Green, Roosevelt converted him, and "the unions were never again unreservedly hostile" to the CCC.[36]

The clear success of the CCC led Roosevelt to announce on August 18, 1933, that he was extending the Corps for a second six-month term, much to the delight of the men in the camps. On January 20, 1934, he once more prolonged its life, this time to April 1, 1935.[37]

Subsequently, a significant expansion of the CCC's work occurred in June of 1934, in response to the devastation of the drought that began to grip the nation. Its baleful effects were especially severe in the Midwest and compounded the unemployment problem. Consequently, FDR sought an additional fifty million dollars for work by the CCC in the stricken areas. Congress concurred and on June 30, the Department of Labor was instructed to select 50,000 additional men to be assigned to drought relief. This expanded the Corps to 353,000 men housed at 1,625 camps. The effort began to succeed, and FDR signed a bill on April 8, 1935, which not only provided for the CCC's retention for two more years, but its expansion to 600,000 men. However, this enrollment figure was not reached. The high mark of 505,000 men in 2,856 camps was attained in 1935.

At this juncture, FDR, because of the development of other programs such as the National Youth Administration (established in late June 1935 to provide employment to youths as an alternative to the CCC), changed fronts, deciding to limit the CCC to 450,000. He hoped eventually that the CCC would be stabilized at about 300,000. In this move, the president came up against concerted opposition even in his own party, especially from politicians seeking reelection in the 1936 elections. After a lengthy battle, FDR was forced to continue the CCC at 400,000 men in 2,158 camps.[38]

In June of 1937, by new legislation the Corps was slated to continue to June 30, 1940. However, henceforth it was understood that the CCC was mainly "for the purpose of providing employment, as well as vocational training, for youthful citizens of the United States who are unemployed and in need of employment ... through the performance of useful public work in connection with the conservation and development of the natural resources of the United States." The new emphasis was therefore away from relieving distress and poverty and placed upon providing work experience and training.[39]

In July 1939, in Roosevelt's Reorganization Plan Number One, the CCC was made a part of a newly created Federal Security Agency, headed by Paul V. McNutt. This grouped together the CCC, the Social Security Board, the United States Office of Education, the Public Health Service and the National Youth Administration under his administration. Though this did not fundamentally alter the corps' structure, it did make for a greater stability, and facilitated a sounder coordination of policy at least for a time. On August 5, 1939, the CCC was again extended, this time to June 30, 1943.[40]

By 1940, the annual expenditures of the federal government in maintaining the CCC amounted to three hundred million dollars. The results had been considerable. With the coming of the peacetime draft in September 1940, and even later, after Pearl Harbor (December 7, 1941), there was an inevitable change in the CCC's focus. To these ends, in June of 1940 Congress enacted Public Law 812 which provided some direction to the responsibilities which the CCC should bear in the National Defense Training scheme then in place. This intended that enrollees were to be trained in "noncombatant subjects" essential to the operations of the Military and Naval Establishments. These might include—but were not restricted to—cooking, baking, first aid, the operation and maintenance of motor vehicles, road and bridge construction and maintenance, photography, signal communications, "and other matters incident to the successful conduct of military and naval activities."[41]

All the while, McEntee among others urged that the CCC be made permanent. The organization was increasingly turning to technical education and work on military bases—relieving soldiers for more pressing duties, he pointed out. In addition, there was a renewed emphasis on firefighting, also a national defense expedient. And, certainly, he noted, "two and a half million girls will get better husbands because of the CCC training that these youths have received." As to the men, "they will be better workers, better neighbors and better citizens," he insisted, but his arguments remained unheeded.[42]

What Congress did agree to in June 1941 was to provide funds for the CCC to maintain 1,236 camps with emphasis on war preparedness training.[43] As the Depression waned with many of the men going into the armed services, the usual enrollment periods beginning every three months were changed in August 1941, to allow continuous enrollment to keep the ranks filled.[44] But enlistments could not be maintained and by November 1, 1941, camps were reduced to about 900, housing less than 200,000 men.[45]

With the coming of the war, in February 1942 the CCC was placed on a wartime footing. Camps were to be mainly engaged in defense training and also involved in such war projects as work on military reservations or the protection of natural resources.[46] However, the continuation of the Corps, often argued for by its leadership, would not be realized. The exigencies of the conflict with its huge demands for manpower, and a preoccupation of the nation with national defense, precluded it. The CCC's *raison d'être* was therefore increasingly questioned, and its fate an oft-debated subject as 1942 unfolded.

When the building of the Alaskan highway was initiated, some CCC leaders hoped that the CCC might be utilized to construct it. "Why wouldn't that be a top-hole job for the CCC?" the corps' national paper, *Happy Days*, asked. It was already trained in construction and had the necessary equipment. Furthermore, it could maintain its own supply lines and if necessary, it was argued, it could "defend itself against anyone who got an idea they might want to prevent the highway being built."[47] Instead, the CCC was ordered to turn over more than 27,000 pieces of its heavy equipment to the Army to assist it in the highway's construction, which was subsequently carried out mainly by the Army Corps of Engineers.[48]

Meanwhile, the CCC had further eroded, and when on May 4, 1942, FDR asked for a new appropriation to maintain 150 CCC camps for the fiscal year 1942-1943, the House Committee on Appropriations demurred. Instead, it voted only to provide a half-million dollars for the Corps' abolishment. When, in a contrary mood, the Senate sought to revive it, the House stood firm but did appropriate additional money to expedite the Corps' liquidation. Not wishing further political battle on the issue, the Senate acquiesced and by the end of June 1942, the CCC had ceased to exist. Its buildings and equipment went mainly to the Army, Navy and the Civil Aeronautics Administration, though some state and local agencies also benefited. There was speculation—and wishful thinking—that the dissolution was only "for the time being," and the CCC would no doubt be revived following the war. This, however, was not to be. In the meantime the CCC's leadership bowed to the inevitable, agreeing to abide by the decision of Congress, which had been "made honestly and in good faith." The nine-year, four-month career of the CCC had ended.[49]

By any standard, the accomplishments of the CCC were impressive. Over 3,400,000 men had been enrolled by the time of its demise and their erosion control projects had benefited approximately forty million acres of farmland. In addition, among other things, 800 state parks were developed, 125,000 miles of roads were built, 814,000 acres of rangeland revegetated, between two and three billion trees planted, and over six million days were expended in fire fighting (in which 29 enrollees lost their lives). The total value of the CCC's work to the nation was estimated to be over two billion dollars, but its worth to the lives of the men that it touched, and the life of the citizenry as a whole, was incalculable.[50]

C.C.C. of U.S.A.

In the hills and vales surrounding you
Came the good old CCC;
And they sent us to the forest
Through the call of Franklin D.
As we chop the trees and burn the brush
Through the hours of the day
We are out to do our very best
For the dear old U.S.A.

Every morning we arise at six
To the heed of the whistle call;
We don our clothes and fix our bunks,
Then march to the dining hall.
To the forest we go out at eight
Without a moment of delay;
And we do the task assigned to us
By the dear old U.S.A.

In the evening as we arrive at camp
When our daily tasks are done;
And we ditch our clothes and wash ourselves,
And go out for a bit of fun.
Some of us go to dance;
Some to the picture plays;
Others recreation grant us
Through the dear old U.S.A.

When our term is up and we must go
Back to our old home town,
We leave behind us memories of
Friends we palled around.
We were loyal to each other,
Not a grudge we would display;
And were proud that we were C.C.'s
For the dear old U.S.A.

—William J. Stunder, *Buffalo Prints*,
Company 2356, Camp Buffalo,
Amherst, Virginia, January 1938

PART I

CCC Camp Papers:
Foundations and Operations

1

The Camp Paper— The Foundations

"Wherever five or six Americans are gathered together, someone starts a newspaper."
—*Happy Days*, July 7, 1934

The *Camp Britton Bug* (Company 1193, Windsor, Connecticut) once exulted in an anonymous poem, that "It's colossal and gigantic/Exquisite and bombastic/It's raved about by every mug/This extraordinary *Britton Bug*." And, not inconsequentially, if perhaps unrealistically, it was alleged that "It makes the girls just squeal and hug/The guys who write the *Britton Bug*."

Indeed, the camp newspaper was often a lively business and, varying with the companies—to a greater or lesser extent—revealed much about a company's life, often serving as a diary and history of its endeavors. In other respects, the camp paper described for people outside the camp the work that was being done to improve the nation's resources. As an important part of its activities, *Happy Days* took an active part— in fact, an almost proprietary interest—in the establishment and nurturing of the camp papers which began to emerge almost from the beginning of the CCC program. "After all," as one observer wrote, revealing impeccable logic: "each camp is a community, a city in itself. And in every community there's news. People make news. News interests people. Newspapers are a part of modern life; therefore they belong in C.C.C. camps." And as the editor of *The Glen* (Company 275, Moravia, New York) stated it, "the camp paper is an interpreter of [its] small world."

The editor of the *Grand Canyon Echoes* (Company 819, Grand Canyon, Arizona) saw additional reasons for a paper: it created a new interest in work and in English grammar; it taught the fellows to observe and reflect upon actual events and life around them; it developed judgment, planning, skill and practice organizing a job; it promoted stability; it appealed to the individual's pride in seeing his work in print; it built a company spirit; and it encouraged originality, the chief essential of a good feature story writer.[1] For *The Harbinger* (Company 698 in Argyle, Wisconsin) the paper was chiefly aimed at the individual enrollee, coming in tired after a day's work, who might "likely ... think that it is a humdrum world he lives in, but if those who are a little more articulate sum up all the things that are going on around this camp and some of the others, we find that all together we are doing something very interesting and very much worthwhile."[2]

To another observer of the camp newspaper scene, the matter was even more pervasive: the armies of Alexander the Great, the Israelites departing Egypt for the Promised Land, Caesar and his Legions, the Crusaders, Napoleon, and others, all had their chroniclers. Indeed, "writing men told the story of these great movements; they told it in song, like the troubadours; they told it in brief, laconic dispatches ... 'I came, I saw, I conquered' ... they told it in swift news stories in tall tales, fact and fiction. But regardless of how—THEY TOLD THE STORY." The CCC could do no less for its own exploits.[3] Thousands of CCC enrollees heeded the call and from the very beginning, the Corps' story was told. With *Happy Days* covering the entire CCC, and the camp newspapers the individual camps, an impressive journalistic combination was in place.[4] It is not clear, however, which camp publication was the first to appear. There are several contenders. One early venture was *The News*, a mimeographed paper first published on April 15, 1933, at Fort Slocum, New York, one week after the first contingent of the CCC arrived at the camp to be processed. There was also the *C.C.C. Bugle*, produced at another Army camp, likewise engaged in the processing of new enrollees, in Brooklyn, New York.

One of the first company papers following the lead of those at the Army camps was the *Booker T. Broadcaster*—subtitled the *Colored C.C. Courier*—of a black company, 1464, stationed at Camp Booker T. Washington, Fort Oglethorpe, Georgia. Its first issue came off the press on May 12, 1933. The paper began with an all-white staff, including Captain Allan W. McComb, a former newspaperman, and two other officers. The first issue announced that when the talent in the company became better known, "the editorial staff would be extended—and 'darkened.'" The paper was destined for a long, creative life of several years.[5] Not far behind the *Booker T. Broadcaster* were the *Smoky Mountain Echo* (Company 1461 at Middle Prong, Tennessee), and the *Trail Blazer* (Company 701 at Ely, Minnesota).[6]

There would eventually be well over 5,000 camp papers published by almost 3,000 of the CCC companies, some of whose publications appeared under more than one title. In a program launched in September 1934 by the director of the University of Illinois library, P. L. Windsor, as much literature as possible pertaining to the New Deal was collected. This included the CCC camp papers, which were regarded as an important component of the gathered materials. By August of 1940, the collection included 3,504 publications from 2,385 different camps. The Library of Congress and numerous state historical societies also accumulated collections. These were eventually taken over by the Center for Research Libraries in Chicago. Subsequently, supported by grants from the National Endowment for the Humanities, as well as the Center's own funds, the papers were preserved in microform, either microfilm or microfiche.[7]

The typical CCC camp paper would have been a weekly with a stylish, colorful cover, well-made-up, and containing clearly written, creative editorials, articles and features focusing on the camp's life and activities, rather than on national or international news. It might include advertising, and would have sections or columns devoted to wit and humor, a coverage of sports and entertainment, and it would likely place some emphasis on the educational program and safety matters. The most frequent publisher was a journalism class created in the company usually by the educational adviser who at times edited the paper. Sometimes, though, frustrated unemployed newsmen, then in the CCCs, saw an opportunity to use their expertise in bringing out a camp sheet.[8]

Some camp papers appeared irregularly, reflecting the difficulties of maintaining a staff, obtaining supplies, or the means of publication, and sometimes further handicapped by pressing work demands, the consequence of blizzards, forest fires, or floods. Papers often had runs of several months or years, sometimes with name changes; others appeared for a much shorter time.

They appeared in many venues from the heights of Glacier National Park to Oregon's Pacific coast; the depths of Death Valley; along dam sites, such as the Boulder Dam project in Nevada; the Red Rocks open air theater in Colorado; and *The 1741 Tabloid*, the weekly of Company 1741 at St. Charles, Arkansas, was published on a houseboat on the White River.

Inevitably, there was a considerable range of standards among the papers. In unexpected ways, even geography entered into the picture. For some reason, an unusually large number of first-rate papers were published by companies in Minnesota, Missouri and California, a fact

April, 1937   Vol. I, Issue 1

The
KEARSARGE
KETTLE

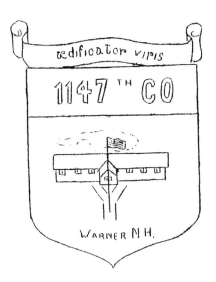

1147th Company, C.C.C. - WARNER, N. H.

Above and opposite: Camp newspapers often changed their titles. *The Kearsarge Kettle* (Company 1147, Warner, New Hampshire) became the *Tory Hill Sentinel* in June 1938.

TORY HILL

SENTINEL

"In the Shadow of Mt. Kearsarge"

Published by

1147th Co., CCC, Warner, N. H.

JUNE, 1938   Vol. I   No. I

at which *Happy Days* repeatedly marveled. *The Sullivanite* (Company 719, Brimson, Minnesota) boasted perhaps the best editor that the CCC produced, at least according to *Happy Days*, in Bob Morin, one of "Minnesota's mighty men." Long regarded as topflight was *The Seagullite* (Company 3709, Grand Marais), once called by *Happy Days* "the snappiest weekly this [paper] ever laid eyes on."[9] There was also the "bellicose" and "warlike" *Walkerite* (Company 3709, Walker). Boasting the motto, "the paper with the punch," it was a sometime critic of *Happy Days*.[10] Companies in Missouri, stung by the praise so frequently accorded Minnesota papers, responded with many of the CCC's outstanding sheets. One of the best—and most controversial—was *Swan Lake Splashes*, published by Company 1727 in Sumner, Missouri. Calling itself "the glamour paper of the C.C.C.," and "the spicy paper of the C.C.C.," it insisted on presenting the lighter side of camp life, eschewing "dull moralizing," which it regarded as all too common in CCC papers. It also caused a furor by publishing a cover featuring a thinly clad belly dancer, thereby pushing the limits of what was acceptable in much of the publishing world at the time. For this, it received a strong scolding from *Happy Days* and numerous scalding comments in other papers.[11] Other good Missouri papers included *Roaring River Ripples* (Company 1713, Cassville), which featured the excellent art work of Tobie Watkins, and another with excellent art, *Chilli Con Chats* (Company 1716, Chillicothe).

California companies also fielded numerous superior papers. One of the most interesting was the *Tabloid Owl*, the brainchild of Company 909, Highland, California. This exceptional, entertaining paper's motto was "a paper for people who think they think." The *Hoy-La* (Company 985, Santa Barbara) was known throughout the CCC for its goofy, highly inventive covers, featuring humorous Rube Goldberg–like inventions and absurd convolutions.

To be sure, sterling papers appeared throughout the 48 states. Several Indian enrollees produced good papers, one of which was the *Wehan-cho-na-que*, the Base Camp No. 1 newspaper of a Zuni Indian Reservation. Some good papers appeared outside of the United States. Company 9502 at Kamuela, Hawaii, brought out *Ka Leo O Ka Makani O Kamuela* ("The Voice of the Wind"). Another rather unusual Hawaiian paper was the *TH-CCC News* (which stood for "Territory of Hawaii CCC News") published as a monthly by the U.S. Department of the Interior, National Park Service, CCC Headquarters, Honolulu, Territory of Hawaii. First appearing on September 1, 1940, it was the united news organ of the CCC in the Territory of Hawaii, and maintained correspondents in each of the Hawaiian camps.[12]

Also noteworthy was *The Alaskan*, appearing in December 1939,

THE SEAGULLITE'S LAST MINUTE FLASH!

it was a lot of fun
GOSH! LOOKS LIKE OUR PAPER'S DONE;
C'MON STAFF, LET'S START ANOTHER ONE!

"SEAGULLITE" PUBLISHED MONTHLY AT CO. 3709. CCC, GRAND MARAIS, MINN. Vo.IV - No 3....

PROJECTS TO BE SUSPENDED JUNE 1

F-55 F. S. PERSONNEL BREAKS UP

A FEW FACTS

ABOUT OUR PAPER

It occupied about all the spare time the staff had....Was run off on a small hand-feed mimeograph...Required 18,000 cranks of the handle... The cover alone required three separate stencils for the color work ...Two colors were run off on some inside pages... But everyone said it was a lot of Jun...And are ready to start another...After getting some sleep...

ABOUT THE EXCHANGES

Our copy of the "LAKESIDE REVIEW" came in with a bang...It featured another one of Jorgenson's color covers..Well, ...WOW!!!

Our neighbor, the "Gunflint Trailer" , has shoved its mimeograph back in the box in favor of a four page printed number...
...LHL...

BROUILLETTE, JACKSON -- TO PRIVATE INDUSTRY

With the orders from the Forest Service authorities to suspend all F-55 projects on June 1, members of its personnel announced their plans for the future. Project Sup't Fred E. Brouillette will enter the employment of John R. Miles of the Oxy..a-tut-ting Welding, Inc. Jr. Forester and Safety Assistant Clayton Jackson will enter parnership with his brother in a Grand Marais, garage. Jr. Forester Herz will be transferred to the Portage River Camp. To nearby Gunflint Camp, (Co. 712) are transferred Lyle Ellis, Jr. Foreman, Oscar Lindskog, Jr. Foreman, Axel Sampson, Mechanic, and Harry Johnson, Shovel Operator. Machine Operator Arno Oftedahl will remain on furlough status until further notice.

TRAIL GETS PRIORTY

LONG SUSTAINING PROJECT
The Gunflint Trail , long the sustaining project of the F-55 setup in this camp is being rushed as priorty project as the date of the suspension of projects was set for June first.

Thaws and rain have raised havoc with the road in places and the man and machine power of the camp is concentrating on having the trail in shape by the deadline.

Sections of the road that have not been completed were also rushed. All other projects are considered as of secondary importance.

TURN PAGE FOR MORE NEWS

"SLIM" LINDSTROM IS BACK

The roving CCC editor, Leonard "Slim" Lindstrom is back again as one of the Army's five exempt men. He will handle the reins of the work-horse "SEAGULLITE" assisted by John Losinski and the staff.

Said Lindstrom on taking over the reins:

"GIDDAP!"

Company 3709, based at Grand Marais, Minnesota, published *The Seagullite,* one of that state's outstanding papers.

Chili Con Chats (Company 1716, Chillicothe, Missouri) invariably featured artistic work, as on this cover of the September 1940 issue.

rather late in the history of the CCC. It was published in Juneau by the CCC Admiralty Division Headquarters of the 6th Corps Area. The first CCC paper to be published there, it "easily lay claim to the distinction of being the northernmost CCC publication." The paper focused mainly on the varied CCC activities carried out in Alaska. Much of the work there served aviation needs, such as building runways and laying telephone lines linking Civilian Aeronautics Administration facilities. Other work was devoted to restoring and preserving Alaska's Indian and Eskimo heritage.[13] Elsewhere, other camp papers were published in the Spanish language. One was *El Verde*, the sheet of the United States CCC Miscellaneous Companies in Puerto Rico, and published in Rio Grande, Puerto Rico. Another Spanish-language CCC paper was the *Ecos del Yunque*, appearing entirely in Spanish except for the sports section. It was published at Palmer, Puerto Rico, by a unit composed of three camps under the direction of the Forest Service.[14]

One matter of perennial concern was the form the papers were to take, and many debates ensued as to the advantages and disadvantages of the mimeographed sheet versus the printed paper. *Happy Days*, the perennial arbiter of the camp papers, favored the mimeographed editions over the far fewer printed ones, insisting that the professionally printed papers detracted from creativity and originality. In addition, they were generally more expensive, always a matter of concern.[15]

Other forms of production were sometimes employed. The hectograph method, with its glycerine-coated layer of gelatin as the basis of the reproduction of sheets, was used by some papers, such as *The Box Canyon Bang* (Company 1339, Escalante, Utah). *The Iron Miner* (Company 209, Cold Spring, New York) used the photo offset method of publication, as did *The Ash Can* (Company 1284, Chatsworth, New Jersey). *The Valley Crier* (Company 317, Hillsgrove, Pennsylvania) was printed in Gothic type using a special typewriter.

Methods of creating illustrations also varied. Numerous camp papers featured art work, often taxing the ingenuity of the editors and art editors. Many of the illustrations were made by the silk-screen method using camp-constructed mimeoscopes. More prosaically, much use was made of linoleum cuts, especially for covers. In some camps, these were produced by a linoleum block-printing class.[16] In another innovation, *The Spillway* (Company 219, Cherry Plain, New York), the CCC's first picture newspaper, adopted the form of the *New York Daily News*, but instead of photographs, all of its illustrations were cartoons. The effect was not only humorous, but also strangely effective. Sometimes photographs were used, however, as by *The Wanless Rip Saw* (Company 703, Schroder, Minnesota), which inserted a separate photo sheet developed and printed by the company's camera club.

A preoccupation with the use of color in producing illustrations was commonplace. *The Keyhole* (Company 432, Stantonsburg, North Carolina) for an Easter number mimeographed the issue on white, blue, pink, yellow and green paper—two pages of each. Another paper, *Peat Smoke* (Company 710, Middle River, Minnesota), sometimes ran short of ink and substituted paint or enamel, "with such gratifying work that we still use both for our color work."

There was wide variation in the frequency of publication and the physical appearance of the camp papers. Some were actually magazines, usually monthlies, and could reach 50 pages or more, typically of mimeographed material. Other papers were published as semi-monthlies, weeklies, or quarterlies. There were a few semi-weeklies, one being *The Kentucky Colonel* (Company 3556, Green River, Utah). Some companies published more than one paper, as did Company 2390, Salem, Virginia. Its monthly mimeographed sheet was the *Triangle Tirade*; its weekly was styled the *Tirade, Jr.* Other companies aspired to produce dailies, but as Nicholas Lucysozyn, the editor of *Red House Eagle* (Company 249, Red House, New York), observed, "putting out a camp daily is no bed of roses," though he thought that it was "the ideal medium for a camp publication." The news was fresh, and he believed that "eventually dailies would replace the multitude of weeklies and monthlies." Nevertheless, dailies remained the exception rather than the rule, though there were some good ones.

The trend in late 1930s America toward digest-sized publications in the magazine field, such as *Coronet* and *Reader's Digest*, was reflected in CCC papers. As small as 5½ by 8½ inches, they were referred to as "the compressed, the small, the intimate," by one observer.[17] Among these were *The Deer Runner* (Company 734, Ellington, Missouri); the *Tide of 3805* (Company 3805, Bartlett, Texas); and the *Camp Canby Transcontinental* (Company 3225, Ilwaco, Washington).

There were other sizes and formats as well. Company 677 of Harrison, Michigan, apparently fielded the first daily "tabloid" newspaper of the CCC, a two-page mimeographed legal-sized sheet, *The Daily Dip*. Another tabloid format sheet was the 7 by 20 inches, two-page paper, the *Beartown C.C.C. C—All*, which served Companies 108 and 112 in the Beartown State Forest near South Lee, Massachusetts.

As to how and where the papers were produced, in Company 1431 in Old Town, Florida, the camp's class in journalism set up and printed the *Suwannee Ripples* on its own printing press. The *Camp Hook News* (Company 172, New Fairfield, Connecticut) was mimeographed at the Danbury Trade School of that city. Numerous others papers used mimeographs and other equipment in local high schools, colleges, and various places of business.

One paper, the bimonthly *Camp Skokie Valley Review,* was unique in that it served 10 companies at the mammoth camp at Glenview, Illinois. Another, the *Beaver Chatter* (Company 754, Beaver City, Nebraska), had two editors: John Wilson, who worked the paper one week; Lloyd Harms, who took over the following one, an effective "Damon and Pythias" arrangement. Company 528 in Bethel, Ohio, had two newspapers: the *Enrollees' Home Journal* and *The Musical Interlude,* the former printed, the latter mimeographed. The *Eleven Ninety News* (Company 1190, Fall River, Massachusetts) organized a journalism council to supervise producing the paper, while the material published in the *Harold Parker Review* (Company 110, Andover, Massachusetts) was selected by an Editorial Page Club. The first issue of *Camp Memoirs* (Company 658, Black River Falls, Wisconsin) was bound in a loose-leaf cover so that subsequent papers might be inserted to develop a complete file.

The camp papers always had to strive to get the men to contribute and otherwise participate in their paper's publication. Indeed, as one observer noted: "There seems to be no definite solution in sight to this ever-perplexing problem that is turning the hair of camp editors gray."[18] The editor of *1845 News* (Company 1845 in Castle Rock, Colorado), Francis Roberts, was keenly aware of the problem, asserting that "we have found that starting a camp paper is like drilling a new oil well in a virgin field. A few men support it until it strikes oil, then everyone is willing to jump in. We struck oil so let's have your support." But perhaps the men could be cajoled into action. The editor of *The Blue Denim Herald* (Company 744, Pinnacles, California) urged his readers to "Get news. If you can't find news, make some!" Another editor took a harder line: "Do you want a camp paper? Then why the hell don't you help in putting it out? Don't pretend you want one. If you don't, say so and we'll quit."

What might be helpful would be to assist the men in determining just what news was. One camp newspaper poet at the *Bitterroot Bugle* (Company 1501, Darby, Montana) thought that he knew: "If you've wrecked a forest flivver/If your pal ate too much liver/If Angel's car picked up a sliver/ IT IS NEWS." In any event, the men were urged to "write them short and write them snappy," because "big long items make us nappy," but in any case, "SEND IN NEWS."[19]

And there might be other expedients. *Happy Days* advised the editor of *Seven-Thirty Edition* (Company 730, Albany, Missouri) to try prizes such as cigarettes awarded for the best short stories, original jokes, or cartoons, a gambit used successfully by *The Yucca Post* (Company 1914, Kaweah, California). *The Ridge Runners' Record* (Company 577, Fairlawn, Ohio) underwrote a trip to Cleveland for dinner and a movie for its best writers.

Other forms of competition were tried. In Company 556, Angola, Indiana, two camp papers, both monthlies, were produced by different journalism classes, evoking an intense rivalry in publishing *The Pokagon Papoose* and *The Pokagon Chieftain*. Competition was also used by *The Old Yorker* (Company 421, Rock Hill, South Carolina). There, each page was edited by a different writer under his own byline. In others, individual barracks produced separate papers, as was done at the District Headquarters Detachment at Fort Douglas, Utah, where *The H Barracks Blah*, was published by Barracks "H" of that unit.

Throughout the life of the CCC newspapers, there was considerable assistance available to the camp editors. In the first place, *Happy Days*, as will be noted below, was a fount of much information and support. In addition, newspapermen in the communities where CCC camps were established often took a paternal interest in the budding camp journalists. For instance, members of Headquarters Company, Sparta District, Wisconsin, were given assistance in absorbing the fundamentals of the printing trade by the Monroe County Publishers, printers of the company's paper, *The Headquarters Star*. This plant turned over their presses to the men as a classroom one evening each week with its regular staffers as instructors. Another professional newspaperman, Don L. Berry, the publisher of the *Indianola Record and Tribune*, taught a journalism class for Company 769 at Indianola, Iowa. He also allowed the men to publish their own camp paper, *The Chief*, as a regular back page feature of the *Tribune*. The reverse was also true. In an attempt to establish ties with the local population, *The Jefferson Excavator* (Company 580, Broadacre, Ohio) produced a column, "The Talk of the Town," featuring community events and personalities. In Horse Shoe Bend, Idaho, Company 4736 maintained a special town correspondent on its staff who wrote a regular page on town affairs for the company's paper, the *Horse Shoe Ringer*.

The staffs of camp papers often visited professional newspaper establishments. Company 528, Bethel, Ohio, sent its Press Club and its "Keeping Up with the News" group which produced the company's paper, *The Enrollees' Home Journal*, to Cincinnati to visit *The Cincinnati Enquirer*. The staff of *The Camp Cross Clarion* (Company 182, West Cornwall, Connecticut) traveled to Hartford, spending an evening as guests of the *Hartford Courant*, the oldest newspaper in the United States.

Opposite: Merle Fearrien was apparently the only woman to edit a CCC camp paper. Her publication was the *Blather-Scatt* (Company 569, Redmond, Oregon). She was, of course, not an enrollee. An example of her work: The October 24 issue of 1941.

BLATHER-SCATT

"Nothing in Excess"

Co. 669 CCC

Redmond, Oregon

S U C C E S S

For success, let's start at the bottom and climb up to the top. Grasping and climbing upward is much better than slipping and sliding downward. Perhaps it will not bring quick success. Go at your work with real and determination to finish. Try to make your work as interesting and entertaining as possible.. Be willing to expend all necessary time and energy required in following every source of information bearing on the problem in your work. Naturally, there will be difficulties. If there were no difficulties, there certainly would not be any real success. The struggle for advancement has led to splendid mechanical inventions. And improvements. It has developed the different resources of all the countries. If we are too easily satisfied with ourselves, we may never acquire success. We cannot do a job better, if we think we have already done it satisfactorily.. For example, when the first automobiles were made, if the manufacturers had thought their work entirely satisfactory, we perhaps would still be riding in open, buggy-like cars with a stick for the steering wheel, going five miles an hour. The really successful ones never, to their own estimation, reach their goal. The more they accomplish, the more they find to be accomplished.--Virginia Park

INSPECTION TOUR

Inspector Watson, his assistant William J. La Pierre, civilian clerk from Headquarters formerly of Whitehall, New York, and Noble B. Martin, Educational Advisor, returned Wednesday from a two-days' inspection tour southeast of here.

"NIGHT-GUARD CLOCK"

The morning after sand was found in the clock two well-known night-guards were heard to be humming "Sand from Havana"!!. Could be? Could be! --"Pie"

THOUGHT FOR THE DAY

To those "Bed Check Missers" and "Late Calisthenics Risers":
Early to bed and early to rise,
Or a private session with Lt. Wise.
--"Pie"

BETTER NOT BET

An argument started on Regulation 67, Page 122, Section 7, paragraph E2134, over the word acute or immediate, and the decision was that it means immediately, if not sooner. Somebody lost five bucks to Lt. Wise, but it can't be collected.

AROUND CAMP

Two cooks, Carpenter and Baker have been seen out picking up spuds. The infirmary is scoring a painting by "The Deacon" in his denims, now getting white!! Two pool tables are being fixed up for the boys; the billiard table is going to Sisters.

URGENT—WHO'LL HELP

HELP WANTED: Dental Assistant wants to join the Navy and needs somebody to take his job over.
HELP WANTED: Need somebody to build fires in "Ed Shack". Don sleeps too much.
HELP WANTED: Somebody to shoot banshees instead of dogs.
HELP WANTED: Special shadowers to be used on Warner and Wiley!!
HELP WANTED: Somebody to help Jack Hardy and Roy Gemmell carry their smiles around for them.

So, Jack Hardy is thinking of joining the "NAVY"?

A farmer was showing a girl visitor from the city around the farm. Suddenly she spied a herd of calves in a field and exclaimed, "Oh, look at the little cowlets!"
The farmer grinned and replied, "Them is bullets."

OCTOBER 24, 1941

The papers helped themselves as well. One expedient was the creation of news services, which copied such professional organizations as the AP and UP. One was for the camp papers of West Virginia organized by *Hardy Life* (Company 1524, Mathias, West Virginia). Another paper, *The Sphinx* (Company 659, Marion, Illinois), set up the Sphinx News Service, which provided free news releases to newspapers of the hometowns of members of the company.

Other help came from interested companies and individuals, often with a vested interest in the production of CCC papers. One was the Chicago Ditto company, makers of mimeograph equipment, which produced a booklet, *Hints For School Newspapers*, widely circulated in the camps as well as in the nation's schools. Another useful book was *Publishing a Camp Paper by Mimeograph* by journalism instructor Charles H. Keedle, of Company 257 in Lake Placid, New York. He himself sold it to interested editors.

Once the papers were produced, circulation, sometimes a problem, had to be addressed. The *857 Log* (Company 857, Denison, Texas) sought to obtain greater circulation by allowing each man two copies of the biweekly—so that one could be sent home—a largess made possible by the considerable purchasing of advertisements by Denison and Sherman merchants. Another plan to encourage the men to send papers home was used by Company 755 at Pawnee City, Nebraska. Its paper, *The Barracks Bearer*, left a blank space at the bottom of the page so that the men could write a short note before mailing it.

Sometimes communities were involved in enhancing circulation. The *Blue Eagle News* (Company 817, Stephenville, Texas) was not only distributed at the camp; the local Chamber of Commerce also disseminated copies throughout the city. In Cascade, Colorado, *Echoes From The Peak*, the weekly paper of Company 802, was forced to increase its circulation from 200 to 325, because many residents of the town developed the habit of strolling into camp every Thursday noon when the paper appeared, collecting copies for themselves.

Even FDR got into the act. In Georgia, the *Meriwether Tri-C News* (Company 1429, Warm Springs) carried a complete account of the president's latest visit to the little White House in December 1933, and his visit to the company, where he enjoyed a barbecue specially prepared for him by the enrollees. In addition, he was presented a copy of the unit's paper, a common practice when he visited CCC camps. For instance, the August 3, 1934, issue of *The Green Guidon*, the "Standard Bearer for C.C.C. activities in the Fort Missoula District, Montana," was dedicated to the president and a copy, reproduced on sheepskin paper with hand-lettered text, was presented to him on his visit to Glacier Park. Another paper with a flair for publicity, *The Harbinger* (Company 698, Argyle,

Wisconsin), sent copies of its paper to the Governor of Wisconsin, Postmaster General James A. Farley, and even Bing Crosby, who answered that he hoped "all the boys are taking every advantage of their opportunities at camp."[20]

Yet other papers resorted to popularizing themselves on the air. One of these—apparently the first CCC camp newspaper to sponsor a daily news broadcast over its own radio station—was the *Daily Dagger* (Company 1229, Machias, New York).[21] Another was *The Lonesome Pine* (Company 2347, Rocky Mount, Virginia), which presented a play, "The Camp Editor," over station WDBJ in Roanoke, Virginia, highlighting the headaches of preparing and publishing a camp paper. Also with a flair for publicity, the editors of *Neighbors* (Company 2388, Marion, Virginia) set up a booth at the Smyth County Fair. Issuing a daily paper from the grounds, they gave the public a close look at their press operations.

One traditional method employed was the exchange list. Typically, *The Catskill Crier* (Company 299, Masonville, New York) was routinely mailed to other company papers, various high-ranking army officers and government officials, *Happy Days*, selected high school papers, the University of Illinois Library, and the *Sidney Enterprise* (the local paper of Sidney, New York). Many papers, including *The Harbinger* (Company 698, Argyle, Wisconsin), printed special pages such as "Links," which analyzed and critiqued other CCC papers obtained in exchanges. In many outfits, these publications were placed in the library for the men to peruse.

The matter of naming the camp papers is of considerable interest. Some companies had difficulties in selecting a title for their sheets. Frequently, contests were held among the camp members to made a decision. In Wellston, Michigan, Company 679's editor made do with *"U" Name It* for the unit's weekly, before calling it the *Hoxeyville Daze*. The original issue of Company 1713's paper in Cassville, Missouri, was temporarily called *The Bugle-News-Star-Post-Chronicle-Bulletin-Times-Dispatch-Herald-Watchman-Examiner*. A contest produced the winning moniker, *Roaring River Ripples*. Some editors, even less certain about a name, used a *"?"* as a title. At least two companies despaired, permanently leaving their papers as the *Nameless News*.

Many titles, in one way or another—and often truncated—embodied the names of the home states of the men in camp, as in *The Alabama-Georgian* of Company 478 of Crawfordville, Georgia. When the camp moved to Bastrop, Louisiana, the paper was renamed *The Alagala*, accommodating the influx of Louisiana enrollees. Yet another move to Florida resulted in the title *Our Fla La Ala Ga*. The whimsical *Arkansawyer* played on the name of the home of the men of Company 4799 involved in the new life of forestry work at Kettle Falls, Washington.

A common device was to focus on the locations and the local predominant weather where the men were stationed. *Airs of Ozone* (Company 1708, of Ozone, Arkansas) is a good example. Others included *The Big Bar Battler* (Company 996, Big Bar, California) and *The Cammal's Hump* (Company 365 at Cammal, Pennsylvania). Reflecting local weather and climate, there was *The Drizzle* and *The Downpour*, the former a weekly, the latter a monthly magazine of Company 2107, Blachly, Oregon. In the depths of Death Valley, California, the men of Company 912 chose the appropriate *Boca del Infierno* to adorn their paper's masthead.

Equally understandable was that many of the papers' titles referred—sometimes with pride—to the specific jobs that the men did. *The Infant Tree* (Company 3882 at Grass Valley, California) had a double meaning: a reference to the quasi-military discipline, and also to the forestry activities (involving the planting of seedlings), with which the men were by then familiar. *The Mononga-Healer* pointed to the conservation work along the Monongahela River carried out by Company 2590 of Neola, West Virginia. The *Sod Saver's Rag* (Company 2737, Fullerton, Nebraska) requires no comment.

Some of the names manifested a certain cleverness, humor, or strikingly coined expressions as in the case of *The Lyman Rickey* (Company 292, Lyman, Washington); the *O'lustee Cheer* (Company 453, Olustee, Florida); and the *Spartan Life* (Company 4474, Spartanburg, South Carolina). Humorous titles included *The Weakly Effort* (Company 835, Mimbres, New Mexico); *The Waggin' Tongue* (Company 910, Soda Springs, Idaho); and *Ink Crumbs* (Company 113, Chester, Massachusetts).

The hard fact of the Depression and its dislocations being met with cheeky, even courageous responses to these conditions, was often reflected in the names. Thus, some papers gloried in the challenges posed by the CCC and contributed to the renewed spirit of "can do" characteristic of the Corps. The sheet of Company 2541, at Kirkland, Arizona, was certain that the CCC was the *Depression Cure*, as its title suggested. The new spirit was also trumpeted in Broken Arrow, Oklahoma, by Company 887's *We-kan-tak-it*, a reference to the CCC's motto, while in Meyers Falls, Washington, Company 602 called its paper *Upanatem*. The *Backbonian* (Company 2366, Swanton, Maryland) similarly manifested a positive attitude, and Company 5463 of Greentown, Pennsylvania, well knew where all the renewed vitality could lead: *The Promised Land-er* held out hope for a bright future for the nation.

The 1930s were dust bowl days which were alluded to in some of the titles as in *Gusts O'Dust* (Company 3827, Springfield, Colorado), located at the heart of that state's dust bowl, and *The Sandpaper*, Company 3811's paper produced in equally dusty Lamesa, Texas. The

In Fayetteville, Tennessee, Company 5428's *The Lighthouse* was one of many camp papers that bore that name.

Erosioneer (Company 1752, Eldora, Iowa) pointed out the effects of the interminable blowing away of the nation's top soil. There were other explanations for titles. *The Wise Quacker*, the paper of Company 952, Brigham City, Utah, was so called because the outfit worked at the Bear River Migratory Bird Reserve. Another company engaged in conservation work, Company 1276 at Hackettstown, New Jersey, called its sheet *The Spawn*, because the company's main job was with a fish hatchery. Another "what's in a name" involved Indian lore. *Thor-Shun* (Company 908, Trona, California) at the Death Valley National Monument, took its name from an Indian word meaning "sunrise."

Some titles reflected historical and literary themes, as did the *Myles Standish News* (Company 103 in Plymouth, Massachusetts); *The Lee-Grant Surrender* (Company 2391 in Appomattox, Virginia); the *Tom Sawyer Journal* (Company 1743, Florida, Missouri); *Tobacco Road* (Company 1156, Chicopee Falls, Massachusetts); *Uncle Sam's Cabin* (Company 3545, Pathfork, Kentucky); and the *Poe Valley Ravin'* (Company 1333, in Coburn, Pennsylvania). Other aspects of the national culture were referenced, as in *Ozark Revener* (Company 1712, Kaiser, Missouri), and *The Captain and the Kids* (Company 374, Cleveland, Virginia).Some names were rather suggestive, even raunchy: *The Hand Shaker* (Company 1162, Ricker Mills, Vermont), which referred to "brown nosing," often said to be a common characteristic throughout CCC life; *The Dixey Doxey* (Company 486, Potts Camp, Mississippi); the *Tally Wacker* (Company 4446, Wilma, Florida); not to mention *The Du Du* (Company 1254, New Augusta, Mississippi).

Beyond their names, considerable attention was given to formulating editorial policies, mottoes and slogans. Walter M. Bury, editor of *The Mocking Bird* (Company 669, Manistique, Michigan), acknowledged that his paper was "not a great city daily with broad, screaming headlines, many pages, scores of pictures, and covered with advertisements, but to us in our forest-surrounded camp, *The Mocking Bird* is to be more or less just what its name signifies. To mock, as does the bird bearing that name, is to reflect, echo, or throw back. In a way, that is what our paper is intended to do." Equally low-keyed was *The Windjammer* (Company 3735, Centerville, Missouri), which shunned such high-flown goals as that of tearing "the scales of blindness from the eyes of justice," the "suppression of tyranny," or mottos such as "with an eye to the right, a hand to the weak, and an ear to the Voice of the Suppressed." Rather, its aims were more modest, and "this twice-a-month struggle," would adopt the simpler procedure of calling "a spade a spade, a shovel a shovel," and, "using no asterisks," would "treat the truth with as much consideration as is convenient."

The Myles Standish News (Company 103, Myles Standish Forest, Plymouth, Massachusetts) did not wish intentionally to hurt anyone's feelings and accordingly, "upon personal matters the *News* will not infringe. However, under no condition will we disregard news that is news," which *Happy Days* thought was a policy "worthy of any newspaper that wants to be a real newspaper."[22] *Hi-De-Hi-De-Ho*, the cheerful paper of Company 4487, a black outfit at Anderson, South Carolina, rather light-heartedly sought "to spread a little laughter, [and] hope [that] it will serve as a vent to our emotions which are sometimes sarcastic, sometimes sad and sometimes happy. It is not copyrighted, not even in Scandinavia, and may be translated into any foreign language including esperanto, without permission."

Many of the papers adopted mottos and slogans, as well as stated policies, which were indicative of what they believed in or cherished, sometimes cast in a humorous vein. In Hillsboro, Ohio, Company 1575's paper, *Rumors*, sought to print "All the rumors fit to print." The *Gallagher Community Weekly* (Company 291, Grimes Pass, Idaho) took pride in its pungent, no-nonsense motto, "Down with Nice Nellieism." *The Peacocker* (Company 1686, Peacock, Michigan) stated that it was "the unofficial and irresponsible publication of Company 1686," and was "entered at the post office as fourth class literature, third class reading matter, second class news and first class scandal." The new *Dugout* (Company 1678, Des Plaines, Illinois) declared that it would not "appoint any colonels nor confer any degrees," while *The Boulder Dam Beacon*, a joint paper of the twin camps occupied by Company 573 and also 2356 in Boulder City, Nevada, took pride in its cheery motto, "The Happiest Camp in the West ... By a Dam Site."

Wittingly or not, certain traditions in American journalism, venerable or otherwise, were sometimes manifested in the camp newspapers. One involved the paper, *The Weekly Call* of Company 1240, which published its 16th issue on board the troop train which carried the company and Company 1246 to Death Valley, California. Previously, it had been the nation's highest CCC camp paper in elevation when it was produced at 12,250 feet at Camp Granite Peak, in Glacier National Park. In its newest location, the paper was renamed the *Death Valley Daze*, and then, at 120 feet below sea level, styled itself "the lowest newspaper in the world." The four-page mimeographed paper thereupon "served the lowest enrollees and the lowest army officers, all of which were lower down than any of their kind in the western hemisphere," the paper proudly asserted.[23] Another paper, appropriately named *The Rambler* (Company 604, of Lowell, Idaho), noted that it was indeed a wanderer. When the outfit was being moved from California to Idaho, the editor busily wrote up an account of the trip, and printed and distributed the paper while the train was en route. These papers' careers recall the odyssey of the *Memphis Appeal* that wandered through the South on board trains in Civil War days. Also harkening back to the Civil War era, *The Little America Flash* (Company 1594, Kurtz, Indiana) used wallpaper, if not for the pages, at least for its covers, which were described as "arty, neat, attractive and different." One wonders if the editors were aware that wallpaper had served some papers, notably *The Daily Citizen* of Vicksburg, Mississippi, as newsprint during the Civil War when paper was in short supply. On another historical note, in Zaleski, Onio, Company 507 decided to upgrade their paper, *Forest Echoes.* They gave up their mimeograph machine in favor of an ancient Washington Press. In mastering it, the paper's staff learned much about earlier methods of putting out a paper, "harkening back to a time when the local publisher was his own reporter, editor, typesetter and pressman."

Elements of continuity were manifested in other ways. Editor DeWitt T. Greenshaw of Company 1826, a veteran's outfit, had been on the staff of the famous American Expeditionary Forces' paper, *The Stars and Stripes,* and no doubt drew upon his experience in editing the company's paper, *The Alibi.*[24] However, the vets of Company 2431, in Lillington, North Carolina, parodied the title of the venerable doughboy sheet, calling their own the *Scars and Gripes.*

The Chieftain, put out by Indian enrollees of the Kiowa Agency at Fort Cobb, Oklahoma, suggests another historical milestone.[25] Though the paper was in English, it harkened back to the time when Shawnee Indians and others of the same area of Oklahoma, in the 1830s and 1840s, had produced the *Shawnee Sun (Siwinowe Kesibwi)* in the native language.

2

The Camp Paper— Operations

Our Paper
Our paper isn't like a deed or draft,
It's a thing we call our own.
With much good sense, and many laughs
Those sheets from off the mimeograph
How dear they have grown.
—Avery John Moffet, the *Stockade*,
Company 2328, Shelocta, Pennsylvania,
January 1938

From early in the paper's history, *Happy Days* devoted considerable time and attention to the camp newspapers, perhaps one of its most enduring undertakings, persisting to near the end of its nine-year career. It sought in numerous ways to assist the camp editors in bringing out the myriad publications that flourished throughout the CCC. By early 1937, about 80 percent of the 2,095 camps published a paper, or about 1,677. Some 50 to 60 of these were printed; the remainder were mimeographed. Four hundred and eighteen other companies did not have a paper.[1]

To start with, *Happy Days* discussed how the camp paper should be established and operated. Reminiscent of an old standard theme of movies and plays, "Let's Put on a Show," a similar question seemed relevant: "Let's Have a Camp Paper." In a series of articles, *Happy Days* outlined the publication steps of a typical, though mythical paper, indicating how it might be created, a staff recruited, and how it should proceed. Continuing for many weeks, would-be camp editors were carried step by step through the process.[2]

Happy Days' efforts were supplemented by elicited views from educational advisers and staffers of the camp newspapers. One adviser, Ben Solomon of Peekskill, New York, thought that the paper should mirror camp activities and the lives of the enrollees. "Too often the officers and advisers do most of the work, most of the thinking and very little of what the enrollees think is visible in the printed result," he argued. The commanding officer of Company 763 in Tecumseh, Nebraska, put the matter succiently in the company's paper, *The Tecumseh Scout*, insisting that it was to be "of the men, by the men and for the men."[3]

Successful camp editors likewise instructed their peers. Jack R. Freiday, the outstanding editor of *The Barracks Bag* (Company 2612, Naperville, Illinois), felt that the "camp paper must be humorous, or educational or thought-provoking," though "the greatest of these is probably humor," he concluded. Lee Evans, editor of *Shell Shocks* (Company 1572, Lebanon, Ohio) concurred, also believing in "good will and good humor." "Since we are full grown men—we hope—our gags may be lusty and at times even salty, yet off-color humor or anything smacking of vulgarity cannot be accepted." This was necessary because "each month many copies may go into the mails; our families read it, and our friends," and at all costs, these must not be made ashamed. Evans also touched on one perennial trouble spot, asserting that "it is our job to waken and revive [the readers] and in so doing we believe our material should be, in so far as possible, original." He further insisted that material derived from other sources be properly credited. *Happy Days* agreed, observing "we'd like to see camp papers use their own stuff. There's no fun in copying somebody's ideas and thoughts. There's no training to be gained by that procedure."[4] Harry Smith, editor of *The Bald Eagle Scream* (Company 1394, Weikert, Pennsylvania), was of the opinion that the camp paper should also develop a "love and devotion for our country and loyalty to those who that land has entrusted with positions of authority." At the same time, publications should encourage artistic talent in the literary and art fields. *Scraps 'N' Stuff* (Company 297, Heppner, Oregon) declared that it would print "cartoons, articles, poetry, satire, art, scraps, music, junk, bunk, and hooey."[5] *The Pyramid* (Company 698, Marion, Illinois) considered whether it should emphasize "Pearls or Ballyhoo?" It was to the credit of the camp, the editor averred, that many enrollees protested the use of too much ballyhoo and wanted more serious reporting. Accordingly, the paper would include some of both.[6]

To further assist in the debate and discussion, *Happy Days* also maintained regular columns devoted to the camp papers. In its December 1933 issue, "The CCC Press" feature was launched. Another early ven-

Many CCC camp papers featured humorous cartoon covers. This one adorned the January, 1939 issue of the *Camel's Hump Barracks Bag* (Company 191, Waterbury, Vermont).

ture was an editorial, "Hints To News-Hounds," containing detailed suggestions about newspapering. This was followed by ongoing columns such as "The Reporter" and "Reviewing New Camp Papers" among others. In the column, "Say the Camp Editors," these scribes were encouraged to send in details as to how their papers were produced and also what they thought about news and other matters. What was sought was dialogue and discussion.[7]

When camp paper editors themselves asked for advice as to how to produce better publications, *Happy Days* responded with the columns, "The Camp Paper," the better-focused "They Asked for This," and later, borrowing a common newsman's term, "The Hell Box." These features were packed with helpful critiques of the camp sheets, often pulling no punches. In general, *Happy Days* observed, too many papers passed up worthwhile news of the camp and devoted their space rather to "almost meaningless items." Humor and personality notes had a place but "should not have all of it." Staffs were urged to spend more time in "digging up the news." More pointedly, some editors were directly assailed: "We don't need much space to criticize your paper, Frank Barone, Company 1229, Republic, Washington.... There isn't very much to say about the *McCann Creek Rippler*, except that we don't like that fancy hand-lettering you used for the headline. Plain letters are much better. It's a newspaper you're printing, not a church program. And you'd better put some larger heads on the inside pages, too, if you want any bouquets from us."[8] *The Petrified Log* (Company 831, Holbrook Arizona) was judged even more harshly: "The entire paper is in need of a complete revamping. It lacks general news, make-up is poor, and the reproduction, likewise. Seems to us that the staff doesn't take much time in publishing the paper."

There were redeeming features for another "terribly printed 4-page daily," the *Educational Department News* (Company 3532, Missouri Branch, West Virginia), which nevertheless earned "our cheers," *Happy Days* declared, because each issue got better, "and any group of men willing to work and sweat to get out a camp daily by themselves deserves a hand."[9] Nonetheless, certain recurring faults were relentlessly excoriated. One was that too many papers appeared with no indication as to company designation, location, and date. These lapses provoked "Shameless Samuel," one *Happy Days* editor who critiqued and discussed the camp papers, to verse: "With vicious thoughts our blurred brain hums/When to our desk a paper comes/Published by some Secretive Scamp/Sans COMP'NY NUMBER, TOWN or CAMP."[10]

Far from resenting sharp criticism, at least some editors were gratified by the attention. When one paper insisted that "a camp paper should be judged only on the basis of its worth to the camp publishing the paper," the editors of the *Frontier* (Company 1256, Moab, Utah)

THE HARD TO GET TYPE

Another "young man's fancy" seemed unattainable, at least to the artist of the cover for *Scraps 'n' Stuff* (Company 297, Heppner, Oregon) for the April 1938 issue. This newspaper also boasted an impressive agenda, as its list of contents suggests.

responded that the competition and comparison engendered by *Happy Days'* efforts were "the two first steps toward perfection. Were there no competitive spirit upon which to build—there would be no need for a camp paper."[11]

Predictably, other staffers were of a different opinion: Vernon Johnson of Company 608 in Glenview, Illinois, a camp paper reporter, was strongly convinced that only "better reporters will make better camp papers," and it was nobody's job to tell another reporter how to write. "According to my experience," he went on, "it can't be done. It should be remembered that a writer clings to his individual style, just as an artist uses the same technique in every painting."[12] Yet *Happy Days* justified its stance, observing that "if you think that our criticism is too severe, remember that it is for your benefit."[13]

Sometimes *Happy Days* encouraged "a fair exchange of constructive criticism between editors": "It's a lot of fun slinging it back and forth," the editor of "The Camp Newspaper" column once asserted. "If you've got something on your mind, spill it." Space would be reserved for any editor "who want[ed] to start something." The subject must, however, be the camp newspaper or the camps themselves. Taking *Happy Days* seriously, one camp paper recorded "how superbly lifted are our spirits when we receive (thru no fault of our own) a copy of the latest _____. By taking one good look at such a dingy paper, ... the staff forgets its weary bones and aching backs, and breaks into peals of laughter and hilarity at somebody's feeble attempt to put out something that might resemble a camp paper." Further ridicule followed, with the observation "that the paper you're putting out won't burn very readily. If you won't change the type of paper, we'll have to find some other use for the copies we receive." *Happy Days* hoped that no one was offended by the comments, which, in truth, "were pretty cheap."[14]

Following other controversies, Herb Harris, the editor at *Happy Days* then working with the camp papers, had had enough, and requested that "please, you hundreds of editors reading this, let's not have any more feuds.... If you must have criticism and must have it quickly, drop us a line and we'll do our best to produce a privately written reply." This seemed especially appropriate when the nation went to war after Pearl Harbor, and Harris hoped that in the future, criticism might "be more gentle than in the past."[15]

The means devised by *Happy Days* to encourage the publishers of camp papers that attracted the most attention and elicited the most comment was a so-called star rating system, though it was some time in evolving. One of the early ventures in rating the camp papers was the First Annual Camp Newspaper Contest, launched in an article in its March 24, 1934 issue. The papers were placed into two classes: camp papers and district publications. They were judged on news coverage, writing, make-up, art work, quality of printing or mimeographing, choice of type faces, choice and writing of heads, the use of halftones and line cuts, and quality of their reproduction.[16]

Then, in the November 23, 1935, issue *Happy Days* launched the star system, which enlivened things considerably. Stars were awarded on a scale of one through four, the results being published in the new "How They Stand" column which now became the center of attention of camp newspaper editors. Another column, "We Liked, This Week," praising the best of camp papers supplemented it. The papers were selected on the basis of what was regarded as successful according to the accepted canons of sound journalism practices including technical matters but also regarding well-balanced, interesting content, attractive makeup, and how effectively the papers communicated. The first paper to attain four stars was *The District Herald* (Ft. Lewis, Washington).

In the May 16, 1936, issue of *Happy Days*, the system was refined. Subsequently, the mimeographed and press-printed camp papers were ranked separately. Other changes followed, most notably in the March 5, 1938, issue of *Happy Days*, when it was announced that five stars would henceforth be the highest rating possible for mimeographed papers, though printed papers could only attain a four-star rating, thus better rewarding the mimeograhed papers favored by *Happy Days*.[17] Certainly *Happy Days* had raised the attainment bar to quite high levels, and the camp papers were well aware what the distinction represented. Subsequently, when a paper attained a five-star rating there was rejoicing in the fortunate camp, and sometimes a banquet was held to celebrate. Ed Chapin, editor of *The Camp Crowder Courier* (Company 773, Trenton, Missouri), acknowledged that "it was the thrill of a lifetime when I finally hit the five-star group. Don't ever let any editor convince you that he doesn't care what rating he makes. All of them would practically give their right arms for five stars. It can be reached only thru hard work and ingenuity."[18]

Nevertheless, some camp editors questioned whether *Happy Days* should be evaluating the papers in this fashion. The editor of *The Indian Trail* (Company 728, Salem, Missouri), for one, was of the opinion that the ratings only reflected the national paper's own standards, which did not perhaps indicate "the value of a particular paper to its particular camp." *Happy Days* was in no position to judge these things, the editor went on. Certainly, *The Indian Trail* worked hard to bring out the best paper possible, stars or no stars, allowing members of the camp to be the final judges. However, "as long as the American people are as they are, we suppose ratings will have to be continued in order to satisfy the vanity of the proletariat," he ruefully admitted.[19] Whatever the merits of the system, which underwent further refinements over the years, the "How They Stand" column was avidly read by camp editors throughout the country.[20]

Happy Days also employed other methods to evaluate and rate the CCC press. For several years, semi-annual "roundups" identified the "cream of the crop of CCC journalism."[21] Then "The Hell Box," in the January 15, 1938, issue of *Happy Days*, "rashly set forth nominations" for a "somewhat dubious journalistic hall of fame" for camp papers appearing from July 1937 to January 1938. This reappeared in the June 18, 1938, and January 21, 1939, issues, apparently undertaken by "Shameless Samuel."

Rather strikingly though perhaps predictably, numerous papers, editors, artists and cartoonists were repeatedly selected for honors. These ranged from *The Quill* (Company 578, Clearfield, Kentucky), often cited for makeup; *Hoy-La* (Company 985, Santa Barbara, California) for the best cover art; while the *Heppner Round-up* (Company 297, Heppner, Oregon) was declared to be the most original sheet. The *Daily Kickapoojian*, (Company 1604, Gays Mills, Wisconsin) was judged the best daily. Often winning for best news style was the *Tabloid Owl* (Company 909, Highland, California). One of the best veterans' papers, guided by one of the CCC's foremost editors, Lee Evans, was the *Vet's Call* (Company 2713, Fairfax, Minnesota). *Hooey* (Company 553, Defiance, Ohio) was considered the most entertaining. Bob Morin, editor of *The Sullivanite* (Company 719, Brimson, Minnesota) and Leonard Lindstrom, of the *Seagullite* (Company 3709, Grand Marais, Minnesota), were given the nod as best editors. The best black papers included *The Big Apple Gazette* (Company 246, Panama, New York) and *The Muskingum Totem*, the "perpetual five-star monthly" of Company 1521, Zanesville, Ohio.

But by all accounts, the paper with the "most spice" was the *Swan Lake Splashes* (Company 1727, Sumner, Missouri). It had also "caused more furor among other editors than any other." While it was not necessarily the best monthly, it was perhaps "the most widely read" by rival editors. It had been the center of heated controversy in numerous camps because, among other things, it had raised fundamental questions as to the purpose of the camp paper. Its critics felt that it evinced too light a touch and that it had not served as "a constructive force in camp life." Its defenders countered that all dull "morale building" copy should be thrown out and papers should in fact concentrate on "being amusing."

Another roundup appeared in the April 12, 1941, issue, by which time "Shameless Samuel" had been replaced by "Fearless Freddie." Arguing that the papers were "just too good to be singled out," and that the competition was too tough, Freddie bemoaned his "thankless job," asserting that he would presume only to select some good examples. He generally

Yellow Springs, Ohio August 28, 1937 Vol. IV, No. 6

Dog Daze!

CCC CAMP SP-16, JOHN BRYAN STATE PARK

Hooey (Company 553, Yellow Springs, Ohio) was one of the CCC's outstanding camp papers. Its clever covers were a staple; the one for August 28, 1937, conjures up the lazy "dog days" of August.

praised camp journalists for making "terrific strides," observing that "one of the most striking features of CCC journalism has been the eagerness of the editors to experiment, to try new layout, new methods of news treatment, novel features and, occasionally, even entire new formats."

MUSKEN

THE NEWS AS IT HAPPENS

GO. 1821   7 \NE=\VILLE. OHIO   SCS-22-0
Volume 1   February 9, 1940   Number 3

Camp To Furnish All Labor To Nursery

Young People's Council Reorganize

Several enrollees were among the thirty-one young people present at the Community Center, Feb. 1, to reorganize the Young People's Council.

(Please turn to page 4)

Company To Give Dance

Camp Muskingum will hold its regular, monthly Company Dance, Friday, February 16.

Plans are being made to recieve a large crowd in view of the successful dance held in January.

Musken Recieves 4 Star Rating

Happy Days, National CCC publication, awarded Musken, this printed newspaper, a 3 star rating on the first issue and a 4 star rating on the second issue.

(Please turn to page 3)

Vast Nursery Program To Use CCC Labor

According to the Camp Nursery authorities, Camp Muskingum will furnish the majority of all labor to be used by the Nursery in their vast program.

Curtailed appropiations make this necessary.

This will be a large responsibility for the camp, and will be a good opportunity to perform a valuable service.

WORK OPENS SOON

As soon as the weather opens up, these operations will go into full swing.

The work will include seeding, lifting, storing counting, and shipping trees that go to five states: Ohio, Indiana, Kentucky, Tennessee and Michigan.

Some papers did not depend on *Happy Days* alone for help. For example, *The Plow Jockey* (Company 1279, Slaterville Springs, New York) improved its articles by correcting, returning and discussing each manuscript with the writer before it was published. Another expedient was tried by a district adviser in Connecticut, James H. Scully, who launched a six-month-long state-wide contest seeking to improve camp papers. The winning paper's staff was "royally feted in Hartford," being treated to dinner, a theater party and a major athletic event.[22]

The editors of *Happy Days* were ever inventive in devising means of instructing, criticizing and encouraging the staffs of the camp papers. For instance, examples of outstanding articles, cartoons, drawings, and front covers appearing in selected camp papers were often reproduced in *Happy Days* as guides, as well as to help fill its own columns. Also recognizing that attention to makeup "can save a paper's face as well as a girl's face," perhaps the best way to teach struggling editors about the subject was to suggest good examples from the field which *Happy Days* repeatedly reproduced.[23]

Happy Days sometimes recruited professional journalists to instruct the camp paper staffers. One was Tom Doerer, who had wide experience as a writer and artist for several prominent national newspapers, including the *Baltimore Sun, Baltimore Post, Washington Star,* and the United Feature Syndicate. He wrote and illustrated sports columns for *Happy Days* which included instruction in both writing and drawing.[24]

Happy Days often lectured camp papers on journalism basics and ethics of the trade. For example, camp editors were instructed in the two major methods of news writing, popularly known as the "circular" and the "diminishing" styles. The circular method consisted of introducing the basic story in lead paragraphs and then returning to these facts, adding more color and detail the second time around. The "diminishing" method was simpler, consisting of leading off with the most important facts and continuing to material of lesser significance. As to ethics, editors were advised that they must never divulge their sources without permission. Indeed, they must stick to this fundamental principle, "cost what it may," as "it is the very foundation of that fourth estate to which we, the CCC editors of America, are devoting the sincerest efforts of our lives."[25]

Opposite: **The *Musken* was the printed sheet of another black outfit, Company 1521, Zanesville, Ohio. It was in the format of a *Reader's Digest*–sized publication of which there were several among CCC camp papers. It was published concurrently with the company's mimeographed *Muskingum Totem* and was produced by the camp's job printing class.**

Where publication of any sort exists there is often the question of censorship. The camp newspapers were no exception, and usually an informal self-censorship was in effect. Bryant A. Long, editor of the *A-1 News* (Company 2301, Beltsville, Maryland), explained certain realities regarding the camp papers: "Here's where you're in a different boat from your brother amateurs in civilian life," he declared. "Your paper is usually subsidized, or at least supervised, by the Administration; and you must avoid all criticism of camp officials and of the regulations which they have established, as much as you conscientiously can. It is your duty to show proper respect to the authorities that be." Similarly, *The Catskill Crier* (Company 299, Masonville, New York) once explained that some articles were not printed because each issue of the paper went to Madison Barracks, Washington, headquarters for the Company. Therefore, the CO should be consulted before critical articles were submitted. Nonetheless, censorship was a not a burning issue and the papers were not primarily instruments of control. Educational advisers and others responsible for the papers' appearance were more intent upon the men's expressing themselves as to what life in the CCC meant to them; more interested in encouraging the men simply to write rather than what they should not be writing about.[26]

Consideration for the sensitivity of individual enrollees also dictated restraint. *The Dam Overflow* (Company 297, Loyston, Tennessee) clearly understood this position, and informed its readers that "if you have contributed some material and it has not been published, then it has been censored for some reason or other. Remember, boys, an editor can't publish everything so when you bring in material, make sure that it doesn't hurt somebody's delicate feelings."[27]

In the perennial struggle to fill their pages, camp editors employed endless expedients. Much more having to do with the content of the CCC press will be presented in specific chapters elsewhere in this study. Nonetheless, a general account seems in order here. Camp paper editors demonstrated considerable ingenuity in developing copy. They ran through the gamut of traditional journalism practices but also introduced innovations of their own.

It was common for camp editors to imitate successful newspaper columnists such as Walter Winchell. Indeed, some editors took Winchell seriously. One of these was Bob Morin, editor of *The Sullivanite*, who praised the controversial newsman as "the purest patriot of his day," who should receive the "deepest thanks for his spirited Americanisms and undying patriotic 'push.'" His weekly reminder of "America's democratic beauty," was helping restore faith in the country and a love of its government, Morin went on. His weekly reminders of America as a most desirable place was in glaring contrast to the "autocratic atrocities known as governments across the sea."

But many camp paper editors simply saw Winchell as someone to imitate. *The Black Rocker* (Company 175, Thomaston, Connecticut) published gossip as "Winchelliana," and *The Wamego* (Company 1662, West Branch, Michigan) gloried in the column, "Vulture Winchell," featuring humor about the camp, and *The Nipmuck Sentinel* (Company 174, Stafford Springs, Connecticut) called its camp gossip column, "Walter Winchbull on Bawdway."[28]

Commanding officers and other officials in the camps seemed to some editors to be likely sources of interesting material. *The Weekly Blabber* (Company 1204, Pulaski, New York), for one, was "thrilling the men of the outfit each week" with a column, "The Skipper Says," recounting his experiences in the Army. Another officer, Lieutenant Ray N. Latimer (jg), who had traveled all over the world, wrote well-received accounts of his experiences abroad for *The Spirit of 740* (Company 740, Litchfield, California). *The Blatter* (Company 1556, Brownstown, Indiana) sometimes included an amusing, readable column, "The Old Timer Says," featuring the philosophic comments of one of the "overhead" at the camp. Presented in a smooth, clear style, it was a favorite with readers. *The Elcho Eagle* (Company 657, Elcho, Wisconsin) published a story by Foreman Earl Wallace, "The Man Without a Soul," and another foreman was featured in a one-act play, "Why Foremen Go Crazy," that appeared in *The Moth* (Company 1166, Belcherton, Massachusetts).

It appeared logical to some editors that their papers should include literary fare. In fact, Company 3204 in Johnsonville, New York, decided to publish a separate publication, *The Literary Quarterly*, featuring stories, poems, plays, drawings, essays and articles. S.D. Markman, the company's educational adviser, also contacted several editors of New York magazines and should the stories in the camp magazine show merit, he would attempt to sell them on the enrollees' behalf. This venture was in addition to the company's regular news sheet, *The Co. 3204 Record*.

Other camp papers sought to enhance the men's literary and cultural awareness in other ways. Many featured substantial book review columns as did the *Stockade* (Company 2328, Shelocta, Pennsylvania), which also discussed movies. The *CCCrier* (Company 892, Cooledge, Texas) similarly included an excellent book review column, some of which excerpted pithy paragraphs from various books, challenging readers to identify them. Robert S. Lawrence, an instructor at Company 1529, Jackson, Ohio, wrote a weekly series of articles on American authors for the company's paper, *The Enrollee*.

The Reveille (Company 1605, Dodge, Wisconsin) included provocative features on psychology, one discussing "those two kin folk," heredity and environment. The *Spring Creek Chronicle* of Company 470, Brinson, Georgia, printed a column, "Sayings of Famous Men," featuring Emerson, Carlisle, Franklin and Thoreau. The *Martin's Gap Messenger* (Company 1381, Huntingdon, Pennsylvania) reproduced by request of the enrollees Kipling's poem "If," which other papers also printed. Sometimes books were reprinted in their entirety as when *The Tommy Hawk* (Company 1608, Tomahawk, Wisconsin) serialized the book *Norfleet*, the story of a swindled Texas rancher who brought the five perpetrators to justice, largely by his own efforts.[29]

Because camp newspapers were intended to assist the enrollees, however, it seemed more desirable to tap their creativity, including fiction writing, thus producing some impressive results.[30] One paper which consistently emphasized this approach was the *Stockade* (Company 2328, Shelocta, Pennsylvania), in one instance publishing a continuing story by Paul Gray, one of the paper's reporters, entitled, "Death Haunts the Arctic." Another reporter and poet, John Susko, created a mystery, "Murder Will Out." Another *Stockade* reporter, John Griffiths, wrote a nonfiction but colorful account of the sinking of the *Titanic*, entitled "Lest We Forget," to commemorate the April 14, 1912, disaster. The paper also opened its pages to the company's educational adviser, Howard D. Blank. His short story, "The Advent of Tony Sarge—Palooka of the CCC," was a humorous dialect piece about a fictitious boxer in the CCC.[31]

The *Stockade* was also inclined to lecture the enrollees regarding proper conduct and sometimes used fiction as object lessons. To these ends, Blank wrote a short story, the theme of which was the job interviews of five boys and why all but one failed to obtain employment.[32] Another short story with an object lesson was by Charles Shubra, the paper's editor. His "Preparation Is the Only Passport to Opportunity," was a fictional account of a CCC boy who took the opportunity to study bookkeeping at the camp school which subsequently won him a good job, as well as the girl of his dreams.

Following the theory that one should write what one knows best, camp authors often described the lives and struggles of enrollees. One good example was a novelette about CCC life appearing in *The Eagle* (Company 598, Emlyn, Kentucky). Some stories were serials, as was the case with "Insurrecto," in *The Seven Thirty* (Company 730, Albany, Missouri). Ghost stories were common. A good example was "The Old Dark House" by Bernard Austin Dwyer, published in *The Blue Mountain Survey* (Company 256, Peekskill, New York). A yarn, "Two-Gun Pete," printed in the *Gasquet Gazette* (Company 5478, Crescent City, California), humorously debunked traditional western heroes.

Detectives, "if any," in Company 2598, Hillsboro, West Virginia, were challenged to do some sleuthing by following a serial mystery story in the camp paper, *The Cannon Ball*, entitled, "Murder in Barrack One." Publication of the solution was withheld for a time so that camp's sleuths could attempt to solve the mystery, and win the dollar prize. Readers were also involved by *The Bag Puncher* (Company 301, Masten, Pennsylvania), which ran a "story-ending contest." The editors began the story, which readers were invited to complete.

Industrious newsmen in Company 390, Fort Wadsworth, New York, for the benefit of the busy men at the camp, copied and mimeographed headlines of all important stories found in daily newspapers on separate sheets for camp-wide distribution. When added to brief stories and reports of their own, the innovators found that the men literally "eat them up." Their counterparts in Company 1219, Panama, New York, who regularly published *The Panama Echo,* also infrequently produced a *CCC Camp Newspaper Digest,* using material from other camp papers.[33]

Another preoccupation, appearing more often than might have been imagined in the CCC press, concerned etiquette. *Ka Hui O Mauna Loa,* the weekly paper put out by enrollees in Hawaii National Park on the island of Hawaii, once featured an editorial on the subject of manners. Similarly concerned with proper behaviour, a book, *CCC Manners,* written by Kathleen Black for men in the Ninth Corps Area, was published in serial form by *The Lynx Creek News* (Company 2855, Prescott, Arizona).

The *Camp Logan Log,* of Company 526, Logan, Ohio, featured a column, "Sports Afield," which printed fishing regulations and material on the lore of fishing, as well as news of the rifle and pistol club at camp. A department in the *Shiprock Cry* (Company 847, Fredonia, Arizona) was a full pager called "C-ciety," devoted to interesting camp personalities. A debate designed to enliven the camp paper was carried by *The Axe and Quill* (Company 126, Danbury, New Hampshire): "Camp spirit— we don't have it; we do have it."

There were specialized columns and features, ranging from music discussions to liars contests. For instance, the *Devil's Track Ripples* (Company 2707, Grand Marais, Minnesota) had a column, "Shoot the Bull," reserved especially for big lies. There were crossword puzzles, some devised by ambitious enrollees. Stories about cigarette moochers, as one in the *Cavern Echo* (Company 574, La Hood Park, Montana), discussed the psychology employed by these common pests. *The Mouthpiece* (Company 837, Jemes, New Mexico) ran a series of stories on "Know the Southwest," describing the struggles of early New Mexico settlers. *The Harbinger* published a listing identifying the camp's most popular enrollee, the worst chiseler, best dancer, best looking, crabbiest, biggest show-off, embryo bridegroom, camp Romeo, biggest hick, worst and best dispositions, biggest pest, most bashful, know-it-all, camp "Gable", and others, including the camp "Trotski" and "Mussolini."[34] There were numerous cartoon strips such as the one in *The Red Rocks Echo,* "Another

Morning in the Twig Army."[35] A popular cartoon feature, "Sub Al Tern" was reprinted many times by *Happy Days* during the seven years that its creator was on the staff of the *Northlander* where it originated.

Even women's topics were not ignored. The *Willoughby Whispers* (Company 121, West Burke, Vermont) featured a "sob sister" column, "The Woman's Angle." The *Pick & Shovel* (Company 1829, Temple, Texas) introduced a ladies' page. Herein, the wives of officers and men at the camp were given space in which "to expedite backyard fence gossip, or what have you."

Opinion polls and interviews made their way into camp papers with greater frequency as time went on. The *CCC Defiance* (Company 3515, Defiance, Ohio), for one, posed questions on the desirability of a third term for FDR, the men responding three to one in favor, while three out of five cast votes against military training in the CCC in another survey. Further polling revealed that Company 3515's favorite movie stars were Spencer Tracy, Mickey Rooney and Tyrone Power, while Nancy Kelly was voted the favorite actress. Jack Benny was their favorite radio personality while the best-liked dance bands included Guy Lombardo, Kay Kyser and Wayne King. *Life* was the favorite magazine and Zane Grey and Sinclair Lewis the authors most often read.

The *Life of Riley* (Company 642, Fifield, Wisconsin) recorded that hamburgers were the favorite food of the enrollees in that camp, with stew being the most disliked. Polka music was the most popular, though the specific songs "Sunrise Serenade" and "Three Little Fishes" garnered many votes. *Life* was their most popular magazine with *Look* second. As to sports, baseball came in first, followed by tennis and dancing. Their favorite job or career choice, by a wide margin, was truck driving. Were they to enter the Army, the majority wanted to drive a truck, though many would elect to be a mess steward or warehouseman. *Life Begins At Forty* (Company 4718, Spivey, Kansas), the paper of a veterans' outfit, initiated a "man in the company street" interview series inquiring as to the men's opinions on the approaching war. One veteran, "Tail Spin" Smith, gave his prophetic views: "I expect [that] all of those old mowing machines, headers, old cars and what have you that we sold to Japan a few years ago as junk will be shot back at us in the form of hot iron, and it certainly is going to be nice to have to pick part of that old header you used to run, out of your epidermis."[36] An inquiring reporter for *The Spotlight* (unknown company) wanted to know, "What Has the CCC Done for You?" Some of the men had learned a trade; others were in better health, had encountered "good companionship," learned to conquer obstacles, had nature opened to them, learned how to be "truly independent," while one credited the CCC with rescuing him from the corner gambling house and beer joints. Another concluded that "the

CCCs [are] making history and I feel proud to help shape its destiny."[37] In another searching poll, *The Cottonwood CCC News* (Company 2714, New Ulm, Minnesota) ascertained that half of the company's men would prefer an immediate job rather than have the assurance of $10,000 in 10 years, or even a college education or a steady girl. Education was ranked second in the poll, and only 16 percent voted for a girl. One asserted that if he had a good job, he would not need a college education, could earn the money, and get a girl, as a matter of course. Others concluded, however, that these goals would be more easily attained if a college education was first accomplished.

Camp papers often attempted to assist the enrollees toward some goal. *The Tannersville Tiger* (Company 291, Tannersville, New York) featured a series of studies to aid its members in preparing for exams for membership in "The Finest," the NYC police force. A page, "The Job," was a regular feature for some months in *The Kanona Daze* (Company 297, Kanona, New York), discussing hydraulics, masonry and photography, and how enrollees might prepare for careers in various fields.

Religion was a topic routinely handled by many camp newspapers. *The Bear Facts* (Company 4727, St. Paul, Minnesota) carried a religious column in each issue written by selected religious leaders from throughout the U.S.[38] The *Stockade* (Company 2328, Shelocta, Pennsylvania) also had a "Religion" page featuring the column "Chaplain's Corner" by the Sub-District Chaplain, Paul L. Giegerich, 1st Lt., Chaplain's Reserve. Another chaplain, Edwin Todd, even produced his own one-man paper, the *Chaplain's Weekly News-Letter*, for camps of the Fourth Forestry District.

Medical matters were not neglected. The *Hackamorian* (Company 977, Canby, California) regularly featured the "Pill Box News," with information from the camp infirmary. The *Stockade* (Company 2328, Shelocta, Pennsylvania) had a first aid page, discussing insect bites, stings, poison ivy, and other hazards.[39] *The Eagle* (Company 120, Becket, Massachusetts) published a series of articles on specific diseases, the first, significantly, on syphilis.

There was a long-standing, lively, informative medical column in *The Bugle* (Company 4468, Barnwell, South Carolina), "Sick, Lame, and Lazy," written by the doctor's infirmary assistant in the infirmary, Clifton Red "Doc" Hammond.[40] The *Crystal Camp Crier* also maintained a regular hospital column, "Hospital Notes," which enabled readers to keep abreast of the general health of the camp. When the company was threatened with a spinal meningitis outbreak, a quarantine was put into effect for forty days. Also to help contain the outbreak, the medical department began testing an anti-meningitis serum, the men being used as "human guinea pigs."[41]

Apparently because they might get out of hand, promote radicalism or even revolution, and perhaps because they could not altogether be controlled by Washington, *Happy Days* sometimes discouraged editorial writing. To be sure, they could be stimulating if not provocative. Consider the anonymous one in the *Crystal Camp Crier* (Company 1742, Tarkio, Missouri), which argued that machinery, while wonderful in many ways, was "slowly defeating the World" by causing technological unemployment. If the world wanted to effect an economic recovery, it must think of its human workers rather than promote its "steel robbers," the writer concluded.[42] Uneasily, *Happy Days* counselled camp editors to soft-pedal such editorials: "Let's not be thoughtful souls this year," it once suggested. "Camp editors, alas, are not usually paid for their thoughts. They may get much personal satisfaction out of printing their mental churnings, but (forgive me) the reader doesn't." The *Happy Days* editor advised that "I believe it would be a good thing for editors to forget for a while the more brilliant facets of their minds. Be a little more earthy, less deep." Editors should therefore "shun the editorial ... and seek out the news. Ignore the ecstacy of the brainwave (it makes wrinkles), and strive for the belly laugh."[43] Yet, *Happy Days* was not always consistent on this score, and praised one of the editors of *The Este Ripples* (Company 2759, Roubaix, South Dakota) for making the paper into "one of the best camp publications in the land," largely because of his editorials.[44]

Borrowing from venerable journalism practice, the camp newspapers often brought out special editions and "extras." Facetiously, the *Pinnacle Press* (Company 1262, Mountain Home, Idaho) once issued a special "Gold Brick Number," in honor of the "work-dodgers," the CCC "leisure class." During a time of vast floods, Company 1397, Johnstown, Pennsylvania, published a daily called the *Flood Relief Bulletin*. The one-pager gave up-to-the-minute accounts of the activities of CCC men engaged in flood relief. When men of Company 1524 in Mathias, West Virginia rescued a family from the turbulent waters, their camp paper, *Hardy Life*, put out a two-page "flood extra" giving the details. When fire raged in the late summer of 1936 in parts of Minnesota, the editors of *The Lone Wolf* of Company 714 in Zumbrota, issued a "fire extra." The camp paper, the *Current Camp Crier* (Company 1366, Reading, Pennsylvania), produced a "Quarantine Number" for the men on quarantine for a time. When smallpox invaded Company 1739 in Willow Springs, Missouri, which normally published the *1739er*, a small, temporary daily, *The Smallpoxonian* appeared to help sooth the victims' suffering.

Christmas was a traditional time for special editions which often featured festive, colorful covers, complete with letters to Santa. Regarding the latter, the subaltern, Lt. Edwards of Company 819, Grand Canyon, Arizona, had one of his printed—probably inserted by one of his enrollees—in the *Grand Canyon Echoes*, asking that Santa "Please send me some good CCC boys that can make their beds properly, [and] keep their lockers clean…. As for myself, well, I don't want much—I would like a new car—but not a Ford. Love, Lt. Edwards. P.S. I would like a new doll that has been to college for about two years."[45]

The Catskill Crier's editors saw no reason why the longed-for monthly payday should not have its "extra," and a special "payday" issue featured a cartoon of enrollees staring up at an eagle in a cage waiting for him to "scream," the classic armed forces' formulation denoting payday.[46] Many camp editors published election extras celebrating FDR's reelection in November, 1936. After the success of Jesse Owens in the 1936 Olympic Games in Berlin, the *Camp Lorain Lantern* (Company 3519, Elyria, Ohio) dedicated an issue to him. *The Ottawa Echo* (Company 663, Gibbs City, Michigan) brought out extras to keep its subscribers abreast of the World Series. Extolling the motto, "support the forces for peace," the editors of *Happy Youth* (Company 4440, Forest, Mississippi) published a special issue dedicated to peace. It contained several features on the subject, one recalling the number of men who were killed in World War I. *The Far East Forester* (Company 192, Princeton, Maine) put out a special Hollywood Edition, the cover depicting Jimmy Durante as a baby—nose and all. Sometimes camp papers went all-out to produce a special edition. One was *The Parisonian* (Company 3747, Paris, Missouri), which published a 49-page magazine commemorating the company's second anniversary. The editors bragged that in completing this task, four pounds of purple ink, one-half pound of silver, 15,000 sheets of paper, and 55 stencils were used. Even more ambitiously, *The Round Up*, the paper of the West Texas District, published a 125-page historical edition, mimeographed with inserts of photographs on glazed paper. Bound in bright yellow covers, this edition, produced "after many weeks of burning the proverbial midnight oil," was widely distributed throughout the state. Often camp papers capitalized on "scoops." *The Sequoian* (Company 915, Three Rivers, California) reported that Ernest Hemingway had visited their camp for several days as a paying guest, seeking rest and relaxation. He had recently returned from Spain. "The writer said the CCC food (for which he paid) was equal to that he ate while observing the effects of a Florida hurricane on a veteran transient camp several years ago."[47]

One characteristic of most of the camp papers was a general lack of awareness or interest in foreign affairs. In the July 15, 1934, issue of *The Jubilee Journal,* in the page headed "Summary of World News" there was a facetious reference to "Adolph [sic] (Oh, you Nazi man!) Hitler." Yet, the paper could be more sober regarding the report of Hitler's assuming full power when Hindenburg died in 1934. There seemed to be few illusions as to what this might mean. A bit later, in the January 1938 issue of the *Stockade*, a poem "The Dictator" by Avery John Moffet of Company 2328, Shelocta, Pennsylvania, seemed more aware of the Nazi threat:

> … … … … …
> Fate chose him as her ally;
> Helping her decide who'll die.
> Hate has marked him for her own;
> Who finds glory in power alone.
> … … … … ….

But, the poet concluded: "Death to the dictator/ Glory in his fall/Forward with democracy/Freedom for all."

Nevertheless, these views were hardly widespread, and *The Harbinger* (Company 698, Argyle, Wisconsin), for instance, in its October 1938 issue, about the Czech crisis and FDR's role in it, observed that he had simply addressed cables to the "Big Four," and "they knew after reading his cables just what they ought to do and they did it in a hurry. Again our President did everyone a good turn," certainly a bit simplistic. But perhaps the reasons for the wishful thinking were clarified by William B. Young, the educational adviser of Company 698, in the paper's next issue. Reflecting upon the meaning of Armistice Day, he observed that the world was in abject fear of another colossal war "which would eclipse the World War." The costs would be prohibitive, profitting no one. "But one thing is certain," he declared, "we shall never again be carried away by such illusions as those 20 years ago." Clearly, isolationism and pacificism were alive and well in the CCC camps as elsewhere in America during these days.

And things did not change rapidly, though by 1940 even the camp papers could not entirely ignore the worsening situation abroad. In the February 1940 issue of the *Tamarack Times* there was the usual editorial on Lincoln, but this time there was a difference. The "Spirit of America," which owed so much to Lincoln, was still a force in the world, the paper believed. It seemed appropriate to compare Mussolini's Italy and America: "Italy through Mussolini, demands an increase in birth[s]; he mobilizes a standing army of every man who can possibly fight including youngsters." By contrast, in America there was no mobilization of youth for war, and through the CCC, the administration was teaching trades instead. In order to insure a perpetuation of this state of affairs, the editor of the *Tamarack Times* (Company 297, Priest River, Idaho) urged that the nation "keep clear of European entanglements," so that no future president would have to use the phrase, "for those who here gave their lives that this nation might live," as Lincoln had done at Gettysburg.[48]

It was not until war came to America following Pearl Harbor that the camp papers assumed a wartime stance, and even this came surprisingly slowly. *The Upshot* (Company 1572, St. Paris, Ohio), the paper of a veterans' company, was one of the first to respond to the Japanese attack. In its issue shortly after the war began, the immediate reaction of the men was recorded: "I'd go as a private," one World War captain in the outfit declared, and most of them accepted that while "it may take a little time to find places for us all," they "must insist that we be given our proper share in the essential work which will be the duty of every citizen to perform. It is no time for holding back. Let's get going and going fast. The CCC is ready for action." These views were no doubt common, especially in the veterans' camps.

Another of the camp papers to respond early to the "Jap slap" was the *Poultney Slate* of Company 2142, in Poultney, Vermont. This monthly, "bright with a Christmas cover that is ironic in these times of no peace on earth, was rolling to press with a slim holiday issue when the news sifted thru from Hawaii," the paper reported. This called for a "hastily remade first page," which carried a statement by the company's commanding officer, Cecil H. Winslow. Headed "Keep Your Shirt On," he counselled the men that there were countless rumors circulating, but no official word had been received as to the status of the CCC. "In the meantime it is foolish to lose your head. If you feel that you must enlist at once, don't go AWOL. Come in and talk it over."

Happy Days agreed, warning in the December 20, 1941, issue that "An AWOL that goes in the book against you when you join the armed service is just as black as an AWOL charged up if you run off with a circus for a job watering the elephants." But from the war-imperiled West Coast, *The Daily Voice* (Company 491, Warrenton, Oregon) subsequently shouted its new slogan in each issue: "One More Day Nearer Victory," while in early 1942, the paper of Company 3336 of Snow Hill, Maryland, a veterans' outfit, changed its name to *The Dive Bomber.*

Having at last been forced to face up to the new conditions some camp papers often went to another extreme: exuding platitudes. One was the *Soil Saver News* (Company 735, Moorhead, Iowa), which early in January urged the nation to gird itself for a bitter struggle, while the churches must instruct the youth in the fear and love of God and help train them in willpower for guidance through a time of trials and temptations. The *Barkshanty Echo* (Company 2336, Austin, Pennsylvania) was similarly inclined, and indicated that all Americans must understand that it was a privilege to sacrifice themselves, bury their differences, and pull and work together, "and remain a shining example of democracy to all the world."[49] Herb Harris, the *Happy Days* editor concerned with the camp papers, was preoccupied with technical matters, urging staffs to continue the papers even in face of paper shortages, making them smaller "but better." They should print on both sides of the paper, for instance, and shun pure "filler," only printing the "best news." They could also eliminate the covers, and reduce their circulation, perhaps to a dozen copies in each barracks and in the camp library.[50]

Yet, for the most part in the new wartime climate, *Happy Days* plainly tired of the camp newspapers. Its criticisms and suggestions became tepid and half-hearted, one commentator simply asserting that the papers in the CCC camps "are growing increasingly more handsome." This indifference in part reflected the fact that many camp paper staffers were by then in the military, some of whom reappeared on the staffs of the newspapers that proliferated in the U.S. armed forces. Among these was the former artist of the *Northlander*, Eddie Mallonen, who turned up at the *The Lock Guard*, publication of the 702nd Military Police unit at Ft. Bradley, Michigan.[51] Another was Billy Bridwell, a camp paper artist who had earlier served the *Arm for News* in Boise, Idaho, and the *Tree Top Tattlers* (unknown company), who emerged on the art staff of the *Rip Cord*, the weekly of McChord Field, Washington. In this way, the experience of the camp papers contributed to the development of the American military press in World War II.

By May 1942, *Happy Days* only rarely rated the CCC papers, though Herb Harris thought it might be of interest to compare the CCC papers with the embryonic Army sheets. Noting that "our intent is not to shatter morale in the nation's Army posts," nevertheless, he candidly stated, "the blunt truth of the matter is that CCC journalism is superior to the mimeographed product of the old cousins in khaki." Subjected to "the same acid test of our torture chamber, fewer Army publications made the five-star grade than camp papers," he concluded. By the time the July 18, 1942, issue of *Happy Days* appeared, however, the column "The Army Press" had supplanted those devoted to the camp papers, which subsequently, for a time at least, were relegated to history's dusty archives.

3

Happy Days—
The National Annals
of the CCC

"The history of *Happy Days* is the history of the CCC. No organization ever had a better organ. Readable and entertaining, it presents news of Corps interest fairly and impartially. Its files are a record of everything of importance that ever vitally concerned the CCC."
— *The Seagullite* (Company 3709,
Grand Marais, Minnesota),
April 25, 1939

The camp newspapers frequently followed the lead of the remarkable national weekly publication, *Happy Days*.[1] A felicitous choice, the title was no doubt inspired by FDR's political theme song, "Happy Days Are Here Again," and it struck a positive chord of hope for all associated with the new organization. As its masthead declared, it was "an independent national newspaper, published every Saturday, in the interest of the Civilian Conservation Corps. It is neither financed by the government, nor circumscribed by governmental dictation. Opinions, when expressed, and not otherwise credited, are those of the editors and do not necessarily reflect opinions of others. Views credited to others are not necessarily those of the editors."[2] Though a private professional venture, the paper was officially authorized, and effectively served as the semi-official voice of the CCC. Widely circulated in all the CCC camps, it was launched on May 20, 1933, about a month following the creation of the Corps, when Volume 1, Number 1 appeared with 12 pages in a five-column printed format. By the autumn of 1934, *Happy Days* had expanded to 20 pages and a bit later, 24.

Its owners were Melvin Ryder, the paper's editor, and Ray Hoyt, the managing editor, both of Washington, D.C.; and the paper's business manager, Theodore Arter, Jr., of Altoona, Pennsylvania. The circulation manager was Lester Lear. Ryder, a regimental sergeant major in the American Expeditionary Forces in France during World War I, had been on the staff—in the circulation department—of the famous, venerable doughboy newspaper, *The Stars and Stripes*. With his knowledge of what men in uniform desired in their newspapers, he was ideally suited to make an instant success of the paper.

The new paper was published by the Happy Days Publishing Company. Its offices were initially located in the National Press Building in Washington, D.C., but were moved in March 1935 to the more modern newspaper building of *The Washington Daily News*, where the paper was already being printed. By July 1933, the paper was printing 500,000 copies per week. The cost of a copy was five cents, three cents in the camps, or one could subscribe for six months for one dollar. The paper was also on sale in all CCC camps and in company exchanges. Some companies ordered several copies per week for their camp libraries or reading rooms. A special form was included in the paper for use by enrollees desiring to send it home to "let the home folks—and the best girl" read it.

Sensing new business opportunities, *Happy Days* branched out into merchandising. Hoyt later wrote a widely circulated, popular book, "*We Can Take It": A Short Story of the C.C.C.*, which he sold through the paper's office. *Happy Days* eventually offered numerous accouterments, souvenirs, and other items for sale. Specially printed books, such as the *Happy Days Cartoons of the C.C.C.*, featuring the art of Wally Wallgren, Grant Powers and Ray Evans, were popular.[3] CCC pennants, various CCC jewelry items, postcard photographs of many of the camps, and much else was available.

Happy Days advanced itself as a model worth imitating by other CCC camp newspapers. It avowed in its initial issue that it had no formal policy, "as other newspapers have, … except the honest policy of being of [good] cheer and giving you the dope." The editors requested letters from the readers, because it "is YOUR paper," and asked for criticisms, because "we can take 'um on the chin."[4] The paper's tone was therefore invariably upbeat and strongly supported the CCC administration's goals. Columns such as "Smiles" and "Toothpicks and Splinters" as well as letters from readers, built upon *The Stars and Stripes'* proven formula of accentuating the positive, but at the same time allowing gripes to be aired and shortcomings to be discussed—though always within limits. This stance and attitude prevailed throughout most of the paper's lengthy career.[5] *Happy Days* ended in August 1942 in an entirely different era, with America at war.

Meanwhile, asking "Brother Can You Spare a Rhyme?", the paper planned to print the best poems of the enrollees, paying five dollars for each one accepted. Soon inundated with responses, the column "Sing You Sinners!", lasting for several years, accommodated aspiring company poets. Though poetry declined in importance in later years, there were always venues for poems. Other poetry columns included "Rhyme and Reason," "Bards in the Woods," and "A Notion of Poetry."[6]

Happy Days also often paid small sums—usually a dollar—for other contributions from enrollees, such as inventions that the men might propose. "For instance," one offer suggested, "if you invent a way to peel potatoes with one hand—or to keep from falling down hill—or to find your way through the woods in the dark," then the paper wanted to know about them.[7]

Regarding potatoes, one is reminded how destitute many people were as the Depression years rolled along. *Happy Days* frequently had much to report about food and how the famished enrollees enjoyed their chow, as well as recording the rapid weight gains that they made. As the second issue of the paper exulted, "Happy Days are here again, we're eating regularly again," and there could only be rejoicing that "that Old Spanish Custom"—eating—had been revived by the CCC.[8] The food, never gourmet, was plentiful and wholesome and generally well prepared, though there were instances of food riots in several camps in years to come. Subsequently, one of the staples of all camp newspapers was the routine printing of detailed holiday menus, as on Thanksgiving Day and Christmas, with commentary on the splendor of the feasts as cooks "pulled out all the stops."

Happy Days, also recognizing that cooks could use some help in purchasing and preparing food for about 200 men, printed suggestions to these ends. In the October 19, 1935, issue, the column "Mess Talk" first appeared. Similar columns included "'Rudy's' Recipes" by Rudolph F. Tschann of Company 3710, Houston, Minnesota, and "CCC Messkit Talks" by "The Old Timer." These normally included recipes and menus based on a 10-day cycle which many camps adopted as a guide for the preparation of their meals.

There was a full complement of cartoons in *Happy Days*. For the first few issues, Ryder drew upon the services of two cartoonists who had been on the staff of *The Stars and Stripes* in France during World War I: A.A. "Wally" Wallgren and Cyrus Leroy Baldridge. Baldridge's first cartoon was "Peeling Spuds," which established some continuity with the World War I military experience remembered by many veterans, that of KP or "kitchen police," sometimes defined as "disrobing potatoes."[9] However, the paper soon employed other cartoonists such as Grant Powers and Ray Evans, many becoming quite skilled and inventive, and the veteran cartoonists withdrew. By early 1935, a continuing comic strip by T.A. Reynolds of Company 305 in Richmond Furnace, Pennsylvania, entitled "Balmy," was introduced. Reminiscent of Joe Palooka, it featured a CCC enrollee and his adventures.

Some of the men who contributed to *Happy Days* were co-opted by the paper. One of these was Marshall Davis, a CCC enrollee who had served as a supply man and storekeeper of Company 1253, Fort Barrancas, Pensacola, Florida. He joined the paper as staff cartoonist, and later had a long and profitable career in cartooning outside the CCC.[10] Other cartoon strips contributed by enrollees included "Curly" by "Zig," and "Slats McGee" by "Hoover and Cade." "Zig" also at times presented a cartoon feature "Odd But True," after the fashion of the ubiquitous Ripley, who was quite popular in 1930s America.[11] By the spring of 1939, Chap Chapman's cartoon strip "The Nutsy Newsreel," featuring "The CCC in Ticklecolor," appeared regularly in the paper.

There was a sports page in *Happy Days* from the outset, with Jerry Dean as the first sports editor. In addition to its usual sports columns, "The Press Box" was launched in the March 17, 1934, issue. This consisted of a series of baseball articles written by David S. Swerdlow, member of Company 269, Miami, Florida, describing the activities of the major clubs in spring training in the state. A later baseball column called "Dust and Diamonds" was written by "Dugout Dan." Beginning in its July 2, 1938, issue, a 12-part series on "How to Play Baseball" was initiated.[12] "The Press Box" was later replaced by "Thru the Knothole," supplemented by yet another column, "From the Stands."

One of the most popular sports throughout the CCC was boxing, which was featured in the column, "Hooks and Jabs." Notably, some camps used the sport as a means of establishing ties with local communities to their mutual benefit. One of these was Company 1204 at Pulaski, New York, which opened its boxing events to the general public at "two bits" a ticket, which proved a considerable "draw."[13]

Other sports were discussed in their own columns. One was "Pigskin Patter"; another was "Sideline Stuff," both reflecting the growing popularity of football, no longer simply regarded as "the sole possession of the Yales and the Harvards." William T. Tilden II was enlisted to contribute to a 12-part series on tennis. Basketball was followed in the columns "Net Results."

There is no doubt where *Happy Days* stood regarding authority—it strongly supported those in charge. In early February 1934, a column "The Brass Hat," featuring news of military officers assigned to the CCC, began. "Sky Pilots in the CCC" was a column for the chaplains, the "circuit riding sky pilots," or "Holy Joes," as they were sometimes rather irreverently called, especially in the veterans' companies. Written by Col. Alva J. Brasted, Chief of Army Chaplains, it featured homilies, such as the one in the July 6, 1935, issue, which emphasized teamwork and the fact that "we are laborers together with God." In later issues, other columns such as "Chaplain's Chats" and "Little Stories from the Bible" were introduced. Thus religion's star was hitched to the CCC.[14]

FDR came in for a large measure of praise in the CCC, much of it heartfelt. His picture often appeared on the covers of camp papers, and *Happy Days* closely followed his genuine interest in the new organization, obviously one of his favorite creations. Lyman Husted of Company 221 at Fort Hancock, New Jersey, in "The 221st Company Psalm," captured something of this special attitude toward the president:

> Roosevelt's my shepherd; I shall not want:
> He maketh me to lie down on straw mattresses;
> He leadeth me inside a mess hall;
> He restoreth to me a job.[15]

Along the same lines, a letter in *Happy Days* asserted: "I thank all those who voted Roosevelt in, because this world was about to come to an end. I vote that our honorable President keeps his seat until Gabriel blows his trumpet."[16] In addition, many of the camp papers, as well as *Happy Days*, had a common desire to honor earlier leaders of the nation, especially Washington and Lincoln. They were prominently featured, especially on covers of the February issues of the papers, and it was *de rigueur* for editorials to commemorate them in traditional ways.

Related to authority was the issue of discipline which had to be addressed. The men were admonished in an editorial in the paper's first issue that "discipline does not necessarily mean giving up our rights—more often it brings a fuller enjoyment of our rights." FDR set the matter in a broader context, noting that "this great group of men have entered upon their work on a purely voluntary basis, with no military training and we are conserving not only our national resources but our human resources." Similarly, Robert Fechner, the CCC Director, observed that, "you are workers. You are not the objects of charity, nor are you in any respect a part of the U.S. Army. You have been given jobs by the federal and state governments to do work that needs to be done." In addition, the men were being given an opportunity of finding themselves, and therefore, "you have been sent into the forests not to just chop around with no effective aim toward a definite accomplishment."

Desertion was another serious perennial problem facing the CCC which *Happy Days* often discussed. Many men became homesick and simply went AWOL. To cope with this "first battle of [the] conservation army," an editorial hoped to convince doubtful enrollees that "to live in the woods with two hundred other men for six months or longer is an experience which relatively few men have enjoyed."[17]

Most CCC papers, following the lead of *Happy Days*, devoted considerable space to safety matters, much of which will be discussed in a separate chapter below. Health was another perennial subject of interest. Diseases, including "the venereal menace," threatening "damaged lives," were usually discussed in articles by camp doctors, appearing both in *Happy Days* and various camp papers. Typical was the feature, "El Medico," co-edited by 1st Lt. Martin Leichter of the Medical Reserve, U.S. Army, and Phillip Ray Rodgers of Company 1965, Green River, Wyoming. It included odd medical facts, safety hints, questions and answers and "those funny expressions heard around the Hospital or camp pertaining to medical care."

The camp papers, reflecting *Happy Days*, also manifested an interest in current trends such as developments in aviation, radio, photography and other advancements, especially in the scientific and technical fields. For instance, the column, "Dots and Dashes," listed CCC ham radio operators with their call signs. Another, appearing for some time in mid–1939 about a favorite pursuit of the CCC, was "Behind the Lens," a "how to" photography column by an expert, Joseph Modlens.

The papers also reveal the pros and cons of the political discussions involving the CCC that waxed and waned in this period. In fact, despite the organization's success, opposition often surfaced. Not everyone in America, after all, supported FDR and his New Deal. In an effort to instruct enrollees about America's political system, *Happy Days* included such columns as "Capitol Hill-Arities" by "Stoney"; "In Washington. News Review of Congress"; and "Our U.S.A." As to national news, "Back of the Headlines" appeared for some time. Though much less emphasis was placed on the international scene in all of the CCC papers, for a time, *Happy Days* did include "The CCC Primer," devoted to foreign affairs, and as the world scene darkened, "This Week in History" ran for many months in 1939 and 1940.

A perennial concern addressed in many of the CCC's papers was naturally unemployment. At times, hiring crusades were launched on behalf of the enrollees, one stressing that there were 400,000 former and current CCC men in the labor pool, all desirable as employees. Typically, in the November 30, 1935, issue, *Happy Days* devoted an entire page to a series of open letters addressed "To American Employers." These emphasized that the CCC man had "learned HOW TO WORK— so that you will not have to stand the expense of so training him."

Enrollees also knew how to "TAKE ORDERS." The average CCC man was ambitious, healthy in body and mind, and had learned how to get along with others. Most enrollees had recognized that "life is a matter of work and human relations," and would take pride in their work, "whether the job is that of digging a hole in the ground, running a machine or keeping a set of books." Most were trustworthy, would be faithful to the job and employers, and had had a fundamental training in good citizenship. Acting as a clearing house between enrollees and prospective employers, *Happy Days* also created a voluminous file recording the qualifications of thousands of enrollees, maintaining it at no expense to either enrollees or prospective employers.[18]

Additionally, numerous articles and editorials instructed enrollees how properly to conduct a job interview, and when they succeeded in landing jobs or positions, *Happy Days* frequently featured them in articles and editorials.[19]

Happy Days took its own advice given to editors of camp papers in that it often varied the paper's make-up, general appearance, and content, and frequently introduced new features and columns. For example, the issue of December 26, 1936, had a crossword puzzle which was not common heretofore. Many of its columns, however, were regular features with longer runs. One of these was "The Camp Site," which was "devoted to the spirit that makes a camp the best camp." It often featured photographs of various CCC camps, highlighting architecture and landscaping. Another, "On the Job," detailed what the men were doing at work. For a time, the column "The Social Whirl" emphasized social life in the camps with a focus on dances, a common feature of camp social activities. One especially interesting, well-written, long-running column was "'Down East' With Domas" by I.J. Domas, devoted to CCC activities in New England. The feature "Between Covers" directed the men's attention to good reading, as in the January 18, 1936, issue, which had much to say about Rudyard Kipling, Carl Sandburg and Walt Whitman. "Recommended Books" was another feature that reviewed books, especially those on self-improvement, public speaking, business and English. By early 1938, another column, "Movie Stuff," discussed the cinema as a major part of the nation's cultural scene. Others included "Arts and Crafts," "The Band Wagon" about music, and "The Voice of the Vet."[20]

On into the summer of 1938, *Happy Days*, always interested in innovation, introduced "On the Odd Side," made up of "strange or humorous, but True" events or circumstances, a feature to which the men were urged to contribute.[21] The long-running feature, "Cob Web Corner," "Where Those Who Think and Those Who Think They Think Can Dust Off the Old Gray Matter," attempted to aid enrollees in spelling, grammar, and math, and included puzzles, brain teasers, and general information. Later innovations included "Strolling Down the Company Street," which focused on the continued developments in the CCC, while the "Tiny Tabloid," evincing a lighter touch, highlighted life's oddities. Professional journalists and writers were also used to help fill the pages of the paper. In the autumn of 1939, William MacLeod Raine, a well-known author of Westerns, contributed the continuing story: "Bucky Follows a Hot Trail." Many camp newspapers—as did *Happy Days*—also borrowed ideas from the working press. For instance, Michael Belloise of Company 1240, Belton, Montana, contributed a column "Sepey's Diary" to *Happy Days*, a parody of the work of the famous columnist, Franklin Pierce Adams [FPA]. Therein, on one occasion, he proceeded through a CCC enrollee's day, recording events of a truck trip into Kalispell, Montana: "A charming damsel passing by and I in hot pursuit. I did chase her ... and chase her ... and chase her, until ... now methinks of it ... she did finally catch me. However, a most gentle creature she ... like a lamb ... always saying 'Bah!' And so to bed—(back at camp)."[22]

Humor was exhibited in *Happy Days*, as well as in most of the camp papers. Several subjects were commonplace such as a preoccupation with the Scots' alleged proverbial stinginess. Blacks came in for their share of jokes, as did women. However, camp members were often singled out, sometimes in special columns devoted to camp gossip. This material featured the relationships between enrollees and the fairer sex in neighboring towns or cities. The peculiar and unusual habits of camp members were commented upon as well. By early 1935, *Happy Days* had introduced the column, "From Grave to Gay," which consisted of humorous bons mot. By the April 9, 1938, issue, there was less humor in the paper, and the column "A Laugh on Us" replaced "From Grave to Gay," which was allowed to lapse. Other humor features that later appeared included "Cream of Wit," by Jim Blancato of Company 256, Peekskill, New York, who admonished his readers not to ask "if it will run cereally." Another was "As Dogs Howl," a column of witty observations presided over by H. Holzinger of Company 1212, Elmont, Tennessee, while Nelson B. Teal of Company 437, Polkton, North Carolina, introduced a similar offering, "On the CCCside."[23]

On November 17, 1934, *Happy Days* introduced "Advice to the Lovelorn" by "Susie Sunshine," aided by Bill Gebhart of Company 294, LaFollette, Tennessee, with such typical fare as: "Dear Susie Sunshine: I'm in a terrible mess. I wonder if you can help me out. I'm going out with two women. They both asked me to marry them. One is young and pretty and the other one has plenty of money but she is homely. Who would you advise me to marry? [Signed] 'Befuddled.'" "Dear Befuddled: Marry the one that is young and pretty by all means.... Send me the address of the other one. 'Susie.'" By end of 1940, the main humor column was "Tri-C Camp Laffs."

All in all, *Happy Days* was an interesting experiment in journalism in that much of it was written by its readers, a considerable portion of the art work was drawn by them, and the poetry and humor was similarly derived. Except for the news which originated in Washington, much of the other material was written by the officers and men in the camps. "Nothing of its sort was ever attempted before, that we know of," the editor surmised.[24] Examples included the regular column "Frankly Speaking" written by Leo Strollo, who also edited *The Millersylvania Grapevine* (Company 1232, Camp Millersylvania, Olympia, Washington). Frank Giordano of Company 301, Masten, Pennsylvania, who also edited his company's sheet, the *Bag Puncher*, presided over the Happy Days column, "Canteen Chatter."

In addition, as the November 18, 1933, issue of *Happy Days* noted, for several weeks it had been carrying editorials from the men themselves. These were often "descriptions of the more intimate feelings and impressions of the men in the camps," and "dealt with the reaction of the men to their work, to their camp, to the other men, and to the environment of nature in which they were living." The paper desired to print more of these, which might feature a "story of a forest fire or a football game," describe "a sunset or the feeling which comes over a fellow as he hears that first call in the morning, or a thought about the homefolks as he sits alone along the road at twilight." Then too, "it might be about the relationship between him and the guy in the next bunk. Something he SEES or FEELS." There was, the editor asserted, "an editorial in every single man of the C.C.C. *Happy Days* should like to print them—if they are good."

And the men responded. Most of the editorials were thoughtful, and emphasized a positive tone. For instance in the issue of December 2, 1933, H.E. Lunsford of the veterans company 1783 at Custer, South Dakota, observed that many men in his company had been overseas in the World War, and "the experiences gained there make it easy for them to gain a true conception of [the CCC]." But in the same issue, Jim O'Neil of Company 530, in Death Valley, California, in his editorial "Shall I Be Ashamed?" inquired provocatively about the activities of the Corps in opening up areas in the natural world that should perhaps best be left unsullied. Indeed, the CCC might be doing as much harm as good to nature, he declared—an environmentalist ahead of his time.

In its continual search for novelty and interesting material, *Happy Days*, reflecting national trends, evinced much interest in contests of various sorts, ranging from the ambitious to the trivial. For example, to obtain the best still photographs and movies from the field, it often used a contest format. In the autumn of 1935, for instance, Company 728 of Salem, Missouri won for its excellent movie of camp life. Not inconsequentially, many of the still photographs provided the paper with a ready-made trove of illustrations which it frequently drew upon.[25]

On one occasion, the paper teamed up with the WPA Federal Theater program for a CCC playwriting contest which produced several hundred manuscripts. The judges were prominent persons in the Federal Theater program. P. Washington Porter of Columbia, South Carolina, was one of the winners honored for his tragedy about the life of blacks, "Return to Death," which presented "the stark truth of a 'Tobacco Road.'" Another winning entry was by George Gill and Bernard Winstock of Company 228, Cohocton, New York; they co-authored a musical entitled simply, "CCC." Both plays were scheduled for production on Broadway by the WPA Federal Theater organization, and the authors were transferred to New York to assist professional playwrights in getting their creations ready for the stage.[26]

Another ambitious contest asked enrollees to select a slogan for the CCC. Contestants were enticed by the prize of $25 dollars, a considerable sum in those days. Though FDR was invited to act as a judge, he declined, perhaps having other things to do, leaving the matter to the enrollees themselves. *Happy Days* hoped that the winning entry would convey the "all-round meaning of the CCC" with "punch," and be brief enough to be used "to advantage." These criteria proved difficult to attain, and the results were often stilted and lacking in imagination. Some suggestions included: "Watch Towers of the Nation," "Woodland Soldiers," "Youth's Light; America's Delight," and the one destined to win, "Builder of Men." Certainly prosaic, it was submitted by Albert Whittaker, Company 3402, Asheville, North Carolina. But *Happy Days*, in its April 10, 1937, issue, included the slogan as part of its masthead as: "The CCC—Builder of Men," which it continued for some time and urged other camp papers to do likewise, though only a few complied.[27]

Another competition elicited examples of "CCC Experiences" from the men. One dollar would be paid for each selection printed in *Happy Days*. One winner was Joe R. Evans of Company 4709 in Wirt, Minnesota, who recounted how the men of his company searched for the body of one of their comrades who had drowned in a nearby lake. Rather better rewarded at $25 was the winner of the contest "On the Fire Line," which asked for "the most vivid, accurate account of fighting a forest fire by a CCC enrollee."[28] Twenty-five dollars was also the prize paid for the winners of the contests, "What I Have Got Out of the CCC Personally," the "Ideal Enrollee," and the best story from anyone getting a job after leaving the CCC with an emphasis on how the CCC experience had enabled him to obtain employment.[29]

Throughout much of 1939, when the contest craze was at its height, *Happy Days* launched a series of events paying five dollars for the best answers to various relevant and timely, if sometimes trivial or humorous questions, presented five at a time, such as: How has the U.S. Army helped to develop the country, aside from protecting it from invasion and fighting its battles? Who is the most dangerous enrollee in camp? Why? Is education the "bunk," and why? Should truck drivers be bunked by themselves? Why? Other questions asked whether health or wealth was more important; most answered health. As to "would you rather be a short man or a tall one?" most responded that tall persons were more fortunate than short ones. Other queries included "What Would You Do With $10,000?" The majority of the contestants indicated that they would buy a farm, though many would tithe, give to the poor, go to college, or marry. In response to the question "Ten Years From Now, What?" the winners had hopes of being salesmen or owning their own farms. No one, apparently, had an inkling about what would most significantly intrude upon their lives late in that decade: World War II.[30]

More seriously, *Happy Days* also provoked and got a substantial debate on the "meaning of democracy," certainly a timely topic. Much discussion ensued concerning the definition of the term, as well as that of a republic, many enrollees concluding that the United States was a republic rather than a pure democracy in the classical sense. Perhaps only in Athens, which founded it, could a true democracy have been established, some argued. Others asserted that America was a "representative democracy." Many emphasized the necessity of responsibility as well as rights and freedoms. Some were cynical: "A democracy is a government where the politicians squabble for a job," one argued, while another insisted that a democracy was "where people can talk freely, worship freely, and where the government is by the people and for them. That's democracy down to brass tacks." Another concluded that "the real meaning of democracy is to live and let live."[31]

Happy Days also took note of a "typewriter picture" portrait of FDR, created by using the "x" key "as the drawing instrument," published in the *Lakeshore Camp News* (Company 1751, Knife River, Minnesota). *Happy Days* saw no reason why this could not be turned into another contest with, appropriately, an Underwood portable typewriter as first prize. Thus "Typeys," the "new art of typewriter drawings," was launched as a contest. The winner, John C. Lynch of Company 2346, Ridgeway, Virginia, produced an impressive, elaborate "Typey" of a Dutch windmill.[32]

Cartoons were also used as the basis for a series of competitions. For one, *Happy Days* printed a cartoon—without the usual voice "balloons"—in which the commanding officer was talking to his startled clerk on the intra-camp phone system. Contestants were to speculate as to what was being said. For each of ten best answers, the paper would pay a dollar.[33]

Though *Happy Days* was a supporter of the CCC's educational programs, it was not until rather late—in early 1938—that the paper began a section concerned exclusively with educational news. Articles were devoted to cooking, agriculture, electricity, diesel engines, and English and vocabulary studies. There was information on the American government and how it worked. Other features discussed "Modern Manners for Men," "Leadership," "Tools: What They Are and How to Use Them," and "Photos: How to Make Them and Why." Basic first aid was covered, horticulture was explained, and a series on typing, not to mention rope tying, was published. A quiz column appeared asking for responses to questions concerning basic English grammar, auto safety, and much else. Camp leaders were encouraged to take enrollees on educational field trips, and in July 1938, *Happy Days* printed a series of outlines to help guide them. Tips were given for a tree identification trip; a visit to a battlefield; a trip to a trial court; visits to art galleries or exhibits. Perhaps the men might visit a prison, a zoo or a natural history museum; the birthplace or boyhood home of some notable person; old estates; study a stream or brook; or maybe look in on a factory or Indian Reservation.[34]

Rather slowly but inexorably, the tone and content, and even the size of *Happy Days* changed as the 1930s wound down and the war years emerged. By mid–1940, *Happy Days* was more often than not a 16-page sheet rather than containing 20 or 24 pages as previously. As of November 22, 1941, its normal size for some weeks was 12 pages, with much less emphasis on humor and sports. One week later, on November 29, *Happy Days* emerged with a changed focus as the "National Weekly Publication of the Civilian Conservation Corps and National Youth Administration," a fact henceforth duly noted on its masthead.

Nevertheless, *Happy Days* did not abandon the CCC. On the contrary, it often stressed its continued importance. A new column, "Coast-to-Coast Comment," by E. Stanton Lay, focused on CCC camps throughout the nation. This was similar to the work then being done by Ernie Pyle roaming about the nation writing first-hand reports on how the nation was faring in the continuing Depression years. Yet there were more important straws in the wind. In 1940 Ryder, sensing another opportunity, launched the *Army Times* to cater to the journalistic needs of the growing United States Army. Thus the Army Times Publishing Company was created, which still publishes *Army Times, Navy Times, Air Force Times,* and *Defense News.*

On every hand, there was a new concentration on military matters which poured over into *Happy Days*. A new column in the issue of July 6, 1940, "What's New in Army News" was introduced. A certain commentator, who styled himself "Dicking," commented on the state of the nation in an article "Mr. Dooley on Defense," which ends: "Oi'm thoroly in accord wit' our furrin policy an' as Oi sid befower, Hinnessy, O'm glad t' see th' Guvernment are beginnin' t' put sum tath into sum o' our policies. Th' sooner we let Hitler an 'ither aggrissors know we mane business th' betther, say Oi."[35] In the November 1, 1941, issue of *Happy Days*, a pinup picture of starlet Georgia Carroll appeared, anticipating a major trend about to surface. In the January 24, 1942, issue the film star Jane Wyman was featured. Dressed in a quasi-military uniform, she had a message to the readers of *Happy Days*: "Hey, there, run, don't walk, to the nearest recruiting station!"

Nevertheless, in other respects, *Happy Days* was rather slow off the mark after Pearl Harbor and for some weeks, there was surprisingly little about the war. There was a political cartoon attacking Japanese in the December 13, 1941, issue. In addition, the paper asked for news of ex-enrollees "distinguished in the armed forces," and would subsequently feature many stories of this sort. A typical letter was printed in the January 17, 1942, issue from a Coast Guard sailor fondly remembering his days in the CCC.

But a more warlike stance was soon evident. In the late 1930s, as war drew nearer, the cartoons in *Happy Days* frequently reflected a martial tone. One example was "Larry Dean: Madcap Ace of the Winged Army" by Dougal Lee, featuring a captain in the airforce of the "United Federation's Winged Army." It was closely modeled on familiar cartoon strips such as "Tailspin Tommy" and "Terry and the Pirates." In the September 9, 1939, issue of *Happy Days*, immediately after Hitler's invasion of Poland, Lee's cartoons began featuring combat operations. In keeping with the propensity of *Happy Days* to use talent from the field, and to help keep the paper fresh and current, a new cartoon strip by R. Lemon, "The Little Sarge," began appearing in the paper on May 6, 1939. This also reflected an emerging military orientation. Similarly, in early 1942, Pvt. Howard Amend, then in the Army, introduced his strip "Beansy O'Brien," depicting the trials and tribulations of young soldiers. "Rear-Rank Ralph" by Joe Bowers also emphasized the foibles of rank and file servicemen in both the Army and Navy.[36]

At the same time, *Happy Days* included many propaganda cartoons targeting Axis nations, and reproduced posters warning about the consequences of loose talk and other matters involving national security. The December 27, 1941, issue published the first silhouettes of military aircraft, both allied and enemy, with emphasis on aircraft spotting. The books being reviewed in late 1941 and early 1942 included those with a war theme: Douglas Miller, *You Can't Do Business with Hitler*, a reprint by Pocket Books, now became popular. Also: *Hi Hattie, I'm in the Navy Now*, included love letters of a "salt to his sweet." Published by M.S. Mill and Company, it included a dictionary of naval slang. More scholarly was Princeton University Press's book, *Army Talk*, a dictionary of military terms.[37]

Happy Days was also sometimes aroused to rally around the increasingly embattled CCC. It became annoyed and even angered that the organization was not being used to full advantage in the nation's war effort. Typically, a front-page editorial by John Pitt in the March 7, 1942, issue noted that the Japanese would certainly know how to make use of the CCC. Indeed, the man who conquered Singapore, Gen. Tomoyuki Yamashita, had visited the USA in 1933 and even then wondered why the CCC was not a paramilitary organization. But America's leaders did not see what Yamashita had clearly apprehended: the potentialities of the CCC in national defense. Unaccountably, some congressmen and senators, and much of the nation's press, were even clamoring for the elimination of the organization. But from its beginnings, Pitt argued, the CCC had trained more men "in the rudiments of military training than the Army, Navy and Marine Corps combined." Indeed, "Nearly 3,000,000 boys were grounded in Army discipline, in living together in camps, in trades and skills as necessary to a modern army as knowledge of firearms and military tactics, and in health and sanitation and love of country." In fact, perhaps one-third of the present-day armed forces were former CCC boys he asserted, and thousands of officers had also been trained in the CCC. What now seemed logical was that about 2,000,000 boys too young for military service should be enrolled and trained by the CCC. Therefore, instead of eliminating the CCC, it should be enlarged to a million-boy strength to train those below the draft age. "From such a CCC," he concluded, "half a million physically fit, well-trained boys could be fed into the armed forces of the nation each year, so long as this war lasts."

But the days of the CCC were plainly numbered, and almost immediately after news of the CCC's termination, *Happy Days* rapidly changed its tack. The last advertisement for *Happy Days* subscriptions appeared in the June 27, 1942, issue, and in the next, the paper noted that it was closing out "our stock of CCC Insignia at slashed prices." Soon thereafter, ads began appearing for subscriptions for the *Army Times*, also—as was *Happy Days*—housed in the Daily News Building in Washington.

Subsequently, news of the military services dominated the pages of the paper, and, with the new infusions, it became a 16-page sheet once more. There were features on military hardware such as the "Jeep," still called in some circles the "peep", and in articles "Know Your Enemy," it was alleged that the Japanese "Zero" fighter was really "not that good," and, while the famed German 88-mm field gun was powerful, it was nonetheless "vulnerable." There was a preoccupation with tanks and paratrooper training, as well as features on the Doolittle raid. The large-scale Carolina maneuvers conducted by the Army were discussed as were new units being formed, such as the 80th Infantry Division.

Happy Days featured articles on such subjects as wartime aviation, including a spread on the "Flying Tigers." Other articles included numerous photos of Allied aircraft, both current and future planes. Army camp life was photographed, often featuring ex-enrollees on active service. Other articles detailed bond rallies being conducted by veterans' companies. One editorial suggested that the CCC camps plant victory gardens, provided that seeds were not wasted and the manpower used did not detract from more serious duties.[38]

Happy Days also joined in the crusade being generally mounted to bring actions and attitudes of the citizenry into conformity with the war effort. Editorials warned against "loose talk," one piece indicating that the Allied strategy to emphasize the European theater as opposed to fighting first in the Pacific was the correct one. To be sure, the editor went on, "honest, enlightened criticism of the war effort is necessary. But it should be made by informed people and considered by informed people. Otherwise it is merely loose talk. Loose talk can make a major contribution to losing the war. No soldier [or civilian] should be guilty of it." In fact, "A good soldier's best bet is to pull his weight and to have confidence in his leaders."[39] Another editorial quoted Congressman Wright Patman from Texas who had advised the men of the CCC to "Look Forward, Not Backward," despite the recent bad war news. America was in fact "a slow-moving giant," which by the middle of 1942 "would be able to extend herself in munitions, ships, arms, tanks, airplanes in a flood," he declared.[40]

In advertising, the tobacco ads always featured men in the armed forces, one Camel cigarettes ad highlighting the Willys-Overland Jeep and its Camel-smoking test driver, Donald M. Kenower. Camels cigarettes began promoting "Camel Caravans," road shows that toured military bases throughout the country. Shoe polish ads were common by now in *Happy Days*. Movies advertising features such as Bud Abbott and Lou Costello in "Keep 'Em Flying," and many others with a wartime theme appeared. Cartoon characters such as "Superman" were enlisted to sell war bonds. Defense contractors, including Martin Aircraft, began to advertise in the paper's pages. As *Happy Days* had earlier sold books concerned with the CCC, the *Army Times* did the same with publications with a wartime emphasis, and many of these in turn were advertised in *Happy Days*. These included *Army Wife; Officers' Guide; Infantry Drill*

Regulations; and the quarterly digest of *War Department Directives. Happy Days* also sold war books, such as Noel Monks' *Squadrons Up!,* about the RAF in France in early 1940, and many others. In the July 11, 1942, issue of *Happy Days* a milestone appeared in the form of an ad for Schlitz beer, the first alcoholic beverage to be advertised in the paper. Pabst Blue Ribbon was not far behind, and one wartime icon, the Zippo lighter, also appeared in ads.

Clearly, by the summer of 1942 *Happy Days* was little more than an adjunct to the *Army Times,* and only a smattering of material appeared concerning either the CCC or the NYA. New columns in *Happy Days* now included "Bliss Bits" from Fort Bliss, Texas; "Croft Capers" from Camp Croft, South Carolina; and "Benning Brevities," from Fort Benning, Georgia. The typical "Take 5" from Camp Roberts, California, edited by Pvt. Joe J. Wilks, contained witticisms and light observations on current affairs and Army life: "Looks as though Il Duce is going the previous Caesars one better—he's going to be a bust during his lifetime." "I'd certainly like to catch up with the guy who said a man is his own boss after he reaches 21." "I hear that the draftee is afraid his pal will take his girl while he's away. Listen, soldier, there really isn't anything to worry about. If Uncle Sam wants your pal, he will be on his way to camp in a few days. If Uncle Sam doesn't want him, neither will your girl." Almost all of the letters and poetry in the July 18, 1942, issue, were from soldiers. Instead of bridge, a new column, "According to Sergeant Hoyle," was about poker, which, as "Hoyle" noted, was "the most distinctively American of all card games."

Army camp humor was a staple in *Happy Days* as formerly had been the case regarding the CCC. There was now the "Army Character": "The Chowhound." The ubiquitous whistle, seemingly being blown nonstop by noncoms to regulate drill, was highlighted in the feature "Nomenclature of the Whistle" by Lt. Charles H. Schraedner and Pvt. Raymond Zaubner in *The Kodiak Bear* from Alaska: "The U.S. Whistle Model M1, is a self-repeating, shoulder strap model. It is lung operated, air cooled, reverberating blast type. The whistle weighed an ounce and a half, and the whistle chain another half ounce."

Even as *Happy Days* had earlier surveyed the camp papers in the column "Camp Paper Comment," a new column, "The Army Press" did the same thing for the new Army papers springing up in great profusion across the nation. Now such papers as the *Falcon* of Fort Bragg, North Carolina; *Shot 'n Shell* at Camp San Luis Obispo, California; and *Flight Time* from Goodfellow Field, Texas, were being critiqued by *Happy Days* as the CCC camp papers had been earlier.[41]

Finally, with the demise of the CCC, *Happy Days* ceased to exist in its original format. Almost with a whimper, the last issue of the paper appeared on August 8, 1942. Continuing as the *Civilian Front* with an entirely different orientation, its long, colorful CCC career was over.

While it lasted, though, *Happy Days* was unquestionably a force of consequence within the CCC and beyond. A typical letter from William Quarry of Company 2206, Speculator, New York, asserted that the paper had interesting cartoons and comic strips, though the most interesting were the editorials. While the poetry was not as popular, still many enrollees agreed that "this page must be carefully watched lest one miss something real good." Much more acceptable was the humor, which was considered "far better than anything in any regular newspaper." The news of the CCC was also important, he continued, the one complaint being that there was not enough of it. Finally, he concluded, "all other features are read even to the smallest ad."[42] Some unknown mother who regularly read *Happy Days* thought it "a great paper for the young men and a greater consolation to Mothers who have sons in the C.C.C. camps to know what they are doing and how wonderful they are being taken care of."[43]

Yet not everyone agreed that the paper was altogether praiseworthy. In a letter to the editor one enrollee, Anthony J. Suroski, took *Happy Days* to task for always focusing on the bright side; for painting life in the CCC as "all roses and cream." But what about when the thorn pricks and the cream turns sour? he asked. Why not sometimes see the "scallions and weeds?" All of the officers, he went on, were not always "the best, most efficient, most humane" imaginable. Surely, he concluded, some were "Simon Legrees or Shylocks."[44]

Much stronger were the criticisms emanating from certain Republican circles, where the CCC papers were regarded as little more than "carrier[s] of propaganda for the New Deal." It was further alleged that the editors of *Happy Days* were employed by the Democratic party, to which those worthies replied, "bunk," insisting that *Happy Days* was in fact politically independent while being "pro CCC." As such, it would assail all critics of that organization, whether Democrat or Republican.[45]

When the (Nebraska) *Omaha Bee News* specifically charged that the CCC was a hotbed of Democratic propaganda and that *Happy Days* was designed to influence the enrollees to be good FDR Democrats, John C. Ivory of Company 793, Hill City, South Dakota, wrote a scathing rebuttal.[46] Marlen E. Pew, editor of the professional journal *Editor and Publisher*, agreed that *Happy Days* was not primarily a political sheet and put it in another perspective. This paper "reminds me of some of the papers that were produced for our armed forces during the World War—a form of journalism that probably contributed as much comfort, information and direction to the fighting forces as any single instrument devised for that great emergency."[47]

In the final analysis, as one observer has remarked, *Happy Days* must be considered "the dean among all publications devoted to the activities of the CCC." It had "won a distinctive place as a skillfully edited and lively organ which has contrived to effect a neat compromise between standard newspaper technique and the special needs and interests of the hundreds of thousands of youths and war veterans who have passed thru the CCC." Its founders, Melvin Ryder and Ray Hoyt, armed with foresight and energy, had "seized Time incontinently by the forelock." Its variety, in both content and makeup, was designed to keep up interest in the paper. In this, it succeeded. Always lively, it effectively served its constituency, only flagging in the last few weeks of the summer of 1942. By the time the editors became preoccupied with military matters, the fate of the CCC was clear, and time and events had overtaken the CCC's chief mouthpiece. *Happy Days* remains, however, much more than a mere historical curiosity: it still evokes the life and times of one of FDR's premier New Deal creations, the Civilian Conservation Corps.[48]

PART II

Chronicle Voices: Life in the CCC

4

Way of Life in the CCC

"A CCC boy is usually a man of few wads."
—*Crystal Camp Crier* (Company 1742,
Tarkio, Missouri), December 7, 1934

"What fools these mortals be, to join the C.C.C."
—*The Kanonan* (Company 297,
Kanona, New York), November 1936

On Thanksgiving Day, 1934, the men of Company 1742 in Tarkio, Missouri, were implored to be especially thankful "for the opportunities granted us when we were able to become part of this real depression-killing army—the CCC."[1] The *Canyon Echo* (Company 819, Grand Canyon, Arizona) further observed that "here in the CCC we are making our start—the first real step in playing the fiddle of life."[2] Such thankfulness and spirit of optimism were a part of the normal way of life in the CCC. When New Year's Day rolled around in 1934, this was plainly apparent to one writer who noted that "before joining the C.C.C. we were, many of us, in the blackest depths of despondency. But now the sky is brighter. Dawn is plainly apparent. The clouds along the rim of the earth are tinged with a rosy pink and a delicate creamy orchid. At any moment the golden disc may slip above the horizon, and we will again be standing in the light of a new day and a new era filled with many wonderful and untold opportunities for us all."[3]

And what was he like, the typical enrollee? Many camp newspapers tell us a great deal about him. The men of Company 1523, Berkeley

Springs, West Virginia, developed a portrait of the average enrollee at their camp. He was nineteen years of age; he had passed the seventh grade in school; he came from a farm or small community—two-thirds coming from a farm center, if not the farm itself—and twenty percent had never had a job. He had been in the CCC for ten months, had usually gained fifteen pounds and two inches in height. The rank and file enrollee was not interested in academic education, "tho he can be reached by vocational and job training classes." He was interested in handicrafts such as woodworking, leathercraft, and photography, and "usually becomes very proficient in the profane languages." His English "was spotty and not to the king's taste," but he had "developed slang that only a CCCer could translate." He disliked wearing a necktie but would don it for retreat and supper because he hated KP duty and spud peeling even worse.

The CCC youth was romantic and his biggest interest was finding out when there was a truck to town so he could see his girl friend. With the girls, however, he was rather bashful, and instead of dancing, spent his evenings at the movies, walking in the park, or holding hands on the front porch. He also carried a picture of his girl back home. He was not a man of wealth, and most of the five dollars that he kept from his pay he spent in the camp exchange. He was not a heavy reader, going in for the funny papers, sport pages, and wild west books. He was keenly interested in athletics though, and usually participated in some of the camp sport activities. All in all, the CCC boy was a "hearty, healthy and happy youth."

He came into the CCC as a boy and went out "pretty much of a man." He had gained in health, had a better conception of citizenship, and had learned to live among other fellows and to depend upon himself. Most of the men had learned a trade and were simply eager to be back into civilian life, get a job, settle down and "become responsible citizens." While in, "they like[d] the CCC, tho among themselves they grouch and crab about everything, but they [were] intensely loyal to each other and to their camps."[4]

The Spirit of 299 (Company 299, Masonville, New York) rounded out the religious and educational picture. Company 299 had 192 men enrolled, the vast majority—150—not yet 21 years of age. Of the total, 59 were Protestant, and 131 were Catholic, with only one Jew and one "other faith." Two had one year of college; 163 had eight years of schooling and up, with 27 having six years to eight. Fifty-two had at least eight years; 31, a year of high school; 35, two years; 19, three years, and 26, four years.[5]

The men came from vastly different backgrounds. In Company 2824 of Wright City, Oklahoma, one enrollee—unnamed—had been reared far back in the hills of the Choctaw country of southeastern Oklahoma. His trip to camp on a truck from Hugo to the camp-site was his first experience riding in a motor-driven vehicle. According to his statement, "that ride was the thrill of a lifetime." He could neither read nor write but after 13 months in camp could do both. He was also one of the most popular men in camp and one of its best workers.[6]

Racial attitudes toward blacks in the CCC will be considered in a chapter below. There were also pronounced anti–Hispanic views, notably in some of the companies in the Southwest. The *Rock Hound* (Company 855, El Paso, Texas, and later Elephant Butte, New Mexico) discussed the matter in an editorial: "Our Spanish-speaking Americans and our English-speaking Americans have been having a few differences. The main trouble, I believe, is the fact that the Mexican boys insist on speaking Spanish. Now our American boys cannot speak Spanish, but our Mexican boys *can* speak English. In order to preserve peace and tranquility, it might be a good idea if we *all* speak English." Indeed, "IN VIEW OF THE FACT THAT THIS IS AN AMERICAN CAMP, AND WE ARE EATING AMERICAN FOOD, AND DRAWING OUR PAY IN AMERICAN MONEY FROM THE AMERICAN GOVERNMENT, IT IS ONLY RIGHT THAT WE SPEAK THE AMERICAN LANGUAGE." Some of the trouble stemmed from the fact that the English speaking boys, "on hearing the Mexican boys speaking Spanish, thought that they were being talked about. In some cases this proved to be true, but as a rule it was not so." Earlier in the company's history, when an enrollee was heard speaking any language other than English, he was fined 25 cents. Many of the Spanish-speaking boys had difficulty speaking English because it was not their native tongue, so it did not seem fair to fine them because they would speak Spanish subconsciously. Nonetheless, "the Mexican boys must realize that they will be among Americans, possibly for the rest of their lives, and that the opportunity they have to learn to speak English fluently, while they are here, may serve them in later years."[7]

Sometimes the men developed favorable views of native peoples encountered near their camps, as did members of Company 819, Grand Canyon, Arizona. They became interested in a local character, "Old Hosteen Yazzie," alleged to be 110 years of age and said to be one of the last Navajo Indians to surrender to Army scout Kit Carson.[8]

Racial aspects were more complicated in the Hawaiian camps, where a rich diversity prevailed. Typically, TH-1 (Territory of Hawaii No. 1) at Wahiawa, Oahu, had of its 93 total: 27 Hawaiians, 15 part Hawaiian, 15 Portuguese, 11 Japanese, 6 Chinese, 9 Filipinos and 10 others. The other Hawaiian camps had similar mixes, and generally prided themselves on their racial integration and harmony.[9]

As to other attitudes among CCC men, Superintendent Leroy A.

Holmberg of Company 2683, Almond, New York, once asked 35 enrollees to respond to several questions. Regarding food, spaghetti and meat balls was their favorite dish, while all hated creamed beef and soft-boiled eggs. To their minds, the most beautiful thing in the world was a woman, yet they preferred to be male rather than female because "women suffer too much." As to how they perceived God, 10 men answered that He was "very good." Four others said that they did not know, and though they believed in God, they had no inkling as to what His purpose was. As to how some men got better jobs, many "banged ears" a great deal, i.e., "browned-nosed," though fitness and ability also counted.[10]

Not everyone thought that the CCC was altogether a desirable place, and the problems of AWOLs and homesickness persisted. *Happy Days* and the camp papers often published letters from those who had gone AWOL and, finding things outside intolerable, wished to be reinstated. Captain Mitchell A. Wackym, commanding officer of Company 420, St. Elmo, Tennessee, received one such letter from a deserter who was remorseful about it: "After I have had time to retrospect [sic] I realize what an ungrateful person I have been." He had thought that he was miserable in camp, but was far more when he realized his failures. It was certainly not the fault of his parents, "because I was raised better." He had joined the CCC of his own free will, and should have been man enough "to have taken my medicine whether I liked it or not." He wanted to return after the holidays to finish his enlistment if possible "so to remove that stigma from my name." Two others, George Worley and Sherman Arwood of Company 1741, as noted in *The 1741 Tabloid*, described themselves as "two sillies," who had gone over the hill and then regretted it. Letters also came in from parents asking for a second chance for their sons. Such requests was sometimes granted.[11]

Would-be deserters were frequently lectured to by both the camp papers and *Happy Days*. The *Camp Spratt News* (Company 467, York, Alabama) editorialized that the men should carefully consider that they were hurting themselves when they went over the hill, because permanent derogatory entries "that you may bitterly regret one day," were added to their records. *The Bugle* (Company 4468, Barnwell, South Carolina) likewise strongly urged the men to refrain from going AWOL, observing that if an enrollee needed either an emergency leave or an honorable discharge, he certainly could get it.[12]

Aware that "there is not a feeling of despair, disappointment or grief quite so impossible to fight down as one of homesickness," the War Department, though rather belatedly, implemented various measures to alleviate it. On July 30, 1937, it issued a directive to Corps Area Commanders to find ways to ease the malady "thru general persuasion and frequent conversations on the part of both company officers and educational advisers with young enrollees."[13] In response, Brigadier General R.O. Van Horn, commanding District "B" of the Fourth Corps Area, ordered the preparation of a booklet which included a detailed description of daily CCC life so that enrollees might know better what to expect before joining.[14]

By late 1938, desertions had markedly decreased; in fact, there was considerable competition for all available slots in the CCC. Rookies were also increasingly eased into the organization by the so-called "Buddy Plan" whereby mature CCC men took new enrollees under their wing and assisted them in finding their way in the unfamiliar surroundings.[15]

Of perennial concern and interest to the men was the matter of their eats. One way that the CCC flaunted the well-being of its enrollees was apparent on holidays, especially Thanksgiving. Camps vied with each other in preparing elaborate meals. On that day in 1933, the U.S. Army Quartermaster Corps reported that the CCC consumed 525,000 pounds of turkey, for an average of 28 ounces per man and at a cost to the government of $131,000. In a column "Pass the Turkey," *Happy Day* gloated about the Thanksgiving meals prepared at various CCC camps, reporting that in some instances, the commanding officer and his staff took over the serving duties for the day in the mess hall.[16] Typically, Company 1617 in L'Anse, Michigan, served roast turkey with sage dressing, mashed creamed potatoes, giblet gravy, nut fruit salad, pumpkin and mince pies, ice cream, coffee, cigarettes, and afterwards staged a dance with lady friends as guests in the Town Hall. In New England "where they invented Thanksgiving," at Company 143, Erving, Massachusetts, the men enjoyed fruit cup Berkshire, crabmeat cocktail, turkey with chestnut dressing, chilled Cape Cod cranberries, baked Georgia yams, mashed Aroostook potatoes, baked Hubbard squash, rose radishes and hot English plum pudding with rum sauce. Almost always, there were nuts and cigars to end the feed.

The feasts were repeated at Christmas and on other holidays, and in a time of widespread hunger, the men of the CCC never tired of emphasizing how well off they were. Both the camp papers and *Happy Days* gloried in food statistics, *Happy Days* recording that camp meals provided on average a generous 4,500 calories each day per man. For the feeding of the 350,000 men in the CCC for ten months, 13,300,000 pounds of bacon from 831,250 hogs would be needed, not to mention the 66,500,000 pounds of beef from 110,826 head of cattle. The men would also consume 6,650,000 gallons of fresh milk; 80,000,000 pounds of flour, the produce of 100,000 acres of wheat; and 66,500,000 pounds of potatoes from 99,950 acres of farm land. Millions of cans of string beans, corn, tomatoes, peaches and other fruit would also be required. Naturally, all of this was a great boon to the nation's well being, and

because much of the produce came from local producers, the presence
of a CCC camp could be of considerable importance to hometown
economies.[17]

These facts were recognized by many camp commanders who coun-
seled their peers on such matters. One of these was Lieutenant (jg) Herbert A. Niemyer, the Commanding Officer of Company 5418 in
Withersbee, South Carolina, an all-black company. He prided himself on
his "tight ship," and his well-run, efficient mess. He observed that but-
termilk was served four times each week: "It is cheap and what a filler it
is. This is usually served at the evening meal because of its sleep compelling effect." And he insisted on the best foodstuffs: "A few rejections
of inferior products will quickly bring the vendors around to observance
of specifications—they want your business, it's just like cash on the bar-
relhead for them and if you don't get first quality products, someone else
will. Insist on the best."[18]

There were various sources for the food in addition to the local merchants. Hunters and fishermen in the camps often supplemented the regular diets by shooting game such as deer and ducks, or bringing fish into
the mess halls in season. Sometimes game wardens donated confiscated
game to the CCC. In Lordsburg, New Mexico, members of Company
843, after catching and killing about 100 rattlesnakes, "got the idea they
were pretty tough [hombres]." "Testing whether this notion would long
endure," Foreman Robert Littell proposed that the crew "emulate the
caveman and eat the kill." This suggestion caused "more or less of a
shock" to the snake-killers, but they pronounced themselves game if their
buddies would go along. Six of the reptiles were prepared, and muster-
ing "what aplomb they could summon," and "with trepidation, then
curiosity, astonishment, and at last, relish, the snakes were downed." The
responses varied: one man asserted that "it was something like chicken....
More like fried eels, claimed another. 'Nahh! Breast of quail,' said a third."
But, in any case, rattlesnake was judged tasty, and the men had "more
respect for the rattler now, and a new interest in killing them."[19] General
Fox Connor, the First Corps Area commanding general, among other
officers, promoted the creation of garden plots within camp areas, con-
forming to a national mania at the time which saw the planting of home
gardens in backyards and even in vacant city lots in great profusion. Gardening might be carried on in conjunction with instruction in elementary plant husbandry, he suggested. Also, local 4-H Club members and
county extension agents were enlisted to help these projects along.[20]

Likewise, as an educational enterprise as well as for profit, a poultry course was introduced at the Stokes side camp in South Carolina.
Thirteen men put up two dollars each for 200 barred rock chicks. Later,
selling their chickens for 20 cents per pound to their company mess, the

men gained a monetary profit as well as a wealth of experience. In a rather different venture, veterans of Company 1755 in Chisom, Minnesota, turned their efforts to picking wild blueberries, both for eating and selling at a dime a quart.[21]

But there were certain eating problems that had to be addressed. Joe Gentile, in charge of the mess of Company 297 in Loyston, Tennessee, writing in *The Dam Overflow*, insisted that the lack of mess decorum must change: "You men come into the mess hall and raise all the hell you can think of. If you want to make a recreation hall out of the messhall, move the piano into the kitchen so I can enjoy myself too."[22]

One way to cope with such behavior was devised by the staff of Company 4468 at Barnwell, South Carolina. The camp there saw a definite "perk up" in manners when they instituted a "hog table" at which men who had not conducted themselves in a mannerly fashion were condemned to eat for a week. This proved embarrassing to many miscreants, effecting their reform.[23]

In some companies, other solutions to mess hall discipline problems were instituted. Numerous commanding officers decided that the men should dress formally for dinner. Such was the case with Company 1727, whose CO, Captain J.J. France, ordered that everyone be shaved, shined and dressed in OD trousers, shirt and tie for dinner. Also required to dress for the evening meal, the men of Company 871 in Hillsboro, Texas, were instructed to call it "dinner" rather than "supper," thereby elevating it to a more formal occasion.[24]

In a further attempt to create a positive atmosphere at mealtime, Company 5418 at Withersbee, South Carolina, an all-black outfit, always sang "a lusty spiritual before every meal in which the entire company takes part." This had "a psychological, as well as a physiological effect, which is good," their commanding officer, Lieutenant (jg) Herbert A. Niemyen, observed. Similarly, it was the custom in Company 299 in Masonville, New York, to have someone say grace before each meal. To encourage this, the company paper, *The Catskill Crier*, published model prayers for guidance.[25]

In addition to eats, the men were interested in their uniforms, with complaints and jokes about ill-fitting clothing being common. Initially, the men were clothed in Army uniforms stored since World War I. But eventually, in the summer of 1936, Fechner authorized the purchase of specific CCC outfits. The new uniforms consisted of long cotton trousers and cotton shirts, with straw or fiber sun helmets issued during the summer months. However, these still smacked too much of the military to suit many. Accordingly, at long last in late 1939, the Corps began to receive more distinctive dress uniforms. Though still of a military cut, they were spruce green and closely resembled U.S. Forest Service dress.[26]

The adoption of badges to indicate rank for assistant leaders and others was also similar to military practice. Eschewing the usual army chevrons—though some companies used them—insignia of rank usually consisted of parallel stripes, green on red, with veterans' companies sometimes adopting yellow on black. In addition, service stripes also emerged. These consisted of green bars embroidered on a red background and worn on the shoulder of the uniform.[27]

But whatever the uniform, most companies insisted upon some attention to their proper care and wearing, in this way again resembling military organizations. For instance, Captain Raymond D. Coltor, the commanding officer of Company 1540 in Henderson, Kentucky, issued orders that no man could leave camp unless he was properly dressed, neat in appearance and clean shaven with shoes shined and hair combed. He must either wear civilian clothes or a uniform, but not a mix. CCC men were regularly inspected and had their clothing and equipment inventoried, losses being charged against delinquents at pay day. The enrollees were not only taught how to dress well; they often received instruction in manners and how to conduct themselves in public. Their courtesy sometimes—though not always—amazed and gratified both "their parents and the many people in their respective communities."[28]

Where the enrollees lived was also a matter of abiding interest. The CCC was often housed under Army tents. But as the organization took on a permanent state, most companies constructed barracks, further emulating the military. But there were innovations. The men of Company 1709, of East Pittsburg, Kansas, for example, lived in a string of boxcars on a rail siding. The men of two companies, 1741 and 731, bunked on houseboats on the White River in Arkansas. A group of 30 Native Americans in Nevada and eastern California lived in a caravan camp of auto trailers—"tents on wheels"—moving from job to job as needed. The camp had a power plant and a 25-watt short wave radio transmitting station, which kept the camp in touch with headquarters. Hot water tanks were also provided, as were refrigerator, kitchen, and dining trailers. In addition, there was a shop with a mechanic, and an office car for the five-man supervisory staff.[29]

When about 200 men from camps in Washington and Oregon travelled to Mt. McKinley, Alaska, for work in the summers of 1938 and 1939, they too lived in primitive conditions. A lack of recreational facilities proved a hindrance, but the Alaska Railroad came to the rescue, giving the men special rates for any point on their lines, allowing many to visit Fairbanks and Anchorage, as well as pan for gold, fish for trout, and participate in athletics in various parts of the Territory.[30]

Another primitive installation was the so-called "spike" camp. These were usually manned by small units stationed in remote wilderness areas

where the men undertook special projects not requiring a company's full
strength. The men often had to improvise to make these habitable. Consequently, they manifested much ingenuity, forecasting similar practices
prevalent among the GIs in World War II.[31] One such camp was located
at Luray, South Carolina. Here the men complained that "girls are rather
scarce, but where there are boys there are apt to be girls." In any case,
some men liked the situation, noting that the "entire camp is like a large
family on a Sunday picnic."

Many of the enrollees went to considerable lengths to make their
surroundings more comfortable and even beautiful. After the men of
Company 2384, Lynchburg, Virginia, saw the film *Lost Horizons* based
on James Hilton's book (1933), they decided to name their camp "Camp
Shangri-La." They also bent every effort to make it a showplace, widely
regarded as one of the most modern and beautiful of CCC camps.[32]
Company 288 of Benning, D.C., boasted a beer garden resembling a
Paris sidewalk cafe at its camp. It also had an installation "rigged out"
in the canteen, complete with the paraphernalia of a modern drugstore.
The clerk, "dressed immaculately in a white jacket," served milk shakes,
hotdogs, coffee and "real ice cream sodas."[33]

Having exerted much effort in improving their camps, many
enrollees deeply resented being transferred to other locales, often in
regions far from their homes. But this, too, had salutary effects, and having learned to adjust to a vagabond existence, many men were pleased
to have had the opportunity of extensive travel. Some companies
recorded odysseys of considerable distances. One of these was Company
1240, which began at Camp Dix, New Jersey, proceeding to Virginia's
Blue Ridge, then to a camp in Montana, finally ending its travels in Death
Valley, California. There is little doubt that the wanderings of the CCCers
often inculcated a measure of patriotism within enrollees that had positive benefits for the nation in the later war years.[34]

Throughout the CCC, considerable pressure was placed on the men
to conform to certain standards. Indeed, both *Happy Days* and various
camp papers were closely involved in what might be called "attitude
adjustment," seeking to boost morale, encourage proper conduct, and
inculcate good citizenship. When the annual All-American football team
was picked in early 1939, adviser Dennis W. Patch of Company 596 at
Redmond, Oregon, made his own selections for the "Big Game of Life"
applicable, he felt, to the CCC milieu. At right end, he chose "Joe Enthusiasm"; right tackle, "Jackhammer Tact"; right guard, "'Horse' Gump-
tion"; at center, "Jake Co-Operation"; left guard "John Guts," because
no character trait was more needed in America then, "than plain un-
adulterated guts," and he would be the team's captain; left tackle, "Dan
Technique"; left end, "Jim Endurance"; quarterback, "Butch Quick-

Thinking"; left half, "George Health"; right half, "Dick Honesty"; full back, "George Fidelity"; all coached by "Bunny Harmony." Could any men in the camp qualify for a spot on the team?, he asked, hoping for a complete squad.[35]

To the ends of good citizenship, the Third District, First Corps Area, provided copies of the "Ten Points of Good Citizenship" for posting in all company areas. These included loyalty, integrity, zeal, cleanliness, initiative, good humor, co-operation, consideration, labor, and obedience.[36]

The *Seven Six One News* (Company 761, David City, Nebraska) went further, clearly identifying what a "true American" was: He was one who cared for his body and mind; learned the "3 Rs"; prepared himself for an honest living; made friends and was a good neighbor; obeyed the laws and respected authority; and "honored God."[37]

Related to the issue of citizenship was the hard fact that democracy was being challenged in many parts of the world in the late 1930s by dictators who were stampeding the young people of other countries "into uncritical acceptance and support of various brands of Fascism." Even at home, patriotism was being discredited by "talkative and mediocre politicians." These threats must be countered, and such papers as *The Pyramid* (Company 698, Marion, Illinois) urged American youths to "school themselves to think deeply and intelligently on public questions, to act fearlessly where the public good is concerned, and to live according to the new standards of unselfish conduct which are being established in this new era of Democracy."[38]

Other areas of attitude and conduct that were subject to manipulation extended to every level of one's person and privacy. One was in keeping one's hair cut to what was regarded as a reasonable length. In one company, a "master-whittler" carved a violin model on which was inscribed: "If you are a fiddler let your hair grow. Otherwise get it cut now!" The violin was given to "anyone seen running around in need of a dog license," with firm instructions to go to the barber shop, where he got "preference over all others in line." Then when he had been sheared, the violin was passed to the next person who needed it. In Company 1407, Lakemont, Georgia, a certain "Curley" Mackendree was tackled and held by members of his forest crew while the barber cut his hair, and "it was a tough blow for 'Curley' as he watched ringlet after ringlet tumble to the earth." Eight men of Company 726, Greenville, Missouri, calling themselves the "Baldy Gang, went to the other extreme and shaved their heads."[39]

But the actions of certain other enrollees seemed more outrageous: "Cold sober, three men of Co. 2704, Minn., went into a town beauty shop and came out with permanent waves. First it was surrealism, now this." This deed was eclipsed by a certain enrollee in Company 299, in Masonville, New York: "Domo has turned pansy just what we thought he was. He let his dame paint his fingernails a very bright red the other night. Shame on you Paul."[40]

Rather sterner was another, perhaps salutary, side of personal intrusion. One form consisted of a vigorous scrubbing by a GI brush applied to those who badly needed a bath. A typical "ceremony" of this sort was staged by Company 802 at Boulder, Colorado: "Nobility has invaded the ranks of Co. 802 at Boulder, Colorado," so read a caption under the picture of a naked enrollee—backside exposed—who was "being initiated into the Royal Order of the Knights of the Bath," by fellow enrollees. The latter were called the "Ten Knights in a Bathroom," and lavishly used GI soap, GI scrub brushes, and large quantities of cold water on their victim. There were two groupings of the Order, the paper explained: the "scrubbee," and the second "and more highly prized," the "disher out." "And 'dishing out' in this society is very, very rough work," the report confided. The *Tamarack Times* of Company 297 reported another "success story" about a man who rarely bathed. At first, he got a hint in the form of an enormous bar of brown GI soap. But when he continued putting off washing, he was summoned to a court hearing. That "legal" procedure "broke his strong faith" about not bathing with the simple implements of a GI brush and soap applied to "his stench marked body.... Today his eyes portray a wariness," the paper noted, and he was occasionally even seen visiting the showers.[41]

Yet there were other effective ways by which the men might be made presentable. *The Kanona Daze* (Company 297, Kanona, New York), suggested that the young ladies of the nearby town of Bath refused to give the men at camp a "tumble" because the men were careless about their personal appearance. Perhaps "if some of 'Nature's Noblemen' would get a shave, haircut, a shoe shine and their clothing pressed, maybe they would get a nod once in a while from the 'fair ones.'"[42]

Rather more serious was the problem of hazing. Initially common, it tended to get out of hand, and official policy soon outlawed it. The new policy emphasized that every effort must be made to make the new men feel at home, thereby cutting down on the AWOL problem which seemed related to it. Fechner instructed all camp officials to "use every precaution against hazing of the newly arrived men, even tho to the older men such play is entered into in the spirit of fun." The new men must be assimilated into the life of the camp as quickly as possible, he insisted, and every effort must be made to "make the early days in camps as pleasant as possible."[43] In Company 1742 at Tarkio, Missouri, to replace hazing, tournaments in checkers, pool and ping pong were held, netting each winner a dollar credit at the camp canteen. In Kanona, New York,

Company 297 often held a "Howl Night," or "Rookie Night," i.e., "supervised noise," as a way of letting off steam.[44]

Nevertheless, the temptations to send recruits to water the flagpole,
find the key to it, and otherwise engage in horseplay, were strong, if atten-
uated in later years. If green enrollees could not be hazed, certainly some
fun could be had at their expense. The editor of Company 299's paper,
The 299th Broadcast, in welcoming a new contingent of 66 rookies from
Camp Dix, New Jersey, hoped that they would not become disgusted if
they had their beds short-sheeted their first night in camp. "After all, the
boys were only having some fun," he declared.[45]

Another perceived problem confronted, but as often ignored, was
that of swearing in camp. Perhaps on occasion hard langauge was understandable, as one poet suggested: "He calls a spade a spade does Joe/Save
when he drops it on his toe."[46] But seeing less humor in profanity, the
editor of Company 4468's paper, *The Bugle*, bluntly asserted that
"roughly speaking, too many speak roughly." The company's chaplain
further commented in a sermon that too many American boys and men
felt that the American spirit demanded that they must "never say die,
[but] say 'damn.'"[47] A writer in *The Catskill Crier* observed that "for
some mysterious reason, there's an idea in the mind of the average person, that in order to be a regular guy and have an aggressive dominat-
ing personality, he always must be tossing around the various four letter
equivalents for the reproductive function, the duties number one and
two, the equivalents for a scion of a female canine, and the offspring of
morganatic associations." While no "little Lord Fauntleroy" himself, he
nonetheless viewed with alarm the amazing amount of profanity and
obscenity that was considered "a substitute for wit and conversational
finesse."[48] Several commanding officers, in addressing the matter, had
recourse to General George Washington's well-known general order
issued in New York in July of 1776, deploring the "foolish and wicked
practice of profane cursing and swearing" being done in the Continental Army. If this attitude was good enough for General Washington, it
was worth heeding by the men in the CCC, so the usual exhortations
went.[49]

The enrollees sometimes responded. In Company 639 based at Win-
netka, Illinois, a "Hide-your-face" club was organized. Members pledged
to "abstain, at all times, and under any circumstances, from the use of
obscene language and vulgar expressions." The guilty party was required
to cover his face with his hands in shame when the rule was broken. If
he refused, he would be dropped from the club and his company would
henceforth be "avoided and his association undesired." The penalty for
profanity in Company 1527, of Sonora, Ohio—though "ordinary swearing [did] not count"—was a swat from each member of the "Anti-

Obscenity Club," using an oak paddle. For every "bad word" uttered by a member of Company 833, Santa Fe, New Mexico, a nickel was forfeited, the offenders in effect buying cokes for others in the company.[50]

The tendency of the men in the CCC to gripe was also addressed. An "old timer" in Company 1173 at Holyoke, Massachusetts, one Charles W. Lemanski, insisted that contemporary enrollees should compare their much better situations with those who enrolled in 1933. Then the men lived under plain canvas tents, yet the shelters were appreciated, even if they did have holes and "we slept in a big puddle when it rained." They often ate in the open, also in the rain, "with beef stew as main dish." The men often took their baths in a mountain brook. Indeed, in those days, CCCers were "men of iron" who had "guts." The *Wind Jammer* (Company 2754, Hot Springs, South Dakota) repeated a homily that seemed applicable: "Do you realize that a mule does not kick when he is pulling— neither does he pull when he is kicking."[51]

Another activity frequently deplored was "brown nosing," identified as "the favorite sport in CCC camps" by *The Dam Overflow* (Company 297, Loyston, Tennessee).[52]

The Field Supervisor of the CCC camps in Hawaii, Everett A. Pesonen, writing in the *Th-CCC News* (Hawaiian Miscellaneous Companies, Honolulu, Hawaii), identified, what to his mind, appeared to be another questionable practice. "Just as Clark Gable and some other movie sheiks have captivated the hearts of American girls, so have the Superman and his like captured the imaginations of our CCC youth," he began. In almost every locker copies of comic books featuring Superman, Dick Tracy, Batman, and many others would be found, he lamented. Indeed, "during their off hours these enrollee readers are living in the land of fancy, saving beautiful girls from savage monsters and villains and performing impossible feats of strength." But they should be aware that most of these publications were "poorly printed and damaging to eyesight. The time spent in reading them, if spent in study of a trade, would pay dividends in later life. By living in a land of wishfulness you are doing nothing to make your real life better," he argued. Insisting that his advice was "not a preachment against reading the comic magazines," he did want to point out "the dangers of over-doing it," the principal one being "that the second-hand thrills you get from reading them come from some imaginary guy's accomplishments—not yours!"[53]

The CCC press, on occasion, stressed manners and the "rules of civility." Accordingly, "Modern Manners for Men," derived from "[George] Washington's Rules of Civility"—which it was said he devised when he was a teenager—was reproduced in *Happy Days*.[54] Even in "the backwoods country of the Kiamichi Mountains," men of Company 310 at Stapp, Oklahoma, enrolled in a course of etiquette led by their educational adviser, Clarence Hunnicutt, using Emily Post's *Blue Book of Etiquette*, as their text. Following this instruction, the Commanding Officer, Captain Edwin C. Holmes, gave a dance, paid for out of company funds, to enable his men to "acquire needed practice in the gentle art of doing right by our Little Nells from far and near." On the eve of the event, Holmes, "fearing the brush hogs had not mastered their eitquet [sic] exercises and might revert to native catch-as-catch-can methods, [delivered] a lengthy lecture to the company." He stressed that "a dance ain't no rasslin' match—nor, furthermore, the warming up exercise for no wrestling match." The men apparently heeded his words, and "done a heap toward putting the social standards of dear old Stapp on a higher plane." Holmes was so pleased that he promised that the men could "throw another dance right away—tho 'throw' ain't the word for the high class dances we have around here now."[55]

Objectionable behaviour seemed all the more reprehensible in the improved circumstances that life in the CCC produced. The editor of *Grand Canyon Echoes* (Company 819, Grand Canyon, Arizona) assailed a rash of thefts in the company, resulting in dishonorable discharges. In addition, some of the boys [had even] been drunk on the job. This was dangerous and would also result in strong disciplinary action.[56]

Religion was frequently used to support good conduct and proper attitudes. Enrollees in Company 855, while stationed at El Paso and later at Elephant Butte, New Mexico, often entertained visitors from town who presented religious programs at the camp. In Littlefield, Texas, a couple, the W. E. Heathmans, conducted sing-songs and held well-attended Bible classes on Sundays.[57]

Wannamaker Teal, the associate editor of *The Bugle* (Company 4468, Barnwell, South Carolina), in his poem "Without God," indicated what religion meant to many enrollees: "A nation without a religion or God/Is like a tree cut loose from the sod/Is as a soldier without his shield/Gone forth for combat upon the field."[58]

There was always discipline to consider. As a help in these matters, Company 855 of El Paso, Texas, set up a Court of Criminal Appeals. Far from being only for amusement, the court addressed serious cases and used a jury picked from men of different barracks, as well as prosecuting and defense attorneys and a judge.[59] Several camps in the Grand Junction District of Colorado adopted a limited city form of self-government. Mayors, councilmen, and other officials, however, remained only an advisory committee for the officers on matters of disciplinary action, improvements, recreation and other phases of camp activity. Nonetheless, the enrollees did have some hand in their camps's governance and became aware of many needs, especially regarding discipline.[60] In Martin, South Dakota, six men of Company 4723, provided with an

"MP" armband, walked the streets of Martin, helping local police look after CCC men in town.[61] In Hawaii, at the TH-7 Waimea (Kauai) camp, good behaviour was encouraged by issuing to about six selected enrollees armbands with a letter "G" thereupon, standing for "Guardian" or "Good Behaviour." The band-wearers patrolled the streets of adjacent communities in part as safeguards "against probable undue 'VOCIFER-ATION' on the part of enrollees when off the camp premises."[62]

Sometimes, however, discipline and proper conduct demanded firmer measures. On one occasion, Captain William J. White, skipper of Company 3206, Manahawkin, New Jersey, had to quell a "mutiny" when a group of 31 enrollees rebelled against orders to go back on the regular work schedule. The men complained that they had not had enough time off between 3 A.M. Tuesday, when they came in from fighting a forest fire, and reporting for work on Wednesday morning. All 31 were given discharges and tickets to their homes. There were also occasional food riots and general mayhem—sometimes making national newspaper headlines—which had to be dealt with. In more extreme cases, even murder was committed in the CCC setting.[63]

As the CCC matured, disciplinary measures to be administered by the CO's were codified. Some of the "authorized punishments" ranged from bawling outs, through limiting privileges and using the miscreants for KP, to loss of pay, capped by the most extreme measure, "the big DD," i.e., a dishonorable discharge. These stemmed from the fact that the commanding officer had the authority to "keep the peace and order in his camp, direct the conduct of the members of his company at all times, and to 'fire' anyone who refuses to do the work expected of him." The enrollee was afforded quick justice, often tempered by "extenuating circumstances," and he also had the right of appeal to the Army Corps area commander in serious cases. By autumn of 1940, the administrative discharge was mitigated to a plain "dismissal." Only in cases of felony or moral turpitude would the CCC enrollees be given discharges with a "dishonorable" designation.[64]

One matter involving discipline at another level concerned the threat of venereal disease. Early in the history of the CCC, the War Department directed that men with such diseases were to be summarily discharged. But it later relented, and ordered that CCC men who contracted syphilis while in the Corps were to be given extended treatment before being discharged. If an enrollee's home state health department would not treat the men, the Army would, for a period of twenty weeks or longer before being sent home. The regulations also required prophylaxis by men exposed to possible venereal disease. Education was also employed to cope with such diseases, one of the common ploys was the showing of a film that made the rounds of the camps, entitled "Damaged

Lives." Medical officers usually concluded the program with appropriate remarks, "in language that every lad could understand."[65]

In general, Army medical and dental personnel took good care of their charges. Most camps had an infirmary with enrollees assigned as aides, which encouraged many to seek medical careers later.[66] Also, as was commonplace during 1930s America, numerous routine appendectomies and tonsil removals were performed, as revealed in the medical statistics of the CCC. Such diseases as mumps, measles, spinal meningitis and others were controlled by the frequent employment of camp-wide quarantines. The enrollees were also a convenient reservoir of guinea pigs used in the development of various sorts of preventative programs, including one for pneumonia. A vaccine for this dreaded disease was experimentally administered by the U.S. Army Medical Corps from 1933 to 1936 to enrollees in the First Corps Area with good results.[67]

The dental staffs were also active. For example, *The Dam Overflow* (Company 297, Loyston, Tennessee) reported that Lt. Hogan, the local dental officer, in a few days' visit to the camp extracted 146 teeth from 64 men, a commentary on their poor dental health.[68]

One matter seemed less pressing in those days than in our present age: the use of tobacco. It was a subject of some discussion, however, as in an article in *The Heppner Roundup* (*Company 297*, Heppner, Oregon), "Tobacco—Is It Harmful?" The general consensus was, perhaps not, because its sedative effects had greatly benefited men in combat in World War I. Because it was a depressant, it also helped people of nervous and irritable disposition, and those on diets were also aided.[69]

Throughout, the CCC enjoyed a remarkable success, as the Army had in World War I, in developing a sense of comradeship and a willingness of the enrollees to assist their buddies. When enrollee Edwin R. Cook of Company 795, then in a hospital in Little Rock, Arkansas, was ill with pneumonia, his campmates provided a ticket for his mother who lived in Bismarck, North Dakota, to travel to his bedside where he was soon recovering. In Company 613 at Marseilles, Illinois, members contributed to a "death fund," which provided transportation home and back for men who had deaths in their immediate families.[70]

The men were not always in camp. It became customary for the enrollees to obtain five-day leaves over either the Christmas or New Year's holiday. This staggered schedules enabled the camps to function, albeit on a holiday routine. The men also had Thanksgiving Day off with pay, but not the day before or after.[71]

Also regarding holidays, anticipating customs prevalent during World War II years and beyond, many CCC camps arranged Christmas parties for children living nearby, featuring "Santa Claus in OD." Company funds and donations made "Christmas a real event in the camp and community." Many companies refurbished old toys for their guests, the veterans' companies especially responding. They all took the lead of *Happy Days*, which urged that the local kids should know that "there is a Santa Claus," and could learn from "a lot of big brothers in the CCC that everything is all right after all." At the national level, on at least one occasion the White House Christmas tree was supplied by the CCC. Cut in the Marquette National Forest, the tree was sent to Washington by the men of Company 667 of Raco, Michigan, "as an expression of their gratitude for the opportunities made available to them by the Government." Mrs. Roosevelt professed to be "delighted."[72]

There were numerous instances of unselfish service throughout the history of the corps. Presaging the "Habitat for Humanity" initiatives, CCC men in Pactola, South Dakota, responded to a program instituted by the civic fathers to assist the local neediest families. Though the men of Company 2748 had little money, they did possess "quite a few strong arms and husky backs," which they employed in building a new home for a Mexican widow and her four small children who had been living in a wretched shack. The new structure had "plenty of windows, a real door that remains shut, and there is even a kitchen wing where a new and bigger stove is installed," one account explained. The men also cut a pile of firewood, which brought "exclamations of shy delight" from the recipients.[73]

CCC men were frequently recognized for acts of courage and derring-do, such as searching for missing aircraft and persons, and once frustrated a kidnapping. Regarding the latter, two CCC men came upon a woman bound, gagged and blindfolded in a car, and released her, foiling the dastardly deed.[74]

In October 1941, Company 126, North Haverill, New Hampshire, aided in the search for five-year-old Pamela Hollingworth of Lowell, Massachusetts, who wandered from a picnic in the forests of Mount Chocorua near Albany, New Hampshire. She was lost for eight days in sleet, rain and snow, and was found alive and reasonably well by Foreman William A. Watson and six other members of the company. The successful rescue received nation-wide attention, and letters of commendation poured in to the company. Duly impressed, *The Boston Globe* issued a special "Pamela's Edition."[75]

But the CCC was sometimes called upon to find missing persons within their own ranks. On several occasions, *Happy Days* published letters from families seeking news of missing members. In a typical query, under the heading, "Anybody Here Seen Kelly?" Mrs. Kate Kelly of Marciline, Missouri, wrote: "Sirs: I am in search of two missing sons, Wilfred William Kelly and James Thomas Kelly. Rumor has it they were in the CCC at one time. Would you ask thru your paper for them to write to me?"[76]

The CCC perhaps most clearly distinguished itself in flood relief and on the fire line. Indeed, it became commonplace for the CCC to be engaged in fire fighting. In August 1939, in the midst of one of the worst fire seasons in years, more than 5,000 CCC men were on the firelines in Utah, Montana, Idaho, California, Oregon and Washington. Some companies gained a considerable reputation as fire fighters. One was Company 297 at Kanona, New York, though its primary job was setting out trees. During one month, it put out two barn fires and five forest fires in and around Bath, New York, "all of which was service rendered gladly to the community." The same company gained further renown when floods ravaged the area, convincing the company paper, *The Kanona Daze*, that the company perhaps should change to a "FFF" company—for "Fire and Flood Fighters"—rather than a CCC organization.[77]

There were, however, tragic consequences for some. For instance, in 1937 in the Shoshone National Forest of northwestern Wyoming, 15 men, 10 of whom were CCC enrollees, lost their lives in the tragic Blackwater fire. The CCC later erected a monument at the site to commemorate their sacrifice.[78]

Matters of safety were among the chief concerns of those in authority. Indeed, the statistics for the first year of the CCC's existence make for sober reading. There had been 417 deaths, of which 69 were work-related. Twenty-three of these were caused by falling objects, while blasting accidents caused eleven. There had been 566 serious auto and motorcycle accidents, of which 119 were fatal. Recreational and "horseplay" accidents accounted for 33 deaths and 384 wounded. Drownings were also all too frequent. Non-fatal accidents included 709 hernias, 534 falls, and 463 handtool mishaps. On average, 1,200 enrollees were injured each week. Many of the accidents were plainly "due to early unfamiliarity of the men with their surroundings and equipment." A few examples clearly reveal that there were many dangers in the camps. When Company 141 in Charleston, Rhode Island undertook to build a baseball diamond, Charles E. Baxter was killed when he fell in front of an improvised roller made of two large mill pulleys. Enrollee Asil Jones of Company 996, Big Bar, California, was fatally injured when a one-ton cement mixer rolled off a truck and crushed him. Gleck Sawyers of Company 1369 at New Castle, Virginia, was instantly killed when he fell beneath the wheels of a fast-moving freight.[79]

And there were other dangers to life and limb. Irvin Mace, a 20-year-old enrollee, lost his life outside the usual line of duty. He was found with his throat cut outside a dance hall at a tavern near Houston, Missouri. The company commander of Company 3741, Hayti, Missouri, according to its paper, the *Hayti Scoop*, warned that the CCC enrollees should steer clear of "common dance halls and other such places to have a 'good' time."[80]

Neither were suicides unknown. Stanley Ziaja of Company 297, on Wednesday, April 3, 1935, stayed in camp because he was not feeling well, but in the afternoon Captain J. B. Jarnagin, the CO, received word that a boy had jumped from Witts Bridge spanning Clinch River near the camp. His clothes were discovered at the bridge, which raised the question: Had he gone swimming or committed suicide? Though a reward was offered by the company for knowledge of his whereabouts or location of his body, he was never found.[81]

Fechner responded to the safety problem on April 14, 1934, by initiating a comprehensive safety and health program followed by a series of bulletins, which *Happy Days* and the camp papers were urged to broadcast widely. In order to hold down vehicle speeds, a major cause of deaths and injury, he stipulated that all truck drivers must be licensed. Governors were ordered to be installed on trucks, reducing their speed to 35 miles per hour. All vehicles were ordered to stop at train tracks; passengers must keep their limbs inside the vehicle, and there was to be no riding on fenders, bumpers, running boards or on the tops of cabs. The men were forbidden to hitchhike or "grab a handful of boxcars," but these prohibitions were widely ignored, and the deaths and injuries that sometimes resulted continued to plague the CCC throughout its life.[82] As a further measure, enrollees were not allowed to keep or operate private autos on camp grounds though some got around these restrictions by garaging them in nearby towns or parking them with friends or family members. As to the railroads, for many years the railroads themselves helped toward a solution of this problem by allowing CCC men to travel at the low rate of one cent per mile. Unhappily, this "so-called charity rate" was rescinded by the Interstate Commerce Commission in December 1938, causing consternation within the CCC, once more throwing many enrollees upon their own devices, sometimes with fatal results.[83]

Education, information and safety campaigns figured in efforts to curtail the dangers of CCC life. Though company papers made their own contributions, *Happy Days* took the lead among CCC publications in publicizing safety issues. It often included an entire safety page, with articles and features on the topic. There were also many columns such as the "CCC Safety Hall of Fame," identifying drivers with good records. Another was "Safety Jingles," featuring submissions from men in the field. One, submitted by Harold Riggott of Company 2105 at Upton, Massachusetts, reads: "Here's the sad story/Of Peg-Leg-Bob—/He tried to split wood/With his foot on the log."

Another, offered by Patrick Dolan of Company 3758, Moberly, Missouri, went: "He could see no reason for goggles/He let his sledge hammer fall/Too late for him now to see reason/For now he sees nothing at all." James D. Diamond of Company 1425, Foley, Alabama, also contributed one: "Tony felt the bandsaw blade/Its tension for to see/Before, he had five fingers/And now he has but three."[84]

Fire safety was front and center of much preventive efforts. "Lest we forget," began one presentation in *Happy Days*, "one tree will make a million matches, but one match may destroy a million trees." Enrollees were frequently reminded that smoking was prohibited while at work in the forests, and consequently, only the old soldier's quid or "chaw" was permitted.[85] The camp paper, *The Puncher Pruff* (Company 798, Fort Robinson, Nebraska) joined in, affirming that "this is God's Country. Don't set it on fire and make it look like hell!"

While accidents continued to plague the Corps to the end of its existence, the concerted efforts of all concerned had some salutary results. By late 1935, Fechner reported that the accident rate was improving and that by that date, the death rate was 2.87 per 1,000 enrollees, compared with the national average of 8.07 per 1,000. Though the causes of enrollee deaths continued to be topped by vehicular accidents, followed by drownings and homicides, these all steadily declined from 1935 to 1941, with deaths from vehicles in 1941 being less than half of those for 1935. Rates for homicide were about two per 100,000 enrollees in 1935, while in 1941, the rate had fallen to less than one per 100,000.[86]

5

The Powers That Be

"This historic, Rooseveltian drama."
—"Lessons From Woodlore,"
Happy Days, June 16, 1934

"Many nations are armed to the teeth but they are not
wisdom teeth."
—*The Bugle* (Company 4468, Barnwell,
South Carolina), April 30, 1937

There seems little doubt that the CCC was one of President Roosevelt's favorite New Deal creations. He visited CCC camps when he could, ventures which he greatly enjoyed, and to which the men warmly responded. His first outing was to five camps near Washington, D.C., in Virginia. The president was "elated" by what he saw: "I wish I could spend a couple of months here myself," he told the men at Big Meadow Camp of Company 350, Skyland, Virginia. "The only difference between us is that I am told you men have put on an average of 12 pounds each. I am trying to lose 12 pounds." At Camp Nira, on the Skyland Drive in the Shenandoah National Park where Company 1316 was based, Roosevelt greatly enjoyed a pageant depicting the demise of "Old Man Depression." Two men, one labeled the "CCC" and another the "NIRA," put the Depression to flight to the warm applause of the audience.[1]

The president later made a great impression on Bill Briggs, of Company 1240 in Glacier Park, Montana, when he visited camps in that remote region. In a guest editorial published in *Happy Days*, Briggs exulted: "I saw the President! For eleven minutes he was with us; blue-eyed, genial, smiling ... his keen eyes flashing over our camp and over us." Though he was a cripple, here was no frail man: "I found a giant with massive shoulders and powerful arms that belied the steel braces on his legs. His face was ruddy and deeply tanned, his blue eyes flashed vigor and good humor, and his shock of iron-gray hair tossed in the wind. He spoke quietly … heartily." Indeed, Briggs felt that "everything about him spoke of power," yet he was serene despite carrying the worries of the nation on his shoulders. "Even the surrounding mountains and green-clad pines must have sensed that a great man was in our midst. Never did they seem so majestic and grand. The air was electric with the sense of a great happening." Briggs had also caught a glimpse of the First Lady and the president's sons, Theodore and Franklin D., Jr., both "blue-eyed powerful counterparts of their famous 'Dad.'"[2]

But the men of Company 1429 at Camp Meriwether near Warm Springs, Georgia, saw the president at least once a year, a "privilege not enjoyed by any other company." This was because the Little White House was "only a stone's throw" away.[3]

One of the president's visits to Georgia especially thrilled Donald Burns, editor of *Pine Mountain Progress* (Company 4463, Chipley, Georgia), who had a "chat" with the president. FDR put him at ease, observing that "I used to be an editor myself—of my college paper." Burns posed a question about the future of the CCC: "Was it to be established on non-relief basis?" he wanted to know. FDR responded that "as long as there are men and boys whose people need relief, they will be given first consideration." Asked if he had read *Gone with the Wind*, he chuckled and said, "Certainly." His secretary, M.H. McIntyre, was nervous at FDR's off-the-cuff answers to this reporter, and asked Burns not "to let this out to any publication but your own…. The President shouldn't have done this," McIntyre grumbled. "He doesn't [normally] give exclusive interviews." He feared that now "every camp and college paper in the country would be writing for one." Burns assured him that this would be an exclusive interview, and took especial note of Roosevelt's final response. The president indicated that there was enough work for three or four more years where Company 4463 was located, and therefore its future seemed secure. "And I thought the President would be a tough interviewee!" Burns exclaimed.[4]

Another poetically inclined enrollee, Christopher Bangert of Company 234, Orange, New Jersey, was likewise worshipful, and in his offering, "The Man of the Hour," noted that "Although a year has passed away/It only seems like yesterday/That from somewhere there came a call/To end the cares and woes of all." There were by then "Three hundred thousand sturdy men" at work, "So Hail the man who ended sorrow/Hail the great man of tomorrow/We'll give him everything we've got/And prosperity is sure to knock."[5]

Enrollee McNiele of Company 914, Nevada City, California, saw

FDR as "a modern Houdini," who pulled forth the NRA, the CWA, the CCC, and other similar agencies from the hat of fate. "While standing on the verge of that ever-widening gulf of unemployment," with his eye on the common man, he strove "with every known power to pierce its mysteries, he studie[d] the troubled horizon and he [had] a strange vision. A cloud of doubt arises before him, [and] in that cloud he sees the soul of the forgotten man and in that soul he finds understanding." This vision was the genesis of the CCC, and its spirit was that "of the Revolutionary Days, [and] the spirit that prompted Abraham Lincoln to take a definite stand." There was a difference, though, he declared: "It is intensified to a degree expected to be attained by this generation." Already, by 1934 at least one CCC enrollee sensed the importance of his peers.[6] Throughout the years of the existence of the CCC, the theme of praise of the president commonly reappeared, as in a poem in *Vets Voice* (Company 1744, Bayport, Minnesota):

> Thanksgiving on the 23rd
> Brings gratitude heartfelt;
> Some are thanking heaven
> And others—Roosevelt.[7]

Annually, the president's birthday (January 30) was the occasion and excuse for special celebrations in CCC companies throughout the country. These regularly featured parties, birthday cakes, and often dances and balls. The celebrations were also frequently coupled with the raising of funds for the Warm Springs Foundation, the president's favorite charity. And naturally poetry was employed to commemorate the day. Ray C. Farmer of Company 1950 in Upland, California, who contributed numerous poems to *Happy Days*, in the January 28, 1939, issue offered "The Enrollee's Tribute to the President..." the people's "Champ" in which he remembered thankfully, "thy happy, natal hour," at which time a tiny baby was born, "Destined, ere selfish greed could kill, devour/Savior, giving hope to those, forlorn." Indeed, "when the knell of revolution came to ear," the election of FDR stilled it, and the nation was on the road to prosperity. Farmer also regarded the president as an international figure of the first rank: "As world leader of sublime democracy/You would safeguard principles of peace," and the "Good Neighbor policy" was solving international problems "till war would cease." Withal, FDR seemed especially close to the Almighty, if not god-like himself.

Another form of homage was the naming of camp papers after the chief executive. An example was the *Rooseveltian* (Company 322 of Edinburg, Virginia). When the men of Company 1652 of Gold Beach,

Oregon launched their four-page weekly, *The Sea Horse*, the premier issue was formally dedicated "to our Commander-in-Chief, His Excellency, Franklin Delano Roosevelt, President of the United States, whose wisdom and love for his fellowmen moved him to found the Civilian Conservation Corps, that we, citizens of this nation whose course he steers, might be preserved from extreme want and from that worse than death— crushed hopes and broken faith in mankind...." Drawings of the chief executive's face also appeared on camp paper covers more frequently than those of any other subject.[8]

And the portrait of the president might be more formally utilized, at least according to the chaplain of District No. 1, New Jersey, D.H. Gerrish. He suggested in a letter to *Happy Days* that a picture of FDR be hung on the wall of every recreation building "in our far-flung CCC." "How President Roosevelt's kindly, courageous face would bolster manhood, and inspire courage!" he unabashedly declared.[9]

There were other ways to recognize FDR's accomplishments. Nicholas Ciorciari, the leader of the Royal Mariners dance orchestra of Brooklyn, New York (a former member of Company 205 in New York), composed one of his most popular foxtrots to honor the president: "Roosevelt's CCC." He also worked up a special arrangement of the piece for the U.S. Army Band.[10]

Roosevelt also normally received widespread support from the CCC in his political campaigns. For instance, *The Bugle* (Company 4468, Barnwell, South Carolina) once stated that the voters must "decide only whether the country made more progress from 1928 to 1932, or from 1933 to 1936," clearly revealing its own position: "We hereby nominate Herbert Hoover for reelection as Ex-President of the United States."[11]

Undoubtedly, then, the most striking aspect regarding officialdom for the men of the CCC was the role of FDR in the scheme of things. His dominance in the country at the time, especially through the New Deal innovations and initiatives, was paramount and the CCCers reflected this. Perceived as the nation's father figure, he was certainly that to many enrollees, who would have agreed with those Americans who regarded him as "the commander in chief of [our] generation."[12]

Appreciative of their interest, the president in his turn undertook to encourage the men of the CCC. In addition to the camp visits, on July 17, 1933, he spoke specifically to them on the radio. Seeking to encourage the work ethic within the Corps, he asserted that "too much in recent years, large numbers of our population have thought of success as an opportunity to gain money with the least possible work. It is time for each and every one of us to cast away self-destroying, Nation-destroying efforts to get something for nothing and to appreciate that satisfying rewards and safe rewards come only through honest work. That must be the new spirit of the American future. You are the vanguard of that new spirit."[13]

But Roosevelt was not the only one in a top position that the men heeded. They naturally paid considerable attention to the director of the organization, Robert Fechner. By the late 1930s, however, the leader had been ailing for some time, and attention was focused on his deteriorating condition. *Happy Days* recorded in 1939 that he had been in Walter Reed hospital for some months but by year's end, was apparently in dire straits. Reflecting this fact, Fechner's short Christmas greetings to the men of the CCC concluded on a solemn note: "I only wish that it were possible for me to talk with each of you in person at this season of the year, when all of us look resolutely toward the future and derive renewed inspiration from the life of Him whose birthday we commemorate on Christmas Day." A few days later—on December 31, 1939—Fechner died, and six enrollees from camps near Washington acted as pall bearers at his funeral. At least one "explanation" for his death came in an editorial in *Happy Days* entitled, "There Must Be Trouble in Heaven," intimating that Fechner's presence was needed to straighten out the chaos: "And if there is any sort of depression up above and de Lawd is worried about what will happen to his younger angels who can't find things to do, it won't be long before Director Fechner has them building terraces in the clouds and cleaning up the celestial forests."[14]

Naturally, Fechner's role in founding and guiding the CCC for many years was emphasized in many camp papers following his death. One was *The Broadcast* (Company 1742, Gallatin, Missouri), which featured him on its January 1940 cover, as well as editorializing about his life, asserting that "we feel that here was a man whom the Creator brought up from the crowd to carry on for awhile in a critical period of American youth."

Predictably, his replacement was James McEntee, who had been the executive assistant director of the organization from its beginning. He was sworn in on March 7, 1940.[15]

Soon memorials to Fechner began to appear, one being the "Robert Fechner Memorial Forest," a part of the George Washington National Forest in Virginia, so designated by FDR. Another, a large rock outcrop, "Robert Fechner Rock" in Shenandoah National Park, also in Virginia, was dedicated by the Secretary of the Interior, Harold L. Ickes. And "Fechner Trees" were planted in numerous camps as memorials to their dead leader.[16]

Despite the preoccupation of enrollees with leaders at the highest level, to many of them, "leadership" meant the commanding officers and the "overhead" staff who were much closer to them in the chain of command. What these did at the lower level was of prime importance in setting the direction that the CCC took, both as to details and its general course. This situation stemmed from the fact of the involvement of the military establishment in the founding and running of the CCC.[17]

Indubitably, the role of the military was central to much of the CCC's efforts and success, with significance beyond its career persisting into World War II. From the outset, the U.S. Army and other military organizations were involved in the work of the CCC, and the camps were under military command. Earlier in the history of the CCC, the military played a greater role than later. This was perhaps inevitable, because it initially seemed necessary to place the men in proven hands. As time went on, the Regular Army had its own agenda and wanted less to do with the CCC. Thereafter, the men from the branches of the regular armed forces were withdrawn, and were replaced by men from the reserve components of the miltary establishment.

Later still, many of the leadership slots were filled by civilians, though reserve military personnel continued to serve in these capacities to the end of the CCC. Throughout, the men and their barracks were regularly inspected as though they were in the Army. They also stood evening retreat formations with the lowering of the flag, and their day's round of activities followed a quasi-military schedule. Late in the life of the Corps, after much debate on the matter, a smattering of drill was introduced into its scheduled activities.

Inevitably, the presence of military officers had direct consequences for the enrollees in the CCC, sometimes to good effect, though not always. In any case, the abilities, attitudes and general competence of the officers could substantially affect how the company functioned. Lieutenant Robert A. Stevens, for one, endeared himself as a junior officer of two companies: 3736 at Canton, Missouri, and 1742 based near Tarkio, Missouri. This led one enrollee of Company 3736 to lament that it was a blue Monday when the outfit learned that Stevens was being relieved from duty, and "I have never seen a more dissatisfied group of boys." Stevens had built up the educational program, had instructed in several of the classes, had greatly improved the company mess and canteen, and was active in sports, being "one of the biggest boosters in this activity."[18]

Indeed, many of the officers met with the approval of their charges. The *Grand Canyon Echoes* (Company 819, Grand Canyon, Arizona) once editorialized that there were rather frequent transfers of officers, part of the "old army game," but "somehow we seldom come out second best. With scarcely an exception all the officers are regular fellows, with wide understanding and with the boys' interests at heart." In like manner, *Buffalo Prints* (Company 2356, Amherst, Virginia) asserted that the company wished "to take this opportunity to express their gratitude to the Officers of this camp for their fair play shown to the enrollees, as a whole.

The company is backing the Officers up in any way they possibly can for the betterment of the camp life."[19]

When Company 299 got a new commanding officer in the person of Captain J.A. Wilson, an instantaneous change was noted. While the former commander, Capt. Ralph Shultz, had treated the enrollees as teen-agers, Wilson regarded them as men. It was all wrong to treat them as mere boys, he declared. "I don't know where the hell you fellows got into the habit! You're men—making your own living, and helping your families along, too. *Boys* nothing!" When floods swept over much of the area near the camp of Company 299, as at Walton, Delhi and Sidney, New York, in appreciation of their hard work in flood relief, Wilson staged a "Howl Night," an "all-company jamboree," so that the men could let off steam, and also provided each member with two bottles of beer. There was a bonfire, singing, boxing matches, three-legged races, and other entertainment. The enrollees were indeed treated like men: like soldiers, in fact.[20]

A measure of how the enrollees felt about their commanding officer was often revealed when the officer obtained a new posting. It became customary for the men to treat their departing skipper to a farewell party, and if he were popular, they sometimes gave him relatively expensive gifts. A new Sam Browne belt was a common present. When Capt. James G. Glass, the CO of Company 360, Cooksburg, Pennsyvlania, accepted a new assignment at Fort Hoyle, his men gave him an elaborate dinner and presented him with an engraved saber. They also voted unanimously to name the camp "Camp Glass" in his honor, because he "did so much for [it] and the fellows."[21]

Unquestionably, though, the military services sought in various ways to influence the men suddenly under their control, which proved to be controversial subsequently. For instance, the magazine *Our Navy* ran ads in *Happy Days* suggesting "all you men who are now in the woods but who will some day be sailing the seas in the U.S. Navy, AHOY!" They were invited to subscribe to the twice-monthly publication for five dollars per year. Rather less subtly, some 45 enrollees of Camp San Jacinto, San Bernardino Forest, California, were escorted by Lt. Macklin, USN, to see the old frigate *Constitution*, then moored at San Diego. They also received a conducted tour of submarines and the submarine tender, the USS *Holland*. Later, hundreds of CCC men from the Fort MacArthur District in California visited the fleet, touring several cruisers anchored in Los Angeles harbor. The visits, intended to acquaint the men with the U.S. Navy and its operations, were no doubt successful, especially later when war clouds gathered. *Happy Days* reported that by the autumn of 1940, about 10 percent of Navy enlistees were former CCC enrollees.[22] Not to be outdone by the Navy, some of the commanding officers of

CCC camps who were in the Army Air Corps likewise sometimes used their skills and positions to impress their charges. One of these was Captain Barber, commanding officer of Company 1901, Yosemite National Park, California. As a reward for having the best-kept barracks at the camp, he took 14 of his enrollees up for a flight—two at a time—in a Waco biplane hangared in Merced. Similarly, Captain Kerr, CO of Company 1210, Ivy, Tennessee, piloted his plane over the camp performing maneuvers at which his enrollees "stared into the air with wild-eyed expressions," and enthusiastically talked about "our flying captain until lights out."[23]

It was indeed difficult for military men to abstain from military-like conduct. Captain James M. Walker, commanding officer of Company 1964 at Milford, Utah, for instance, awarded medals to four enrollees of his company "for outstanding service for the fourth enrollment period." Exactly what sort of decorations these were is not recorded. In the Third District, some camps designated certain men "CP's," denoting "Camp Police," to help maintain discipline. The men with blue arm bands with white letters, "CP" had regular beats in nearby towns much as the "MPs" did in the Army.[24]

As time went on, more and more military rank and speciality insignia appeared for first aid men, leaders, truck drivers, company clerks, storekeepers, mess and canteen stewards, buglers, and mechanics, among others. Shoulder patches were often affixed to uniforms indicating "U.S. CCC." More familiar were rank chevrons, usually embroidered green on red background.[25]

The flag formations in the mornings, and the standing of evening retreat, were reminders that the CCC bore at least a faint aura of the military, which, however, favorably impressed some of the enrollees. One man—unnamed—of Company 3439, Sparta, Georgia, admitted that "when in the mornings we are summoned out to witness the raising of the flag, the bugle sounds its silvery notes and the banner begins its ascent, there stirs within me emotions of honor, patriotism and respect that are difficult to control." The strains of the bugle conjured up for him the sound of many of "the long-dead voices of ancestors who lived and died for this country." They compelled him to live the coming day in "a manner that befits a son of [this] America." The unfurled flag, therefore, signified that "our country has embarked upon yet another day's voyage, and it rises to receive the blessing of the morning sun." To him, it stood for the "inestimable privilege of living and functioning in a free nation."[26]

As part of the command structure, the chaplains likewise naturally attempted to exert some influence on their charges. Among avenues utilized were columns both in *Happy Days* and in various camp papers. One chaplain, Captain Charles M. Kinard, in a short column "Chaplain's Chats" in *Happy Days*, sought to silence "gripers" and "grouches" who were a "nuisance and a bore," and who were a "constant stream of poison in our spring of life." He recommended that the grouches adopt the slogan: "KWITCHERBELLIAKEN."[27]

It is therefore readily understandable why many observers considered the CCC to be at least partially militarized. To others, however, it was not militarized enough. In the circumstances, the question of whether or not the CCC was indeed part of the military establishment—or should be—was a subject of considerable interest and discussion within the Corps and the nation at large. Persisting for most of the CCC's existence, the substance of the often intensive debates poured out in the pages of the CCC papers.

There were some mistaken notions, for instance, that if a lad enters the CCC, then Uncle Sam "'has him by the short hair' and will try to make a soldier out of him whether he likes it or not, just because he has signed up in a government organization." But such was not the case, so an editor of the *TH-CCC News* explained.[28] While it was true that the enrollees "must obey the will of the superior, otherwise we would have no discipline nor coherence in the CCC, or any organization," another paper, *The Tumbleweed* (Company 3802, Littlefield, Texas) argued, yet, "within the limits imposed by their orders, there is still a great field for the exercise of individual initiative. Obedience we must have, but it should be reasoning and intelligent obedience, [and] not the blind obedience of dumb animals." Another enrollee, speaking out in the *Stockade*, insisted that the CCC, while administered by the Army, did not bear "even a suggestion of military discipline. There is discipline, but it is the friendly man-to-man sort of thing which no sensible person can resent." The only thing compulsory was to work on the work projects. All the rest, such as the educational projects, for instance, were voluntary. He had found the Army officers quite congenial, and had heard of no complaints from his fellows. There were no doubt some slave-driving officers, but he had no personal knowledge of any.

Captain Homer Dye, of the Arkansas District of the Seventh Corps Area, compared and contrasted the concept of discipline in the Army and the CCC. In the Army, the skipper of a regular Army outfit had some "inexorable rules and impressive traditions" to assist him in maintaining discipline and respect of the men in his command. "The oath that the recruit takes at the time of enlistment is something of an awe-inspiring mouthful, and once it is taken, there are teeth in it. [There was] the firing squad at sunrise, in the final extremity." But this did not apply in the CCC. He noted that the military officers in the camps must learn how to lead without recourse to such traditional aids of command as the salute, standing at attention, and other "habits of deference and respect for the superior officer [which were] products of ages of Army experience in dealing with masses of men."[29]

Because many of the enrollees were favorably impressed by their contact with the military, they often requested military training in their camps, a stance that was variously embraced in some quarters in the nation. A letter in *Happy Days* explained: "In our hitch in the CCC we have come in contact with and learned to know numerous officers of the U.S. Army with pleasing personalities, high standards of morality and very influential men. It has always been our ambition to impersonate them," and hence the enrollees desired more contact with officers with an eye to becoming involved in the military themselves.[30]

Indeed, military training in the CCC was the crux of the matter. Company 299's paper, *The Script*, interviewed several enrollees on the subject. Claire Sinner felt that such training would help the nation prepare in case war should become inevitable. Also, the physical conditioning would be beneficial. Harry Schwarts was in favor if the Air Corps were involved, and with flight training widely given, "because the next war will be fought in the air," he declared. William Pratt was opposed, however, because "we have enough work to do as it is." Also other countries would think that the USA was secretly preparing for war, regarding the CCC as a "hidden army," which notion would be greatly intensified if CCC adopted military training. William Bouchard was not in favor because military training only promoted war, which was "a gross waste of human life and materials." In the future, the nation might need a large military force, but "in war even the winner loses horribly. To promote progress we must take every step to prevent war so [we must] carefully avoid any military formations."[31]

Happy Days, at least initially, stressed the role of the U.S. Army in the nation's affairs, but it eventually became ambivalent on the subject of military training in the CCC. Naturally disposed towards the military, it nonetheless was also in tune with the Corps' management, the Roosevelt administration, and the Army high command, none of which was interested in making the CCC an adjunct of the Army. It accordingly served as a more-or-less neutral voice, sounding board and clearing house for the debates that swept the nation on the subject.[32]

Those who favored military training in the Corps never lacked suggestions as to how military training might be implemented. Lon M. Sniffen, of Company 1797, Seneca, Kansas, thought that ROTC and CMTC units might be created at CCC camps. This would take care of military training and allow only those interested to participate. These programs would be part of the educational curriculum the same as other classes. Joseph P. Bitzer, District Headquarters Company, Ft. Des

Moines, Iowa, suggested that selected CCC camps be strictly designated for military training and that all members of the CCC attend a Citizens Military Training Camp one month a year while continuing to draw their CCC pay. One unnamed veteran wanted the vets to train other enrollees: "We Vets are not too old to help…. We are not all washed up as most people think."[33]

Proponents of the negative side were equally outspoken. One veteran of the Great War, Thomas T. Tanous of Company 1920 at Willows, California, was strongly opposed to anything redolent of the military: "I saw morgues with caskets piled full of dead awaiting burial," he recalled. His personal advice was for the CCC to "forget military training," and also to "forget war and all it stands for." The men, rather, should "ponder on some constructive possibilities, such as finding a new and easier method of reforestation, soil erosion and flood control, something that will benefit humanity, and make this country a paradise on earth." He was loyal to the nation's flag, but could see no reason for the needless sacrifice of lives. If enrollees wanted the military, they should enlist in the regular services. J.E. Kimes of Company 2823, Morris, Oklahoma, argued that military training on a part-time basis would not justify its extra time and expense, and "we already have an Army, why create another?" The nation's natural resources were, in any case, "our greatest bulwark … against any enemy whatsoever," and the CCC was specifically created for this purpose alone. To Bernard Harkness, a foreman in Company 275, Moravia, New York, military drill and the CCC mission were "an oil and water combination" that simply would not mix. There were too many rush projects under way and too many dams to be poured, and he wanted the army "heartily [to]subscribe to a policy of hands off the CCC."[34]

Other stances in the nation which spilled over into the CCC and its papers, and which had a bearing on the arguments about military training, were pacifism and isolationism. Many Americans clung to the notions once advanced by William Jennings Bryan, that "should war be forced upon America, a million men would spring to arms overnight, prepared to smite the enemy hip and thigh," though not before. Charles W. Dexter, of Company 2335 in Waynesboro, Pennsylvania, agreed, observing that one could not extinguish a fire with more fire; could not stop hate by hating. The opposite was true. Therefore, America should "fight war with peace." It had been proved that to fight "A War to End All Wars" was folly, and the United States could "do more for the world by remaining neutral and non-aggressive, and proving the profits of peace and the greater losses of war." Many enrollees of Company 2328 at Homer City, Pennsylvania, and no doubt elsewhere, strongly supported Anne Morrow Lindbergh's views as expressed in her book *The Wave of the Future*, in which she argued that America should avoid entanglements in "hopeless" crusades abroad to "save civilization." Americans should instead engage in a peaceful reformation at home.[35] George Abalan, of Company 2137 in Centennial, Wyoming, concurred and asked in his poem, "Not For Us," why should Americans fight across the sea and bring despair and misery to the land? He advised remaining neutral, "and leave war alone."[36]

Jimmy Doyle, a member of the veterans' unit, Company 1561 in Nashville, Indiana, in his "Yuletide," added his two cents' worth. He advised that especially in the spirit of the season, Americans should stay "right here for Christmas," and "glorify the Lord," the Prince of Peace who came to earth to bring good will to man, "And didn't use a sword."[37]

All of these were certainly beautiful theories, the critics of pacifism admitted, but they glossed over the fact that it would be extremely cruel to send unprepared youth into battle. Theodore Doiron of Company 4403, Lafayette, Louisiana, for one, vociferously insisted that America would not be well served by the kind of man who "sit[s] near the flag and preach[es] pacific doctrines," but rather by those "who are alert, prepared, and willing to sacrifice everything in its defense."[38]

One area in the CCC which did more than talk about military training in the camps was Hawaii. This, no doubt, reflected the sense in the Islands that they were more directly exposed to threats of war, as events indeed bore out. For whatever reason, the Hawaiian CCC press reveals that the enrollees there were simply more war-conscious, and a good deal more overtly patriotic, than elsewhere in the CCC. In addition to the morning calisthenics which were then being conducted throughout the CCC, at the Territory of Hawaii Camp Nine on Molokai, "the world's smallest CCC Camp," and at other sites, the enrollees voluntarily agreed to put in 30 minutes of close-order drill each afternoon after supper. Beyond this, they began using the local National Guard Armory for an extra weekly hour of intensive drill. One enrollee at the CCC camp at Waimea on Kauai, Mumo Sakauyue, rather fancifully described these events: "With an eye for soundness of body and coordination of mind, the enrollees of this camp are daily going through their calisthenics. As the tropic sky tinges with the coloring rays of dawn, the barking command of Project Assistant Elsie Enriquez can be clearly heard as it is carried on the morning breeze. The blue and white of clean undershirts and denims blend well with Old Glory who waves approvingly overhead."[39]

A sampling of opinion among the enrollees of Territory of Hawaii Camp Seven at Waimea, Kauai, reveals a great deal about the patriotism then current there. D.S. Ramos observed: "We should consider it a privilege to serve our country in these troubled times." Archie Masuda stated that "An American is not afraid to stand at the front rank to defend the

Stars and Stripes against any foreign foe!" As to the prospects of war, Mume Sakauye noted that conflicts were "the remains of barbaric instinct and as long as such remains in the heart of mankind, we will have wars!" Therefore, Hawaiians should be among those prepared for the inevitable coming conflict.[40]

Whatever the arguments about militarizing the CCC, there were strong, decisive centers of opposition. One of the most important was the Army itself. Brig. Gen. George P. Tyner, of the War Department, asserted that the Army had never advocated military training for the Civilian Conservation Corps for several reasons. In the first place, the training of a soldier was a full-time job and part-time training was simply too costly. Work project time must not be abridged by military training. Often overlooked was that one third of all CCC enrollees were under 18 years of age. Finally, he declared, "these boys are being of great service to the country now. Why make them double up on their work?"[41]

Maj. Gen. H. A. Drum, commanding the Sixth Corps Area, in a circular letter to his CCC camp commanders, set forth key objectives of the CCC as viewed by the Army high command. Camp commanders should see that enrollees were taught citizenship, with an emphasis on duty, service and patriotism. There was to be consideration for the "dictates of comradeship, team play, proper reasoning and attention to duty, and with a consideration of the needs of others and demands of authority." In addition, high ideals and performance of duty were demanded, and loyalty should extend "from the officers and leaders to enrollees, and from enrollees to the leaders and officers under whom they serve." The men were to develop mental and moral courage, emphasizing firmness, fearlessness, straightforwardness, and honesty. Physical fitness and alertness were further goals. Consideration for others and resourcefulness would be inculcated as well. Purity, both "inside and out," would be the result of clean living and clean thoughts, capped by a neat, "manly" appearance. Finally, "no enrollee should complete his enrollment without acquiring the fundamentals of some useful trade to assist him and his family in his normal life." Conspicuously absent was any mention of military training as one of the CCC's goals.[42]

General George Catlett Marshall, Chief of Staff of the U.S. Army, asserted that "the CCC, as it is, is of inestimable benefit to the Army," being "admirably suited to our noncombatant needs." Lauding the work of those companies which had been transferred to military reservations for such work as clearing land for rifle ranges, and for other projects, he concluded that "we have actual troops in training," and therefore have no need to instruct CCCers in military matters.[43]

In response to the calls for military training in the CCC, Robert Fechner, the corps' director, never varied his views. In a speech delivered at Atlantic City on September 11, 1939, entitled "Our Kind of War," the CCC's chief clearly indicated that he hoped that America would stay out of the conflict by then raging in Europe. He reflected on the "vastly different kind of war which this nation, thru the Civilian Conservation Corps, has been waging for the past six and a half years—a war of reconstruction; not a war of destruction." Steadfastly maintained as a civilian institution, the CCC had made the nation stronger. In many European nations, labor camps had been instituted, in most of which military training had been instituted. In at least one nation—he no doubt was referring to Germany—the youth camps were "maintained largely for pre-military training purposes." But in the CCC, the young men were taught not the military arts, but self-discipline. "While a young man in the CCC camps learns many things and gains bodily strength and health which would be of great value to him and to his country in the event he ever went to war," he would not be drilled "in the gentle technique of shooting people.... It is not possible under present laws for the Civilian Conservation Corps to be inducted into the United States Army as a body," he declared. A CCC boy was a civilian, and would remain so. Even in time of war his status would be that of any other civilian, "because enrollment in the CCC was not enlistment in a military organization of any kind."[44]

Fechner's attitudes were seconded by James J. McEntee, acting director of the CCC, who was aware that the War Department, FDR, the CCC Advisory Council, and the Labor Committee of House of Representatives were all opposed to a militarization of the Corps. There should be no attempt to take advantage of the "captive audience" of enrollees to force them to take a course in military training, he insisted. This would especially discriminate against the poor. "You have no right to select a group of boys from poor families" and in this way, to defend the country, which was "the responsibility of everyone, not particularly that of boys from families in reduced circumstances."[45]

Another powerful—and decisive—opponent of the militarization of the CCC was the president himself who wanted it to remain essentially a civilian agency. In 1939, these views and other reasons resulted in his ordering that all appointments to camp jobs, including commanding officers, henceforth would be civilians. This move answered "to a great extent, the demand of the intelligent public for divorce of the CCC from the military," as one writer put it. Reserve officers then on CCC duty would be permitted to serve out their respective tours, but all must be relieved from duty under their commissions by December 31, 1939.[46] In the event, however, the new appointments would still be drawn from the active duty lists of the Officers Reserve Corps of the Army, Navy and Marines, or from the ranks of reserve Coast Guard warrant officers. Only when there were no eligible applicants from these categories would Corps Area commanders be permitted to appoint persons who did not hold reserve commissions.

Henceforth all appointees would be civilian employees of the War Department and given civil service classification, and the Department would still retain its full authority in administering the CCC camps. Subsequently, there would be considerably less emphasis on the military mode. Gone would be the use of Army titles of rank, for instance. As civilians, appointees in charge of a CCC company would have the designation "Company Commander," and their assistants "Subaltern" and where appropriate "CCC Physician" and "CCC Chaplain." They would be addressed as "Mr." rather than by military rank. New uniforms were also prescribed but paid for by appointees. But more importantly, the pay scales were lower than for reserve officers.

Predictably, FDR's decision caused much consternation and heated debate. Characteristically, *Happy Days* thought that the new system deserved a debate and asked for opinions. One disgruntled Army wife declared that "being reduced to a civilian status makes us ill with disappointment, shame, a feeling of being degraded, and a sense of unfair treatment."[47]

But developing events were destined to sweep away or alter many of the concerns about military training in the CCC. One was the coming of America's peacetime draft when the first drawing of numbers was held on October 29, 1940. On that occasion, Secretary of War Henry Stimson drew the first of 10,000 numbers to determine the order in which the men would be called into military training. Initially drafted for one year's service, 800,000 men were to be taken before July 1, 1940. Many of these would be from the ranks of the CCC, and they would certainly then, at last, get their military training.[48]

In addition, the matter was solved for many by the greatly increased demands for trained military personnel, or those desiring to be trained, as the maw of war opened ever wider, and many CCCers volunteered for duty with the armed forces or accepted jobs in the burgeoning defense industries. By the autumn of 1939, for the first time, certain areas in the country had a shortage of men wanting to enroll in the CCC.[49]

Beyond this, more and more former CCC enrollees were being commissioned as officers in the armed forces. In addition, the worried Army wives who had been concerned when their officer spouses had to be addressed as "Mr," soon found them being called to active duty. By 1940, indeed, the Reserve Corps officers engaged in CCC work were being summoned in such numbers that many subalterns for the CCC camps would henceforth be appointed from civilian lists.[50]

As to the Corps itself, in mid–August 1941, orders at last came down from the War Department stipulating that marching and simple formation drill would be conducted for 15 minutes a day, five days per week. This had long been resisted, but when it came, its stated purposes were to contribute to "better discipline and more orderly conduct, as well as better company appearance," which were more easily obtained "when members of an organization moving in groups follow some set procedure." James J. McEntee, earlier opposed to any military training in the CCC, acquiesced, noting that while the outdoor work was doing wonders with building up the men physically, "it does not tend to improve their posture." Thus "it is believed that addition of marching to the basic training program of the Corps will improve the general physique and carriage of enrollees and increase their employability." Officials hoped that this explanation would make military training acceptable to the American public, many of whom were still firmly opposed to war, if not openly flirting with pacificism.[51]

Though never its primary goal, obviously the CCC provided a training ground for the Army's administration, and for military officers, whether regular or reserve, in an era when military expenditures were severely curtailed and command opportunities limited. Likewise, the rank and file obtained some military exposure, and at the same time emerged in better health, while learning how to live and work together in an organized fashion, all of which served the nation well in the challenging years ahead.

In many ways, then, as the men of the CCC interacted with various levels of officialdom from FDR on down, they were conditioned to accept a measure of leadership, with themselves being more or less willingly led. This formative pattern would be instituted much more significantly subsequently in the military setting of World War II.

6

The CCC in
the Community

"It is fitting and proper at this time to express our deep appreciation for the most loyal support and good feeling which we ... have
received from the natives of Assonet [Massachusetts]. They have ...
made us quite at home in this little village."
— *The Harold Parker Review* (Company 110,
Assonet, Massachusetts), September 16, 1935

"'I didn't raise my daughter to be fiddled with,' said the pussy
cat as she rescued her offspring from the violin factory."
— *Mountain Yodel* (Company 1653,
Mountain, Wisconsin)

While passing by a mountaineer on their way to work one morning,
a truckload of men of Company 1539, Frenchburg, Kentucky, in a jeer-
ing way, called out, "'Hi, Buddy. Is that a good gun?' The man didn't
enter into their fun, and took their humor for ribbing." Therefore, "he
raised the gun in question and took a pot-shot at the crew, winging three
of the men," two receiving shot in their faces and a third in his legs. They
were treated at their company infirmary and returned to work, "sans wise
cracks." In another incident, one Anthony "Qui-Qui" Porcelli, of Company 299 encamped at Masonville, New York, received a "juicy black
eye," when a young citizen of Rockrift hurled a stone into the passing
truck. "Must not call out nasty names, Qui-Qui—it makes 'em sore," the
company's paper advised the wayward enrollee.[1]

Clearly, the CCC was not always welcome. In fact, there was a perennial concern within the Corps as to what the public thought about their

121

presence. The men of Company 299 were reminded in their company paper, *The Spotlight*, that "the morbid curiosity of the public is focused directly on us wherever we go, and our behavior in town is of titanic importance." In other words, "we still are on trial," and the men were urged to behave themselves.[2]

Similarly, a writer in *The Ozark Oracle* (Company 1731, Winona, Missouri) advised its readers that the CCC truck driver was "an ambassador to the public." It was the truck driver more than any other man in camp who gave the public its opinion of the Corps, he declared. If he drove carefully, was considerate, wore his uniform well, and was concerned with his personal appearance, he could give a good impression of the CCC. *The Harbinger* (Company 698, Argyle, Wisconsin) cautioned the men that if one got "tight" and became obnoxious by extremely loud talking and swearing, then the entire company and the Corps itself lost standing.

There was a problem with wearing the CCC uniform in some communities, and enrollees often complained that "it is a well-known fact that you are forced to wear civilian clothing to town if you want to be treated like a human being." The reduced rate for theater tickets that CCC men paid led movie personnel to wear "a look of either tolerance or anxiety" when enrollees entered the theater. Indeed, "we have often been greeted in a manner which was patently one of concern." *The Indian Trail* (Company 728, Salem, Missouri), however, grumbled that "the most distasteful thing about this difficulty is that it is no fault of the members of the corps." While it was generally understood by "non-prejudiced observers" that the conduct of the CCC men was "on a par with any other group of young men outside of the organization"—though to be sure, there were examples of "a few law violations by CCC men," for which the men were willing to take the consequences—often they were confronted with "unfair discrimination whenever in disputes with civil authorities."[3]

Related were concerns with members of the nation's armed forces mainly because the CCC enrollee's $30 per month pay exceeded the $21 paid to an Army private. These attitudes were clearly reflected in a derisive poem by an unnamed Army officer at Fort Benning, Georgia:

> Mama, put out your service flag
> Your man's in the C.C.C.
> He's S.O.L. but what the hell!
> He's gone to plant a tree.
> He'll make the sylvan forest bloom
> And save the army cut,
> Providing that the hungry squirrels
> Don't take him for a nut.[4]

Indeed, though the CCC was one of the most highly praised of the New Deal programs, its relations with the public, and how it was viewed in the country, remained problematical. While the Corps received much support from both political parties, it came in for its share of scrutiny and criticism, as was the case with all of FDR's programs. Some journalists, editors and politicians were opposed to everything derived from the New Deal, including the CCC. One of the perennial detractors was the governor of Georgia, Eugene Talmadge. In an address before the American Legion in Atlanta, he described CCC men as "those bums and loafers," who were "running around in the woods." This led to a spate of letters descending upon the governor from many men in the CCC, among them the boys of Company 272, Boston Corners, New York, who mounted a systematic writing campaign to flood his office. Huey Long, U.S. Senator from Louisiana, another vitriolic FDR baiter, once stated that "he [would] eat all the trees that live that are planted by the Civilian Conservation Corps," a sally which immediately gave rise to a plethora of angry retorts.[5]

Sniping was continual in the national press, notably in such publications as the perennial anti–New Deal *Chicago Tribune*, Colonel Robert R. McCormick's notorious sheet. Among other things, the paper focused on the alleged sprees that were typical following paydays in at least some CCC camps. Such charges were not groundless, as *The Jubilee Journal* (Company 698, Oak Hill, Illinois) admitted. "Some of our men, new to the ways of Bacchus, spend part or all of their monthly allowances upon sprees," and "occasionally confirmed drinkers have come into this company," but, the paper explained, these had usually "been elbowed out by the men themselves" or summarily dismissed by the commanding officers. In fact, the editor went on, the men in the company tended to spend their five dollars a month on education courses, and on clothing and other such "luxuries," and some even sent the money home to their families. Therefore, the CCC was clearly "not a drinking fraternity of spoiled scions rolling in luxury, liquor, and lassitude."[6] In like manner, the editor of *The Marion Honker* (Company 3723, Marion, Iowa) deplored that "a [certain] neighborly newspaper" had asserted that "we have nothing to do but eat three meals a day, rest and sleep said meals off and take life easy." Of course, this was reprehensible—and inaccurate. And "if anyone wishes to determine the honest value of the CCC to the nation let him wipe the film of political prejudice off his glasses and view all the phases of the program."[7]

The nation's magazines sometimes joined the fray, *Today* once charging that discipline in many of the camps was poor, and some of the men were doing almost no work of value except improving their own camps. In addition, the working hours were too short and in some camps only about five hours of real work was being done, the remainder of the time being consumed in marching to and from the tents or barracks. The editor of *The Script* (Company 299, Masonville, New York) retorted that the CCC had the 40-hour work week in place since the beginning. He also felt that this criticism was a poor way to show proper feelings toward a group of youths who were forced to accept this mode of living. To be sure, not all of the boys were as good as they should be, but many townspeople's boys were undoubtedly worse. In the Masonville camp, at least, there had not been complaints forthcoming from the officers of the law locally. "So we hope there will not be any bad feelings between Sidney [New York] townspeople and our boys."[8]

More damaging was an article in *Field and Stream* insisting that the CCC was harmful to wild life, and quoting William N. McNair, the mayor of Pittsburgh, who claimed that a recent disastrous flood in the area was caused by the CCC. He contended that the CCC boys had denuded the forests of brush wood, which allowed the waters to run unimpeded. Joe Norton of Company 1328, Burgettstown, Pennsylvania, took the mayor to task, wanting to know where the CCC was when the disastrous Johnstown flood of 1889 occurred.[9]

In other quarters, a furor was aroused by Professor M.L. Fernard, a botanist and director of Harvard's Gray Herbarium. In a speech delivered in Philadelphia, he characterized the CCC as composed of "misguided and enthusiastic young men" engaged in faulty conservation practices that were upsetting the "natural equilibrium of nature." His remarks set off a furious debate in the nation's press. A letter in the *New York Times* deplored Fernard's remarks and *The Brooklyn Citizen* averred that even if the professor was right, which was arguable, "we should still favor the CCC." But *The Salem* (Oregon) *Journal* agreed with the professor: "There is a good deal of truth in what the professor says," the paper declared. There had been a concerted effort "to make a formal garden out of our forests and by making the wilds easily accessible, to exterminate not only natural vegetation but wild life along with it." Backpedaling, the professor responded that he had been misquoted, noting that he was not against much of the good that the CCC accomplished but his learned paper was an "expression of grief of those who value the preservation of the rarer and more sensitive [natural] types that the encroachment upon their preserves by large groups of men and boys with high motives but not always with full understanding of the problem, is bound to kill them out." He insisted that his remarks were "purely scientific," and not polemical as some news accounts indicated.[10]

Ministers of the gospel were often self-appointed watchdogs of the CCC, and did not refrain from sharp criticism. One of these was Ted Mariano of Chicago, Illinois, who strongly complained about the men's profanity. "Believe me," he said, "the Marines and the Aviation Corps put together could not compare with the vocabulary of the boys who recently have returned from the CCC camps. It is strong enough to give a minister concussion of the brain." He wondered if the CCC could not go into a campaign to curb some of it. "I hope you don't think that I am a reformer or an angel, but too much is too much, and I don't mean maybe."[11]

A private citizen, James H. Baker of Monrovia, California, was concerned about other matters. In an irate letter to the Department of Interior, he deplored the fact that the enrollees in the work camps had developed an "obnoxious custom" of "stripping their bodies to the waste line [sic] when engaged in most any kind of work." He did not think that ladies visiting work projects should have to be subjected to viewing half-naked men. "Men employed by the government should KEEP THEIR SHIRTS ON," he concluded. He was answered by James J. McEntee, then the assistant director of the CCC, asserting that he did not feel that "one should adopt the habit of advising what others wear, and why." Furthermore, there was apparently no concern about men being even more scantily dressed at the beach, though those in charge of the CCC camps "are careful to see that common decency in dress is observed."[12]

But far more ominous for some was that the CCC was allegedly a hotbed of communist activity, fears which many in the U.S. Army shared. There were a few incidents that fueled their concerns. One of these occurred at Trout Creek, Michigan, about eight miles from Camp Jumbo near Kenton. There Company 1612 was visited by an assembly of communist "agitators," which, however, was forcibly dispersed by men of the company, following which "an enjoyable evening was had by all."[13] Communists, in turn, charged that American capitalists were seeking to transform CCC enrollees into "shock troops of fascism in the struggle against American workers," as an article in the *Daily Worker* asserted. It was also alleged that the CCC was being militarized, blacks were being discriminated against, and that the conditions in the camps were deplorable. These allegations were strongly rebutted in *Happy Days*, which published several letters from irate readers on the subject. Michael C. Maras, of Company 549, Ironton, Ohio, for one, reported that in one mixed company in which he had served, 18 colored enrollees "shared with us equally every and all privileges and facilities in camp, and at no time did we have racial dissension." In addition, Maras had seen no military activity in the two camps where he had been. He contended that in fact, "we have received fair treatment; that we have plenty to eat, a good place to sleep, have our opportunities to improve ourselves mentally and physically, and that we are happy to be able to live like men instead of tramping the streets like we used to before we joined." Another enrollee writing in the

Stockade (Company 2328, Homer City, Pennsylvania) admitted, that while occasionally a newcomer might rebel against conditions—that was perhaps natural—"I can say honestly I have known no one who after living in camp a while was inclined to radical agitation. In my camp the 'Red Menace' was a myth."

When Roger Babson, a well-known statistician, attacked the CCC camps as being "hotbeds of radicalism," Lieutenant James J. Corbett, a chaplain for Company 312 at Waterville, Pennsylvania, maintained that he had encountered thousands of the CCC boys and had yet to see a radical. He himself had "lived under the hammer and sickle for six years," and knew something of the "mechanics of revolution and the bloody interpretation of the Marxian philosophy." He was certain that in the CCC camps, "the 'comrades' would get little consideration." In fact, far from being radicals, more typical was the case with the men in Company 896 in Lindale, Texas, who on Tuesday and Thursday evenings were studying such topics as "Our Constitution," "Courtesies Due Our Flag," or "American Citizenship and its Privileges," under the direction of the commanding officer.[14]

The problem of communism was coupled in some minds with anti–Semitism, it being understood that many communists were Jews. To guard against "the poison of these notions," the *Stockade* (Company 2328, Homer City, Pennsylvania) drew upon the views of Msgr. Fulton J. Sheen for guidance: "I must remember that not all Jews are Communists," he declared, and furthermore we must consider that "we cannot be anti-semitic without insulting the parentage and lineage of Jesus and His disciples." Another point to ponder, he went on, was that "common justice and fraternity is guaranteed to them by our Constitution."[15]

In the event, company commanders took firm measures to squelch anything that might smack of communism or radicalism. When Company 1190 in Fall River, Massachusetts, worked out a plan for self-government, providing for a camp mayor elected by the enrollees and a community council made up of four representatives elected by each of the barracks, their CO, Captain A.E. Arnold, moved quickly to block these notions. Deciding that the plan was not feasible, he categorically stated that the camp would only be operated according to the rules and regulations issued by the War Department.[16]

Some of the reasons for the anti–CCC feeling grew out of a misunderstanding as to what the organization was supposed to accomplish. In a letter to Jesse M. Wood, Judge of a Criminal Court of Atlanta, Georgia, the commanding general of the Fourth Corps Area, Major General George Van Horn Moseley, took strong issue with the judge's attitude toward the CCC. The judge had ruled that one youth convicted of stealing radiator caps, and sentenced to twelve months on a chain gang, would have the penalty suspended if he were selected by the Local Relief Committee for the CCC. The general was outraged, maintaining that the judge was clearly unaware of what the CCC was—and was not. "In no sense is it a corrective institution," he protested. "On the contrary, it is made up of those lads whom the depression left unemployed on the streets of the nation. It was no fault of theirs that there was no demand for their strong bodies and their willing hearts." Those selected for the CCC were, in fact, to be of good character, and "where local committees have attempted to do what you apparently have done and pass on to us a lad of bad character, he is discharged as soon as discovered." The general suggested that the judge modify the picture that he evidently had regarding the Civilian Conservation Corps, and "the fine lads who compose it."[17]

Certainly, the need for favorable publicity to counter the substantial negative stream of criticism was one of the aims of the camp papers. Some concentrated on this more than others. One was *The March Field Courier*, of the March Field District in California. Lt. Col. Henry H. Arnold, U.S. Army Air Corps, commander of the District, and slated later for the much loftier office of commander of the entire Army Air Forces, complimented the staff for its efforts along these lines, noting that "the problem of public relations is an important one, because there is constant need of information and interpretation to the public, of an organization such as the C.C.C."[18]

Another paper, *The Mo-Kan*, publication of the Missouri-Kansas district, urged both the camp overhead and the rank and file of the camps to do some intelligent "handshaking" to assist in cementing relations between camps and towns. Officers especially were urged to join civic organizations, golf clubs, and lodges, as well as participate in churches and their work.

One shrewd expedient calculated to enlighten local communities as to how much the CCC camp might mean to their economy was adopted by many company commanders who paid their men in silver dollars. The unfamiliar coins soon showed up in the cash registers of merchants who could, in a concrete way, note the immediate positive effect of the presence of the enrollees.[19]

Overall, the supporters of the CCC outnumbered the critics, and much of the nation's press was in favor and urged its continuation, as a survey conducted by *Happy Days* revealed.[20] In the spring of 1936, when the American Institute of Public Opinion polled the nation's voters on the desirability of retaining the CCC, 82 percent were in favor, which included 67 percent of the Republicans polled. Among those who warmly praised the organization was Dave Brown, who as a staffer of the *Louisville Courier-Journal* visited several Kentucky camps. "It's no skylark," he admitted, observing rather that "[the CCC] is a program of definite and worthy achievement." Another admirer was Susan T. Towles, a librarian in Henderson, Kentucky. In an article written for the *Cromwell Cardinal* (Company 1540, Henderson, Kentucky), she indicated that "rarely does a detachment of men, stationed near a town, make the good impression on the community that the CCC Camp has made on Henderson people.... This most satisfactory condition is due, of course, not only to the boys but to the institution of the camp, to its discipline, its educational system, to its general conditions."[21]

Henry Horner, the governor of Illinois, was similarly impressed, declaring that he was "enthusiastically happy to have the Civilian Conservation Corps in our State," and to his mind, the benefits of the program "have been so definite that it is no longer a social and economic experiment, but a proved and tremendous success."[22] When the city of Sebring, Florida, was faced with the prospect of losing Company 453, the city fathers accepted a U.S. Government proposition that they could keep the company otherwise slated to be transferred if they would provide a new camp site. The city council, the county commissioners and other interested bodies promptly raised $1,700.00, and the company remained.[23]

In fact, when times of trouble came, many communities were not reticent in seeking help from local CCC camps, no matter how local sentiment might regard the Corps. When Walton, New York, experienced severe flooding, the men of Company 299 were called upon for assistance. Miss Margaret Schlafer, a resident of the town, was sufficiently impressed by their unstinting work to suggest that "CCC" should henceforth stand for "Cheerfulness, Consideration and Competence." Also following the men's 11-day flood cleanup in the villages of Walton, Delhi and Sidney, New York, the Delhi and Walton Kiwanis clubs sent warm letters of thanks. The relief work of the men also seems to have changed the minds of the citizens of Sidney, who had earlier refused the men the use of the school gym. Subsequently, by a vote of 78 to 34 the townspeople agreed that the men could henceforth use the facility.[24]

The CCC's leadership, at all levels, then, paid considerable attention to cultivating public opinion. To help in putting their best foot forward, CCC leaders took advantage of special occasions such as the great exposition "Century of Progress" held in Chicago in the autumn of 1934. Thousands of CCC men in companies within a 100-mile radius of Chicago were allowed to attend, using CCC trucks for transportation. For others, special train and bus fares were negotiated. The men who participated were sternly warned that they represented the CCC and must be on their best behaviour. Apparently few if any cases of misconduct occurred, and the CCC obtained much favorable publicity from the event.[25]

Happy Days also used the radio network to create national public-ity on behalf of the Corps. On August 17, 1933, on a nation-wide NBC hookup, it sponsored an hour-long show featuring addresses by Fechner and other officials. Several bands peformed, including the U.S. Army Band, Jack Denny and his orchestra from the Waldorf-Astoria hotel, and Eddie Holtz and his band from the Hotel Lexington in New York. Also featured was the Hill Billy Band of Company 334, Skyland, Virginia.[26]

Some companies—though not all—carefully cultivated close rela-tions with the communities. One outfit with a good relationship lasting for many years with its local area was Company 1742 at Tarkio, Mis-souri. On one occasion, its commander, Capt. Glenn L. Riddle, invited about 60 members of the Tarkio Chamber of Commerce to the camp on a Thursday in January 1938. The enrollees put on a special feed with veal chops, mashed potatoes, gravy, olives, celery, bread, butter, jelly dressing, peaches with whipped cream, coffee and cigars. The evening was an informal social affair enjoyed by all. In another instance—as reported in the camp paper, the *Broadcast*—a quartet of singers from the company took first honors at an annual singing contest sponsored by the school board, and they were subsequently scheduled for various perfor-mances, including one on the radio.[27]

The men of this company also worked closely with the local high school, and some men signed up to complete their public school educa-tion while at the camp. Area ministers often preached at the camp. In addition, the camp was the site of various soil conservation and farm-ers' meetings. On February 8, 1936, men of the Company assisted in dig-ging a snow plow and four railroad coal cars from a snow drift near the town. W.F. Giles, superintendent of the Chicago, Burlington and Quincy railroad sent a fulsome letter to Lt. M.N. Huston, then the CO, thank-ing the enrollees for their valiant action. Later repeating their heroics, in July 1938 the boys of Company 1742 were drawn upon "on a[n other-wise] peaceful Sunday" to assist in flood control at the request of farm-ers living near Langdon. Working around the clock, they and others, filling 100,000 sacks with soil, helped hold the dike. Later, as a "good will offering," farmers brought 30 gallons of ice cream to the camp.[28]

Sports were the vehicles used by some companies to insinuate them-selves within communities. The men of Company 1742 at Tarkio, Mis-souri, often played on independent baseball teams in the area. In addition, bowling teams challenged their town counterparts, and the camp's bas-ketballers were invited to practice at the local Tarkio College gym. In another sign of the times, when more and more Tarkio-area men joined the armed forces, Company 1742's team, outfitted in the town club's uni-forms, was asked to represent the community as its official softball club in the summer of 1941. Not inconsequentially, at about the same time the pages of their paper, *The Broadcast*, were filled with accounts of many of the enrollees marrying local girls, no doubt reflecting the persistence of the draft and the hint of war.[29]

Numerous CCC men developed close ties with certain merchants in their local communities. For example, men of Company 855 at Hot Springs, New Mexico, took a special liking for the Buckhorn Cafe, the scheduled meeting place of the company's social organization "The Rio Grande Jolly Club." Similarly, the men of Company 297 in Kanona, New York, frequented the coffee shop of one Joe Miller in Bath, a long-standing "favorite with the boys."[30]

Sometimes the camp papers attempted to address—or redress—relations with local communities. *The Dynamo* (Company 134, Warren, New Hampshire) designated June 27, 1937, as the beginning of a "Goodwill Week" in an effort to get people from the community to visit the camp for entertainment and refreshments, thereby getting better acquainted with the enrollees. Such camp visits were nation-wide affairs on the celebration of the CCC's birthday each April. In what became a national tradition, and a great aid in cementing good community relations, elaborate open houses were scheduled at the camps, events that were attended by surprisingly large numbers of people. Some of the visitors arrived out of curiosity; others came for the entertainment; but obviously most came for the food served in huge quantities, certainly a welcomed "feeding of the multitudes."[31]

There were other dimensions to community relations. Though one company—Company 4727 at St. Paul, Minnesota—named its camp the "Eveless Eden," it should not be assumed that there were no contacts between the CCCers and local girls. Indeed, these were naturally of continual, widespread interest. The *Hooey* (Company 553, Yellow Springs, Ohio) once produced a fanciful "love bug" cover—with the love bug "magnified 100 times"—which the editor explained was featured because "the love bug causes more fatalities in the CCC than from all the diseases, snakes and black widows combined." And the song writers were right, he concluded, "Love IS Everywhere." Proof of this occurred when Wilburn Chunn, an enrollee in Company 490, Dyer, Tennessee, while surveying spied a girl through his surveyor's transit, and calmly announced that she would be his wife. He made her acquaintance and in a few weeks, had indeed married her.[32]

It worked both ways, and girls caught up in the often dull, boring, Depression years, suddenly finding a CCC camp in their neighborhood, were hardly indifferent and their excitement frequently palpable. This

Opposite: **Another *Hooey* cover, for the March 1938 issue, welcomed spring when a "young man's fancy...."**

The flowers that bloom in the Spring (tra la) have a lot to do with the case.

was manifested for example, in the Ozarks of Arkansas. There it was noted that girls from a radius of 150 miles regularly attended dances of Company 1740 held at Camp Taft, Arkansas, located on the banks of the "beautiful Mulberry River." The camp was also the destination of flocks of visitors, which certainly included many girls who came every Sunday, often staying for dinner or supper. In another instance, *Happy Days* printed a letter from a girl desperately wanting to locate one Winton (Cotton) Parker, the heavyweight CCC boxer of Oregon: "Send me his address, please, please, please, immediately." It was signed "A C.C.C. sweetheart, Mary."[33]

Three girls of Dolores, Colorado (Thelma Boyd, Peg Baxstrom and Almeda McEwen) in a poem "The Return of the C.C.C.'s." made clear what they thought of "the forest lads": "Once again the old town's a-humming/ for the C.C.C's are here/Grey skies have vanished and blue ones appear." They were more than gratified to see them "stroll down our 'main-drag' in their nifty OD's," all the more acceptable because "They 'trip the light fantastic' in every imaginable way/ [And] say, we would choose a CCCer any old time of day/And we think the army trucks are the grandest of cars/With their many bent-up fenders, and old patched-up tires."[34] Even grammar school girls at Ft. Payne, Alabama, noticed the extent to which men of Company 472 married local girls and settled down there, one third grader writing a jingle on the subject: "When you get grown/Don't marry a tramp/Marry a boy/From the CCC camp."[35]

Matters were no different in Pennsylvania: "Moon over Shelocta/ Shine on the Boys and me/So we can stroll along the road/Of the Happy C.C.C.'s." The Shelocta girls knew what they were waiting for: "The monthly dance or for a chance/To step inside the Rec. hall door."[36]

Certainly the CCC men responded to such attention. A dozen or so excited CCC enrollees of Company 1390, Green Bay, Virginia, as recorded in a *Happy Days* article, "CCC Gigolos in Demand," were selected by the educational adviser Booker Smalley to fill the request of a local boarding school for a "dozen nice men" to act as escorts for the institution's fair damsels at their annual junior-senior prom. The enrollees at the Beltsville Camp in Maryland also proved to be acceptable dance partners for coeds at the University of Maryland, who undertook to teach them how to "tap dance in G.I. [shoes]," certainly a noteworthy feat.[37]

When *The Turkey Run Flash* (Company 2580, Marshall, Indiana) asked about ideal girls, one man desired "a chubby little rascal, plenty of good looks, pleasant voice and disposition." Another indicated that he liked any girl, "providing she isn't a blond," while yet another stipulated that "she must have the face of Hedy Lamar, the legs of a Dietrich, a brain slight inferior to mine, the virtue of a Madona. To other men she must be as friendly as an irritable pit bull."[38]

One of the bachelors at Camp Pack, a black outfit, was looking for a girl Indian Brown in complexion; five feet, nine inches tall; 26" waist; hair long and black; age 18 to 25; type, conservative; eyes, black; profile, beautiful; personality, fascinating; and education, junior high grad. Anyone knowing whereabouts of such girls was asked to address Mr. William A. Hall at the Matrimonial Bureau, Camp Pack, New Lisbon, New Jersey.[39]

But if desirable as companions, girls were also the common butts of jokes, both in *Happy Days* and other camp papers. Clichés and stereotypes abounded: "First Devil: 'Ha! Ha! Ha!' Second Devil: 'Why the laugh?' First Devil: 'I just put a woman in a room with a thousand hats and no mirror.'"[40] Others joined in the fun, as did the *Cub Reporter* (Company 1506, Preston, Idaho) which informed its readers that "when a girl shows her true colors it's because she's run out of rouge," further observing that "it takes a lot of pluck for a girl to keep her eyebrows in shape." *The Saltkehatchie Pow Wow* (Company 4468, Barnwell, South Carolina) lampooned the popularity of women's bridge clubs in the 1930s: "Man: 'I don't know where my wife is, but wherever she is I'll bet she has a cigarette in one hand and a weak no-trump in the other.'"

Women also bore the brunt of some of the rather suggestive offerings so common in CCC camp papers, as one example appearing in the *Broadcast* (Company 1742, Tarkio, Missouri) illustrates: "Gently he pushed her quivering shoulders back against the chair. She raised beseeching eyes in which vain hope and fear were struggling. From her parted lips the breath came in short, wrenching gasps. Reassuringly he smiled at her. B-z-z-z-z-z-z went the dentist's drill." *The Bugle* (Company 4468, Barnwell, South Carolina) similarly joked: "He: 'Let's go up to my apartment. I want to show you a wonderful antique bed I have.' She: 'Not on your life, I don't fall for that old bunk.'"[41]

Sometimes, the jokes revealed women as the enrollees hoped that they might be, including a bit of wishful thinking in *The Bugle* (Company 4468, Barnwell, South Carolina): "She—'You remind me of Nero.' Adams—'Really, why so?' She—'Well, here I am about to burn down and you just keep fiddlin' around.'"[42]

Not infrequently, a harder edge was noted, as in a poem in the *Roaring River Ripples* (Company 1713, Cassville, Missouri):

Little Miss Muffet
Decided to rough it
    In a cabin quite old and medieval.
An enrollee espied her
And plied her with cider
    And now she's the forest's prime-evil.[43]

Even more extreme was a decidedly anti-woman stance which was sometimes manifested in the CCC press. Tony March, a sometime columnist in *Happy Days*, was another avowed anti-feminist who made no apologies for his views. One on-going topic of interest among CCC boys was the appearance of so-called "She-She-She" camps. There were some camps in existence, though they were usually part of the NYA Work Program rather than part of the CCC, and for a time there were 28 camps with an enrollment of about 1,900 girls. March visited one at Ailanthus Hall near Parsippany, New Jersey, condescendingly reporting on his visit in *Happy Days*. He noted that the camp director had concluded that "girls cannot be regimented. They find it hard to work together toward a common end. The director must do it for them." The camp had a paper, he reported, noting that "I looked over a few copies and found them surprisingly well done. They were sprightlier than many in the CCC, and were outspoken in many ways." But, perhaps inevitably, he sneered, "there was an article in one of the papers on the science of make-up."[44]

Contrastingly, women were often idealized and sometimes put on a pedestal. Pinups were also introduced in the CCC in various camps, long before their being institutionalized in World War II. Ginger Rogers was one of the first, emerging as the "moving spirit" of Company 677 in Harrison, Michigan. The commanding officer of the company had been a one-time business associate of the actress, and she sent a personally autographed picture to the outfit in response to his request.[45]

Charles Rinehart of Company 562 in Prichard, Idaho, in his poem, "Hollywood Flower Garden," recognized the perennial appeal of movie queens, ranging from the description of Mae West as "a prickly cactus flower/That thrives 'neath desert skies," and Joan Crawford as "a buttercup, a flower blest by God," to "a cute gardenia—So lovable and sweet," that was Alice Faye.[46]

Though *Happy Days* sometimes revealed an anti-feminist stance, the paper also pushed for education and instruction on what it regarded as a proper moral stance regarding women and the family. It strongly advocated that educational advisers, "by means of formal and informal instruction and guidance," instruct enrollees on issues of "marriage and citizenship." It no doubt approved of the concerted efforts of such papers as the *Stockade* (Company 2328, Shelocta, Pennsylvania) to encourage proper attitudes and conduct toward women advising the company's enrollees to familiarize themselves with the West Point *Manual of Courtesies and Customs of the Service*, which forthrightly addressed such matters: "Nothing so quickly discloses the presence or absence of breeding in a man as does his attitude toward women. In polite society a lady's person is inviolate. To touch her except in dancing or other entirely acceptable purpose is inexcusable rudeness." Lamenting the prevalent custom "in many college circles" of "mauling and necking," the CCCers should rather practice "a nice fastidiousness," because petting was "evidence of lack of discrimination and taste." In its health page, the paper discussed the subject of "Reproduction in Animal Life," with a section on the human sex instinct and the necessity of controlling it. The situation was analogous to fire, normally a great blessing to mankind, but when it ran wild, it became a destroyer. Yet another health page focused on "The Young Man's Relationships to Girls," insisting that women be treated as befitted future mothers of the race.[47]

When many enrollees of Company 1742 at Gallatin, Missouri, seemed prone to date women judged either too young or too old, their company paper, the *Broadcast,* was horrified: "Boys!! Please!! Pick a companion near your own age, not over 50 or under 12. You will look and feel better by it." Rather less serious was a problem noticed by *The Bugle* (Company 4468, Barnwell, South Carolina): "Certainly people back in 1910 thought that kissing was more like a turkey pecking up corn than vulcanizing." Where there were dances, there was the potential of unpleasantness and accordingly *The Saltkehatchie Pow Wow* (Company 4468, Barnwell, South Carolina) was disposed to praise the company members when they were well behaved, observing that certainly the company was determined to keep these entertainments on the highest plane so as "to build up a reputation for CCC dances that no mother would have any apprehension about her daughter attending." The dances were usually chaperoned, typically by the military overhead and perhaps their wives.[48]

Indeed, the wives of the leadership personnel often contributed considerably to the well being, good order and stability at the camps, the presence of the boys sometimes bringing out their maternal instincts. One who responded was Mrs. George W. Crawford, wife of the commanding officer of Company 4468, Barnwell, South Carolina. She devoted much time to teaching the three R's in camp for the men struggling to learn how to read and write. Mrs. Walter J. Rymer, the wife of the commanding officer of Company 819 at Grand Canyon, Arizona, enjoyed "making ... curtains and doing little things to improve [the] camp." She was not forgotten by the enrollees at Christmas, who took up a collection to buy her a "lovely manicuring set and gorgeous box of candy." Another case was Mrs. Ralph Shultz, the wife of the commanding officer of Company 299 at Masonville, New York, who repeatedly "proved that the best way to a man's heart is through his stomach." On one occasion the company enjoyed "home made cupcakes accomplished by her culinary skill," while on another, as the company paper appreciatively reported, "she made a sweet-tooth of German nature and although the name is hard to pronounce it did not spoil the good taste of the dish. We didn't know that 'Mother' was proficient in the art of 'Black Magic' yet the company certainly enjoys these pleasant surprises."[49]

Sometimes the camp papers admitted the company wives into the hallowed precincts of their papers with their own space, sometimes a page or so, called in the *Pick and Shovel* (Company 1829, Temple, Texas), "The Silent? Partner." There were many others, including *Willoughby Whispers* (Company 121, West Burke, Vermont), which labelled its "sob sister" column "The Woman's Angle."

Finally, the CCCers revealed a closeness to their mothers, though not to the extent manifested by the doughboys in the Great War. For example, ads in *Happy Days* hawked Mother's Day gifts; there were frequent special issues of camp papers commemorating the occasion; and if the men failed to respond otherwise, they were officially reminded, as in May 1935, that "it [was] the desire of the Secretary of War that each officer, enlisted man, and member of the Civilian Conservation Corps write a letter to his mother on Mother's Day ... as an expression of the love and reverence we owe to the mothers of our country"[50]

Whatever the results of the contacts of CCC enrollees within their local communities, certain it is that they more often than not made a lasting impression, whether for good or ill.

7

The Veterans

Posterity

The old man plants a tree;
With pain, now, does he bend
And kneel to spread the roots. Not he
Nor any of his age shall spend
One single hour beneath its shade
Nor eat its fruit that is to be,
For soon he shall be subject to the spade
Yet graciously the old man plants a tree.

—*The Veterans' Voice,*
Company 1774, Rochester,
Minnesota, December 1937

Likkerish

I wish I had a likker locker
To lock some likker in,
I wish I had a lotter likker
To place therein.
Because I am a likker liker,
Fond of Scotch and Gin,
I wish I had a likker locker
For me and my frin.

—"Jonesy," *Tamalpais Fog Horn*
(Company 1921, Mill Valley,
California) November 1938

Writing in *Collier's,* Walter Davenport once highlighted the problems of one category of CCC enrollee, the "indigestible veterans of the Great War." They were often victims of "veteranitis," he declared, which

137

he defined as a point of view in which "today and the future [are] not nearly so important as the past." Furthermore, they were given to "too much grousing and too little enthusiasm for hard work." In fact, he concluded, not altogether accurately, "[the CCC was] a young man's chance ... and not a veterans' revival."[1] *The Blatter* (Company 1556, Brownstown, Indiana), a veterans' outfit, was one of several that responded to Davenport's remarks. Apparently what Davenport meant, *The Blatter* writer imagined, was that the vets were not fit to be employed on the outside. However, no one who was associated with them held this notion; rather, the common view was that "there were no better workmen, nor a better behaved group of men nor a better or more conscientious class of citizens anywhere in th' world than these—'INDIGESTIBLE VETERANS.'" Certainly, the veterans were not put off by such slanders because the veteran had instilled within himself on the battlefields of Europe a perfect faith in himself as a "MAN—WHAT NO AMOUNT OF MUDSLINGING WILL EVER OVERCOME."[2]

Unquestionably, the approximately 28,000 veterans enrolled in the CCC's veterans' companies at any given time formed a distinctive part of the Corps' program. Their collective experiences and relative maturity required the CCC leadership to treat them in ways quite distinct from the so-called "junior" enrollees. Among other things, it was recognized that they should be led by more mature officers, usually captains and majors, themselves veterans of overseas service in the World War. One of these was Captain Lyston Black of Company 1760 at Somis, California. He had earlier commanded five junior camps, but "I'll Take the Vets," he said. "For one thing," he explained, "there is more excitement in veteran camps. When a vet blows off steam, he lets go a lot. Their problems are more complex than junior's, even if they come in fewer bunches." The veterans were more experienced, "know all the answers and some of the questions too, have been thru war, depression, even domestic troubles. They have a wholesome regard for their country and its institutions."

"The problem in a veteran camp is to get the men to think life begins after forty. The men were rapped hard when young by a war, and just when some of the harsher effects began to disappear a depression came along and set them back again." Another commanding officer of a vets outfit, Capt. Warren H. Plasters of Company 1774 in Minnesota, was also aware that the veterans usually had a more difficult adjustment to make to the CCC environment, because for those who had gone through camp life under the stress of war time, "another camp life experience means only a necessary expedient in a grim battle with economic depression." By way of contrast, the junior enrollees usually found that camp life was "a romp and full of romance."[3]

No doubt, veterans often came into camp with excess baggage. The Depression had hit many of them particularly hard. They entered the camps only as a last resort, often temporarily leaving their families behind. Others had never been able fully to adjust to civilian life. Though some had a measure of success in establishing themselves in the 1920s, they found themselves unemployed and destitute with the coming of hard times in the next decade. As Arthur J. Waldron of Company 1118, Waterbury, Vermont, surveying a veteran's contingent explained, "their sacrifices were forgotten in the turmoil of readjustment after the war." Subsequently, all too often they were clad in threadbare clothing, ill from hunger and exposure, disillusioned and embittered "toward a thankless country, standing in breadlines asking for food or a night's shelter."

Gilbert W. Cass, writing in *The Veterans' Bugle* (Company 2775, Mandan, North Dakota) rather long-windedly observed that "the greater number of us are ... in the C.C.C. because we have found it afforded one means of retaining our self respect in some degree in our struggle against most adverse conditions, industrially, politically, and otherwise, to keep a roof over our heads and to provide food and clothes for [our families] without publicly passing the hat or Gold bricking on [the] W.P.A." Some people tended to think of the veterans' CCC camp as "nothing more or less than a transient Camp ... sorts maintained by a benevolent government to keep habitual drifters off the streets," and, to be sure, the conduct of some of the "careless enrollees" did create an adverse and unfavorable impression. Yet, the average vet maintained an "implicit faith in the future," and foresaw that better times were in store "for all of us who continue in our effort for self improvement. We still believe this great Country of ours was good enough to fight for and to live in."[4]

But not all vets were so sanguine; apathy was also present. The *Vet's Call* (Company 2713, Fairfax, Minnesota) observed that the malady was a highly contagious disease with which most of the men in the company were stricken, and even more worrisome, were passing on to others. All too many had "no other hope in life save that the mess hall will not burn down." They were under the delusion "that a man past forty years of age is thru, washed up and unemployable." The men stricken in this way "sadly shake their heads, feel sorry for themselves and accept the mythical condition as a fact." The antitoxin was "will-power and right thinking." In fact, it was not true, as was often alleged, that they could not compete with young men just out of school for jobs. These boys had not yet learned how to live and cope. The vets, on the other hand, had "been thru the mill. We've learned to work, to give and to receive orders. We've learned human nature." Therefore, "if we try and keep on trying there's a good chance of success."[5]

Similarly, *The Veterans' Voice* (Company 1774, Rochester, Minnesota) reminded its readers that the time of the Depression was simply another ordeal. Soon a "cosmic resiliency" would kick in, and the "age-old cycle" would once more reassert itself. What was forgotten, the *Vet's Call* (Company 2713, Fairfax, Minnesota) reminded its readers, was that numerous major businesses had likewise gone under, and though many veterans in the CCC camps seemed to be failures, it was through no fault of their own.[6]

Some of the veterans were alcoholics, and drink was a problem even for those not addicted. The veterans' camp newspapers did not soft-pedal the issue, but also professed to see a lighter side. At Company 1921 at Fairfax, California, the *Alpine Echo's* editor of long standing, Eugene E. "Tailspin" Tailfer, in his gossip column "Tripewritings" and on a joke page "Jeepers Creepers Finders Keepers" kept the matter of alcohol in the jocular vein: "Dutch: 'Yep, pardner, I agree with you, rum *is* a curse. That's why I drink beer.' Watson: 'Goodness me, my friend, beer is also a curse!' Dutch: 'That's right, pal. But beer is only a mild sort of curse— like 'Goodness me!'" And the *Vet's Call* (Company 2713, Fairfax, Minnesota) could similarly find humor in drinking: "Skipper: 'Oh ho, what's this? I thought you said you had nothing but clothing in your foot locker!' Unperturbed Vet: 'Why uh, yes, sir—uh, that's my night cap.'"[7]

There was a more serious dimension to alcoholism, of course, and "Liquid Notes," a column in *Tamalpais Foghorn* (Company 1921, Mt. Tamalpais, California), lectured the vets, observing that there was often mention of how a man treated alcohol when job qualifications came up. "If he could only handle his liquor he would be a good man for the job," was a typical comment. Often jobs were available, "if the man could only stay sober." This was a matter of greatest concern to all who sought employment, and many men confessed: "Yes, I can do so and so as well as any man in the business but the minute I get a pocket full of money I know right where it is going...."

Drinking also spilled over into camp situations, as *The Veterans' Voice* (Company 1774, Rochester, Minnesota) once observed: "What barracks, formerly referred to as 'The Ole Maid's Club,' is now called 'The Gas House Gang'? This unenviable distinction was brought about by the acquisition of a bevy of hard-riding and heavy-drinking galoots during the past few months." The men's conduct in town, frequently conditioned by hard drinking, also caused concern—though the junior enrollees could create similar problems—and the commander of Company 1921 in Fairfax, California, warned that if his men insisted upon painting the town red, he would bar offenders from leaving camp for 30 days. It was regrettable, the *Vets Lament* (later paper of Company 1921) asserted, "that the Captain has to admonish us so often on our downtown

THE
VETERANS'
VOICE

VOL. 3 NO. 3
VCCC.Co.1774
Rochester,Minn.

MARCH ISSUE
1938

The Veterans' Voice, Company 1774, Rochester, Minnesota) invariably featured artistic work, as on this cover of the March 1938 issue.

conduct. It's the old, old story of sailors ashore being unable to behave themselves." But being confined to camp was not enough, apparently, and the skipper was later compelled to impose a fine of three dollars for drinking.[8] In Middletown, New York, veterans of the Third Sub-District were formed into a police force trained by the district provost marshal. They proved effective, and "their long arms have already extracted many a peavie from difficulty or carried him over the hard bumps ahead of many a week-end excursion." These man saw to it that all CCC men on a pass in town behaved themselves and acted in a manner that would "reflect nothing but credit upon the corps."[9]

Drinking was not the only abuse associated with the veterans. Their propensity to loaf or "gold brick" was also often commented on as in the column "Hospital Notes" in the *Alpine Echo* (Company 1921, Fairfax, California): "GEORGE WOLFE, the sailor-lumberjack, was restored to duty after the powers that be had decided that his back was not broken and changed the diagnosis to a case of malingering." *The Vets Voice* (Company 1774, Rochester, Minnesota) addressed the matter poetically: "The Goldbrick is a mighty man/With muscles large and fat/And neck that's very husky too/From looking where the leader's at."[10]

The men were sometimes labeled whiners as well, and one old North Dakota veteran, in a poem "That's That" advised the veterans to cease whining and have faith that the government would come through: "So let's all stick together and be fair/And I am sure our Government will treat us square."[11]

The veterans, then, differed from the junior enrollees. For instance, they had their own views regarding religion. This was a well-known fact, at least to the veteran chaplains, the so-called "Holy Joes," an appellation carried over from the World War. Typically, one district chaplain, a Captain McKerlicher, on several visits to the camp of Company 1921 in Fairfax, California, entertained the men with motion pictures on such topics as game and wild life in the United States, hunting in the Far North, FDR's first inaugural, and even "Felix the Cat." On another occasion, the chaplain "was a witness to the destruction of some 'Christmas Cheer' collected during the holiday festivities." Another district chaplain, Lieutenant Robert L. Dougherty, visiting the same company, agreed with this approach, asserting that "[his] time devoted to this camp would be concentrated on furnishing entertainment." Nonetheless, one local cleric of Fairfax was more forthright and traditional in his weekly services to the camp, declaring that "after observing some of these gents who are unable to shed their skid row manners, we suggest a glimpse into the other side of life—the spiritual side."[12]

Leisure time and recreational activities of the veterans' companies were also distinct from that of the younger men. The *Alpine Echo* reported that the veterans at Fairfax actively participated in a particular "ancient and honorable game": "Bingo thrives as a popular indoor sport. It's a good way for a lot of healthy brutes to entertain themselves without any mental strain even if you won't get rich." To be sure, more active activities such as softball, and volleyball were also indulged in, and many camps boasted their own bowling alleys. The veterans of Company 2775 at the Mandan, North Dakota, camp also staged variety softball games, such as the "Clowns" versus the "Bloomer Gals" at the Veterans Circus in Mandan. On another occasion, ballgames were held between the fat and slim men, with the slim men usually winning. Leisurely horseshoe pitching contests were more common, though, and more common still were the incessant card games such as blackjack, "smear," "fan-tan," and cribbage. Whist and pinochle tournaments were also scheduled. The men of Company 2775 at Mandan, North Dakota, further noted with pleasure the arrival of new checker boards, which would "be the source of a lot of fun during the coming winter."[13]

In other activities beyond their work hours, many veterans participated in local veterans' organizations. For example, men of Company 1774 provided the entire membership of the Parks Sylvester Post 2720 of the Veterans of Foreign Wars in Rochester, Minnesota.[14]

Whether in difficulty with alcohol or given to discontent, the vets could also exhibit gratitude for the opportunities that the CCC afforded. One vet asserted that the CCC was the "smartest thing [the] president has done." Indeed, the Corps was a manifestation of "the Spirit of 1917" which had miraculously reappeared, and the war veterans could rally "themselves around the old flag again," and, not incidentally, be provided with "some plentiful eats" as well.[15]

At Christmas time in 1939, the men could also help others. The familiar veterans' activity, the "toys for tots," program, was under way in the shops of Camp Alpine Lake, Company 1921, Fairfax, California, and elsewhere. But if they played the role of Santa Claus, as an anonymous poem in the December 1939 issue of the *Vets Lament* (Company 1921, Fairfax, California) revealed, they certainly received as much as they gave: "Some say there aint no Santa Claus/But sitting as I am—/I claim we Vets have a Santa Claus/His name is Uncle Sam." Another, reflecting upon his improved lot in the CCC, observed that "in the first place, there aren't any more cooties, practically no hard-tack, only an occasional ration of goldfish, and our corned willie is now a delicacy." Even more noticeable was that there were no more squads right, reveille, retreat, and taps; no more MP's, patriotic speeches, or Sophie Tucker. Certainly, when many of the veterans compared notes with their buddies outside the Corps, "we gain much consolation in the undisputable fact that we are a hundred per cent better off than many people on the outside."[16]

To many veterans the CCC became a new way of life, and it was commonplace to remark that many had found a new home in the C's as the Army had been to some previously. An expression often heard was that they were now "making a [life] study and career of the CCC." Sometimes the veterans would leave the camps, only to return after a time "and seemed glad to be [back]."

Perhaps the men should stay in camp until they had found something definite outside, they were sometimes advised. After all, the "work in the field or in camp is not too laborious and the mess is good so make the best of the prevailing conditions and add to the morale of every one here." The infirmary was a refuge for some, especially those suffering from alcoholism, who occasionally assumed the form of a "mummy sleeping in for a few days."[17]

As regular as the seasonal ebb and flow, the arrival of fall and winter caused vet enrollments to increase throughout the CCC. Such was the case with Company 1774 at Rochester, Minnesota, for instance, which late in the year of 1937 attained its full strength of about 200 men. As the company paper explained, "the advent of cold weather has caused many to 'join up' so as to ensure themselves of a warm, clean place to spend the winter and the assurance of getting mulligan, coffee and cakes till the birds start chirping next spring."[18]

But some of the veterans were concerned that they and their buddies were tempted to consider the CCC a permanent home, while it should be regarded only as a temporary refuge. The men should earnestly seek to better themselves, they often read in their papers. They must continue the fight in what sometimes seemed "an eternal losing sturggle." Indeed, the use of the CCC as a permanent refuge aroused the ire of the editor of the *Tamalpais Foghorn* (Company 1921, Mill Valley, California), who suggested that after two years of service in the CCC if the vet had some money on deposit and was in good health, he ought to get out and "give other waiting veterans a chance." It was most certainly annoying "to see these old homesteaders living so smugly here, at peace with themselves and supremely happy."[19]

But throughout, the veterans did not lack defenders. One woman, Elsie Smith-Parker, otherwise unidentified, writing in fulsome praise of Company 2775 in Mandan, North Dakota, sought to rebut the criticisms leveled against the veterans. To her, these men—and their families—were genuine heroes, who had endured "the cruel lashes of The War God; of famine, poverty and disease," and were now "attempting to hold back the juggernaut," a fight in which "the dice were loaded against them." To her mind, it seemed only proper, then, to honor these veterans then engaged in "the bravest battle that ever was fought."[20]

If unlike the junior enrollees in many ways, the veterans joined them in publishing camp papers. As a group, these were generally considerably better than those of their younger peers. After all, the older members had much more experience with life, and the camp scene was hardly a new experience for them. *Happy Days*, in a reference to *The Bass River Veteran* (Company 2201, New Gretna, New Jersey), acknowledged that it was a good representative veterans' newspaper, and "written by men well up in their years, the news stories and features reveal a keen sense of understanding. It is devoid of the impetuosity that is evident in papers published by junior outfits. Instead it is characterized by mellowness and experience." In one of its "Hell Box" columns, a *Happy Days* editor further commented: "Juniors are so earnest!"

"I believe that if all the sweetness and light contained in Junior camp papers were thoroly [sic] absorbed we would fall just a mite short of Utopia. Frankly, I don't want it and neither do you. It's fun to be a little bit bad—in whatever direction we tend to lean." Uplifting sermons and editorials were "definitely futile, simply because they set out so passionately to reform people." The vets, "being at that time of life when they're what they will be till death takes them," recognized the eternal truth that "any attempt to change another's opinion is a thankless task." The vets therefore usually embraced a "live and let live" philosophy. For this reason, the vets' papers were "relished" above the junior papers, and the editor admitted "that there is more actual enjoyment to be gained by reading them."[21]

Among the outstanding veterans' papers was the optimistic *Life Begins at 40* (Company 4718 in Spivey, Kansas), which accentuated the positive aspects of CCC life as experienced by the former soldiers. The *Vets Echo* (Company 1327, Lancaster, Pennsylvania) featured excellent art and makeup, and *Happy Days* once referred to *The Ponderosa Veteran* (Company 2936, Usk, Washington) as "'Public Inspiration No. 1' in CCC journalism." Guided by its editors, the three "Wizards of Usk"—the "Three Musketeers"—and printed by the veterans in their own print shop, *The Ponderosa Veteran* was the first printed paper to win five stars. Characteristically, it was consistently "right up at the top in all departments," though this took hard work and careful planning "rather than magic." *Happy Days* recommended that the magazine-style monthly "be on hand to demonstrate the ability of C-vets to do professional work— if there are any scoffers left."[22]

Veterans of Company 1924, Avery, Idaho, called their eight-page mimeographed sheet the *Bath Tub Leaks*, while Company 2414 of Sumter, South Carolina, named their mimeographed weekly *Vingt Ans Apres*—"20 Years After"—in reference to the war years. *The Dugout* (Company 2625, Hales Corner, Wisconsin) was a bright, sprightly paper that had been published since January 1938, winning the praise of General John J. Persh-

T.S.

Veterans' papers were often better produced than those of junior enrollees' companies. The stately *Arcadia Veteran* (Company 1116, Hope Valley, Rhode Island), in its commemorating Mother's Day, May 1939, is a good example.

ing, American Legion leaders, senators, representatives, and other high officials. Also seeking to "produce a full mirror of camp life," which they succeeded in doing on a high level, were *The Stockade* (Company 4719, Ottawa, Kansas); the *Pick and Shovel* (Company 1829, Temple Texas); and the redoubtable *Alpine Echo* (Company 1921, Fairfax, California).

One attribute of the veterans' papers was their propensity to challenge *Happy Days*. One of these papers with "zing," and "our constant critic," as *Happy Days* ruefully observed, was the *Vets Voice* (sometimes *The Veterans' Voice*) of Company 1774, of Rochester, Minnesota. Often displaying hilarious covers and thoughtful editorials and articles, it criticized *Happy Days* for various reasons, such as its generally uncritical support of authority, and its alleged prudishness. Other veterans' papers which sometimes took on *Happy Days* included the *Vet's Call* (Company 2713, Fairfax, Minnesota) and the *Mohican News* (Company 1570, Loudonville, Ohio).[23]

Related to the criticisms of *Happy Days* were considerations of what the role of the veterans' papers should be and how they should be managed and edited. *The Veterans' Voice* was among those with decided opinions on these subjects. As the editor of that paper, Eugene E. Tailfer, noted, "when we set about turning out our monthly blatter the idea we have in mind is to put out a sheet that will be amusing and informative to the members of V.C.C. Co. 1774, the fellows we live and work with. We run off a hundred or so extra copies and mail them out to other outfits, because we believe an interchange of ideas is a good and wholesome thing, but we don't distribute our sheet with any idea of smarting off or trying to outdo the efforts of the '*Podunk Mudslinger*' or show up the '*Bowstring Bitcher.*'" Tailfer evinced a lighter touch, especially in such pages as "The Old Hokum Bucket," and "Good Gags From Other Rags," scissored by him as "A Slight Case of Larceny," though he was careful to give credit and deplored "the lifting of gags from this rag without a snitch of credit being mentioned," which was all too common. The paper had some handicaps, he admitted, but "we've always maintained that a camp paper is all out of focus if it pretends to be but a newspaper. The modern grapevine system is so perfect in its dissemination of information that it would be futile to try and compete with it." In fact, "more news is circulated during one crowded latrine sitting than you could pack on one printed page of any camp paper." What the camp paper should be, then, was a magazine, and "otherwise nuts with news coverage. We say it's spinach and to hell with it!"[24]

Another characteristic of veterans' papers was their keeping close tabs on their peers, often ignoring the papers of the junior enrollees, though exceptional sheets that the youngsters put out were sometimes warmly praised. For example, *Vets Voice* once observed that one of the "grabbed-first-to-look-over" camp papers was the *Swan Lake Splashes* (Company 1727, Sumner, Missouri), and thought that they were probably right to call themselves "the glamour paper of the CCC." In the exchange column, "A Gander at Our Contemporaries," *The Veterans' Voice* (Company 1774, Rochester, Minnesota) often commented on its

Humor regularly appeared in veterans' sheets. Here is a cartoon appearing in the *Veterans' Voice* in November 1938.

peers. Once analyzing the *Lakeside Review* (Company 3710, Waterville, Minnesota), it stated that "we like your 'rag' a helluvalot more since you went back to the mimeograph. More individual." But when fellow editors seemed to function below par, they were just as quickly lambasted. The editor of *Vets Lament* (Company 1921, then at Camp Calaveras Big Trees, Big Trees, California), in critiquing *The Pickup* (Company 1396, Farrandsville, Pennsylvania), pulled no punches: "We don't like the face on the Statue of Liberty on the cover of your July [1940] issue. Looks like the mumps to us."[25]

One matter of considerable interest and concern to these men was the veterans' bonus. Previously voted by Congress, those who had served in World War I were to receive payments to recompense them for their sacrifices. Originally, however, these payments were not due until 1945. But in view of the pressing demands of the Depression, veterans strenuously lobbied for immediate payments. In 1936, over FDR's veto Congress responded, and provided the vets with two billion dollars in bonds to be paid out in short order. The veteran CCC press and *Happy Days* naturally closely followed developments, and *Happy Days* exultantly announced in its June 6, 1936, issue that the 27,000 veterans in the CCC would soon be receiving nearly fifteen million dollars as their share of the two billion total. Each eligible veteran would receive an average of $550 in bonds, with deliveries to begin on June 15, 1936. This gave *Happy Days* the excuse to poll the veterans' contingent, wanting to know what the men would do with the from $40,000 to $80,000 that would come into each company.

Just to consider the size of such a windfall seemed delicious. Would the men leave the CCC? Would they stay in and put the money away in a nest egg? Or would "they spend it on wine, women and song, or on a wife, farm and back debts?" In answering, between 15 and 20 percent of the veterans stated that they would leave the CCC and attempt to make it outside, and if they once more failed, they would simply return to the fold. Over 25 percent planned to buy farms. Ten percent wanted to go into business for themselves, such as barbering or blacksmithing. Seven percent would buy homes; 13 percent would save for interest payments; 10 percent would pay their debts; while 21 percent remained undecided. In any case, most of the men planned to take a five- or ten-day leave, and most of their camps planned elaborate celebrations. For instance, a dance was scheduled for Company 2690 in Michigan; a banquet was held for those leaving Company 2418 in Georgia; other companies planned smokers; and "a party of 'real' veterans" was held in Company 390 at Wadsworth, New York, in competition with a "farcical party" being organized by those left out of the vets' celebration, and who styled themselves "the veterans of future wars." But in the main, as the skipper of Company 1351 in Virginia noted, "the men in general assume[d] a very sensible attitude toward receipt of their bonus."[26]

The payment of the bonus did have an effect, at least temporarily, on the total number of veterans in the CCC. These figures dropped from below 30,000 to about 25,000, the numbers of junior enrollees correspondingly being increased by 5,000.[27]

The humor that was a common staple in all of the CCC papers was especially noteworthy in veterans' camp sheets, and they were more inclined than the junior enrollees to push the limits of good taste, propriety and the risqué. *The Veterans' Voice* (Company 1774, Rochester, Minnesota) was well aware of these tendencies, the editor once observing that "some of our 'cracks' wouldn't set well in a *Campfire Girls'* magazine, but you must remember we're grizzled old vets and we're sorta used to calling a spade a lousy shovel. We probably got that way from reading *The Stars and Stripes* paper when we were over in France."[28]

When *The Veterans' Voice* (Company 1774, Rochester, Minnesota) in its August 20, 1938, issue published a "Fantasma" cartoon focusing on a grotesque "nude" dancer that had been the center of attention at a recent carnival "girlie" show, the paper was roundly reprimanded by *Happy Days*. Thus, as the editor noted, we were given "a verbal spanking for running a cartoon last month which they considered too pornographic." The *Voice* did promise to "mow him down," that is, cartoonist R.J. Weidlich, "if he ever goes on such a rampage again."[29] However, numerous camp papers thought that the drawing was amusing, and "we still wonder," the *Voice* continued, "how our fellow vets in their *In-Zane Monthly* (Company 1575, Bellefontaine Ohio) got by a short time ago with their cartoon showing a line-up of camp inmates with their step-ins dropped down to their ankles preparatory to being physically inspected by the camp croaker [the doctor]. Maybe MADAM GRUNDY wasn't on duty that week in the *Happy Days* office."[30]

In retaliation for *The Veterans' Voice* being "chided no end for not laundering some of our recent gags and cartoons," the paper presented its own idea "of the cleanest drawing we can possibly conceive, and it is ardently hoped that it will receive the hearty approval of our dear public." It consisted of a framed-in white space: "A Neo-Modernistic Impression of a White Swan Eating a Mess of Marshmallows With Whipped Cream in a Snow Storm"—the ultimate in minimalistic art.[31]

The fact remains, however, that *The Veterans' Voice* (Company 1774, Rochester, Minnesota), was consistently among the most active in pushing the accepted limits of the risqué such as the article suggestively entitled: "Camp Builds Cat House," but the reference in fact was to the

Typical vets' humor appearing in *The Veterans' Voice.*

construction of a garage to house the company's Caterpillar tractor. Or in the form of an anonymous poem:

> A giddy young gal from Saint Paul,
> Wore a newspaper dress to a ball;
> The dress caught on fire
> And burned her entire, sport section,
> Front page and all.

And on the page "A Slight Case of Larceny: Scissored Snickers," the comment, "Good girls are born, not made" was lifted from the *In-Zane Monthly*. The *Voice* also once "borrowed" a joke from the *Flickertail Crier* (Company 2763, Salmon, Idaho): "'Let's play automobile.' 'Okay—but how do you play it?' 'You be the gears and I'll strip you.'"

The *Veterans' Voice*, on occasion, published blatantly offensive racial material passing as humor. One piece described a black Easter Day service. Strongly resented by a staffer of *The Quill* (Company 578, Morehead, Kentucky), this had an immediate effect on the newly-named *The Vets Voice*: "We received a terrific burn," the editor admitted, and promptly responded: "If the colored preacher piece was offensive to the Blue Grass people or anyone else, we abjectly apologize for running it. If we had reread the squib with any thought, we would have refrained from using it. Fact is, we culled it from a trade journal that has national circulation, so they are even more culpable than we are."[32]

Even more distressingly racist was an article in the *Voice* entitled, "Signs of Progress." This strongly deplored that the Minnesota state legislature had recently recessed, and citizens had turned out en masse, when "dusky, dead-panned Joe Louis recently visited Minneapolis. Just why all this fanfare and bally-hoo should accompany Mr. Louis' advent to the Minnesota metropolis is more than we can understand. Outstanding characters of a far larger calibre than Mr. Louis have been accorded a much milder reception than was the coffee-colored Number One citizen of Detriot and ex-pickaninny from Alabama." At best, the article went on, all that Mr. Louis had done "for suffering humanity was to furnish temporary amusement for a host of yokels—many of whom paid forty bucks for the privilege of watching him discombooberate [sic] a few doddering derelicts who masqueraded under the guise of prizefighters. The sole asset of Mr. Louis (whose real name is Joe Barrow) is, or rather was, a pulverizing punch which knocked his opponents for the well-known row of something or another. Those who went down before his murderous onslaughts included such set-ups as Primo Carnera, Kingfish Levinsky, Pauline Uzcudum, and the Livermore Laugh—better known as Max Baer. And there isn't a one of these hombres who ever possessed the qualities of a first-class fighter. Strangely enough, Mr. Louis lost much of his invincibility and his punch was shorn of most of its lethal properties when Max Schmeling entered the picture. Incidentally, the Herr Maxie was, until that time, the only man who had guts enough to climb into the ring without admitting defeat before the imbroglio got under way. All of which is away off the subject. We started out to wonder why 'dead-panned' Joe should be given such a royal reception."[33]

Of course, not all of the wit pushed the limits of good taste. *The Veterans' Voice* could be more sedate, as a potpourri drawn from its various joke columns such as "Shredded Wit," "Dipsy Noodle," and "Laff Durn Yuh," reveals: "Ed Adviser: 'What is a naturalist?' No So Bright Pupil: 'I dunno—unless it's a guy who's always throwing sevens and 'levens'"; "Dizzy Definitions": "Thomas Jefferson, though born a gentlemen, turned out to be the first Democrat;" "The only difference between this new jitterbug dancing and wrestling is that some holds are barred in wrestling;" "Shakespeare a La CCC": "As the first cook said when he tasted the T-bone steak he cooked for himself, 'What foods these morsels be!'" "Two pints make one cavort and four quarts make one gallant"; and the definition of "Dressed lumber": "Charlie McCarthy."

In the late 1930s, the worsening international situation and the outbreak of armed conflicts were sometimes lightly dismissed, even in the veterans' camps. The *Vets Voice* once quoted a disgusted traveling salesman returning from an unproductive trip: "If Hitler wants more territory, he can have mine." Another writer declared in *The Veterans' Voice* that "after reading the war news in the Far East during the past several months, it would seem that the Japs have made a hobby of collecting China."[34]

Some veterans, however, were more thoughtful. Adviser R.M. Herriott of Company 3818 at Brownwood, Texas, warned that with a possible war coming, industry should already be hiring men aged 40 and over in key positions, so that it could immediately move into full wartime production. Obviously, veterans could be used in this expanded workforce.[35]

But there was fatalism too, regarding the worsening situation. The editor of the *Alpine Echo* (Company 1921, Fairfax, California) once wrote that even if FDR would keep the U.S. out of war for a year or so, "we'll get suckered in finally and the same old gags, dressed up a bit, will work just as well as they did twenty years ago." Thus, he advised his readers, "eat, drink and be merry lads, while you've still got the chance." Indeed, as a *bon mot* had it, "war determines not who is right but who is left." Maybe the proper stance was on a firm "Americanism," defined by several veterans' organizations, which the *Alpine Echo* endorsed, and reminded the men "lest we forget," that "Americanism is an unfailing love of country; loyalty to its institutions and ideals; eager to defend it against all enemies; individual allegiance to the flag and a desire to secure the blessings of liberty to ourselves and posterity."[36]

Similarly, Jack J. London, writing in his company's paper, the *Bull's Eye* (Company 2930, La Mesa, California), urged all citizens to pull together as one person because "Hitler desires nothing more than to have men going around the country creating disunity and misunderstanding." But the president and his organization heads knew what was going on in the world and "how best to cope with the chaotic world conditions," and had sources of information at their disposal, which no single person or small group of persons had. Therefore, it was expedient for "all true Americans" to "follow our great leaders chosen by the people and of the people of the U.S.A."[37]

The Veterans' Bugle (Company 2775, Mandan, North Dakota), unlike many camp papers, was more inclined to keep abreast of the international scene. An editorial once observed that the democracies were being challenged by autocracies, and the issue may well be that "democracy is finished"; it "had had its day." What could democracies do to counter the threat? They must do "only the things any law-abiding citizen could do, when gangsters are breaking the peace," e.g., "keeping within doors, arming himself, and preparing for defence." As early as February 1938, one of the paper's writers, Gilbert W. Cass, warned that the nation must be prepared for a surprise attack, because "closing the door after the horse has been stolen is, we know, an idle gesture at best." Johannes Hanson, a camp poet at Mandan, recognized something of the magnitude of Hitler's threat: "Upon My great 'I Am' I stand/I am the first soldier of my land/Millions, others, have no choice/I am the brain, I am the voice." But Hanson warned that when the "mind of man becomes obsessed with conceit/The great 'I am' soon spells defeat."[38]

But the veterans, as did many other Americans, sometimes embraced pacifism and isolationism. The *Vets Voice* (Company 1774, Bayport, Minnesota) observed in the autumn of 1939, shortly after Hitler's invasion of Poland, that "from an alphabetical standpoint, we think we are all better off with a million men in the CCC than in the AEF again." And: "It used to be 'Hold 'er Newt,' but now it's 'Hold 'er Neutral!'" These sentiments were echoed in an editorial in the same paper by Eugene E. Tailfer entitled "Wonderful Thing, Peace." Therein, he acknowledged that yet another war was in evidence, that "experience may be the best teacher, but how teach a pupil who won't learn? Most veterans, members of this company, having seen war at close range, know how dreadful and ugly—and futile—it is. There is nothing more desirable and valuable than Peace. God bless Peaceful America and keep us peaceable and peaceful."[39]

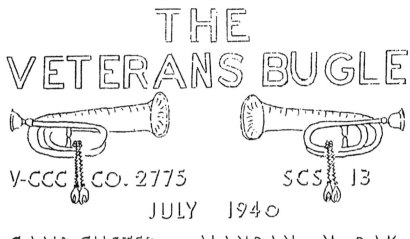

The Veterans Bugle, of Company 2775, Mandan, North Dakota, was one of the vet's better papers.

Sometimes veterans because of their ethnic origins or for other reasons supported embattled nations abroad, seeking to arouse interest in foreign conflicts. One of these was Carl H. Watson, on the staff of *Vets Voice*, who prepared an extensive article on the Finnish Republic then under attack by the Soviet Union. And in other instances, the commanding officers of the veterans' companies actively sought to keep their members more closely attuned to developing events. Company 1921, at Camp Calaveras Big Trees, California, had such a skipper in Capt. John P. Youngman who, in his own "Skippers Page" in the camp paper, *Vets Lament*, in view of the worsening situation abroad advised his charges to "be on your toes, keep your record clean, improve yourself, and be ready to be recommended to the multitude of duties your government may need you for again in the near future." The paper's editor agreed, urging the men that it was necessary "that we quit using the 'Ostrich' philosophy of burying our heads in the sands of false security," and "face twentieth century reality."[40]

In like manner, the skipper of Company 2775 at Mandan, North Dakota, Capt. D. K. Scruby, much earlier than in most other companies, saw to it that his veterans were more actively involved in discussing world affairs. He established evening "Town Hall Open Forums," sometimes with "standing room only," which continued for many months. Typical of the fare was a presentation by an Army officer, Captain James M. Hanley, Jr., who spoke on the Spanish Civil War, then in its last stages. Another timely subject was "The Place for the Veteran in the Defense Program." Strong sentiment was expressed that veterans could be used as hospital attendants, cooks, bakers, or clerks, serve in the Quartermaster Corps, or perhaps be employed as military instructors in the cantonments, freeing up younger men for more pressing duties.[41]

With the coming of the war the veterans as a whole, rallied to the nation's plans to pursue the struggle vigorously. The time for talk had passed, they felt; how about some action that would make use of their high resolve and past experience? Yet there was to be continuing frustration in these matters. *The Vets Voice*, in an article "Too Hard to Explain," forlornly asked "why most of the Vets are finding their places in the Defense Program on 'de fence.'" Also deplorable was that, while junior companies had increasing difficulty in obtaining enrollees, the opposite was the case with the veterans' companies.[42]

Among those eagerly seeking to be used were veterans of Company 2448 in Lexington, Tennessee. Their educational adviser, Samuel C. Finch, noted that while one often read of bitter, disillusioned World War veterans, there was in fact no more loyal group of men in the nation, and "if you think they are relieved that the draft age leaves them out, you just don't know your World War veteran." Many thousands of them wanted to return "to finish what we started last time." Likewise, veterans of Company 1327 in Lancaster, Pennsylvania voted to offer the services of the entire outfit, the only limitation being physical unfitness. Many of the men began getting themselves into condition by "doing a little boxing," exercising, and getting their teeth in proper shape "so they [would] not be turned down [for] poor teeth." "We want action," they said; "we got it before; we want it again."[43]

In the meantime, vets of Company 1115 at East Brewster, Massachusetts, set up a pigeon loft for training pigeons as military messengers. They were aided by Major Robert Milne, the company's subaltern, who, as a captain in World War I, was in charge of 304 "homers" in France. The veterans were aware of famed carrier pigeons of that conflict and opined that the lives of "some future vets may depend on how well these homers are cared for and trained." At least this was something they could do for the moment, pending a more substantial demand upon their services.[44]

In the end, their being kept on the sidelines never did seem right somehow; many veterans were never reconciled to being left out as a group. Though numerous individuals were able to make contributions to the nation's war efforts, many more in the 75 veterans' camps that still existed in the country by early 1942, continued to chafe that there was simply no satisfactory disposition and collective use of their training, energy and willingness to be employed in the conflict. *Este Ripples* (Company 2759, Roubaix, South Dakota) clearly summed up the situation: "The veterans would like the chance to make a recognized contribution to our war efforts and they can efficiently function as company units in fields that are closed to them as individuals."[45]

8

The Blacks:
Their Life in the
CCC and Their
Company Newspapers

"Since I made my trek across this terra firma to this domicile of the C's I have found it as sweet as the bee's product."
—Leonard "Conkie" Wright,
The Trojan (Company 2694,
Harrison, Michigan),
October–November 1940

Happy Days was frequently preoccupied with discovering all manner of "ests" in the CCC, e.g., the shortest, the tallest, the oldest, and the like, a proclivity that it shared with its World War I predecessor *The Stars and Stripes.* Once, when recording the apparent shortest and tallest men in the Corps—a man over seven feet tall and another shorter than five feet—the editor observed, "If nothing else, this ... proves that there's no discrimination in President Roosevelt's conservation corps." Such was certainly the case as to height; such was not regarding race. The CCC did, it is true, accommodate black enrollees, either in their own segregated companies, or sometimes in mixed companies. The officers were usually white, though there were notable instances when black officers were in charge, and others served on the medical staffs and as chaplains. These cases were deemed newsworthy and were often reported in *Happy*

Days, and in the many camp newspapers produced by the black companies.[1]

Initially, the usual—often negative—attitudes regarding blacks that prevailed in the nation were manifested in *Happy Days*. In early June 1933, soon after the paper began, a condescending article by Lieutenant R.F. Twinam of the 317th Field Artillery commented on the morale at Booker T. Washington camp, Fort Oglethorpe, Georgia. He noted that when he asked how the men were feeling, a grin dawned "like the moon coming up over a persimmon tree," and a man with a "dusky good-natured face" elaborated: "Oh, yessuh, you bet dey is [fine]. Us gets treated more better than in many a day. Them ossifers seem like nice genmen, an' we ain' been work half so hard as we is been eating." Twinam concluded: "Bad as this good-natured giant may pine for Beale Street over in old Memphis town, his contentment and wholesome spirit are typical of the selectees in Camp Booker T. Washington." A colored lad in an Arizona camp similarly expressed his satisfaction with the CCC: "'Lawdy,' he said, 'I'se ridin' on de gravey train, an' Roosevelt's pushin.'"[2]

Another article in questionable taste, entitled "Was It a Weird Love Call That Echoed Thru the Night?" appeared in *Happy Days* under the byline of its author, Captain John S. Moran of Company 891, Camp Leonard Wood, Woodville, Texas. It recounted that a plaintive call, which often echoed through the night causing apprehension in the camp, was identified as from an aged black, "howling his weird notes onto the night air.... The darkey, age eighty years, was a slave and for years had given this call at night, thinking that some of his old slave friends will hear him."[3]

But men of Company 361, a black company, in a letter to the editor took strong exception to the piece, labeling it "an insult to our race, and feel that all colored American citizens are concerned. We also demand an apology. We trust that you will see the great wrong you have done us, and that we will receive your acknowledgement soon." All that was forthcoming, however, was an explanation that it "'Twas All in Fun."[4]

Veterans' companies, in particular, were often offenders in racial matters, though junior companies were not exempt, as a joke which appeared in numerous camp papers, reveals: "One of the boys wanted to know if they used white ink when they fingerprinted the colored companies."[5] Sometimes, though, even the black papers participated in poking fun at themselves and their stereotypes as in the poem, "The Preacher in the Graveyard," by Ivy Williams, the social editor of *The Border Tab* (Company 2924, Jamul, California):

An owl hooted and the preacher jumped
And his eyes alighted on a real white stump.
The Preacher whirled, bent low to the ground
And dug up dirt like a whippet greyhound.
He was traveling pretty fast when he passed his gate
And he glimpsed his house just a little too late.
There was a barbed wire fence, strung in eight
Stretched across the lane supposed to be a gate.
The preacher hit the wire just a little below the slack
Staples began to fly and I heard some posts crack.
But the preacher kept going about ninety miles flat
Hurdled the next one and didn't even look back.[6]

Protests by black CCC members were one form of countering the anti-black bias then endemic nationwide. Another development tending to these ends was the influence of numerous newspapers of the black companies, several ranking at the top of those produced by the Corps. *Happy Days* once praised them for being "up to the standards of many papers with less handicaps." One of those which kept "well to the fore in the ranks of better camp papers," was *The Muskingum Totem* (Company 1521, Zanesville, Ohio). Called by *Happy Days* a "Humdinger," and one of the best black camp papers in the U.S., it was edited by Herman O. Baines and his staff artist Don Lewis. When the sheet won a five-star rating in the August 12, 1939, issue of *Happy Days*, a sumptuous banquet was held in celebration.[7]

The Big Apple Gazette—its title derived from Harlem slang—was another good paper, published by Company 246 at Panama, New York. It was singled out for praise by *Happy Days* on several occasions. *Ditch Dots and Dashes* (Company 517, Portland, Indiana) and *Little Ethiopia* (Company 5418, Witherbee, South Carolina) also enjoyed a measure of success, while the perky *Hi-de-hi-de-ho* revealed the high spirits of the men of Company 4487 in Anderson, South Carolina. Other outstanding sheets included the *Pine Needle*, a mimeographed bimonthly produced jointly by two companies, 235 and 237, both based at Camp Pack near New Lisbon, New Jersey; *The Border Tab* of Company 2924 at Camp Minnewawa near Jamul, California, another five-star paper; and the *Battlefield Echo* (Company 1355, Gettysburg, Pennsylvania).

Undoubtedly, one of the most successful of the black papers was *The Trojan* of Company 2694, based at Camp Walkerville near Bitely, Michigan. First published on October 9, 1936, it was a neat bimonthly. Set up by the educational adviser, Bret M. Miller, there was a full staff including artists; a society editor; and a radio, stage and screen editor, Ulus Davenport, who had a passion for swing music. There was a

COMPANY
2694
CCC

MARCH
APRIL
MAY
*
EDITION

A PAPER WITH A PURPOSE

VOL. 4   HARRISON   MONTHLY   MICHIG   NO. 3

COMPANY SENDS
EXHIBIT TO DETROIT

MELVIN BUTLER REPRESENTS COMPANY AT EXPOSITION

(SDM--5/28/40) Instructions were issued from District Headquarters in April that Camp Houghton Lake, Camp Bitely and Camp Stronach were expected to contribute a display to the "75 Years of Negro Progress Exposition" in Detroit, May 10 - 19. A-long with these instructions was the statement that one enrollee from each of the three companies would be selected to accompany the exhibit. While preparing the ex-hibit the problem of what enrollee to nominate for the trip became acute. The idea was suggested that we run an essay contest on the theme the exposition was celebrat-ing. The matter was discussed with the Company Commander, and he thought it was a good idea.

EDUCATIONAL
COMMITTEE
VISITS   DAM

(PJ--5/28/40) On the 23rd of May the Camp Edu-cational Committee, com-posed of Lt. MacDonald, Mr. Cline and Mr. Hughes, visited the first pouring of concrete at the Mus-kegon Dam Project. Mr. Cline was anxious to get pictures of the activi-ties, so both Lt. Mac-Donald and Mr. Hughes came prepared and took some very good pictures.

An interesting story of this particular project will appear in the June issue of the TROJAN. Watch for it.

-----o-----

The contest was an-nounced to the company, and the subject was to be "What 75 Years of Freedom Has Meant to the Negro." Many started and lost heart, but six enrollees came through with flying colors. They were Aubrey C. Agee, Melvin Butler, Fredrick Cureton, Emanuel Houston, Mike Lawton and Connell Mitchell.

(CONTINUED ON PAGE 4)

The Trojan, the mimeographed monthly of Company 2694, at Harri-son, Michigan, was one of a number of outstanding black papers. This is the cover of the combined March/April/May 1940 issue.

reporter for each of the four barracks at the camp. The reporters took
their responsibilities seriously, as did the one for Barrack "B": "We challenge the company at large at Bridge or Whist. (Bring your own dice)."
The *Trojan's* publication policy asserted that it intended to print news
"from an optimistic point of view," and eschewed articles that might
endanger the "feelings and morale of its readers."[8]

In many respects the black papers had much in common with their
white contemporaries. There was a great deal of information about the
recreational and cultural activities scheduled in the black companies, as
was true of most of the CCC camps. For example, many camps—black
and white—were included on the circuit for plays developed by the
Drama Department, United States Works Progress Administration of
New York City. Between October 25, 1934, and November 5, 1935, the
twin camps 235 and 237 attended the performances of 14 plays—though
some were repeats. These included among others *The Whole Town's Talking*, performed by Vaudeville Unit #1; *One of the Family*; *The Late Christopher Bean*; *The Taming of the Shrew*; *Skinner's Dress Suit*; *Your Uncle
Dudley*; *Believe Me, Xantippe*; *The Fall Guy*; and *Friendly Enemies*. The
Pine Needle warmly saluted the New York Drama Department, which
had amply demonstrated that New York thespians "Could Take It," as
could the CCC. Though the plays were discontinued in the winter
months because of transportation and weather problems, they were sorely
missed because they "had offered an enjoyment that was never before
realized in camp and created an entertainment that only a cast of professionals could render."[9]

The *Pine Needle* included safety reminders, as was customary with
all CCC papers, often using crude cartoon drawings making the point
that "an ounce of safety is worth a pound of luck," and urging all to "realize that safety is a part of your job."[10]

Similar to CCC camp papers generally, the *Pine Needle* often emphasized humor and the common touch. Bernard Macfadden, in his column
"Thoughts" suggested that the men keep their troubles to themselves,
"or tell them to a policeman if you must talk about them." The paper's
general policy was upbeat, and an on-going local camp gossip column
"Night Owl" was dedicated to light-hearted jests, as: "Why does Shim
Sham call C.B. his friend and then trys to take his girl?" And: "What
young Romeo lost his girlfriend Tuesday night in the movies?" And elsewhere: "Boys, you know that xmas is almost here, so it will pay to fall
out with your 'chicks.'" The paper's "Humor Column" often included
suggestive poetry: "When Jack and Bill/Go up the hill/To see the farmer's
daughter/You can bet your life/That Jack and Bill/Arn't going after
water."[11]

The blacks did have their own attitude toward women—a rather macho one. "The Phantom Speaks," in *The Trojan* (Company 2694, Bitely, Michigan), noted that each month there would be the announcement of the "Sheik of the Month," defined as the man "who plays the weaker sex the hardest from the fifteenth of one month until the fifteenth of the next." The first winner's attainments were described: "By playing frails in London, Detroit and Kalamazoo he has earned this honor." The man in second place, "Old Folks" Alfred Gaye, was not first because "rumor has it that his Ardine is playing around with another 'square' while Gaye is typing reports until 9:45 nightly. Which reminds me of the old saying: 'Absence in love is like water upon fire; a little quickens, but much extinguishes it.'"[12]

Many CCC papers emulated Walter Winchell, the *Pine Needle* being no exception, sometimes calling its gossip column "Walnut Witchazel." One item from the column entitled "My Dream Girl" reads: "She stands before me, nude, the whole day through/Her body shedding light where there is dark/But still, there's really nothing that I can do/For she's just a statue in my city's public park." Lovelorn columns also appeared, one called, "Behold Venus Pigeons," which gave humorous, questionable advice to lovesick supplicants.[13]

Homesickness was color blind, and black companies were not exempt. The *Pine Needle* commiserated with the men so afflicted but, taking a stern stance, insisted that the new enrollees must henceforth realize that "your Maternal care you will find in the Army, and the Paternal care you will find in the Forestry." And: "We that are hearing your moans nightly feel for you but we cannot reach you."[14]

Blacks, like whites, were concerned perennially with the job situation in the world beyond the camp walls. Exhortations often warned the men not to desert but to stay in camp so that "Old Ruco"—a term for the "wolf at the door" or "unemployment"—would not capture them: "Because old Ruco is waiting/Yes the wolf is on the scout/ And Old Ruco will get *you*/If you don't watch out."[15]

Correspondingly, one of the fates of many men in the CCC was that they would be unwillingly discharged but most would take their medicine in the spirit of cooperation, determined to return to public life knowing that they were better prepared to assume their duties at home. As the *Pine Needle* expressed it, "the Government has done its full share," and the men must now contribute in turn to their various communities.[16]

But if the black camp papers resembled those of the CCC in general, more striking were the ways in which they were dissimilar. The humor and gossip material deviated, sometimes subtly, from that in the papers of the white camps. *The Pine Needle* often manifested this in "The Informer" column. The writer, recognizing that the men about camp especially liked having their names in the paper, obliged, often in jivy rhymes: "Mr. Carl Mitchel better known as moonglow/Words from his tongue glibbly flow." And: "Mr. Harold Caines better known as Picolo Pete/With the musical feet." And: "Mr. Walter Morrow a snake fearing man/When one he sees he is an also ran." Other columns to these ends included humorous listings of "Who Who's" in Companies 235 and 237, such as "greatest playboy," "greatest lover," "the egoist," "biggest John," "most studious," "most unfortunate," "the most dutiful," "the jiver," "the agitator," and many others. The "Night Owl" column of *The Pine Needle* likewise named names: "Can it be that Dudly doesn't know any better or is trying to be a modern Don Juan? I happen to know that he is trying to play L. W., E. W., M. B. and M. C. all at the same time. My what a foolish boy." Another column, "About the Boys," featured one-liners descriptive of the enrollees soon to leave the camp: John Blow, "bow-legged but well liked"; Harry Claireborne, "puzzling but true to his friends"; and Leonard Giles, "one of Mussolini's staunch supporters." Also in the *The Trojan*, a cartoon page, "The Cat's Corner" by staff artist John Allen depicted zoot suiters and other "cats."[17]

Black slang, which the blacks themselves gloried in, attracted considerable attention in the CCC newspapers, and lists were compiled from time to time. One was by Eugene Watkins, the post exchange steward of Company 246, at Panama, New York, a black outfit. Some examples: salty—angry or disgusted; hard rubber—new or flashy auto; copping a deuce—to make an excuse or to lessen the meaning of a statement; weed, rope, or white boy—cigarette; dig—do you understand or to look; so you collar the riff—do you understand the conversation? cut out—let's go or get away from me; solid—right; hipped—experienced or wise; jive the man—confidence in a person; unhipped—inexperienced or not alert; unhipped lame—entirely green; scratch—money; Big Apple—Harlem; that man—anyone in authority; wolfing—loud talking; stiffing—going through the motions of working; front—best suit of clothes; mellow as a cello—excellent; frame—a person's baby. That many of these are now familiar, at least in American usage, is testimony as to how thoroughly they were subsequently absorbed into common parlance.[18]

Other examples appeared in the column "Jive Around the 'Lake'," in the form of a "letter" to "All Hep Cats in Swingology," by a columnist of *The Trojan*, Leonard "Conkie" Wright: "If any of you cats are ever visiting the Lake [Camp Houghton Lake], you must drill into the Bomcile's castle. It is under the care of Count Frazier and his cats. These cats get their knowledge box charged with swing jive from the swing box over W.M.A.Q. every bright [day]. Since Ole man Climate has come on with his cool products, which get the cats together every 7th bright to out tell the others weird tales. These 'five canaries' come on with some fine chirpin.' They have let their jive cords trilly all around the Lake and down to Harrison and back. These cats are coming on and do bear watching, Jack…. Well, cats, 'Conkie' will bring his verbal pow-wow chin session to a sudden stop. Be on hand next time as I bring you jive as you like it." *The Border Tab*, a bimonthly mimeographed sheet of Company 2924, Camp Minnewawa at Jamul, California, sometimes featured a page "The Hipped Cat," signed "Yours diggingly." A sheet filled with gossip presented as jive talk, its author warned men at the camp that "I am the most hipped cat in these parts. I do no harm, I only let the world know what you are doing. So I tell you now if you don't want it printed don't do it, for I know all and see all." The column also gave the men advice as to their conduct: "Vile language and uncouth actions don't harmonize with our beautiful landscape—and the Captain loves his flowers—ya get it?"[19]

More seriously, the CCC press, both *Happy Days* and the camp newspapers, reported on the progress being made in the CCC by black enrollees and officers, and the black papers were often preoccupied with self-esteem and attempts to improve the status of blacks in American society. FDR had called for the employment of black military officers to take their places of responsibility in the growing Corps. One of the first black medical officers appointed was Dr. Maurice E. Johnson, a First Lieutenant in the Medical Corps Reserve, who was sent to an all-white outfit, Company 1334 at Goshen, Virginia. Other black medical officers soon followed. In addition, by September 1935, 70 black educational advisers and four chaplains had been assigned to black CCC camps.[20] The first black officer to command a CCC company was Captain Frederick Lyman Slade of Washington, D.C., placed at the helm of Company 1354 at Gettysburg, Pennsylvania. Company 1251 in Elmira, New York, a black outfit, was an early example of a camp commanded entirely by black officers. *The Trojan* (Company 2694, Harrison, Michigan) also sometimes featured black military leaders, presenting them as role models for men in the company.[21]

The black camps often discovered ways to advance black awareness, a perennial theme well developed in the black CCC press. For example, Negro History Week was widely celebrated in the black CCC camps. The men of Company 235, New Libson, New Jersey, were urged to recognize that "faith in God" was fundamental to their future progress. A survey of Negro History was presented; interpretations of the Negro in art, music and entertainment were made by several members of the company; and a group of visiting girls sang spirituals and popular songs.[22]

The Border Tab (Company 2924 at Jamul, California), in its ongoing page "Who's Who in Colored U.S.A," often stressed the importance of blacks in U.S. history and culture, featuring such personalities as the popular singers Marian Anderson and Dorothy Manor. In addition, prominent blacks in business, education, and in the Catholic Church were discussed, as were Negro soldiers in the Revolutionary War. In a time of growing interest in the military, one article focused on the life and career of Brig. Gen. Benjamin O. Davis, the first black to hold the rank of general. Other high-ranking officers in the U.S. military establishment were also discussed.

There were features in *The Muskingum Totem* (Company 1521, Zanesville, Ohio), such as its page "It's True That—" filled with facts and oddities regarding the black race. Similarly, the *Battlefield Echo* (Company 1355, Gettysburg, Pennsylvania)featured "The Negro in Our History," and *The Trojan* of Company 2694, Bitely, Michigan, included articles on the history of the blacks and their rightful place in American society. In the column "Assorted Facts That You Should Know," excerpts from papers such as the *Pittsburgh Courier,* the *Detroit Free Press,* and the *Indianapolis Recorder* were printed, emphasizing the accomplishments of Joe Louis and other blacks.

At a time when aviation was all the rage, the blacks went on record that they were not to be counted out. Articles featuring the training of black airmen by such institutions as Howard University and Tuskegee Institute appeared in some of the camp papers. Indeed, the aviators then involved in training would be heard from later in World War II, gaining their own measure of fame.

Booker T. Washington and Frederick Douglass were often featured, the latter frequently sharing billing with Lincoln and Washington as three of "February's Immortals." Typical of the pieces on Booker T. Washington was a column in *The Pine Needle* by Eugene Holmes. Washington was praised for his founding of National Negro Health Week in 1915, with its emphasis on the famous four "H's": Head, Heart, Hand and Health. An account of his life detailed his struggles as a boy and how he had overcome adversity in founding the Tuskegee Institute. It seemed only fitting, therefore, that such a clear role model for all blacks, he would be given a postage stamp in his honor. Another paragon was Mary McLeod Bethune, president of Bethune-Cookman College at Daytona Beach, Florida. She was recognized for having built the institution by money earned, among other things, from the sale of sandwiches and cakes. Thus, "in her desire to lead her race out of darkness she strove to build a castle of education and understanding and let others share it with her."[23]

As did newspapers generally, the black papers paid considerable attention to FDR, the *Pine Needle* once expressing "our appreciation to our beloved president, Franklin Delano Roosevelt, for all that he has done for us." If white CCC companies rarely had much say about Eleanor Roosevelt, such was not the case among black enrollees. Her "highly publicized solicitude" toward minorities was well known and appreciated.[24]

Another theme common in the black CCC company newspapers was the need for black enrollees to take advantage of their opportunities in the Corps. While this was a usual approach in white CCC papers as well, there nevertheless seemed to be a greater urgency manifested by the black company papers in this regard. Black enrollees were especially urged to improve themselves through education; the development of a work ethic; and attention to personal conduct, health and general appearance. Two of the papers most active in education were *The Pine Needle* in New Jersey and *The Trojan* in Michigan. In both cases, active educational advisers and commanding officers mobilized the papers to advance learning. Indeed, the only thing remaining, the papers asserted, was the enrollee's "own interior disposition and thirst for bettering himself, his own perseverance in showing the proper attitude and spirit that will not only enable him to carry on but which will increase his own proficiency, emphasizing his own willingness to take advantage of a real opportunity for self-education."[25]

Yet, as always in the CCC, there was considerable difficulty in obtaining the men's support for education and betterment programs. It was acknowledged that it was surely a hardship for the tired enrollee to direct his footsteps toward the educational room after a hard day in the field, but this was required if one was to expect progress. Indeed, "we expect a large percentage of you gentlemen to show more signs of ambition and hope," *The Pine Needle* scolded.

Nevertheless, out of a total enrollment of about 400 men in the twin camps of Company 235 and 237, only 13 were enrolled in English and public speaking; 10 in journalism, mainly the staff of the paper; 7 in a debating society; 19 in history; 16 in geography; 23 in math, and 9 in first aid. Predictably, enrollments were higher in the technical courses, with 35 taking classes in auto mechanics. As might be expected, greater numbers participated in recreational pursuits. There were 42 enrolled in dramatic and musical clubs; 37 came out for football; 24 for basketball, 29 for baseball; while 20 participated in boxing and 12 in track.[26]

Nevertheless, educational advisers often exerted themselves to make education more palatable to the men. For instance, at Company 2694, Camp Houghton Lake, Harrison, Michigan, Richard M. Hughes set up a Correspondence Study Center, creating thereby "a University of Michigan outpost in our camp," as he enthused, though only a few men took advantage of it. More effective was the scheduling of classes at the camp from 7:00 to 7:45 A.M. between breakfast and work call, with the pointed proviso that those not attending classes had to "answer to the police call and must tour the entire camp area picking up all paper and rubbish and deposit[ing] it in the waste cans."[27]

If education was a major emphasis, moral and spiritual concerns, as well as health and general well-being, were not neglected in the black camps. In fact, religion, as "an indispensable element in any great human character," was regarded as a necessity and not an option in many black companies. One chaplain, 1st Lt. John Samuel, for instance, addressing the men of Company 2594 in his regular feature in the company's paper, *The Trojan*, advanced religion as a shield against the discrimination common in the day against blacks. "No one can degrade me; I alone can do that," he declared, and enjoined his readers to "look to Almighty God to impart such strength to us as will make us Conquerors in all the tests of life." At Camp Pack in New Jersey, home of companies 235 and 237, the religious needs of the enrollees were addressed by theology students at Princeton Theological School who periodically visited the men in camp.[28]

There were various other expedients to help the men establish some sense of self-worth. In California, *The Border Tab* encouraged the men of the company to write essays in which they expressed themselves positively about their work and the specific jobs that they did, with the end in view of inculcating pride and in establishing the work ethic so essential to success. Similarly, *The Pine Needle* instructed the men of Companies 235 and 237 that they must "keep the habit of being on time, retire on work days at a reasonable hour, remember to be courteous to your superiors and elders, keep care of your bodies and strive to retain the health and safety precautions learned in camp, don't neglect going to church, and above all keep out of difficulty with law enforcers and out of the courts and prisons."

Proper conduct and good manners were also calculated to enhance self-esteem. To help matters along, Robert Anderson, news editor of *The Pine Needle*, penned a lengthy article on "Etiquette" in which he lectured the men about their conduct at the movies, they should not smoke, stand in the aisles, nor talk during the movie. They should as well refrain from loud laughter and the making of "bad remarks." It was also not good manners, he went on, to "discuss the movie with a friend or tell what will happen soon for it will spoil the entertainment for others." In short, they should be generally courteous to all, especially to the ladies. In addition, remarking that "it is said that a loan often loses both itself and [the] friend," the men were urged to promptly pay their debts, which could also help keep their heads held high.[29]

Health problems were frequently discussed as well, *The Pine Needle*, reporting that the men of Companies 235 and 237 had been addressed by their camp physician in a "plain but forceful heart-to-heart talk" on the perils of venereal diseases. Some 57 rookies were sufficiently impressed to submit to Wassermann tests. Less spectacularly, if still important, the camp's dentist sometimes submitted articles to *The Pine Needle* on the necessity of dental hygiene.[30]

Sports and music were two areas that attracted considerable attention in the black camps, and these avenues also contributed to the development of self-worth. The overhead often used sports figures as role models for their enrollees and sometimes had exceptional opportunities to do so. Such was the case with Company 235. In the summer of 1938, Eugene Mickens, a veteran professional boxer, became an enrollee at Camp Pack. Enlisted by *The Pine Needle* to encourage the men, he advised them to take advantage of the camp's considerable educational facilities, and its opportunities for "wholesome work and recreation." In addition, he warned "against too much vulgarity and not enough politeness." Eulace Peacock, a sprinter on the famed 1936 U.S. Olympic Team, reinforced Micken's exhortations. Making a personal appearance at Camp Pack, he encouraged the enrollees to establish their own programs of health and physical development.[31]

Boxing, baseball and basketball had devoted followings within the black companies. Company 2694, for a time based at Camp Kalkaska, Kalkaska, Michigan, was fortunate to have Captain C. A. Gerfen as their commanding officer. For a number of years he had been the manager of a baseball team in Battle Creek, and his presence gave considerable impetus to that sport. As to boxing, the Golden Glove program provided challenges to black CCCers. *The Trojan* often featured boxing heroes. Joe Louis's bout with Max Schmeling was avidly followed, the results being acclaimed because he had "stopped the only man who ever marred his professional record." *The Trojan* also followed the careers of other outstanding black athletes, including Jessie Owens, as well as college stars. "All of these young men have paved a way for others to follow," the paper declared, also recognizing that there were many good black athletes in their own camp. The latter were urged to work hard at their chosen sports, aspiring "to be the best in the game." The road was often tough, but it was worth the effort, and even Joe Louis had had to struggle to make it to the top.[32]

The men of Company 2924 in California enjoyed considerable success in basketball, winning the Los Angeles District Championship Basketball trophy in early 1940. They had worked hard for their success, their company paper, *The Border Tab*, maintained, noting that while "the wanting was easy, the getting was hard." Indeed, the fast-paced game was instructive for larger endeavors: "Events happen just as fast in life," the *Tab* contended, "and in life also, the victory goes to the best-trained man."[33]

Music was another area of great interest in the black companies. For a time, Company 2694 in Michigan had as company commander Captain Joe A. Martin, who had a long career on the stage with a famous saxophone group and, in addition, was a music teacher in the public schools of Battle Creek, Michigan. He set up music classes for the company each Tuesday morning before work, teaching trumpet, violin, saxophone, and other instruments. In California, Company 2924 gained fame for its glee club which often entertained at schools, colleges, and service clubs, as well as in churches in the San Diego and Los Angeles areas. Similarly, the two CCC companies at Camp Pack, Nos. 235 and 237 at New Lisbon, New Jersey, each month staged the Camp Pack "Scandels" [sic], a variety show featuring the "Pine Needle Four," a quartet; a comic act, instrumental numbers, dancing and other numbers. Camp enrollees also performed in nearby towns, such as Camden and Burlington, New Jersey, and elsewhere in the Second Corps Area, "carving themselves a place in the entertainment world."[34]

To be sure, the black experience was not all sports and music. They also came in for their share of serious trouble, though this was hardly confined to black companies. Albert W. Jernberg, a commander of a black company, in his book, *My Brush Monkeys: A Narrative of the CCC,* has much to say about the difficulties of commanding blacks, noting their tendency to rowdiness and being difficult to control in general, though he was also favorably impressed by the many accomplishments of black CCCers.[35]

One serious event involving black CCC enrollees occurred when a long smoldering animosity between members of a black company and black youths of Chestertown, Maryland, erupted in violence. As a CCC glee club was leaving a church prayer meeting, a burst of shotgun fire wounded 17, sending 10 men to a hospital. More seriously, Lt. Paul E. La Masters, the commanding officer of a black outfit, Company 2664 at Mt. Carroll, Illinois, was killed in his office by two young bandits. These were John Collins, aged 17, a former member of the company who had been discharged earlier, and his 15-year-old brother. The pair made off with the monthly payroll totaling about $1200, though they were soon apprehended.[36]

On the larger stage, there was often tension between CCC enrollees and townspeople. As was common with many CCC camp papers, it was often necessary to lecture enrollees on their conduct when outside the limits of the camp. The *Pine Needle* advised its readers that "our conduct makes us welcome in most towns," but not all of the CCC enrollees were so regarded. One of the main complaints was "the public use of vile language. It is said that the culprits seem to amuse themselves, to the discomfort of the spectators and when chastised, often want to engage in an altercation with the Chastiser." The men were urged to join in a general campaign to stamp out these undesirable conditions, though it was recognized that while "we can give advice, ... we can't give conduct."[37]

Sometimes the grounds for complaint went well beyond the mere matter of profanity. Certain men of Camp Pack had allegedly been involved in a disturbance at the "Green Goose" establishment in Camden, New Jersey. As a result, nine were arrested and tried, though they stoutly maintained their innocence. Found guilty, the boys were barred for a time from setting foot in Burlington, Mill's Dam Park and Camden, all near their camp.[38]

Other sensitive issues involved the womenfolk of communities where CCC camps existed. Pulling no punches, Teddy Greene, an acting editor of the *Pine Needle*, reported that he heard an enrollee state that "the CCC has wrecked many a happy home," proceeding to describe what he meant. There was the case of enrollees who met "small town women and immediately seek an opportunity to do away with lonesome hours." Typically, one would meet a female, make his identity known (mostly fictitious), and flatter her "as no man has ever done before. [And] mind you, this woman is married, yet our CCC boy is able to fill her head with such tales as to make her think him a Clark Gable or a modern Don Juan. Poor little Lass! Little does she know that she is playing with fire." Then, "not being able to withstand his ardent and passionate love-making, she meets him willingly and repeatedly." The inevitable result: the woman grows tired of her husband and seeks to take up with her CCC lover. But what does she find? "'Tis simple, the Don Juan is no longer interested in her." In fact, she was never anything to him but another adventure. The results: a heartbroken husband; a shamed and disillusioned wife; and the CCC boy who goes on his way "just as happy as before." Who was to blame? "She for believing or he for deceiving?" Certainly food for thought, Greene concluded.[39]

If the CCC boys came under suspicion and encountered opposition in the larger community, many enrollees—in both black and white companies—complained that they were sometimes unfairly discriminated against by civil authority. *The Indian Trail* (Company 728, Salem, Missouri), admitted that on occasion the CCC boys did cause some disturbances in towns where they sought recreation. They were more or less willing to take responsibility for such actions. However, the paper strongly protested that there were many instances when CCC men were accused by civil authorities of things which they had not done, which "far exceed the actual violations." The reasons might be politically inspired or for some other reasons the CCC boys were forced "to take the rap" for things that they were not involved in. This was a "most despicable police practice conceivable and under no circumstances is it justifiable." The CCC boys should not be at the mercy of the unscrupulous "copper" nor of the "unjust judge."[40]

Despite the troubles in black companies, they were also frequently looked upon favorably. This was especially true of their firefighting activities. Company 2924 at Camp Minnewawa put numerous men on a fireline to battle successfully a five-day forest fire in California in the summer of 1940, winning them renown. Indeed, CCCers seemed perennially attracted to flames. Thus it was only natural that 36 blacks from Company 237 in New Jersey were ordered by Major Doncal C. Hawley, the commander of the Trenton District, to Lakehurst on May 6, 1937, the date of the *Hindenburg* airship disaster, to help in relief and rescue operations, for which they were officially commended.[41]

Meanwhile, lowering clouds on the international scene, the related problems of isolation, pacificism and the issue of military training in the CCC in the late 1930s, had a measurable impact on the black companies as on the white CCCers. Foremost was a consideration of what the fate of black Americans might be if another war came. Frank Wilson, writing in *Happy Days*, reminded readers of the lapse in promises made to blacks in the World War that if the men would fight, "on our return home we would find a new America for all, regardless to color, race or creed." Paul Lawrence Dunbar, in a poem in *The Pine Needle* for Memorial Day, 1938, called attention to what blacks had accomplished in that struggle:

If the muse were mine to tempt it
And my feeble voice were strong,
If my tongue were trained to measure
I would sing a stirring song.

I would sing a song heroic
Of those noble sons of Ham
Of the gallant colored soldiers
Who fought for Uncle Sam.[42]

Notwithstanding their having served with distinction, the lot of blacks had not improved. Accordingly, Henry Holmes of Company 3308 in Reedsville, Pennsylvania, thought that the blacks' role in the event of another conflict was a matter of some urgency which Congress should seriously consider. Would the black be allowed to fight or only carry a pick and shovel on his shoulder "as he did in the late World's War?" he asked. Were blacks merely to be "laborers and servants dressed in soldiers' and sailors' uniforms?" Times had changed since the war, Holmes declared, and "negroes have cultivated self-pride and they have developed along the lines of economy wonderfully, and they feel that should America be forced in the present holocaust, their desires are to serve in all branches of the service, just as the colonials serve France." Malcom W. Bingay, writing on "The Negro's Plight" in *The Detroit News*—in an article reprinted in *The Trojan*—concurred. He insisted that "we will learn that we cannot neglect one portion of our community, our state and our Nation without having all of them affected. Intelligent selfishness, if nothing else, demands justice for the Negro."[43]

Despite misgivings about military service, many blacks saw it as a a means of gainful employment. *The Pine Needle* thought that CCC men might consider enrolling in the Regular Army, which was "an excellent chance and opportunity ... to receive training for citizenship under Regular Army discipline." There were other benefits: "A man who enters the Army of the United States for two or three years will have the opportunity of his life to see the world and learn the real significance of life and will increase his degree of intelligence far over that of the average man without an opportunity for such training as that one may receive from the Army of the United States of America." Indeed, "military training makes for quick action and a keen mind which prepares a person for the highest type of services. No American citizen should ever look upon military training as preparation for War. It is preparation for peace and, [it] may be added, preparation for life."[44]

Whatever their views on the subject of black involvement, the imperatives of war began to impinge on blacks in the CCC as on everyone else in the nation. Conditions in the world had deteriorated by the autumn of 1941, and the subaltern of Company 2924 based at Jamal, California—Lieutenant Henri C. Holgate, writing in *The Border Tab*—urged the men to turn from speculation about their anticipated roles and carry their share of the load at camp, "and to get on the tail of the fellow that 'don't.'" This was necessary for "Uncle Sam has a lot of worries these days," because "some little squirt with a black mustache over there across the pond is raising hell." Indeed, "'He don't [sic] give a Hoot' about regulations either and Uncle Sam is out to give him a little extra duty. Maybe Uncle will give him a [dishonorable discharge] and if he gets a D.D. from Uncle Sam you can bet Ruco's last dollar that he won't be able to get another job for a long time."[45]

After Pearl Harbor, as the reality of war hit home for the men at Pine Valley in war-sensitive California, Holgate emphasized the need for calm and self-discipline, further urging that every effort be made to prepare for the dangers to come. All must participate, he concluded, because "cooperation has never lost a war."[46]

Though *The Border Tab* continued with its usual features, as was the case with many CCC papers, it now had to take into account many new challenges. Consequently, considerable information was forthcoming as to how to respond to possible air raids and gas attacks. Throughout, as the camp commander Lieutenant Fred W. Palmtag noted, the men were to do their best as part "of that great army working behind the lines for and with our armed forces." Indeed, "we have a job to do, a big job. Let's do it right, do it willingly and DO it good." And the company's educational adviser, James O. Whaley, further urged the men to save sugar and take better care of their clothes. Specifically regarding black enrollees, he reminded them that "drape suits are out—you know. After May 9th, certain styles are forbidden. No cuffs on pants. No extension waist bands. No pleats. No unusually wide knees. No patchpockets. No coats longer than standard length and no vest with a double breasted suit. [Have] you given this a thought? Fellows, WE ARE AT WAR." The men should also work harder, get up a few minutes earlier, and limit their individual desires. In short, he concluded, "we must begin now to sacrifice."[47]

The record of the black companies in the CCC, as mirrored in the pages of their company papers, reveals, as one might expect, a mixed bag. Near the end of the CCC's career, *The Border Tab* recorded that 250,000 colored youth served in the CCC since its founding. For the past year, $700,000 a month had been allotted by colored CCC boys to their parents and dependents at home. Other statistics revealed that some 130 black college graduates were serving CCC camps as educational advisers. In addition, 1,200 part-time, experienced WPA teachers were instructing colored enrollees. Twenty-five colored medical reserve officers and chaplains were on active CCC service. Four colored engineers and six technical foremen were on duty in Pennsylvania camps, and at Gettysburg, the superintendent was a black.[48]

At the personal level, numerous blacks attested to what the CCC experience had meant to them. John Roundtree, his company's first sergeant, recounted that the CCC had taught him how to type, get along with others, and work hard, "the forerunner of all success." But "one of the greatest and most impressive things in the CCC is working in the fields. Traveling by truck for many miles into the far recesses of the forests is an opportunity that many people from large cities would not ordinarily have," he declared. "There it was," he continued, "that I first saw life in its primary stages. Thousands of birds, hundreds of rabbits, deer by the herd and porcupines and other wildlife filled the forests. Life is observed in its most primitive state with you serving in the capacity of an audience. This experience tends to make you more aware of the fact that you are only a very small and inconspicuous part in a world of immensity." Matured in mind and body, he found that a busy life was a satisfying one, and he thanked the CCC for its manifold benefits.[49] When the Rev. John W. Wright of Company 237 in New Jersey bid a farewell to the CCC, he admitted that "never at any time have I been very fond of it. I didn't come to camp because I would enjoy being here, but because conditions forced me to place myself therein." Yet he acknowledged its advantages, and concluded that if anyone wished to better his character, "the CCC camp is the place for the test."[50]

The Border Tab, drawing upon the comments of Oliver B. Witherspoon, the paper's associate editor, perhaps spoke the last word for many black CCCers. Reflecting upon the passing of Robert Fechner and the legacy of the Corps, it was, in Witherspoon's view, forever beyond doubt that "to some youngsters, spending a period in the CCC simply spells the difference of a life filled with shame and dishonor and one of unquestionable repute."[51]

9

Education

I know a little history,
Some verses, too, by heart.
I know a little science,
I know a little art.
I know a little Latin,
I know a little Greek.
He runs a little restaurant
Where I eat every week.
                    —*The Bugle Call* (Company 1728,
                                      Liberty, Missouri)

"I will study and get ready, [for] some day my chance will come."
[A thought attributed to Abraham Lincoln].
                    —*Pine Needle* (Companies 235 and
                           237, New Lisbon, New Jersey),
                                      February 26, 1936

As always in America, where education is involved, there is controversy, the educational aspects of the CCC being no exception. Throughout, the educational component of the CCC was often featured in the camp papers, both as to content and as promotional material. These media also illuminated developments on the general American educational scene in the 1930s.

In the first place, many of the officials associated with the CCC insisted that the organization was primarily to be engaged in work and would only seriously consider education which was mainly "on-the-job training." Many in the Corps saw it as a "college" of a practical type, dealing primarily in the arts of human relations, work and discipline.[1] The instructors desired were in the main the foremen, who taught the men skills having to do with their immediate work. It did not require much training to learn to use the basic tools of planting trees or making fire trails, park roads, or small check dams. Brawn, not brains, was the main prerequisite. Accordingly, even many of the early commanders and other men in charge of the camps were opposed to formal education, and substantial numbers of the enrollees were in complete agreement. After all, many had dropped out of school precisely because they were bored and saw no reason to further their education. As it had long ago been observed by Alexis de Tocqueville on his famous journey to America in the 19th century, "for most Americans ... 'the pleasures of the mind' did not constitute 'the principal charm of their lives.'"[2]

Yet many others saw the CCC as a splendid opportunity to introduce more formal education, and eventually this view prevailed, though always with considerable opposition and limited success. As early as May 18, 1933, W. Frank Persons, head of the CCC's selection process under the United States Employment Service, had attempted to convince Robert Fechner to launch a much more elaborate educational scheme than he was then contemplating. However, Fechner demurred, apparently seeing little need of education in the Corps as he had little formal schooling himself—he had not completed high school—and did not see the CCC as an appropriate agency to embark upon such an undertaking. His attitude continued to be a problem, as he remained convinced that the CCC should concentrate on unemployment relief and conservation projects. In this, he was initially strongly supported by the Army, "whose fear of radical and leftist infiltration of the camps colored its whole attitude to educational work."[3]

But Fechner was deluged by requests from state selecting agencies demanding a comprehensive education program. The newly-appointed federal commissioner of education, George F. Zook, was also strongly in favor, and he and Persons developed a comprehensive scheme which was presented to Fechner on November 2, 1933. Meanwhile, FDR became convinced, and on November 22, 1933, accepted a plan for a Washington-directed CCC education service. Congress responded and in early 1934 earmarked $1.3 million for education in the Corps for the first half of 1934. Prior to this time, educational work had been entirely at the discretion of each camp commander. The Army under General Douglas MacArthur, the Army Chief of Staff, thereupon changed its tactics and now sought to control the program which, however, it failed to do.

On December 29, 1933, Dr. Clarence S. Marsh, dean of the evening college at the University of Buffalo, became the Director of CCC Camp Education. He selected the company educational advisers from unemployed teachers and university graduates, often involving the Work Projects Administration (WPA) and the Federal Emergency Relief Administration (FERA) in his endeavors. Fifteen hundred full-time civilian educational advisers were initially appointed to the camps, charged with coordinating and supervising the educational and training programs. By June 1934, the program was in full swing.[4]

At first, Marsh warmly embraced the new venture, seeing it as "a great American folk school movement," an educational enterprise "growing out of the natural culture of the young men who want to learn the things which are of most interest and importance to them." The program would emphasize folklore and history, "not as something highbrow and musty, not as treaty facts and meaningless dates to be memorized— but instead, as something that's already in the blood of every fellow in camp." In this context, history was "the story of the land he played baseball on, the story of the rivers he's fished in, and the story of his own family and his campmate's families." Furthermore, men in the colored CCC companies would study Negro literature and the contributions of blacks to American music, specifically their spirituals and jazz.[5] One key aspect was that CCC education was not compulsory and would emphasize individual instructional methods aimed at "meeting the needs and interests of the men." Marsh identified three aims: education for work, for culture and for play. Education for work would be vocational in nature. As to culture, something was meant "as far from 'high-hat' as a man's boots are," he declared. Finally, education involved how the men played and what they learned in the process.[6]

Subsequently, however, in January of 1935 Marsh, despairing of operating a satisfactory education program in the CCC, resigned from "the School of the Forest," becoming associate director of the American Council on Education under Dr. George F. Zook, its head. He was replaced by Howard Oxley, a former educational adviser to the Liberian government. Under Oxley's leadership, the educational momentum within the CCC continued apace to the end of the CCC's career despite all opposition to it and the difficulties which it never altogether overcame.[7]

Certainly, the educational challenges in the CCC were formidable. Some 250,000 youths and men from widely divergent backgrounds and with varying skills, aptitudes and desires—many of them illiterate—had to be instructed. The adviser worked in primitive conditions, at least in the early days, and often did not have an office or classroom. Consequently, most of the instruction was done in mess halls or barracks. Library facilities and equipment were either rudimentary or nonexistent. The camp commander's attitude was crucial, and this ranged from outright hostility to some cooperation, though rarely wholehearted. Even the Corps commanders, such as General Fox Connor, refused, for instance, to have "cultural courses" taught, which limited the classes offered in his First Corps Area. Army officers also sought to discourage discussion of social and political issues, fearing a radicalization of the camps or a breakdown of discipline.

Something of the magnitude of the educational task can be seen by examining the educational levels of the men in the CCC. The educational "attainments" of Company 1224 in Lewes, Delaware, were perhaps more or less typical: out of 195 men, one had a BS degree; another was a graduate of a junior college; eight had some college work; 32 had graduated from high school; 65 had attended a high school but had not graduated; and grammar school graduates numbered 51, with the remainder below these levels. Veteran Company 2420 of Chatom, Alabama, however, retorted in early 1934 that several doctors, lawyers and professors were represented on their rolls, an indication of the depth of the Depression at that time. As late as May of 1939, one commentator noted that the average educational level in the CCC was about eight and one-third years of education, or a third of the way through the first year of high school. Just over 12 percent of the enrollees had a high school education; a little over one percent had done some college work. Out of 271,800 junior enrollees analyzed, only 67 had college degrees.[8]

Meanwhile, the battle won as to whether or not the CCC would have an educational dimension, the conflict shifted to what type of education would be provided. Throughout, the edge always seemed to be with the technical and practical devotees. It seemed logical to many educational theorists that the men in the CCC were "hand" learners rather than "book" learners: "They like action rather than study and learn more readily by doing than by reading or hearing. By both desire and aptitude, they are more fitted for manual jobs than for professional or highly technical trades." But this was not necessarily a negative attribute. Some men were illiterate as to "book minded" matter; others were illiterate as to "hand minded" matters. In the industrial age, was it not "just about as shameful for a man to be mechanically illiterate as it is for him to be unable to read and write?" *Happy Days* asked. Certainly the CCC had gone a long way "toward removing some of this mechanical illiteracy." While the CCC "discovered" some exceptional enrollees who went on to college-level work, "on the whole, it would seem that the enrollees are well suited to the types of jobs now pursued in CCC camps."[9]

Indeed, there was no reason to conclude that manual work was not as "enobling" as college was usually considered to be. "Working one's way thru the CCC, and taking advantage of what it offers, is every bit as admirable and rewarding as 'working one's way thru college,'" the editor of *Happy Days* once declared. Formerly, "education [was] perhaps the one achievement which was, until recently, most admired by Americans. The village orator, who could spout Latin and Greek quotations by the dozen, was a great man, destined for Congress and beyond." Times had changed, however, he insisted, "and the scholar, unless he does something with his scholarship, is no longer the great man." While "not exactly a pioneer in this trend," one of the strongest proponents of it was the CCC.[10]

Joe D. Cellman of Company 783, Leon, Iowa, for one, appreciated the new state of affairs. Elaborating in a guest editorial in *Happy Days*, he emphasized that learning was not absent in the CCC but rather it was distinctive. "Washed free of staid theorists and traditional educational practitioneers with high noses and hard rulers, comes a refreshing, promising, tidal wave in learning." The old system was eclipsed as "a happy by-product of the CCC." In the new practical setting, as the boys worked and lived with regular hours, meals and medical care, they, being "healthy, happy, congenial," manifested "an instinctive desire to explore, learn and prepare for life."[11]

This being the case, one editor of *Happy Days* observed that "if the CCC ever offers a degree, it would no doubt be a 'Master of Labor.'" The men awarded such a degree would be those "who recognize the value and dignity of the ordinary must-stick kind of labor." The new degree would not "mean that he can conjugate a Latin irregular verb. But it will mean that he can do an honest day's work and that he considers an honest day's work worth doing."[12]

But many professional educators, such as those associated with the National Education Association, were strongly opposed to the CCC's initiatives. One of the most outspoken was Dr. George D. Strayer of Columbia University who regretted the tendency of the CCC and other agencies "to take over the functions of education." As he explained, "we want to control and administer education as such and don't want it turned over to an army officer or a welfare worker. We believe that those services of education wherever they are offered should be distinctly under control of educational authorities." Perhaps, though, he admitted, the public school educators might find something in the CCC "brand of education which could be used to advantage in their own schools."[13]

The critics, however, were answered in detail by Vestie G. Steele, company clerk of Company 759, Mitchell, Nebraska, among others. Professional educators had no monopoly on education, he declared. But CCC was more than willing to cooperate with established school officials, schools and colleges. Indeed, only a small number of CCC camps did not do so. While it was well to consider that education was "a very valuable commodity," nevertheless, there was no danger of the supply being exhausted, and therefore, it should be obtained where possible. His views were echoed by P. Everett Sperry, project manager at Potawatomi Indian Agency, Horton, Kansas, who had spent 19 years in the teaching profession. He agreed that the educational setup in the CCC was certainly not on par with universities in America, "especially good old Columbia University." Nevertheless, he felt that "some of our professors become so absorbed in what they are doing themselves in those universities that they lose the human side of life and become biased in their thinking." Certainly the CCC had no desire to take over the universities "nor encroach upon their territory." The university remained the desired place for an education, but many people could not pursue it through that avenue, and anything that a CCC staff could do should accordingly be encouraged.[14]

Educational ventures in the CCC sometimes ran afoul of religious institutions. When one educational adviser, George A. Hagen of Headquarters Company, Camp Custer, Michigan, discussed the success of a class in social relations with emphasis on marriage and matters of sex and venereal disease, the Catholic church objected. Hagen had stated that "a reputable physician may perform an abortion if necessary to save the life of the mother." But the Catholics advised Hagen that his views were "absolutely contrary to Catholic teaching on the matter," and abortion was also illegal in several states of the union. On the matter of birth control, which had been treated as a matter open for discussion in the class, the Church was emphatic: "It is not open for discussion in the Catholic Church."[15]

In a blend of the old and the new educational settings, many of the camps sought to transform their educational programs into pseudo-universities and colleges. Company 843, Red Rock, New Mexico, called its school "Yucca University" and rather ambitiously planned to carry out all the activities of a modern university as far as possible. Company 739 at Almaden, California, created "Almaden University," issuing a lengthy catalogue describing 44 academic and vocational subjects taught by 25 regular instructors, supplemented by on-the-job training and correspondence courses. The catalogue appeared as a 10-page section of the semi-monthly camp paper, the *Mt. Madonna Miner*. Other companies adopted the idea of a "Rainy Day University" dedicated to turning days of inclement weather into study days.[16]

In no other area of life in the corps, then, was there a wider variation in endeavor, points of view and procedure than in the educational arenas. The attempts to make education interesting and appealing to the enrollees continued to the end of the CCC's career, and those responsible for education tirelessly put forth innumerable expedients and programs. Schemes were instituted only to be abandoned with others substituted, unendingly seeking the right formula. Therefore, educational ventures in the CCC remained problematic. The initiatives, attitudes and endeavours of individual commanding officers, educational advisers, and other members of the overhead, as well as those of the individual enrollees or groups within a company at any given time—not to mention accidents of locale and opportunity—all seemed to have varying influences on the success or failure of education in the CCC.

Blandishment was a common approach taken in the camp papers and in *Happy Days* to convince enrollees of the need to participate in educational ventures. *The Broadcast* (Company 1742, Gallatin, Missouri) deplored that "we just about have to grab some of you young rascals by the nap of the neck and drag you down to Old Grand College [the camp school's name] where you will gain a little more knowledge—if you don't go to sleep." And the educational adviser of Company 299 at Masonville, New York, declared that "you can lead a horse to water, but a jackass doesn't even know he's thirsty."[17] "Red Sez," a commentator in *The Kanona Daze* (Company 297, Kanona, New York), elaborated, embracing Aristotle's dictum that education was mankind's "best provision for old age": "Most of us will live fifty years or more. Fifty years is a long time. We shall have to spend it in our own company. The educated man is good company for himself and for anyone else. THE EMPTY MINDED MAN seeks corner gossip, drink, gambling or whittling wood, … [and] in old age he is dredfully [sic] alone."[18]

In an effort to create more interest in the educational programs, Company 2716 at Maquoketa, Iowa, grouped its enrollees with common educational interests together. Thus, every barrack became a classroom. Barrack one, for instance, became "Vocational Hall," while barrack two was styled the "Engineer Billet."

Other incentives included awards and rewards. The *Tamarack Times* (Company 297, Priest River, Idaho) noted that two packs of cigarettes awaited each man who received a certificate for class work or for the completion of a correspondence course. Also to enhance the appeal of educational programs, the staff artist of *Happy Days*, Marshall Davis, produced an elaborate educational certificate designed by Colonel W.H. Waldron, district commander of the Charleston (West Virginia) District and adopted by the companies in his district. Similar certificates were prepared for use in other districts and Corps areas.[19]

There were other available sources to stimulate educational efforts. The 1930s was a time when training films and documentaries appeared in vast quantities, and the camps were frequently inundated with reels from the Department of Agriculture, the Park Service and other agencies, which were often reviewed by the papers. The men of Company 1742, Tarkio, Missouri, for example, on their regular Thursday evening showings, viewed films from the Navy Department such as: "Jack Wins his Wings," and "The Gray Armada," illustrating the U.S. Fleet in action. They also saw films from the Department of the Interior including "Glimpses of National Parks," "Seeing Glaciers," and "Natives of Yosemite." Other agencies provided the "Romance of Rayon," the "Panama Canal," and "Lubricating Oil," not to mention "Duck Farming," and "How to Get Rid of Rats." *Happy Days* frequently printed motion picture film directories listing free films, as well as those for rent or sale available from various agencies and outlets both for instructional use and for entertainment.[20]

Another aid to education was the development of clubs. Polls from time to time in *Happy Days* indicate that photographic clubs headed the lists in popularity with drama and service clubs next in importance. Handicraft clubs also, steadily grew, as did social, rifle, archery and model aircraft organizations. In addition, numerous journalism groups put out their company papers. In the radio clubs, many enrollees studied radio sufficiently to obtain government radio operator's licenses.[21]

When possible, among the instructional initiatives employed were attempts simply to make education entertaining. The men in the camps of sub-district No. 2, San Antonio District (Texas), once staged combined brain and brawn contests, featuring spelling, writing, essay writing, arithmetic, extemporaneous speech, typewriting, first-aid; and athletics incuding volleyball, playground ball (soft ball), races and jumping. Many camp papers joined in similar activities. The *Crystal Camp Crier* of Company 1742 at Tarkio, Missouri, for one, published a "Game of English," in which readers were invited to test themselves on their command of the language.[22]

Sometimes unusual educational opportunities presented themselves. In April 1939, a one-year sea training program to involve 250 CCC men was launched by the U.S. Maritime Service. Each enrollee had to have served in the CCC for one year to be eligible. The training, to be conducted by U.S. Coast Guard officers, would send the men to sea for a six-month stretch on one of two ships: the *American Seaman* or a sailing vessel, the *Joseph Conrad*, based at St. Petersburg, Florida. *Happy Days* closely followed their training careers, which were sufficiently successful to encourage the Maritime Service to recruit a total of 1,000 CCC men for the program.[23]

On other occasions, CCC education was a matter of serendipity, and educational advisers were quick to "seize the day." When a swarm of bees arrived in the camp of Company 2328, Shelocta, Pennsylvania, they were provided with a box to convert into a hive. The men soon had honey with their flapjacks, and the camp paper, the *Stockade,* lost no time in turning its nature page over to the subject of the honey bee. The veterans of Company 2775 at Mandan, North Dakota, also became interested in beekeeping and bought a two-pound package of bees complete with queen, establishing them in hives constructed at the camp. They were rewarded with a harvest of over a hundred pounds of honey. This impressive production encouraged the men to intensify their practical education in farming and gardening. As 1938 rolled around, their paper, *The Veterans' Bugle*, reported that seventeen enrollees were taking correspondence courses in these fields, eight in poultry, four in beekeeping, four in farm lighting, and one in pork production.[24]

On another occasion, the men of Company 2328 at Shelocta, Pennsylvania, were entertained by a troupe of five American Indians who performed tribal dances and conducted adoption ceremonies for camp members. Later, the men of the company enjoyed a half-day holiday, proclaimed by the company commander on September 17, 1937, to commemorate the 150th anniversary of the signing of the U.S. Constitution. A special dinner with a guest speaker was arranged, providing an occasion for instruction on that document and its purpose and meaning.[25]

When men of Company 2113 in Heppner, Oregon, unearthed the skeleton of a long-dead Indian—perhaps of a Columbia River Indian tribe—they were given permission to clean up the bones and wire them together for a camp museum exhibit. The educational adviser, M.E. Dixon, took advantage of the find to instruct the men in archeology and anthropology. The location of camps often contributed to educational initiatives. Company 819 at Grand Canyon, Arizona found itself in such a place. The company's paper, the *Grand Canyon Echoes*, frequently published accounts of the canyon's colorful history, and encouraged the men to study its geology and its richly varied plant and animal life.[26]

The problem as to when education would be conducted was at times a pressing one. Though a common occurrence, the scheduling of night classes remained controversial. The practice was often excoriated because the men had already put in a long, hard day's work and should not be tormented further in night school. The enrollees were already doing what the CCC was designed to accomplish, in any case, the argument went. Nonetheless, the evening hours remained the most convenient for many of the instructors employed, such as WPA teachers, local college students, the CO, the subalterns, the project superintendent or his staff of foremen, and the camp doctors who were employed in the teaching role.

To get around some of the complaints and difficulties associated with night schedules, some company commanders altered work schedules so that field work was completed by noon and the afternoon could be devoted to classes. Such was the case with Company 1742, Tarkio, Missouri, for instance, though the men did have to get up early for this to be possible.[27]

Farther reaching was an arrangement in Nebraska where many companies established a compulsory educational program for the winter months of 1938, according to which the men were in classes rather than going to the fields at all. Classes were 45 minutes, and in the mornings were specified as to subject matter, the enrollees studying soil conservation, job training, language usage, and arithmetic. In the afternoons, vocational subjects of individual choice were undertaken.[28]

Similarly, in Company 3802, Littlefield, Texas, there was a considerable struggle on the part of educational advisers to involve the men in educational pursuits. There, the attitudes of the enrollees were major stumbling blocks to the establishment of an effective program, as revealed in the pages of the company paper, *The Tumbleweed.* "Manhood, not scholarship, is the first aim of education," one enrollee declared, but the men could be appealed to by mounting field trips. Excursions were taken to Carlsbad, New Mexico, to visit the famous caverns, and in October 1936, 12 men from the camp joined a group of 700 schoolchildren and townspeople from Littlefield for a special excursion conducted by the Santa Fe line to Dallas to attend the Texas Centennial Fair.[29]

Indeed, among the reasons for an emphasis on practical matters was the presence at CCC camps of competent, well-educated leaders. Typical was the Forestry Superintendent of Company 299 at Masonville, New York: Royal G. Bird, a role model for many of the enrollees in his outfit. He had a BS degree in forestry from Cornell with a year's graduate work in forest management. In sports, he had rowed for the university, and had as hobbies reading, stamp collecting and camping. He had served in the 20th Engineers in France during the World War, and after the war had worked for large paper companies. He thought that more attention must be paid in the CCC to specialized training in commerce and business, though some general education might be emphasized. Among the lessons that he passed on to the enrollees in his company was the necessity for them to complete at least a high school course "at any cost." Another was from Shakespeare's lines in Hamlet: "'This above all: to thine own self to be true, And it must follow, as the night the day, Thou canst not then be false to any man." Typical technical training might involve learning how to run a bulldozer, which McEntee, the head of the CCC, suggested should "be one of the emblems of the CCC," so important were these machines in getting the organization's work done. Certainly, a man who learned how to run a bulldozer would have no trouble in getting a job later. In addition, he would be a valuable man to the nation in time of war, because a man who could operate a bulldozer could certainly operate a tank.[30]

Many among the CCC leadership personnel agreed with this general approach. C. E. Ward, educational adviser of Company 1252 at Mariou, Virginia, presented a course in "Vocations," in which he polled the class, asking what they wanted to be in 10 years. Of 35 men queried, eight chose auto mechanics, and others with high numbers were: mason, civil engineer, athletic coach, landscape gardener and office worker. Many of these choices reflected what the men had been exposed to in the CCC. Only a few chose aviation, preaching, or consular service. Almost none selected a profession, such as lawyer, doctor or professor. Along these lines, enrollees in all of the camps in the Seventh Corps Area were required to attend classes in "occupational adjustment," with an emphasis on the opportunities offered in the business world and associated job and educational requirements. The men of Company 2328 in Shelocta, Pennsylvania, were likewise instructed by their company paper, the *Stockade*, in such matters, which sometimes included a special page on "Careers." Therein, the men were urged to learn to use the telephone and were given tips on how to conduct a successful job interview.[31]

In other instances of functional education, sometimes WPA teachers were attached to the camps. Two arrived at Company 2328 in Shelocta, Pennsylvania. J.L. Brilhart, who taught elementary and commercial subjects, while Larry Edwards, a sign painter, interior decorator, and show card writer, taught courses in commercial art. In short order, they considerably bolstered the company's educational effort. Neither was the embryonic television industry ignored by men of the company. One issue of their paper, the *Stockade*, focused on developments in the new medium and what it could mean for the future.[32]

Company 297 at Priest River, Idaho, included instruction in radio operation and broadcasting, practical logging, truck driving, wood working, practical arithmetic, photography, spelling, geography, shorthand, and carpentry. As was common during these years within the CCC, no doubt because of the popularity of the FBI in hunting down the flamboyant criminals of the day such as John Dillinger, there were courses in finger printing.[33] At Company 299, Masonville, New York, a radio class was taught by a former wireless operator in the Merchant Marine, as were other practical subjects. The boys also took courses at the local high school joined by interested townspeople, though the CCCers seemed to be attending one paricular night class there in unusual numbers: a course in home-making, no doubt "for the chow and feminine company!" Such cooperation with interested people in communities was hardly unique. In another case, the owner of a large electrical shop at Henderson, Kentucky, on three nights a week turned his shop over to men from Company 1540 to work on projects and study shop techniques.[34]

The educational program at Company 4468, Barnwell, South Carolina, included Saturday morning field trips to dairy, turkey, hog, and cotton farms arranged in cooperation with the county agent of Barnwell County. These featured instruction in tractor driving and the use of farm implements. The junior officer of the company, one Lt. Pardue, who was a professional in woodworking, made shop work a popular course as well. Another educational and practical instructional tool at the camp was its short wave radio setup. This was part of a 10-camp short wave radio net which one of the districts in the Fourth Corps Area established, presided over by 1st Lt. T.B. Winstead of the Signal Corps at Fort Moultrie, South Carolina.[35] But the focus on skill-oriented education was not confined to individual camps. In District E of the Fourth Corps Area, each month 35 members from each of its camps spent 30 days of intensive training at headquarters, Camp Beauregard, Alexandria, Louisiana. This work prepared them for key positions in camp administration and maintenance.[36]

Another practical area was that of health. Both *Happy Days* and the camp papers took it upon themselves to instruct the enrollees about such matters. Much of the material tended to be a bit pedantic and "preachy." The *Stockade* of Company 2328 in Shelocta, Pennsylvania, decided to inform its readers regarding "The Truth about Lady Nicotine," emphasizing its harmful effects. The tobacco industry sought to counter such ploys. To these ends, a Mr. Treharn, representing the American Tobacco Company, entertained members of the company in a program featuring a humorous skit about a tobacco salesman. But the *Stockade* was not deterred by such opposition, and forthrightly took on another health threat in an article "Thumbs Down on John Barleycorn," warning the men that "toxic" meant poison; consequently, "intoxicate" meant to poison one's body.[37]

The *Crystal Camp Crier* (Company 1742, Tarkio, Missouri) was another sheet preoccupied with health, and frequently devoted entire pages to certain diseases such as lobar pneumonia, ringworm and syphilis. Regarding the VD menace, the *Stockade*, typically of many of the camp papers, on occasion reviewed books that might help enrollees guard against the usual sexual temptations.[38]

Nor was mental health ignored, being addressed in various ways. The educational advisers of many companies administered the Stanford Achievement, the Hemnon Tests or the Otis intelligence tests to their enrollees. In what would in the present day be considered a violation of rights of privacy, the results of the tests were often printed in the camp newspaper. For example, when the Otis test was given to men of Company 2328 in Shelocta, Pennsylvania, the educational adviser, one Harold B. Hudson, published the names of the 20 enrollees scoring the highest. At the head of the list was one Paul Gray, with an IQ of 113. The remainder of the list of 20 ranged from 103 through 112. In a later Otis test given to 126 enrollees in the same company, the IQs extended from 70 to 119 for the 77 men given the "higher form" of the test, and for the remainder, given the "intermediate form," the scores varied from 50 to 97.[39]

The *Stockade* (Company 2328, Shelocta, Pennsylvania) was more inclined than many camp papers to exhort enrollees to develop their minds and personalities. To these ends, the sheet's book review page often featured self-help and inspirational books such as Orison Marden's *The Secret of Achievement* and William S. Walsh, M.D., *Making Our Minds Behave* in which, among other things, he discussed superstitions. The American Red Cross routinely began to present their standard course in First Aid at many CCC camps. The Metropolitan Life Insurance Company sent a complete set of its health booklets, including *Swimming and Life Saving, First Aid,* and *Milk: An All-round Food,* among others, to all CCC camps.[40]

Chief among those desiring practical instruction, as opposed to purely academic programs, were the veterans. The CCC leadership recognized that the veterans needed special consideration, though it was not until September 1939 that a man, Russell Cook, was appointed research assistant to the director of CCC education and placed in charge of war veteran education. Cook, a reserve officer, had served in various capacities in the CCC, at one time being the commanding officer of Company 1537, White Sulphur Springs, West Virginia. He coordinated his efforts with the American Legion, which rather belatedly developed an interest in veterans' education, only appointing a representative to the CCC Educational Office in 1939.[41]

Even before these initiatives, astute educational advisers working with the vets recognized their special needs and desires. One of these was H. T. Schell, adviser to Company 1774 in Rochester, Minnesota. Writing in the company's paper, *The Veterans' Voice,* he observed that while it might be true that "you can't teach an old dog new tricks," at least the "old dog" should retain the tricks he once mastered, "or he soon is slipping below the average."[42]

Indeed, the presence of knowledgeable, thoughtful educational advisers and first rate teachers could make a major difference in any CCC company, but these could be especially effective in the tougher educational climate of the veterans' companies. This was well illustrated in Company 1921 based at Camp Calaveras Big Trees, Big Trees, California. Many of the vets in the company were plainly apathetic toward education, the educational adviser acknowledged, and there was, for instance, little response when the local high school's shops were made available to the men. Even a new camp educational building did not excite them. Many veterans possessed skills which they thought were not being used in the Depression era, and so why gain others or, indeed, acquire any learning? they asked. Nonetheless, courses such as woodworking and cabinet making, radio, photography, criminal investigation, and mathematics, enjoyed some popularity. On the job, many of the men took considerable interest in blasting, surveying, masonry, carpentry and concrete construction. The vets also responded to programs of self-education through selective reading, and many of the men availed themselves of correspondence courses of a practical nature available free of charge from the California State Department of Education.[43]

But what made the educational program of Company 1921 first rate for some years was the presence of a remarkable professor, Ludwig H. Schwiers, an inspiration to "his many eager listeners," a man who had "endeared himself to all that know him." He had first introduced a class in astronomy, which started with only two men, but the word got around concerning the interesting manner in which the class was conducted and soon 15 men were enrolled. Schwiers then introduced several classes in foreign languages, "far and away" the most popular courses in camp. French, German, Spanish, Portuguese, and Russian were scheduled, as well as Danish, taught by 1st. Lt. Ray Duss, the company adjutant, and Japanese, taught by an enrollee, one McIntosh. The teaching of Japanese was not understood by men of another veterans' outfit, Company 1774 in Rochester, Minnesota, which jeered at the California camp, wondering "what you're going to do with it if and when you learn it. Uncle don't 'low no Geisha gals hangin' round' over here—so you can't try your Nippon dialect on them, and Tokyo is so danged far away!" To the veterans' great sorrow, Schwiers departed the company to teach mathematics at Hamilton Field for the U.S. Army Air Corps, sorely missed by his numerous former students.[44]

Among the CCC's most effective practical educational programs were those in the area of remedial education. One of the goals of the CCC was to see to it that every illiterate enrollee master the basic three "R's" by the time that he left camp. By 1940, about 85,000 men had been helped to attain these ends. In addition, the drive toward getting CCCers to obtain their eighth grade and high school diplomas was on-going. Typical was the situation in Company 1742 in Tarkio, Missouri. A complete course of eighth grade subjects was offered for those who had not completed their elementary work. Those who satisfactorily finished were issued a county graduation diploma. "Boys should be overjoyed at being able to complete this work while in camp since the lack of at least an eighth grade graduation will mean a great handicap in future life toward getting a job," their paper, the *Broadcast,* declared. Indeed, it became a feat of sorts for numerous CCCers to obtain this distinction, and *Happy Days* often featured successful enrollees.

If there were numerous courses and programs leading to the attaining of the eighth grade diploma, the educational aspirations of those at higher levels were also addressed. One method was through correspondence work. *Happy Days* reported that by the spring of 1934, some 1,187 correspondence courses were being offered by the famous International Correspondence Schools of Scranton, Pennsylvania, and certain universities and colleges. The University of North Dakota mounted the most elaborate program of any American university, persisting to the end of the CCC's career. Its offerings cost 25 cents per credit hour, though books and paper costs were extra. A typical course was the popular offering on diesel engines which consisted of 30 lessons for three hours of credit. The Moody Bible Institute of Chicago offered 15 correspondence Bible courses. In all, about 40 universities and colleges offered correspondence work to CCCers, and 28 more scheduled extension classes.[45]

Where the camps were near enough to campuses, many CCC enrollees obtained scholarships, their work schedules being arranged to accommodate their studies. For instance, two men from Company 1223, Mill Creek, Washington, were given scholarships by Whitman College, Walla Walla, Washington. Similarly, men of Company 3355 went to the campus of New Mexico State College in Las Cruces for their college work. Twelve enrollees from Company 4703 in Council Grove, Kansas, traveled 31 miles—one way—three days a week to Kansas State College at Emporia. There they took a full course load of from 12 to 15 hours. "They say traveling 62 miles a day in a G.I. truck isn't exactly a pleasure trip, but it's worth it," one student declared.[46]

But there were always strong currents in the CCC educational stream insisting upon much more than merely technical, vocational and other so-called practical training. Caught up in the battle of education, *Happy Days*, while supporting the practical approach, often argued that too much emphasis was being placed upon "the objective of making an individual more capable of earning more money. Too little of learning has been directed toward affording an individual the enjoyment of other things—things which have little to do with the winning of bread and cheese."[47]

Taking their cue from *Happy Days*, many camp papers stressed traditional educational initiatives. Reading was recognized as essential, and the men of Company 2328 in Shelocta, Pennsylvania, under the leadership of Harold B. Hudson, their educational adviser, were asked, "suppose we had nothing really good to read—nothing well written. Life would be pretty dull." The *Stockade* also regularly reviewed books, and helped sponsor a book reading contest. For a time, five books were selected every month and contestants were examined on their reading by the commanding officer, Lt. Herbert R. Watson. Contest winners would receive one dollar's worth of merchandise from the camp canteen. For example, the books for December 1937 included the books of Esther and Ruth in the Bible; Van Etten's *I Am The Fox*; Max Miller, *The Great Trek*, recounting the real-life adventures of nine men following a herd of 3,000 reindeer across 1,000 miles of Canada and Alaska; and Joseph Conrad, *Lord Jim*. Another educational adviser, in an attempt to help the men steer through the maze of reading matter available, recommended that the men read two good newspapers daily, including *The New York Times;* steep themselves in the Bible, Shakespeare and the novels of Dickens; and spend 15 minutes per day with some standard dictionary. Another company which stressed reading was Company 819, Grand Canyon, Arizona. There a monthly tally was kept of the numbers of books read by the company's enrollees. In one instance, Fred Kersch read seven books in one month, out of the total of 96 read by the entire company, a figure which the outfit's paper, *Grand Canyon Echoes*, thought impressive.[48]

The educational advisers were often the staunchest supporters of a time-honored academic approach, though well aware that they faced substantial challenges. Their expedients were many and varied. The educational adviser of Company 1209 of Raritan, New Jersey, for example, posted a copy of *The New York Times* in each barracks with a list of pertinent questions and page references. During the evening, he visited the barracks, sparking debates on current events and other topics.[49]

Indeed, few avenues for education remained untried. One company, No. 669 stationed near Manistique, Michigan, with an enrollment of 100 percent in its educational programs, conducted a course on marriage and the family, with emphasis on "personal magnetism, courtship, and marriage." However, because they were "buried in the heart of the Hiawatha National Forest," 22 miles from town and snowbound much of the time, any practical application of the subject matter would have to wait: "But when the spring thaw melts the snowdrifts on that 22-mile stretch to town, the enrollees will be in fine shape to strut their stuff."[50]

Some educational advisers were of the opinion that the men themselves should be recruited to assist in bearing the burden of instruction. John P. King, Jr., of Company 4468, Barnwell, South Carolina, for instance, organized a select group of enrollees, assigning each man a class or project to develop. "The value in this system ... teaches them more about their own subject through teaching, and facilitates the efforts of the Educational Department in reaching every man in camp," King explained.[51]

Partisans of traditional education often thought that company thespians should be encouraged, helping the men to develop both knowledge and acting skills. They were aided by the creation of the Drama Division of the Civil Works Administration headquartered in New York City. The division created a circuit involving numerous camps, especially active in the Northeastern part of the country. These staged plays which often included enrollees as temporary cast members. Company 274 of South Huntington, New York, went further, creating a large dramatic club. Under the direction of William Howard of the Federal Writers Project of New York, a volunteer dramatic instructor of the camp, the men wrote and produced an original play, "He Who Brags," the men of the company also serving as actors and the audience.[52]

The men of Company 1742 in Tarkio, Missouri, were fortunate that the superintendent's wife, Mrs. Clarence E. Moyer, had a deep interest in drama. The author of a novel about CCC life, *Some Find a New Dawn*, she was thoroughly grounded in the CCC scene and knew how to interest the men. She had also written several plays and had previously taught dramatics and was therefore well qualified to take over the company's dramatic program. She soon created a troupe, that staged several productions, including a minstrel show with the cooperation of the Christian Church of Tarkio, some members of which were also performers. Some educational advisers led the men in developing radio skits and programs. Often featuring musical groups and portraying life in the CCC camps, such programs were frequently broadcast over the radio locally or regionally.[53]

The gathering of war clouds was destined to have a considerable impact on CCC education, moving it into new channels. Radio and aviation were perennial areas of interest, which was intensified in the late 1930s by being relevant to military operations. Where the men could find instructors, they made considerable progress in these technical fields. Short wave radio enthusiasts, including those in Company 398 at Spencer, Massachusetts, maintained contact with the explorers then at the South Pole. Far more numerous were enrollees interested in aviation. Air-minded members of Companies 1709 and 1715 at Toronto, Kansas, studied aerial navigation, aerology, and airplane construction and operation under the instruction of Zeno Rogers, a former Army pilot. In Company 1268 at High Bridge, New Jersey, an aviation class tore down an old aircraft and its engine, overhauled and reassembled it, and readied it for flight. The district educational adviser of the Littleton, Colorado District, a Captain Hunter who was an active pilot in the Colorado National Guard, often used an aircraft to fly throughout the state to instruct his far-flung charges, frequently lecturing on aviation. Likewise, in Company 2770 at Red Wing, Minnesota, Olav Fostervold, one of the few licensed pilots in the CCC, conducted a class in elementary aeronautics for 25 men in the company. When the national championship model airplane meet was held in St. Louis in June of 1935, many CCC enrollees participated.[54]

However, it was in the area of mechanics and aircraft construction—

which fascinated many staffers of the camp papers—that the CCC made its most notable achievements in aviation. In the late summer of 1939, the Piper Aircraft Company in Lock Haven, Pennsylvania, employed 31 former CCC enrollees from nearby companies. These men had completed ground school classes at their camps, in addition to a 90-hour aircraft welding course conducted at the Piper plant. Much more ambitious was the program established for the men of Company 2948 at Camp Vista, California. There, 44 enrollees received a 600-hour intensive course in aviation mechanics. Classes were held three hours each night Monday through Thursday for 10 months at Escondido High School. George Irvin, former head of a San Diego aircraft school, was chief instructor. Also, the Navy Department provided the camp with four aircraft engines and other equipment to assist the program. Graduates were promptly hired by the Consolidated aircraft plant in San Diego, which eagerly sought as many additional CCC graduate mechanics as it could find. Other California CCC camps, notably those at Cuyamaca Rancho, Camp Dalton Canyon, and Pine Valley, soon followed suit. Subsequently, many graduates of these programs were hired by Douglas, Ryan and other California aircraft companies.[55]

CCC education in general, and especially its emphasis on the practical, took new directions when the CCC began to be turned toward the nation's concern with national defense. In FDR's developing schemes in the spring of 1940, the CCC was slated to participate in training in skilled jobs regarded as desirable in peacetime but vital in wartime. The CCC was to focus on automotive operation and repair, short-wave radio operation, photography, road and bridge building, telephone line construction, cooking, baking and first aid.[56]

In mid–1940, FDR asked Congress for 250 to 400 million dollars for training in "non-combatant skills" in the CCC, while continuing to reject the introduction of military training in the camps. In the event, FDR got 280 million for these purposes to extend to July 1, 1941. This would ensure the continuation of 1,500 CCC camps during that period.

By the autumn of 1940, plans were in place for implementing the new educational proposals. Beginning on October 1, 1940, three main types of training were to be undertaken in the CCC: training for service operations of direct military value, training for employment in industrial production, and training for food production in agriculture. The U.S. Office of Education was charged with providing the defense training facilities to all CCC camps.[57]

In early 1941, as the CCC training program shifted to vocational training, the War Department indicated that it would permit a five-hour per week reduction in work hours for enrollees who would devote at least 10 hours per week on their own toward non-combatant vocational training. By the Spring of 1941, McEntee reported that the reduction plan had been a great success. By that time, nearly 25,000 men were participating in national defense vocational training. As of June 30, 1941, *Happy Days* reported that 77,582 men, most trained in some trade, had left the Corps during the fiscal year 1941 to enter employment, often in defense plants, with an additional 14,291 men making their way into the armed forces. Thus, "with war over the horizon, the CCC is becoming an increasingly vital force in National Defense."[58]

Meanwhile, by late 1940, scores of educational advisers had resigned to accept active duty with the U.S. Army or to become CCC subalterns or commanders. In order to deal with the paucity of junior officers, subaltern training schools were set up in each Corps area with most of the candidates having been leaders, senior leaders, clerks, or canteen stewards in their respective camps. By April 1941, there were more than twenty subaltern schools throughout the nation.[59]

By this time, however, the CCC's efforts had peaked, and by the autumn of 1941 it began steadily to decline, its strength being about 200,000 men in 1,130 camps. Nonetheless, new educational ventures continued to be launched. In September 1941, the first of 50 or more automotive mechanics schools, such as the ones at Circleville, Ohio, and New Brunswick, New Jersey, were opened. These operated in connection with the 55 CCC Central Repair Shops. Created to repair the 45,000 pieces of automotive equipment used by the Corps, each was manned by about 25 experienced mechanics to whom enrollee-students were assigned for instruction.

Whatever might be said about CCC education—and much was—it did enjoy a measure of success despite its many failures and shortcomings. *Happy Days* and many of the camp papers often reported on successes that could be attributed to the various educational ventures in the Corps.[60]

There were also often articles in *Happy Days* and in the camp papers describing how CCC training prepared enrollees for Army careers. Indeed, "if the United States ever has to go to war the ranks of the Army undoubtedly will be filled with CCC-trained men," *Happy Days* declared. "They will [have] the jump on most of their non–CCC brethren when it comes to qualifying for the Army jobs which call for experience or training." So it transpired, and thousands of former CCC enrollees—as they still attest—got a "leg up" in the military services, a direct result of their training, education and general experiences in the CCC.[61]

From its uncertain beginnings, education in the CCC evolved in breadth and depth. With its emphasis on technical and practical training, it helped prepare many men for the intense and elaborate technical training initiatives in the armed forces and for employment in the nation's war industries in the years to come.

10

Culture, Words,
Wit and Wisdom

A bunch of boys were whooping it up
In the Lanesboro saloon.
The kid who twisted the radio dials
Had captured a jig-time tune.
When suddenly out of the ether there came
A program they all deemed dandy.
And cards were dropped as Rookies stopped
To listen to Amos 'n' Andy.
—*The Spotlight* (unknown company)

"You know, you look like Helen Black?"
"Yes, but I look worse in white."
—*The Heppner Roundup* (Company 297,
Heppner, Oregon), December 1937

"'I hear that your girl is so intellectual she spends all her time reading the classics.'
'Yes, but what can I do about it?'
'You can squeeze the Dickens out of her.'"
—*Vets Lament* (Company 1921, Fairfax,
California), November 1940

"FIVE PROMINENT SEXPLORERS GO BIG DAME HUNTING."
—*The Weakly Effort* (Company 835,
Silver City, New Mexico)

The men of the CCC participated in the culture of the 1930s both as creators and consumers, aspects that were chronicled in their press, thereby providing additional insights into CCC life. The music scene was of paramount interest to many enrollees. The CCC seemed a logical subject for new music, and many anthems and marches were composed with it in mind. One who contributed was Nicholas Ciorciari of Brooklyn, New York. Having served in the CCC, he returned home to his own dance orchestra, the "Royal Troubadours," which he conducted, and which had a slot on a New York City radio station. "I have our President to thank for giving men an opportunity to get away from the city, and it was the money alloted to me that has started me on the road to success," he wrote in a letter to *Happy Days*. He used the money earned while an enrollee to publish a song he composed, which was dedicated to FDR. Other compositions came from Clive Kilgore of Coraepolis, Pennsylvania, the father of an enrollee. He produced two numbers, "Working For the C.C.C." and "Hooray for the C.C.C," pieces which he hawked through CCC camp canteens.[1]

Another enrollee, Bryant Alden Long of Company 2301 at Beltsville, Maryland, who confessed to being "guilty of both words and music (an attempt at snappy march tempo)," of another piece, hoped that it would be adopted as the official CCC anthem. Its refrain concluded:

> For C—C—C—We'll always be
> Grateful to our Nation and her Chief;
> As woodsmen true we bring to you
> A loyalty and love beyond belief![2]

When the Texas CCC District decided upon an official march, however, it stuck with a recognized master, adopting John Philip Sousa's last composition, "The Northern Pines." Though the original title was not appropriate, "the swinging cadence of the music [was] so in keeping with the spirit of the C.C.C.," that it was decided to adopt it anyway, retitling it "The Texas C.C.C. March." But to copy someone else did not appeal to Colonel Converse R. Lewis, CO of the Third CCC District, First Corps Area. He insisted that "The Third" must have its own march, and selected Second Lieutenant Harry J. Jenkins, an organist and composer of radio and theater fame, then in Company 128 at North Adams, Masachusetts, to compose the "Third C.C.C. District March."[3]

Another piece of music already in existence, U.S. Army Field Artillery March, also seemed to lend itself well to the CCC's activities. Company 565 of Highland, Californa, kept the tune but altered the words:

Over hill, over dale, as we hit the dusty trail
     It's the CCC that still carries on.
Smeared with mud, filled with grub, we're the bunch that
     takes the rub,
It's the CCC that still carries on.[4]

The tune "My Maryland" also seemed a natural for a CCC composition, at least to J. B. Robertson, the educational adviser of Company
415 at Mt. Sterling, North Carolina:

Our search for work became a roam,
     CCC, my CCC.
You took us in without a home,
     CCC, my CCC.[5]

Naturally, sweethearts of the CCC were commemorated in music.
Parker Lowell was one enrollee who wrote a piece along these lines, the
words and music of which were published in *Happy Days*. It began: "Two
bits once a month for a movie/On hot dogs and hamburgs we dine/She
knows I've no money/But still she's my honey/That CCC Sweetheart of
mine."[6]

In a scathing commentary on the contemporary music scene, Anderson M. Scruggs of Company 1592 in Croydon, Indiana, a lover of classical music, deplored the craze for swing in his poem "Meditation on
Swing," concluding that as far as he was concerned, the men might enjoy
their brand of music: "Long may they swing, is my earnest hope/Accom-
panied by a tree and rope."[7]

Most CCC camps had radios or other means of producing music.
The Pine Needle recorded that Company 237 possessed a Nichelette electric music box, but the powers that be decided that the records would
be censored. The recording "Let Me Feel Your Leg," was removed, "for
it was restricted in Harlem for being too vulgar." On the other hand,
Count Basie's "Swinging at the Woodside," being "solid," passed muster.[8]

The omnipresent polls were often employed to determine what
music the enrollees liked best. *Happy Days* often conducted these, and
recorded the results in its column "*Happy Days* Hit Parade." One of
these in mid–1936 listed such favorites as "Tavern in the Town!" and
"On Treasure Island." John Moody of Company 3844 at Redvale, Colorado, in a clever article "Swing Song Fever" reflected further on hits
of the day: "I'll Sing You a Thousand Love Songs," for "The Way
You Look Tonight," will lead to "A Fine Romance." And: "Sophisticated
Lady," "You Turned the Tables on Me," but "I Can't Escape From You,"
because "When I'm with You" "Happy Days Are Here Again" and "I

Feel a Song Coming On." But "If You Don't Love Me" "I'll String Along with You" anyhow, "Until the Real Thing Comes Along."[9]

The marathon dance craze sweeping the nation also gripped CCC enrollees when they had the time and energy to devote to it. Company 1267 at Bassett, Virginia, fielded ten teams. Dancing to the recorded syncopation of Rudy Vallee, Guy Lombardo, Cab Calloway and Fred Waring, the winners were awarded cigarettes, a common prize for many endeavors in those days.[10]

Radio was popular in the CCC as throughout the nation, and it remains one of the most pervasive avenues to the nation's popular culture of the times. Many CCC newspapers reflected this. Regarding one icon of the era, Orson Welles' famous radio program depicting invaders from Mars, the men of Companies 235 and 237 in New Jersey, near the site of the alleged horrifying events, reacted as many citizens did. "Radio Drama Scares Camp," the camp paper, *The Pine Needle* (Companies 235 and 237, New Lisbon, New Jersey), admitted a few days later, describing the local scene: Initially, many men turned out of the barracks in a panic, and "the camp's Paul Revere, Leonard 'Muzzy' Giles, even smelled poison gas and ran to each barrack yelling warnings. What he smelled was only fumes when he passed the oilhouse." Another "made famous" by the scare was Fred Smith, who cried, "'We are without any soldiers. They have all been killed.' 'Pig Meat' and Peguese led a prayer meeting in the mess hall. Gilbert ran all over the camp yelling 'the end is here.' … Galloway declared 'My folks are only 5 blocks from the Pulaski Highway,'" at the center of the alleged events. Mr. Coleman, the camp's educational advisor, arriving in camp from New York, was amazed at the many tales that the men, crowding around, regaled him with, since he had just passed through "the destroyed sections" including Trenton, without noticing any Mars warriors. But then he had missed the broadcast; he was listening to Charlie McCarthy.[11]

Apparently many others might have been as well, because the wooden dummy was second only to "Amos and Andy" in popularity. When the editor of the *Blue Creek Bulletin* (unknown company) asked his readers to respond to the question, "Who's the greatest blues-chaser in the country?" most readers answered: "Charlie McCarthy." The editor decided accordingly to dedicate one issue to "the wooden-head comedian," and another company's paper jokingly asked: "What is meant by dressed lumber?" The answer: "Charlie McCarthy."[12]

Some of the men's reading material interested certain "watch dogs." One target was the tiny lascivious comic books common in the 1930s. At least one chaplain, Davis C. Sullivan of Company 2105 at Westboro, Massachusetts, headed a campaign in the First Corps Area to persuade the enrollees to sign pledge cards promising not to "buy, read, keep in possession or distribute magazines, joke books or pictures of unclean, immoral or of the spicy nature." A total of 15,000 cards were signed— representing about 90 percent of the enrollees of the area.[13]

Men in the CCC—like men in the armed forces—were addicted to regular comic books. Many CCC canteens stocked them, notably some which seemed commendable such as *True Comics* and *Real Heroes*, both of which were not "kid" comics but sources of "true stories about real people." Featuring such "heros" as FDR, General George Marshall, General Chiang Kai-shek and General MacArthur, they were in fact, "swell comics about men who have done big things," or so *Happy Days* thought.[14]

But the War Department did what it could to place more substantial periodical literature in the men's hands. It normally requested bids for subscriptions for specified periods of several months. For example, from April 1 to June 30, 1937, it asked suppliers for two copies each of *Colliers, Liberty, News Week,* and *The Saturday Evening Post* for every CCC camp, and one each of 38 other titles, including *Argosy, Aviation, Baseball, Current History, Detective Story Magazine, Field and Stream, Literary Digest, National Geographic, Popular Mechanics, Radio News,* and *Western Story.* In addition, the magazine *Opportunity* was provided for the 189 black companies then in existence.[15]

The War Department was no doubt guided in its selections in part by what the men wanted to read, according to the polls. In one survey, *Life* "won in a fairly easy walk," followed by *Reader's Digest* in second place, judged "the closest to being the perfect publication for those who demand the best of reading, in a compact form." It was many magazines in one, the poll analyst suggested, and it was cheap. Boasting no advertising, it covered a wide range of subjects aimed for all peoples in all walks of life. Also favored were *Time* and *News Week,* the latter because it published significant news and was written in an "intelligent, authoritative style." No one voted for *The Saturday Evening Post, Esquire,* or *Collier's,* however. Another prominent choice was *Ken,* which was liked because of its "open denunciations of foreign tyrants and dictators and their exposures of the manner in which these dictators are trying to undermine democracy." Black CCC men liked *Service,* "one of the best colored magazines we as a race have," John Taylor of Company 1251 at Fishers Landing, New York, declared, for it gave a running account of the "progress we have made and also our outstanding people." *American, Liberty,* and *Cosmopolitan* were selected as favorite magazine sources for fiction.[16]

Polls similarly indicated which books and poetry were most popular, Edgar Guest being probably the CCC's favorite poet. His poems were reprinted by the dozen in camp papers. As to books, *Happy Days*

sometimes coupled typical polling questions with a contest in which contestants were asked to indicate why their favorite book was the one preferred. The winner of the $5 first prize was Wayne Berkshire of Company
793, Hill City, South Dakota, who indicated that the Bible was his favorite
because it was "my mother's," and accorded with his own wish that he
might develop a more wholesome, sincere and faithful religion. Others
who won prizes selected *Lost Horizon*, because "of its unreality in a world
of realities"; Theodore Roosevelt's biography, *A Typical American*,
because the reader learned something of "true patriotic sportsmanship";
Carnegie's book, *How to Win Friends and Influence People*; Pearl Buck's
The Good Earth; Sinclair Lewis, *Arrowsmith*; and Gene Stratton Porter's
Freckles, because "it gives an excellent insight into the beauties of nature."
Other favorites included *The Nine Tailors* by Dorothy Sayers; Margaret
Mitchell's *Gone With the Wind*; while some enrollees liked the encyclo-
pedia. Surprisingly, others, indeed "more than one might imagine,"
entranced with words, doted on the dictionary. Rather facetiously, one
enrollee, a certain Twykmon of Company 3482 in Alabama, stated: "My
favorite book is the CCC Regulations. I like it because it is full of variety. I never finish reading it. I never reach the climax. It is a wonderful
story.... It keeps the nights filled with interesting and exciting dreams."
A more honest answer came from another enrollee named Casey of Company 1733 at Ava, Missouri: "I like a canteen [coupon] book because I
don't have to read it." But nobody, apparently, "had a kind word to say
for Shakespeare."[17]

Many enrollees aspired to write novels about CCC life. One was
Eddie C. Hall, editor of *The Harmony Star*, paper of Army Camps 1 and
2, Fort Benning, Georgia. Less desirable as to creative writing in the
CCC, at least in the view of *Happy Days*, was an attempt by the editors
of *Champion Youth* to elicit from interested enrollees stories of the CCC
that cast the organization in a bad light. *Happy Days* urged its readers to
ignore the appeal, and shun the communist-inspired magazine that
launched it.[18]

The movies captured the men's enthusiasm and polls sought to
determine their most popular movies and movie stars. In 1938, for
instance, a survey of various camp papers revealed that the movie, "Boy's
Town," starring Spencer Tracy, was the movie most commented on in
their pages. When *The Cottonwood CCC News* (Company 2714, New
Ulm, Minnesota) ran a camp poll regarding the most popular actor and
actress, the winners were Alice Faye and Spencer Tracy, the latter picked
for "his humanism, realism and versatility." His movie *Dawn Patrol* was
voted the best for its thrilling action and "lack of feminine characters."
Also regarding movie queens, one CCC paper was ahead of the military
on a certain matter: the *Partridge Newsette* (Company 2767, Allen,

Minnesota) selected Betty Grable as the CCC girl of the month in its November 1941 issue. Artist Reesman Kennedy performed "a labor of love" in tracing a full-page portrait of Miss Grable, to whom the November issue of the paper was dedicated: "To Betty Grable and her particular brand of youthful, wholesome American Girl beauty, we humbly dedicate this issue of the *Newsette*." She was "cute, cuddlesome and cozy," and therefore merited the attention.

Neither was art ignored. Albert Gregory Hull, enrollee-artist of Company 2656, Rock Island, Illinois, painted a mural, 8 by 18 feet. for the local arsenal museum, the mural attracting considerable notice. He had previously worked on murals with Grant Wood, and had completed several murals for national park buildings in Oklahoma. Another CCC artist, Friedolin Kessler of Company 739 at Camp Mt. Madonna near Almaden, California, had some of his outstanding work featured in *Happy Days*. Hoping to tap the aristic skills of enrollees, the National Park Service sponsored a poster contest on the subject of fire and forest safety. The three winners went to Washington to prepare their posters for printing by the Service.[19]

There were other dimensions of CCC life alluded to by an event far from the USA. At the funeral service of the Irish writer James Joyce, in Zurich on January 15, 1941, the British minister to Bern, Lord Derwent, stated: "Of all the injustices Britain has heaped upon Ireland," he said, "Ireland will continue to enjoy the lasting revenge of producing masterpieces of English literature."[20]

At the heart of that literature would certainly be a preoccupation with words, how they could be used to best effect, and if necessary, as in Joyce's *Finnegans Wake*, the invention of new ones. If not at those lofty levels, at least some men of the CCC were similarly preoccupied with words, often cleverly used, with new twists and meanings and frequently with a great deal of verve and versatility. Indeed, the *Tamalpais Fog Horn* (Company 1921, Mt. Tamalpais, California) noted that "the potentialities of the English language will never be known until serving a hitch in the CCC." As Dard Albritton of Company 848 in Tucson, Arizona, observed, "CCC-Ology," though not taught in CCC schools, nonetheless existed as a fact of its institutional life. Scholars also recognized this truth, one being Allegheny College's dean of men, J. R. Schultz, who, certain that the CCC was having a hand in "forming the English language," began a collection of words, expressions and abbreviations relating to the it.[21]

Verve and cleverness characterized some of the writing appearing in the camp newspapers, whether original or borrowed. An essay on the apple published in the *Transcontinental* (Company 3225, Ilwaco, Washington) is a good example: "Apples are born on trees, spend a large part of their lives in barrels, and are buried in pies." A poem in the *Crystal Camp Crier* (Company 1742, Tarkio, Missouri) by Lee Esser might be included as well: "The wanton hills lie naked to the breeze/The woods and thicket now are all unfrocked/Bare are the limbs of the shameless trees/No wonder that the corn is shocked."[22]

A feature article appearing in the *Broadcast*, paper of Company 1742 at Gallatin, Missouri, could be mentioned: "A boy who had left the farm to get a job in the city wrote a letter to his brother (who had stayed on the farm) telling him the joys of city life. In it he wrote: 'Thursday we autoed out to the Country Club where we golfed until dark then motored to a nearby beach where we week ended.' The brother [on the farm] wrote back ... 'Yesterday we buggied to town and baseballed all afternoon. Today we muled out to the cornfield and geehawed until sundown. Then we suppered and piped for awhile. After that we staircased up to our room and bedsteaded until the clock fived.'"[23]

The *Tamalpais Fog Horn* (Company 1921, Mt. Tamalpais, California), one of the more innovative and livelier of the CCC papers, often included humorous pieces such as one entitled, "So Sorry": "During a recent tong war in San Francisco's Chinatown, a neutral member of a participating tong was clipped behind the ear with a .45 pellet. At his funeral later in the week, was delivered a floral piece with the following inscription: 'We wanted Lee Wing/But we winged Willie Wong/A sad but excusable/Slip of the tong.'"[24]

The *Alpine Echo* (Company 1921, Fairfax, California), in its "Sense and Nonsense" column, urged its readers to: "Be kind to all dumb animals/And give small birds a crumb/Be kind to human beings, too—/They're sometimes pretty dumb."[25]

Slang was another prominent CCC characteristic which the organization also shared with other social groups of the 1930s. That decade, in general, produced much distinctive jargon. For instance, the all-too-common subculture of hobos had their own talk, the "lingo of the road." In this argot, "yard bulls," were railroad detectives; "shacks," cops; "town clown," local cop; "stemming the drag," panhandling on the main street; "Jesus stiff," anyone eating at the Salvation Army (Sally's); "road hog," large engine on a full train; "riding the blinds," riding in a blocked doorway of the first car behind the coal car of a passenger train; "riding the rods," an obsolete term for riding underneath a freight car; "crummy," a caboose; "on the fritz," broke; and "misery" was coffee. Also during this time, the term "bindle stiff" replaced the obsolete "hobo."[26]

Slang also appeared almost immediately in the CCC, and various camp papers, in addition to *Happy Days*, published glossaries of the new language. "To bang," for instance, meant to bum, as a smoke. "That Man" referred to the army. "Kick" was a reference to a dishonorable discharge. "Stroll" meant going AWOL. "An extra" was a handout. "A stroke" was to put something over on someone. An extra detail was "wedged." "Bat" was your buddy's best girl and "take five" was a five-minute rest break, now commonly used in the American idiom. "Whing-ding" was a spree, and "mildew" meant to linger, to hang around, as in, "let's go to town and mildew awhile."

"Screech" was to squeal on someone. "Shug" was a very sweet girl. "Eagleday" was payday. "Jones Boy" was no person in particular, some-times used when addressing strangers. "Popeye" was spinach; "mellow" was anything good, such as a piece of music. A "crum" was one who was lax. "What's doin'" was a synonym for "good morning," "good night," or "how are you?" "John L's," were winter underwear; "sweat pads," hot-cakes; and "brush-batty" was someone mentally overwrought. "Dog ken-nels" were heavy shoes; a "greaseball" was a truck driver; "hayloft," a bed, bunk, or sleep-sack. "Logging" meant walking, while "zoom" meant to walk fast. "O'Connors" were potatoes; "pontoons," snow shoes, and "sawdust (tobacco) with blankets (papers)" were the "makin's" or "rollin's" for a cigarette; to "crank one up" was to roll a cigarette, while a "stiffy" was a ready-made or tailor-made smoke; "submarine turkey" was salmon. It was also clear that by the summer of 1937, the term "GI" was well established, as in "GI truck."[27]

Black companies developed their own distinctive patois: as, for exam-ple, the term "go fruiting," which meant to go looking for girls, as did also the term "johning," both with sexual overtones. Black enrollees leav-ing the CCC were said to be "going on the hard turf." Blacks were also credited with the development of "jive" talk, but this phenomenon was not confined to blacks only. As one observer noted, philologists and other workers "in the vineyard of American idioms, could do worse than study the department called 'Gossip and Jive,' which appears each month in *The Turfnocker*," the camp publication of Company 1269 [a white com-pany] in Absecon, New Jersey. The column was written by Clifford Phillips, who affected an expert's knowledge of "so-called 'jive' jargon to relate the lowdown on his fellow enrollees." As he explained in a typical column: "Sam is laying it on a certain nifty down in A. C., who wears cheaters, but he ain't nowhere with that hen. Stop gumbeating to Phillips that you linger with her, Sam, because that chick called up one night and got you all straight about that." Translation: "this means that an enrollee named Sam is pouring honey words (presumably by mail) into the ear of a bespectacled damsel who lives in Atlantic City, but all in vain. Phillips is irked by Sam's claims that he is her favored suitor and demands that he cease making such remarks, reminding Sam that the femme aforesaid told him on the telephone that she cared for him less than a little. Do you cats dig the story, or are you solid squares?"[28]

Veterans developed their own distinctive lingo, often with ethnic overtones, which was characteristic of these companies in general. For example, "Chinese jello" was rice pudding, and "Polish pop" or "old joy" was gin. Other terms included "gookum" for pancake syrup; "red lead" for ketchup; and "goo-goo" for gravy. An expression sometimes substituted for "that takes the cake," was: "that takes the rag off'n the bush."[29]

But such ethnic usage was common throughout the nation in those days. Lee Lorenz, writing in *The New Yorker* on the subject of media humor, asserts that "up to the Second World War, ethnic humor, sexual jokes, and the free use of racial and sexual stereotypes were staples of popular humor." Even *The New Yorker* "made little effort to screen out such stuff," he observed. "Almost every issue published prior to 1940 contains something inimical to felicitous intergroup relations—rapacious Jews, ten-watt blonds, no-account blacks, shrewish housewives, and so on." Thus, it might be said, the 1930s was an era of "extreme incorrectness." Certainly, in many of the bolder CCC papers this description was apt.[30]

Throughout, a major characteristic of the camp papers was a focus on humor. In this, as in other things, *Happy Days* led the way. One of its typical columns was "Silly as It Seems," which often featured rhymes, a common form of humor: "The ice man has a happy life/His job is very slick—/While other guys have but one wife/The ice man has his pick."[31]

Similarly, in the column "At The Keyhole" appearing in a typical camp paper, *Think Nothing of It!* (Company 232, Bountiful, Utah) was a comical poem about a certain boss's typist:

> My typust is on her vacation
> My tripist's awau fpr a week
> My typaut us in her vscarion
> Wgile thsee daamb key plsy
> hude and seej
> Choris:
> Breng bock, bfing bzck
> Oy, brung becj MuB onnie ti
> my tp.mr;
> Br&ng b4xj be-ng bicz
> Oj, brong bosk m% BeLnio-1
> my-oh helK![32]

The column "Canteen Chatter" appearing in *Happy Days* and presided over for some time by Frank Giordana of Company 301, Masten, Pennsylvania, often featured humor. A typical entry concerned food:

"Our Cook: 'That oyster we've been using is beginning to get worn out. What shall we do for soup today?' Mess Sergeant: 'You ought to know. Use the old bean.'"[33]

Following *Happy Days'* lead, the average camp paper had its own offerings of wit, humor or "advice," as with the "Drops of Wits-Dumb" column in the *The Harbinger*, paper of Company 698 in Argyle, Wisconsin. The same company's earlier paper, *The Jubilee Journal*, often included a "Ho Hum Department," featuring light camp gossip presented in a humorous fashion: "Tanglefoot Twirp, our most promising rookie, remarks that digging diversion ditches may be diversion for some people, but to him it's just plain, ordinary hard work." And: "When 'Lindburgh' Holley of the Harlen crew boasted of having taken a correspondence course in aviation, one of his companions remarked, 'Well, if you're an aviator, let's see you make that dirt fly.'" The column was continued when the paper changed its name to *The Pyramid. Happy Days* once warmly praised this feature, usually edited by "Tarzan," but which also included "Uncle Oswald's" advice: "Dear Uncle Oswald 'What can I do for that tired feeling?' (Mr. Morton Seidman). 'Dear Morton: Go rest, young man, go rest.'" Another humor department was "Bosh & Bosh, Inc.," appearing in *The Clipper* (Company 3502, Wilmington, Ohio). The paper of Company 297, *Scraps 'N' Stuff* (Company 297, Heppner, Oregon) often included a column, "Wit and Witout," while the *Rock Hound's* venue of wit was called "Around Our Kennels" with such offerings as: "Mike Krause, the camp Romeo just went out and bit Charlene, the camp dog, so that the editor would have some news."[34]

Many CCC papers, especially magazines, were entirely devoted to humor. One educational adviser, Robert G. Winters, who served in several CCC companies, was praised by *Happy Days* as one who had "probably done more for the CCC humor magazine than any other person." He first brought forth that style of paper with *Hooey* (Company 553, Defiance, Ohio), later introducing *Whozit?* (Company 1519, Nigh, Kentucky), then the *Rattler* (Company 564, McKee, Kentucky). He concluded by founding the *In-Zane Monthly*, published by Company 1575 in Bellefontaine, Ohio.[35]

One characteristic of camp paper jokes was that they frequently appeared in a succession of publications, often being "borrowed" without attribution. One of the jokes which made the rounds was: "Were you excited when you asked your husband for money? No, I was calm—and collected" (*Lawrence Lookout* [Company 549, Ironton, Ohio]). Another went, "'Pink elephants,' claims Bill Allen, 'are nothing but beasts of bourbon'" (*Grand Canyon Echo* [Company 819, Grand Canyon, Arizona], February 1940).

Sometimes *Happy Days* borrowed from the camp papers, as its editors once admitted: "We swipe most of our jokes from *Alpine Echo* and tell 'em to friends over at Harry's Bar. They're always good for a drink." Long before the days of "political correctness," as has been noted, ethnic jokes abounded in the CCC press as elsewhere. One went: "A Swede having heard much about the Bible, bought one. 'Yee Whiz,' he said to his friend Ole, 'Ay ban read for months now. It tells all about St. Paul but not wan t'ing about Minn-e-apoolis.'"[36] There were anti–Semitic jokes: "'Teacher: 'Isaac, what is the difference between electricity and lightening?' Isaac: 'Ve dun't have to pay for lightning.'"[37]

The Scots and their proverbial stinginess were frequently featured: "A Scotchman left a tip for a waitress. He had been eating asparagus" (*The Watch Tower* [Company 1296, Fort Niagara, New York]). Another: "A scotchman and a dozen friends had just finished dining when the waiter arrived with the check. 'Give it to me, I'll pay it,' came in loud tones from the scotchman. The following day in the newspapers headlines appeared stating: 'Scotchman kills ventriloquist'" (*Vets Voice* [Company 1774, Bayport, Minnesota], June 21, 1940).

Cheap shots at blacks were also common, though they were not regarded as such, so common were they in the culture at the time: "'Brethern and Sistern,' the colored preacher began, 'Ah has here a $5 sermon, a $2 sermon and a $1 sermon. Will the deacons please take up the collection so's I can tell which one you wishes to heah?'" (*Kiamichi Forester* [Company 876, Nashoba, Oklahoma]).

Risqué and suggestive jokes, and raw, barbed humor of questionable taste—at least as regarded in some segments of society—were a mainstay of many sheets: "While returning home from work last Friday evening Ida Wanna had her handbag snatched away from her by a holdup man. In it was her pay envelope as well as her Aunt Fannie's pay envelope. She hurried back to town and entered the police station yelling, 'Oh, I've just been robbed of my pay and my aunt's pay.' "'Calm yourself, lady,' answered the night sergeant, 'cut out the hog latin and tell me what happened'" (*Oregon Forest Log* [unknown company] quoted in *Happy Days*, May 15, 1937). "A pal of ours landed a soft job. He's in a bloomer factory now pulling down a couple of thousand a year" (*The Pine Bur* [Companies 1805 and 1811, Bastrop, Texas]). "Little Audrey was walking in the wood when she saw a man with his arms around a tree. But Little Audrey just laughed and laughed because she knew only God would make a tree" (*Happy Days*, December 18, 1937). "George Buitron (Reading letter from home.) 'My gosh! if this letter is an "o" my brother shot himself, but if it's an "i" he didnt'" (*The Rock Hound* [Company 855, El Paso, Texas], March 22, 1935).[38]

The veterans' companies were more inclined than were the junior enrollees' papers to push the limits of the questionable: "The abolish-

The title of *The In-Zane Monthly* (Company 1575, Bellefontaine, Ohio) is a play on the word "insane," but also commemorates Zane Grey, one of the CCCers' favorite authors, who was a native of Ohio.

ment of corsets has promoted better feeling all around" (*Alpine Echo* [Company 1921, Fairfax, California], January 1937). Another: "'I think Bill and I will go to Bali when we're married and see what it's like.' 'Don't be silly. It's the same everywhere'" (The *Tamalpais Fog Horn* [Company 1921, Mt. Tamalpais, California], August 1938). The *Rock Hound* (Company 855, Elephant Butte, New Mexico) was especially given to printing risqué black ethnic jokes including: "The darkey shiek was making love to his fair Sheba. 'Honey, can't you all see the love light shining in my eyes?' 'Go 'way now, Moses. You knows that is nothing but a tail light.'"

Women in general were considered fair game, and jokes regarding them touched on numerous subjects: "Here's to the greatest gambler of all times—Lady Godiva. She put everything she had on a horse" (The *Alpine Echo* [Company 1921, Fairfax, California], October 1937 issue under the heading, "That's Not Saying Much"). "Sometimes a girl is like a typewriter keyboard. If you touch the wrong places you get terrible words" (*Co. 299 News* [Company 299, Masonville, New York], November 22, 1934, issue). The *Alpine Echo* once printed a joke about some elephants that had escaped from a circus: "A small Middle-Western town was visited for the first time by a circus. During the parade the elephants stampeded and ran loose around the town. One housewife had never seen an elephant before and phoned to the Sheriff frantically: 'There's a large animal in my yard and it's pulling up all my cabbages with its tail.' Sheriff: 'What's it doing with 'em?' H.W. 'If I told you, you would never believe me'" (Company 1921, Fairfax, California, October 1937). Another pointed out a certain "truth": "As the birdies well know, many a love nest is built on no stronger a foundation, than a cute little limb" (*Vets Voice* [Company 1774, Bayport, Minnesota], January 1940).

Relations between the sexes was also common fare: "The average man is a dame fool," *Vets Voice* (Company 1774, Bayport, Minnesota), in its June 21, 1940, "Freshly Laid Eggs" column opined. *Flying Chips* concurred: "Some men fall to their knees when they propose; others are able to hold their liquor" (*Flying Chips* [unknown company]). An anonymous poet recorded that, "In the dark he split the kindling wood/By the light of his darling Maude/For he was hatchet-faced you see/And she was lantern-jawed" (The *Jolly Griper* [Company 752, Hebron, Nebraska], January 31, 1935). There were many others concerned with gender: "'I'd like a couple of hard-boiled eggs to take out,' said the camp vet to the girl at the lunch counter. 'All right,' replied the waitress with a smile, 'but you'll have to wait. Me and Mamie don't get off until ten'" (*Vets Voice* [Company 1774, Bayport, Minnesota], January 1940).

Lawyers, judges and the legal system were fair game: "Lawyer: 'Here's my bill. $100 down and $25 a week.' Client: 'Sounds like buying

Cartoon appearing in the *Vets Voice*, January 1940.

a car.' Lawyer: 'I am'" (*Trout Creek Mountaineer* [Company 803, Buena Vista, Colorado]). "Judge: 'Do you wish to challenge any of the jury?' Prisoner: 'Well, I think I can lick that little guy on the end'" (*Happy Days*, February 20, 1937).

Cruelty jokes were rather common. Many focused on "Little Audrey" who appeared in numerous camp papers: "Little Audrey took her little brother to the top of the Empire State building, and in looking over the edge, little brother fell over. Little Audrey laughed and laughed because she knew her little brother didn't have another dollar to come back up" (*Chat Chatter* [Company 1995, Chatcolet, Idaho]). A rage sweeping the country, "Knock, Knock" jokes crept into every corner of the USA and even into the camp papers, as in *The Pine Bur* (Company 1811, Bastrop, Texas), which once published an entire page of them.

Road safety could also be humorous: "Ruth rode in my new cycle car—/In the seat in back of me—/I took a bump at fifty-five/And rode on ruthlessly" (*The Survey* [unknown company], quoted in *Happy Days*, October 20, 1934).

Jokes about nature, the human condition or the current scene were common: "They laughed when I walked to the piano, but they were right. I couldn't move it" (*Happy Days*, April 24, 1937). "And now what our five-cent cigars need is a good country" (*The Forest Log* [unknown company]). "The favorite song of the CCC cigarette moocher is 'Let the Rest of the World Go Buy'" (*Camp Cascadia Cannonade* [Company 2907, Cascadia, Oregon]). Another admitted: "I'm as pure as snow, but I drifted." And: "He who laughs last is very dense." The "Are You Having Any Fun" column of the *Vets Voice* reported on a failed business deal: "Movie Actress: 'I'll endorse your cigarettes for no less that $50,000.' Advertiser: 'I'll see you inhale first'" [*Vets Voice* (Company 1774, Bayport, Minnesota], January 1940). Liquor and drunks were perennial subjects for jokes, such as the one that went: "Make mine a whiskey and sofa" (*Vets Voice* [Company 1774, Bayport, Minnesota], January 1940). And: "There was the man who gave up drinking for the sake of his wife and kidneys" (*Indian Creek Ripple* [Company 4776, Monticello, Utah]). "Flap: 'My grandfather lived to be over ninety, and never used glasses.' Dab: 'Well, a lot of people prefer it out of a bottle'" (*Triangle Review* [unknown company]).

Not the least of the offerings of the camp papers were the wit, wisdom and humor that they contained. Reflecting the optimism of often irrepressible, exuberant enrollees, their humor suggests a verve and dynamism that would help carry the nation through the often harrowing crises of the 1930s and 1940s. While revealing that CCC enrollees mainly participated as consumers in America's cultural life, CCC journalism also indicates that they were capable of making their own contributions.

11

All Work and No Play: Recreation and the Great Outdoors

"In the spring a young man's fancy may turn to love—but his heart turns to baseball."

— *The Stockade* (Company 2328,
Shelocta, Pennsylvania), April 1938

A CCC boy, on observing a passing storm: "I thought of God who gave me life/And these things to see and enjoy/I thought of the time that fate made me/A happy CCC boy."

— *The Pine Needle*
(Company 235 and 237, Camp Pack,
New Lisbon, New Jersey), August 1937

From the outset, recreation was regarded as essential to the CCCer's well being, another central theme in the camp papers. Under the recreational plans drafted by the War Department in May 1933, Brig. Gen. James F. McKinley, adjutant general of the Army, was given the job of taking care of this end of camp life. He placed Major Joseph J. Teter in charge of directing a diversified program. Major Teter's first efforts were in equipping each company with athletic supplies. The first teams fielded were from Company 322, Edinburg, Virginia; the men of the original camp, Camp Roosevelt at Luray; Company 315, Medix, Pennsylvania, and Company 306, Loganton, Pennsylvania.

By the end of 1933, $365 was made available to each camp for ath-

211

letic equipment. Uniforms appeared and the list of additional sports that
were supported grew ever longer—no doubt in part, to stem popular
gambling games, which were illegal but widespread. Golf, tennis, shooting, and camp track and field events became common, and in the West
mountain climbing was introduced.

While *Happy Days* focused on sports in the national arenas, camp
papers, including the *Alpine Echo* of Company 1921, Fairfax, California,
a vet group, emphasized local events. In its pages, W.T. Jordan, for one,
had some comments on sporting events, "Behind Barracks 2":

> As you read the sport sheet over
> Of the things the big shots do,
> All about Joe De Mag, the "Huskies"
> And their crew,
> Have you ever stopped to notice
> Our volley ball team at play?
> Why brother—you ain't seen nothin
> Them big shots fade away.[1]

Indeed, many camps took athletics at the local level seriously. One
of these, Company 2356, made up of a large number of men of Polish
descent, excelled in baseball and boxing. They took pride in calling themselves "Fighting Hunkies"—well before the days of "political correctness"! Even when the company moved from Amherst, Virginia, to
Whitewater, New Mexico, in the summer of 1938, they continued their
success and by early fall, had beaten four other CCC camps in the New
Mexico area to win the Silver City Sub-District baseball title.[2]

Many of the camps undertook extensive building projects to further
their recreational programs. Company 1291 at Fillmore, New York,
decided to form the "Lost Nation Country Club" dedicated to "the recreational and cultural advancement of the enrollees." It featured an outdoor dancing pavilion, a swimming pool and extensive athletic fields,
including tennis courts, a track, courts for volleyball and horseshoe pitching and softball fields. The camp also had a "top-hat band," the "Lost
Nation Troubadours," which furnished music for dance programs. The
men of Company 327 at Conrad, Pennsylvania, constructed their own
swimming pool, as did many other camps.[3]

Some camps extended the range of their recreational activities by
using municipal or school facilities in nearby towns and villages. Camp
baseball and softball—often called "kittenball" or "mushball"—teams
often played in local leagues, and many CCC camps extended their
influence in this fashion. The men of Company 4468 at Barnwell, South
Carolina, obtained permission to use the municipal swimming pool but

because the pool's bottom was silted up, they first had to clean it up as their price of admission.[4]

The enrollees of Company 299 at Masonville, New York, were not as fortunate, because the nearby Sidney, New York, board of education "acted very unAmericanly in depriving us of their gym," they complained. This led to the development of other amusements and forms of recreation, such as ping-pong, pinochle, and bowling which could be pursued at camp. Company 2328 at Shelocta, Pennsylvania, got around the difficulty with the local Elderton high school gym by simply renting it once a week for the use of the company's basketball team.[5]

Certainly *Happy Days* needed no convincing as to the importance of play and devoted considerable space to recreational ventures throughout the CCC.

One of its preoccupations was baseball, and it kept its readers informed in such columns as "From the Stands," presided over by John H. Stoneburg, Jr., formerly of Company 941 in Glenville, California. Stoneburg had come to the attention of the paper's editors for the excellence of his writing and was subsequently attached to the paper as a sports writer.[6]

Taking some initiative in baseball as early as June 1933, *Happy Days* quizzed men in the camps seeking to locate the top CCC players. The aim was to identify men for CCC All-American teams at the national level. This venture matured when cooperation with major league baseball teams evolved. By the summer of 1936, educational advisers, athletic officers, and commanding officers were routinely asked to turn in information and photographs to the paper of outstanding baseball players in their camps. It seemed reasonable that "when three men can agree on baseball talent it usually means that the youngster in question has something on the ball," the paper declared. The player data was then turned over to major league clubs.[7]

Indeed, it was apparent to big league baseball scouts almost from the outset that baseball prospects of a high order might turn up among CCC enrollees. As early as the 1934 season, out of the 19 players on the Camp Skokie Valley baseball team, 17 were selected to play professional ball in the minor or semi-pro leagues, and two were signed by the majors. Other discoveries included Charles "Chink" Vanatta, star pitcher of Company 2729, Centaur Station, Missouri, who after being spotted by scouts, was sent to a farm team of the St. Louis Cardinals at Springfield. Afterward, these events became commonplace. For example, Hadley Brown and Edward Cuthrell, who played CCC ball with Company 424 at Swanquarter, North Carolina, were seen by Nap Tucker, "famous ball scout," who signed them to long-term contracts with the Atlanta Cracker League. Another was Hugh Carroll "Cunnie" Wilson, formerly of Company 747, Eagleton, Arkansas. His story was typical: He left camp after a Cincinnati Reds scout saw him fan 17 men in eight innings. He was sent to Peoria in the Three-Eye League for seasoning, and then to the Waterloo Reds, another Cincinnati farm club. He was then moved up to the pitching staff of the "Cincinnati." Later, "Duke" Finocchiaro, a former enrollee in Company 2729, was signed to play for the Chicago White Sox after working with a farm team. Likewise, James D. Bromlee, former catcher for Company 1491, Provencal, Louisiana, where he "slapped the pill around with gusto," was drafted to play for Monroe in the Cotton States League.[8]

Rarely allowing any opportunity to encourage CCC baseball players to go untapped, when Robert "Bob" Feller, the Cleveland Indians' pitching sensation burst upon the baseball scene, *Happy Days* asked him for an interview. Feller, then all of 17 years of age, obliged: "I have never been in the CCC. That's my tough luck. It might have made my fast ball faster. But those fellows who hit against me say it could not be much swifter. So maybe it wouldn't have. But I've played against the CCC fellows—and they are tough to beat. Three meals a day, hard work and plenty of old fortitude on the playing field makes them give you a run. I like 'em much."[9]

Undoubtedly, baseball was a great stimulus to the CCC recreational calendar. It was the dominant sport in the Hawaiian camps, for example, and inter-island tournaments were common, though TH-9 on Molokai, "the world's smallest CCC Camp," could not field a team and accordingly, "they were thinking of issuing a Hula challenge or a calisthenics competition." Rather less serious, was a venture of the athletes of Company 4468 at Barnwell, South Carolina, who played a game of donkey baseball with the Barnwell boys, the proceeds benefitting the Barnwell Chapter of the American Legion.[10]

One characteristic of the American athletic scene in the 1930s, colorful sports writing *à la* Grantland Rice and Ring Lardner, overflowed into the CCC press. One of the *Stockade's* sports writers, Victor "Cotter-pin" Minarik, could not resist a story "The Baseball Game," featuring a play on words according to which, "cigar was in the box with lots of smoke" and the umpire, Apple, "who was rotten," while naturally "the crowd cheered when Spider caught the fly." Nor could a writer in *Happy Days* avoid hyperbole when reporting on the prowess of a certain young pitcher, Archie Templeton of Winston-Salem, North Carolina, identified as an 18-year-old youth "who toes the slab for the Methodist Children's Home," and who had fanned 68 would-be batters in 32 innings. "Not only does this youngster pitch a wicked spheroid, but he also puts the wood on the horsehide *à la* Gehrig."[11]

Though baseball received much of the sports attention, at least in

Happy Days, it was hardly the only sport featured. Boxing was popular, and as early as June 1933, such camps as the one at Plattsburg, New York, boasted that Joe Desmond, "one of the classiest amateur lightweights in New York State, [was appearing] as a CCC boxer, fighting under colors of the Plattsburg camp." He also coached others who later became outstanding CCC fighters. The year 1934 also saw the emergence of CCC Golden Glovers, and four members went to the finals in Chicago's "Battle of Champions." When commanding officers had special expertise in sports, it could make a difference in camp athletics. Such was the case with Captain Ralph F. Miles of Company 3354, Fort Stanton, New Mexico, who had earlier boxed as "Red O'Brien." He coached the camp's boxing team with considerable success.[12]

With the teams sometimes playing in improvised uniforms, football also made an appereance, as many men well able to "boot the ovoid," were naturally present in the CCC as well. One of the early good teams was fielded by Company 974 of Idyllwild, California. Another early venture was launched when a former Rutgers University football star and New Jersey state forester agreed to coach a team for Company 218 in Branchville, New Jersey.[13]

Less strenuous were the football pools conducted by some companies with prizes usually being cigarettes, tobacco or ice cream (for non-smokers). In some instances on Saturday afternoons, as at Ohio State in Columbus, men of nearby CCC companies were invited to see university football games as guests of the school.[14]

But not all recreation involved sports. The boys of Company 4468 at Barnwell, South Carolina, for instance, apparently enjoyed dancing even more than baseball. So as to be present for these events, they decided not to participate in an extensive district baseball schedule that had been arranged because many of the venues were too far distant and the boys did not to wish to be far from camp on weekends.[15]

Thespians, both members of individual camps and others drawn from various circuits established by the federal government to benefit unemployed professional actors, appeared on the often-makeshift stages in CCC camps. Typically, the men of Company 299 saw the farce *Baby Mine*, and *The Whole Town is Talking*, a "hilarious comedy," followed by *Your Uncle Dudley*, and later a production of *Mable Looks Ahead*. Nor was vaudeville ignored, and in August of 1938, a variety show was presented to the veterans of Company 1921 at Mt. Tamalpais, California, by a troupe of players from the Federal Theater Project. Other veterans were pleased that Elsie Janis, the famed entertainer who had been the "Sweetheart of the American Expeditionary Forces" in France in the World War, still had the boys' interests at heart. She visited several companies, including men of Company 1668 at Hinsdale, Illinois.[16]

But local talent was encouraged also, and minstrel shows were popular. One, "Under a Spanish Harlem Moon," put on by Company 903 at La Canada, California, was warmly praised by a representative of the Federal Theatre Project who enthused that "never have I seen a more spontaneous performance." Company 299 of Masonville, New York, was apparently the first camp to receive a regular dramatics instructor, Robert Harper.[17]

Lecturers and speakers abounded, and the enrollees of Company 1921 at Mt. Tamalpais, California, listened to Colonel Nelson M. Holdeman, the Commandant of the Veterans Home of California, tell the story of the "Lost Battalion" of World War fame. Later men of the company heard a former member, one Hans Amlie, regale them with details of his adventures while serving with the Loyalist International Brigade in the Spanish Civil War.[18]

Even the commonplace game of bingo was important in some CCC companies. W. T. Jordan of Company 1921 at Camp Mt. Tamalpais near Mill Valley, California, a vets organization, captured something of its appeal in his poem "Bingo," which urged the men, "When you are craving some excitement/And camp life seems quite tame," to join in one of "Toothpick Charlie's" bingo games.[19]

Enrollees often took advantage of the numerous fairs, expositions and similar attractions that dotted the nation in the 1930s. When the Golden Gate International Exposition opened on Treasure Island, San Francisco, on February 18, 1939, the men of many of the camps in the area were able to attend. In the autumn of 1936, men of Company 4468 in Barnwell, South Carolina, went by truck to the State Fair in Columbia on a company holiday.[20]

In many instances, recreation and education were intertwined. Company 1848 at Morrison, Colorado, staged an amateur night using the format of the popular Major Bowes Amateur Hour, uncovering a wealth of camp talent. The camp also boasted a group styled *The Camp Players*—later the *Red Rock Players*—which staged plays, such as the one-act production "Abie Eats," presented in the form of a three-man radio skit. In July 1936, a large group of Camp Morrison enrollees journeyed to Denver's Cheeseman Park for an outdoor production of "The Vagabond King" produced by local talent. On another occasion, a large group from the camp took a recreational trip to Pike's Peak.[21]

The 1930s witnessed a great popular interest in the radio, and CCC camps participated in the national craze. *Happy Days*, well aware of the great interest in the maturing medium, often featured columns, such as "Let's Get on the Air," which began in the May 25, 1935, issue, to keep the CCC men informed of developments. Camps with short-wave radio stations were encouraged to listen to special CCC news bulletins, supplied by *Happy Days*, broadcast by WLW [Cincinnati] every Friday night at 7 and 10 P.M. EST on 6990 and 3497.5 kilocycles. WLW was the Net Control Station of the Army Amateur Radio System.[22]

During this period, ham radio and camp radio messages were the e-mail of their day. Typical was the case of Camp Isle Royale, an isolated winter camp in upper Lake Superior. There the men broadcast a regular program every Sunday afternoon over stations in Duluth, Hibbing, and Virginia, all in Minnesota, and over a short-wave station in Superior, Wisconsin, thereby keeping in touch with the outside world.[23]

Talented men of the CCC were often featured on commercial radio programs. For example, the glee club of Company 1371, Alexandria, Virginia, made frequent public appearances as well as being broadcast over selected NBC stations.[24]

Aviation provided another means of recreation for enrollees of a technical bent. When men of Company 350 of Big Meadows, Shenandoah National Park, Virginia, prepared a local landing field to host a National Glider Meet, the officials of the Soaring Society of America rewarded them by establishing gliding classes, and providing two gliders for use in their flight training.[25]

In a time when home movies were increasingly popular, it was inevitable that films of the men's lives in the CCC would be made. The commanding officer of Company 985, Santa Barbara, California, was one of the enthusiastic amateur movie producers. He systematically filmed the daily camp life of his men, and prepared a film—dedicated to FDR—entitled: *Young America Conserves—Rebuilds*. Fox Movietone newsreels also sent a crew to shoot the activities of Company 531 at Lone Pine, California; Fox was preparing a film for national distribution. Six hundred other CCC men selected from a dozen camps across the nation, especially from the Yellowstone and Grand Teton area, were also featured in an episode of *March of Time* devoted to the CCC and its history. Paramount Films went even further, making a feature in early 1936 entitled *It's a Great Life*. Its plot revolved around the life and adventures, as well as the romances, of CCC enrollees. It starred Joe Morrison, Paul Kelly, Rosalind Keith and William Frawley, with Charles (Chic) Sale in a comedy role. In the following year, another feature-length production, *Blazing Barriers*, appeared, starring Edward Arnold, Jr., a "son of the well known movie star." Its story also revolved around life in the CCC with a forest fire as its dramatic climax, in which hundreds of CCC men participated. The filming was done on Hollywood backlots, but also at several nearby California CCC camps.[26]

More passively, the CCC men naturally saw films in great numbers. Cut-rate tickets for movies in local theaters for enrollees were soon the norm throughout the country. Camp newspapers often included theater bills for local theaters, noting their 10-cent and 25-cent tickets. Also at the movies in 1930s America were the popular "bank nights" at which ticket stubs were drawn to select winners. CCC enrollees sometimes emerged with impressive prizes. One was Ernest Walstrom, a rookie of Company 2754, Hot Springs, South Dakota, who won $200. He intended to throw a party for all the men in his barracks with some of the proceeds, he declared, but as to the remainder, "guess I'll leave it in the old sock."[27]

Music provided a natural outlet for many talented men in the CCC, and choirs and choruses were organized as were camp orchestras and other musical groups. Many companies boasted resident musical directors. One of these was Company 299 at Masonville, New York. Though musical instruments were scarce, some of the men rented their own, ending the era when "shoe horns [were] the only ones in camp." The director also focused his attention on choral groups and harmonica players, and provided those interested with a printed set of chords, enabling them to "fake" it at the piano. A "hill-billy" contingent was also active.[28]

Sometimes CCC musical talent was discovered in unusual ways. Enrollee Daniel Goduto of Company 677 at Irons, Michigan, had the habit of singing while working in the woods. He was heard by trout fishermen fishing along the Little Manistee River. Greatly impressed, they persuaded him to perform on local radio stations. He was soon recognized as a budding talent and made an appearance in Orchestra Hall in Chicago. There, impressed musicians planned to see to the furthering of his career.[29]

As the CCC matured, clubs began to form. These included AEF clubs for veterans; forestry clubs; at least one "sunshine club" formed to help members in case of need or distress and as a social committee; chess and card clubs; Bible clubs often dedicated to systematic group Bible study; and the Holy Name Club, of Companies 219 and 205, Cherry Plain, New York, held communion breakfasts each month. The "Anti-Chiselers Club" of Company 182, West Cornwall, Connecticut, had its members swear never to chisel or to pass out anything to chiselers. There were numerous reading clubs, and Company 1699 at Milwaukee, Wisconsin, launched a "New-Word-a-Day" club. Its purpose was to learn the definition of a new word posted on the bulletin board each day; a quiz was held every 30 days to see who had learned the most words. Gun clubs were popular, and many CCC camps boasted firing ranges.

One common dimension of the CCC experience, in addition to a preoccupation with recreation, was the enrollees' encounters with the natural world. Many of the men hailed from urban areas and had little knowledge of, or previous contact with, nature. The experience—often confrontational—provided the newspapers with much copy. *Happy Days* anticipated these experiences early in its career, and included articles in a regular column—appearing for a time—"Outdoor Neighbors." In such articles as "Mister Screech Owl" and "Mr. Wild Turkey" by an author styling himself "Titwillow," enrollees were introduced to the wonders of their natural environment. The paper also printed features on the National Parks with emphasis on the indigenous animals. Typical of the camp papers in this respect was *The Harbinger* (Company 698 in Argyle, Wisconsin), which regularly published pages on wildlife.[30]

Indeed, the contact with nature seemed to release deep emotions of the men, which, as the editor of *Happy Days* once remarked, among other things resulted in the flood of poetry pouring into the paper's offices. Thus, he observed, "the outdoors seems to make a fellow FEEL more," and many who had not previously given nature a second thought were deeply affected. One of those was E.D. Rennacker of Company 1921 in Fairfax, California, whose poem "Return to Nature" clearly illustrates the point:

> … … … … … … … … …
> The sun is setting as I rest
> Upon a hillside, Nature's guest:
> Who in our moment's of despair
> Or ecstacy, seems glad to share
> Our inward thoughts: and like a friend,
> No interruption does offend.
>
> The quiet hills and deep ravines
> Revive my memory of scenes
> I had forgotten in the strife
> Of civilization's noisy life
> Above, there spreads a huge oak tree,
> Years older by many seasons than me;
> And as I lean against its bark,
> I have no fear of the gathering dark.
> … … … … … … … … … … … …[31]

Philip A. Smith of Company 1614 in upper Michigan also caught the spirit of the great outdoors: "The pioneering spirit is just realistic enough to bring out the ruggedness in us. Already we have a wilderness-fever that is like a drug," he declared. "The whole thing grows right in you and it's hard to break away." Anthony Yourch of Company 130 at Baxter State Park, Maine, was in awe of Mount Katahdin, and wished that he possessed "power over words great enough to cause another individual the same pleasure which was my good fortune to experience as I marveled at the view from Mount Katahdin." Truxton Hosley of Company 295, Camp Walker River, Nevada, in his poem "The Lonesome Pine" praised a stately pine "unharmed, lonesome and free." Noting that "Its sight has thrilled me thru and thru/Its beauties never die," he roundly cursed anyone who might fell or harm it. Even swampland could have this effect, and *The Southern Pine Whisper* (Company 1414, Soperton, Georgia) published a "swell article" by James M. Lawton, "The Spell of the Swamps," which exuded "atmosphere and plenty of it."

The contact with nature not only evoked a new appreciation for the natural world; it also awakened a concern with how it was treated, complete with cautionary tales as to where abuse might lead. Gerald J. McIntosh of Company 1780, a veteran outfit at Mt. Nebo, Arkansas, was one who was given pause by a scene common in America: the sale of Christmas trees. When he heard "A huckster loudly cry/Through snow and cutting sleet/Christmas trees for fifty cents.... My mind went out to stately trees/Back in the forest green/That I had left the day before—/May God preserve that scene!" He strongly deplored that "trees of beauty, made by God/Were piled upon the ground," and "butchered cruelly thus," were now sold for only fifty cents.[32]

Another poet, writing in the *Stockade*, was similarly moved to address the matter of animal extinction: "Mine Will Never the Privilege Be": "Mine was never the privilege to see/A great cloud of Passenger Pigeons passing over me," nor would he have the privilege to feel "A game grayling gripping my reel." He hoped that humankind would take steps to save other animals from the same fate.[33]

But to some of the men this adoration of nature went too far in one respect, at least: There were simply too many reprintings of Joyce Kilmer's poem "Trees." One result was a spate of spoofs, such as one by Jim Duffy of Company 366 at Elimsport, Pennsylvania, entitled "Trees—An Irreverent Parody." He confessed that he did not know why the poet raved about trees, Duffy calling their roots "hungry mouths," for instance. "I wish [he'd] try to dig 'em out," he opined, and as to "nests of robins" in their hair, who needed that?[34]

Nature sometimes exacted tolls; it had its harsher side which sometimes struck down the unwary, the careless, or simply the unlucky. Snakes were a threat that many enrollees encountered for the first time, sometimes with unfortunate results. To instruct the men in his area about dangerous reptiles, a doctor in Pennsylvania captured two live rattlers for display. In another camp, where the enrollees seemed less fearful, a rattler was regarded as the camp mascot until it nipped the finger of one of them, "and thus signed its own death certificate." In another incident, Kenneth Bacon of Company 901, Pine Valley, California, was bitten twice within the short span of a few days, though he recovered "nicely."[35]

To be sure, the preoccupation with rattlesnakes produced much misinformation and many myths about them, some of which were even perpetuated by forest rangers. A debate ensued in the pages of *Happy Days* on the matter, and hopefully many errors were rectified.[36]

Not all of the men feared the vipers, however; snake hunters soon learned "what swell souvenirs the rattles make," and the skin could be fashioned into belts, which were often featured in arts and crafts projects. The men of Company 1448 at Okefenokee Swamp, Georgia, were also not over-awed by rattlesnakes and often held snake fights in the company street as a Sunday afternoon diversion, featuring king snakes vs. rattlesnakes. "Everyone knows that the king snake is a sure bet to win," one account in *Happy Days* explained, "but nevertheless it is interesting to watch the writhings and contortions until the king snake gets a strangle hold on the rattler and slowly applies the pressure until the rattler ceases to breathe." While it might be acceptable to engage in this pastime, when the men of Company 1791, Custer, South Dakota, pitted a badger against a dog, the local Humane Society protested. Nevertheless, the camp commander insisted that "the camp was a military reservation," and continued to allow such encounters.[37]

Other contacts with nature were of a different sort. In some of the western states, prairie dogs were destroyed in large numbers as vermin; the men spread poisoned oats over wide areas to control their numbers. Another animal that did not fare well at the hands of the CCC was the porcupine, regarded as "the greatest [animal] enemy of the pine forests," exceeded only by fire. Therefore, the CCC was sometimes engaged in porcupine eradication programs.[38]

Other extermination activities concerned the cordially hated mosquito. In many camps where these were present, they were collected and sent to the U.S. Army Medical Corps or the Department of Agriculture for scientific study. These agencies also planned to prepare the first complete map of their range throughout the country.[39]

Another side of nature concerned violent storms which often damaged or destroyed CCC camps. For example, in late August 1933, major tempests racked camps in Pennsylvania, Maryland and Virginia, wholly or partly destroying nine of them by flood and wind, and killing one man. Lightning took an additional toll; a strike on a recreation tent of Company 132 in Lewiston, Maine, killed four men and injured 20 others. In October of 1934, a tornado hit the barracks of Company 1773 in Maryville, Missouri, killing five CCC enrollees, injuring others, and virtually destroying the camp.[40]

Pets were part of the natural world as well, and where there are boys, there are usually dogs. Inevitably, therefore, most CCC camps boasted of their canine inhabitants. When Company 297 departed New York for

Heppner, Oregon, a dog of the outfit, "Hungry," had an adventure recorded in two of the outfit's subsequent papers, *The Heppner Roundup* and *Scraps 'N' Stuff.* It transpired that when a train stopped in La Junta, Colorado, "Hungry" left the train and failed to reboard. A wire sent back to the station revealed that he was indeed there, and that it would cost $13 to ship him on to Oregon. A collection was taken up, and their pet was soon again in their midst.[41]

Transcending the negative side of nature, an awakened awareness of the country and its natural wonders among CCCers undoubtedly contributed to the development of patriotism and a recognition of an investment in the nation earned by their own toil on its land and in its forests. To some extent—if not usually recognized or expressed as such—former enrollees on active military service later apprehended more fully why they fought, and the environmental movement also no doubt benefitted therefrom.

12

Advertising

"Don't patronize our advertisers; they quit us."
— *The Cheningo Clarion*
(Company 1264, Truxton, New York)

Unlike *The Cheningo Clarion*, however, *Happy Days* was decidedly of another opinion. The national paper strongly urged the men to support patrons who advertised in the paper because they were interested in the CCC, "quite apart from the return they get from their advertising. They think it's a great movement and deserving of what support they can give it by way of advertising in ITS newspaper." Many camp papers did likewise. In some Corps areas, commanding officers forbade ads by their interpretation of Army regulations which seemed to prohibit them, but this interpretation was not universal. In some areas, the matter was left in the hands of individual company commanders, and "what he says goes."[1]

The ads were often crudely drawn illustrations in hand-written or hand-printed script, and in content were typical of those appearing in the national press. Yet there were some notable innovations and initiatives. Some of the camp papers enjoyed close relations with local merchants, selling a fairly extensive array of advertising. Typically, *The Catskill Crier* (Company 299, Masonville, New York) asked readers not only to patronize advertisers, but to thank them for their ads as well, because merchants made it possible for the company to purchase rebuilt typewriters and educational equipment and other things. Some papers found that advertising enabled them better to relate to local businesses and communities. Most ads were for cleaning establishments, barbers, cafes, and other shops, but occasionally advertising for alcoholic beverages appeared, a rarity in CCC papers: "Specify Ramshead Ale, The Aristocrat of Ales Exclusively Distributed by Orange-Crush, Binghamton Bottling Corp." More traditional was an ad for Serling's Market, Binghamton, New York, where the men were urged to "Meat Me For Meat." Another carried the boast of Spencer's Dairy of Sidney, New York: "We milk our COWS not our CUSTOMERS." Short notices were common, such as: "Compliments Dr. D.S. Grant," or "Compliments Taylor's Hardware." *The Bugle* (Company 4468, Barnwell, South Carolina), as did other papers, also employed clever slogans: "Come clean with us and we will treat you white," was the promise of the Stark Empire Laundry in Augusta, Georgia; and "We minister to soles in need," was the lofty mission of the Williston Shoe Shop, apparently of Barnwell. And an ad for Ida's Cafe appearing in the *Chanticleer*, (Company 4725, Alcester, South Dakota) read: "Come in and see our waitress. We also have tasty food."[2]

Happy Days, not being an official paper, was under no restrictions by the Army nor anyone else, and entered fully into advertising from the outset, though it was not until the autumn of 1935 that it included a classified section. And it had something to sell to advertisers. It reached a rather large market of almost 300,000 men with new needs and outlooks that might be exploited.

One of the paper's significant innovations in advertising grew out of the establishment of camp exchanges or canteens which furnished simple articles of personal needs to the enrollees. Usually managed by enrollee canteen stewards, these emporia had been in existence since the very beginning. No federal funds were used in their establishment and operation, nor were they officially sponsored, but, as Robert Fechner once observed in testifying before the Congress, "we think they have contributed substantially to the welfare of the boys and to the morale of the camps." The canteens' profits indeed underwrote much activity at the camps, making it possible to rent motion pictures; buy camp athletic equipment, radios, pianos, ping-pong and pool tables; and furnish recreation halls. In some camps, canteens also supported company dances, paid for visiting entertainers, and supported the publication of the company paper. Impressed by their activity, *Happy Days* created a long-running feature "Behind the Counter" to support them, and which coincidently assisted *Happy Days* in its development as an advertising medium.[3]

Ever mindful of the CCC's role as educator, *Happy Days* recognized that the canteens provided an excellent opportunity to instruct and encourage young men in commercial pursuits, good business practices and the art of advertising. "The customer is always right," one column reminded canteen stewards, noting that this formulation had originated in the adjustment department of a large store organization, the adjusters being told to see that every customer was satisfied, and instructed to make whatever "adjustments were demanded without argument." This view was sound, the column went on, because the "customer is the boss with power of life and death over any business," and "should be treated that way." Even if customers were unreasonable—"not to mention inconsiderate and ungrateful"—"that's all right, too," because "they still have the money to spend and they can spend it with you or with some other storekeeper. Therefore, don't treat [them] rough ever."[4]

As to ads, they were "simply a part of the process of selling the products of every industry," and "the results of any advertising campaign depend entirely on what the customer decides to do about it." Ads informed customers about merchandise as well as stimulating their desire to buy. Simply because people were able to buy, they might not do so, the stewards were reminded. They had to be constantly pressed to use their purchasing power. Stewards were advised that canteens were "to sell goods, not to be a warehouse," and "when you run out of things to advertise it's time to advertise your business for sale."[5]

"Behind the Counter" was often used to alert camp canteen stewards to the arrival of new products and how to feature them. They could also reap the benefits of national advertising; it was recognized that about 90 percent of the products sold in the camp canteens were promoted nationally. For instance, 1935 was a banner year for the introduction of new candy bars as chocolate manufacturers sought to take advantage of the fact that five million candy bars were sold each month in CCC camps. The new products included Old Nick, "America's Outstanding Nut Roll"; Bit-O-Honey, "The Candy Delight for the Grownup Appetite"; and the Jack Dempsey Chocolate Bar, featuring Jack Dempsey's picture on the wrapper, and his quote: "I've tried them all—this is the best." The latter went head-to-head with "Walter Johnson's Heavyweight Champ," the quarter-pound Power House, truly "A Husky Candy Bar for Husky Men." In 1937, the Curtiss Candy Company brought out a new offering, Baby Ruth, followed by Peter Paul with its Mounds and Dream bars. These new arrivals openly challenged an older favorite, O'Henry, which, aware of the new threats, stepped up its advertising. But *Happy Days* advised that the keen competition could work to the advantage of the camp canteens. For instance, because "most fellows like to try something new," an "on-the-ball canteen" might treat enrollees to taste tests, publicizing the results.[6]

There were other treats. Planters began advertising Planters Salted Peanuts in *Happy Days* in early 1937. At about the same time, Mail Pouch, the first chewing tobacco to do so, began advertising in the paper. Wrigleys Spearmint Gum began an advertising campaign in the paper also in early 1937, the company being well aware that the average chewing gum sales per month were over $10 per camp, making a total of over $21,000 throughout the CCC, a market worth cultivating.[7]

Happy Days decided that its propensity to stage contests could be extended to the area of advertising. In the spring of 1937, the paper introduced a contest with the substantial first prize of $10 to be awarded for the best paragraph, poem or story using the names of the major products sold in CCC canteens and advertised in *Happy Days*. The winner was Agnar Swanson of Ft. Snelling, Minnesota, who worked the names of the products into an account of a baseball game entitled: "What a Game." This involved a pitcher, "'Pudge' Planters," on the "Mounds"; a deficient fielder, "Butterfingers"; a fine hitter, "Heavyweight Champ"; and a man, who if he had the "Wings" of an angel, could steal bases with ease.[8]

Though the column "Behind the Counter" was terminated some time before the CCC or *Happy Days* ended, it remained for a number of years an outlet for information and instruction in the arts of good business and sound fiscal practices, as well as the finer points of advertising.

Much of the advertising in *Happy Days* was typical of that appearing in the nation's papers of the period. The national news magazines also advertised heavily in the CCC papers. *Argosy*, for instance, announced that its issue of September 23, 1933, included a complete novel by F.R. Pierce, *Wooden Soldiers*. Hailed as "a palpitating, thrilling yarn of how a Reforestation Buddy bucked the depression singlehanded," it seemed most appropriate for CCC enrollees.

Happy Days, on occasion, advertised booklets and leaflets available to the enrollees at nominal sums to cover postage and handling through its Washington Service Bureau. Some titles were: *Stamp Collecting, Correct English, Indian Names, Etiquette for Everybody, Favorite Poems, Popular Screen Stars, Bible Facts*, and information on birds and animals, education, science, aviation and radio.[9]

Certain books seemed appropriate to the CCC setting. Patriotism was a concern of many within the CCC and *Happy Days* thought that a 50-cent book by Colonel William H. Waldron, U.S. Army, *Flags of America*, including color pictures and histories of each of the nation's flags, might be of help. Or, for a quarter, enrollees could buy from *Happy Days* the publication *Your Army*, a short informative book describing the U.S. Army, which might have encouraged enlistments. Rather less martial was the book *Manners for Millions* [author unknown], costing enrollees 89 cents per copy.[10]

When war loomed in the late 1930s, and fears of spies and fifth column activity became almost a national mania, *Happy Days* strongly recommended that "everyone in the CCC" should read George Britt's *The*

Fifth Column Is Here. The book directly addressed a nation-wide scare, widely reported in the nation's press, that there would be a major sabotage plot triggered on Memorial Day 1941. Britt's book included "amazing, blood-chilling facts" on the matter and even "dared to name NAMES!" Some important people in the movement "[held] important executive jobs," Britt—an early-day Joseph McCarthy—maintained. Indeed, some were "heads of key industries," he charged, while "others were installed in high American political and military circles."[11]

With many members of the CCC engaged in feeding the men, knowledge of chow preparation seemed necessary, and *Happy Days* was more than happy to instruct them. The publication *Army Mess Management Simplified* by Major E. A. Hyde, U.S. Army, was advertised as a "must" for CCC messes. When Captain Clifford Allen Kaiser of the Field Artillery Reserve published his appropriately named *Group Feeding*, which included details on operating a company mess, *Happy Days* likewise strongly recommended the 400-page book, though it cost a rather hefty three dollars and fifty cents.[12]

In addition, many of the ads in *Happy Days* had to do with food and its handling and preparation. Food companies found a readily exploited field in the Corps. In one issue of *Happy Days*, Kellogg's Wheat Krispies presented a page-long ad announcing cash prizes restricted to CCC men with the first place being a substantial $50, second, $20 and lesser awards for 27 others. Contestants were to write a paragraph on "Why I Like Kellogg's Wheat Krispies," a recently introduced cereal. One winning contestant appreciated the cereal because when "You're out achoppin' brush/Or swinging on a pick/Their goodness seems to stick."

The firm Seidel and Sons of Chicago, makers of griddle cake and buckwheat pancake mix, offered to provide samples to any company mess officer requesting them. In addition, the firm presented a copy of the Constitution of the United States to each CCC company "as a slight contribution on our part to the greatest of all peace time movements—the Civilian Conservation Corps."[13]

Other food companies tried to make themselves useful to the CCC while advertising their goods and services. One of the most aggressive in this regard was General Foods, which ran an ongoing advertising feature "On the Range with Sam Skillet," a "Dope Sheet" published monthly in *Happy Days* for a number of years. Therein "Sam" suggested 10-day menu schedules which included special holiday menus. Each menu was calculated to feed 100 men; cooks could adjust the menus to their own needs. "Sam" was aware of the special needs of the CCC camps and his noonday offerings were "designed to be transported wherever your crews are working … [while] night meals are correspondingly heartier and supply food elements that are necessary to balance the day's ration." The noon repasts might feature sandwiches and perhaps lamb goulash or soup, while the evening meals included omelets, salmon dishes, or veal cutlets. All of his menus naturally suggested General Foods' products.[14]

It was not until near the end of the long run of *Happy Days* that alcoholic beverages were advertised, but certainly these restrictions did not apply to soft drinks. Thus, the familiar Pepsi-Cola cops "Pepsi and Pete" graced the pages of *Happy Days*, as did Moxie soda, that peculiarly New England drink bottled by The Moxie Company in Boston.[15]

Tobacco companies sensed a golden opportunity with the appearance of the CCC. By 1936, "Behind the Counter" calculated that sales of cigarettes within the camps reached 300,000 cartons per month, with perhaps another 100,000 bought outside. Of course, this was not much of the total market (it was estimated that Americans smoked 150 billion cigarettes in 1936), but it was nevertheless well worth some advertising in the CCC press. Consequently, tobacco companies remained among the most active of *Happy Days*' advertisers. Undoubtedly, tobacco was one of the major drugs of choice during these years, extending into the years of World War II. Aware of its addictive properties, Leland E. Rice of Company 1633, Doty, Washington, in a *Happy Days* column "Vagabond Vagaries" bemoaned the fact that "even though we often belittle Lady Nicotine with the most unfriendly names, we are never quite ready to call it 'quits.'"[16]

The tobacco companies certainly hoped that, far from calling it "quits," CCC enrollee smokers would increase exponentially. To these ends, for many years Chesterfield—manufactured by the Liggett and Myers Tobacco Company—reserved the bottom half of the last page of *Happy Days* for its advertising. The paper once paid a "sincere tribute" to the company for being "our first advertiser," providing monetary support in the early days, enabling the paper to increase in size and expand its operations "until other advertisers recognized the importance of the CCC market and placed their advertising in *Happy Days*." Chesterfields continued to advertise in the paper until the September 27, 1941, issue. The company apparently decided subsequently to concentrate on the growing military establishment, an even more fruitful field for the investment of its advertising dollars.[17]

In January 1935, the R.J. Reynolds Tobacco Company, makers of the popular Camel brand, entered the picture to challenge Chesterfields. Camel ads, in the national press as well, featured prominent men of science, sportsmen, race car drivers and, seeking to capitalize on the avid interest in aviators in the 1930s, focused on such stalwarts as Col. Roscoe Turner, famed "ace of the skyways," who won several aviation awards such as the Bendix Trophy. Baseball stars, including the "Friendly Enemies," hitter Joe DiMaggio of the New York Yankees, and William

"Bucky" Waters, pitcher of the Cincinnati Reds, who met in the 1939 World Series, claimed to be "Camel fans." Chesterfields also emphasized well-known personalities in its advertising, once highlighting the "famous movie couple," Ronald Reagan and Jane Wyman.[18]

As new brands of cigarettes came onto the market, their ads duly appeared in *Happy Days.* Among these were Wings, Old Golds, Domino, and Marvels. Later, Philip Morris began advertising in *Happy Days,* adding its rather "splashy" ads to the others in the paper. However, Philip Morris was a 15-cent cigarette, unlike the many others selling for 10 cents per pack, and did not gain as much popularity as a consequence.[19]

In the January 11, 1936, issue of *Happy Days,* the "Behind the Counter" column reported that Prince Albert tobacco was scheduled to begin advertising in the paper and that exchanges should be ready to exploit the new opportunities. By April, the advent of the new product led to an interesting innovation: pipe-smoking contests, which were "springing up in the CCC." Company 1189 of East Brewster, Massachusetts, seems to have begun the fad. *Happy Days,* desiring to standardize similar contests throughout the 2,158 CCC camps then in the country, asked the company for its rules. Free to use any type of pipe, each entrant was given the same amount of tobacco, and all pipes were inspected to ensure that they were empty. At a given signal, all pipes were lighted; all had to be lighted in the first 15 seconds, after which no second attempts were allowed. The winner was the enrollee who kept his pipe going the longest. The brand names or brand name of tobacco might be determined by the managers of each contest. Canteen stewards were urged to point out that "none can be a CCC champion pipe smoker without training and at least some natural abilities along smoking lines. You might point out these facts to your customers and urge them to spend all their leisure hours smoking your pipes and your tobacco in preparation for the camp contest."[20]

The first record, placed on the books by Company 1189, was 52 minutes, but Company 1171, North Adams, Massachusetts, claimed a new one of 62 minutes, only to have Company 1189 return with yet another of 67 minutes, 25 seconds, held by "Pop" Goff, who, for the moment at least, was the undisputed "U.S. CCC Pipe-Smoking Champion." This certainly was "something that you cannot take away from him without a lot of huffing and puffing," the paper declared.[21]

By early 1941, cigarette advertising in *Happy Days* became increasingly slanted toward the military, as when Camel cigarettes sought to tie together two generations of soldiers—fathers and sons. These ads stated that Camels were smoked by doughboys in the World War and now their sons, entering military service in ever-increasing numbers, were doing so as well.[22]

Clothing firms such as Stetson and Miller hats were also prominently featured in *Happy Days* and camp newspaper advertising. Other ads from clothiers enticed CCC men to wear tailored cloths in camp, at a reduced rate for themselves, or free clothes, and take orders from other enrollees. "Papa" Danko, a supply clerk, wrote a "memoir" in his company paper, *The Harbinger* (Company 698, Argyle, Wisconsin), in which he recalled the three years that he had spent in the CCC, and "with moist eyes," closed his account "with feeble hands and wavering voice, using not the words of Omar Khayyam, but my own, I am asking: 'Have you seen my latest samples in the Three Star Clothing lines and the Mason Shoes?'" *Happy Days* was pleased to report that hundreds of CCC men like "Papa" Danko had received practical experience and training in salesmanship under plans offered by such clothing firms as Progress Tailoring Company, Jim Foster, Inc., and Three Star Clothes, all of Chicago. As a consequence, having graduated to full-time jobs in the tailoring business, former enrollees were "making good."[23]

Numerous other companies sought to capitalize on the CCC market by recruiting men to serve as "authorized agents." Among these was Brown and Company featuring engraved Christmas cards; various radio companies pushing radios and radio kits; Gemsco of New York City with a complete line of emblems, ornaments, pillow tops and insignia; Everlast Pens; and even one company featuring leather ties. The latter were definitely "something new," and, looking like silk, the ties sold "on sight;" in fact, if the ads were to be believed, they were "sweeping the country." The ubiquitous pillows and pillow cases on fine satin or sateen, decorated with portraits of Roosevelt, the ideal Mother, or CCC emblems, intended for sending home to "Mom" were featured. These were especially pushed when Mother's Day rolled around, a tradition that prevailed in the armed forces later. *Happy Days* itself became a huge emporium for CCC merchandise: company flags and guidons, lapel buttons, stick pins, watch fobs, shoulder insignia, service stripes, felt and paper pennants, tie clasps, CCC commemorative coins, portrait rings, license plate holders for autos, embossed CCC Christmas cards, and much else.

Other firms sensed opportunity in the appearance of the CCC. A.G. Spalding and Brothers, a major manufacturer of athletic equipment, created a special Civilian Conservation Camp order department to handle the sales of its special sports kits designed for the camps. The most common kit, costing $89.25, consisted of basketballs; goals; footballs; playground balls; volley balls; playground bats; boxing gloves and punching bags; and horseshoe sets. Special kits included the boxing kit for $41.90, a volley ball kit for $12.30, and others.

The appearance of camp newspapers led to ads for gelatin and stencil duplicators by the Heyer Corporation of Chicago and others. With the popularity of typing as a subject of interest in the CCC camps, the Royal Typewriter Company widely advertised its products. Featuring the touch typing system, it offered free copies of its instructional handbook to members of camp typewriting classes. Similarly, the Gregg Publishing Company pushed its Gregg typing and shorthand systems, complete with appropriate books and manuals. Though many CCC enrollees were still too young to shave, nonetheless Gillette and Gem razors were regularly featured.

Another company which detected a wonderful business opportunity in the CCC program was the Brunswick-Balke-Collender Company of Chicago, makers of billiard tables. The company wanted "to do our part to help increase your recreational facilities" by making pocket billiard (pool) play possible "right in your own Camp for those who now are missing the chance to keep up their skill." To these ends, the company offered to provide reconditioned tables to the camps at a greatly reduced price. "They're not 'stylish'," the company admitted, "but they're good playing tables—substantial, well built and come complete with full equipment."[24]

The music business also bought considerable advertising space, ads ranging from harmonicas to music lessons and song books. The Rodeheaver Company of Philadelphia, for one, offered its songbook *Sociability Songs*, featuring stunt, pep, folk, patriotic, sacred, and black music. Along similar lines were ads for minstrel costumes, theater equipment and "plays of distinction for every need," as well as materials for arts and crafts and related projects so prevalent in the camps. Naturally, "Behind the Counter" got into the act, urging the enrollees to develop their musical talents, and for good measure, sought to ascertain the most popular song in the CCC. "Home on the Range" was apparently the winner.[25]

Hohner Harmonica appealed to individuals seeking to master a musical instrument, but also hoped to interest the camps in forming harmonica bands. The firm's widely circulated free book, *Harmonica Playing Made Easy*, was a likely means of opening the sales doors. On a grander scale, the James and Holstrom Piano Company of New York City, "realizing the importance of relaxation and diversion, and how vital a Grand Piano and Music is to increase the spirit of happiness amongst C.C.C. workers, in the fine construction work they are doing for the Nation," decided to make the camps a special offer: They would sell their specially-created Model "C.C.C. Premier" grand piano for $345. In this way, "the C.C.C. [would be] right up to date on its piano fashions." *Happy Days* also sought to encourage the men's piano talents by publishing illustrated lessons.[26]

Ever on the lookout for talent to both encourage and exploit, *Happy*

Days identified several cartoonists who contributed work to the paper who were then enabled to profit from their talent. One was Tom Doerer, who prepared a 20-lesson publication on modern cartooning published by the National Arts Guild, Washington, D.C., that the men could purchase "for less than you pay for your 'smokes.'" In this way, they could prepare for "a fascinating and profitable job with a newspaper, a syndicate, or in advertising."[27]

Films were a natural subject of considerable interest in the CCC and were often featured in advertising. One of the most active firms in this field was the Herman A. DeVry company of Chicago, which vowed to "Bring Broadway to Bull Creek." The Kodascope Libraries of New York City created a special CCC department to make films available for use in the camps. Not to be outdone, MGM made first-run films available to CCC camps at a special low rental rate.[28]

Unaccountably, other companies which might have profited from entry into the CCC market only belatedly, if at all, made a bid for the Corps' patronage. One was Greyhound Bus Lines. Only in 1939 did ads for the company appear in *Happy Days* and then only briefly.[29] Also late in appealing to enrollees were the catalog emporia such as Sears, Roebuck, and Company. That firm, however, did decide in the fall of 1938 to enter the CCC market, doing so with its customary verve and energy. In a splashy, full-page ad, Sears jumped in with both feet: "The Finest Thing in America … make no mistake about it … is still AMERICAN MANHOOD," this offering began, and concluded that "as fine American manhood as the world has ever seen is being made, right now, in the CIVILIAN CONSERVATION CORPS." Consequently, Sears wanted to keep in touch with the dynamic organization, and to do so, was "sending a spic and span new SEARS CATALOG to every C.C.C. camp in the United States," asking the company commander to put it in the camp library. Advising the men "never put off till tomorrow what you can order today," the firm promised that special attention would be accorded CCC enrollee orders: "we mean to fill [them on] the same day [they are] received."[30]

There was also improbable advertising in the camp papers and *Happy Days*. Luxury hotels and other establishments in New York City and elsewhere, no doubt wishing to associate their names with the successful CCC rather than seriously expecting business from enrollees— much as firms did during World War II when their products were temporarily off the market because of wartime priorities—often bought advertising space in CCC sheets. Among the New York City hotels featured were the Manhattan Towers and the Hotel Governor Clinton, the latter with daily rates of three dollars featuring bath, radio, a Servidor, and "circulating ice water." The Roosevelt at four dollars and up was pricier, but featured "rooms delightfully furnished in the early Colonial period." For entertainment, the vacationing CCC enrollee might like to drop in at The Wivel, "New York's Glamorous Scandinavian Cabaret," with its three nightly shows and wine, dinner and dancing, with no cover charge. CCC men finding themselves in Atlantic City, New Jersey, could stay at The Breakers, an ocean front hotel with rooms priced at six dollars per day with meals and private bath. In Baltimore, the Mount Royal Hotel was a bit more affordable, with its rooms at $2.50 per day on the European plan. The Corona Hotel in Montreal, Canada, likewise joined the parade, though how much CCC business it generated, probably very little, was not recorded.[31]

13

Conclusions

"Where there is no vision, the people perish."
—Proverbs 29:18

"The history of every nation is eventually written in the way in which it cares for the soil."
—FDR, as quoted in *The Harbinger*
(Company 698, Argyle, Wisconsin),
November, 1938

"The CCC ... is a 14 Karat opportunity."
—Humphrey Bogart, letter to *Happy Days*,
published in the March 7, 1942, issue

Placing FDR's CCC initiatives in historical perspective, an associate editor of *The Bugle* (Company 4468, Barnwell, South Carolina), W.A. Boyne, observed that the dark clouds of 1929 and 1930 had plunged many young men into despair, their ambitions "crushed by old man depression." Crying youth, "members of the lost generation," had filled the streets and highways, with only one prayer on their lips: "Give us a chance." But the only answer from those in power was that "we are afraid to take a chance." Crime intervened, the youth were forgotten and only the strong held on with faith in themselves and God. Their steadfastness was rewarded when President Roosevelt established the Civilian Conservation Corps. Instead of despair, any boy subsequently discharged from the CCC left "with a light of hope in his eye, and the faith that spell[ed] success."[1]

Three themes stand out regarding the CCC as revealed in the camp papers, all reinforced and borne out in contacts with CCC alumni. One

234

was evident early in the Corps' history: that of the almost immediate improvement in the conditions of the lives of the average enrollee. The men recognized the effects, a pattern that is even more easily appreciated from the vantage point of the present.

The men were at once grateful for, and proud of, their encounter with one of Roosevelt's most successful New Deal programs. Interviews with alumni of the CCC, and innumerable accounts in the contemporary CCC press, reveal that they were profoundly touched by their experiences. Entering the organization as boys, almost invariably they emerged as men—and to this day, they never tire of recounting the details. In some ways, it seems, CCCers who are still around cherish their experiences in the camps even more highly than their later military service. The reasons are not difficult to find: Their needs were greater in the 1930s, they were younger, and in many cases, the CCC was their first experience away from home, their first great adventure.

The CCC's way of life produced many testimonials appearing in both the camp papers and *Happy Days*. In a guest editorial in *Happy Days*, entitled, "I Struck a Home," Bill Briggs of Company 1240 in Death Valley, California, asserted that his CCC experiences had been salutary for him and his family: the rent had been paid at home, and as for himself, he had greatly improved his health. Similarly, James W. Danner styled himself a former "97-Pound Weakling [who turned] into [a] 'Bruiser.'" When he enrolled, he was "underweight and only partly recovered from a nervous breakdown ... he put on pounds, rose to senior leader and left the corps almost reluctantly to attend college." Company 297's *Tamarack Times* devoted space to paragraphs from representative members of the camp describing the benefits of the CCC. Nick Santullo had learned about mechanics and electricity, while Orlando Rocco admitted that "I came to the CCC for the adventure it promised ... and I got adventure all right." From Delaware he had traveled to the Pacific coast. Charles Williams, then first cook, had filled many CCC jobs, including generator man, electrician, first cook, and projection machine operator. He was accordingly assured that "there's a new life outside of camp and camp has given me the confidence to meet it." Malcolm Baucum, who served in Company 808 at Sulphur, Oklahoma, enjoyed another sort of triumph: He was subsequently elected to the Oklahoma State Legislature.[2]

To war veterans, the CCC was a safe haven in a time of dire economic and social dislocations. Regarded in some circles as disreputable, the vets—of whom almost 250,000 were eventually enrolled—sometimes battling alcoholism and much else, often found their footing again in the CCC. One of their number, Gilbert W. Cass, writing in *The Veterans' Bugle* (Company 2775, Mandan, North Dakota), concluded that the vets were "maintaining implicit faith in the future; we believe better times are in store for all of us who continue in our effort for self improvement. We still believe this great Country of ours was good enough to fight for and to live in...."[3]

Enrollees in the black companies, often guided by inspired educational advisers, sensed opportunities in the Corps to better themselves. Accordingly, they used the organization to good effect. Black enrollees, totalling over 200,000, also seized the opportunity to improve communication skills and develop an awareness of their race and the role that they should henceforth play in the nation's affairs.

An anonymous poet of Company 280 at Augusta, Montana, voiced his homage to the CCC and its role in his life. Writing in *The Drifters*, and using as a springboard Bob Hope's famous theme song, he well summed up an attitude common among the rank and file:

> Thanks for the memories,
> Of hash and beans and such,
> Those foods I wouldn't touch,
> Until the Conservation Corps
> Had changed me, oh, so much;
> How lovely it was.[4]

A second theme was a parallel betterment of the nation's physical condition, the consequence of the collective work projects undertaken. It was widely recognized that the CCC's program was largely two-fold in nature, and that "we are building good timber both on our hills and among our youth."[5] Ray D. Smith of Company 991, Feather Falls, California, elaborated, observing that in the early 1930s throughout the country he had witnessed young men with "the mark of shattered ambitions and blasted hopes written in their faces ... the result of fruitless tramping of the city streets showing in every stride." Appearing in the CCC camps, this "discouraged horde" had been inserted "into the life-giving, wine-laden air of the mountains for a fresh start." The results had been spectacular, and "this defeated army [had] been regenerated into a compact group which cannot and will not recognize defeat." Physically and morally rejuvenated, the men were proud of their work, all the while being "profoundly thankful to a generous government for the opportunity it has given [them]," a new beginning resting upon the fundamental foundation of "swinging the pick and shovel for a dollar a day and 'found.'"[6]

The men of the CCC gloried in their work projects, which, despite criticism from many quarters, were numerous, varied and often strikingly successful. By any standard, the accomplishments of the CCC were impressive. A profusion of sources reveal a convergence of views as to its importance. The *Wall Street Journal*, for one, opined that "the CCC is one part of the New Deal that we can all heartily approve." Over 3.4 million men had been enrolled by the time of its demise, and their erosion control projects had benefited approximately forty million acres of farmland. In addition, among other things 8,000 state parks were developed; 125,000 miles of roads were built; 814,000 acres of rangeland revegetated; between two and three billion trees were planted; over five million check dams and almost 50,000 bridges were built. The total value of the CCC's work to the nation was estimated to be over two billion dollars.

The CCC expanded its activities in the early summer of 1934 by establishing new camps in 22 drought-stricken states including South Dakota, Texas, Utah, Nebraska, New Mexico, Oklahoma, and Wyoming, when Congress appropriated fifty million dollars from drought relief. These included many veterans' outfits. Working under the U.S. Bureau of Reclamation of the Department of the Interior, as the dust bowl grew in intensity more and more CCC camps were earmarked for service in the plains states. One of their activities was the planting of shelterbelts of trees to help hold the soil in place.[7]

As time went on, the CCC was acclaimed for its willingness to fight forest fires. But such work was dangerous, and the CCC national headquarters designed a Certificate of Valor which Fechner on occasion awarded to members of the CCC for outstanding service, especially in flood rescue operations and for exceptional work in the burning forests. In all, over six million days were expended in fire fighting, in which 29 enrollees lost their lives.[8]

Where there were not fires, there was often too much water. The decade also witnessed major flooding in the United States. Many of the CCC companies were involved in much of the work of flood control by building dams and dikes, and also cleaning up after the floods had receded.

The scope, complexity, and often quite substantial undertakings of CCC projects were striking. In Stephenville, Texas, for instance, a 50,000-cubic-yard earth dam was built by CCC men working in double shifts. Company 1848 in Morrison, Colorado, undertook the massive task of constructing Red Rocks outdoor theater, still in use. Details of its activities were recorded in the pages of the company's paper, the *Red Rocks Echo*. Enrollees of Company 814 at Sandia Park landscaped the University of New Mexico campus at Albuquerque. Company 1908 at Montgomery Creek, California, built a major highway bridge. Sometimes, in emergency situations such as in blizzards in the winter of 1936, the CCC was called upon to feed endangered cattle and wildlife. Company 1741 at Mound City, Missouri, was designated a biological-forestry camp and worked on fish shelters.

Other enrollees on the White River in Arkansas helped to create the White River Migratory Waterfowl Refuge. Still others built quail and wild turkey hatcheries. The most important battlefields of the Civil War were restored as state and national parks. Other CCC camps were in the front lines against gypsy moth and blister rust infestations, as well as Dutch elm blight, not to mention a plague of Mormon crickets in Nevada, the latter fought by erecting miles of steel fences and constructing pit traps. Though there was already a monument to seagulls in Salt Lake City to commemorate earlier saviors against a similar plague, perhaps it was time for another to be dedicated to the CCC in Nevada, so *Happy Days* opined.[9]

Much of the work was routine, such as controlling the shifting sands on Hatteras Island, North Carolina, but other activities were more exotic. One involved about a hundred volunteers who accepted extreme cold temperatures, as well as being cut off from the remainder of the country, at a winter camp on Isle Royale, a remote, isolated island in upper Lake Superior. Under the direction of the National Park Service, the men cut out burned-over parts of the island, which a major forest fire had recently denuded, and in addition trapped moose for removal to the mainland in the spring.[10]

In Puerto Rico, one of America's territories, about 2,400 men were employed in forest conservation work. There also one of the outfits located, recovered and restored the wreck of an ancient Spanish galleon, buried beneath the sands at a site on Mona Island. In the Virgin Islands, enrollees were engaged in soil conservation programs and also drained numerous malarial swamps. In Alaska, facilities were constructed in support of military and civilian aviation. Many Eskimos and Indians were also engaged in archaeological evacuations and in the restoring of important parts of their heritage such as totem poles. CCCers in Hawaii's six camps planted over a million trees and also removed wild animals, including sheep, goats and pigs that had overrun the national parks, and built fences to keep them out. In addition, the camps also trained men for defense work, many of them eventually being engaged in the greatly expanding naval construction at Pearl Harbor.[11]

Pride in their accomplishments was considerable, as the poetry in numerous camp papers reveals. One example was by a friend of the CCC, Gretchen E. Green, who addressed the matter in a lively poem published in *Smudge,* the paper of Company 219 stationed at Shaker Place, New York:

Oh, East side, West side,
All around the town.
Boys from all the city
Most of whom were down.
Joined the C.C. Corps,
Without a lot of talk.
Chased Old Man Depression,
From the Sidewalks of New York.

An anonymous poet, writing in the *The Little Village Torch*, had further provocative comment:

Hordes of gullies now remind us
    We should build our lands to stay,
And, departing, leave behind us
    Fields that haven't washed away.
When our boys assume the mortgage,
    On the land that's had our toil;
They'll not have to ask the question,
    "Here's the farm, but where's the soil?"[12]

Something of the scope of their attainments was rather more fancifully described by a writer in the *Thousand Islander* (Company 1249, Fishers Landing, New York). Entitled "The Parable," his piece concerned a CCC enrollee who failed to get into heaven and was sent, instead, to hell. But there, he applied modern techniques to revamping it: he harnessed the fiery furnace for light and power; cooled the place with artificial refrigeration; drained the Brimstone Lake; flung bridges across the bottomless abyss; bored tunnels through the Obsidian cliffs; paved the streets; created gardens, parks and playgrounds, as well as lakes, waterfalls and beautiful rivers. "In fact he's been raising hell in Hell ever since he got there." His new creation led many of the "heavenly denizens" to begin to ask for transfers to the inferno.[13]

The third theme which emerged later but was no less striking was the preparation of the enrollees, the military, and other individuals and agencies for the nation's involvement in World War II. It is frequently alleged that the United States was ill-equipped for the waging of the war when it burst upon the nation after Pearl Harbor. In many respects, this was true, but partly because of the establishment and development of the CCC, the nation was in better shape than has been generally recognized. The Depression was one of the major defining events in the first half of the twentieth century for the United States. The historian Eric Bergerud elaborated: "The generation of young that fought World

War II was extremely well suited to the task. The formative event of their time was the Great Depression. Although a dreary period of history in almost every respect, the Depression helped mold a generation of youth uniquely qualified for war."[14]

FDR, in his Philadelphia speech accepting the Democratic renomination on June 27, 1936, prophetically noted that "there is a mysterious cycle in human events. To some generations much is given. Of other generations much is expected. This generation of Americans has a rendezvous with destiny." Indeed, it has been said that from those to whom much is given, much will be required. But what of a generation to which little was given yet much was also expected? From one perspective, the Depression experience seemed almost necessary as a "conditioner" for the nation's preparation for the far greater exertions and harsher demands of World War II, facts well documented in the CCC press. In a gritty, harsh, depressing decade, which sometimes bore out the truth of Thomas Hobbes' observation about life being "nasty, brutish and short," the CCC helped prepare for a time when his insight would be even more relevant.[15]

More to the point, writing in *Look* magazine, Major Leonard Nason of the Army Reserve forthrightly declared that "the basis for our new army should be the Civilian Conservation Corps which is now assigned to tasks of primarily non-military character ... [and was] a going, successful concern...." The CCC administration, he went on—which included many Army personnel—"knows more about camp sites, about procurement of supplies, about making cooperative teammates out of civilian youth than any other department of the government. They are practical men, solving problems daily with American youth—our great military potential, our manpower."[16]

When the draft was instituted, other military spokesmen recognized that the Army's experience in transporting and caring for large numbers of CCC enrollees would "prove extremely valuable in handling this [same] problem" created by the conscription law. Estimating that about 30,000 reserve officers had been involved, *Happy Days* editorialized that "the War Department ... soon recognized in the CCC ... a chance to teach many things a young officer should know ... handling men, running a mess, becoming acquainted with paper work, getting to know the ways, whys and hows of practical Army work. Also, Regular Army officers got a chance at experience with an 'army' in the field," and the Quartermaster Corps, The Medical Corps, and those in charge of finance and transportation, not to mention the Corps area commanders, and other high-ranking officers, obtained practical command experience.[17]

The man destined to be the Army Chief of Staff during the war, General George C. Marshall, in 1933 as commander of a battalion of the

8th Infantry and later the Regiment's commander at Fort Sereven, Georgia, and Fort Moultrie, South Carolina, was caught up "in a New Deal measure for which he developed and retained a great enthusiasm all his life—the Civilian Conservation Corps." Later as a brigadier general in command of the 5th Brigade of the 3rd Division stationed in Vancouver Barracks, Washington, he continued his work with the CCC. Thereby "mobilizing unlikely youths into effective work forces," he was well aware that these men would make promising soldiers. He "enthusiastically praised the CCC publicly as 'the greatest social experiment outside of Russia'," and described it as "a splendid experience for the War Department and the Army."[18]

General Douglas MacArthur, the Army Chief of Staff in the early 1930s, saw considerable value in the Army's involvement in the CCC. This had, he reported, "given renewed evidence of the value of systematic preparation for emergency, including the maintenance of trained personnel and suitable supplies and the development of plans and policies applicable to a mobilization."[19]

General Malin Craig, Army Chief of Staff in the later 1930s, identified other dimensions. Addressing the graduates of the U.S. Army Medical Field Service School, Carlisle Barracks, Pennsylvania, in 1938, he pointed out that one of the most difficult assignments given to Army medical men was in providing CCC enrollees with medical care; keeping camps sanitary and "free from contagious disease" was a challenge. But the low sick rates for the camps and the fact that the men returned to their homes "tremendously improved in health and physique," indicated that medical personnel were successful. Such improvements in the health of soon-to-be servicemen, as well as experience gained by medical personnel, were a boon to the country.[20]

Numerous testimonials and accounts affirmed these realities at various levels. For one thing, the CCC developed a sense of comradeship. The editor of *The Broadcast* (Company 1742, Gallatin, Missouri) asserted that the value of its group associations was a factor often overlooked. Men were accustomed to living and working together—an essential attribute of military life. In a letter, a former assistant leader of Company 2328 at Homer City, Pennsylvania, then in the engineers at Ft. Belvoir, Virginia, attested to the truth of these views, asserting that his time in the CCC had been beneficial because, "I learned discipline, to speak when spoken to, to be alert; to shower, shave, and shine my shoes every day. I learned table manners and learned not to loan or to borrow from anyone."

After the draft took effect, *Happy Days* was pleased to report that one out of six men drafted had CCC training, and they were making the best soldiers. Another highly placed observer, the Adjutant General of the Army, Major General James A. Ulio, concurred, noting that by early 1942 "hardly a large unit in the Army is without key men who owe their important assignments either in whole or in part to the training they had in the CCC." His assertions are strongly supported by innumerable interviews with CCC veterans who often stress with eloquence the role of the CCC in preparing them for their military service. Added to this was a sense of nationhood that the CCC had inculcated often by its transfering men to and fro throughout the United States. This is also borne out by this author's interviews with CCC veterans.[21]

While the CCC did not "teach soldiering," clearly it did give its members "a discipline combined with self-reliance that makes them readily convertible into good soldiers." As Robert Mueller, editor-in-chief of *Spruce Lake Splash* (Company 3707, Two Harbors, Minnesota) put it, the CCC was primarily to learn how to work, "and not fight." But "if on the other hand Uncle Sam decides we should learn more about war ... we will gladly do his bidding." They would subsequently prove this in unstinting measure.[22]

Despite their achievements, conversations with surviving enrollees frequently reveal fears that with their demise, all knowledge of their organization's accomplishments and their own considerable attainments will be forever lost. To these ends, they often strongly support the current AmeriCorps and Job Corps programs, regarding them as heirs, and continually renew appeals that the CCC be revived.

There are many reasons, however, why they will not be forgotten. For one thing, in 1977 the National Association of Civilian Conservation Corps Alumni was founded specifically "to remember and celebrate the efforts of the Civilian Conservation Corps." Headquartered at Jefferson Barracks in St. Louis, Missouri, it currently has over 140 local chapters with more than 7,000 members. There is a large museum and research center at the headquarters, and it issues a monthly publication, the *NACCCA Journal,* which serves as a clearing house for much information on the CCC, and frequently publishes rememberances and memoirs of former enrollees.

Nationwide, reunions at various levels and venues are scheduled, and many CCCers are active in erecting statues, plaques and other memorials to commemorate the organization's activities. Also former CCC camps and structures are being renovated as living reminders of past ways of life and accomplishments. This activity is supplemented by programs and exhibits of many state and local CCC museums and other institutions. No doubt to the great satisfaction of veteran CCCers, the U.S. Senate on March 15, 2002, passed Senate Resolution 207 declaring March 31 as "National CCC Day."

In addition, there are numerous accounts and sources delineating the details and essentials of the organization. Among those largely ignored are the CCC newspapers—the repositories of contemporary voices preserved in the printed word—which appeared in the thousands during this era. Prescient librarians at the University of Illinois and elsewhere in the country, with dedication, industry, and a clear vision, established the foundations for this rich archival source.

To be sure, the camp papers frequently were poor productions indeed, though *Happy Days* rarely was. Never mastering the use of mimeograph, some editors produced pages that were so faint as to be illegible. Other sheets were merely cobbled together, lacking sound makeup. In others, articles and editorials were inane and commonplace; poetry was beneath the level of doggerel; cartoons little more than stick figures; and the wit heavy-handed or sarcastic as authors unsuccessfully strived for irony.

Nevertheless, they include useful information and readers learn about daily life in the camps: what enrollees did; how they worked, what they thought, ate, wore; how they conducted themselves. Their choices of books, music, movies; what sports they played; how they worshipped God; these are all present. The details of their work and educational projects are recounted. The papers also served as safety and health bulletins. Furthermore, the CCC papers suggest something about the attitudes of enrollees, providing a means of probing those years when despair gave way to a guarded hope that "happy days" might indeed be close at hand.

In addition, outlets were provided for the men to express their deepest sentiments: their hopes, dreams, fears, aspirations and desires—and learn something about writing the English language in the process. In this regard, the *Echoes from the Valley* (Company 1697, Coon Valley, Wisconsin) once averred that no one "is really educated unless he has the power to express himself, and it has been generally conceded that a newspaper is the best medium of expression in the world today." Most of the CCC journals endeavoured to build camp morale, and served as diaries and repositories of the histories of certain individuals and companies. To some enrollees, the simple fact of the publication of their names and activities in their local sheets was a boon not to be denied.

The William Spratt News (Company 467, York, Alabama) saw other dimensions: The general public could be informed about the CCC, enabling it to form a balanced view of the organization. In addition, camp papers often "play[ed] up [the] success of men in jobs received thru training in the CCC." The editor of *The Bugle* (Company 727, West Plains, Missouri) also noted that the papers had a tendency to destroy cliques in camps, and by fostering a strong civic spirit encouraged cooperation between camps and communities.[23]

Certain it is that the papers were well received by many of their readers. A member of Company 1414, Soperton, Georgia, finding himself in the hospital, received a copy of the company's paper the *Southern Pine Whisper*, and wrote the editor, "If you had sent me an ounce of gold, it wouldn't have been more appreciated than *The Whisper*."[24]

The good work done by camp papers was sometimes recognized and acknowledged. Captain J.A. Wallace, the commanding officer of Company 874 in Tempe, Arizona, who was returning to regular army duty, attributed "the present high standards of conduct and performance in this company," to the excellent material in the unit's paper, *Snappy Daze*. "I have been in a position to know that the paper was frequently produced under the most trying circumstances but always without complaint and in accordance with the best traditions of the press."[25]

It was also well-known that being on the camp newspaper staffs could result in employment outside the CCC, and editors especially tended to "make good" in the larger world of journalism. When the *Valpariso News*, a weekly paper of Valpariso, Florida, went out of business, the men of nearby Company 1402, Niceville, Florida, decided to take it over and run it. Two ex-editors from the top-flight paper, *The Genessee Gazette* (Company 201, Castile, New York), Bob Feeney and Franch Recchio, both landed positions as reporters, Feeney with the *Buffalo Evening News* and Recchio at the *Batavia* (New York) *Weekly*.

Rather more impressive was the case of L.H. Lindstrom, outstanding editor of several first-rate CCC papers, who became the editor of *The Walker Pilot* at Walker, Minnesota. The CCC gave him his chance, he acknowledged, explaining that "those camp papers over which I had spent so many weary hours of labor to produce were an open sesame into professional newspaperdom. The fact that I was not a college graduate was overlooked." Indeed, he declared, he would not trade his seven years in the CCC for a four-year college education.[26]

What the camp papers were all about to many staffers was expressed poignantly in a comment in *Happy Days*: "[That] 'printer's ink never wears off,' as the old phrase has it, is an almost infallible truth. Whatever the victims wind up doing in the long run they always remain lushly sentimental about their days of intimacy with the printed word, however brief the association or obscure the journal."[27]

The CCC camp papers were lacking in subtlety, manifesting a basic, raw honesty in reporting details of the conditions in the CCC, evoking the plainness and straightforwardness of life as it was lived, often conveyed in a free-wheeling style. There was little sham; much came from the heart and the often immature minds of the enrollees—all decades before "political correctness" was even heard of. Instead of PC, indeed, they manifested "VC"—verve and candor. Therefore this journalism conveyed how CCCers truly and honestly felt, producing a panorama of life in the round of daily endeavors, and revealing the way enrollees truly were—peccadillos, blemishes, major faults and all. After all, editors and reporters had only themselves and their peers to dazzle; only their buddies to impress. Newspapers mimicked what they were familiar with as to ads, columnists, and sports for example, but beyond that, spoke with their own distinctive voices whether veteran, black or other benighted youth of the era. They were plainly inspired by a leadership empowered by an administration that saw their needs and sought to remedy the faults and failures of preceding governments and men in government accustomed to *laissez faire*, clearly appreciating and understanding that something must therefore be wrong with *laissez faire*.

The CCC made a timely arrival, helping to pull the U.S.A.—phoenix-like—out of the Depression years. Having been involved in their nation at the basic levels of soil, bedrock, forests and fields, CCCers additionally drew upon shared experiences lived in close-knit groups accustomed to functioning as a team in their peer societies. The men rallied to each other in a rough and ready *camaraderie*. Often far from home and its comforts, they built their own universe and depended on each other as they later would on the globe's far-flung battlefields. These conditions produced greatly valued and useful attitudes about the country and themselves, and predisposed responses to the unexpected, often horrific, challenges of the ensuing conflict, responses which proved to be a prescription for success in World War II. The CCC also helped resurrect America's military forces in the nick of time to begin the exacting of a terrible vengeance on one of the most massive threats ever posed to Western civilization: the collective power of Nazi Germany, Fascist Italy and the militarists of Japan. The camp newspapers provide students of the era of the Great Depression and World War II with unique avenues into this developmental process, while remaining a key "primary documentation of the day-to-day activities, amusements and musings of the young men who participated in one of the most extensive social relief programs in U.S. history."[28]

Chapter Notes

Preface

1. Abraham F. Cohen, "A Tribute To The Civilian Conservation Corps," *The Alaskan*, April 20, 1940.
2. The CCC program extended from April 5, 1933, to June 30, 1942.

Introduction

1. The paper was so named because the company was then stationed at Kanona, New York.
2. Guest editorial by Paul A. Coleman, Company 1329, Salisbury, Pennsylvania, in *Happy Days*, May 9, 1936.
3. The verve of the CCC experience was contagious. Robert Fechner, head of the CCC, in early July 1933 informed the President that the success of the early phases of the program was assured, and *Happy Days* happily informed its readers, the "first bridge to span what seemed a bottomless pit of unemployment and dejection," was now in place, and the great hosts of the unemployed were prepared to march "over [that] bridge of cheers and smiles that marks the first big span across the abyss of dank depression." *Happy Days*, July 8 and July 15, 1933.
4. As quoted in James J. McEntee, *Now They Are Men: The Story of the CCC* (Washington, D.C.: National Home Library Foundation, 1940), p. xii. McEntee, Fechner's assistant from the beginning, was the second director of the Civilian Conservation Corps, taking over following Fechner's death on December 31, 1939.
5. *Ibid.*, p. 1.
6. There was little provision for women and girls. There were a few experimental camps created, such as Camp Tera, On-The-Hudson, a camp set up by The Emergency Relief Asociation—hence Camp Tera—by the initiative of Mrs. Roosevelt for 200 needy New York City girls. Other camps also existed for a time. They were facetiously referred to as "She-She-She" camps by their male contemporaries. See lengthy article on Camp Tera in *Happy Days*, August 12, 1933.
7. McEntee, *Now They Are Men*, pp. 1–8. There have been numerous studies of the CCC. These include the standard work by John A. Salmond, *The Civilian Conservation Corps, 1933–1942: A New Deal Case Study* (Durham, North Carolina: Duke

247

University Press, l967); Leslie Alexander Lacy, *The Soil Soldiers. The Civilian Conservation Corps in the Great Depression* (Radnor, Pennsylvania: Chilton Book Company, 1976); John D. Guthrie, *Saga of the CCC* (Washington, D.C.: American Forestry Association, 1942); and an extensive report by the American Youth Commission, *The Civilian Conservation Corps* (Washington, D.C.: The American Youth Commission, 1940). A pictorial presentation of interest is Stan B. Cohen, *The Tree Army: A Pictorial History of the Civilian Conservation Corps, 1933–1942* (Missoula, Montana: Pictorial Histories Publishing Company, 1980). A useful bibliography has been compiled by the Office of the Director, Civilian Conservation Corps: *Civilian Conservation Corps Bibliography. A List of References on the United States Civilian Conservation Corps* (Washington, D.C.: Office of the Director, Civilian Conservation Corps, 1939). The major archival source for study of the CCC is Record Group 35, located in the National Archives, Washington, D.C. The basic finding aid is: Douglas Helms, *Preliminary Inventory of the Records of the Civilian Conservation Corps* (Washington, D.C.: National Archives and Records Service, General Services Administration, 1980).

    8. See series of articles entitled "The March into the Forests," in *Happy Days*, September 30; October 7, 14, 21, 28; November 4, 1933, which outline a history of CCC, and the roles played by the major departments and agencies.

    9. As quoted in McEntee, *Now They Are Men*, pp. 9–10.

    10. Details of the debates surrounding the creation of the CCC are summarized in Salmond, *The Civilian Conservation Corps*, pp. 13–23.

    11. See Kenneth Holland and Frank Ernest Hill, *Youth in the CCC* (Washington, D.C.: American Council on Education, 1942), note 2, p. 7. Though commonly referred to as the Civilian Conservation Corps from the outset, it was not until June 28, 1937, that the Congress officially recognized this name.

    12. This Act is reproduced in Ovid Butler, ed., *Youth Rebuilds. Stories from the C.C.C.* (Washington, D.C.: The American Forestry Association, 1934), pp. 188–89.

    13. Some of their stories and reflections are recounted in *ibid.* and other sources.

    14. There is a discussion of these two men in Salmond, *The Civilian Conservation Corps*, pp. 27–29. See also in Ray Hoyt, *"We Can Take It": A Short Story of the C.C.C.* (New York: American Book Company, 1935), p. 19. Fechner and McEntee ran the CCC from its inception to its dissolution. Fechner himself had gone to work when he was 16, and had been a member of the machinists' union for 37 years. As a railroad machinist, he had traveled over a large part of the United States and Mexico, and in Central and South America. Since 1914, he had been a member of the General Executive Board of the International Association of Machinists. He had played a prominent part in the 1901 fight for a nine-hour working day, and in 1915 for the eight-hour day. He had lectured on labor economics at Harvard, Brown, and Dartmouth. He first met FDR in Washington in World War I.

    15. The Office of the Director was located at Washington, D.C., and consisted of the Divisions of Selection, Investigations, Safety, Planning and Public Relations, Research and Statistics, and Automotive and Priorities. Liaison officers and special investigators made up the field staff.

    16. McEntee, *Now They Are Men*, pp. 26–27. After May 15, 1939, the Director's Office took over the supervision of selecting enrollees from the Department of Labor. As to the men themselves, and their expected attitudes, see anonymous editorial in *The Pyramid* (Company 698, Oak Hill, Illinois), April 21, 1934, entitled "Your New Opportunity."

    17. See pictures of the nine Army Corps commanders in *Happy Days*, May 20, 1933.

    18. For details of these operations, see Holland and Hill, *Youth in the CCC*, pp. 25–42.

    19. These details are in McEntee, *Now They Are Men*, pp. 54–56; Holland and Hill, *Youth in the CCC*, pp. 29–36.

20. See account in *Happy Days*, April 25, 1936.
21. See in Salmond, *The Civilian Conservation Corps*, p. 45. See *ibid.*, pp. 26–45, for a detailed discussion of the mobilization of the CCC. General Douglas MacArthur, the Army Chief of Staff, also praised the nine Corps area commanders upon their completing the initial task of getting the men into the forest camps. Seventy-three conditioning camps on military reservations throughout the U.S. had been employed in the work. MacArthur in official boiler-plate had this to say: "Only a high morale, spirit of cooperation, pride of service, and devotion to duty could have accomplished such splendid results. I extend to you and all members of your command my sincere appreciation of this great accomplishment. It was well done, Army." *Happy Days*, July 8, 1933.
22. See articles in *Happy Days*, August 5 and September 30, 1933.
23. Initially, there were 72 camps on the reservations. See article in *ibid.*, May 20, 1933.
24. See Holland and Hill, *Youth in the CCC*, note 5, p. 32.
25. In later years, the family allotments were reduced with the enrollee keeping a greater share. See in McEntee, *Now They Are Men*, p. 34; *Happy Days*, November 9, 1940, and February 14, 1942.
26. The leadership positions were created on June 17, 1933. See discussion in *Happy Days*, June 17, 1933. The rated men often wore badges to indicate their rank. See in *ibid.*, September 23, 1933.
27. Naturally, there was a latrine, which some called "the house of commons" because "there's so much arguing always going on there." *Ibid.*, September 9, 1933.
28. At the General Staff, Colonel Duncan K. Major, Jr., was in charge of the Army's participation in the work. See article in *ibid.*, May 20, 1933.
29. McEntee, *Now They Are Men*, pp. 32–33.
30. Initially 169 Naval medical officers were selected. See in *Happy Days*, May 20, 1933. On June 17, 1933, a first call of 130 chaplains was made.
31. For additional details on this subject, see Chapter V below.
32. CCC enrollment did not exempt the men from compulsory military service when the draft was instituted in 1940.
33. McEntee, *Now They Are Men*, pp. 38–39, and article in *Happy Days*, May 20, 1933. This uniform was introduced into the country section by section over a rather long period of time.
34. *Happy Days*, May 20, 1933.
35. See Frank Ernest Hill, *The School in the Camps: The Educational Program of the Civilian Conservation Corps* (New York: American Association for Adult Education, 1935).
36. Salmond, *The Civilian Conservation Corps*, p. 47.
37. *Happy Days*, August 26, 1933 and December 29, 1934.
38. Details of these battles are in Salmond, *The Civilian Conservation Corps*, pp. 58–70. In late June 1935, the National Youth Administration was created by FDR by executive order. Coming under the Works Progress Administration, the NYA also emphasized training and educational initiatives.
39. Discussion in McEntee, *Now They Are Men*, p. 52.
40. *Happy Days*, April 29, May 6, and August 5, 1939; McEntee, *Now They Are Men*, p. 53.
41. See this law as quoted in McEntee, *Now They Are Men*, pp. 65–67.
42. *Ibid.*, pp. 67 and 69.
43. *Happy Days*, May 24 and June 21, 1941.
44. *Ibid.*, August 2, 1941.
45. *Ibid.*, October 4, 1941.
46. *Ibid.*, February 7, 1942.
47. *Ibid.*, February 21, 1942.

48. *Ibid.*, March 14 and April 11, 1942.
49. See *Congressional Record*, 77th Congress, 2nd Session, Vol. 88, Part 4, p. 5789; *Happy Days*, July 4, 18, 25; August 1 and 8, 1942.
50. For statistics of the CCC's accomplishments, see Stan Cohen, *The Tree Army: A Pictorial History of the Civilian Conservation Corps, 1933–1942* (Missoula, Montana: Pictorial Histories Publishing Company, 1980), passim.

Chapter 1

1. *Grand Canyon Echoes*, November 1, 1936. See brief account of the camp newspapers in McEntee, *Now They Are Men*, pp. 40–41.
2. *The Harbinger*, September 11, 1936.
3. *Happy Days*, November 24, 1934.
4. *Ibid.*, January 12, 1935.
5. See discussion in *ibid.*, June 6, 1936.
6. Rather unusually, the *Smoky Mountain Echo* was edited by the company's commander, Captain Allan W. McComb.
7. *Happy Days*, November 17, 1934; January 26, 1935; and February 24, 1940. Wayne S. Yenawine, the assistant director of the Illinois library, wrote a master's thesis in 1938 on "CCC Camp Papers," based on the 3,000 camp papers in the collection at the time. See report in August 31, 1940 issue of *Happy Days*. The task of microforming was accomplished between July 1, 1988 and March 31, 1991. An excellent, detailed finding aid was also prepared: Marlys Rudeen, comp., *The Civilian Conservation Corps Camp Papers: A Guide* (Chicago: The Center for Research Libraries, 1991). See also Marlys Rudeen, et al, "Final Performance Report CCC Camp Papers Project" (Chicago: Center for Research Libraries, 1991), p. 1. Two other collections of CCC camp newspapers which were not included in this project are located at The Idaho State Historical Society, Boise, Idaho, and The Nebraska State Historical Society, Lincoln, Nebraska.
8. Typical was Frank Kalasz, a former police and news reporter for the *Toledo Blade*, who was on the staff of the *Thistle Downs Tops* of Company 3501, Mt. Vernon, Ohio. Arthur Hahn of Company 1953, King City, California, who guided the destinies of the company's *The Quail Call*, had been a sports writer on the *Los Angeles Examiner* and rewrite man at the *Los Angeles Times*. He had also worked on other camp papers. See account in *Happy Days*, November 28, 1936.
9. *Happy Days*, November 19, 1938.
10. *The Walkerite*'s editor was L. H. Lindstrom, who had edited several outstanding CCC papers including *The Sea Gull Times*, *The Seagullite*, and *The Deer Lake Echo*. In his view, his long experience as a camp editor was better than a four-year college education. See *Happy Days*, June 1, 1940, and discussion in *The Seagullite*, April 25, 1939.
11. The debated cover appeared on the *Swan Lake Splashes*, August, 1940.
12. These included: TH-1, Wahiawa, Oahu; TH-3, Keanae, Maui; TH-7, Waimea, Kauai; TH-8, Kokee, Kauai; TH-9, Molokai, then the smallest CCC camp in the U.S., and the HNP (Hawaii National Park) camp, which concentrated on road construction at Hilina Pali and work on roads and parkways. Unlike the camps in the United States, these camps had directors, not commanders. The paper also supported the notion that Hawaii should become a new state, but as it once lamented, "Hawaii is just a baby state wot's havin' one helluva time findin' its daddy!"
13. The situation regarding the CCC in Alaska was distinctive. By December, 1939, there were 783 men in 43 camps located from Ketchikan to Fairbanks. Two types of camps were maintained: camps of the usual sort where men were housed and fed; the other type was for the per diem men who lived at home and fed and clothed themselves and received an allowance or per diem. All native and a few white

crews were handled on the per diem basis. See *The Alaskan,* January 20 and October, 1940.

14. The December, 1939, issue of *El Verde* included verses, an article on first aid, sports accounts, a brain teaser, and an article on soil conservation. *Ecos del Yunque* placed great emphasis on safety, and several cartoons illustrated the dangers of blasting and quarrying. There was also a comic strip depicting the vicissitudes of the life of a rookie.

15. *Happy Days,* July 5 and December 6, 1941.

16. For good examples of linoleum work see the *Deep Creek Chronicle* (Company 1216, Bryson City, North Carolina); *The Lucky 13* (Company 1370, Crewe, Virginia); and *The Pine Cone* (Company 798, Halsey, Nebraska).

17. One paper was smaller yet, a pocket magazine measuring 4¼ by 5½ inches, but as *Happy Days* observed, "as a novelty it's nice, but its practical usefulness is debatable." *Happy Days,* July 30, 1938.

18. *Ibid.,* December 5, 1936.

19. *Ibid.,* May 10, 1941.

20. *The Harbinger,* September and October 1939.

21. This began on March 14, 1938. The station was W8QVD at 7045 kilocycles.

22. *Happy Days,* July 28, 1934.

23. *Ibid.,* January 12, 1935. The paper also bragged that it had traveled 30,000 miles in its wanderings throughout the country since its foundation in May of 1933.

24. A sergeant from the 835th Aero Squadron, Greenshaw had been in the mailing department of the *Stars and Stripes.*

25. A typewriting class produced the paper as a class project. Its co-editors were H.W. Lookingglass and Amos Toahty.

Chapter 2

1. *Happy Days,* January 23, 1937. In the April 2, 1938, issue of *Happy Days,* there is an article reviewing the history of the camp newspaper.

2. For example, the role of advertising was discussed, for which see *ibid.,* August 17, 1935.

3. *Ibid.,* June 6 and 13, 1936.

4. *Ibid.,* June 13, 1936; June 28, 1941.

5. *Scraps 'N' Stuff,* April 1938.

6. *The Pyramid,* March 17, 1934; May 1, 1935

7. *Happy Days,* April 13, 1935.

8. *Ibid.,* August 11, 1934; August 3, 1935.

9. *Ibid.,* June 26, 1937.

10. A good example is in *ibid.,* July 28, 1934; another is in the November 25, 1939, issue.

11. Letter in "They're Telling Us" column in *ibid.,* January 7, 1939.

12. *Ibid.,* November 10, 1934.

13. *Ibid.,* June 8, 1935.

14. *Ibid.,* January 14, 1939.

15. *Ibid.,* October 11 and December 27, 1941.

16. *Ibid.,* April 28, 1934; June 1, 1935.

17. *Happy Days* did seek to assist editors in attaining five stars by giving tips in the issue of March 19, 1938.

18. The November 23, 1940, issue of *Happy Days* had a photo of the editor of *Quail Call* (Company 1953, King City, California), cutting a "five-star cake." See also *ibid.,* October 11, 1941.

19. Criticized because he did not know what editors had to contend with, "Shameless Samuel" noted that in 1934 he had produced the *Ridge Runner Record* for Com-

pany 577, and therefore had "sacrificed our share of mutilated stencils on the sacred altar of CCC Camp Journalism."
    20. See excerpts from four critics and responses in *Happy Days*, July 12, 1941.
    21. In fact, this remains a useful guide to students of the CCC papers as to which were the best of the lot during these years.
    22. Details in *The Spectator* (Company 180, East Hartland, Connecticut), and in *Happy Days*, December 10, 1938.
    23. *Happy Days*, August 21, 1937; April 29, 1939; February 24, March 23 and April 27, 1940.
    24. *Ibid.*, September 5, October 24 and 31, 1936. Doerer's articles began with the January 4, 1936, issue and ran for many more.
    25. *Ibid.*, May 11, 1935; July 16 and 23, 1938.
    26. *The Catskill Crier*, March 28, 1935.
    27. *The Dam Overflow*, April 22, 1935.
    28. *Ibid.*, May 30 and June 7, 1934.
    29. J. Frank Norfleet, *"Norfleet"*: the actual experiences of a Texas rancher's 30,000-mile transcontinental chase after five confidence men. (Fort Worth: White Publishing Company, 1924).
    30. To help matters along, *Happy Days* published a bulletin on short story writing—which it characteristically sold for five cents. See also "Camp Paper Fiction Swells Output of Creative Writing," *ibid.*, November 7, 1936.
    31. *The Stockade*, March and April 1937; April and October 1938. Other Sarge stories followed. See the November and December 1938 issues for examples.
    32. *Ibid.*, February 1939.
    33. Mimeographed, this publication measured 5 by 8 inches with usually 30 or more pages per issue.
    34. *The Harbinger*, April 30, 1936.
    35. See in initial issue, *The Red Rocks Echo*, February 21, 1936.
    36. This appeared in the December 6, 1941, issue of *Happy Days* "Camp Paper Comment" column.
    37. *The Spotlight*, February 7, 1935.
    38. See in the August 29, 1936, issue of *Happy Days*, in "Press Room Chatter" column.
    39. See the *Stockade*, June 1936, for example.
    40. See discussion of him in *The Bugle*, July 2, 1937.
    41. *The Crystal Camp Crier*, May 20 and 26, 1935.
    42. *Ibid.*, August 14, 1936.
    43. "The Hell Box" column, January 8, 1938, issue of *Happy Days*.
    44. *Ibid.*, March 14, 1942.
    45. *Grand Canyon Echo*, December 25, 1936, issue.
    46. *The Catskill Crier*, August 23, 1935, issue.
    47. As quoted in *Happy Days*, August 14, 1937.
    48. *The Tamarack Times*, June 1, 1940.
    49. *Happy Days*, December 20, 1941; January 3 and May 16, 1942.
    50. *Ibid.*, May 23, 1942.
    51. His cartoon character, "Sub Al Tern" was often reprinted by *Happy Days* during the seven years that Mallonen was on the staff of the *Northlander*.

Chapter 3

    1. Microfilmed collections of *Happy Days* are in the Library of Congress, Washington, D.C.; Hoover Institute Library, Stanford, California; and The State Historical Society of Wisconsin, Madison, Wisconsin.
    2. *Happy Days*, April 10, 1937.

3. New York: American Book Company, 1935. The 32-page book sold for 15 cents per copy.
4. The first column of letters was entitled simply, "Questions and Answers," though the first questions seem to have been "planted."
5. See Alfred E. Cornebise, *The Stars and Stripes: Doughboy Journalism in World War I* (Westport, Connecticut: Greenwood Press, 1984).
6. *Happy Days*, July 20, 1935; November 25, 1939; and December 2, 1939, issues.
7. Throughout its career, *Happy Days* paid a dollar or sometimes five dollars for such things as: "the what-how-why" of smiles; the best photos of camp sites; and a nickname for the CCC, the winning name was "civies," though another suggested, "peavie", a tool with an iron hook used in the forests to handle logs, came into general use. "Civies" was largely ignored, and enrollees were often called "peavies." Some of the names rejected included: "Sapling Soldiers," "Doughless Boys," and "Roosevelt's Timber Tailors." Songs were desired, especially devoted to the CCC, with the paper suggesting a possible title: "We don't have to say Buddy Can You Spare a Dime Anymore." Mottos for the CCC were considered also. The winner: "We can take it." In addition, the paper sponsored contests seeking to locate the best athletes in the camps, as well as the tallest, shortest, oldest enrollee, and which company could boast the youngest commanding officer. These matters had earlier concerned the readers of *The Stars and Stripes* during the World War.
8. *Happy Days*, June 3, 1933.
9. See in *ibid.*, May 20 and June 3, 1933.
10. His first effort was in charcoal, crayon and ink, and was entitled "In the Forest Legion." See *ibid.*, November 18, 1933, and November 10, 1934.
11. For an example, see *ibid.*, February 1, 1936.
12. As in May 13, 1939, issue of *Happy Days*.
13. *Ibid.*, October 20, 1934.
14. Colonel J.E. Yates, earlier the Chief of Chaplains, U.S. Army, observed in a letter that he was gratified to see the new paper, noting that as soldiers had been cheered up in France by *The Stars and Stripes*, CCCers would be similarly encouraged by the new sheet. See in *Happy Days*, June 10, 1933.
15. *Happy Days*, June 10, 1933.
16. Letter from James A. Spencer, Company 611, Estacada, Oregon, in *ibid.*, July 29, 1933.
17. *Ibid.*, June 3, 1933.
18. *Ibid.*, September 2, 1933. This piece set forth a model letter of application which might include the statement: "Whatever the job is, Mr. Employer, I am fitted for it. I have been fitted for it here in the forests.... That's what I am offering you. A real man, for a real job. A man who knows how to 'take it'." See also *ibid.*, November 23, 1935.
19. *Ibid.*, January 4, 1936.
20. *Ibid.*, May 25, 1935.
21. *Ibid.*, August 6, 1938, for example: "What's in a Name?" noting that Lieut. Jack Hammer was commanding officer of Company 1998, Thompson Falls, Montana. Also: Enrollee John Gear drove a truck for Company 1641, Peebles, Ohio, while in Camp Zig-Zag, Vancouver Barracks District in Washington, Stanley Hash was second cook.
22. *Ibid.*, July 13, 1935.
23. Good examples are in *ibid.*, October 27, 1934.
24. Editorial in *ibid.*, January 6, 1934.
25. *Ibid.*, September 28 and October 26, 1935; October 30 and November 13, 1937.
26. *Ibid.*, October 3, 1936; April 3, 1937.
27. List in *Happy Days*, December 5, 1936. See also November 7 and December 12, 1936; January 9 and April 10, 1937 issues.

28. *Ibid.*, February 13, 1937; January 7, 1939.
29. *Ibid.*, February 27 and April 3, 1937; December 31, 1938.
30. *Ibid.*, December 31, 1938; January 7 and 14, February 4, April 1, 1939; July 13, 1935; May 20 and August 19, 1939.
31. Printed in *ibid.*, March 25, 1939.
32. *Ibid.*, November 28, 1936; January 2, 1937.
33. *Ibid.*, July 23, August 6 and 20, and September 3, 1938.
34. *Ibid.*, February 5 and 26, 1938; April 9, 1938; July 2, 9, 16, and 23, 1938.
35. *Ibid.*, October 25, 1941.
36. Lee's strip began in the April 29, 1939, issue.
37. These are reviewed in *ibid.*, January 24, 1942.
38. *Ibid.*, February 21, 1942.
39. *Ibid.*, February 28, 1942.
40. *Ibid.*
41. *Ibid.*, July 18, 1942.
42. *Ibid.*, July 13, 1935.
43. *Ibid.*, December 1, 1934.
44. *Ibid.*, November 10, 1934.
45. *Ibid.*, September 5, 1936.
46. *Ibid.*
47. *Ibid.*, November 25, 1933.
48. *Ibid.*, February 4, 1939. In this issue, a National Park Service employee, Mrs. Lillian P. Sartain of the regional office staff, published a study of camp papers in Region One, including a brief history of *Happy Days*.

Chapter 4

1. *Crystal Camp Crier*, November 26, 1934.
2. *Canyon Echo*, January 1940.
3. *Happy Days*, January 20, 1934.
4. *Ibid.*, July 30, 1938.
5. See chart in *Spirit of 299*, August 1934.
6. *Happy Days*, April 10, 1937.
7. The *Rock Hound*, August 4, 1934; February 22, 1935.
8. *Grand Canyon Echoes*, June 15, 1937.
9. See chart the *TH-CCC News*, June 1941.
10. *Happy Days*, February 25, 1939.
11. *Ibid.*, September 2, 1933; January 8, 1938.
12. *The Bugle*, January 31, 1938.
13. *Happy Days*, August 14, 1937.
14. This area included camps in Georgia and North and South Carolina. See discussion in *ibid.*, July 24, 1937.
15. For instance, the motto of Company 3222, based at Wyoming, Delaware, emphasized that the rookie was to be "A full-fledged member in 24 hours." *Ibid.*, March 4, 1939.
16. *Ibid.*, December 2 and 9, 1933.
17. *Ibid.*, September 5, 1936.
18. *Ibid.*, April 23, 1938.
19. *Ibid.*, July 23, 1938.
20. *Ibid.*, May 4, 1935.
21. The *Bugle*, August 12 and 19, and October 21, 1936; *Happy Days*, September 7, 1935.
22. *The Dam Overflow*, November 29, 1934.
23. *The Bugle*, October 28, 1936.

24. *Happy Days,* December 30, 1933; September 14, 1935. At least one rookie in Company 299 in Masonville, New York, professed to like the custom of formal dress for dinner, "for I believe it helps to keep us civilized." *The Catskill Crier,* May 1935.

25. *Happy Days,* April 23, 1938; *The Catskill Crier,* April 1935.

26. *Happy Days,* May 2, 1936. The new spruce green uniforms were first issued in October 1939 in some Corps areas, initially to the First, Second and Third. See *ibid.,* January 7 and 28, and October 7, 1939.

27. *Happy Days* was more than happy to sell such accouterments to the men and did a thriving business in such throughout its career, as the many advertisements in the paper indicate.

28. *Ibid.,* August 24, 1935.

29. *Ibid.,* January 22 and November 12, 1938; December 5, 1936. Appropriately, the floating camp of Company 1741 at St. Charles, Arkansas, was commanded by a naval officer, Lieutenant James V. Metcalfe, USNR. The Native Americans' traveling camp is described in detail in *Happy Days,* December 3, 1938. Some 77,416 Indians had been enrolled in the CCC from April 1935 to June 1938, about an average of one person for each Indian family in the USA. See discussion in *ibid.,* October 29, 1938.

30. Account in *ibid.,* September 10, 1938.

31. See accounts in *The Bugle* (the company paper), January and July 15, 1936.

32. *Happy Days,* July 30, 1938.

33. *Ibid.,* November 17, 1934.

34. *Ibid.,* November 3, 1934. Ellis Tietze of Company 277 in Salinas, California, emphasized the broadening aspects of travel in a guest editorial in *Happy Days:* "In days gone by," he noted, "lucky was the man who had even reached the Mississippi during the course of a lifetime." And his CCC company had already "bathed in the rough surf of both the Atlantic and Pacific Oceans and have traversed 13 states in the course of our travels." "So let's hang on, fellows," he enthused, "and give thanks to Roosevelt and our glorious country. We're CCCing America First!" *Ibid.,* December 7, 1935.

35. *Ibid.,* January 7, 1939.

36. *Ibid.,* July 27, 1935.

37. *Seven Six One News,* December 1940.

38. *The Pyramid,* November 19, 1934.

39. *Ibid.,* March 17, 1934; photo and poem in *Happy Days,* November 9, 1935.

40. *Happy Days,* February 27, 1937; *The Catskill Crier,* late April, 1935.

41. *Happy Days,* April 6, 1935; the *Tamarack Times,* June 1, 1940.

42. Discussions in *The Kanona Daze,* August 1936, and *The Kanonan,* October 1936.

43. *Happy Days,* December 14, 1935; November 20, 1937; February 3, 1940.

44. The *Broadcast,* October 1938; *The Kanonan,* February 1937.

45. *The 299th Broadcast,* October 10, 1934.

46. *Happy Days,* December 9, 1933.

47. *The Bugle* July 16, 1937, and *The Saltkehatchie Pow Wow,* June 3, 1938. This paper replaced the earlier *Bugle.*

48. *The Catskill Crier,* October 18, 1935.

49. See, for instance, "The CO's Page," by Lt. Ellis R. Ates, in *The Broadcast* (Company 1742, Gallatin, Missouri), July 1941.

50. *Happy Days,* November 18, 1933; January 12, 1935; April 17, 1937.

51. *Ibid.,* January 23, 1937.

52. *The Dam Overflow,* February 22, 1935.

53. *Th-CCC News,* November 1, 1940.

54. *Happy Days,* February 5, 12 and 26, 1938.

55. Article, "Oklahomans Doff Hayseed, 'Go for' Emily's Etiquet [sic]," in *ibid.,* January 22, 1938.

56. *Grand Canyon Echoes,* June 15, 1937. Company 299 at Masonville, New York,

had similar problems as reported in its paper, the *299 Lowdown*. See in the September 25, 1934 issue.

57. The *Rock Hound*, August 4, 1934; August 16, 1935. The *Tumbleweed*, May, and August 17, 1936. The *Rock Hound* also often printed a short weekly sermon.

58. The *Bugle*, November 18, 1935.

59. *Happy Days*, August 25, 1934.

60. *Ibid.*, December 19, 1936.

61. The enrollees themselves had suggested their use. *Ibid.*, September 30, 1939.

62. *TH-CCC News*, October 1, 1940.

63. *Happy Days*, May 30, 1936. The *Barracks Bearer* (Company 755, Albion, Nebraska) recounted that a food riot had occurred in the company when, "after a particularly skimpy breakfast, the company refused to go to work." The officers could do nothing, and when district headquarters at Eugene, Oregon was informed, the orders came down to "feed 'em again," which was done, solving the problem. See issue for October 1935.

64. *Happy Days*, March 31 and April 7, 1934; September 28, 1940.

65. *Ibid.*, December 31, 1938. See, for example, an account of the film's viewing by Company 4468 in Barnwell, South Carolina, in *The Saltkehatchie Pow Wow*, May 10, 1938. *Happy Days* also ran a series of articles, "From Me to You—Diseases We Catch from Humans," the one devoted to gonorrhea appearing in the July 23, 1938, issue, and syphilis on July 30, 1938.

66. At least one enrollee patient appreciated the care that he received. See his article, "Ten Days in the Infirmary or How Many Fly-specks on the Ceiling?" in *The Catskill Crier* (Company 299, Masonville, New York), August 1, 1935.

67. *Happy Days*, October 2, 1937. The ethics concerning the use of such "guinea pigs" were apparently of no interest to those involved.

68. The *Dam Oveflow*, November 29, 1934. Dentists routinely visited each camp every six months or so, staying for about two weeks at each. Account in the *Crystal Camp Crier* (Company 1742, Tarkio, Missouri), December 14, 1936.

69. The *Heppner Roundup*, December, 1937.

70. *Happy Days*, December 29, 1934.

71. In some camps, as in Company 727, West Plains, Missouri, lotteries determined which holiday each man would take.

72. *Happy Days*, January 2 and November 27, 1937; December 16 and 23, 1939.

73. *Ibid.*, March 11, 1939 issue.

74. *Ibid.*, June 2, 1934.

75. The *Boston Globe*, October 15, 1941; *Happy Days*, October 25, 1941.

76. *Happy Days*, May 7, 1938; October 16, 1937.

77. The *Kanona Daze*, August 1936; The *Kanonan*, September 1937.

78. This was dedicated on August 20, 1939, with appropriate ceremonies. There is a photo of the memorial in *Happy Days*, August 19, 1939. See also *ibid.*, August 26, 1939, for further discussion of fire-fighting activities of the CCC.

79. *Ibid.*, April 28, 1934. Sawyers had been on a weekend pass to his home in Bedford, Virginia. See *ibid.*, March 20, 1937.

80. Quoted in the *Crystal Camp Crier* (Company 1742, Tarkio, Missouri), December 1937.

81. The *Dam Overflow* (Company 297, Loyston, Tennessee), April 22, 1935.

82. *Happy Days*, July 8 and October 7, 1933; April 14, June 16, July 28, and August 11, 1934; July 27, 1935.

83. *Ibid.*, December 17, 1938; The *Buffalo* (Company 753, Tekamah, Nebraska), August 1, 1935, and the *Jolly Griper* (Company 752, Hebron, Nebraska), November 14, 1934.

84. *Happy Days*, June 5, 26 and July 24, 1937. The paper often paid a dollar for each jingle published.

85. *Ibid.*, June 3, 1933; January 12, 1935.
86. *Ibid.*, January 4, 1936; January 3, 1942.

Chapter 5

1. *Happy Days*, August 12 and 19, 1933; December 29, 1934. On the occasion of Roosevelt's visit to the Virginia camps, *Happy Days* featured a pencil sketch of the President on its cover, copies of which—suitable for framing—the men could obtain for 10 cents in stamps.
2. *Ibid.*, August 18, 1934.
3. *Ibid.*, November 9, 1935.
4. *Ibid.*, May 8, 1937.
5. *Ibid.*, April 21, 1934.
6. *Ibid.*, September 29, 1934.
7. *Vets Voice*, November 1939.
8. *Happy Days*, February 17, 1934; February 27, 1937.
9. *Ibid.*, March 17, 1934.
10. Ciorciari claimed that he had sold more than 10,000 copies of the work by May of 1934. *Ibid.*, May 26, 1934.
11. *The Bugle*, October 7, 1936; August 2, 1937.
12. Michael E. Parrish. *Anxious Decades: America in Prosperity to Depression, 1920–1941* (New York: W.W. Norton and Company, 1992), pp. ix–x. The enrollees often sought to produce something tangible to show their "sincere appreciation of the New Deal and the opportunity given [them] by the President through the C.C.C." For Christmas 1933, for instance, men of Company 817, Stephenville, Texas, designed a special Christmas card signed by members of the company and dispatched to the White House. Because it was well known that FDR collected ship models, enrollees of Company 1276 in Hackettstown, New Jersey, built FDR a large replica of Donald McKay's three-masted, square-rigged clipper ship. See accounts in *Happy Days*, January 13, 1934, and February 10, 1940.
13. *Happy Days*, July 22, 1933.
14. *Ibid.*, December 9, 16 and 30, 1939; January 6, 1940.
15. FDR nominated him on February 15, and the Senate unanimously confirmed his appointment on February 26. See in *ibid.*, March 9, 1940.
16. *Ibid.*, April 13, 1940; March 1, 1941. In a further honor, in 1943 a Liberty ship, the *SS Robert Fechner*, was launched at the Southeastern Ship Yard in Savannah, Georgia. See details in the *NACCCA Journal*, Vol. 24 no. 11, November 2001, p. 7.
17. See Ann Thedford Lanier, "The Civilian Conservation Corps, 1933–1942: Organizational Structure and Social Effects," unpublished MA Thesis in Sociology, University of Colorado, Boulder, 1983, pp. 128–145; Charles W. Johnson, "The Army and the Civilian Conservation Corps, 1933–42," *Prologue*, Vol. 4 no. 3 (Fall 1972); and a Communist pamphlet by James Lasswell, *Shovels and Guns: The CCC in Action* (New York: International Publishers, 1935). Albert W. Jernberg, a reserve U.S. Army Air Corps officer who commanded several CCC companies, including a camp for black enrollees, has presented a vivid account of his four years of service in *My Brush Monkeys: A Narrative of the CCC* (New York: Richard R. Smith, 1941), which contains much information on the military's involvement. A useful semi-fictitious, but generally accurate, unpublished narrative by another officer, which emphasizes the military dimension, entitled "Naturally," is located in the Edwin W. Jones Papers, U.S. Army Military History Institute, Carlisle Barracks, Pennsylvania.
18. *The Broadcast*, Company 1742, November 1938.
19. *Grand Canyon Echoes*, March 1, 1936; January, 1940; *Buffalo Prints*, May 1938.
20. *The Harbinger*, October 1938; *The Catskill Crier*, August 1, 1935.
21. *Happy Days*, June 29, 1935.

22. *Ibid.*, March 3 and December 15, 1934; April 27, 1935; October 19, 1940.
23. *Ibid.*, June 29 and September 14, 1935.
24. *Ibid.*, September 14, 1935; January 4, 1936.
25. These were for sale by *Happy Days*. See ads in February 2 and April 13, 1935, issues, for example.
26. See letter to *Happy Days*, March 25, 1939. The flag received considerable attention in the CCC press. See editorial in the *Seven Six One News* (Company 761, David City, Nebraska) June 1941 issue, which stated that the flag meant: "America first; it means an undivided allegiance. It means America united, strong and efficient, equal to her tasks."
27. *Happy Days*, June 29 and August 10, 1935.
28. *TH-CCC News* (Hawaiian Composite Companies, Honolulu, Hawaii), October 1, 1940.
29. *Happy Days*, October 12 and November 30, 1935; the *Stockade*, January 1936.
30. *Happy Days*, May 25, 1935.
31. *The Script* (Company 299, Masonville, New York), December 20, 1934.
32. *Happy Days*, March 4 and October 7, 1939. *Happy Days* also published ongoing polls on the subject of military training. In the spring of 1936, the American Institute of Public Opinion [the Gallup Poll] found that 77 percent of the American public thought that military training should be part of CCC training, with 80 percent of Democrats and 74 percent of Republicans being in favor. Predictably, only 43 percent of socialists agreed. In repeated polling, the Institute found that the figures held firm throughout the mid–1930s, though by 1939, 90 percent were in favor of some sort of military training in the CCC, but on a voluntary basis.
33. *Ibid.*, October 24, 1936; January 9, 1937; February 25, 1939.
34. *Ibid.*, January 7 and February 25, 1939; September 28, 1935; November 21, 1936.
35. *Ibid.*, February 4, December 9 and 30, 1939; the *Stockade*, October 1940.
36. *Happy Days*, November 18, 1939.
37. *Ibid.*, December 9, 1939.
38. *Ibid.*, January 21, 1939.
39. *TH-CCC News* (Hawaiian Composite Companies, Honolulu, Hawaii), October 1 and November 1, 1940.
40. *Ibid.*
41. *Happy Days*, February 4 and 25, and March 4, 1939.
42. See Circular Letter No. 1 to his CCC camp commanders which *Happy Days* published in its June 25 and July 2, 1938, issues as an editorial, and *ibid.*, September 2, 1933.
43. Marshall made these statements on April 17, 1941. See *ibid.*, April 19, 1941. But if the top brass was opposed to military training in the CCC, such was not the case with one of the nation's celebrated military heroes, Sergeant Alvin York. He became involved in the work of the CCC, being appointed a project superintendent for Company 3464, in Cumberland Homesteads State Park near Crossville, Tennessee. York insisted that the normal work day of seven hours be shortened by an hour a day to devote to military training. He added, "defense, rather than aggression," however, "should be the keynote of this training," certainly a politically astute position to take at the time. The famous former sergeant of the 82nd Division had another camp in Tennessee named for him: that of Company 1475 in Sewanee. See in *ibid.*, November 11, 1939; August 2, 1941.
44. *Ibid.*, September 16, 1939. See also discussion in the *Seven Six One News* (Company 761, David City, Nebraska), September 1939. Fechner also stated that "we venture that if war should ever come to these shores the young graduates of the corps would be among the first to come forward to defend their country. But meantime their patriotism will not be used to whip up war fervor in America."

45. *Happy Days*, February 25, 1939.
46. *Ibid.*, June 17 and July 1, 1939.
47. *Ibid.*, June 24, August 12 and 26, and October 21, 1939.
48. *Ibid.*, October 26, 1940. This issue also contained details of the draft law and its implementation.
49. *Ibid.*, October 14, 1939.
50. *Ibid.*, September 28, 1940.
51. *Ibid.*, August 16, 1941.

Chapter 6

1. *Happy Days*, January 12, 1935; *The Catskill Crier*, October 18, 1935.
2. *The Spotlight*, February 7, 1935. More than half the members of Company 1731 wanted to be truck drivers, he went on. Thus, they should be fully aware of their responsibilities. See in *The Ozark Oracle*, quoted in *Happy Days*, June 8, 1940. *The Harbinger*, June, 1939. Good conduct would prevent people from calling the camp as soon as some violation of the rights of others had been committed, the editor observed.
3. *The Dynamo* (Company 134, Warren, New Hampshire), n.d.; *The Indian Trail* as quoted by *Happy Days*, June 26, 1937.
4. This poem first appeared in "The Flare," a column in the [Fort] *Benning Herald* [no date given] and was reprinted in *The Sentinel*, July 8, 1933, the troop newspaper of the 15th U.S. Infantry Regiment, then stationed in Tientsin, China. The poem also refers to the propensity of Congress frequently to cut military appropriations in the 1920s and 1930s and the role of the CCC in saving the jobs of many military officers ordered to CCC camps. Many military personnel would have preferred other, more martial employment, but took what was offered if not always with good grace.
5. *Happy Days*, July 8 and September 23, 1933.
6. See discussion in *ibid.*, September 29, 1934. To be sure, the enrollees did drink on occasion, one anonymous poet commemorating moonshine in his poem, "Arkansas Corn" which went in part:

> Made in rusty tubs of iron,
> buried from the sight of law
> In the sandy, rocky hillsides,
> Is the corn of Arkansas.

But the poet recognized its baleful effects, and swore off, fervently cursing the hard liquor. See in the *Jolly Griper* (Company 752, Plainview, Arkansas), September 17, 1934.
7. As quoted in *Happy Days*, June 26, 1937.
8. *The Script*, December 7, 1934.
9. *Field and Stream*, March 1936; *Happy Days*, March 14 and April 18, 1936.
10. *Happy Days*, June 11 and 25, 1938.
11. Letter in *ibid.*, November 30, 1935.
12. *Ibid.*, August 11, 1934.
13. *Ibid.*, September 16, 1933.
14. *The Daily Worker*, June 8, 1935; *Happy Days*, April 27, May 25, August 3, 1935; the *Stockade*, January 1936; *The Philadelphia Record*, April 24, 1935.
15. *The Stockade*, January 1941.
16. *Happy Days*, November 23, 1935.
17. *Ibid.*, June 16, 1934.
18. *Ibid.*, December 8 and 15, 1934. *The March Field Courier* was issued from Company 908's camp at San Bernardino, California.
19. For one example, see account regarding Company 1101 of West Campton, New Hampshire, in *Happy Days*, June 4, 1938.

20. *Ibid.*, May 5, 1934.

21. *Ibid.*, December 22, 1934; June 22 and August 3, 1935. Further to ascertain the truth about local sentiment, the editor of *The Musical Interlude* (Company 528, Bethel, Ohio) sent one of its reporters into the community to take a poll of 10 people, using the format of a "Man on the Street" interview. The locals were asked to respond to two questions: "What is your opinion of the camp?" and "What is your opinion of the behavior of the men?" Eight citizens responded favorably; the other two were noncommittal. *Happy Days*, December 8, 1934.

22. *Happy Days*, August 18, 1934.

23. *Ibid.*, September 5, 1936. Camp papers frequently included testimonials as to how communities and officials regarded local CCCers. When the Rotary Club and the chamber of commerce of Valentine, Nebraska, praised the men of Company 753 stationed near there, the company's paper *The Buffalo* was gratified to record it: "Upon [the camp's] establishment much doubt and skepticism was evident. There was the thought, that the city might be overrun with rowdies and there might be much dissatisfaction resulting from the closeness of the camp to the city." But daily contact with the personnel had indicated that the original anxieties were unfounded and the camp proved to be "a decided asset to the community." See in the November 1936 issue.

24. *The Catskill Crier*, August 1 and October 18, 1935.

25. *Happy Days*, September 29 and October 13, 1934.

26. *Ibid.*, August 19, 1933.

27. *The Broadcast*, February 1938.

28. *Crystal Camp Crier*, March 14, 1936; *The Broadcast*, April and July 1938.

29. *The Broadcast*, June 1941 and passim.

30. *The Rock Hound*, March 22, 1935; *The Kanonan*, January 1937.

31. See *Happy Days*, June 25, 1938, for an account complete with photographs of the crowd of over 3,000 visitors to Company 788 in Farlington, Kansas, enjoying the chicken dinner served to "all comers."

32. *Ibid.*, January 15, 1938.

33. *Ibid.*, November 11, 1933; January 20, 1934.

34. *Ibid.*, September 8, 1934.

35. Quoted in *ibid.*, June 21, 1941.

36. Beatrice Litzinger and Evelyn McGregor, the *Stockade* (Company 2328, Shelocta, Pennsylvania), September, 1937.

37. *Happy Days*, February 2 and 9, 1935; May 22, 1937.

38. As quoted in *ibid.*, February 18, 1939.

39. The *Pine Needle* (Companies 237 and 235, Camp Pack, New Lisbon, New Jersey), October 31, 1935.

40. *The Hayden Hollow* (Company 562, Coeur d'Alene, Idaho).

41. The *Broadcast*, May 1939.

42. *The Bugle*, November 18, 1935.

43. As quoted in *Happy Days*, February 2, 1935.

44. *Ibid.*, May 22 and August 7, 1937. March later wrote that he had refused to read the novel *Gone With The Wind*, thereby bucking a national trend. He explained: "The most important reason for my not reading the book lies in a very narrow-minded (I'm happy to say) prejudice I've always had. And that is, no lady novelist—even Miss Mitchell—could ever beguile me into reading 300 of her pages, let alone a thousand or more. Because lady novelists seldom say anything worth listening to, and they say it at great length."

45. *Ibid.*, March 16, 1935.

46. *Ibid.*, June 4, 1938.

47. *Ibid.*, April 25, 1936; the *Stockade*, April 1939; May and June 1940.

48. The *Broadcast*, June 1940; *The Bugle*, November 28, 1935; *The Saltkehatchie Pow Wow*, May 10, 1938.

49. *The Bugle*, April 2, 1937; *Grand Canyon Echoes*, December 25, 1936; *The Catskill Crier*, April 11, 1935.
50. See, for example, notice in the *Super Snooper* (Company 758, Alma, Nebraska), May 10, 1935, and in numerous other camp papers.

Chapter 7

1. Article, "Boys in the Woods," *Collier's* (May 22, 1937), pp. 12–13, 70–72.
2. This was reprinted in "Voice of the Camps" column in *Happy Days*, June 19, 1937.
3. *Ibid.*, May 29, 1937; *The Veterans' Voice* (Company 1774, Ely and Rochester, Minnesota), April 20, 1935.
4. *Happy Days*, November 30, 1935; *The Veterans' Bugle*, March 1938.
5. *The Vet's Call*, September 1937.
6. The *Veterans' Voice*, February 1939; the *Vet's Call*, as quoted in *Veterans' Voice*, May 1939.
7. The *Alpine Echo*, December 1936; January 1937; the *Vets Lament*, July 1939; the *Veterans' Voice*, April 20, 1935; September 1937; November 1938; *Vet's Call*, reprinted in the column, "Easy Pickings. Good Gags From Other Rags," in the *Veterans' Voice*, January 1939.
8. The *Tamalpais Foghorn*, March 1939; *The Veterans' Voice*, January 1939; *Vets Lament*, May 1939.
9. Picture and article, *Happy Days*, August 15, 1936.
10. *Alpine Echo*, December 1936; *The Vets Voice*, April 1939.
11. *Happy Days*, January 13, 1934.
12. The *Alpine Echo*, November 1937; January 1938.
13. *Ibid.*, *The Veterans' Bugle*, July and September 1940; *Vets Voice* (Company 1774, Bayport, Minnesota), passim; *The Veterans' Voice*, October 31, 1937.
14. *The Veterans' Voice*, November 1, 1936; February 28, 1937.
15. *Happy Days*, May 27, 1933; June 23, 1934.
16. *The Veterans' Voice*, November 1, 1936; *The Veterans' Bugle*, August 1938.
17. *Alpine Echo*, February and April 1938. This paper often included a sprightly column, the "Sick, Lame and Lethargic," reporting on the various casualties in camp.
18. *The Veterans' Voice*, November 1937.
19. *Alpine Echo*, Company 1921, Fairfax, California; January 1938. *Tamalpais Foghorn*, September 1938. His remarks produced much adverse comment from irate veterans.
20. *Happy Days*, February 16, 1935. As Elsie Smith-Parker had remarked, the wives of many veterans often became involved in the work of their husbands. Some 30 wives of men of Company 1780 at Mt. Nebo, Arkansas, for example, rented a cottage near the camp, set up housekeeping, and resumed their wifely duties. They also created a social club as an auxiliary of the CCC, calling it the "Veter-Annes." *Ibid.*, April 21, 1934.
21. *Ibid.*, November 27, 1937; October 22, 1938.
22. *Ibid.*, October 14, 1939; March 30 and May 4, 1940; April 12, 1941. *Happy Days*, in its May 4, 1940 issue, published several pictures of the "Three Wizards of Usk": John G. Powell, pressman; George Young, compositor; and Errol M. Sweet, editor and carver of the linoleum block prints that decorate the paper.
23. *Veterans' Voice*, October 20 and December 1938.
24. *Ibid.*, March 1938; February 1939.
25. *Vets Voice*, September 20, 1940; *Vets Lament*, May 1939 and July 1940. See also *The Veterans' Voice*, April and December 1938.
26. *Happy Days*, June 13, 1936, issue. The vets were also lectured to as to what they should do with their windfall. The commanding officer of Company 2745 at

Minatare, Nebraska, for one, noted that it might be "a long, long time before Uncle Sam sees fit to do anything more for us." The men were advised to "salt away [the] bonus," and stay with the company, as "it doesn't take long to spend five or six hundred dollars. Think it over. Take a look before you leap." See in the *Lake Minatare Breeze*, January 1936.

27. It was decided about this time (June 1936) that the strength of the CCC would be maintained at approximately 350,000 total in 2,000 camps until March 31, 1937, the end of the then-currently authorized life of the CCC. See statistics and discussions in *Happy Days*, May 23 and June 27, 1936. There is a useful listing of all veteran camps as of mid–1938 in *ibid.*, May 7, 1938.

28. *The Veterans' Voice*, December 1937.

29. Ray J. Weidlich, the cartoonist of *Vets Voice*, Company 1774, Bayport, Minnesota, was a 1st Lieutenant in Coast Artillery Reserves and would soon be a captain. He was a senior foreman and had drawn many cartoons for the paper, which had been praised by many other camp papers. He departed on January 4, 1941, for Seattle and a job with Boeing as a draftsman in the engineering department. See in the *Vets Voice*, January 1941.

30. The *Vets Voice* is referring to the so-called "short arm" medical inspection of the male sex organ common in military and CCC camps. *The Veterans' Voice*, earlier paper of the same company, in its November 1937 issue, had already referred to the procedure under the topic "Meat Inspection," which noted: "Of all the inspections held in this camp every month, the one held by doc has got them all skinned."

31. The cartoon was by the beleagured artist R. J. Weidlich. *The Veterans' Voice*, September 1938.

32. *Ibid.*, February 1939.

33. *Ibid.*, January 28, 1937.

34. *Ibid.*, March 1938; *The Vets Voice*, July 23, 1940.

35. *Happy Days*, December 11, 1937.

36. *Alpine Echo*, November and December 1937.

37. *The Bull's Eye*, October 1941.

38. *The Veterans' Bugle*, September 30, 1937; February and September 1938.

39. *The Vets Voice*, October and December 18, 1939; January 25, 1940.

40. *Ibid.*, January 25, 1940; *Vets Lament*, August 1940.

41. *The Veterans' Voice*, January 1939; *The Veterans' Bugle*, January and February 1941.

42. *The Vets Voice*, February 13, 1942.

43. *Happy Days*, January 31 and February 14, 1942.

44. See long account in *ibid.*, March 7, 1942, which also included details of famous pigeons of World War I and their exploits.

45. As quoted in *ibid.*, June 13, 1942. Among the individual veterans who "made good" was Elmer C. Paterson, who departed Company 2775 at Mandan, North Dakota, for employment with the firm "Contractors, Pacific Naval Bases, Wake Island," engaged in the construction of a naval base and airfield there. He most certainly was destined shortly to be killed or captured when the Japanese overran the island. See accounts of his early activities on Wake Island in *The Veterans' Bugle*, September and October 1941.

Chapter 8

1. *Happy Days*, June 3, 1933. See also Olen Cole, Jr. *The African-American Experience in the Civilian Conservation Corps* (Gainesville, Florida: University Press of Florida, 1999). This useful study focuses on black enrollees in California.

2. *Happy Days*, June 10 and September 9, 1933.

3. *Ibid.*, March 3, 1934.

4. *Ibid.*, March 3 and 17, 1934.

5. For one of those papers, see *The Saltkehatchie Pow Wow* (Company 4468, Barnwell, South Carolina), April 9, 1938.

6. *The Border Tab*, April 1942.

7. *Happy Days*, June 5, 1937; July 15 and August 12, 1939.

8. *The Trojan*, October 9, 1936, and August 1939.

9. The *Pine Needle*, November 15 and 30, 1935.

10. See example in *ibid.*, November 15, 1935.

11. *Ibid.*, October 31, November 15, and December 15, 1935.

12. *The Trojan*, June 1938.

13. The *Pine Needle*, November 30, 1935; February 1939.

14. *Ibid.*, November 15, 1935.

15. *The Trojan*, February, combined March-April-May issue, and August 1940.

16. The *Pine Needle*, August 1937.

17. *Ibid.*, November 15 and December 15, 1935; the distinctive column, "The Jive Box," in August 1938; March 1939. *The Trojan*, June 1938.

18. Reprinted in *Happy Days*, June 5, 1937.

19. *The Trojan*, October–November 1940; *The Border Tab*, June 17, July 20, and November 15, 1938; November 1940.

20. *Happy Days*, August 31, September 14, and November 30, 1935.

21. *Ibid.*, April 24 and May 15, 1937; *The Pine Needle*, April 1937; *The Trojan*, January 15, 1939.

22. The *Pine Needle*, February and March 1937.

23. *The Border Tab*, February, March, and November 1940; August 1941; *The Trojan*, February 15 and December 1939; *The Pine Needle*, September 1938; February 1939. For a history of the black aviators, see Stanley Sandler, *Segregated Skies: All-Black Combat Squadrons of World War II* (Washington, D.C.: Smithsonian Press, 1992). Mary McLeod Bethune was a member of the unofficial "black cabinet," which sometimes advised the government on black affairs. See discussion in Michael E. Parrish. *Anxious Decades: America in Prosperity and Depression, 1920–1941* (New York: W.W. Norton, 1992), p. 378.

24. *The Pine Needle*, December 15, 1935; *Happy Days*, March 18, 1939. See also discussion in Parrish, *Anxious Decades*, p. 285.

25. *The Pine Needle*, November 15 and 30, 1935.

26. *Ibid.*, February 26 and March 23, 1936. If the admonitions of those in command perhaps had little influence on the men, maybe a former enrollee might succeed. Accordingly, a letter from a former member of Company 237, Victor L. Washington, then enrolled in Virginia State College at Ettrick, Virginia, was printed in the *Pine Needle*. He greatly regretted the hours that "I sat on my Camp cot twiddling my thumbs," he admitted. "This world has something for all of us," he advised the men, "so let's get it." *Ibid.*, March 23, 1936.

27. *The Trojan*, October 15, 1938; January 15, March 15, September and November 1939.

28. *The Pine Needle*, December 15, 1935; July 1937; *The Trojan*, May 15 and June 1938.

29. *The Pine Needle*, June 1937; September 1938; March 1939.

30. *Ibid.*, May 1938; April and May 1939.

31. *Ibid.*, August 1938.

32. *The Trojan*, May 15 and June 1938.

33. *The Border Tab*, March 1940.

34. *The Trojan*, November 15, 1938; October–November 1940; *The Border Tab*, May and June 1940; *The Pine Needle*, October 31 and November 15, 1935.

35. Albert W. Jernberg, *My Brush Monkeys: A Narrative of the CCC* (New York: Richard R. Smith, 1941). There is a review of Jernberg's book in *Happy Days*, July 26, 1941.

36. *Happy Days*, December 17, 1938; April 1, 1939.
37. *The Pine Needle*, March 23, 1936.
38. *Ibid.*, December 1938; January 1939. Despite the Camden affair, Camp Pack was rated the "Superior Camp" of the Trenton District for the month of March 1939. In addition, the Reverend Joseph W. Bowers of the Oakland Branch of the Orange, New Jersey, YMCA, stated that his branch was "happy to extend them free privileges in all activities because of their fine sense of community values." See in *The Pine Needle*, April 1939.
39. *Ibid.*, April 27, 1936.
40. Article from *The Indian Trail* reprinted in *The Pine Needle*, June 1937.
41. See accounts of the company's action along the U.S-Mexican border in 1938 in *The Border Tab*, December 16, 1938. For other activities, see *ibid.*, July 1940; *The Pine Needle*, June 1937.
42. *The Pine Needle*, May 1938. The paper followed up in November with a notice of Armistice Day commemorations of the 92nd and 93rd Divisions of the AEF, made up of colored troops. *Ibid.*, November 1938.
43. *Happy Days*, March 18 and October 7, 1939; *The Trojan*, April 1942.
44. *The Pine Needle*, July 1937.
45. *The Border Tab*, September 1941.
46. *Ibid.*, December 1941.
47. *Ibid.*, March, April and May 1942.
48. *Ibid.*, April 1942.
49. *The Trojan*, February, combined March-April-May issue, and August 1940.
50. *The Pine Needle*, May 1938; March 1939.
51. *The Border Tab*, January 1940.

Chapter 9

1. *Happy Days*, July 1, 1933.
2. As quoted in Michael E. Parrish, *Anxious Decades: America in Prosperity and Depression, 1920–1941* (New York: W.W. Norton and Company, 1992) p. 184.
3. Persons, who had worked with the Red Cross during World War I, had been appointed by Secretary of Labor Francis Perkins. Salmond, *The Civilian Conservation Corps*, pp. 27 and 48; *Happy Days*, December 29, 1934.
4. *Happy Days*, October 28, 1939. Much later, in October 1939, educational advisers were authorized to wear a distinctive uniform, using as their insignia "the well-known lamp of learning."
5. See for an example the program in Company 580, Broadacre, Ohio, discussed in the column "Chalk Talk," *Happy Days*, January 26, 1935.
6. *Happy Days* included a special section—pages 5–10—November 24, 1934. For enrollee debates on the nature of education in the CCC, see for example Company 299's paper, *The Reflector*, January 25, 1935.
7. *Happy Days*, January 26, 1935.
8. *Ibid.*, February 3, 1934; July 20 and August 17, 1940.
9. *Ibid.*, June 29 and July 6, 1940; October 4, 1941.
10. *Ibid.*, April 12, 1941.
11. *Ibid.*, September 14, 1935.
12. *Ibid.*, January 13, 1940.
13. *Ibid.*, March 4, 1939. The NEA attacked the government for what its Educational Policies Commission called "paralleling the state public educational systems by making an educational institution of the Civilian Conservation Corps and the National Youth Administration," and frequently demanded their abolition. See one of McEntee's strong responses in *ibid.*, January 31, 1942.
14. *Ibid.*, March 18, 1939.

15. *Ibid.*, August 8 and September 5, 1936.

16. *Ibid.*, November 3, 1934; January 26, 1935; June 5, 1937. In some CCC camps, the advisers took the educational milieu quite seriously. In Company 2356 at Camp Buffalo, Amherst, Virginia, J.B. Garnett introduced a Camp Yell on the collegiate model: "Hoorah ... Hoorah!!!! Sis Boom Bah!!! C.C.C. Camp, Rah! Rah! Rah!" See in *Buffalo Prints*, February 1936.

17. See in *The Script*, December 20, 1934; *My Own Camp News*, November 1934; *The Courier*, January 10, 1935; *The Broadcast*, September [August] 1940.

18. *The Kanona Daze*, March 1936.

19. The *Tamarack Times*, August 1940; *Happy Days*, May 16, 1936. By the spring of 1938, certificates for the completion of educational work were being printed by the Government Printing Office for general distribution throughout the CCC. Public schools and state educational agencies also awarded certificates for the completion of study programs. See discussions in the *Broadcast*, Company 1742, Tarkio, Missouri, April 1938 and March 1939; and the *Stockade*, Company 2328, Shelocta, Pennsylvania, January 1939.

20. The *Crystal Camp Crier* (Company 1742, Tarkio, Missouri) April 8, 1935; May 14, June 14, September 14, 1936; February 14, 1937.

21. For typical club activities see *The Jubilee Journal* (Company 698, Oak Hill, Illinois) September 21, 1934; *Happy Days*, August 18 and 25, and September 8, 1934.

22. *Happy Days*, March 13, 1937; the *Crystal Camp Crier*, March 14, 1936.

23. *Happy Days*, September 16 and November 4, 1939; February 17 and May 25, 1940.

24. *The Stockade*, October 1937; *The Veterans' Bugle*, January 31, 1938.

25. *The Stockade*, December 1936; September and November 1937.

26. *Happy Days*, August 1, 1936; *Grand Canyon Echoes*, March 1 and December 25, 1936.

27. The *Crystal Camp Crier*, July 10, 1935; June 29, 1936.

28. *754 Cornhusker* (Company 754, Humboldt, Nebraska), winter 1938 issues, passim; *The Broadcast* (Company 1742, Tarkio, Missouri) January 1938.

29. *The Tumbleweed*, November 25, 1935; August 17 and 29, and October 23, 1936.

30. *The Courier*, January 10, 1935; McEntee, *Now They Are Men*, pp. 48–49.

31. *Happy Days*, April 28, 1934; *The Broadcast* (Company 1742, Gallatin, Missouri) June 1940; the *Stockade*, October 1936; September 1937.

32. The *Stockade*, February and October 1937.

33. *Tamarack Times*, February, June and July 1940.

34. *The Catskill Crier*, September 19, October 18, and November 15, 1935; *Happy Days*, May 15, 1937.

35. *The Bugle*, February 19, May 14 and 21 and August 2, 1937.

36. *Happy Days*, April 15, 1939. *Happy Days* contributed to practical educational emphases by including advertisements for the correspondence courses of the Floyd Gibbons School of Broadcasting in Washington, D.C., and others such as the popular Gregg shorthand and Gregg typing courses of the Gregg Publishing Company.

37. The *Stockade*, October and November 1937; January 1938.

38. *The Dam Overflow*, March 22 and April 22, 1935; *Crystal Camp Crier*, June 1937; the *Stockade* October, 1937. To be sure, an emphasis on the practical in the health field might be taken too far. One can only wonder about the educational methods employed by one Dr. Sangmeister, the camp surgeon of Company 1324 in Scotland, Pennsylvania. Seeking the ultimate in realism, as *Happy Days* recounted it in an article "Fido's All Cut Up as Anatomy Class Studies Structure," he "put a stray dog out of his existence of misery in order to show his class in anatomy just how the higher animals are hung together." Thus an end came to "poor Fido, or maybe it was Rover," as Sangmeister "showed the boys exactly how dissection is done in medical colleges, and explained, as he worked, the similarities and differences between Fido's anatomy and that of man." *Happy Days*, June 5, 1937.

39. *The Broadcast* (Company 1742, Gallatin, Missouri) April 1940; the *Stockade*, March 1937; August 1940.

40. The *Stockade*, August 1937.

41. *Vets Voice* (Comany 1774, Bayport, Minnesota) December 18, 1939.

42. *The Veterans' Voice*, September 1937; January and February 1938; the *Vets Voice*, January 25, 1940.

43. *Tamalpais Fog Horn*, March 1939; *Vets Lament*, September 1939, and June and July 1940. The educational program of Company 1921 had to share with the exposition that opened on nearby Treasure Island in early 1939. The men took advantage of its proximity in full swing for nine months to enhance their recreation as well as their education.

44. The *Alpine Echo*, March 1938; the *Tamalpais Fog Horn*, December 1938; *The Veterans' Voice*, January 1939; *Vets Lament*, January 1940.

45. *Happy Days*, November 24, 1934; November 21, 1936; May 22, 1937; the *Crystal Camp Crier* (Company 1742, Tarkio, Missouri), July 14, 1936.

46. The *Stockade*, January 1937; *Happy Days*, November 2, 1935; February 22, 1936; April 22, October 7, and November 11, 1939.

47. *Happy Days*, November 11, 1933; November 30, 1935. *Happy Days* often included special sections on education, and frequently published statistics regarding these endeavors.

48. The *Stockade*, September and December 1937; January 1938; *Grand Canyon Echoes*, July 1, 1936; the *Buffalo Prints*, February 1938.

49. *Happy Days*, March 17, 1934; and November 30, 1935.

50. *Ibid.*, January 19, 1935.

51. *The Bugle*, April 23, 1937.

52. *Happy Days*, June 5, 1937.

53. The *Crystal Camp Crier*, November and December 1937.

54. *Happy Days*, August 25 and September 8, 1934; February 16, March 23, and November 30, 1935; December 24, 1938; January 14 and February 25, 1939.

55. *Ibid.*, August 5 and September 30, 1939; January 27, February 24, and March 9, 1940; January 11, 1941.

56. The desires of the Army were usually considered in establishing what training and deployment would be made of the CCC. *Ibid.*, May 25 and June 1, 1940.

57. *Ibid.*, October 12, November 30, and December 7, 1940. By December 1940, some 41 states and the District of Columbia were granting elementary and high school credits for classwork done in CCC camps.

58. *Ibid.*, March 8 and 22, April 5, and August 23, 1941.

59. *Ibid.*, December 7, 1940; January 11, February 1 and April 5, 1941.

60. *Ibid.*, May 15, 1937.

61. Many former CCC enrollees have informed the author in personal interviews that their CCC training and education often prepared them for immediate promotions, or their being placed in responsible positions, when they entered military service. The *NACCCA Journal*, the monthly publication of the National Association of Civilian Conservation Corps Alumni, is also filled with articles and features regarding the results of CCC educational initiatives.

Chapter 10

1. *Happy Days*, November 4, 1933; May 26, 1934.

2. *Ibid.*, June 2, 1934.

3. *Ibid.*, December 15, 1934; March 16, 1935.

4. *Ibid.*, February 16, 1935.

5. *Ibid.*, July 20, 1935.

6. *Ibid.*, March 2, 1940.

7. *The Candlelight* (Company 1592, Bluffton, Indiana) as quoted in *Happy Days*, April 12, 1941.
8. *The Pine Needle*, December 1938.
9. *Happy Days*, August 1 and November 28, 1936.
10. *Ibid.*, December 15, 1934.
11. *The Pine Needle*, November 1938.
12. The *Stockade* (Company 2328, Homer City, Pennsylvania) January 1941.
13. The text of this card read: "I sign this pledge of my own free will because I wish to have a clean, pure, healthy mind in a healthy body and I know that indecent literature is like a deadly poison." *Happy Days*, October 1, 1938. This literature is discussed in Bob Adelman, Richard Merkin and Art Spiegelman, *Tijuana Bibles: Art and Wit in America's Forbidden Funnies, 1930s–1950s* (New York: Simon and Schuster, 1997).
14. *Happy Days*, February 28, 1942, and passim.
15. See a complete list in *ibid.*, March 20, 1937.
16. *Ibid.*, March 18, 1939.
17. *Ibid.*, February 27, 1937; February 11, 1939.
18. *Ibid.*, February 27, 1937.
19. *Ibid.*, July 17, 1937. There are examples of Kessler's work in *ibid.*, August 7 and 21, 1937.
20. Brenda Maddox, *Nora: The Real Life of Molly Bloom* (Boston: Houghton Mifflin Company, 1988), p. 345.
21. *Tamalpais Fog Horn*, July 1938; *Happy Days*, March 3, 1934, and January 30, 1937.
22. *Crystal Camp Crier*, November 26, 1934.
23. *The Broadcast*, September 1940.
24. *Tamalpais Fog Horn*, November 1938.
25. The *Alpine Echo* January 1937.
26. John Toland, *Captured by History* (New York: St. Martin's Press, 1997), p. 68.
27. *Happy Days*, February 16 and March 9, 1935, and passim. See, among many others, the *Barracks Bearer* (Company 755, Albion, Nebraska), May 18, 1935.
28. *The Pine Needle* (Companies 235 and 237, New Lisbon, New Jersey), March 1939.
29. For representative examples, see the *Vets Voice* (Company 1774, Bayport, Minnesota) February 22, 1940.
30. *The New Yorker* (December 15, 1997), p. 124.
31. *Happy Days*, October 21, 1933.
32. As quoted in *ibid.*, October 21, 1933.
33. *Ibid.*, November 11, 1933.
34. *The Harbinger*, October 9, 1936; *The Jubilee Journal*, August 6, 1934; *Happy Days*, Christmas 1934; The *Rock Hound* (Company 855, El Paso, Texas), June 9, 1934.
35. *Happy Days*, March 12, 1938.
36. *Ibid.*, December 18, 1937; *Vets Voice*, October 23, 1940.
37. *Varieties* (Company 2957, Three River, California).
38. There were a few papers styling themselves scandal sheets, but these were normally short-lived because of opposition from someone in authority, usually the CO. One good example was the *Bung-Hole Droppings*, a weekly "unofficial" two-page publication of Company 763, Tucumseh, Nebraska. This appeared for only a few issues, though specifically why it was terminated is not clear. See typical bon mot in the May 21, 1937, issue: "Christenson says his girl is a virgin but for how long, we wonder?"

Chapter 11

1. The *Alpine Echo*, April 1938.
2. The *Prairie Times*, Whitewater, New Mexico, August and September 1938; *The Camp Crier*, June 1939.
3. *Happy Days*, May 27, 1933; June 13, 1936.

4. *The Bugle*, May 28, 1937.
5. *The Script*, December 7, 1934; *The Catskill Crier*, February 20 and August 23, 1935; the *Stockade*, April 1938.
6. *Happy Days*, August 27, 1938.
7. *Ibid.*, June 13, 1936.
8. *Crystal Camp Crier*, August 14, 1936; *Happy Days*, May 1 and October 2, 1937; April 22 and August 26, 1939.
9. *Happy Days*, August 29, 1936.
10. *TH-CCC News*, October 1, 1940; *The Bugle*, October 21, 1936.
11. The *Stockade* (Company 2328, Shelocta, Pennsylvania), March, 1938; *Happy Days*, May 1, 1937.
12. *Happy Days*, October 28, 1939.
13. *Ibid.*, October 5, 1935.
14. The *Crystal Camp Crier* (Company 1742, Tarkio, Missouri), October 14, 1936.
15. *The Bugle*, May 28 and June 11, 1937; *Co. 299 News*, November 22, 1934; the *Buffalo Prints*, August 1936; April 1938.
16. *My Own Camp News*, November 1934; *Co. 299 News*, November 22, 1934; *Tamalpais Fog Horn*, August 1938; *Happy Days*, May 8, 1937.
17. *Happy Days*, June 13, 1936; *The Catskill Crier*, June 13, 1935.
18. The *Tamalpais Fog Horn*, August and October 1938.
19. *Ibid.*, July 1938.
20. *The Bugle*, October 21, 1936.
21. *The Red Rocks Echo*, July 3, July 10, August 7 and September 22, 1936.
22. *Happy Days*, May 18, 1935.
23. *Ibid.*, January 16, 1937.
24. *Ibid.*, May 18, 1935.
25. *Ibid.*, October 27, 1934.
26. *Ibid.*, February 2 and September 21, 1935; January 11, 1936; April 24, 1937. The screen play for "Blazing Barriers" by Edwin C. Parsons was later serialized in *Happy Days*.
27. *Ibid.*, March 13 and May 1, 1937.
28. *The Catskill Crier*, August 1, 1935.
29. *Happy Days*, February 5, 1938.
30. *Ibid.*, May 27, June 3, September 16 and 23, 1933; *The Harbinger*, September 1936.
31. *Vets Lament*, February.
32. *Happy Days.*, December 8, 1934.
33. The *Stockade*, February 1938.
34. *Happy Days*, October 21, 1933.
35. *Ibid.*, September 2, 1933.
36. *Ibid.*, September 9 and 30, 1933.
37. *Ibid.*, July 8 and 22, 1933; November 3, 1934; March 13, 1937; June 3, 1939.
38. *Ibid.*, July 1, 1933; July 7, 1934.
39. *Ibid.*, July 1 and September 2, 1933.
40. *Ibid.*, July 29 and August 5, 12, and 26, 1933; November 3, 1934.
41. *The Heppner Roundup*, February 1938; *Scraps 'N' Stuff*, April 1938

Chapter 12

1. *Happy Days*, January 20, 1934.
2. The *Rock Hound*, February 22, July 26, and August 9, 1935; *The Catskill Crier*, April, May, June 27 and August 1, 1935; *The Bugle*, September 23, 1936.
3. *Happy Days*, September 12, 1936; May 1, 1937. Some states attempted to tax canteen sales but this was not justified, Fechner insisted, and he asked Congress to forbid the practice, which it did.

4. *Ibid.*, June 3, 1939.

5. *Ibid.*, August 3 and 10, 1935; October 31 and November 14, 1936; July 16 and 23, 1938; June 3, 1939. Ever on the lookout for aids to the canteen stewards, *Happy Days* informed them that the Merchants Service Office of the National Cash Register Company in Dayton, Ohio, had prepared a booklet, *Better Retailing: A Handbook for Merchants,* which the stewards could procure to aid in developing marketing skills. In addition, "Behind the Counter" published its own special bulletin sent out to all camp canteens containing much information about how to run a canteen.

6. *Ibid.*, January 5 and August 10, 1935; April 25, 1936; February 13 and 27, 1937.

7. *Ibid.*, February 27, March 13 and April 3, 1937.

8. *Ibid.*, March 27, April 17 and 24, 1937.

9. Various issues of *ibid.*, March 1936.

10. *Ibid.*, February 22, 1941.

11. *Ibid.*, May 31, 1941.

12. *Ibid.*, October 9, 1937.

13. *Ibid.*, August 3, 1935; November 14, 1936.

14. The ads began in *ibid.*, August 31, 1935, the last "Dope Sheet" appearing in the August 6, 1938, issue. There was also a specially prepared camp cook book, *Come and Get It,* that General Foods distributed to CCC companies.

15. *Happy Days.*, June 3, August 19, and October 7, 1939.

16. *Ibid.*, January 20, 1934; September 26, 1936.

17. *Ibid.*, August 10, 1935; March 27, 1937.

18. *Ibid.*, January 19, February 9, and October 12, 1935; October 7, 1939; June 7, 1941. The paper recorded that Chesterfields and Camels were the leading cigarette brands sold in CCC canteens.

19. *Ibid.*, August 10, 1935; January 16, 1937; May 13, 1939.

20. *Ibid.*, April 18, 1936.

21. *Ibid.*, February 8 and April 11, 1936. So that smokers might light up with greater ease, including its own special CCC cigar which appeared on the market, *Happy Days'* advertising also featured a new "flameless mystery cigarette lighter" both for auto use and for the individual's pocket.

22. *Ibid.*, April 19, 1941.

23. *The Harbinger,* October 23, 1936; and January 29, 1937. The programs of the firms were similar. They provided each of their CCC salesmen with a zippered leather carrying case and a free sample line of their made-to-measure suits, selling from about $14.00 each. A free suit was given to the salesmen for each four sold as their payment.

24. *Happy Days,* January 26, 1935.

25. *Ibid.*, April 18, 1936.

26. *Ibid.*, October 27, 1934; April 18, 1936.

27. *Ibid.*, February 6, 1937.

28. *Ibid.*, October 16, 1937.

29. *Ibid.*, August 26, 1939.

30. *Ibid.*, September 3, 1938, and passim.

31. See typical ad in *ibid.*, October 19, 1935

Chapter 13

1. *The Bugle,* October 7, 1935.

2. *Happy Days,* July 21, 1934; March 23, 1935; December 6, 1941; February 20, 1937. The *Tamarack Times,* January 1940.

3. *The Veterans' Bugle,* March 1938.

4. Poem quoted in *Happy Days,* November 16, 1940. "The memory of the associations formed in the CCC will be one that the boys will cherish all their lives," one writer concluded, which has proved to be the case. See in *Happy Days,* March 1, 1941,

and April 4, 1942; the *Stockade*, December 1940 and March 1941. To be sure, the fraternity of CCC alumni nowadays tend to dwell upon the positive side of life during the Depression, sometimes ignoring or glossing over the harsher aspects of the times they lived through.

5. The *Stockade* (Company 2328, Shelocta, Pennsylvania) October 1936.

6. *Happy Days*, August 12, 1933; January 27, 1934.

7. *Ibid.*, June 30 and December 22, 1934; May 11, 1935. For statistics of the CCC see Stan Cohen, *The Tree Army: A Pictorial History of the Civilian Conservation Corps, 1933–1942* (Missoula, Montana: Pictorial Histories Publishing Company, 1980) passim, and *Happy Days*, November 2, 1940.

8. In addition, three foremen, a forest ranger, and a civilian workman died. *Happy Days*, August 28 and October 2, 1937.

9. *Ibid.*, July 21, 1934; October 5, 1935; February 22, June 20, and November 21 and 28, 1936; May 29, 1937.

10. *Ibid.*, July 25 and November 7, 1936.

11. *Ibid.*, June 8 and October 5, 1935; November 28, 1936; May 15, 1937; January 15 and November 19, 1938; January 4 and March 8 and 29, 1941; and the *TH-CCC News* (Hawaiian Miscellaneous Companies, Honolulu, Hawaii) June 1941.

12. Company 1229, Machias, New York.

13. As quoted in *Happy Days*, November 28, 1936.

14. Eric Bergerud, *Touched With Fire: The Land War in the South Pacific*. (New York: Viking, 1996) p. 153.

15. Numerous World War II memoirs and studies make the point that the CCC helped toughen and otherwise prepare American's military forces for war. See, for example, Gerald Astor, *Crisis in the Pacific: The Battles for the Philippine Islands by the Men Who Fought Them—An Oral History* (New York: Donald I. Fine, 1996) pp. 188, 356, 372 and passim, discussing servicemen with CCC backgrounds.

16. *Look*, July 30, 1940, as reported in *The Alaskan* (Admiralty CCC Division, Juneau, Alaska) August 20, 1940.

17. *Happy Days*, November 9, 1940.

18. Forrest C. Pogue, *George C. Marshall: Education of a General, 1880–1939* (London: MacGibbon and Kee, 1964) pp. 292, 317, 324. It is significant that Marshall welcomed these contacts with citizen soldiers from which he drew his faith in the value and effectiveness of a citizen army. From the same experience he became familiar with the civilian point of view in a way rare among professional military men. A member of his staff later commented that "he had a feeling for civilians that few Army officers ... have had.... He didn't have to adjust to civilians—they were a natural part of his environment.... I think he regarded civilians and military as part of a whole."

19. Ed Cray, *General of the Army: George C. Marshall, Soldier and Statesman* (New York: W.W. Norton and Company, 1990) pp. 115 and 125, the Annual Report of the Army Chief of Staff 1933, and discussion in *Happy Days*, December 2, 1933.

20. *Happy Days*, June 4, 1938.

21. *The Broadcast*, November 1939; *Happy Days*, October 26, 1940.

22. *Happy Days*, September 28, 1940; May 7, 1938; *Th-CCC News* (Hawaiian Composite Companies, Honolulu, Hawaii), October 1, 1940; June 1, 1941.

23. *Happy Days*, June 1, 1935. See useful article on the function and role of the CCC camp papers in *The Harbinger* (Company 698, Argyle, Wisconsin) September 11, 1936.

24. *Happy Days*, November 4, 1933.

25. *Snappy Daze*, December 16, 1933.

26. *Happy Days*, June 1, 1940.

27. *Ibid.*, March 29, 1941.

28. Rudeen, *The Civilian Conservation Corps Camp Papers: A Guide*, p. v.; Rudeen, "Final Performance Report," p. 1.

Selected Bibliography

This study is largely based on an extended microfilmed run of *Happy Days* located at The Hoover Institution, Stanford, California, supplemented by rolls from the State Historical Society of Wisconsin in Madison. In addition, hundreds of CCC camp newspapers were perused on microfilm or microfiche obtained from the Center for Research Libraries in Chicago. The excellent guide to these sources is: Marlys Rudeen. *The Civilian Conservation Corps Camp Newspapers: a Guide.* Chicago: The Center for Research Libraries, 1991. Additional microfilmed camp newspapers came from the Nebraska State Historical Society, Lincoln, Nebraska. The finding aid for records of the CCC, especially Record Group 35 located in the National Archives in Washington, D.C., is: Douglas Helms. *National Archives (U.S.). Preliminary Inventory of the Records of the Civilian Conservation Corps.* Washington, D.C.: National Archives and Records Service, General Services Administration, 1980. Also of major importance were the numerous interviews and other contacts with members of various chapters of the National Association of Civilian Conservation Corps Alumni throughout the nation, and also members of the staff of that organization located at Jefferson Barracks, St. Louis, Missouri. Finally, much material was obtained from the internet, the online sources provided by the Library of Congress being especially useful.

Selected Books and Articles:

Adelman, Bob, Richard Merkin and Art Spiegelman. *Tijuana Bibles: Art and Wit in America's Forbidden Funnies, 1930s–1950s.* New York: Simon and Schuster, 1997.

American Youth Commission. *The Civilian Conservation Corps.* Washington, D.C.: American Council on Education, 1940. This book contains the educational recommendations of the American Youth Commission of the American Council on Education.

271

Barber, William. *Designs Within Disorder: Franklin D. Roosevelt, the Economists, and the Shaping of American Economic Policy, 1933–1945.* New York: Cambridge University Press, 1996.

Bauman, John F., and Thomas H. Coode. *In the Eye of the Great Depression: New Deal Reporters and the Agony of the American People.* De Kalb: Northern Illinois University Press, 1988.

Butler, Ovid, ed. *Youth Rebuilds: Stories from the C.C.C.* Washington, D.C.: American Forestry Association, 1934.

Cohen, Stan B. *The Tree Army: A Pictorial History of the Civilian Conservation Corps, 1933–1942.* Missoula, Montana: Pictorial Histories Publishing Company, 1980.

Cole, Olen, Jr. *The African-American Experience in the Civilian Conservation Corps.* Gainesville: University Press of Florida, 1999. One of the few accounts of the blacks in the CCC, this useful study focuses on black enrollees in California.

Dearborn, Ned Harland. *Once in a Lifetime: A Guide to the CCC Camp.* New York: Charles E. Merrill Company, 1935.

Eliot, Thomas H. *Recollections of the New Deal: When the People Mattered.* Boston: Northeastern University Press, 1992.

Fenwick, Robert W. "They took to the woods ... and came out men." *Empire Magazine* (June 20, 1965) pp. 6–9. Several photos of CCC activities.

Gallup, George H. *The Gallup Poll: Public Opinion, 1935–1971.* New York: Random House, 1972.

Guthrie, John D. *Saga of the CCC.* Washington, D.C.: American Forestry Association, 1942.

Hanson, James A. "The Civilian Conservation Corps in the Northern Rocky Mountains." Ph.D. dissertation, University of Wyoming, 1973.

Hill, Edwin G. *In the Shadow of the Mountain: The Spirit of the CCC.* Pullman, Washington: State University Press, 1990.

Hill, Frank Ernest. *The School in the Camps: The Educational Program of the Civilian Conservation Corps.* New York: American Association for Adult Education, 1935.

Holland, Kenneth, and Frank Ernest Hill. *Youth in the CCC.* Washington, D.C.: American Council on Education, 1942.

Hoyt, Ray. *"We Can Take It": A Short Story of the C.C.C.* New York: American Book Company, 1935.

Jernberg, Albert W. *My Brush Monkeys: A Narrative of the CCC.* New York: Richard R. Smith, 1941.

Johnson, Charles W. "The Army and the Civilian Conservation Corps—1933–42." *Prologue*, Vol. 4 no. 3 (Fall 1972), 139–156.

_____. "The Civilian Conservation Corps: The Role of the Army." Ph.D. dissertation, University of Michigan, 1968.

Kennedy, David M. *Freedom from Fear: The American People in Depression and War, 1929–1945.* New York: Oxford University Press, 1999.

Kornbluh, Joyce L. *A New Deal for Workers Education: The Workers Service Program, 1933–1942.* Champaign: University of Illinois Press, 1988. For women's programs akin to CCC.

Lacy, Leslie Alexander. *The Soil Soldiers: The Civilian Conservation Corps in the Great Depression*. Radnor, Penn.: Chilton Book Company, 1976.

Lanier, Ann. "The Civilian Conservation Corps, 1933–1942: Organizational Structure and Social Effects." MA Thesis, University of Colorado, 1983.

Lasswell, James. *Shovel and Guns: The CCC in Action*. New York: International Pamphlets, 1935. Rabid anti–CCC tract from the point of view of American communists.

Lyons, Thomas, ed. *1930 Employment 1980: Humanistic Perspectives on the Civilian Conservation Corps in Colorado*. Boulder: Colorado Division of Employment and Training, U.S. Department of Agriculture—Forest Service, and the Office of Youth Programs, U.S. Department of the Interior [1980].

McEntee, James J. *Now They Are Men*. Washington, D.C.: National Home Library Foundation, 1940.

Merrill, Perry Henry. *Roosevelt's Tree Army: A History of the Civilian Conservation Corps, 1933–1942*. Montpelier, VT.: P.H. Merrill, 1981.

O'Hearon, Maide [Mrs. C.E. Moyer]. *Some Find a New Dawn*. Aurora, Missouri: Burney Brothers Publishing Company, 1936(?). This book was by the wife of Clarence E. Moyer, superintendent of CCC Co. 1734, and was based on a year's collection of material concerned specifically with eight CCC boys. Moralistic in tone, the book was published under her maiden name.

Oliver, Alfred E., Jr., and Harold M. Dudley. *This New America: The Spirit of the Civilian Conservation Corps*. London: Longmans, Green and Co., 1937.

Parham, Robert Bruce. "The Civilian Conservation Corps in Colorado, 1933–1942." MA Thesis, University of Colorado, 1981.

Parrish, Michael. *Anxious Decades: America in Prosperity and Depression, 1920–1941*. New York: Norton, 1992. Useful survey.

Salmond, John A. *The Civilian Conservation Corps, 1933–1942: A New Deal Case Study*. Durham: Duke University Press, 1967. Classic historical account of the CCC. Indispensable.

United States. Civilian Conservation Corps. *Woodsmanship for the Civilian Conservation Corps*. Washington, D.C.: U.S. Government Printing Office, 1938.

_____. Soil Conservation Service. *The CCC at Work: A Story of 2,500,000 Young Men*. Washington, D.C.: U.S. Government Printing Office, 1941. Many good photographs and an elementary text.

Uys, Errol Lincoln. *Riding the Rails: Teenagers on the Move During the Great Depression*. TV Books, 1999.

"Volcanic Editors: The CCC Newsmen Work on Edge of Crater and Everywhere Else." *The Literary Digest*, Vol. 123, No. 24, June 12, 1937, p. 32.

Wallgren, Abian. *Happy Days Cartoons of the C.C.C.* Washington, D.C.: Happy Days Publishing Company, 1934.

Yenawine, Wayne S. "CCC Camp Papers." MA thesis, University of Illinois, 1938.

Your CCC. A Handbook for Enrollees. Washington, D.C.: Happy Days Publishing Company, n.d.

Index

275

Harris, Herb (*Happy Days* official) 48,
  63–64
Hartford (Connecticut) *Courant* 34
Hawaii 12, 87, 99, 116–117, 214, 238
Hayti Scoop (Co. 3741, Hayti, Mis-
  souri) 102
The Headquarters Star (Headquarters
  Company, Sparta District, Wiscon-
  sin) 34
Hemingway, Ernest 61
Heppner Round-up (Co. 297, Heppner,
  Oregon) 50, 100, 195, 222
Hi Hatti I'm in the Navy Now (book) 78
Hi-De-Hi-De-Ho (Co. 4487, Anderson,
  South Carolina) 41, 160
Hindenburg (airship) 172
Hints for School Newspapers (Ditto
  Company) 36
Hitler, Adolf 61–62, 77, 78, 153, 154,
  245
Hooey (Co. 553, Defiance, Ohio) 50,
  51, 130–131, 205
Hoover, Herbert 108
Horner, Henry (Illinois governor) 128
Horse Shoe Ringer (Co. 4736, Horse
  Shoe Bend, Idaho) 34
*How to Win Friends and Influence Peo-
  ple* (Dale Carnegie) 200
Howard University 166
Hoxeyville Daze (Co. 679, Wellston,
  Michigan) 37
Hoy-La (Co. 985, Santa Barbara, Cali-
  fornia) 28, 50
Hoyt, Ray (*Happy Days* managing edi-
  tor) 66, 82

I Am the Fox (Van Etten) 191
Ickes, Harold L. (Secretary of the Inte-
  rior) 109
Indian Creek Ripple (Co. 4776, Monti-
  cello, Utah) 210
The Indian Trail (Co. 728, Salem, Mis-
  souri) 49, 122, 171
Indianapolis Recorder 166
Indianola (Iowa) *Record and Tribune*
  34
The Infant Tree (Co. 3882, Grass Valley,
  California) 38
Infantry Drill Regulations 79–80
Ink Crumbs (Co. 113, Chester, Massa-
  chusetts) 38
International Association of Machinists
  9
International Brigade (Spain) 216

International Correspondence Schools
  190
In-Zane Monthly (Co. 1575, Belle-
  fontaine, Ohio) 150, 152, 205, 207
The Iron Miner (Co. 209, Cold Spring,
  New York) 31
"It's a Great Life" (CCC documentary
  film) 217

Janis, Elsie (entertainer) 215
Jefferson, Thomas 153
The Jefferson Excavator (Co. 580,
  Broadacre, Ohio) 34
The Jolly Griper (Co. 752, Hebron, Ne-
  braska) 208
Joseph Conrad (U.S. training ship) 183
Joyce, James 201
The Jubilee Journal (Co. 698, Oak Hill,
  Illinois) 61, 123, 205

Ka Hui O Mauna Loa (Co. 9502,
  Hawaii National Park, Hawaii) 57
Ka Leo O Ka Makani O Kamuela (Co.
  9502, Kamuela, Hawaii) 28
Kai-shek, General Chiang 199
Kanona Daze (Co. 297, Kanoa, New
  York) 6, 59, 95, 102, 182
The Kanonan (Co. 297, Kanona, New
  York) 85
Kansas State College 190
The Kearsarge Kettle (Co. 1147, Warner,
  New Hampshire) 26
Keedle, Charles H. (author) 36
Kelly, Nancy (actress) 58
The Kentucky Colonel (Co. 3556, Green
  River, Utah) 32
The Keyhole (Co. 432, Stantonsburg,
  North Carolina) 32
Kiamichi Forester (Co. 876, Nashoba,
  Oklahoma) 206
Kilmer, Joyce 220
King, Wayne (band leader) 58
Kipling, Rudyard 56
Kyser, Kay (band leader) 58

Lakeside Review (Co. 3710, Waterville,
  Minnesota) 149
Lamar, Hedy 132
Lardner, Ring 214
Lawrence Lookout (Co. 549, Ironton,
  Ohio) 205
Lee, Dougal (cartoonist) 77
Lee-Grant Surrender (Co. 2391, Appo-
  mattox, Virginia) 40

Turner, Colonel Roscoe (aviator) 228
Tuskegee Institute 166
The 299th Broadcast (Co. 299, Masonville, New York) 96
Tyner, General George P. (War Department official) 117
A Typical American (Theodore "Teddy" Roosevelt) 200

"U" Name It (Co. 679, Wellston, Michigan) 37
Ulio, General James A. (U.S. Army Adjutant General) 242
Uncle Sam's Cabin (Co. 3545, Pathfork, Kentucky) 40
United Press (UP) 36
United States Army 177, 194
United States Army Air Corps 112, 189
United States Army Band 129
United States Army Corps of Engineers 10, 19
United States Army Medical Corps 221, 240
United States Army, newspapers of 64
United States Army Office of Chief of Finance 10
United States Army Quartermaster Corps 240
United States Bureau of Animal Industry 10
United States Bureau of Entomology and Plant Quarantine 10
United States Bureau of Plant Industry 10
United States Bureau of Reclamation 10
United States Coast Guard 183
United States Congress 8, 9, 17, 18, 19, 149, 177, 193
United States Department of Agriculture 6, 8, 9, 10, 14, 182, 221
United States Department of Labor 8, 9, 17
United States Department of the Interior 8, 9, 10, 12, 14, 183
United States Employment Service 177
United States Federal Security Agency 7, 17
United States Fish and Wildlife Service 10
United States Forest Service 6, 8, 31, 91
United States General Land Office 10

United States Grazing Service 10
United States Maritime Service 183
United States National Park Service 10, 16, 182
United States Navy 111–112
United States Navy Department 10, 18, 182–183, 193
United States Office of Education 13, 17, 193
United States Public Health Service 17
United States Senate 242
United States Social Security Board 17
United States Soil Conservation Service 10, 16
United States War Department 8, 9, 10, 80, 99, 118, 119, 193–194, 199, 211, 240
United States Works Progress Administration 178, 184, 186
United States Works Progress Administration, Drama Department of 162
University of Illinois 2, 25, 37, 243
University of North Dakota 190
Upanatem (Co. 602, Meyers Falls, Washington) 38
The Upshot (Co. 1572, St. Paris, Ohio) 63

The Valley Crier (Co. 317, Hillsgrove, Pennsylvania) 31
Valpariso (Florida) *News* 244
Veterans 11–12, 137–157; bonus 149–150; education and 188–189
The Veterans' Bugle (Co. 2775, Mandan, North Dakota) 139, 154, 155, 184, 235
The Veterans' Voice (Co. 1774, Rochester and Ely, Minnesota) 137, 140–141, 147–148, 150–151, 152–153, 188
Vet's Call (Co. 2713, Fairfax, Minnesota) 50, 139, 147
Vets Echo (Co. 1327, Lancaster, Pennsylvania) 145
Vets Lament (Co. 1921, Fairfax, California) 140, 143, 156, 195
The Vets Voice (Co. 1774, Rochester and Bayport, Minnesota) 142, 147, 152, 153, 156, 206, 208, 209, 210
Vingt Ans Apres (Co. 2414, Sumter, South Carolina) 145
Virgin Islands 12

The Waggin' Tongue (Co. 910, Soda Springs, Idaho) 38

Judith Gentleman

Mexican Oil
and Dependent Development

PETER LANG
New York · Berne · Frankfurt am Main

Library of Congress Cataloging in Publication Data

Gentleman, Judith, 1950–
  Mexican Oil and Dependent Development.

  (American University Studies.   Series X, Political
science; v. 2)
  Bibliography: p.
  1. Petroleum industry and trade – Mexico.   2. Mexico –
Dependency on foreign countries.   I. Title.   II. Series.
  HD9574.M6G46   1984   338.2'728'0972   83-48896
  ISBN 0-8204-0063-7
  ISSN 0740-0470

CIP-Kurztitelaufnahme der Deutschen Bibliothek

Gentleman, Judith:
Mexican Oil and Dependent Development / Judith
Gentleman. – New York; Berne; Frankfurt am Main:
Lang, 1984.
  (American University Studies: Ser. 10,
  Political Science; Vol. 2)
  ISBN 0-8204-0063-7

NE: American University Studies / 10

© Peter Lang Publishing, Inc., New York 1984

Printed by Lang Druck, Inc., Liebefeld/Berne (Switzerland)

Table of Contents

List of Tables

Preface

This study was conceived as an opportunity to examine the impact that the condition of dependency would have upon Mexico's effort to develop its huge petroleum resources in the mid 1970s. What follows is hardly a pleasant tale and one that provides little encouragement for those searching for solutions to underdevelopment within the contemporary Mexican political setting. Despite the fact that the study details a failed development project, the alternative to the model in place is far from obvious, as painful as that observation may be. Indeed, the failure of the development project and the analysis presented here of that failure is not directly suggestive of a preferable development alternative. While a "socialist" model is usually implied by dependency analysis, the socialist alternative frankly provides little guarantee of a prospect of long term viability, self-directed development and essential political and human rights to oppressed people.

The completion of the study was supported by the Geneseo Foundation of the State University College of New York at Geneseo. A summer research grant from the Foundation provided financial support for which I am most grateful. Thanks are due especially to Gary Hoskin, James Petras, Claude E. Welch, Jr. and Voytek Zubek for comments upon an earlier version of the study.

x

The State and Dependency

CHAPTER I

Like Iran, Venezuela, Nigeria and other oil rich states before it, in the late 1970s and early 1980s, Mexico embarked upon its own project of "sowing" revenues earned from its enormous oil resources. Plagued by an array of serious economic, social and demographic problems. Mexico stood at a crucial juncture in its development. The ramifications of Mexico's oil development policy and the uses to which revenues generated by the resource would be put were of the most profound importance for Mexico's ensuing development. As one astute observer noted, the "oil may enable Mexico to slip away from the IMF but not from history."[1]

By 1983, Mexico ranked fourth in proven reserves and production among world oil producers. Its proven reserves of oil and gas were put at seventy-two billion barrels. The most optimistic assessments put Mexico's reserves at a potential 700 billion barrels and suggest that its reserves may in fact be equivalent to the entire Middle East.[2]

The Mexican government maintained that the oil bonanza would permit the country to accelerate its development project while enabling it to overcome negative aspects of the economic and social order such as external dependence, internal inequalities and regional imbalances. Mexico, it was argued, would be able to disentangle itself from the web created by its dependent state status and to create a previously unknown level of prosperity that would extend to all Mexicans. The serious structural problems within the economy that posed the most difficult challenges in the long run could now be met because petroleum development would provide greater revenue to the state.

During this period, Mexican policy-makers evidenced considerable sensitivity to the negative outcomes that had resulted in other oil rich economies. Certainly, the Iranian Islamic revolution and its precipitants provided food for thought for Mexican elites. While the Iranian experience was not usually alluded to directly, the point was not lost on policy-makers that the continued marginalization of the bulk of the population could portend calamitous developments. At a less catastrophic level, the Venezuelan experience suggested that care had to be taken to avoid excessive dependence upon the petroleum sector. The experiences of other oil-based economies illustrated the impact of the inflation generated by the development of enormous oil resources in already fragile economies. Fear of such outcomes led to a substantial new planning effort and the design of what was argued to be a program for balanced development that would incorporate previously excluded population groups, regions and economic sectors and would prevent the onset of the types of economic problems in which the program could easily become ensnared.

Yet some analysts argued that the nature of Mexico's development model in fact would preclude the attainment of the ends stipulated by the regime. Moreover, it was argued that paradoxically, the petroleum resource in essence would only compound existing problems by providing short term panaceas to symptoms emerging from structurally rooted problems. More importantly,

oil revenue would shore up the specific network of internal and
external relations that have inhibited real development in Mexico while encouraging economic growth that has been distorted by
virtue of its dependent character and that has failed to meet
societal needs.

The specific pattern of economic growth in Mexico may be
argued to resemble closely Fernando Henrique Cardoso's model of
associated dependent development wherein economic growth in aggregate terms is registered - and in the case of Mexico has even
been fairly spectacular - but development in a fully articulated
sense has not been achieved. Instead, in this perspective, economic growth is argued to have been conditioned by the requirements of the center state(s) economy thereby distorting development in the periphery. The model suggests that the relationship
that has been forged between elites in center and periphery in
the international system has determined for whom the peripheral
economy exists, in its most fundamental sense, and who has benefited from the system of production.

Mexico's petroleum resource, considered to be a national
inheritance, is managed by the state sector under the auspices
of the state petroleum enterprise, Petróleos Mexicanos (Pemex).
With the exception of secondary petrochemical production, the
bulk of Mexico's oil, gas, petrochemical and fertilizer industry
falls within the state sector. As a result, the petroleum development project was expected to expand significantly the state's
critical role within Mexico's economy. These developments have
invited examination of the process and consequent impact of the
expansion of the state's activity in hydrocarbon resource development and in other areas upon Mexico's development program.
Two related areas of theoretical concern - the nature and
function of the state in societies characterized by associated
dependent development and the "theory" of dependency itself have
framed our consideration of Mexico's petroleum development.

The study addresses the question of whether the expansion
of the state sector and the consequent maturation of Mexican
state capitalism have resulted in substantial changes for Mexico
with regard to its dependent character either at the level of
international exchange or at the level of internal class relations. The study seeks to discover whether the process of associated dependent development has demonstrated an ability to
transform Mexico's oil, clearly an asset in objective terms,
into tangible benefits for the mass of the population. Have
Mexican elites succeeded in circumventing those aspects of the
growth model that tend to preclude adequate distribution of
wealth and tend to produce serious economic distortions? Some
have argued that the oil-fueled growth of the state would enable
the state to enjoy a degree of autonomy that would free it to
devise a progressive set of development policies addressing
those areas of society and economy long neglected or disadvantaged by the development model. This study examines the contention advanced in some quarters that within a state capitalist
model of development, and specifically in the Mexican case,
enhanced autonomy financed by oil revenues would enable the

state to adopt a more "neutral" character. In this view, the newly financially independent state could be expected to arrogate to itself ever increasing responsibility for the central entrepreneurial function in society, thus unchaining itself from the dominant class in society, ultimately creating a truly independent state sector that would act in the "common" interest.

The emergence of a strengthened state capitalist regime would result not simply from the availability of additional revenues but would stem as well from several other outcomes of the hydrocarbon development program. The state would need to effectively confront problems emerging from the development model that could be aggravated by the petroleum boom. Almost inevitably, the state would seek to enhance its planning and management capability to meet this need and to plan for the investment of petroleum resources. In addition, in state capitalist regimes, the tendency over time has been for states to attempt to improve upon the terms of the dependency relationships. In the wake of Mexico's petroleum development, it was expected that the state would attempt to profit from anticipated bargaining advantages in order to strengthen its position vis-à-vis foreign capital.

The study addresses the question of whether such efforts have indeed been undertaken and further, attempts to ascertain whether the relationship of dependency has been modified in any fundamental sense as Mexican elites suggested would be possible. Has the petroleum boom intensified Mexico's long-standing dependency or has it facilitated national development?

Dependency Theory

Born out of contradictory intellectual traditions, dependency theory is an umbrella term that has sought to explain the causes of poverty, immiseration and failed economic programs in the Third World. Its critics emanate from a variety of theoretical backgrounds ranging from the classic desarrollista or developmentalist position to that of orthodox Marxism. Yet despite pronouncements regarding its death, its obsolescence or misguided emphasis, it continues to be regarded as having considerable heuristic value for the study of underdevelopment.

The British political economist E.V.K. Fitzgerald notes that early dependency writing concentrated on international exchange and the "excessive export of surplus" rather than "production or accumulation."[3] Those who engaged in this early strain of work have been termed the "surplus extractionists", and include such writers as André Gunder Frank, Paul Baran, Paul Sweezy, Samir Amin, Arrighi Emmanuel, Immanuel Wallerstein, Ruy Mauro Marini, and even Raúl Prebisch.[4] Some authors like Prebisch, writing from the developmentalist perspective, and others like Frank, writing within a Marxist tradition (although hardly orthodox in his approach), concluded that underdevelopment was caused essentially by the extraction of surplus in various forms by the industrialized states.

Early theorists within the dependency framework argued that the problem of underdevelopment was one fundamentally rooted at the international level and suggested that national development could take place if the condition of dependency at the level of international exchange could be remedied. Essentially the challenge was that of overcoming "dependency within capitalism."[5] A critique of the international system emerged which attempted to explain how it was that autonomous national capitalist development had been stymied. As a direct result, Third World ruling groups launched what proved to be a frustrating attempt to establish a New International Economic Order in hopes of achieving a redefinition of the terms of their dependence. It soon became apparent that the early analyses were essentially nationalist in orientation and placed "nations and regions" rather than classes at the core of the analysis of dependency as the "ultimate actors,"[6] a quality which some found disturbing.

Surplus extractionists such as Baran and Frank, as well as the structural reformists at ECLA, were criticized for focusing almost exclusively upon international exchange to the detriment of consideration of what Richard Fagen, for example, terms the "logic of capitalist production and distribution at the national level."[7] Cardoso also condemned the early emphasis upon surplus extraction, terming it the "vulgar current of dependency theory" that "regarded imperialism and external economic conditioning as the substantive and omnipresent explanation of every social and ideological process that occurred."[8] While some came to regard this early tendency as a fatal flaw within the framework, interest in the approach has been sustained.

Despite the enormous gulf that separates the work of individual theorists loosely grouped within the dependency approach, some consensus regarding the conceptual core of the framework appears to have emerged around the following points:
- Underdevelopment cannot be understood as strictly a national problem; development in the periphery is viewed as essentially reflexive in nature. As a result, dependent economies develop critical distortions.
- Unequal exchange characterizes the interaction between core and periphery in the international system.
- Peripheral social formations are functions of the core - periphery relationship in the international system.[9]

Dissatisfaction with the early work pursued within the dependency approach inevitably spawned efforts to correct errors of focus and emphasis in seeking to explain the sources of underdevelopment while relying on core elements of the approach. World systems theory[10] and the concept of the internationalization of capital are representative of these efforts.[11] Cardoso's model of associated dependent development represents still another variant and it is to a consideration of this model that we now turn.

Associated Dependent Development

Cardoso has been erroneously classified by some as a member of the surplus extractionist school of dependency theorists and has also been accused of heretical eclecticism as well as the violation of numerous sacred orthodoxies. His analysis of underdevelopment is actually based upon a two-pronged approach: first, the nature of exchange between core and periphery and secondly, the analysis of the domestic social relations spawned by the internationalization of peripheral economies. While some argue that the study of domestic social relations should constitute the primary focus of the study of underdevelopment, Cardoso's approach also includes analysis of the core-periphery relations which provide the context in which domestic social relations are immersed. Focusing exclusively upon domestic social relations can provide only partial results in the study of underdevelopment and therefore should not be relied upon to the detriment of other considerations.

Within the dependency framework, Cardoso's formulation of the concept of associated dependent development has proved to be an important advance over earlier works by others who tended to conceive of dependent economies only in terms of those characteristics that pertained to the most rudimentary enclave, primary-product-reliant types of economies. Cardoso refutes the idea of the impossibility of development in the periphery and with it the assumption that dependence necessarily implies stagnation. The antiquated depiction of the establishment of enclave economies established for the export of raw materials or minimally processed goods no longer accurately describes the range of Third World economies within the international system.[12]

His work suggests that in contrast to earlier types of dependency, in many instances, the foreign internal market, however limited, has taken on a new importance with the expansion of capitalism essentially relying upon a degree of prosperity in markets such as Mexico's, particularly with the heavy involvement of transnational corporations (TNC) in manufacturing for internal consumption by middle and upper classes.[13] Increasingly, transnational subsidiaries in Latin America especially depend upon host country markets for the bulk of their sales.[14]

In fact, Cardoso asserts that the internal markets of dependent states such as Mexico have in essence been "internationalized" as

> part of the industrial system of the hegemonic countries
> (has been) transferred, under the control of international corporations, to countries that have already been
> able to reach a relatively advanced level of industrial
> development.[15]

As the work of Theodore Moran, Raymond Vernon and the Harvard Business school project, along with the work in Mexico of Newfarmer and Mueller,[16] has shown, direct foreign investment (DFI) in the contemporary period has most frequently involved the mobilization of host country capital resources rather than transfers of surplus capital to peripheral economies from the center states. As has been the case in Mexico, capital has been mobilized by means of the takeover of local enterprises in defense of TNC market shares, most commonly following the adoption of protectionist barriers against imports in order to protect domestic infant industry. As has been widely noted,

direct foreign investment along with royalty payments, licensing
fees, debt servicing and amortization, intra-TNC transfers and
exorbitant profit-taking have resulted in net transfers of capital to the center nations.[17]
    Cardoso argues that:

> After an advanced capitalist sector is implanted, its
> dynamism (which could have benefited in the initial
> phase from reserves of labor and pockets of poverty)
> no longer depends on the development of underdevelop-
> ment but, on the contrary, requires the real creation
> of a capitalist consumption market. This market is not
> simply comprised of the consumption of workers, but
> also that of capitalists, and, more especially, of firms,
> the state, and the classes linked to the tertiary sector.[18]

Cardoso does not deny the existence of restrictive markets or
distortions in productive capacity but he argues that these conditions do not render capitalism unviable. An important difference does exist, however, between capitalism in center and
periphery:

> ...competition between capitalists...leads - in the
> case of dependent economies to an increase in the
> demand for the production of capital goods in the
> central economies, and considering the deterioration
> of the terms of trade, also leads to increasing
> foreign indebtness.[19]

    Lying at the heart of the process of dependent development
is the fact that the cycle of capital accumulation must be completed at the international level. Cardoso and Faletto argue
that "a system is dependent when the accumulation and expansion
of capital cannot find its essential dynamic component inside
the system."[20]

> ...capitalist accumulation in dependent economies does
> not complete its cycle. The accumulation, expansion
> and self-realization of local capital requires and
> depends on a dynamic complement outside itself: it
> must insert itself into the circuit of international
> capital.[21]

    Cardoso and Faletto's work suggests that in the case of Mex-
ico, for example, the economy simply does not have the ability to
"enlarge the scale of capital" which is a process that is reliant
upon control over and creation of new technology and the "continuous expansion of the production of 'capital goods'."[22] Thus, as
a dependent state, Mexico's economic structure would have its
"main features determined by the phases and trend of expansion of
capitalism on a world scale."[23]
    The maintenance of an acceptable level of economic growth
would require that the level of the import of capital goods be
maintained if not expanded. Fundamentally, however, the fact

that the capital goods sector along with the infrastructure supporting technical innovation in that sector resides in the center
states (primarily the U.S.) means that "the dynamism deriving
from investment in the domestic market spreads to the center..."[24]
That is, instead of a "deepening" of the Mexican industrial
structure, one would expect to see little progress in the production of intermediate and capital goods. As José Serra has noted,
the "highly regressive distribution of income" spawned by dependent capitalism produces a market structure which can only be
served by the continued importation of high technology capital
and consumer goods.[25]

Venezuela's development pattern, despite its oil riches,
constitutes a classic example of just such outcomes. Petras,
Morley and Smith found that:

> Little effort has been directed toward long-term, large-
> scale projects in basic industry; even less attention
> has been paid toward fostering innovation, research, or
> the design of new technology. By demanding and getting
> government subsidies and protection, extremely high
> profit margins are maintained, which in turn allow the
> private sector to pay royalties to foreign manufactur-
> ers in order to borrow technology and designs or to
> import semi-finished goods.[26]

For elites in Mexico and other dependent societies, the
dilemma of associated dependent development is essentially that
contradictions emanating from the internationalization of the
economy may eventually defy solution. The structuring of the
most dynamic sectors of the economy on the basis of external
variables yielding employment and production profiles inconsistent with the needs of the mass of peripheral populations and producing financial insolvency may _eventually_ render a marginally
viable form, unviable. The continued linkage with "market,
investment and decision-making structures located outside the
dependent country"[27] can produce contradictions, (for example,
the employment minimizing character of capital intensive center
state technology), that are not amenable to solution by elites in
the periphery.

The model suggests that the internationalization of the
economy is achieved largely by means of the relationship that
exists between elites in center and periphery. Thus, the Mexican
class structure is rooted in the "coincidences of interests
between local dominant classes and international ones..."[28]
Cardoso argues that the study of internal class relations must be
understood within the context of how "internal social groups
defined the outward directed relations implicit in underdevelopment."[29] Thus, the composition of Mexican elites would be understood as having been critically affected by the dynamic of dependency and continually conditioned by their insertion into the
international system. At the same time, these classes are con-
tinuosly engaged in a process of redefining the external linkage
within certain parameters, an activity that generates their own

transformation and more specifically, as we shall see in our discussion of the state, the realignment of groups within the dominant sector in terms of relations with the state and transnational actors. As Cardoso notes "the relation of dependence does not
mean that national history in dependent nations will simply
reflect changes in the hegemonic center..."[30] Instead, analysis
of dependency should be based on "the relations between different
social classes within the dependent nations themselves."[31] The
"processes of domination"[32] in Mexico must thus be analyzed by
examining not only the external as well as the internal components of the dependency process.

Of course, while it is not the dependency per se that causes
the exploitation of one group by another, and while exploitation
exists in non-dependent contexts it is in fact the condition of
dependency that defines the specific nature of the relationship
that currently exists between groups in Mexico.

Contemplating the Outcomes of Associated Dependent Development

Within the framework of associated dependent development,
the program of development itself is based upon a strategy of
"duplicating the existing consumption structures of the developed
world."[33] The growth of transnational corporations has enabled
the developed states to "(standardize) consumption patterns
across as many markets as possible."[34] Control over technology
is primarily maintained, however, by means of "preventing the
dispersion of R&D operations."[35] These tactics allow TNCs to
pursue what Peter Evans calls a "global strategy" which bears
little relationship to the objectively determined needs of the
host country.[36]

It has become commonplace for states to seek to mitigate
some of the more negative aspects of the presence of TNCs by
placing various restrictions upon TNC activity. Where DFI brings
with it direct capital, technological, managerial and marketing
dependence, countries have attempted instead to obtain capital
through financial markets, access to markets through bilateral
governmental negotiations and access to technical and managerial
services through licensing and direct payment for technical
services.[37] What results, however, is continued dependence upon
capital, technology, management and market access from abroad
despite the modifications in the relationship. This continued
dependence, coupled with the need to produce goods for export
that will be competitive in the international market insures that
the homogeneity of the international production structure is
maintained.

When direct foreign investment is sought, dependent states
will attempt to the extent allowed by their specific bargaining
power,[38] to modify the terms of such investment by mandating
local majority equity participation, for example, or by establishing local content requirements. Further, states may reserve
entire sectors for local private or state investment only.

In James Petras' view, such "nationalist" policies are essentially designed to "allow the national private sector to capture and control a substantial part of the new industrialization in order to be able to associate with foreign capital on an equal basis."[39] Although equal participation may clearly be desirable, its achievement remains unlikely. The point to emphasize, however, is that efforts to achieve equal participation can only serve to shore up the prevailing techno-production structure.

A final constraint operating upon the production structure in dependent states such as Mexico is the fact that resources in the market context flow to areas of highest profitability that have tended to be luxury consumer goods since the prices charged for mass consumption items are frequently regulated by the government and show a low profitability potential. Moreover, the low level of effective demand characterizing the mass of the population tends to propel new investment into areas which do not serve mass needs. As a result, Barkin argues that strict reliance upon a market mechanism which is conditioned by the process of dependency results in a failure to meet fundamental social needs.[40]

In examining the Brazilian case, Peter Evans has further commented in this regard, arguing that:

> ...whether products were developed locally or abroad, by multinationals or local firms, they were developed in response to perceived opportunities for profits, which given the skew of Brazilian income distribution, is hardly synonymous with the satisfaction of needs.[41]

In Venezuela, for example, oil revenues have "forced" a resort to overseas investment due to the limited nature of the internal market, severe income inequalities, and the saturation of high income markets.[42] The "sowing" of Venezuela's oil revenues has been less than successful in terms of any deepening of the industrial structure and instead, major growth has been noted in services, imports and commerce.[43]

Dependent development has produced serious distortions then, in the production structure as the result of having been based upon a highly skewed distribution of income.[44] As noted before, it has also been characterized by foreign domination of the most dynamic sectors of the host economy. DFI provides the investor, even in minority equity situations with "power over where equipment and inputs are bought, what products are produced, how the process of production is organized, where and to whom goods are to be sold and so on."[45]

Certain structural differences have been noted as well that differentiate locally initiated activity and DFI. Evidence suggests that local capital tends to be less concentrated, less technologically or capital intensive and tends to respond to demand emanating from lower income groups. Foreign controlled enterprise, on the other hand, tends to be more highly concentrated, more highly capital intensive, tends to serve higher income groups both domestically and for export, and tends to occupy a strategic position in the producers' goods sector.[46]

Thus it is the most advanced sectors of the economy that are directly linked to the international economy.

But while trade, investment and imports of capital continue to be important indicators of the outcomes of the process of dependency and the internationalization of peripheral economies, dependent states are hardly static in that social and economic relations evolve in both center and periphery resulting in modifications in the forms of the dependency.[47]

In terms of the political expression of the state within the context of dependency, that expression in Cardoso's view cannot be reduced to an "epiphenomenal" level because there exists no one regime type for any particular platform of development.[48] While the state is capitalist and dependent, the regime may be authoritarian, fascist, corporatist or even democratic, essentially depending upon the ease with which social conflicts have been managed. Where those conflicts have been most volatile, as in Argentina and Brazil, for example, bureaucratic authoritarian states have emerged.[49] In other states such as Mexico, where societal antagonisms have been managed through corporatist organization and cooptative ideology, a less draconian regime type has been sufficient to contain conflict.

The management of conflict, it may be argued, in associated dependent states is made more difficult than would otherwise be the case because of the variety of factors which condition the productive system. The structure of dependency not only intensifies those problems normally generated by a market mechanism but removes key decisional loci from the national system rendering those loci less susceptible to moderating influences that would attempt to mitigate the effects of those problems.

The irony of this situation is that while center state elites are obviously interested in maintaining viable economies in the Third World, the relationship of dependency and concomitant relationship that inheres between dominant classes in center and periphery renders peripheral systems more susceptible to radical transformations in the long run than would otherwise have been the case, especially given the tendency for dependency to heighten generic systemic contradictions.

State Capitalism

Mexican state capitalism is the political response to problems that have arisen within dependent capitalism.[50] As Elizabeth Dore notes, in state capitalism the "state's economic function is not determined *directly* by the needs of capital", as expressed by specific economic interests but instead is determined by contradictions emerging from the system.[51] Its emergence signals a response to the problem of conflict between different economic interests in society. This conflict takes on a more acute form in peripheral societies, a fact that propels the state into a preeminent position in the society. Elites in dependent states have increasingly come to view state capitalism as potentially providing a solution to the problems of economic development, industrialization, equity and national independence which more traditional forms of organization have failed to manage.[52]

In both the developed and dependent capitalist states, "the state and public sector (have acted) as mechanisms for the socialization of the risks and losses of the largest enterprises."[53] The cost of this social absorption of risk is paid for by the competitive sector (non-monopoly) and by the "middle and popular classes through direct and indirect taxes, credit, and inflation."[54] Moreover, in peripheral economies, the state has performed a number of other important functions beyond the development of infrastructure and an assortment of financial services. The state has also acted as the "agent of the dissolution of old forms and structures of domination."[55] Specifically, the state has aided in capital's consolidation by engaging in the liquidation of precapitalist forms through land reform and political and administrative reform, and has provided support for those sectors of the economy that are more fully integrated into the international economy.

In dependent states, the private entrepreneurial sector has traditionally been quite weak both in terms of its position domestically and certainly with respect to the international economy. As a result, state power has often emerged as the chief vehicle of economic development. In many quarters, state capitalism has come to be viewed as the "last possibility of capitalist development in the Third World."[56] Studies that have dealt with the emergence of state capitalism have shown that rather than resulting from techno-bureaucratic impulses or the alleged interests of some elites in engaging in "state-building", in conditions of dependent development, state capitalism has emerged as a response to a vacuum that exists in the economic order.[57]

Petras, Morley and Smith found that nationalization and state capitalism became, in the Venezuelan context, "the only means to overcome the inadequate resources and capabilities of strictly private sector activity."[58] The state entered the production process thus departing from more traditional activities, specifically because of the size of the capital requirements of new industrial activity and the inability of the private sector to respond to the challenge. The state in Venezuela has in fact expanded its activity into a range of productive areas including petrochemicals, basic metals, iron, steel, aluminum, cement, pulp and paper and has, in the opinion of some analysts, become the principal actor in the development process.[59]

State capitalism differs from regimes where there is substantial state intervention in that the state comes to play the pivotal role in the reproduction of the economy. Thus, as Dore notes, it is incorrect to label regimes as "state capitalist" simply on a quantitative basis. What may actually exist is a high level of state intervention in economy and society, but not state capitalism per se. The state in state capitalism occupies a dominant role in four key areas of the economy: 1) planning, 2) investment, 3) production, 4) labor mediation. These activities remain circumscribed, however, by their immersion in the context and process of dependency.

Within state capitalism, although the state clearly comes to play the role of the major entrepreneur in society, the intention is to nurture private capital by means of this role rather than to undercut it. Fitzgerald underscores this point and notes that in Latin America as a whole, the public sector, in addition to normal infrastructure

> controls two-thirds of merchant shipping tonnage, half the airline traffic, the bulk of petroleum production, three-quarters of electric power generated, half of steel production and possibly as much as half of investment finance. When this is set against the domination by foreign enterprises of much of the dynamic large-scale branches within the modern final production sector, as well as mining and finance, it is difficult to disagree with the ECLA view, however guarded: 'The traditional idea of conflict between the public and private sectors ceases to have any meaning in many cases...because...the real choice is between public and semi-public enterprises and foreign or international enterprises. At the same time...the existence of the state enterprise sector has definitely had the effect of helping the private sector to extend its operations'.[60]

The state has sought to bolster the private sector and to in a sense, create the national entrepreneurial sector. Further, the state has sought to undermine pre-capitalist forms which it viewed as negative forces in the development of national capitalism. Neither theoretically, nor empirically can state capitalism be viewed as constituting a political-economic form that is antagonistic to private capital.

The issue of state autonomy is of crucial importance in the consideration of state capitalism because some theorists have argued that by means of the emergence of a "state bourgeoisie", the state can achieve a degree of autonomy that will free it to serve A) the "common interest" or B) its "own" interests. In either case, the suggestion is that the interest being pursued is not allied with the interests of the private sector. Yet, the goal is not socialism - hence the term "intermediate regime." Analysts such as Petras, Hussein, Kalecki and Fitzgerald to name several, argue that such an eventuality is indeed possible.[61] Implicit in their conceptualization is the thesis that a newly emergent state bourgeoisie, largely comprised of techno-bureaucrats with petit-bourgeois backgrounds, will develop and pursue its "own" class interest. Petras argues that these are transitory regimes that ultimately lead back to neo-liberal regimes. Yet the point remains that we should expect some degree of independence to be exercised by the state bourgeoisie in the interim.

This perspective is of crucial import in the examination of Mexico's development as it suggests that in the Mexican case, as the state acquires greater autonomy, chiefly as a result of its increased oil based revenues, an increase in managerial expertise

and competency in technical planning, and the consequent increase
in state intervention and growth of state enterprise, it will be
freed to pursue policy options that will serve the "common good".
Advocates of this position would therefore suggest that the
growth of state capitalism, in the Mexican context, could be
expected at least in the medium term, to enable the state to
somehow assume a new role in society, not only one that allows it
to better handle emerging contradictions in society but more significantly, to move beyond its fundamental role as the guardian
of those conditions that facilitate capitalist production.
    Nora Hamilton's observation calls this assertion into
question:

> The basic contradiction inherent in the conceptualiza-
> tion of the autonomous state operating within a system
> of capitalist production relations resides in the
> attempted segregation of political power from economic
> power.[62]

Studies such as that done by Peter Smith in the Mexican context
clearly demonstrate the network of relationships that exists
between capitalists and the state apparatus as well as the tendency of members of the state apparatus to use political office as
a stepping stone to participation in capitalist enterprise.[63]
    Peter Evans, for one, rejects the notion that members of the
state sector constitute a new "class" or social force. He asks:

> Can there be a 'state bourgeoisie?' A bourgeoisie by
> definition appropriates surplus to itself, yet as part
> of the state apparatus, managers of state enterprises
> are supposed to be directing the process of accumula-
> tion in the general interests of capital as a whole,
> and not in their own particular interests.[64]

The Triple Alliance

    The crucial relationship that remains to be explored is that
which exists between the state, national capital and foreign
capital within state capitalism. Within dependent state capitalism, these three sectors are seen as being essentially cooperative in their relationship, and as such, Peter Evans has coined
the term "Triple Alliance". Many observers have noted that
although the state pursues "nationalist" policies and endeavors
to support the private sector, economic growth continues to be
conditioned by the internationalized character of the dependent
state's economy and continues to seek advanced technology, R&D
support, and financial support from external sources.
    The state adopts what appears to be a "nationalist reorien-
tation"[65] in order to compensate for the weaknesses in dependent
economies. Such a reorientation enables the dependent state to
attempt a redefinition of its condition of dependency and to
compete more effectively with other peripheral states which share

similar positions within the international division of labor.

Domestically, the emergence of state capitalism, endowed with a frequently flamboyant "nationalist" component, has proved to assuage for a time the resentments of disadvantaged groups that have been engendered by the development process. Blame for systemic shortcomings is focused exclusively upon structures and interests external to the nation.

Within the Alliance, tension frequently surfaces as state and local private interests feel genuine displeasure over a variety of aspects of their dependent status. Paradoxically, however, as the discontented members of the alliance are directly linked to elites in the developed countries and depend upon them, radical changes in the relationship become unlikely.

However, given the tension in the relationship, nationalist policies have emerged. Such policies in their more extreme forms have been described by Petras.

> The state-capitalist regime attempts to redefine the
> terms of dependency and to contain labor demands to
> favor nationalist capitalist accumulation. The forms
> of national-state-capitalist accumulation include a
> variety of policy instruments: initially it can involve
> increasing tax revenue from the earnings of imperial
> firms; extending ownership to include management rights,
> limiting foreign capital activities to the external
> sector (commerce), fragmenting their operations (explora-
> tion rights, management contracts)...limiting access to
> local capital, directing foreign-owned industries to
> export, etc. It culminates in measures involving
> varying degrees of nationalization.[66]

Despite what would appear to be a full range of nationalist defensive options, the outcomes of such policies have been less than successful. In the Venezuelan case, state support of the private sector has not been able to erode the "lack of indepen-dence and initiative"[67] evidenced by the private sector. More-over, in the wake of the nationalization of the Venezuelan oil industry, it was found that in fact, an even more pervasive network of linkages developed between the members of the "triple alliance" than had previously existed.[68] The emergence of the "joint venture" as a response to the negative results of one hundred percent foreign ownership has most commonly resulted in the absorption of even greater levels of risk by the state while private local and foreign capital have earned greater profit. Thus, increased participation by the state within the context of the joint venture has directly served private interests.

Cooperation between the three sectors is also seen as the state enters the production arena and typically maintains low pricing structures (state enterprises being infamous for their lack of profitability), enabling local private and foreign inter-ests to obtain inputs at low prices, boosting the profitability of their operations. In this way, as the state occupies a more central role in the production area, greater and greater amounts

of surplus tend to be circulated <u>back</u> to capital in the form, for
example, of cheap credit, investment incentives, and low cost
inputs. One seldom finds that state policies discriminate
against TNCs in credit, subsidies, low cost inputs, precisely
because the presence of the TNCs is viewed as an intrinsic part
of the development project.

As planning and budgeting increasingly take hold in the burgeoning state sector, increased surpluses from state enterprises
are utilized in ways which mesh with the internal logic of the
development model. There exists no theoretical or empirical
basis for the argument that the tendency for surpluses to be
transferred to the private sector will be upset. Although
state capitalism adopts an array of "'socialist forms' - political (one party state, socialist rhetoric, etc.) and economic
(state ownership, planning, etc.)"...the purpose is to support a
capitalist model of development.[69]

Does state capitalism, then, provide a solution for the
problems emerging from the model of associated dependent development? Has Mexican state capitalism evidenced a capacity, during
the course of the hydrocarbon development project, to effectively
overcome critical contradictions emerging from the process of
dependent development? Has oil development compounded the
problem of the marginalization of the bulk of the population?
Has this development experience under the aegis of state capitalism enhanced the strength of private entrepreneurs? What has
greater autonomy for the state meant for Mexico's development?

The Organization of the Study

Our discussion of dependency and state capitalism raises a
number of questions about Mexico's recent experience with hydrocarbon development. First of all, in dependent states such as
Mexico, the cycle of accumulation is dependent upon and in fact
must be completed at the international level. In the absence of
an internal dynamic component within the internationalized Mexican economic system, have Mexico's efforts at oil-fueled industrial revitalization led to an even greater internationalization
of the economy?

Has the process of oil-fueled development led to a "deepening" or substantially increased vertical integration of the
industrial structure or are benefits being derived from this
process of industrial revitalization by the center states in the
form of increased opportunities for investment as well as
increased sales of technology and capital goods?

The model of associated dependent development suggests that
instead of pursuing a more autonomous path of development, the
Mexican state could be expected to seek increased direct foreign
investment and international finance capital. Any increase in
bargaining leverage achieved by Mexico as a result of oil would
be used then to encourage "desirable" types of investment from
abroad and favorable terms of credit but would not lead to any
fundamental change in Mexico's position in the international
environment.

What impact would the development process have upon internal class relations? Given the tendency for the development model to produce increasing maldistribution of wealth over time and to perpetuate and aggravate the marginalization of substantial portions of the population, the Mexican oil development program could be expected to reinforce these already well established tendencies. What impact would oil development have upon the state itself? Would we see the emergence of an "autonomous" state bourgeoisie acting in the "common" interest (benefiting those previously marginalized), or its "own" interest? Would the state continue in its previous patterns of activity, encouraging private entrepreneurs, facilitating local-private and international capitals' cooperation, and attempting to maintain an acceptable balance among state, local and foreign capital?

Would the state's anticipated enlargement of its activities in planning and production constitute a challenge to the preeminence of national and foreign capital in the production arena? Or, would the state's more ambitious program be formulated as a response to systemic contradictions, primarily deriving from the national entrepreneurial class' inability to successfully introduce and sustain the initial phases of the new development program, that of export-led industrialization? Would the new phase of development conform to the contemporary outlines of the expansion of capitalism on a world scale ? Would the pattern of development in any sense reflect the specific domestic requisites of the Mexican population? Finally, would Mexico's oil-based bargaining leverage enable the nation to redefine the terms of its position within the international capitalist system and to substantially overcome its condition of dependency?

We begin in Chapter II with an examination of the empirical manifestations of dependency and state capitalism in Mexico at the outset of the petroleum development project. This foundation will provide a basis for assessing the nature and rate of change seen during the late 1970's and early 1980's in terms of the role of the state and the character of dependency relations.

In Chapter III, we discuss how Mexico's specific dependent state configuration accounts for the precise energy exploitation pattern that emerged and consider how this impacted upon the larger development project. We review the dimensions and characteristics of Mexico's petroleum resources but more importantly, we evaluate these resources in terms of their strategic and economic importance as a world resource particularly with respect to U.S. interest in Mexican supplies.

Chapter IV examines the means by which petroleum has impacted upon the state sector and the specific policy direction that developed during the period. Did the oil boom in any sense radically alter the pattern of development?

Chapter V examines Mexico's relationship with its dominant metropolitan partner, the U.S., at the level of international exchange. The analysis focuses specifically upon two key issue areas: trade and labor. In this section, attention will be focused upon the major issues that have been on the U.S.-Mexican bargaining table throughout the preliminary period of oil development. We examine these areas in order to monitor any shift in the nature of the relationship between the actors or in the bargaining structure. Further, we examine the concept of the "North American Common Market" which was discussed in the U.S. at a variety of levels of government and by elements of the private sector. This response will be evaluated on the basis of declaratory policy, concrete policy overtures and policy outcomes.

Finally, in Chapter VI, we assess Mexico's financial crisis of 1982 as well as the longer term prospects for development in Mexico. We conclude with a discussion of the implications of the study for the larger question of the role played by state capitalism in the management of contradictions generated by associated dependent development.

NOTES

[1] Richard Fagen, "The Realities of U.S. Mexican Relations," Foreign Affairs, v.55, n.4 (July,1977), p.698.

[2] William Metz, "Mexico: the Premier Oil Discovery in the Western Hemisphere," Science, v.202 (December 22, 1978), p.1261.

[3] E.V.K. Fitzgerald, The Political Economy of Peru, 1956-78, (Cambridge: Cambridge University Press, 1979), p.15.

[4] Elizabeth Dore, "The State and Dependency Analysis: A Critique," Paper presented at the 8th National Meeting of the Latin American Studies Association, April 5-7, 1979.

[5] Timothy F. Harding, "Dependency, Nationalism and the State in Latin America," Latin American Perspectives, Issue 11, v.III, n.4 (Fall, 1976), p.7.

[6] Augustín Cueva, "A Summary of 'Problems and Perspectives of Dependency Theory'", Latin American Perspectives, Issue 11, v.III, n.4 (Fall, 1976), p.13

[7] Richard Fagen, "A Funny Thing Happened on the Way to the Market: Thoughts on Extending Dependency Ideas," International Organization, v.32, n.1, (Winter, 1978), p.289. Also see Elizabeth Dore, "The State and Dependency Analysis: A Critique;" Elizabeth Dore and John Weeks, "International Exchange and the Causes of Backwardness," Latin American Perspectives, Issue 21, v.VI, n.2 (Spring, 1979), pp.62-87; F.H. Cardoso, "Current Theses on Latin American Development and Dependency: A Critique," New York University, Ibero-American Language and Area Center, Occasional Papers, n.20, May, 1976, p.1.

[8] F.H. Cardoso, "Consumption of Dependency Theory in the United States," Latin American Research Review, v.12, n.3, (1977), p.12.

[9] Richard Fagen, "Studying Latin American Politics," Latin American Research Review, v.XII, n.2 (1977), p.25; Ronald Chilcote, "A Question of Dependency," Latin American Research Review, v.XIII, n.2 (1978), pp.55-68. Also see Thomas Angotti, "The Political Implications of Dependency Theory," in Dependency and Marxism. Toward a Resolution of the Debate, ed. by Ronald Chilcote, (Boulder, CO: Westview Press, 1982), p.126; Ronaldo Munck, "Imperialism and Dependency: Recent Debates and Old Dead-Ends," in Dependency and Marxism. Toward a Resolution of the Debate, ed. by Ronald Chilcote, pp. 162-179.

[10] See for example Immanuel Wallerstein, The Capitalist

World-Economy, (London: Cambridge University Press, 1979.)

[11]David Barkin, "Internationalization of Capital, An Alternative Approach," in Dependency and Marxism. Toward a Resolution of the Debate, ed. by Ronald Chilcote, pp. 156-161.

[12]F.H. Cardoso, "Imperialism and Dependency in Latin America," in Structures of Dependency, ed. by Frank Bonilla and Robert Girling, (Stanford, CA: Institute of Political Studies, 1973), p.11.

[13]F.H. Cardoso, "Dependency and Development in Latin America," New Left Review, 74 (July-August, 1972), p.90; Cardoso, "Imperialism and Dependency in Latin America," p.12.

[14]Ricardo Ffrench Davis, "Foreign Investment in Latin America: Recent Trends and Prospects," in Latin America in the International Economy, ed. by Victor L. Urquidi and Rosemary Thorp, (N.Y.: John Wiley and Sons, 1973), p.183.

[15]F.H. Cardoso, "Associated-Dependent Development: Theoretical and Practical Implications," in Authoritarian Brazil, ed. by Alfred Stepan, (New Haven: Yale University Press, 1977), pp.156-157.

[16]Raymond Vernon, Sovereignty at Bay: The Multinational Spread of U.S. Enterprise (N.Y.: Basic Books, 1971); U.S. Congress, Senate, Committee on Foreign Relations. Multinational Corporations in Brazil and Mexico: Structural Sources of Economic and Non-Economic Power. Report to the Subcommittee on Multinational Corporations, by Richard S. Newfarmer and Willard F. Mueller, 94th Congress, First Session, 1975.

[17]Harry Magdoff, The Age of Imperialism (N.Y.: Monthly Review Press, 1969); Ronald Mueller, "Poverty is the Product," Foreign Policy 13 (Winter, 1973-74), pp.85-88.

[18]Cardoso, "Current Theses," p.9.

[19]Ibid., pp.10-11.

[20]F.H. Cardoso and Enzo Faletto, Dependency and Development in Latin America, translated by Marjory M. Urquidi, (Berkeley: University of California Press, 1979), p.XX.

[21]Cardoso, "Associated-Dependent Development," p.163.

[22]Ibid., See also F.H. Cardoso, "El desarrollo en el banquillo," Comercio Exterior, v.30, n.8 (agosto de 1980), pp.846-860. See especially pp. 852-853.

[23]Cardoso and Faletto, p.XXIII.

[24] F.H. Cardoso, "The Originality of a Copy: CEPAL and the Idea of Development," CEPAL Review, (1977, Second Half), p.35.

[25] José Serra, "Three Mistaken Theses Regarding the Connection between Industrialization and Authoritarian Regimes," in The New Authoritarianism in Latin America, ed. by David Collier, (Princeton, N.J.: Princeton University Press, 1979), p.112; also David Barkin, "Summary Notes," in Latin America in the International Economy, ed. by Urquidi and Thorp, pp.26-34.

[26] James Petras, Morris Morley and Steven Smith, The Nationalization of Venezuelan Oil (N.Y.: Praeger, 1977), p.78.

[27] Cardoso, "Associated-Dependent Development," p.146.

[28] Cardoso and Faletto, p.XVI.

[29] Ibid., p.17.

[30] Ibid., p.173.

[31] Ibid., p.22.

[32] Ibid., p.X.

[33] Barkin, "Summary Notes," p.28.

[34] Peter Evans, Dependent Development: The Alliance of Multinational, State and Local Capital in Brazil (Princeton, N.J.: Princeton University Press, 1979), p.203.

[35] Ibid.

[36] Ibid., p.276.

[37] Ffrench Davis, "Foreign Investment in Latin America: Recent Trends and Prospects," in Latin America in the International Economy, ed. by Urquidi and Thorp, pp.180-181.

[38] Theodore Moran, "Multinational Corporations and Dependency: A Dialogue for Dependentistas and Non-Dependentistas," International Organization, v.32, n.1 (Winter, 1978), pp.79-100.

[39] Petras, Morley and Smith, p.61.

[40] Barkin, "Summary Notes," p.28. Also see David Barkin, "Internationalization of Capital: An Alternative Approach."

[41] Evans, p.288.

[42] Petras, Morley and Smith, pp.75-77.

22

[43] Ibid.

[44] Cardoso, "Associated-Dependent Development," p.149.

[45] Evans, p.80.

[46] Ibid., pp.116-118.

[47] Cardoso and Faletto, p.X.

[48] Cardoso, "On the Characterization of Authoritarian Regimes in Latin America," in The New Authoritarianism in Latin America, ed. by David Collier, p.39. Also see Cardoso, "The Originality of a Copy," p.852.

[49] Guillermo O'Donnell, Modernization and Bureaucratic-Authoritarianism, Institute of International Studies, Politics of Modernization Series, No. 9, (Berkeley: University of California, 1973.)

[50] E.V.K. Fitzgerald, "The State and Capital Accumulation in Mexico," Journal of Latin American Studies, v.10, n.2 (1978), pp.263-282.

[51] Dore, "The State and Dependency Analysis," p.18; Also see Alex Dupuy and Barry Truchil, "Problems in the Theories of State Capitalism," Theory and Society, v.8, n.1, (July, 1979), p.14 and 32.

[52] Fitzgerald, The Political Economy of Peru, p.11.

[53] Marcos Kaplan, "El leviathan criollo: Estatismo y sociedad en la América Latina contemporanea," Revista Mexicana de Sociología, v.5, n.3, (1978), p.803.

[54] Ibid.

[55] Florestan Fernandes , Revolucao Burguesa no Brasil (Rio de Janeiro: Zahar Editores, 1975), p.308 cited in Evans, p.42.

[56] James Petras, "State Capitalism and the Third World," Journal of Contemporary Asia, v.6, n.4 (1976), p.433.

[57] In particular, see the work of Fitzgerald, Petras, Morley and Smith, Perez-Sainz, Bamat, Munck and Kaplan.

[58] Petras, Morley and Smith, p.73.

[59] Juan Pablo Perez-Sainz and Paul Zarembka, "Accumulation and the State in Venezuelan Industrialization," Latin American Perspectives, Issue 22, v.VI, n.3 (Summer, 1979), p.20.

23

[60] E.V.K. Fitzgerald, "Some Aspects of the Political Economy of the Latin American State," Development and Change, v.7, n.2 (April, 1976), p.122. For an interesting comparison, see Berch Berberoglu, "State Capitalism and National Industrialization in Turkey," Development and Change, v.11, n.1, (January, 1980), pp.97-122.

[61] Petras, "State Capitalism and the Third World," pp.432-443; Mahmoud Hussein, Class Conflict in Egypt 1945-1970 (N.Y.: Monthly Review Press, 1973); Michal Kalecki, "Observations on Social And Economic Aspects of Intermediate Regimes," in Essays on Developing Countries, (N.J.: Humanities Press, 1976), pp.30-39; For an application of this notion see Kenneth Jameson, "An Intermediate Regime in Historical Context: the Case of Guyana," Development and Change, v.11, n.1, (January, 1980), pp.77-95; also Thanos Skouras, "The 'Intermediate Regime' and Industrialization Prospects," Development and Change, v.9, n.4 (October, 1978), pp.631-648; M. Kalecki and M. Kula, "Bolivia - An 'Intermediate Regime' in Latin America," Economía y Administración, 16 (1970), pp.75-78; E.V.K. Fitzgerald, "The Limitations of State Capitalism as a Model of Economic Development: Peru 1968-1978," No.27 Working Papers, Latin American Program, The Wilson Center, Washington, D.C., p.3; Kalecki, Problems of Financing Economic Development in a Mixed Economy (Cambridge: Cambridge University Press, 1972.)

[62] Hamilton, "The Limits of State Autonomy," p.100.

[63] Peter Smith, The Labyrinths of Power. Political Recruitment in Twentieth Century Mexico, (Princeton, N.J.: Princeton Univeristy Press, 1979), p.204.

[64] Evans, p.46.

[65] Pérez-Sáinz, "Towards a Conceptualization," p.60.

[66] Petras, "State Capitalism and the Third World," p.441.

[67] Petras, Morley and Smith, p.40. Also see James Petras, "Class and Politics in the Periphery and the Transition to Socialism," Review of Radical Political Economy, (Summer, 1976), pp. 20-35.

[68] Petras, Morley and Smith, p.114.

[69] Petras, "State Capitalism and the Third World," p.437.

Mexico Before the Oil Boom

CHAPTER II

xico's programs of Stabilizing Development and Luis
s Shared Development had generated an economic crisis
.ed to a major devaluation of the peso, capital flight
of an imminent military coup. The economy had come
ning halt and the "Mexican Miracle" had seemingly run
           . All aggregate indicators of economic life reflected
the crisis that had beset the economy. The IMF Stabilization
Program of 1976 that was instituted as part of a program to cure
Mexico's economic malaise was condemned by many for exacting
unfair "sacrifices" from precisely those groups in society that
had failed to benefit from the fruits of the Mexican miracle.

It had become evident that something was seriously wrong
with the economy. Some charged that Echeverría's increased
governmental activism had ruined the economy by accumulating
huge and insupportable deficits in the public sector and by in-
timidating the private sector to the point that its investments
had fallen off to a mere trickle and instead had been channelled
outside of the country.

It is against this background of economic impasse that we
begin our examination of the Mexican model of economic development, the structure and process of dependency in Mexico, and
attempt to ascertain the point to which Mexico's associated
dependent development had led the country. In addition, we shall
examine the state's role in the development of Mexico's economy
and society. We shall assess its relationship with private local
and foreign capital and attempt to explain its position as the
primary actor within the Mexican economy.

By 1976, the Mexican economy manifested all of the classic
symptoms of a state characterized by associated dependent development and found itself confronted with a range of serious structural problems which were not easy to overcome. The most dramatic indictment of the model was its failure to provide opportunities for meaningful employment for over half of the population.
The emerging structure of the economy, coupled with alarming
demographic trends, suggested that the problem was only likely
to become more severe rather than improve in years to come.
Since 1950, the population growth rate had hovered at a worrisome
3.2 - 3.3 percent.[1] These two factors were major contributors to
the worsening of the distribution of wealth that had been seen in
Mexican society in recent years.

Population Growth, Employment, and the Distribution of Income

By 1977, Mexico had registered a population figure of 62.3
million persons, 40% of whom were under the age of 15. The population was expected to reach 72 million by 1980, and registered
an astounding birth rate of 3.6 percent per year between 1970 and
1979,[2] (compared, for example to the Philippines' birth rate of
2.4 percent, Asia's most rapidly growing nation).

Despite some success in family planning activities begun in
1972, it was expected that the population would reach 120 million
by the year 2000, nearly doubling the population in only a
twenty-five year period. Questions arose, however, regarding

Mexico's ability to make significant reductions in population
growth rates given the youthful skew of the total population.

As a result of such accelerated growth rates, the economically active population (EAP) was expected to double between 1980
and 2000, increasing the number of job seekers by 20 million
persons.[3] Furthermore, the labor supply would largely be
comprised of unskilled workers given the fact that by 1977, the
average Mexican adult had 3.6 years of schooling while only 3
million persons had more than an elementary school education,
with only 300,000 having graduated from universities.[4] Compound-
ing the problem further was the fact that the slowing of the
birthrate would tend to increase participation by women in the
labor force thereby increasing pressure in the employment arena.[5]

The Mexican government defines the EAP as "Those between 12
and 65 currently employed or having been 'recorded as having
applied for a job in the two months before a special census.'"[6]
Naturally, this excludes those who would be potentially employed
who have found only frustration in their efforts to find employment and have "dropped out". By 1976, the EAP was thus put at
16.7 million persons of a total population of 62.3 million.[7]

Unemployment/underemployment as a single category reached a
level of 50% in 1977, up from 45% in 1970 and was based on a
definition of employment that considers occupied persons as
those having been paid for one hour of labor or having accumulated 15 hours of unpaid work in the week prior to the census.[8]
Official government figures put the unemployment rate at approximately 9%.[9] Moreover, beyond the 50% un/underemployment rate,
much disguised unemployment could be found in the agricultural
sector due to the seasonal nature of the occupation.

Employment itself grew at a laggardly pace throughout the
post-war period. During the 1950s, it grew by 2.9%, during the
1960s, it grew by only 2.1%, and finally, during the period 1970-
74, employment grew by only 1.6% annually, trailing far beyond
the population growth rate.[10] In fact, by 1974, the country
needed, according to Banco de Comercio, to create 685,000 new
jobs per year, yet in that year, only 125,000 jobs were created.[11]
In fact, the expectation by the mid-1970s was that the economy
would somehow have to create 700,000 new jobs per year just to
maintain what were then current levels of unemployment. Since
WWII, employment has tended to shrink in agriculture, growing
only at a paltry rate in manufacturing and at a more rapid clip
in the service sector. Table 2-1 compares the growth in employment and sectoral share of Gross Domestic Product (GDP).

Although the agricultural sector still supported 40% of the
population, its share of GDP had dropped to less than 10%, impact-
ing severely upon rural incomes. At the same time, population
moving to urban areas found little employment increase in the
manufacturing sector where heavy investment has been concentrated,
and instead entered the service sector which includes large
numbers of "jobs" of a marginal character such as domestic help,
street vending and day labor. Not only had the manufacturing
sector failed to produce substantial employment opportunities,
the most dynamic sectors which accounted for two-thirds of manu-

Table 2-1

Comparison of Sectoral Product and Employment Shares,

1950-75
(percentages)

	1950		1960		1970		1975	
	GDP	EMP	GDP	EMP	GDP	EMP	GDP	EMP
Agriculture	22.4	58.3	16.1	49.4	11.8	40.9	9.8	40.9*
Manufacturing	21.0	14.8	19.2	17.2	23.4	21.8	23.9	24.0*
Services	56.6	26.9	64.7	33.4	64.8	37.3	66.3	35.1*

*estimates

Source: Statistical Yearbook for Latin America, 1968 and 1978, various tables. 1975 figures are estimates from Mexico, Profile of Labor Conditions, U.S. Dept. of Labor, 1979, based on International Labor Organization data.

facturing output employed only one-third of the labor force.[12]

Total employment grew only at a rate of 2% p.a. between 1950 and 1960 and only by 2.5% p.a. between 1960 and 1970, clearly falling far behind the growth in EAP. As a result of shrinking employment possibilities, explosive growth rates and concentration in industry, the distribution of income had worsened over time, leaving many in more tenuous straits than had previously been the case. According to a U.S. government report, fully a third of the population was worse off by the late 1970's than they had been ten years earlier.[13] Table 2-2 illustrates the distribution of income as it had developed since 1950. Clearly, the bottom half of the population had found its position to have deteriorated relatively as a result of the development process. While yielding somewhat different percentages, Hernández Laos' and Córdova Chávez's study reveals the same tendency for the poorest sectors to be disadvantaged.[14]

Although growth in the GDP had slipped by the mid 1970's following an expansionary period in the 1960s and early 1970s (Table 2-3), on balance the Mexican economy had been characterized by impressive growth rates during the post-war period. Yet despite this success, the inequality in society produced by the model of development has been characterized even by conservative observes as severe.[15] In terms, however, of real increases in GDP, the picture was less spectacular as shown in Table 2-4.

The difference in the two estimates can essentially be accounted for by the factoring of the impact of inflation in Table 2-4. Figures shown in Table 2-3 are, however, those most commonly used in public assessments of the health of the Mexican

Table 2-2

Percentage Distribution of Family Income After Tax,

1950-1975

	1950	1958	1963	1968	1975
Poorest 20%	6.1	5.0	4.2	3.7	4.1
30% below median	13.0	11.7	11.5	10.7	10.1
30% above median	21.1	20.4	21.7	22.5	19.4
Richest 20%	59.8	62.9	62.6	63.1	66.4

Source: Wouter van Ginneken, "Socioeconomic Groups and
Income Distribution in Mexico," International Labor Review,
v.118, n.3 (May-June, 1979), Table 1, p.332.

Table 2-3

Gross Domestic Product, 1961-1976

(percentage growth per annum)

1961-65	1966-70	1971-74	1975	1976
7.2	6.9	6.1	4.1	2.1

Source: IDB, Economic and Social Progress in Latin America,
1979, Table 1-2, p.8.

economy by the government. In terms of GDP per capita, inflation also accounted for what would appear to be fairly rapid
growth in per capita income evidenced by the jump from US $438
in 1960, US $622 in 1970 to US $1,113 in 1977.[16] In fact, as
shown in Table 2-5, real growth in GDP per capita had been
stymied in the 1970's. Actually after 1970, the growth rate in
GDP per capita had fallen off substantially. (Table 2-6)
   In addition to the pressures placed upon the distribution

Table 2-4

Trends in Gross Domestic Product
% Real Increase

(in 1970 dollars)

1972	1973	1974	1975	1976
3.8	3.9	2.2	0.7	-1.8

Source: Economist Intelligence Unit, Quarterly Economic
Review of Mexico, Annual Supplement, 1978 (London, 1979),
p.6 and "Documento: La evolución económica de México en
1978," CEPAL, Comercio Exterior, v.29, n.7 (julio de 1979),
Table 1, p.787.

Table 2-5

GDP per capita, 1973-1977
(in constant 1970 dollars)

1973	1974	1975	1976	1977
720	735	740	727	723

Source: "Documento: La evolución económica de México en
1978," CEPAL, Comercio Exterior, Table 1, p.787.

Table 2-6

Growth Rate of GDP per Capita, 1960-1976

(percentage per annum)

1960-65	1965-70	1970-75	1976
3.7	3.5	2.2	-1.4

Source: ECLA, Statistical Yearbook for Latin America, 1978,
Table 47, p.66.

Table 2-7

Cultivation of Basic Crops, 1974-1977

(hectares)

	Rice	Maize	Beans	Wheat
1974-75	125,367	682,887	227,264	541,126
1975-76	61,589	565,228	170,687	689,159
1976-77	99,810	907,446	128,476	502,900

Source: William Chislett, "Agriculture in Poor Shape,"
Financial Times, (January 11, 1980), pp.50-51.

of income by the population growth rate, much of the problem was
due to what van Ginneken identified as the tendency for productivity in the so-called modern sector..."to rise faster than in
traditional sectors."[17] Robert Looney has also noted such a
tendency operating in the Mexican economy.

> Not only has industrial production become more concen-
> trated, but since 1940 all categories of income (wages
> and salaries, self-employed income, rent, and interest)
> have declined as a percentage of GNP, with the highest
> loss (27 percent) experienced in wages and salaries.
> This decline in wages and salaries was reflected in the
> percentage gain in profits, whose share of GNP increased
> from 29 percent in 1940 to 34 percent in 1966. Although
> their percentage share of GNP declined during this
> period, real wages in manufacturing still grew by 23
> percent, while output per worker increased by 64 percent.
> Accordingly, labor cost per unit of manufacturing output
> fell by 26 percent.[18]

Concentration and capital intensivity have also meant that
any wage gains accrued through gains in productivity have been
passed on only to the limited number of workers employed in the
relatively small number of firms occupying the more dynamic
areas of the manufacturing sector. In enterprises employing 100
or more workers, salaries were approximately 42% higher than
those received by workers in enterprises employing between 26
and 99 workers. Furthermore, workers in enterprises employing
from 1 to 25 workers earn two and one-half times less than
workers in the 26-99 category.[19]

By 1977, the rural population had reached a total of 23
million persons, 41% of Mexico's total population. Ten million
are currently in enclaves of under 500 inhabitants with a total
expected by 2000 in such enclaves of 23 million persons. Of the
present total of 23 million, 20 million lack any health care,
and at least 15 million have no potable water, education, or
electrification. Ninety-six percent of the total rural pre-
school population has been deemed malnourished.[20]

The situation in Mexico's rural areas has only worsened over
time. Between 1950-1975, the poorest 40% of the rural population
had experienced a drop in real income of 38%.[21] As a result of
such deterioration in incomes in the countryside, an out-migra-
tion of rural population to urban areas in Mexico and to the U.S.
labor market was stimulated. It was estimated that between the
period 1940-1975, three and one-half million Mexicans had migra-
ted to the U.S. both legally and illegally.[22] The increased
migration to the U.S. was due not only to the desire for work
that was unavailable in Mexico, but also was stimulated by the
wage differential existing between the U.S. and Mexico estimated
at 7.4 to 1 in 1977, and ranging in certain cases as high as
13:1.[23] In fact, Reynolds estimated that by 1975, the total
number of Mexican workers in the U.S. (having arrived since 1940),
equalled one-fifth of Mexico's EAP.[24]

Pressure on wages in Mexico emanated, of course, not only from a desire to maintain hefty profit margins and the availability of a huge reserve of unemployed, but also from wage structures prevailing in other economies occupying a similar position in the international division of labor. Mexico's manufactured and agricultural exports would naturally be severely prejudiced should the wage structure change inordinately.

Agriculture

During the period 1966-1976, agricultural production had grown at an annual rate of 2.3% far below the population growth rate. Between 1970 and 1976, agricultural production increased by only 1.6% p.a. and in 1975 and 1976,[25] the actual volume of output fell, reflecting the fact that the amount of land in production had actually fallen despite the burgeoning population and resultant internal demand for food.[26] Moreover, much of the growth that had been seen in the 1970s in agriculture had been in cattle raising and did not represent increases in food supplies for internal consumption but rather for export. Cattle raising had become especially attractive because of the limited labor factor, because the major capital investment are the cattle themselves, and because prices were not subject to government ceilings.[27]

The agricultural sector managed to retain a positive balance in commercial trade due to the heavy commitment of land to production for export.[28] A full 35% of the value of Mexican exports emanated from the agricultural sector. Eighty percent of the exports were accounted for by only five products--coffee, tomatoes, beef, shrimp and cotton.[29] At the same time, however, Mexico's self-sufficiency in agriculture had begun to erode very seriously. In 1970, the country had been self-sufficient in foodstuffs, but by 1973, agricultural imports, principally of basic grains and oils, represented a full 22.5% of Mexico's balance-of-trade deficit.[30] Food imports jumped to $400 million dollars in 1976, $770 million in 1977 and were expected to reach as much as a disastrous $4 billion in the years ahead.[31]

This situation had been brought about by a confluence of several factors: first, nearly all capital investment in recent years had been put into irrigation for commercial farming for export.[32] Little effort had been made to support the less concentrated and less mechanized farming sector which produced for the internal market at low costs. Second, the restrictive nature of internal demand based upon serious inequities in the distribution of income had caused some producers to curtail production (Table 2-7) and had caused others to engage in the production of more profitable crops, mainly for the export market where profits would not be constrained. Third, the presence of TNCs in agriculture aggravated the export orientation of production, concentrated income and capital and exacerbated unemployment problems in the countryside, in addition to monopolizing productive land and much of the available credit and irrigation investment funds. Fourth, the productivity of small cultivators fell due to increased population pressures on land and lack of access to credit, extension services, and irrigation. These factors brought the Mexican agricultural sector to the point of producing a smaller and smaller proportion of the GDP while continuing to be the locus of employment for forty percent of the population. Continuing negative terms of trade[33] between the "modern" sector of the economy and agriculture jeopardized any hopes for substantial improvement even with substantial government investment. As a result, government spending for subsidies to producers of basic commodities and for imports of basic commodities had increased over time, placing increasing strain on budgetary resources. These increases which would only grow in the future could not easily be sustained.

The Internationalization of Mexican Industry

The distortions that characterize associated dependent economies are many, but one of the most fundamental is the failure of industrialization programs to result in the vertical integration or "deepening" of that structure. The Mexican case represents one of the most extreme cases in the industrializing world of this phenomenon. As with many other economies, the policy of import substitution industrialization (ISI) that had been pursued expecially after WWII had reached an impasse in the 1960s when the next logical stage for substitution was that of capital and producers goods. This stage followed on the heels of successes seen in the substitution of consumer durables and some intermediate goods.

Frequently, the term "exhausted" is employed to describe the bankruptcy of the ISI strategy, yet, the fact is that the process is anything but "exhausted." The problem is that taking the next step necessitates a willingness and a commitment to moderate the economy's degree of reliance on management, technologies and marketing emanating from the central industrialized economies. In the Mexican case, such autonomous paths were consistently rejected and in fact, the World Bank has noted that Mexico is "unique among the more advanced industrializing countries in its almost total reliance on (capital goods) imports."[34] The Bank continues:

> A comprehensive program of support, in the form of developing strategy and financial incentives would be essential[35].... lack of any independent indigenous technological capability represents a critical weakness in the manufacture of capital goods.[36]

The Bank notes that presently in that sector, there is almost complete reliance on foreign technology and research and development. In fact, the Bank argues that there is virtually no chance for Mexico to develop "appropriate technology" (technology geared specifically to the Mexican context) as there is "no corresponding R&D activity to expand on acquired knowledge." The state organization established in the early 1970s to advance

Mexican R&D, the National Council for Science and Technology (CONACYT), was charged with the responsibility of doing so, according to one observer, by essentially acquiring "foreign scientific and technological know how."[37]

Specifically, when we speak of capital goods in the Mexican context, we are referring to the following groups of goods that are fairly rudimentary and do not include items of advanced technology: 1) Plant equipment (non-electrical power equipment, steelmaking equipment, chemical industry equipment), 2) Machine tools (metal-cutting machines, metal forming machines), 3) Heavy industrial machinery, 4) Heavy electrical equipment such as generators, transformers and switchgears.[38]

By the mid 1970s when compared with Brazil, for example, Mexico was extraordinarily dependent upon foreign suppliers in this regard.

Table 2-8

Machine Tools Production,
Comparison of Mexico and Brazil, 1970-1975
(Millions of US dollars)

	1970	1975	1975 GDP
Mexico	5.0	4.5	$69.1 billion
Brazil	33.8	137.0	$121.8 billion

Source: IBRD, Mexico Manufacturing Sector, Table 4, p.127.

In comparing Argentina, Brazil and Mexico, a similar pattern of extreme Mexican dependence was evident. In recent years, the import of capital goods accounted for fully 40% of the total value of Mexico's imports.[39] Much of this import activity was accounted for by the presence of TNCs in the most dynamic sectors of Mexican industry and the import intensivity of their activity.

Direct Foreign Investment

Mexico's industrial sector has traditionally been highly protected by a system of tariffs and import licensing which has been criticized by Mexico's major trading partners, particularly by the U.S. Protectionism has, according to many analysts, yielded an industrial structure characterized by high costs, an inability to compete in the international market, and a nearly exclusive emphasis upon consumer durables and assembly components imported from abroad.[40] Neoclassical diagnoses of Mexico's econ-

Table 2-9

Capital Goods Imports, Industrial Machinery,
Comparison of Argentina, Mexico and Brazil

(as a percentage of internal demand)

Argentina		Brazil		Mexico	
1970	1973	1970	1973	1970	1974
34.6	19.4	26.6	29.7	44.7	48.7

Source: IBRD, Mexico Manufacturing Sector, Table 9, p.130.

omic ills have tended to ignore, however, the serious and systematic impacts of TNCs in dependent economies. TNCs, as we noted
in Chapter I, pursue a number of policies which produce just such
results. They frequently restrict utilization of state-of-the-
art technology by subsidiaries, emphasize assembly operations and
production of consumer durables and generally inhibit the competitiveness of exports.

Protectionist policies in fact encouraged DFI by challenging
TNCs to defend market shares that had previously been maintained
through exports from center to periphery. Once in the country,
TNCs then benefited from protectionism as did national interests.
These policies, in the Mexican context, actually served to protect
such "infant industries...as Ford and G.E."[41] René Villareal
argues that the protectionist structure, coupled with the limited
nature of the internal market spawned a monopolistic structure
which in turn was ultimately dominated by TNCs and oligopolist
Mexican firms or grupos.

But the history of foreign investment in Mexico antedates
the tremendous growth seen in the postwar period. At the time of
the Mexican Revolution, clearly two-thirds of all investment in
Mexico had come from foreign sources.[42] Foreign investors controlled 76% of all major corporations in Mexico including 100%
of the oil, 98% of mining, 96% of agriculture, and 89% of industry.[43] Moreover, more than 40% of all of Mexico's agricultural
land was in the hands of American interests.

In the aftermath of the revolution and particularly during
the nationalist Cárdenas period, much of foreign investment was
nationalized. Yet with the pursuit of industrialization in the
post-war period, foreign interests once again emerged as dominant
actors in the economic arena. In a reversal of the pattern prevailing during the Porfiriato, DFI came to be concentrated in
industry and commerce more than in primary activities. By the
1970s, almost 90% of DFI was located in these areas.[44]

Table 2-10

Distribution of Foreign Investment, 1975
(percentage of total)

Manufacturing	75%
Commerce	11%
Services	7%
Mining	6%
Others	1%

Source: Consumer Markets in Latin America, p.148.

Table 2-11

Comparative Rate of Return on Investment, 1970s
Selected Latin American Countries

(by percentage)

Argentina	11.9	Mexico	18.3
Brazil	13.4	Panama	13.0
Central America	4.6	Peru	9.4
Chile	15.7	Venezuela	15.1
Colombia	13.7	Others	17.5

Source: "New Enthusiasm for Latin America," LAER, (16 November, 1979), p.32. Rate of return includes income from dividends, interest, fees and royalties, calculated as a percentage of the book value of investment.

Table 2-12

Sources of Foreign Investment in Mexico by Nation, 1975
(by percentage)

United States	72.2	Japan	1.9
W. Germany	5.8	Holland	1.5
U.K.	4.7	France	1.5
Switzerland	4.2	Italy	1.5
Canada	2.0	Other	4.7

Source: Mexico: Business Opportunities, Metra Consulting and
International Joint Ventures (London, 1977).

By the mid 1970s, Mexico had become the most profitable[45] country
in Latin America for foreign investment despite its relatively
"high" labor costs (as compared to other dependent states).

Moreover, between 1971 and 1977, the rate of return on
investment actually grew by 50%.[46] By 1975, the U.S. accounted
for the bulk of DFI in Mexico (unlike the period before the
revolution when the U.S. had a 38% share, Great Britain 29% and
France 27%).[47]

Between 1971 and 1977, Mexico absorbed almost US$1.9
billion in DFI, principally from the U.S. By 1977, the accumulated value of DFI had grown to US$5.384 billion.[48] Increas-
ingly, however, the numerical value of DFI has come to be viewed
as an inefficient indicator of the extent of TNC control. As
Chumacero and a host of others have noted, DFI has increasingly
been based upon capital generated in the host market and such has
been the case in Mexico.[49] TNCs tend to provide only seed
capital in new ventures while most funds are obtained locally.
Further, during the early 1970s, 75% of all new foreign investments came in the form of acquisitions, a pattern that the state
later moved to reverse.

In Mexico as in many other countries, DFI has resulted in a
net-decapitalization of the economy on a systematic basis.[50]
Moreover, writing in the early 1970s, Newfarmer and Mueller
reported that

by almost any measure, substantial industrial denationalization occurred in Mexico during the sixties. Moreover,
the tendency shows no signs of abating. Through their
control over vital industries, leading firms, and a
substantial share of the national market, MNCs exercise
a great deal of influence over the Mexican economy, and
their conduct is crucial to its performance.[51]

Even at the beginning of the 1960s, of the largest 400 enterprises in Mexico (which accounted for 77.26% of total national income), fully 54% of the income from that group was produced by enterprises either totally controlled by TNCs or with strong foreign participation.[52]

By the mid 1970s, foreign investment had reached the following proportions:

- 50% of the top 300 firms in manufacturing were controlled by TNCs.
- 35% of total industrial production controlled by TNCs.[53]
- 61 of the top 100 manufacturing firms were U.S. controlled.[54] This accounted for fully three-quarters of the top 300 firms' assets.
- In 11 of 18 industrial sectors, TNCs controlled majority shares of capital while Mexican firms led in only four sectors: textiles, food, non-metallic mineral manufacture, leather.[55]

Predictably, these Mexican dominated sectors were "less technologically advanced and more competitive."[56] Fully 75% of foreign capital, thus, tended to be located in the more dynamic, technologically advanced and non-competitive industrial sectors.[57] TNC affiliates on the average were 50% larger than Mexican competitors[58] and profits in the non-competitive sector were 400% higher than in competitive sectors.[59] Mexico's market concentration level actually equalled that of the U.S.[60] Investments have flowed into the following areas: electrical machinery, non-electrical machinery, transport equipment, rubber, chemicals, lumber, paper, tobacco, fabricated metals and precision instruments.[61]

The implications of such concentration within a context of dependency are that administered prices will tend to further concentrate income and reduce the chances, however slight, for any local innovation, R&D, or for local needs to be factored into the product-mix of the TNC subsidiary. The pernicious effects of market concentration and super-concentration profiled in the industrialized states are simply intensified.

Along with increasing concentration in the economy, we have witnessed increases in the utilization of capital rather than labor in Mexico's most dynamic sector slowing down employment growth in the industrial sector.[62] The standard contradiction brought about by the internationalization and concentration of peripheral economies is that as technology is introduced in order to boost productivity, the economy experiences a "reduction in the capacity of the market to expand due to a slowing down in the utilization of labor."[63] Mexican industry is in fact more capital intensive than Taiwan, Hong Kong, or South Korea[64] at least in part because of the relatively higher labor costs.

Mexico was not able to maintain the early success achieved in the growth rate of value added in industry during the early 1960s. By 1976, that figure had dropped by nearly 50%. Especially compared to Brazil, the growth rate was lackluster. What increases that were registered were in an important way accounted for by the development of the Border Industrialization Program in 1965.

Table 2-13

Growth Rate in Value Added in Manufacturing Sector,
Comparison of Mexico and Brazil, 1971-1976

	1961-65	1966-70	1971-75	1976
Mexico	9.2	8.8	6.2	4.7
Brazil	4.2	10.2	11.8	10.5

Source: IDB, Economic and Social Progress in Latin America,
1979, Table I-10,p.20.

In an effort to expand employment opportunities, Mexico in
cooperation with the U.S., initiated a Border Industrialization
Program in 1965 that was designed to attract foreign investment
chiefly from the U.S.[65] By 1977, the program had grown to include
500 enterprises and employed 85,000 persons. The program had
catapulted Mexico to third place in world ranking after West
Germany and Japan "in terms of value added as a processing
platform for the United States."[66] The program was expected to
supply upwards of 110,000 jobs in Mexico by 1979 and perhaps as
many as 300,000 by 1983.[67]
Essentially, the program was designed to allow TNCs to
import assembly components to their Mexican subsidiaries on a
duty free basis. Finished products would then be exported back
to the U.S. with tariffs applied only to the portion of "value-
added" derived from Mexican assembly operations. The program is
based on a system of paired or twin plants located on each side
of the border. Despite protests from labor interests in the U.S.,
it has been estimated that for every job created by the program
in Mexico, two new jobs are created at U.S. plants. Moreover,
for every dollar equivalent in pesos earned by Mexican workers,
30¢ is spent in the U.S. thereby benefiting Southwestern states'
economies.[68] TNC interests benefit, of course, from Mexico's
reduced labor costs. In addition, the program has been exempted
from standard DFI regulations as well as patent and other
transfer of technology restrictions. Little investment is
required--an average of only $700 per job[69] (compared to $36,500
in iron and steel in Mexico).[70] Enterprises in the program are
generally 100% foreign owned. Finally, unlike other areas of
manufacturing investment by TNCs, virtually nothing of what is
produced by border industry is for Mexican consumption. Primary
areas of manufacture include assembly of electronics, communications equipment and clothing.[71] By 1975, the plants produced
fully 50% of the value of Mexico's manufactured exports.[72]

Trade

    As with foreign investment, by the mid 1970s, Mexico had
developed a very close trading relationship with the U.S. Despite
Mexico's refusal to join the General Agreement on Tariffs and
Trade   (GATT), Mexico continued to enjoy Most Favored Nation
(MNF) status with the U.S., unlike two other regional oil producers, Venezuela and Ecuador, largely because of its failure to
join OPEC. Although Mexico's protectionist policies had been
viewed by the U.S. as being inconsistent with the principles of
GATT, Mexico was nonetheless accorded privileges (again, unlike
Ecuador and Venezuela) under the Generalized System of Preferences (GSP) of the Trade Act of 1974, a program developed under
international auspicies to assist developing countries in the
export of manufactures.[73]
    Although trade with Mexico as percentage of total U.S. inter-
national trade accounted for only 3-4% at the beginning of the oil
boom,[74] Table 2-14 shows the importance that the U.S. market held
for Mexican imports and exports. After 1960, efforts to boost the
value of manufactures as a percentage of total exports had
achieved some success, growing from 20.8% in 1960 to 34% in
1977.[75] At the same time, the composition of the exchange between
the U.S. and Mexico followed the standard pattern of periphery-
center relations with Mexican exports primarily of an unprocessed
character with little value added while U.S. exports to Mexico had
high value added. The only Mexican exports that enjoyed any sort
of advantage within the context of international trade were
"building materials, furniture, household items, metal products
and parts and assembly activities, perishable food, fashion sensitive clothing."[76] The process of ISI had, by the mid 1970s,
fully substituted consumer goods as has been the traditional
pattern.[77] By 1977, consumer goods accounted for only 8% of total
imports. Imports, however, had grown much more rapidly than had
exports between 1960 and 1975.

The Growth of Mexico's Debt

    The 1970s saw worrisome growth in Mexico's trade deficit and
at the same time, between 1971-76, the average growth in capital
inflows, primarily accounted for by loans, increased at 47% p.a.
Foreign loans to the public sector grew from US$280 million in
1971 to US$3.054 billion in 1975.[78]
    Mexico had begun to engage in heavy borrowing in the 1960s,
but between 1970-76, the external debt actually rose from US$3.8
billion to US$17.973 billion.[79] Mexico thus became the second
most highly indebted country in the world to U.S. commercial
banks.[80] Major U.S. commercial lenders to Mexico included the
Bank of America, Chase Manhattan, Chemical, Manufacturers Hanover
Trust, Morgan Guaranty Trust and Citicorp International Group.[81]
    Public external debt had grown during the period of 1965-76
at an average annual rate of 18.3%. By 1976, interest on the
public external debt equaled 12-15% of total public expenditures.[82] Although public sector debt had shown a sharp increase

42

Table 2-14

Mexican Trade with the U.S., 1975-1977
(billions of U.S. dollars)

	1975	1976	1977
Imports, total	6.6	6.0	5.5
Imports from U.S.	4.1 (62.1)	3.8 (63.3)	3.5 (63.6)
Exports, total	3.3	3.8	4.6
Exports to U.S.	2.1 (63.3)	2.4 (63.1)	2.4 (52.2)

Source: U.S. Department of State Bulletin, v.79, n.2024,
(March, 1979), p.58.

Table 2-15

Composition of Mexico's Trade with the U.S., 1977

Mexican Exports to U.S.		Mexican Imports from U.S.	
Agriculture	34%	Intermediate Goods	46%
Petroleum	22%	Capital Goods	36%
Metals & Minerals	7%	Consumer Goods	8%
Industrial Goods	3%	Other	10%
Other			

Source: U.S. Department of State Bulletin, v.79, n.2024,
(March, 1979), p.58.

in this period, the overall structure of Mexican external debt
was dominated by loans contracted by the private sector. Private
sector debt grew 747% (including inflation and devaluation)
between 1965-75, while public sector debt increased by a more
modest 282%. Rapid increase in the debt meant that the debt
service ratio (ratio of service payments to export earnings)
worsened over time. Expressed as a percentage of the GDP, Mex-

Table 2-16

Comparison of the Growth of Imports and Exports

1960-1975

(billions of U.S. dollars)

	1960-65	1965-70	1970-75
Imports	6.4	10.7	21.2
Exports	8.0	7.9	16.9

Source: ECLA, Statistical Yearbook for Latin America, 1978,
Table 48, p.66 and Table 50, p.67.

Table 2-17

Mexican Foreign Trade Profile, 1965-1976

(billions of U.S. dollars)

	IMPORTS			EXPORTS	BALANCE OF TRADE
	Total	Private Sector	Public Sector		
1965	1.559	1.302	.256	1.113	-.445
1970	2.326	1.769	.557	1.281	-1.045
1971	2.254	1.800	.453	1.363	-.890
1972	2.717	2.072	.645	1.665	-1.052
1973	3.813	2.590	1.227	2.070	-1.742
1974	6.056	3.854	2.202	2.850	-3.206
1975	6.580	4.082	2.498	2.869	-3.721
1976	6.029	3.875	2.154	3.315	-2.713

Sources: "Indicadores Económicas," Comercio Exterior, v.VI,
n.10 (septiembre de 1978), Table IV-2, p.65, and Economist
Intelligence Unit, Quarterly Economic Review of Mexico, Annual
Supplement,1978, p.22.

44

Table 2-18

Ratio of External Public Debt Service
to the Value of Exports of Goods and Services,
Comparison of Mexico, Argentina, Brazil, 1961-1976

	1961-65	1966-70	1971-75	1971-76
Mexico	19.3	22.9	23.0	32.5
Argentina	21.0	25.3	19.3	18.6
Brazil	28.8	17.8	14.1	17.5

Source: IDB, Economic and Social Progress in Latin America,
1979, Table III-26, p.101.

Table 2-19

External Public Debt as a Percentage of National Product,
Comparison of Mexico and Brazil, 1970-76

	1970	1972	1973	1974	1975	1976
Mexico	12.2	12.8	17.0	20.7	24.0	29.6
Brazil	11.6	12.3	12.7	13.7	14.6	16.8

Source: IDB, Economic and Social Progress in Latin America,
1979, Table II-23,p.97.

ico's external public debt rose substantially from 1970 and even
exceeded Brazil's ratio.

If we examine the Echeverría period, however, we find that
borrowing in the public sector outpaced that of the private
sector. In 1976, for example, of a total of US$2.930 billion,
fully US$2.701 billion was committed to the state sector.[83]

In the Latin American region as a whole, bank credits sur-
passed DFI as a share of total capital inflow during the 1970s
and Mexico proved no exception. Increasingly, ISI was financed
not through DFI but through external sources of credit. In Mexico, DFI represented 34% of total capital inflow during the 1960s.
By 1970 it reached 40% but a dramatic increase in borrowing
reduced DFI's share to only 9.3% of total external capital flows
by 1975.[84]

A major reason for the growth of the debt was the rising
imbalance on commercial account and the need to cover such def-

icits. The growth in imports from the inflation wracked industrialized countries boosted the deficit. Moreover, as Mexico
turned increasingly to the Eurocurrency market and the U.S. commercial market, the terms of credit became less favorable with
higher interests rates and shorter periods for repayment.

The situation had become so destabilized that by 1976, the
International Monetary Fund (IMF) granted a credit of US$1.2
billion to Mexico to support its deficits. This "Extended Fund
Facility" credit was funded by the IMF and the U.S. Treasury on
a 50-50 basis. Moreover, a European consortium added a $800
million eurodollar credit for additional support.[85] The "Facility" itself was to be disbursed over a period of three years but
the disbursal was predicted upon Mexico's having met the goals of
the IMF Stabilization program that Mexico was "required" to
accept.[86]

During 1977, Mexico was to have been limited to only US$3
billion in net new borrowing and US$2 billion in 1978. Mexico
had received a grace period of three years to establish "external
and internal equilibrium".[87] As with most IMF Stabilization
Programs, the principal prescriptions included cuts in government
spending and a general contraction of the economy. Typically,
this has meant an increase in unemployment and a curtailment of
services of a social welfare character.[88] The expanded activities of the state were viewed as the primary culprit in the
generation of the 1976 crisis. Although the specifics of the
program were not disclosed for a full year after an agreement was
reached with the IMF, the details were eventually made public and
included the following points:

1) Economic growth should register 4% in 1976, 5% in 1977,
   6% in 1978 and 7% in 1979.
2) Capital formation was to equal 26% of GDP in 1977, 27%
   in 1978 and 28% in 1979. This requirement sought to
   address Mexico's failure to mobilize domestic savings
   which might be utilized as an alternative to external
   financing. Moreover, the IMF preferred private to
   public savings and went so far as to specify the ratios
   for the three year period.
3) The public sector budget was to drop from 25.9% of
   GNP in 1976 to 24.5% in 1979.
4) The balance of payments deficit on current account was
   to drop from -2.3% of GNP in 1976 to positive 0.6%
   in 1979.
5) Public sector savings were to rise from 0.5% of GNP
   in 1976 to 5.5% in 1979.
6) Restrictions were placed on international borrowing.
7) Growth in public sector employment was restricted to
   a maximum of 2% per year.
8) The public sector deficit as a proportion of GNP was
   to drop from 10% in 1976 to 2.5% in 1978.[89]

Clearly, restrictions upon the state sector coupled with a
virtually assured worsening of the Mexican employment profile
would prove troublesome.

The State in Mexico Before the Boom

In the aftermath of the Mexican Revolution, the Mexican state played a critical role in the strengthening of the Mexican entrepreneurial class which in 1920 was small and weak.[90] Acting on behalf of private capital, during most of the post-revolutionary period, the state shunned the accumulation of profits and revenues in order to engage in transfers to the private sector through extensive direct and indirect subsidies in order to assist in the capital accumulation process.[91]

As a result of the weakness of the entrepreneurial class, the state engaged in the direction of Mexico's constitutionally mandated "mixed" economy, and its industrialization program "generated both industrialists and bankers as major power groups."[92] Nora Hamilton terms the state's participation in the formation of contemporary capitalism in Mexico "extensive."[93]

In a study of the development of three of Mexico's major grupos (financial and investment groups) including Garza Sada, Aaron Saenz and Banco Nacional de México, Hamilton found that the state provided not only the standard liberal-state services of infrastructure, incentives and protection, but had also engaged in the promotion and financing of specific firms within the private sector through loans, securities purchases, investment and "facilitation of foreign loans."[94]

In "late industrializing" or associated dependent states, the size of the state apparatus as measured only by employment or contribution to GDP, for example, has tended to be a poor indicator of the state's role in society.[95] Instead, the participation of the state in capital formation has been of crucial import. Characterizations of the state as an intervener of "last resort," while perhaps accurate in specific cases of direct investment,[96] obscure the central role of the state in the evolution of society. In fact, the Mexican state, in quantitative terms (compared to the U.S., for example or other industrialized countries where state sector activities account for at least one-third of the GNP) by the mid 1970s carried an intermediate ranking,[97] although substantial growth was seen during the Echeverria period. By 1976, 2 million people[98] were employed by the federal state and the total number of public or mixed public-private enterprises had jumped from 400 in the early 1970s to 845 in 1976.[99]

Throughout Mexico's industrialization, the state has occupied a central coordinating and promotional role. During the first phase of ISI, (1945-1954), the state aided the private sector through: 1) tariff protection, 2) licensing arrangements, 3) government tax incentives and subsidies, 4) the establishment of public enterprises in key sectors, and 5) the provision of electric power, roads, communications systems and "fuel at subsidy prices."[100] The state absorbed risk for private capital and acted as a "partner and expediter whenever bottlenecks had to be broken or excessive risks reduced."[101]

During the period of "Stabilizing Development" (1955-1970) or the second phase of ISI, the government acted "to stimulate the capitalist sector to invest through maintaining very low rates of effective direct taxation of incomes and profits," and generally acted to create a favorable climate for private and foreign investment.[102] Looney argues that it was during this period that state development policy

> favored the formation of a completely distorted market, i.e., an appendage of the productive consumer structure of the Western capitalist economy, particularly the United States, was superimposed upon the traditional Mexican economy.[103]

Also during the second phase, the increasingly internationalized and complex economy had spawned the development by the state of a rudimentary planning capability. An increased level of state investment had been seen during the López Mateos period (1958-64) which complemented private sector growth and made evident the need to provide greater coordination of public investments.[104]

During the third phase of ISI, the state's activity grew substantially in response to a recognition that Mexico had arrived at the standard ISI impasse. This impasse was produced by the failure of consumer products and intermediate goods substitution within the context of dependency to yield backward linkages leading to a deepening of the productive structure. Essentially, these linkages failed to materialize because national entrepreneurial interests accustomed to state absorption of risk and costs and oriented toward the international economy as a source of industrial inputs (including technology), did not respond to linkage signals from the market.[105]

It was state activity during the third phase that sustained growth in the economy as this impasse emerged.

> ...the growth of the industrial sector was maintained only by the expansion of state sector enterprises including petrochemicals, electricity, and in later years, oil.[106]

Mexico's industrialization project would have ground to a halt had the state not pursued substantial investment.

Public Investment

State sector investment as a percentage of total investment has been substantial. Between 1940 and 1970, the state sector share of total investment was 40%[107] and by 1976,[108] the state's share had jumped to 56%. As a share of gross fixed investment, state sector participation had reached 80% in 1975.[109] The growth rate in public investment between 1965-1976 outpaced that of the private sector as seen in Table 2-20.

Of total public sector investment between 1965-1976, 40% was committed to industry for the most part import substituting, and 13% to agricultural and rural development. Petroleum and petrochemicals development alone accounted for 20% of total investment.[110] During the period 1971-1977, some increase was seen in agricultural investments while industry maintained its 40% share. (Table 2-21)

Table 2-20

Growth Rate in Investment, 1965-1976

(averages, percentage per annum)

	1965-70	1971-76
Public sector	3.0	15.3
Private sector	13.5	4.0

Source: Examen de la Situación Económica de México, v.LII, n.616, (marzo de 1977), p.106.

Although by 1972, state firms controlled only 9% of the 300 largest manufacturing firms,[111] the World Bank reported that during the period 1971-75, fully 57% of investment in manufacturing had originated in the public sector compared to 31% in the late 1960s,[112] with the bulk of the latest investment directed at automobiles and steel.[113] Thirty-four firms accounted for nearly the total public sector manufacturing investment. Moreover, the top 15 firms accounted for 90% of that investment. The top five recipients included Sicartsa (steel), Altos Hornos (steel), Guanomex (fertilizer), Diesel Nacional (motor vehicles), and Constructora Nacional (railroad equipment.) Of the top 34, investment flowed to the following sectors: steel - 58%, autos - 22%, chemicals - 13%, sugar - 5% and machinery - 2%.[114] In the crucial steel industry, government participation was substantial. (Table 2-22).

Clearly, the state has expanded beyond the traditional boundaries of the liberal state and is firmly entrenched in productive sectors. Still other areas of investment include pulp and paper, films, textiles, food, beer, cement, glass, metal-working and hotels.[115] Investment by the state has taken the form of minority, joint venture, and majority equity in addition to 100% state ownership. Joint ventures have occurred in conjunction with both private local and foreign capital. As we have noted previously, the issue of ownership vs. control is an important one and it is reasonable to suggest that state and foreign minority equity participation in firms formally registered as national-private may understate the importance of the role played by these actors in determining corporate policy. Moreover, state financing and credit heavily influence investment decisions made by the private sector.

Financial assistance to industry has been channelled principally through the Bank of Mexico and Nacional Financiera (NAFINSA), the central development arm of the state. By the end of the 1970's, the state had created an elaborate network of institutions and programs designed to assist the private sector with its development activities.

Table 2-21

Composition of Public Investment, 1971-1977

(percentages)

DEVELOPMENT	78.4
Agriculture	17.0
Agriculture	15.1
Livestock	0.7
Forests	1.1
Industry	40.3
Energy	30.3
Steel	4.7
Mining	0.2
Other	5.1
Communications and Transport	21.1
SOCIAL WELFARE	19.2
Public Services Urban, Social	9.5
Hospitals	3.6
Education and Research	6.0
ADMINISTRATION AND DEFENSE	2.4

Source: Ifigenia Martínez Hernández y Gildardo López Tijerina, "El Sector Público Federal en México, Su Importancia y Control," El Economista Mexicano, v.XIII, n.6 (noviembre-diciembre, 1979), p.63

50

Table 2-22

Steel Production, 1977

Company	Ownership	% of Production
Altos Hornos	State	39.8
Hojolata y Lamina	Garza-Sada	22.9
Cía Fundidora de Monterrey	Banco Nacional de México	12.2

Source: Economist Intelligence Unit, Quarterly Economic Review of Mexico, Annual Supplement, 1978, p.14 and Barkin, "Mexico's Albatross," p.68.

Chief among the development assistance arms of the state that had been developed as the oil boom exploded were:

BANCO DE MÉXICO:

1. FONEI: (Fund for Industrial Equipment). This program was established in 1973 to assist enterprises engaged in import substitution or export. Between 1973 and 1978, FONEI was budgeted at approximately P5 billion. The bulk of the funding was directed toward intermediate and capital goods.[116]
2. FIRA: (Financing for Agricultural Related Enterprise). FIRA was designed to aid small and medium-sized enterprises and has been funded by the Banco de México along with the World Bank, the Interamerican Development Bank and Chase Manhattan Bank. [117]
3. FOMEX: (Fund for the Promotion of Manufactured Exports). Budgeted at P17.7 billion in 1977, FOMEX was largely internally funded (82.4%) and was designed to foster import substitution and export growth. At the same time, however, FOMEX funds have been used to support imports by Pemex and CFE.[118]

The other arm of support to industry was the NAFINSA, an organization that embraced a full range of programs. Since 1950, NAFINSA has provided between 33% and 50% of the financial sector's financing for industry.[119] Its programs include the following:

NAFINSA

1. PAI: (Program for the Integrated Support of Small and Medium Sized Industry.) PAI has provided technical assistance and in particular supported pre-investment studies.[120]
2. FOGAIN: (Fund for the Promotion of Small and

Medium-sized Industry) Established in 1954, FOGAIN commanded the largest resources and had spent P85.6 billion by 1978. FOGAIN had provided support for training for industry and provided loans for plant infrastructure as well as debt restructuring.[121]

3. FONEP (Fund for Pre-investment Studies) Established in 1967, FONEP has supported pre-investment studies for both private and public capital.

4. FOMIN (Fund for Industrial Promotion) Established in 1972, FOMIN has provided support for the establishment of new enterprises and the expansion and modernization of industrial plant through stock acquisition . FOMIN engages in high risk investment.[122]

5. FIDEIN (Fund for Industrial Site Development) Established in 1970, FIDEIN was designed to absorb initial site development costs for private enterprise.[123] While industrial decentralization was to have been one of FIDEIN's primary goals, the World Bank noted that little success had been achieved.

6. FONTUR (Fund for Tourism) FONATUR has absorbed a variety of costs for tourism ventures initiated by private capital, frequently in conjunction with foreign interests.

Investment and credits have also been channelled through over thirty public credit institutions.[124] Included among the largest were BANOBRAS, BANCOMEXT, Banco Pesquero, Banco Nacional del Ejército y la Armada, Banco Nacional de Crédito Ejidal and Banco Nacional Agrícola. Even by the late 1960s, a third of all assets in the financial sector were controlled by state financial institutions.[125]

The state has also provided subsidies to capital through tax incentives and in fact had maintained one of the lowest tax rates in the developing world. Subsidies to business through favorable pricing of goods and services produced in the public sector amounted to a figure equalling 40% of total annual public investment by the mid 1970s.[126]

Between 1970 and 1975, federal expenditures rose from US$3.2 billion to US$12 billion. Table 2-23 presents a breakdown of central government expenditures including capital and current accounts for 1977.

Central government expenditures, however, represent only a portion of total public spending as investment in public enterprises and their costs of operation are excluded. Thus, the commitment to "social development" is greatly overstated while expenditures for industry and economic development generally, are greatly understated. By 1977, total public sector spending reached a figure of P697.2 billion while central government expenditures amounted only to P295.5 billion.[127]

Including all government spending, the state sector share of GNP rose to 25.9% in 1976. (Table 2-24) At the same time that public sector spending rose at a rapid pace, the costs of government operation absorbed all available resources and rising deficits were financed by credit, increasingly obtained from

Table 2-23

Central Government Expenditures by Main Sectors, 1977
(excluding public sector enterprises)
(by percentage)

Social Development	30	Interest on External Debt	8
Industry	24	Transport & Communication	7
Administration	14	Trade	6
Farming	11	Tourism	.003

Source: Calculated from data in Economist Intelligence Unit,
Quarterly Economic Review of Mexico, Annual Supplement, 1978.

Table 2-24

Total Public Sector Spending as
a Proportion of GDP, 1952-1976

1952	1960	1970	1975	1976
4.1	11.0	13.0	22.0	25.9

Source: 1952 & 1970: Looney, Mexico A Policy Analysis, p.43;
1960: John B. Ross, The Economic System of Mexico,(Stanford,
CA: Stanford, 1971), p.103; 1975: Martínez Hernández and
López Tijerina, p.46; 1976: "Características..." Comercio
Exterior, pp.355-356.

international sources. Credits to the government from the
Central Bank tripled during the period 1971-76 while credit to
the private sector remained constant.[128] Leading recipients in
the public sector of long term foreign financing included the
Federal District, the Federal government, Pemex, CFE, Telemex,
Ferrocarriles, and CONASUPO.[129] As of December 1976, CFE alone
accounted for 23% of Mexico's total public foreign debt. CFE's
operating losses which mandated such heavy borrowing, in addition
to normal capital requirements, stemmed from subsidies provided
to industrial users via nominal rate schedules for electricity.
CFE's subsidy to industry in 1976 was estimated at US$3 bil-
lion.[130] Subsidies from a variety of state sectors benefited
not only private capital but foreign capital as well.

Mexicanization and the Triple Alliance

In the post revolutionary period, Mexican business interests found themselves to be vulnerable to international capital despite nationalist animosity toward encroachments by the colossus to the North.

> The class which emerged in power after the Revolution was a new industrial bourgeoisie whose conflicts with imperialism were not over the further development of capitalism--that issue was settled--but over who would control that development and how its benefits would be divided. But as a class the new bourgeoisie was weak and its emerging state still unstable. The only forces upon which it would have depended in an all-out confrontation with the U.S. were the working class and peasantry. And while the new state attempted to build a base of support among these classes through agrarian reforms and progressive labor legislation, the bourgeoisie feared the uncontrolled power of the popular classes more than it feared imperialism. In the end, its relative weakness forced it to accept accomodations with foreign capital which left the U.S. monopolies in the saddle of key industries...[131]

As a result, despite the new Mexican elite's abhorrence of Díaz's "sell-out" to foreign interests, cooperation between the central state and Mexican elite interests became more clearly complementary rather than antagonistic.

Especially since the Cárdenas period (1934-1940), however, the Mexican state has sought to assist local business interests in redefining the terms of the dependency relationship. The state has done so by entering infrastructural and productive areas in order to absorb costs and risks that local private interests could not or would not absorb and that otherwise would have become the domain of foreign investment. In other cases, the state acted to facilitate local private sector joint investments with foreign capital through both direct and indirect means.

By 1930, banking[132] and railroads had already been "Mexicanized". During the 1930s, electric power and petroleum resources were added to the list with further efforts being directed at the full Mexicanization of rails.[133] By the 1970s, a variety of other activities had become the province of the state--including basic petrochemicals, nuclear energy, and the mining of radioactive materials. In 1972, the state declared that firms engaged in the manufacture of auto parts would have to be converted to at least 60% Mexican equity while telecommunications, urban, air and maritime transport, forestry, and natural gas distribution would all be 100% Mexicanized.[134]

In 1973, all previous Mexicanization provisions and new provisions were codified into a series of laws which also created a National Commission on Foreign Investment as well as a Registry of

Technology Transfer.[135] The National Commission on Foreign
Investment was to address the problems of denationalization, concentration, balance of trade effects, employment, and regional
distribution[136] in considering whether applications for new DFI
(and expansions of existing plants) should be approved. The
Registry of Technology was similarly charged with evaluating the
impact of technology transfer on employment, exports and other
factors.[137]

Sectors that would be entirely closed to DFI were to include,
in addition to major sectors listed earlier, insurance, all financial services, all communication, transport and fishing. Sectors
requiring majority ownership included: steel, cement, glass, fertilizers, cellulose, aluminium, chemicals (basic), and rubber.[138]
In the automobile industry, autos for export would require 40% of
their components to have been manufactured in Mexico while autos
for domestic sale would require a factor of 60%.

As a mechanism for assuring national control over industry,
Mexicanization has been criticized by those who argue that even
when foreign equity is reduced to a minority share, TNC subsidiaries remain dependent

> ...on the parent for supplies, technology, long term debt
> capital and export markets and the past centralization of
> decision-making within the MNC organization.[139]

Furthermore, even where majority local ownership is mandated,

> ...foreigners often have decisive influence over company
> policy because domestic equity ownership is dispersed
> and minority stock ownership is concentrated...[140]

Thomas Biersteker has identified a variety of strategies
that have been employed to circumvent the intent of such legislation. These include:
1) dispersing shares through public sale thereby preserving foreign control
2) negotiation of exemptions
3) technical service contracts
4) "fronting" through selection of managerial personnel
5) change in voting rules
6) diversification of the corporation: where a corporation includes processes or activities that require
   100% national equity, these processes may be split
   from the larger corporation thereby evading full
   indigenization of the enterprise. Similarly, a
   corporation may be divided so that the resulting two
   corporations, for example, ('A' with 60% foreign
   control, and 'B' with 40% foreign control) will both
   be managed by 'A'.[141]
To cite only a few cases, Ralston Purina, Firestone, Hart Schaf-
ner & Marx and Scott have utilized stock diversification strategies to insure the "widest possible distribution of stock ownership" designed to retain management control. Ralston Purina

also consolidated its subsidiaries into a holding company, and
through a complicated series of maneuvers, was able to maintain
centralized management of its subsidiaries.[142]

In those areas where indigenization has been successful, the
primary result has been an increase in the economic power of a
few Mexican investment groups, thereby exacerbating the problems
produced by concentration such as inordinate profit-taking and
non-competitive production. Moreover, the policy has in fact
improved relations between local private and foreign capital.
Because the state recognizes the economic contradictions that
have been and will continue to be produced by this alliance, it
has begun to seek to contain the dimensions of this new cooperation in the interests of system stability as a whole.

> The policy of Mexicanization has resulted in a striking
> increase in the economic power of a small handful of
> industrial and banking grupos de poder (power groups),
> and a strengthening of the ties between this dominant
> segment of the national bourgeoisie and multinational
> corporations. Our evidence indicates that the illogic
> of Mexicanization has become apparent to those govern-
> ment officials responsible for the administration of the
> policy, and that they have begun to use the policy in a
> wholly different way. Instead of trying to induce Mex-
> icanization of foreign-owned firms, they appear to be
> using the threat of Mexicanization to bargain for directly
> desirable outcomes (e.g., more exports by subsidiaries of
> MNCs.)[143]

The private sector has supported Mexicanization and the continuance of foreign investment, essentially because DFI is viewed
as providing access to export markets and advanced technology.[144]
More fundamentally, these linkages are supported because of the
links senior Mexican financial and entrepreneurial actors have
with international business. The state's behavior generally
conforms, then, with Peter Smith's assertion that the state acts
to eliminate "excessive international competition" but at the
same time acts as a facilitator of foreign capital's participation in the economy.[145]

The State and Labor Mediation

Unlike the old style authoritarian regime, the Mexican state
has adopted a "non-military and inclusionary type of regime" that
exhibits "greater capacity for endurance by giving social roots
to an authoritarian system" than for example, does the bureaucratic-authoritarian form found in South America.[146] The dominant classes in Mexico have "solved" the problem of labor control
for the time being at least, and did so prior to the emergence of
contradictions stemming from the model of associated dependent
development.[147] With great skill and political sophistication,
the Institutional Revolutionary Party (PRI) has achieved "control
of labor".[148]

The regime has been described as "patrimonial" in nature, taking responsibility for labor control as well as for the provision, however limited, of "welfare services, often provided in the absence of overt popular demand..." Such efforts are undertaken principally as a means of preempting the expression of such demands which could have destabilizing consequences.[149] The state has successfully maintained control over labor by incorporating union leadership and labor as a whole into PRI, by squelching attempts at independent labor organization, by persecution of non-conformist labor leadership, and by strictly controlling organizing activities especially in the agrarian sector.[150] Presently, industry-wide bargaining in textiles, electronics, films, rubber, sugar, mining, rails, petrochemicals, cement, and steel (in addition to public sector enterprises' labor questions) is managed by the federal government as provided for in the constitution. Government also heavily influences wage policy by setting minimum wages and setting precedents in labor negotiations in the public sector.[151]

Roughly 50% of the employed portion of the EAP (50% being un/underemployed) is organized with the highest rate in the industrial sector.[152] High levels of labor organization coupled with state control of much of that organization and the organization of business interests into two principal chambers, the Confederation of Industrial Chambers (CONCAMIN) and the Confederation of National Chambers of Commerce (CONCANACO), facilitate the state's mediation of labor conflicts. Moreover, the corporatist approach to labor management has served system stability.

> The organized labor movement plays an institutional role within the Government. Top leaders are consulted on major decisions at the highest political levels. Labor leaders serve with government representatives and employers on official bodies at all government levels. The union movement has seen steady advances in living and working conditions of urban workers over the years, and usually cooperates with the Government to achieve mutual goals.[153]

Although some urban workers have benefited from the model of development, such cooptation has allowed the regime to pursue policies that on the whole, have resulted in the reduction over time of wages' share as a proportion of GDP and severe un/underemployment.

By contrast, Roger Hansen concludes that

> ...no other Latin American political system has provided more rewards for its new industrial and commercial agricultural elites...It is hard to imagine a set of policies designed to reward private entrepreneurial activity more than those of the Mexican government since 1940.[154]

Table 2-2

Major Mexican Labor Organizations

Organization	Membership
CTM Confederación de Trabajadores (state) de México	2-3 million
FSTSE Federación de Sindicatos de (state) Trabajadores al Servicio del Estado	½-1 million
CROM Confederación Regional Obrera Mexicana	150,000
CROC Confederación Revolucionaria de Obreros y Campesinos	150,000
CGT Confederación General de Trabajadores	30,000

Source: U.S. Department of Labor, Mexico Profile of Labor Conditions, p.5.

The state has consistently and systematically pursued a policy of substantial rewards for business to the detriment of labor, in particular, unorganized labor.

Conclusion

By the mid 1970s, the Mexican state had matured substantially in the exercise of its post revolutionary role as "manager and designer of a new society",[155] and over time had taken upon itself increased responsibilities in the areas of investment, production, planning and labor mediation in pursuit of the principal objective of capital accumulation. Because of the acute structural disequilibria produced by the model of development, the state had developed a greater presence in the productive areas of the economy, not as a result of necessarily imperial motives on the part of state operatives. Instead, the state's managerial responsibilities compelled the state to confront emerging contradictions.

Reflecting upon these developments, David Ibarra Munoz, Secretary of the Treasury and Public Credit (SHCP) during the López Portillo sexenio, identified several specific obligations that had evoked greater activity by the state in the productive

sector:
1) defense of "national autonomy"
2) the need to take risks and provide capital for private
interests when the capital required was "too" great or
the payback period was too long
3) the need to open up opportunities for private investment through state investment
4) the need to save weak enterprises in order to avoid
reduction in employment
5) the need to regulate and even break up certain private
monopolies
6) the need to augment the technical level of Mexican
industry
7) the need to accelerate regional investment[156]
Heightened unemployment, technological and other forms of
dependence and structural blockages in the path of future development, pressed the state to pursue efforts

> ...not only to increase production but also to find
> appropriate channels for cooperation with private enter-
> prise in order to diminish external dependency and at
> the same time to find more just means of distributing
> the fruits of economic development.[157]

Recognition of inequalities and patterns of marginalization which
could be threatening to the system as a whole moved the state
during the "Shared Development" administration of Luis Echeverría
to engage not only in increased investment and direct participation in the productive sector but also in increased social
welfare spending.[158] Given the nature of the model of associated dependent development and given the state's refusal to pursue
fiscal reforms, increased spending, as we have noted earlier, led
to a greatly increased "foreign debt, inflation and a trade
deficit"[159] that only promised to become more severe.
By the end of 1976, inflation raged at 60%, capital flight
had reduced private investment to a trickle, exports had fallen
off because of inflation and inefficiency which had rendered them
less competitive, and finally, the peso was allowed to float
leading to a substantial devaluation.[160] International and
domestic private interests argued that economic recovery could be
achieved through 1) a reduction in labor costs, 2) a curtailment
of state intervention, 3) a liberalization of trade, 4) liberalizing rules for private foreign investment, and, 5) a moderation
of plans for state spending in the petroleum sector.[161] In addition, the government was advised to place greater direct emphasis upon the private sector in its planning. The standard
requirement that the state remain fiscally responsible and resist
excessive state sector spending (that is argued to fuel inflation) is reflective of an important contradiction. In effect,
while international financial and business interests demand
fiscal responsibility from dependent states, the model of development advocated by these interests provokes disasterous state
sector deficits over time.

Implicit in the prescribed recovery package is the suggestion that the state is somehow acting at cross purposes with
private capital and that the state is in fact infringing upon the
private sector's terrain. Rather than a deliberate obfuscation,
this argument results from the observation of real conflicts that
emerge among different business interests and between the state
and various segments of the elite regarding the appropriate means
for pursuing developmental goals.

The Echeverría administration, for example, complained in
1976 that a

> ...lack of understanding (had been) shown from the begin-
> ning by certain business groups regarding the new guide-
> lines set up to sustain the country's development impetus
> in terms of social justice.[162]

Efforts by the state to restrict excessive profits, to provide
subsidies for basic commodities (CONASUPO has been a favorite
target), and to shore up an eroding wage structure in the interests of the ultimate stability of the system had been resisted by
a variety of business groups,[163] in particular, by the Monterrey
group which had chosen instead to adopt the rather quaint "company town" approach to labor management.[164] Thus, there were real
conflicts within the economic elite over the specific configuration of the development project and over the necessity of responding to emerging contradictions. In fact, there was real
disaffection in some quarters for the growing responsibilities of
the state.

Continued state efforts toward resolving systemic contradictions were, of course, dependent upon the state's ability to
finance such efforts. As long as the state had to compete with
private interests for investment capital and considered pressing
the private sector for increases in operating revenues, elements
of the private sector would balk at the activities of an activist
state. If an independent funding source should materialize, however, the private sector could be relied upon to easily shelve
its objections. Essentially, these objections were not questions
of principle as much as questions of short and medium term expe-
diency.

Impasses in the model had become so severe by the mid-1970s
that two analysts were led to conclude that "a policy of primary
reliance on the private sector seems to be severely threatened at
this point in Mexican history,"[165] and without recourse to international financing (that had become increasingly difficult to
obtain due to the level of Mexican indebtness) that would facilitate greater activity by the state, the Mexican "Miracle" might
well be permanently stalled.

Instead, however, Mexico's geologic history would provide a
solution to the dilemma, enabling Mexican state capitalism to
more fully mature and to attempt to grapple with systemic contradictions.

60

NOTES

[1]United Nations, Economic Commission for Latin America, ECLA, Statistical Yearbook for Latin America, 1978 (New York: United Nations, 1979), Table 1, p.3

[2]Interamerican Development Bank, (IDB), Economic and Social Progress in Latin America, 1979 (Washington, D.C., 1980), p.309.

[3]Clark Reynolds, "Labor Market Projections for the United States and Mexico and their Relevance to Current Migration Controversies," Stanford Food Research Institute, 1979. Printed in U.S. Congress, Senate, Hearings before the Committee on the Judiciary, Immigration and Nationality Efficiency Act of 1979, S.1763, 96th Cong., 1st Session, October 17 and 26, 1979, p.226.

[4]Robert E. Scott, "Politics in Mexico," in Comparative Politics Today: A World View, 2nd ed., ed. by Gabriel Almond and G. Bingham Powell, Jr., (Boston: Little, Brown and Co., 1980), p.452.

[5]Reynolds, p.278.

[6]"Mexico Launches Ambitious Programme to Create Jobs," Latin America Economic Report, v.VI, n.25 (30 June 1978), p.200.

[7]Consumer Markets in Latin America, (London: Euromonitor Publications Limited, 1978), p.144, and "Mexico Launches Ambitious Programme to Create Jobs," Latin America Economic Report.

[8]Edwin P. Reubens, "Surplus Labor, Emigration and Public Policies: Requirements for Labor Absorption in Mexico," in U.S.-Mexico Economic Relations, ed. by Barry Poulson and T. Noel Osborn, (Boulder, Colo.: Westview Press, 1979), p.130.

[9]The problem of the reliability of Mexican statistics should be noted. Economists from the National Autonomous University of Mexico (UNAM) and El Colegio de México have commented "...the economic reality of the country is not correctly represented by the current statistics because of failures in the organization of statistical data collection." Specifically, they note that inflation and unemployment statistics are inaccurate. Clearly, political concerns as well as technical problems underlie the issue. The 50% figure has been "informally" attested to by Labor Ministry officials. El Sól, (julio de 1978), U.S. Department of Labor, Mexico, Profile of Labor Conditions, 1979, p.3.

[10]Stephen R. Niblo, "Progress and the Standard of Living in Contemporary Mexico," Latin American Perspectives, Mexico: The Limits of State Capitalism, v.11, n.2, (Summer, 1975), p.114, and Antonio Yunez Naude, "Política Petrolera y Perspectivas de Desarrollo de la Economía Mexicana. Un Ensayo Explorativo," Foro Internacional, v.XVIII, n.4 (1979), p.619. Yunez uses data from Nacional Financiera (NAFINSA). Niblo uses Mexico's Department of Labor data.

[11]Niblo.

[12]David Barkin, "Mexico's Albatross: The U.S. Economy," Latin American Perspectives, Mexico: The Limits of State Capitalism, v.11, n.2 (Summer, 1975), p.66.

[13]U. S. Congress, House, Committee on Science and Technology, Subcommittee on Science, Research and Technology. U.S./Mexico Relations and Potentials Regarding Energy, Immigration, Scientific Cooperation and Technology Transfer. 96th Cong., 1st Sess., 1979, p.119.

[14]Enrique Hernández Laos y Jorge Córdova Chávez, "Estructural de la distribución del ingreso en México," Comercio Exterior, v.29, n.5 (mayo de 1979), Table 4, p.507.

[15]Marcelo Selowsky, "Income Distribution, Basic Needs and Trade-offs with Growth: The Case of Semi-Industrialized Latin American Countries," World Development, v.9 (1981), pp.73-92.

[16]Rodrigo Botero, "Relations with the United States: a Latin American View," in Latin America in the International Economy, ed. by Urquidi and Thorp, p.285; Peter Smith, Mexico, the Quest for a U.S. Policy (N.Y.: Foreign Policy Association, 1980), p.29.

[17]van Ginneken, p.331.

[18]Robert Looney, Income Distribution Policies and Economic Growth in Semi-industrialized Countries. A Comparative Study of Iran, Mexico, Brazil and South Korea (N.Y.: Praeger Publishers, 1975), p.117.

[19]Scott, p.131.

[20]"Pasado y presente del indigenismo," Comercio Exterior, v.29, n.6 (junio de 1979), p.626. Also see Selowsky.

[21]"Pasado y presente del indigenismo."

[22]Reynolds, p.220. The issue of precisely how many Mexican undocumented workers are in the U.S., how many are permanently residing or temporarily residing in the U.S., is a difficult

62

one that will be treated in detail in Chapter V. The Select
Committee on Immigration and Refugee Policy reported in 1981
that there were an estimated 3.5 million to 6 million undocumented workers in the U.S., half of whom were thought to be
Mexican. Robert Pear, "Panel Asks Rise in Immigration with
Tighter Law Enforcement," New York Times, (February, 27, 1981).
pp. A-1 & B-5.

Reynolds, p.223.

Ibid., p.220.

Alan Robinson, "Foodstuffs Program Not Yet Complete,"
Journal of Commerce, (May 21, 1980.)

[26]Examen de la Situación Económica, v.LIII, n.619 (junio
de 1977), p.234.

[27]Arturo Warman, "Desarrollo capitalista o campesino en
el campo mexicano," Comercio Exterior, v.29, n.4 (abril de
1978), p.401.

[28]"Mexico Puts Pragmatism Before Rhetoric on Land,"
LAER, v.VI, n.35 (8 September 1978), p.276.

[29]Examen de la Situación Económica, v.LII, n.624,
(noviembre de 1977), p.517.

[30]Niblo, p.120.

[31]U.S. Congress, Senate, Committee on Energy and Natural
Resources, The Western Hemisphere Energy System, 96th Cong.,
1st Sess., 1979, p.117.

[32]Economist Intelligence Unit, Quarterly Economic Review
of Mexico, Annual Supplement, 1978, p.8.

[33]Reubens, pp.137-138.

[34]IBRD, Mexico Manufacturing Sector: Situation Prospects
Policies, A Country Study (Washington, D.C.,March, 1979),
p.147.

[35]Ibid., p.134.

[36]Ibid., p.138.

[37]Hadad Fardovie Oveisi, Entrepreneurial Activities of
the Public Sector in the Economic Development Process, (unpublished dissertation, Unitersity of Texas at Austin, 1979),
p.191.

[38]IBRD, Mexico Manufacturing Sector, p.124.

[39] Bank of London and South America Review, v.12, n.4/78 (4/78), p.207.

[40] Olga Pellicer de Brody,"La crisis mexicana: hacia una nueva dependencia," Cuadernos Políticos, v.14 (octubre-diciembre,1977), p.46.

[41] René Villarreal, "Import Substituting Industrialization," in Authoritarianism in Mexico, ed. by José Luis Reyna and Richard Weinert (Philadelphia: Institute for the Study of Human Issues, 1977), p.46.

[42] Judith Adler Hellman, Crisis in Mexico (N.Y.: Holmes & Meier Publishers, 1978), p.2.

[43] Peter Baird and Ed McCaughan, "The Electrical Industry. What Price Power," NACLA, North America and Empire Report, v.XI, n.6 (Sept.-Oct., 1977), p.5.

[44] Hellman, p.27.

[45] Angela Delli Sante,"The Private Sector, Business Organizations and International Influence: A Case Study of Mexico," in Capitalism and the State in U.S.-Latin American Relations, ed. by Richard Fagen, p.79.

[46] Antonio Chumacero, "Consideraciones sobre la política mexicana en materia de inversiones extranjeras," El Economista Mexicana, v.XIII, n.6 (noviembre-diciembre, 1979), p.93, and F. Fajnzylber and A. Martínez, Las Empresas Transnacionales, (Mexico City: Fondo de Cultura, 1976).

[47] Baird and McCaughan, p.5.

[48] Chumacero, p.93.

[49] Newfarmer and Mueller, p.15.

[50] Barkin, "Mexico's Albatross," p.75.

[51] Newfarmer and Mueller, p.63.

[52] Pablo González Casanova, Democracy in Mexico, (N.Y.: Oxford University Press, 1970), Table 10, p.211.

[53] Richard S. Weinert, "The State and Foreign Capital," in Authoritarianism in Mexico, ed. by Reyna and Weinert, p.113.

[54] Newfarmer and Mueller, p.62.

[55] Ibid., p.54.

[56] Ibid.

[57]José Luis Reyna, "Redefining the Authoritarian Regime," in Authoritarianism in Mexico, ed. by Reyna and Weinert, p.157.

[58]Newfarmer and Mueller, p.62.

[59]U.S. Congress, Senate, Committee on Foreign Relations, Market Power and Profitability of Multinational Corporations in Brazil and Mexico, by John M. Connor and Willard F. Mueller, 95th Cong., 2nd Sess., 1977, p.6.

[60]Ibid.

[61]Ibid., p.23.

[62]Selowsky, Table 4, p.78.

[63]Carlos A. Rozo and Raul A. Livas," The International-ization of U.S. Capital in Mexico," in U.S. - Mexico Economic Relations, ed. by Poulson and Osborn, p.163.

[64]Reubens, p.135.

[65]Raúl Fernandez, The United States-Mexico Border (Notre Dame, Indiana: Notre Dame University Press, 1977), especially pp. 131-148.

[66]Reynolds, and Edward L. McClelland, "U.S.-Mexico Border Industry Back on Fast Growth Track," Voice of the Federal Reserve Bank of Dallas, (July, 1979), p.3.

[67]U.S. Congress, House, Committee on Foreign Affairs, North American Energy Cooperation, Hearings before the Subcommittee on Inter-American Affairs and on International Organizations, 96th Cong., 1st Sess., Part I, September 27, 1979, p.20.

[68]McClelland, p.3.

[69]Reynolds.

[70]Reubens, p.136.

[71]See Donald W. Baerresen, The Border Industrialization Program of Mexico (Lexington, MA: Lexington Books, 1971), and Baerresen, "Unemployment and Mexico's Border Industrialization Program," Inter-American Economic Affairs, 29,2 (Autumn, 1975), pp.79-90.

[72]IBRD, Mexico Manufacturing Sector, p.2.

[73]CECON Trade News, v.II, n.5 (May, 1977) p.11. On the whole, the Trade Act of 1974 angered Latin America. The U.S. had excluded, despite the intentions of the United Nations

mandate, some of Latin America's most important manufactured exports from GSP coverage. See Gordon Connell Smith, "Latin America and the Carter Administration," Bank of London and South America Review, v.12, (June, 1978), p.294.

[74]Smith, Mexico, the Quest for a U.S. Policy, p.10.

[75]Economist Intelligence Unit, Quarterly Economic Review of Mexico, Annual Supplement, 1978, p.21.

[76]IBRD, Mexico Manufacturing Sector, p.15.

[77]See Timothy King, Mexico: Industrialization and Trade Policies Since 1940 (London: Oxford University Press, 1970). See also "Medición del Comercio Intraindustrial entre México y Estados Unidos," Comercio Exterior, v.28, n.10 (octubre de 1978), pp.1243-1262. An itemized listing of the types of goods traded between the U.S. and Mexico reflecting the international division of labor quite graphically can be found in "United States Trade with Major Trading Partners," Overseas Business Reports, (May, 1980), Table 11, pp.33-35.

[78]U.S. Congress, Joint Economic Committee, Recent Developments in Mexico and their Economic Implications for the U.S. , Hearings before the Subcommittee on Inter-American Economic Relationships. 95th Cong., 1st Sess., January 17 and 24, 1977, p.51.

[79]IDB, Economic and Social Progress in Latin America, 1979, Table III-22, p.95.

[80]"Mexico," Euromoney, (May, 1977), p.93.

[81]Rosario Green, "Mexico's Public Foreign Debt, 1965-76," Comercio Exterior, v.24, n.1 (January, 1978), p.20

[82]"Mexico," Euromoney, p.90; also see U.S. Congress, International Debt, the Banks and U.S. Foreign Policy, 95th Cong., 1st Sess., August, 1977.

[83]Hamilton, "Limits of State Autonomy," p.24.

[84]U.S. Congress, Joint Economic Committee, Recent Developments in Mexico and their Economic Implications for the U.S., p.36.

[85]"Características del crédito otorgado a México por el FMI," Comercio Exterior, v.30, n.4 (abril de 1980), p.355.

[86]O'Donnell and Frenkel argue that "it is simplistic to believe that 'somebody' imposed these programs from abroad. But it is also simplistic (or diplomatic) to assert that a

given government freely elected a certain program that was
later approved by the IMF. What we really are facing is a
convergence of determinations, or better still, a case of
overdetermination." Roberto Frenkel and Guillermo O'Donnell,
"The 'Stabilization Programs' of the International Monetary
Fund and their Internal Impacts," in Capitalism and the State
in Latin America, ed. by Richard Fagen, p.199.

[87]"Mexico. Industrial Investment Stressed in 'Alliance
for Production,' " Commerce America, v.II, n.3 (January 3,
1977), p.11.

[88]Frenkel and O'Donnell, pp.171-212, and "La Reconquista
de la estabilidad," Progreso (julio-agosto de 1978), pp. 35-38.
Laurence Whitehead, "Mexico from Bust to Boom: A Political
Evaluation of the 1976-1979 Stabilization Programme," World
Development, v.8, n.11 (November, 1980), pp. 843-864.

[89]"Características..." Comercio Exterior, pp. 355-356,
and "Aspectos financieros del sector presupuestario en 1979,"
Comercio Exterior, v.30, n.9 (septiembre de 1980), pp. 937-944.

[90]Douglas Bennett and Kenneth Sharpe, "The State as
Banker and Entrepreneur," Comparative Politics, (January, 1980),
p.183 and 166; Reyna, "Redefining the Authoritarian Regime,"
p.158; Walter Goldfrank, "World System, State Structure and
the Onset of the Mexican Revolution," Politics and Society,
v.5, n.4 (1975), p.424.

[91]Baird and McCaughan, p.7.

[92]Fitzgerald, "Capital Accumulation in Mexico," p.410.

[93]Nora Hamilton, "The State and Class Formation in Post-
Revolutionary Mexico," Paper prepared for presentation at
the joint National Meetings of the Latin American Studies
Association and the African Studies Association, November 2-5,
1977, Houston, Texas, pp. 33-34.

[94]Ibid.

[95]Rolando Cordera Campos, "Estado y economía, Apuntes para
un marco de referencia," Comercio Exterior, v.29, n.4 (abril
de 1979), p.415.

[96]Bennett and Sharpe, "The State as Banker and Entrepreneur," pp. 176-179. They cite the cases of state investment in Altos Hornos in the 1940s and investment in Diesel
Nacional (DINA) and in SOMEX. Vernon also adopts this perspective in The Dilemma of Mexico's Development: The Roles of
the Private and Public Sectors (Cambridge: MIT Press, 1965).

[97]Cordera Campos, p.416.

[98]Scott, p.447.

[99]Douglas Bennett, Morris Blachman, Kenneth Sharpe, "National and International Constraints on the Exercise of Power by the State: The Echeverría Sexenio in Mexico," Paper presented at the National Meetings of the Latin American Studies Association, April 4, 1979, Pittsburgh, Pa.; and Roger D. Hansen, The Politics of Mexican Development (Baltimore: Johns Hopkins University Press, 1971), p.44.

[100]Robert E. Looney, Mexico. A Policy Analysis with Forecasts to 1990 (Boulder, Colo.: Westview Press, 1978), p.14.

[101]Vernon, The Dilemma of Mexico's Development, p.108.

[102]Looney, Mexico. A Policy Analysis, p.17.

[103]Ibid., p.27.

[104]Vernon, The Dilemma of Mexico's Development, pp. 115 and 119.

[105]Bennett and Sharpe's study of the automobile industry in Mexico is highly instructive in this regard. At the time that an indigenous industry could have been developed, the Mexican business community preferred to pursue TNC investment in assembly of center state autos in Mexico because of their consumer orientation toward products from the center states, and because of their linkages with center state business interests. See Douglas Bennett and Kenneth Sharpe, "Agenda Setting and Bargaining Power: The Mexican State Versus Transnational Automobile Corporations," World Politics, v.XXXII, n.1, (October, 1979), pp.57-89. See especially p.76.

[106]Rogelio Ramirez de la O., "Industrialización y sustitución de importaciones en México," Comercio Exterior, v.30, n.1 (enero de 1980), p.34. See also Normand E. Asuad Sanén, "La intervención del estado en la economía mexicana de 1917 a 1974 y sus antecedentes," El Economista Mexicano, v.XI, n.5, (marzo de 1977), pp.111-128, and Carlos Tello, La política económica en México, 1970-1976 (Mexico City: Siglo XXI Editores, 1979).

[107]Frederick C. Turner, The Dynamic of Mexican Nationalism, (Chapel Hill, N.C.: the University of North Carolina Press, 1968), p.154, and Villarreal, p.98.

[108]Bennett, Blachman and Sharpe, "National and International Constraints," p.19; Also see Oveisi, Table 4, p.103.

[109]Ibid.

68

[110] "La política económica para 1980," Documento de la Secretaría de Presupuesto y Programación (SPP) y la Secretaría de Hacienda y Crédito Público (SHCP), Comercio Exterior, v.30, n.1 (enero de 1980), p.71.

[111] Newfarmer and Mueller, p.54.

[112] González Casanova, p.54.

[113] IBRD, Mexico Manufacturing Sector, p.29.

[114] Ibid.

[115] Economist Intelligence Unit, Quarterly Economic Review of Mexico, Annual Supplement, 1978, p.18. See also "Registro de la Administración Pública Paraestatal," El Mercado de Valores, v.XXXVIII, num. 41 (9 de octubre de 1978), p.833-844; Barkin, "Mexico's Albatross," p.68.

[116] Arturo García-Torres y Manuel Serdán Alvarez, "Apoyo Crediticio del Gobierno Federal a la Industria Nacional," El Economista Mexicano, v.XIII, num. 5 (septiembre-octubre, 1979), p.90.

[117] Ibid., p.92.

[118] Ibid., pp.93-95.

[119] Bennett and Sharpe, "The State as Banker and Entrepreneur," p.176.

[120] García-Torres y Serdán Alvarez, p.97.

[121] Ibid., pp.98-99; IBRD, Mexico Manufacturing Sector, p.112.

[122] García-Torres and Serdán Alvarez, pp.100-101, and IBRD, Mexico Manufacturing Sector, pp.115-116.

[123] IBRD, Mexico Manufacturing Sector, pp.111-117.

[124] John F.H. Purcell and Susan Kaufman Purcell, "Mexican Business and Public Policy," in Authoritarianism and Corporatism in Latin America, ed. by James M. Malloy, (Pittsburgh, PA.: University of Pittsburgh Press, 1977), p.193; Looney, Mexico. A Policy Analysis, p.34.

[125] Bennett, Blachman and Sharpe, "National and International Constraints," p.19.

[126] Cordera Campos, p.417.

[127] "Documento: La evolución económica de México en

1978," CEPAL, Comercio Exterior, p.797, and IMF, Government Finance Statistics Yearbook, v.IV, 1980, (Washington, D.C.: IMF, 1981), Table C, p.273.

[128] Leoncio Durandeau Palma, "The Sources of Recent Mexican Inflation," in U.S.-Mexico Economic Relations, ed. by Poulson and Osborn, p.41.

[129] Bank of London and South America Review, v.11, n.8/77 (August, 1977), p.436.

[130] Baird and McCaughan, pp.10-11.

[131] Baird and McCaughan, p.6.

[132] Department of the Treasury, Report to Congress on Foreign Government Treatment of U.S. Commercial Banking Organizations in International Financial Conditions, Hearings before the Subcommittee on International Finance, Committee on Banking, Housing and Urban Affairs, U.S. Senate, 96th Cong., 1st Sess., December 12 and 14, 1979, (1980), p.529. By 1976, the only foreign bank operating in Mexico was Citicorp's First National City Bank which conducts limited operations under a "grandfather" clause. Five hundred foreign banks were registered with the Ministry of Finance as "representatives." Economist Intelligence Unit, Quarterly Economic Review, 1979 Annual Supplement, p.19.

[133] Ross.

[134] Newfarmer and Mueller, p.58.

[135] Alonso Aguilar M. et al, Política Mexicana Sobre Inversiones Extranjeras (Mexico City: UNAM, 1977.)

[136] Weinert, pp.119-120.

[137] Ibid., p.122.

[138] Ibid., pp.119-120.

[139] Newfarmer and Mueller, p.59.

[140] James O'Connor, "The Meaning of Economic Imperialism," in Readings in U.S. Imperialism, ed. by K.T. Fann and Donald Hodges (Boston: Porter Sargent, 1971), p.53.

[141] Thomas J. Biersteker, "The Illusion of State Power: Transnational Corporations and the Neutralization of Host Country Legislation," Journal of Peace Research, v.XVII, n.3 (1980), pp.215-217.

[142] "Mexicanization via the Stock Market," Business Latin America (June 28, 1978), pp.201-203.

70

143Douglas Bennett and Kenneth Sharpe, "Controlling the Multinationals: The Ill Logic of Mexicanization," in Global Dominance and Dependence. Readings in Theory and Research, ed. by Lawrence Gould Jr. and Harry Torg (Brunswick, Ohio: King's Court Communications, forthcoming), p.9 of pre-publication manuscript.

144U.S. International Communications Agency, "U.S. Investment in Mexico: Attitudes of Key Mexican Elite Groups," Research Report R-29-78, October 18, 1978, pp.2-3.

145Smith, Labyrinths of Power, p.205.

146Cardoso, "Characterization...", p.36.

147Guillermo O'Donnell, "Change in the Bureaucratic-Authoritarian State," Latin American Research Review, v.XIII, n.1 (1978), p.28.

148Smith, Labyrinths of Power, p.205.

149Merilee S. Grindle, Bureaucrats, Politicians and Peasants in Mexico: A Case Study in Public Policy (Los Angeles: University of California Press, 1977), p.5.

150James Cockcroft,"Mexico," in Latin America: The Struggle with Dependency and Beyond, ed. by Ronald Chilcote and Joel Edelstein (N.Y.: Halstead Press, 1974), pp.292-99.

151U.S. Department of Labor, Mexico. Profile of Labor Conditions, p.4.

152Ibid.

153Ibid., p.5.

154Hansen, p.85.

155Miguel de la Madrid H., Secretario de Programación y Presupuesto (SPP), "La regulación de la empresa pública en México," Comercio Exterior, v.30, n.3 (marzo de 1980), p.216.

156David Ibarra Munoz, "Reflexiones sobre la empresa pública en México," Foro Internacional, v.17, n.2 (1976), pp.142 & 149.

157Editorial: "Nueva presencia del estado en la economía," Comercio Exterior, v.25, n.10 (octubre de 1975), p.1072.

158Alonso Aguilar Monteverde, "La fase actual del capitalismo en México," Economía y Desarrollo (enero-febrero de 1978), pp.85-109.

[159] Olga Pellicer de Brody, "La crisis mexicana," p.46 and Bank of London and South America Review, v.12, n.10/78 (October, 1978), pp. 528-538.

[160] IBRD, Mexico Manufacturing Sector, p.35.

[161] IBRD, Estudio especial de la economía mexicana: políticas y perspectivas para 1977-82 cited in Rafael Rodríguez Castaneda, "Aplica el gobierno las directrices del Banco Mundial," Proceso, p.5, and Dwight S. Brothers, "Mexico-U.S. Economic Relations in Historical Perspective," in U.S.-Mexico Economic Relations, ed. by Poulson and Osborn, p.18.

[162] Mexican Newsletter, Office of the Presidency, (February 29, 1976), p.2.

[163] Susan Eckstein, The Poverty of Revolution. The State and the Urban Poor in Mexico (Princeton: Princeton University 1977), p.16; Bennett and Sharpe, "The State as Banker and Entrepreneur," p.183.

[164] "Mexico, Crisis of Poverty/Crisis of Wealth," Los Angeles Times,(July 15, 1979), p.13 (special supplement.)

[165] Bennett and Sharpe, "The State as Banker and Entrepreneur," p.187.

Hydrocarbon Resource Development within the

Context of Dependency

CHAPTER III

> If there are no internal resources and none coming from
> anywhere else, all hope is crushed, and I do not wish
> to lead a people for whom all hope is lost.[1]
>
> José López Portillo
> Speech to Petroleum
> Workers, March 30, 1978

Recognizing that the society had by the end of 1976 arrived
at a serious developmental impasse, President López Portillo immediately began to pursue Mexico's oil option, arguing that the
development of the resource provided the only alternative to the
loss of all hope for the future.[2] As the son of an oil engineer
himself, the President was no stranger to Mexico's oil sector or
to the state enterprise sector, having once headed the huge electric monopoly, the Federal Electric Company (CFE). As a former
Secretary of the Treasury in the Echeverría government, he was
also well aware of Mexico's precarious financial situation and
began to pursue what was then termed an "interim" solution to the
financial dilemma.

López Portillo appointed his close friend, an oilman himself,
Jorge Díaz Serrano, of whom one noted scholar said, "I swear,
Díaz Serrano is practically a Texan,"[3] to head the state's oil
monopoly, Petróleos Mexicanos (Pemex.) Díaz Serrano, a self-made
millionaire, had lived and worked in the U.S. and had long been
involved in the Texas oil community, having been a chief executive officer in a company whose vice president at the time had
been George Bush who was later to become Vice President of the
U.S. Díaz Serrano came to the position as a powerful advocate of
the rapid development of the resource as opposed to espousing a
more modest, conservative approach.

López Portillo thus had named a man rich in experience in
the world petroleum community and one with whom he had a warm
personal relationship to head Pemex, although Díaz Serrano had in
the past only served as a private contractor to Pemex. Even by
1977, Pemex had become the largest corporation in Latin America.
Moreover, it carried the distinction of being the world's third
oldest national oil company (the Soviet Union and Bolivia having
been first and second respectively).[4]

Oil in Mexican History

José López Portillo would in fact preside over Mexico's
second oil boom, the first having occurred under Anglo-American
management during the early part of the twentieth century.
During the 1920s, Mexican production supplied fully 25% of the
world's supply of petroleum[5] although Mexican petroleum exports
accounted for only 40% of the value of total Mexican exports,[6]
(unlike the 1980s when that figure was to rise to over 75%).
Mexico ranked second following the U.S. in world oil production
during the first boom period.

Control over the Mexican enclave oil industry shifted

between British and American interests during this period. In 1927, the U.S. controlled 77% of all production and 80% of total reserves. By 1936, the British share of production had jumped to 71% with control of reserves reaching 64%. This shift was due principally to the rapid exhaustion of American held reserves and the discovery of new reserves by British interests.[7]

At the height of the first oil boom, Mexico produced .549 million barrels per day (mbd). By 1931, that figure had plummeted to only .039 mbd. Lagging investment and production in the industry beginning in the early 1930s was due principally to the heightened interest of the foreign oil companies in Venezuelan prospects. Venezuela appeared to be a comparatively desirable site for investment due to the less active character of the Venezuelan state, a more quiescent labor force and a more favorable tax climate. Moreover, Article 27 of the Mexican constitution conferred ownership of all subsoil rights within Mexican territory to the Mexican state, labelling them Mexico's national "patrimony" or inheritance. Venezuelan law provided no such challenges to TNC interests.

Although the nationalization of foreign oil interests in 1938 was precipitated by a labor conflict involving petroleum workers and the foreign oil companies, subsequent handling of the labor issue by the Cárdenas regime, coupled with the nationalist-activist character of that regime, suggests that the nationalization would in all probability have occurred even without the specific precipitant labor strife. The wanton exploitation of

Table 3-1

Mexican Oil Production Prior to the Boom,

1921-1976

(millions of barrels per day)

1921	.549	1970	.487
1931	.093	1972	.507
1938	.106	1973	.525
1941	.119	1974	.653
1950	.202	1975	.806
1960	.298	1976	.897

Source: David Fox, "Mexico. The Development of the Oil Industry," Bank of London and South America Review, 10/77, v.11 (October, 1977), Table 1, p.521.

Mexico's reserves had provoked criticism of the totally foreign control of the sector as had the influence of the oil companies in Mexico more generally, including allegations concerning their involvement in the revolution itself. The act of nationalization

on March 18, 1938 was interpreted by the regime and perceived by
the population as a virtually unparalleled revolutionary act in
Mexican history and is to this day revered as one of the nation's
most notable events and has been accorded the status of a national holiday.

The nationalization itself provoked protests from the U.S.
government and a full rupture of diplomatic ties with Britain.
The more serious reaction came, however, from the oil companies
themselves. Despite assurances of just compensation for the
nationalized properties, the oil companies responded with a
series of retaliatory acts that seriously disrupted Mexico's
industry in the immediate aftermath of the nationalization. Mexico experienced a loss of foreign markets, embargoes on crucial
petrochemical, technical and other material supplies and an international campaign of harassment orchestrated by the oil companies.
Moreover, the companies sought to undermine and destabilize the
regime by supporting a rebellion in Mexico under the leadership
of an avowed fascist, Saturnino Cedillo.[8] Cardenas was able to
quash the revolt, however, and the program of destabilization
and export interruption was laid to rest principally because of
the outbreak of war in Europe. Although Mexico had established
alternative export markets in Germany and Japan following the
cut-off of market access to the Western democracies, Mexico
remained close to the West and with the entry of the U.S. into
war and the settlement of claims, Mexico once again became a
preferred supplier to the U.S. and Britain.

The state oil company was established June 7, 1938. The new
management soon found that in addition to the injurious overproduction of Mexican reserves, the foreign oil companies had left
the industry "in a state of decay."[9] Investment in new equipment
had been at a minimum in the latter years as corporate attention
had shifted to Venezuela. The inferior technical condition of
the industry was compounded by acts of sabotage committed by the
retreating oil companies. Although the state company suffered
initially from a shortage of skilled technical and managerial
personnel, it proved to be fully capable of operating the industry.[10]

On the most serious problems facing the new management was
the fact that the industry had a pronounced "enclave" character
and had been developed for export activities.

>...the industry--geared for export--had yet to integrate
>itself with the local economy. Pipelines ran down to the
>Gulf instead of to the potential industrial, residential
>and governmental customers in major inland cities.[11]

The export orientation of the industry was clearly felt to be un-
satisfactory by the new management group that later came to be
known as Pemex's "Generation of '38". With regard to the previous
overproduction of the resource, the "Generation of '38"

>...consistently advocated conservation of Mexico's
>national patrimony lest output again plummet, as it
>did following the 1921 production peak, or the indus-

try once more would become the focus of foreign aspirations.[12]

Thus, as domestic demand rose and the more conservationist and nationalist philosophy prevailed, Pemex shifted its emphasis from exports to domestic supply to avoid any further squandering of the national inheritance.[13] The government's conservative oil policy resulted in a fairly static reserves picture (Table 3-2) and a moderate exploration and drilling program through the mid 1970s. Although the period 1958-1964 was an especially active drilling period, production itself increased only by 25%.[14]

With internal demand rising and reserves stagnating, by 1968, Mexico had become a net importer of hydrocarbons although Mexico's first petroleum trade deficit was actually incurred in 1970.[15] By 1973, Mexico was importing 65,000 bd,[16] of which approximately 50,000 bd were imported from Venezuela. In 1974, Mexico's petroleum import bill was substantial US$382 million.[17] Even prior to the oil embargo of 1973-74, the administration of Luis Echeverría set in motion programs geared toward boosting proven reserves and supporting accelerated domestic demand and export sales. Important discoveries were made in 1972 in the Villahermosa area and in the Reforma area of Chiapas state,[18] and were suggestive of the petroleum bonanza whose full dimensions still remain to be determined.

Prices which had been frozen in the domestic market since 1958 were increased in 1974 and again in 1976,[19] in order to defray the greater financing requirements of the program. Increased prices in the domestic market were also a reflection of the post-embargo increases in world prices. The price freeze in the domestic market for Pemex products had acted as a constraint upon Pemex's growth by curtailing revenues while providing tremendous subsidies to the domestic economy. In the aftermath of the boost in prices, Pemex's capital spending jumped from US$370 million dollars in 1970 to US$1.25 billion in 1976.[20] This increased activity and emphasis upon development and export marked an important shift from the emphasis in the philosophy of the "Generation of '38." Increases in the foreign debt, balance of payments problems and the allure of heightened revenues that could be earned in the international market in the wake of the creation of OPEC and the rocketing upward of world prices, propelled Pemex into activities it had previously deemphasized.

As a result of the development initiatives of the Echeverría administration, Mexico by 1975 had once again become a net exporter of oil.[21] Production nearly doubled during the 1970-76 period although official reserve figures showed only marginal increases. Yet the central activity of the state monopoly during the post-expropriation years was clearly of a domestic orientation. Table 3-3 reveals the shift in focus in the disposition of production from the 1922 period to the 1938-76 period.

Production nearly doubled during the 1970-76 period although official reserve figures showed only marginal increases. Although during the preponderance of the post-expropriation

Table 3-2

Mexican Petroleum Reserves,* 1938-1983

(billions of barrels)

Year		Proven	Potential	Reserves/Prod-uction Ratio
1938		1.276	-	-
1950		1.608	-	-
1960		4.787	-	-
1970		5.568	-	-
1976		6.350	-	18
1977	(Jan.)	11.160	120	25
1977	(end)	16.001	120	30
1978		40.194	200	60
1979		45.803	200	60
1980		60.126	250	-
1981		67.800	250	-
1983		72.008	250	52

* (66% crude and 33% gas)

Sources: Grayson, Politics of Mexican Oil, p.239; Alan Riding, "The Mixed Blessings of Mexico's Oil, " New York Times Magazine, (January 11, 1981), p.22; General Accounting Office, Prospects for a Stronger United States-Mexico Energy Relationship, (May 1, 1980), Table 3, p.35; José López Portillo, "Tercer Informe", Hispano, v.LXXV, n.1949 (10 de septiembre de 1979), p.14; "Energéticos y petroquímica básica," Comercio Exterior, v.33, n.10 (octubre de 1983), p.907; "La actividad de Pemex en 1982," Comercio Exterior, v.33, n.4 (abril de 1983), p.292.

period Pemex had served a supply and subsidy function and was not specifically concerned with accruing profits and foreign exchange for the state, Pemex nonetheless did provide more resources to the state than had the foreign oil companies. Within seven years of the nationalization, Pemex had earned an amount that equaled the amount paid in taxes during the entire period of foreign domination in the oil industry.[22] With the advent of the second oil boom, however, Mexico's policy regarding oil revenues and their role in development would undergo a major change.

The Second Oil Boom

At the outset of José López Portillo's administration (1976-1982), Pemex was immediately catapulted into a more central posi-

Table 3-3

Disposition of Petroleum Production

(percentages)

Year	Domestic Market	Export Market
1922	1.0	99.0
1932	37.5	62.5
1938	40.0	60.0
1941	62.0	38.0
1976	89.0	11.0
1977	81.0	19.0
1978	73.0	27.0
1979	68.0	32.0
1980	63.0	37.0
1982	46.0	54.0

Sources: 1922-41: Meyer, Mexico and the United States in the Oil Controversy, 1917-1942, Table 1, pp.8-9; Rippy, pp.270 and 282; 1970s figures based on data in Table 3-6. 1980 data from Table 3-6 and 1982 figure from "La actividad de Pemex en 1982," Comercio Exterior, v.33, n.4 (abril de 1983), Table 2, p.293.

tion within Mexican development strategy. The secretive and conservative oil policy of the Echeverría administration was overturned and within weeks of López Portillo's accession to the Presidency, Mexico officially raised its reserve figures by 76% although the presence of such reserves and even potentially larger reserves had been suspected earlier. First official Mexican government notices of the huge potentials were floated in 1972 and again in 1974. U.S. President Gerald Ford reportedly talked with Echeverría in October of 1974, and at that time obtained the Mexican leader's promise that Mexico would not join OPEC as well as assurances that the U.S. would indeed have ready access to Mexican oil.[23] According to a U.S. government report, the U.S. "knew of Mexico's potential energy reserve level at a very early stage,"[24] and even by 1976, the U.S. estimated Mexico's reserves at 20 billion barrels compared to Mexico's official estimates of 11.16 billion barrels.

The apparent reluctance of the Mexican government during the Echeverría period to reveal the full extent of what were known to be large resources has been explained by one observer as a result of nationalist fears concerning possible U.S. responses to news of the reserves at its doorstep.

> ...the first several years of Mexican oil policy (1972-76) was characterized by a defensive secretive stance designed

to obscure and confuse facts and figures on reserves and
production. The Mexican government was fearful of the
'envy and rapacity' of the United States and played down
the potential richness of the finds.[25]

Yet there was little secret in informed circles concerning the
dimensions of the reserves. By early 1979, former U.S. Energy
Secretary James Schlesinger was quoted as saying that "the Mexican oil reserves prospectively (are) as great as those of Saudi
Arabia."[26]

The Mexican government shifted away from its conservative
and secretive approach to oil policy at least in part because the
López Portillo administration was in a position to substantially
boost investment in oil (aside from the necessity of doing so)
without incurring political liabilities. The Echeverría administration had poured fully half of all public investment during the
1973-75 period into agriculture and social services.[27] Within
the Mexican system, balance is maintained through a rather orderly
and predictable alternation between so-called populist (e.g.
Echeverría) administrations and more "pragmatic" business oriented
administrations (e.g. López Portillo).[28] Thus, huge investments
in petroleum development conveniently came at a time when the
logic of the system would have prescribed a swing away from populist social spending.

Further, as Echeverría's six-year term drew to a close and
serious economic dislocations were encountered, the new administration would have to bear the responsibility for fashioning a
new oil policy as innovations in policy-making traditionally are
made during the first four years of the presidential term. Moreover, the Mexican government would have to engage in substantial
new planning for the development of the resource given its dimensions. With only 10-15% of Mexico's potential hydrocarbon territory, (fully 80% of the national land area),[29] having been ex-
plored, planning for development of the resource and for the utilization of revenues would have to be excessive.

The state would have to ensure that potentially rising expectations regarding the domestic results of the mining of the "black
gold" would be adequately managed so as not to produce any destabilization in the society. Clearly, one obvious strategy that
might be employed to insure that the population would coalesce
behind the state's development strategy would be to invoke the
specter of the energy-starved colossus to the North and present
thinly veiled suggestions regarding U.S. plans for the reserves.
Particularly in light of Mexican intentions to pursue an export
intensive strategy, any nationalist posturing would help to
deflect the inevitable criticism by the Left and by members of
the PRI seeking political advantage. Finally, it is apparent
that the more conservative posture was abandoned as the Mexican
state sought to demonstrate to the international financial community its enhanced credit-worthiness and to emphasize the viability and attractiveness of the Mexican economic environment.

As early as 1978, observers put potential reserves at 200

billion barrels and by 1979, the potential reserves figure had
grown to between 500 billion and approximately 700 billion
barrels. The U.S. government reported in 1980 that Mexico had
the hydrocarbon resource capacity to become leading world producer by 1990.30 Pemex publicly admitted to having a potential
reserve figure of only 250 billion barrels, but declined to
confirm the 500-700 million barrel estimates and for good reason.
First, such an announcement would surely have had a depressing
effect on world prices and Mexico had consistently supported
OPEC's pricing policy and had even exceeded average OPEC prices.
Second, the management of domestic expectations would be sorely
tested by an announcement that Mexican reserves were equivalent
to Middle Eastern proven reserves. The Middle Eastern oil producers, for example, have consistently shied away from publicizing the full extent of their reserves in order to provide
support for the petroleum price structure. Thus, Mexico would
have had little incentive for prematurely tipping its hand.

Mexico's Resource in the World Energy Context

Whatever the final figures prove to be, Mexico's reserves
now put at 72 billion barrels (proven), are very substantial. By
the early 1980s Mexico had become the world's fourth largest producer of crude oil and in terms of proven reserves, Mexico had
moved into fourth place. Mexico's reserves far exceeded dwind-
ling U.S. reserves.
Ultimately recoverable world oil resources are estimated at
1 trillion barrels with approximately 652 billion barrels proven
in the early 1980s, down from 675 billion barrels in the mid
1970s. Of the world's proven reserves, fully 360 billion barrels
had already been produced by the late 1970s. Outside of Mexico,
the brightest prospects for the discovery of new oil have been in
the OPEC nations. The Saudis, for example may well have deposits
totalling 300 billion barrels while Iraq has been involved in a
huge secret drilling program.
Mexico's oil was viewed with particular interest by the U.S.
where the results of ambitious programs in the 1970s proved dis-
couraging with U.S. reserves dropping 16.2% since 1970 despite
the high drilling rate.[31] The U.S. Geological Survey estimated
that the U.S. had anywhere from 143 billion barrels to 46 billion
barrels yet to be discovered with a probable figure closer to 89
billion barrels. Other major oil countries such as Venezuela,
Nigeria, Indonesia and Algeria are thought to be near or already
past their peak production period. U.S. output of crude was
expected to drop from a 10 mbd production figure to 7.84 mbd in
1985[32] and according to one analyst, U.S. reserves of convention-
al oil would be seriously depleted by the year 2000.[33]
As a reflection of the U.S. domestic shortfall, imports had
doubled between 1973 and 1979 with imports constituting fully 50%
of oil consumed.[34] Some success was registered by the U.S. and
other major consuming states in curtailing imports in the latter
part of the 1970s and this trend was in fact continued but news

of Mexico's reserves was nonetheless received with elation.

The dimensions of Mexico's reserves thus became known at a time when the world oil supply was entering a downturn period, or what some have termed the latter stages of the petroleum era. By the latter part of the 1970s, the world shortfall had been forecast at 4 mbd by 1985, 10 mbd in 1990 and a sizeable 28 mbd shortfall in the year 2000. New Mexican resources, the continued availability of Soviet petroleum exports (about which doubt had arisen in the late 1970s), oil shale, tar sands, and hydrocarbon based synthetic fuels production brightened the energy horizons to some degree. Yet the prospect of politically induced supply interruptions and shortfalls rendered Mexico's resource, situated within a relatively stable political environment, terribly attractive to the industrialized countries. In the late 1970s, oil imports accounted for a substantial portion of total energy supply for these countries. (Table 3-5)

Table 3-4

Net Oil Imports as a Percentage of Total Energy

Consumption in Major Industrial Countries, 1978

U.S.	22.0	W. Germany	53.3
Japan	73.4	Italy	68.0
France	60.0	U.K.	21.4

Source: Morgan Guaranty Trust, World Financial Markets (February, 1979), Table 4, p.6.

By the end of the 1970s, the U.S. was still receiving 78.5% of its imports from OPEC although in real terms, the U.S. was much less import dependent than Japan or France, for example. It was hoped by the energy pressed industrialized West that Mexico would be producing 10 mbd by 1990 with exports of 4-5 mbd thus providing a relatively secure non-OPEC supply source. Customers could, however, expect to pay OPEC level prices. Such hopes notwithstanding, Mexico's development and production policy would provoke consternation among potential customers and would stimulate competition among the industrialized countries for Mexican exports, even for the 1-2 mbd in exports projected for 1985, a figure which would amount to only 3-4% of free-world import demand estimated at 34-44 mbd for 1985.35

Mexico's Oil Development, Production and Export Policy

Major areas of new discoveries in the early part of the 1970s, as was noted earlier, included the Chiapas-Tabasco region. During the latter half of the 1970s, additional exploration produced major finds in four principal areas: Reforma, Campeche Bay, Chicontepec and Cuenca de Sabinas in Coahuila.

As new discoveries continuously pushed up figures for proven and potential oil and gas, Mexico proceeded with a development program formulated in 1977 at the outset of the López Portillo sexenio that was later to undergo moderate revision. The program of exploration, development, production and export was based upon the fear that without substantial effort, Mexico might become a net importer once again[36] and the belief that without significant oil development, Mexico's larger economic problems might not be amenable to solution at all.

Initially, López Portillo declared that he would not make petroleum development "the axis of national development" but that instead, the oil would be used to solve what he termed a "transitory problem,"[37] (i.e., the financial impasse that had resulted in the IMF Stabilization program.) As was patently clear, however, the problem was hardly of a transitory nature and López Portillo quietly and quickly abandoned such pretense. Instead, he began to advance the argument that oil would enable Mexico to overcome the country's "fundamental problem...the financing of development."[38] "Oil is our chance for self determination because it will allow us to be less dependent on external financing and will improve our international economic relations."[39] In 1978, López Portillo projected that by 1980, Mexico would in fact no longer be reliant upon external financing for its development because of expected oil revenues.[40] Moreover, he maintained that "Mexico has no intention of becoming a typical oil country which imports resources and exports capital. We intend to use oil income for rational development which will avoid converting our country into an exporter of capital."[41]

But the central role in development that the oil would play was reflected in a report from the Ministry of National Properties and Industrial Development (SEPAFIN). In the beginning of the sexenio

> ...the oil was, before anything else, a financial instrument that was used to cover deficits in the balance of payments and in public sector accounts. In the second stage, the petroleum became an instrument to be used in the structural transformation of the economy.[42]

Oil would become the basis for "self sustained industrialization" which would end unemployment by the end of the century.[43] Oil development would provide stimuli for the development of the capital goods industry and in general for Mexican exports.[44] The oil development project was billed as having the capacity to double industrial capacity in only seven years,[45] generating a

10% annual growth rate for the economy.

As an interim financial mechanism, the oil quickly strengthened Mexico's negotiating position with the IMF and restored the waning confidence of international creditors.[46] In addition, as we shall see in Chapter IV, oil served to free López Portillo's hand vis-à-vis the IMF Stabilization agreement, enabling the state to avoid the potentially politically destabilizing consequences of a contractionist policy while satisfying the overall intent of the agreement.

In sum, oil was seen as the means of emancipation from international economic subordination and as one leading Mexican economist argued, oil would effectively remove externally imposed constraints upon development. "The external constraint will cease to be the principal restraint upon efforts to promote sustained economic development."[47]

Officially, Mexican oil development policy came to embrace three formal orienting principles:
1)   production to be based upon the economy's ability to absorb resources that would be generated;
2)   rational use of non-renewable resources;
3)   desire to avoid inducing uneven and distorted development in the economy.[48]

Theoretically, these principles would assist state planners in determining answers to several questions that would form the basis for an oil policy. 1) How rapidly should development be pursued? 2) Should development primarily serve the domestic market or the export market and what would be the appropriate mix? 3) How should the development be financed? 4) What emphasis should be put on the production of crude oil, petrochemicals and refined products?

Despite the seemingly judicious and prudent character of the set of guiding principles that were officially espoused, it appears, as Turrent Díaz has argued, that a decision was made to pursue a vigorous development policy not only because of the obvious financial requisites of the economy but also because there was no reason to pursue a conservationist policy for a resource that would be "technologically replaced in the future."[49] This perception was expressed in detail by Pemex director Jorge Díaz Serrano early in the López Portillo sexenio and we shall quote here at length.

That is to say, the world can be sure of some twenty more years living in the petroleum era, and Mexico has this time to generate wealth by taking advantage of high demand levels, and the high prices paid at present, which will doubtless continue to rise as we approach the end of the century. We need,therefore, to reach the production level of which we have spoken (production of 2.2 million barrels per day in 1982, duplication of refining capacity and triplication of our basic petrochemicals industry) in an extremely short space of time, in order to benefit from these twenty years when the

great volume of demand for energetics (sic) for transport
and the generation of electricity will look to hydrocarbons for its satisfaction. Afterwards, it is possible
that the demand for energetics (sic) will become diversified; at the present time, world use in the petrochemicals
industry accounts for only between 5% and 7% of production
and, while it is possible that this proportion may rise,
this industry will never be able to absorb the volumes
which would be freed by the development of alternative sources of energy. Mexico will participate on a
massive scale in the growth of petrochemicals, but its
great short and medium-term capacity for the generation
of wealth lies in energetics. (sic)

The petroleum business, as we know it at present,
will change by the end of the century, especially in its
economic aspects. Without losing a sense of proportion,
we may point to other good businesses which have been
lost to us in other areas, when artificial substitutes
were found for cochineal, dogwood, natural rubber and in
recent years cotton and sisal. There are only about
twenty years when we can be sure to benefit from hydrocarbons to such an extent that we can cover the country's
necessities for a much longer period than that...

Both domestically and abroad Mexico will be stronger
politically to the extent that it manages to increase
the power of its petroleum industry, but we should not
forget that this is a race against the clock...

The social cost of our failing to follow a dynamic
production policy will be very great. Every industrial
development program for primary and secondary petrochemicals and associated manufactures will be slowed down
in the short and medium term; not only will we be unable
to catch up with the developed countries and fight our
way into the respective markets, but we shall see other
developing nations which are also oil producers and which
are working in the same direction we are, and with greater
resources, inevitably catch us up, thus, making our
position very difficult and blocking our ambition of
becoming, for many, many years, a power in the petrochemicals world...

I cannot think that the alternative is very difficult
to see. We need to produce more crude, more refined, more
petrochemicals, more liquified gas and more natural
methane gas, and we need to trade these products with
those who will pay the best price for them, without distinction of ideology, or preferences for particular
groups. The interest of Mexico demands this.[50]

Díaz Serrano's compelling argument was for the most part accepted as a fair interpretation of reality and the Mexican government did in fact opt for a vigorous development program that
would have a significant export component (although not of the

dimensions hoped for by the industrialized states).[51] This
marked a formal shift away from the conservative domestic market
policy orientation that had been the benchmark of Mexico's nationalist oil policy. No longer would the industry be viewed primarily as a source of domestic subsidy to industry. Instead, the
foreign exchange that could be earned through the export of crude,
product and petrochemicals would, it was thought, provide sufficient capital for Mexican development such that external constraints could be eliminated.

Significantly, early intentions to export refined product
were quickly abandoned[52] and development planning would emphasize
the intensive export of crude because of pressing near term domestic financial requirements and the expense involved in developing
increased refining capacity. For the 1977-1982 period, crude oil
production was to be doubled, gas production would reach 4
billion cu. ft. per day, and oil exports were to increase sixfold.
Refining capacity was to be doubled by 1982 and petrochemical
capacity was to triple. Initial plans provided for exports of
1.105 mbd of oil by 1982 with domestic demand estimated at 1.137
mbd.[53]

Through accelerated exports, the Mexican government sought
to transform the oil into a negotiating chip. As Díaz Serrano
noted:

> When oil is under the ground, it has no strategic value.
> It loses its meaning and becomes only a reason for other
> countries to envy us. On the other hand, if the oil is
> put into production and is a source of wealth, it acquires
> a strategic value in negotiation and a real economic value
> for Mexico.[54]

While the oil was viewed as a useful resource domestically (the
economy could rely upon a plentiful, secure supply of oil and
would be spared the financial burden of costly oil imports, so
damaging to other Third World states), its "real" value would be
realized in the international arena, not only because of the
domestic price structure but because of the overall development
model that would become even more import intensive than had previously been the case. Díaz Serrano openly acknowledged at a
conference of European industrial and banking leaders in 1978,
that the development project spawned by the oil reserves would
require the importation of unprecedented amounts of heavy equipment and finished products,[55] and as a result, the externally
oriented facet of the oil industry would be of vital importance.

The total projected cost of investment required to reach
these goals during the period was initially put at US$15 billion,
five times the investment of the Echeverría period. This projection was quickly upped to US$17 billion, however, due to the
addition of plans for a US$2 billion pipeline for gas exports to
the U.S.[56] Total spending for the six year plan was estimated at
US$45 billion. Gross earnings were calculated at US$54 billion.[57]

The intention to pursue steady but measured growth in pro-

Table 3-5

Projected Distribution of Pemex Spending, 1977-82

(percentage)

Development	46
Exploration	8
Refining	15
Petrochemicals	17
Distribution & Transport	13

Source: Fox, pp.528-9; GAO, <u>Prospects</u> <u>for</u> a <u>Stronger</u> <u>United</u> <u>States</u>-<u>Mexico</u> <u>Energy</u> <u>Relationship</u>, p.41.

duction grew out of Mexican policy-makers fears that an overly accelerated pace would simply generate revenues that would be undigestable for the Mexican economy, provoking a high rate of inflation that would be injurious to the domestic economy and would impact negatively upon other Mexican exports. The inflation would affect export prices, rendering them uncompetitive in international markets, worsening the already aggravated balance of payments situation.[58] Both production and exports tended to outpace Pemex's planning projections (Table 3-7) but rapid development of the resource was viewed as critical for the financial solvency of the economy.

Export earnings reached an impressive US$10.3 billion dollars by 1980 and rose to US$16.594 bn in 1982 as shown in Table 3-8. By 1982, fully 94% of Mexico's petroleum export earnings were derived from the sale of unrefined crude oil alone, up from 90% in 1979.[59] Petroleum exports developed enormous influence as a share of total Mexican exports. By 1982, the figure had risen to 78.4%, up from only 4.3% in 1974. When we compare the significance of Mexican oil exports as a share of total exports with Venezuelan exports of oil, for example, Mexico's petroleum dependence appears quite striking. In 1978, Venezuela's petroleum exports accounted for 60.8% of the value of total exports, a figure significantly less than that of Mexico's petroleum exports given the relative infancy of the industry. (We can use the term infancy here in the sense that Mexico is a relative newcomer to the inner circle of major oil exporters.) Moreover, Venezuela's industrial sector is relatively less developed and thus one would expect to see a greater rather than a lesser share for petroleum exports. Petroleum dominance in the export sector had come to represent exactly the outcome that Mexico had hoped to avoid. World price increases (with which Mexico kept pace), coupled with greater than initially planned-for production and weak performance in other export sectors resulted in

Table 3-6

Comparison of Planned and Actual

Oil Production and Exports

(millions of barrels per day)

	Production		Exports	
	Planned	Actual	Planned	Actual
1977	.953	1.086	.153	.202
1978	1.246	1.330	.336	.365
1979	1.522	1.638	.568	.532
1980	1.781	2.2	.770	.827
1981	2.028	2.3	.960	1.098
1982	2.242	2.748	1.5	1.5
1983	-	2.748	1.5	1.5
1985	3.5	-	-	-
1990	4.1	-	-	-

Sources: Planned production and export figures for 1977-82 from
Fox, Table 2, p.529. Planned production figures for 1985 and
1990 from "Mexico's Energy Programme Limits Oil Exports to
Meet National Needs," Latin America Weekly Report (28 Novem-
ber, 1980), p.1. Actual production figures for 1977-79 from
Abel Beltrán del Río, "El sindrome del petróleo mexicano,"
Comercio Exterior, v.30, n.6 (junio de 1980), Table 1, p.557.
Actual production figures for 1981-82 from "La actividad de
Pemex en 1982," Comercio Exterior, v.33,n.4 (abril de 1983).
Actual export figures for 1977-81 from Banco de México, "La
actividad económica en 1982," Comercio Exterior, v.33, n.5
(mayo de 1983), p.462. Actual export figure for 1982 and
1983 from Mario Ramón Beteta, "La necesidad de estabilizar
el mercado petrolero," Comercio Exterior, v.33, n.11 (noviembre
de 1983), p.1032.

Table 3-7

Comparison of Pemex's Domestic and

Export Earnings, 1977-1982

(percentage)

Year	Domestic	Export
1977	70	30
1978	58	42
1979	45	55
1980	28	72
1982	15	85

Source: "Informe de Petróleos Mexicanos, 1979," Comercio Exterior, v.30, n.4 (abril de 1980), p.392. "La actividad de Pemex en 1978," Comercio Exterior, v.29, n.5 (mayo de 1979), p.561. "La actividad petrolera de México en 1980," Comercio Exterior, v.31, n.4 (abril de 1981), p.452. "La actividad de Pemex en 1982," Comercio Exterior, v.33, n.4 (abril de 1983), p.295.

Table 3-8

Pemex Export Earnings, 1974-1982

(billions of dollars)

1974	.123	1978	1.887
1975	.460	1979	3.986
1976	.544	1980	10.401
1977	1.018	1981	14.585
		1982	16.594

Sources: 1974 & 1975: Mexican Newsletter (February 25, 1976), p.10. 1976: Latin America Weekly Report, (6 March, 1981), p.9. 1977-1981: Banco Nacional de México, "La actividad económica en 1982, Comercio Exterior, v.33, n.5 (mayo de 1983), p.462. 1982: "La actividad de Pemex en 1982," Comercio Exterior, v.33, n.4 (abril de 1983), p.293.

90

Table 3-9

Pemex Exports as a Share of Total Exports, 1974-1982
(percentage)

1974	4.3	1979	49.0
1976	13.1	1980	65.0
1977	24.8	1981	75.0
1978	31.5	1982	78.4

Sources: 1974: Beltrán del Río, Table 5, p.560. 1976-77: Gutiérrez R., Table 5, p.841. 1978: Bank of London and South America Review, 5/79, v.13 (May, 1979), p.311. Grayson, "Oil and U.S.-Mexican Relations, Journal of Interamerican Studies and World Affairs, v.21, n.4 (November, 1979), p.445. 1980: "Rising Oil Exports Fail to Prevent Mexican Trade Deficit," Latin America Weekly Report, (27 February, 1981), p.1. 1981: Alan Riding, "Mexico's Economic Imbalances," New York Times (April 6, 1981), p.D-1 and D-6. 1982: "La balanza de pagos en 1982," Comercio Exterior, v.33, n.5 (mayo de 1983), p.400.

Mexico's transformation into a nation heavily dependent upon the export of oil and thus extremely vulnerable to changes within that single market.

Financing Oil Development

Estimates at the outset of the sexenio put the foreign financing requirement for new Pemex investment at the 50% mark for the 1977-82 period,[60] and in fact they proved to be accurate. Despite Mexico's avowed intention to pursue autonomous oil development, Pemex became one of the world's premier borrowers in international markets.[61] Between 1976 and 1978, Pemex's foreign debt doubled.[62] In fact, in the period 1979-80, Pemex ranked as the world's second largest borrower after the Bank of China. (The Federal Government of Mexico ranked 8th in the world while Mexico's CFE ranked 10th).[63] Pemex's total external borrowing for the 1977-82 period was estimated at US$16 billion dollars.[64] Mexico did attempt to diversify its lending sources by moving vigorously into the Eurocurrency market and by seeking Japanese funds, but its reliance upon U.S. financing remained substantial and in fact, the U.S. remained Mexico's single largest source of external financing.[65]

Total spending by Pemex for the period 1977-82 was estimated at US$40 billion.[66] Naturally, Pemex commanded large shares of

Table 3-10

Pemex External Borrowing, 1977-1980

(billions of dollars)

1977	1.2
1978	2.25
1979-80	5.084

Sources: 1977 and 1978: Bank of London and South America Review, 5/79, v.13 (May,1979), p.311; 1979-80: Euromoney Annual Financing Report, (March, 1981), p.4.

Table 3-11

Pemex Budget as a Share of

Total Public Sector Budget

1975-1980

(percentage)

1975	10.0	1978	30.0
1976	13.5	1979	33.0
1977	20.0	1'980	20.0

Sources: 1975-1976: Fox, pp.525-6; 1977: Edward Williams, "The Agricultural Sector, Unemployment and Petroleum Earnings in Mexico: Policy Prospectives for the Medium Range, mimeo; 1978: Proceso (8 de mayo de 1978), pp.10-11; 1979: U.S. Department of Commerce, Foreign Economic Trends, (June,1980), p.4; 1980: "Shah Kept Out by Internal Pressures," Latin America Weekly Report (7 December, 1979), p.62.

92

Table 3-12

Pemex Federal Budgetary Allocations, 1976-1981

(billions of dollars)

1976	.652	1980	17.700
1977	.900	1981	23.000
1979	9.500		

Sources: 1976-1977: Williams, "The Agricultural Sector,"
1979: "Pemex Still the Big Spender in Mexico's 1979 Budget,"
Latin America Economic Report (8 December, 1978), p.375; 1980:
"Oil-fired Wealth and Controversy," Latin America Weekly
Report, p.9; 1981: Alan Riding, "The Mixed Blessings of
Mexico's Oil," p.25.

the public sector budget during this period. Pemex commanded
almost 35% of all state investment in the period 1977-1981, up
from an average of 17.5% in the 1971-76 period.[67] Similarly,
Pemex commanded a substantial share of the entire public sector
budget. (Table 3-11.) Pemex was in fact transformed into the
nation's largest industrial investor. Clearly, the tremendous
emphasis upon oil investments would constrain investment in other
sectors. Unfortunately, the intensive investment was not offset
by the revenues garnered through oil sales. In 1980, for example,
Mexico's total debt repayment bill came to US$9.4 billion,
a figure uncomfortably close to oil export earnings of US$10.4
billion.[68] By 1982, Mexico's external debt profile had deteriorated to the point where even earnings of over US$16 billion
were insufficient to satisfy repayment obligations. It was also
the case that the import intensity of the petroleum development
project further aggravated the external sector of the economy by
provoking unprecedented current account deficits.[69]

Pemex Revenues to the State

Pemex's earnings for the state are collected by means of taxation on production and exports. As is shown in Table 3-13, the
1980s marked a substantial increase in the taxation rates for the
industry. Pemex revenues as a percentage of public sector income
amounted to 12% in 1975, 17.8% in 1978, 21.4% in 1979 and 30% in
1982.[70] By 1982, Pemex accounted for 10.2% of the GDP, and over
78% of the value of all Mexican exports.[71] The combined impact

of a higher taxation rate, and increased production and sales resulted in a tremendous increase in revenues to the state by the early 1980s. The state had clearly become increasingly dependent on oil revenues yet the state had hardly been "emancipated" by the increased revenue base. Even with earnings of over US$16 billion in 1982, revenues to the state seemed almost insignificant when contrasted with the financial impasse that had emerged. With exports projected through the 1980s and 1990s in the 1.5-2.5 mbd range,[72] petroleum revenues were expected to play an important role in domestic development but would not provide a magic cure-all for the economy despite the early optimism of Mexican planners.

Table 3-13

Rate of Taxation on Pemex Activities, 1976-1981

(percentages)

		Petrochemicals	Exports
1976	16	12	n.a.
1977	16	12	n.a.
1978	17	12	n.a.
1979	18	13	50
1980	27	15	58
1981	27	15	58

Source: "Aspectos de la política tributaria y cambios fiscales para 1981," Comercio Exterior, v.31, n.2, (febrero de 1981), Table 7, p.140.

Table 3-14

Taxes Paid to the Federal Government by Pemex, 1976-1980

(millions of pesos)

1976	9,682	1979	47,014
1977	19,764	1980	162,400
1978	30,283		

Sources: 1976-1978: Grayson, The Politics of Mexican Oil, p.242; "La actividad petrolera de México en 1980," p.451 for 1979-1980.

Technical Dependence and Oil Development

Pemex has frequently been depicted as an example of the growth potential that awaits enterprises in dependent states where a nationalist posture has been adopted. It has been variously described as the world's only fully integrated oil company and as the world's largest drilling company, all which is meant to suggest that dependence is by no means unavoidable or that center states do not hold a monopoly upon successful enterprise. Pemex itself became a "TNC" of sorts, operating a joint venture drilling enterprise, the Mexican Exploration Company, in Costa Rica.[73]

From the beginning of the petroleum development project, Pemex argued that it would be fully capable of designing and managing a project of the dimensions it proposed to undertake, and that it would need little foreign assistance. In fact, Pemex proved to be quite successful in limiting the direct participation of foreign contractors. By 1979, according to the then Pemex Director Díaz Serrano, Pemex was doing 93% of its own engineering and 100% of its own construction.[74] While the latter figure was almost certainly inflated due to Pemex's lack of expertise and technology in the area of offshore operations (the U.S. held a virtual monopoly on the technology,) which are extensive in the Bay of Campeche,[75] on balance, it may be said that Pemex was fully responsible for the overall management of the development program and carried out virtually all of the onshore development.[76]

Pemex, however, according to one observer, made "extensive use of U.S. consultants and companies that provide technical support services."[77] The U.S. engineering firm of Brown and Root was contracted, for example, to

> ...coordinate the engineering work, construct required
> land based facilities, and oversee the purchasing of pro-
> duction platforms, pipelines, and gathering mains to
> initiate large scale operations in the Campeche Sound.[78]

In addition to offshore operations, Pemex contracted with foreign firms in the development of the US$2 billion 48" gas pipeline from Tabasco to the Texas border as well as in the petrochemicals area.[79] Pemex deliberately sought to minimize public awareness of the participation of foreign contractors, however, and Díaz Serrano, for example, claimed that there were only "100" foreign workers involved in Mexican petroleum development at any one time,[80] clearly an understatement of the case.

Despite Pemex's competence, the development project was seriously dependent not only upon foreign financing, but also upon the importation of capital equipment and technology. In a stinging indictment of the technical maturity and scientific sophistication of the Mexican petroleum industry, Leopoldo García-Colín Scherer, subdirector of the Institute of Mexican Petroleum (the research and development arm of the petroleum industry),

argued that in fact, the Mexican petroleum industry was almost
totally dependent upon foreign technical innovation, and lacked
the capability to develop or even adapt available technology.[81]
Further, he argued that the industry was particularly weak in its
ability to handle imported software.

The most serious deficiencies were to be found in the petrochemical industry. "In the entire country, there is not one
institution in which there are solid and objective research
programs in any area of petrochemicals."[82]

> Currently, we totally lack any scientific infrastructure
> in this area, a fact that puts us almost unconditionally
> into the hands of foreign licensors of petrochemical
> processes.[83]

García-Colín Scherer maintained that Mexico was a "prisoner
of technological colonialism" in the petroleum era.[84] The technological dependence characterizing the petrochemical industry
particularly undercut Mexico's ability to fulfill its intention
to become a fully independent world class producer of petrochemicals. While Mexico was in fact able to achieve ambitious
production levels, the industry itself remained dependent upon
foreign technology not only in the secondary petrochemicals area
where TNC participation has been permitted and even encouraged,
but also in the basic petrochemicals located in the state sector.

From the outset of the petroleum development project, the
level of dependence upon the importation of capital equipment was
significant. While officially the intent was always that the
capital equipment requirements of the project would spur the
domestic production of such inputs, in fact, no provision ever
was made by the state sector for such backward linkages. The
rapid pace of the project outran the domestic industry's ability
to achieve a production capability sufficient to meet the demand.
Conceivably, had the development pace been slowed, greater participation by domestic industry might have been seen. Instead,
any linkages that were produced by the oil development project
were of a secondary nature. Oil revenue based state spending in
other areas created new demand which domestic producers sought
to respond to but could only satisfy over the long term. Even
for such basic supplies as steel and cement, the petroleum industry had to turn to foreign suppliers.

During the period 1971-1976, Pemex imported 43.6% of its
capital goods.[85] For the period 1977-86, however, the figure
would rise to over 50%.[86] By 1979, fully 75% of Pemex's capital
goods were imported from abroad.[87] Particularly in refining and
petrochemicals, the level of import dependence was extreme. For
the period 1977-86, Pemex estimated that only 23.13% of necessary
capital goods for these sectors would be of domestic origin.[88]
In petrochemicals, the industry which Díaz Serrano and others
labeled the cornerstone of industrial development, only 19.6% of
required capital components were to be acquired domestically.[89]
Indeed, it would be years before industries such as basic metals,

metal products, and electrical and non-electrical machinery would be affected by Pemex's development.[90] Instead, capital goods demand would spur activity essentially in the U.S. economy which supplied 70-80% of Pemex's foreign capital goods requirements.[91] Foreign spending for capital goods rose by 1979 to US$1 billion, a figure that amounted to more than half of Mexico's total spending for capital and technology abroad.[92]

Direct foreign investment in the petroleum industry was, of course, prohibited as it was in basic petrochemicals. In secondary petrochemicals, however, foreign participation was permitted to rise to 40% and the strength of that participation was augmented by the particular degree of technical dependence present in the process which would require licensing. While organized labor pressed for the closing of secondary petrochemicals to foreign interests,[93] the sector remained open and Pemex's plans for petrochemical development were viewed most favorably by TNC interests.[94] Basic petrochemicals production which was expected to jump from 5.2 million tons in 1977 to 23.8 million tons in 1985,[95] would provide, at a fraction of world prices, excellent and cheap feedstocks for TNC secondary production. Even in basic petrochemicals development within the state sector, development involved reliance upon licensing agreements. One such case was that of the 100,000 ton per year propylene plant at Allende, Veracruz, under license from Mitsui Petrochemical Industries of Japan.[96] Thus, while Mexico could be said to have made tremendous strides in petrochemical production and had become self-sufficient in all basic petrochemicals, the industry itself developed as a highly technologically dependent sector.

Exporting the National Inheritance

As was noted earlier, plans called for modest growth in exports during the sexenio. The entire subject of exports proved to be a subject of controversy for the state inasmuch as criticism from the left such as Herberto Castillo, an engineer and head of the small Mexican Workers Party, charged that the national patrimony or inheritance would be squandered under the administration's plan. Yet despite initial flurries of protest activity, for the most part limited to street demonstrations in Mexico City, and considerable discussion within the press, the plans for petroleum exports proceeded apace. The greatest rancor was generated, however, by plans for natural gas exports to the U.S. as we shall see later.

To begin with, Pemex faced a severe shortage of export facilities to handle its shipments. It had no deep water ports to handle supertankers and had only one buoy capable of loading a 250,000 ton tanker. During the period 1971-1977, its tanker fleet had grown from 19 to 30 vessels achieving a total tonnage capacity of 654,000 tons. Yet plans for the 1977-82 period called for an increase to 930,000 tons.[97] No major plans were formulated for the development of a super-tanker fleet, the workhorse of the international petroleum industry. Although

major efforts would be undertaken in the area of port construction, these efforts would not be sufficient to alleviate the
monumental congestion at major ports that developed during the
boom. Lack of storage facilities and lack of containerization
capacity produced serious bottlenecks not only in crude exports
but also in the processing of imports which had grown tremendously as a result of agricultural shortfalls and new import requirements for accelerated development. As a result, in 1979, exports
reached only .532 mbd although .778 mbd had been projected in a
revision of early projections. Between October of 1980 and February of 1981, Pemex was only able to export 1 mbd although it
had commitments totalling 1.2 mbd.[98]

Despite these obstacles, Mexican leaders pursued the export
market and maintained that Pemex would not compete with established producers and would develop its own markets.[99] It
intended to diversify its markets and avoid dependence upon any
single country, in particular, the United States. Prices would
follow OPEC's lead although Mexico chose not to join the organization. Claiming that it preferred to guard its sovereignty by
remaining independent, Mexico's decision not join OPEC constituted a rather pragmatic response to two serious concerns. First,
Mexico desperately needed to assure itself of a stable and predictable source of export revenues because of its serious economic difficulties and wanted to avoid involvement in politically motivated embargoes. Secondly Mexico feared that the U.S.
would withhold Most-Favored-Nation status in the trade relationship as it had done with Venezuela and Ecuador, both OPEC members,
an eventuality which Mexico could expect to be very damaging.

By the early 1980s, Mexico had achieved considerable diversity in its export market despite an early tendency to rely upon
the U.S. market. The purpose of market diversification was of
course to reduce the nation's dependence and to utilize the
resource to obtain the widest possible range of commercial advantages.

In virtually every case of the sale of oil to the developed
countries, with an exception of the U.S., Mexico endeavored to
obtain the world price per barrel plus guarantees of access to
financing and technology from the purchasing state. In effect,
Mexico has used the exports not only to generate revenues, but
has also used it to broaden its technical dependence. In the
case of sales to France, for example, in exchange for a guarantee
of a supply of 100,000 bd, France agreed to build de-sulphuring
plants for low pollution oil processing, to construct an enriched
uranium reactor, and to provide access to other capital goods and
technology.[100] In exchange for an agreement to sell 50,000 bd to
Canada, Mexico obtained a commitment for a full range of industrial development assistance. Canada was to undertake joint
ventures in Mexico, transfer technology, and provide credits
totalling US$430 million to finance the importation of capital
equipment. Canada would thus be participating in mining, aluminium manufacturing, communications, transport, oil and gas equipment manufacturing, forestry, pulp and paper, urban planning and

Table 3-15

U.S. Shares of Mexican Petroleum Exports, 1976-82

(percentages)

1976	90.0	1979	86.0
1977	90.0	1980	53.0
1978	86.8	1982	49.8

Sources: 1976 calculated on the basis of data found in Williams, The Rebirth of the Mexican Petroleum Industry, pp.52-53; 1977: Williams, "Oil in Mexican - U.S. Relations: Analysis and Bargaining Scenario," p.208; 1978: GAO, Prospects for a Stronger United States-Mexico Energy Relationship, p.55; 1979: calculated on the basis of data reported in "Oil Export Rise Seen in Mexico," New York Times, (August 2, 1979), p.D-3; 1980: Business Latin America, various issues; 1982: "La activ-idad de Pemex en 1982," Comercio Exterior, v.33, n.4 (abril de 1983), p.294.

Table 3-16

Mexican Petroleum Export Structure, 1982

(percentages)

U.S.	48.9	United Kingdom	5.6
Spain	11.4	Israel	4.7
Japan	7.6	Central America	3.7
France	5.7	Others	12.4

Source: Mario Ramón Beteta, "La necesidad de estabilizar el mercado petrolero," Comercio Exterior," Graph 3, p.1035.

port development as a direct and deliberate result of the oil trade agreement.[101]

Negotiations with Japan, however, were most extensive. Japan aggressively sought to obtain commitments for exports of 300,000 bd. At the same time, Japan sought a reduction in the price of Mexican oil because of the additional transport costs involved. Heavily dependent upon the Middle East for its oil imports, Japan preferred to obtain Mexican oil, believing it to be a more secure supply even given the fact that it would have to pay approximately 40¢ more per barrel than it had been paying Saudi Arabia,[102] its major supplier, due to added transport costs Mexico refused to accede to the request for a reduction, and

instead suggested that an oil trade and economic cooperation
package might smooth the way for Japan to obtain the quantities
of oil it desired.[103] For example, Japan would be "invited" to
assist Mexico in the construction of a deepwater port on Mexico's
Pacific coast that would help to lower transport costs.

Essentially, Mexico succeded in gaining access to unprecedented amounts of Japanese capital and technology in exchange for
oil exports, ultimately expanding Mexican technological and financial dependence. In November of 1978, Japan provided Mexico with
two loans totalling over US$1 billion. The first loan totalling
US$600 million was the largest loan without any strings attached
ever put together by Japanese banks for a foreign country.[104]
The remainder was tied to the importation of machinery and technology for Pemex, CFE and Nafinsa.[105] Projects included were the
construction of port facilities, the so-called Alpha-Omega
project involving road, rail and pipe facilities in the Isthmus
of Tehuantepec, and finally, petrochemicals.[106] Prior to this,
twenty-one Japanese banks had floated a P6 billion loan for
Nafinsa in July of 1978.[107] In addition, the Japanese Export-
Import Bank provided a loan of US$265 million dollars at favor-
able interest rates to finance the construction of the Salina
Cruz Pacific port and an expansion of the state steel works "Las
Truchas" at Lazaro Cárdenas on the Pacific Coast.[108]

During 1979, Japanese banks received permission to open
branches in Mexico[109] and later, a consortium of thirty-six
leading Japanese oil companies, trading companies and banks
formed the Mexican Petroleum Import Co. to facilitate oil imports
and economic assistance. At that time, Japan received a commitment of 100,000 bd in exchange for a US$500 million package of
assistance, principally for oil development projects.[110] By 1980,
Japan finally secured the larger commitment for oil exports that
it had sought in exchange for an additional US$204 million in
financial aid.[111]

Mexico's efforts at diversifying its oil export markets have
also included exploratory trade and technical exchange negotiations with a number of other countries. Refining agreements have
been concluded with Rumania and Spain. Negotiations for a variety of commercial arrangements were undertaken with a host of
countries including Bulgaria, Poland, China, Yugoslavia, Czecho-
slovakia, West Germany, Finland, Italy, the Soviet Union, Vietnam,
the United Kingdom, virtually all the OPEC states, and all of the
Latin American states.

The export "chip" enabled Mexico to attempt to exert some
leverage in the unstable Carribbean area. Under a Venezuelan
initiative now known as the "San José Accord," Mexico and Venezuela agreed to provide petroleum supplies to nine Carribbean and
Central American states at subsidy prices.[112] A commitment to
provide a total of 196,000 bd was made by the two countries, 50%
each.[113] The countries receiving the oil were to pay 70% of the
normally posted price while the remaining 30% would be treated as
a long term loan payable at only a nominal interest rates.[114]

The U.S. remains Mexico's most important customer, however,

receiving nearly half of Mexico's petroleum exports. The proximity of the huge American market makes the U.S. Mexico's most "logical" customer essentially because of the minimal transport costs involved. More important in the export equation, however, is the fact that Mexico's sizeable trade deficits with the U.S. coupled with Mexico's level of indebtness to the U.S. and the 1982 financial bailout of Mexico by the U.S. have compelled Mexico to maintain fairly high export levels to the U.S.

The Natural Gas Export Controversy

One of the most politically troublesome issues to have emerged from the petroleum development project for the Mexican regime concerned that of the export of natural gas. In August, 1977, Mexico signed a Memorandum of Intentions to sell natural gas to six U.S. pipeline companies. The negotiated price of US$2.60 per thousand cu. ft. was rejected by the U.S. government as it proceeded through the regulatory process, and the Memorandum was allowed to lapse in December, 1977 in the wake of U.S. concern for the price of the imported gas.[115]

Some charged that the price constituted a threat to the U.S. administration's natural gas regulatory reform proposals which were pending in Congress although Mexico would have only supplied the U.S. with 4% of its natural gas needs according to the terms of the Memorandum. Charges emanated from both sides of the border regarding the reasons for the collapse of the deal, but the U.S. denied that there had been any last minute deceits or surprises involved in the negotiations as the Mexican had charged. U.S. Department of Energy (DOE) officials had supposedly warned the Mexican negotiators "well in advance" that there were problems.[116] At that time, Mexico was informed that there were three coequal problems: price, length of contract and the nature of the price escalator clause.

State Department officials in the U.S. suggested that informed circles both in Mexico and the U.S. were well aware that the agreement would not fly but that López Portillo may not have been informed early enough by the Mexican bureaucracy, hence creating a situation in which the Mexican President was "embarassed" and "resentful"[117] when the deal collapsed. Whether or not such early warnings had in fact been given, López Portillo certainly found himself in a difficult situation as negotiations were terminated because he had for some time been publicly stating that only alternative to selling gas to the U.S. was to burn it off and waste it which infuriated those already skeptical of the heavy export component of the petroleum side of the development project. López Portillo was roundly criticized by the Left for this approach to the disposition of Mexico's national inheritance. Herbert Castillo, expressing the displeasure of many, argued that López Portillo had been sadly mistaken in thinking that a satisfactory arrangement could be arrived at, all the while "proclaiming to the four winds" that Mexico wasn't sure about what to do with the gas..."Either we sell it, or we burn it or we reinject it."[118]

Clearly, the question of what to do with the tremendous amount of gas that is found in association with oil had become an explosive political issue. Approximately 77% of Mexico's gas was found in association with oil.[119] After considering a variety of alternatives such as liquid natural gas (LNG) production, reinjection, and the curtailment of oil production, but importantly not domestic utilization, Pemex opted for gas exports to the U.S. Liquid natural gas (LNG) delivered in Rotterdam would yield revenues of only US$.27 per thousand cu. ft. compared to the asking price of US$2.20 per thousand cu. ft. for natural gas delivered at the Texas border. Moreover, the tremendous capital outlays required for LNG production would severely curtail expected revenues which were sorely needed for petroleum and other development projects.

Pemex director, Díaz Serrano, defended the plan to the House of Deputies where he was called to testify following public outcry over alleged U.S. duplicity and Mexican gullibility in the collapse of the deal.[120] The Director argued that there was plenty of gas available to meet Mexican needs even after exports, that the ammonia market was well supplied and ought not to be over-supplied, and that reinjection was both too expensive and not income producing. It was not until after the U.S. rebuff that Mexican policy makers seriously considered possibilities for domestic consumption of the gas. As is typical of export-led dependent economies, the immediate inclination was to export the gas in order to earn vital foreign exchange.

A variety of unexpected events further contributed to Mexico's failure to close the deal. At the time of the original agreement, Pemex officials were fairly certain that Canada would not undercut their position with its own gas pricing policies in the export market,[121] however, to Mexico's dismay, Canada's gas export price consistently undercut Mexico's price demands despite assurances that such would not be the case.

While a U.S. Commerce Department official went so far as to call the Mexican "foolish" for having asked the price they did when they did,[122] (at the time of the natural gas battle in the U.S. Congress in the late 1970s) it appears that the timing was in fact poor. Pemex hoped that the U.S. public would pressure the U.S. government into accepting the price in exchange for a hedge against cold winters ahead.[123] On the other hand, the U.S. pipeline companies wanted to use the Mexican price to pressure Washington on the issue of deregulation.[124]

There was considerable dismay in some quarters in the U.S. over the failure by the U.S. Department of Energy to conclude a deal with the Mexicans. Some argued that a resolution of the gas controversy would free tremendous new quantities of Mexican oil that would then be committed to export.[125]

Complicating matters further was the fact that rumors (which were widely publicized in Mexico) abounded that U.S. Energy Secretary James Schlesinger had told Mexico's foreign Minister Roel and Pemex Director Díaz Serrano that a deal could be worked out if Mexico were to publicly accept the U.S. government's newly unveiled undocumented workers plan[126] although this charge was hotly denied by U.S. officials.

Despite Schlesinger's bullishly impolitic statement that "sooner or later they (Mexico) will have to sell it (the gas)," the Mexican Secretary of National Properties announced in February of 1978 that if the U.S. would not buy the gas, it would be used domestically as a substitute for oil in power generation and petrochemicals, thereby freeing oil for exports. Plans were developed to transform Mexico into a leading world producer of ammonia.[127] The US$2 billion gasoducto was conveniently rechristened the Troncal Nacional and diverted from export service to the meeting of newfound domestic needs. Pemex actively pursued offshore development where less gas is found in association with oil and where peasant-state disputes over land could be minimized although gas offshore would be lost due to the lack of transmission facilities to the mainland. Newly available natural gas would be employed in petrochemical production and by CFE to generate electricity.[128] Within the context of its industrial decentralization plan, the López Portillo administration offered a 30% reduction over the already de facto subsidized price of the domestically sold natural gas to companies that would agree to locate in one of the new regional development zones in Tamaulipas, Veracruz, Salina Cruz, Oaxaca and Guerrero.[129] A gas export line to Costa Rica was also considered but financing remained a problem.[130]

The decision by Pemex, however, to put the Chicontepec basin into production, despite the difficulty of recovery, and to refrain from capping some associated southwestern wells or to cut back on northern gas well production and well development suggested that increased flaring would be difficult to avoid. Mexican claims that it no longer had gas to export because of the change in its priorities were clearly unfounded and were chiefly designed to quell domestic discontent over Mexico's apparent humiliation by the U.S. Because of the political sensitivity of the gas flaring issue, reports of the actual amount of gas being flared have varied substantially. Table 3-17 reveals the discrepancies in reporting. While U.S. government statistics may overstate the amount of flaring, it is undoubtedly the case that Pemex understated the amount. By 1982, Mexico was flaring 638 mcf per day or 15% of its production.[131]

The accord that was finally reached in the Fall of 1979 followed a series of diplomatic pirouettes designed to make each side appear to be the sought after party. The agreement itself represented a substantial setback for the argument that Mexico's hydrocarbon resources would confer new advantages to it in bargaining situations with the U.S. Not only was the starting price desirable from the U.S. perspective but Mexico also failed to obtain the specific price escalator clause it sought that was central to the contract.[132] By 1983, Mexico was exporting 9% of its natural gas production to the U.S. or 233 thousand cu. ft. per day.[133]

Despite the fact that the natural gas affair produced a

Table 3-17

Mexican Natural Gas Flaring, 1976-1980

Comparison of Estimates

(Millions of Cu. ft. per day)

Year	Source	Amount
1976	U.S. Govt.[1]	765
1976	Pemex[2]	444
1978	U.S. Govt.[1]	500
1978	Pemex[3]	80
1979	U.S. Govt.[5]	700
1979	Pemex (official)[4]	120
1979	Pemex ("off the record")[7]	500
1980	Pemex[7]	446
1980	Pemex[8]	260

Sources: 1) GAO, Prospects for a Stronger United States-Mexico Energy Relationship, p.39.
2) Pemex figure reported in "Vast Hydrocarbon Wealth is the Cornerstone of Mexico's Energy Plans," Business Latin America, p.243.
3) Díaz Serrano cited in Latin America Economic Report, v.VI,n.37 (September 22, 1978.)
4) Financial Times, (January 11, 1980) cited in ISLA, v.20, n.1 (January, 1980), p.43.
5) U.S. Congress, U.S./Mexico Relations and Potentials Regarding Energy, Immigration and Technology Transfer.
6) Latin America Economic Report, v.VII, n.15 (April 13, 1979.)
7) "Mexico's Latest Plan Sets Conservative Course for Energy Development," Business Latin America (November 26, 1980), p.382.
8) Alan Robinson, "Mexico to Increase Production Ceiling," Journal of Commerce (March 20, 1980) cited in ISLA, v.20, n.3 (March, 1980), p.10.

104

great deal of public discussion, in particular within the media,
the Left and among more nationalist, conservation oriented
members of the PRI, the intent of the state to earn export revenues from the sale of gas was never thwarted as a result of internal discord. The temporary interruption of plans for gas exports
did, however, inadvertently compel the state to pursue new policies geared toward the domestic consumption of the gas although
Díaz Serrano and others made it clear that internal consumption
was not the ultimate goal but rather the intent was the freeing
up of petroleum based fuels for the export market. The affair
did, however, spur the development of expanded internal distribution networks which undoubtedly would have proceeded, if at all,
at a more laggardly pace.

Reassessment of Petroleum Development Policy: 1980 the Platform
Year

     At the outset of the sexenio, 1980 was designated the pro-
duction platform year in which a major reassessment of production
and development policy would be undertaken. Throughout the
period, Mexico experienced rising internal demand as the economy
recovered from the mid-decade collapse, and, fueled by petroleum
development, grew at a rapid clip. Internal demand for petroleum and petroleum products grew at a 10% per annum rate between
1977-81, slipping to only 2.6% in 1982.[134] Plans had called for
only a 7% per annum growth in domestic demand.[135] Importing
countries expressed concern that with such tremendous growth in
demand, Mexican exports might dry up completely by
     Pemex later revised its estimates for the year 2000, pro-
jecting that fully a quarter of Mexico's requirements would be
covered by nuclear power with the construction of twenty plants.[136]
Yet by 1980, Mexico did not have any nuclear plants operating
with the first expected on line in 1983. By 1979, energy derived
from hydrocarbons provided 92% of all energy consumed.[137] Little
interest had been shown in alternative energy forms and despite
the availability of coal reserves (1.07 billion tons), quite
understandably, in view of Mexico's oil riches, infrastructural
support for the coal industry was at a minimum.[138] Thus, for the
medium term, hydrocarbon based energy would continue to supply
the bulk of Mexican energy regardless of official intensions to
diversify.
     In 1979 and 1980, the petroleum based electrical industry
began to experience radical shortfalls and consumers suffered
lengthy cutbacks in electrical supply as demand outpaced the
infrastructure's ability to provide sufficient energy. These
problems were compounded by raging inflation to a large extent
fired by the petroleum boom, concern for the continued preeminence of the U.S. as Mexico's premier oil customer, and for what
some feared was an overly rapid production pace.
     It was against this backdrop that in November of 1980, the
Mexican government revealed its National Energy Plan which set
goals for the nation through the year 2000. A ceiling on exports

for 1982 was placed at 1.5 mbd. No more than 50% of its petroleum exports could go to any one country and Mexico would refuse
to provide to any country over 20% of its oil imports.[139]
Imports to the U.S. would thus have a ceiling of approximately
750,000 bd. In the future, production and sales decisions would,
however, be geared to limiting the "deficit on current account of
the balance of payments to 1% of GDP,"[140] (clearly a mechanism
designed to legitimate substantial export increases when deemed
advantageous.) The value added component of petroleum exports
was to increase and exports would be used to support Mexican
manufactured exports and in general to support Mexico's international economic position. Energy efficiency would be stressed
in order to stem the growth of internal energy demand.[141] The
plan projected a production total of 4.1 mbd, 2.6 mbd of which
would be absorbed domestically for 1990.

The plan called for domestic prices to be brought more into
line with international prices. Diesel and industrial products
would rise to 70% of their export value. Natural gas, priced
only at 10% of the export value would also rise 2.5% per month
through 1982,[142] and on the average, domestic prices for petroleum products were to rise to 50% of the world level by 1982 and
to 80% in 1985.[143] In so doing, domestic demand would hopefully
be curtailed and the policy of providing inordinately generous
subsidies to large consumers including TNCs would be moderated.

The new policy had been the subject of an ongoing and intensely heated debate between liberal and conservative factions
of the PRI.[144] Díaz Serrano and the more liberal faction argued
that production should be boosted and that an expansionary policy
be adopted in order to cope with the mounting costs of development and the continuing squeeze on the balance of payments.[145]

The more conservative position was espoused by key memebers
of the López Portillo "economic cabinet" (an inner circle within
the larger group of ministers) including José Andrés de Oteyza,
the Secretary of National Properties and Industrial Development,
David Ibarra Munoz, the Secretary of Finance and Public Credit,
Miguel de la Madrid Hurtado, Secretary of Programming and Budgeting, and Jorge de la Vega Domínguez, Secretary of Commerce.
Technically, the responsibility for the coordination and planning
of energy policy was the province of the Secretary of National
Properties and Industrial Development. An interagency body established in 1973 which included the directors of Commerce, National Properties, Pemex, CFE, the National Institute for Nuclear
Energy, Agriculture and Water Resources would also play an advisory role but in effect, in Mexico's executive-centered system,
ultimate responsibility would rest with the President.[146]

The moderates held that Pemex had become a state-within-a-
state that was no longer responsive to the requirements of the
overall development project. As early as 1979, Ibarra Munoz had
advised López Portillo that there was a "shortage of good
projects to spend large amounts of money on." and that a slowed
pace for oil development would be preferable in order to avoid
becoming a "net exporter of capital."[147] Mexico had climbed to
the position of one of the world's leading exporters but had

incurred serious inflation, crippling bottlenecks (in ports and in the provision of industrial inputs), a striking import bill, lagging capital goods development and a worsening of the distribution of income.[148] One oil analyst has argued that such developments are symptomatic of what he has called the "petroleum syndrome,"[149] typically experienced by other Third World oil exporters with a diversified economy.

Díaz Serrano's expansionary position was ultimately rejected and his more favorable attitude toward large exports to the U.S. was also overruled although he maintained his position as Pemex director and appeared to have survived the defeat. Within six months of the announcement of the new policy, a series of events led to the ouster of Díaz Serrano.

In April of 1981, Pemex announced that its export prices would be cut by an average of US$4 per barrel[150] as a response to the intra-OPEC squabbling that, along with conservation measures on the part of the industrialized countries, had led to a glut of oil in the international market. In so doing, however, Mexico had become the first of the major oil producers to announce a price cut, reportedly because it had experienced cancellations of orders in the U.S. market. Moreover, by cutting prices, it hoped to pressure Libya and Nigeria into similar price reductions.[151]

Díaz Serrano's rationale for the price cut was the fact that OPEC had failed to agree on a production curb and in the face of surplus oil, Pemex would have to reduce its prices in order to guarantee stability in its revenues. Observers felt that the reduction in oil earnings would compel Mexico to significantly exceed its announced export ceiling of 1.5 mbd if contraction in government spending were to be avoided. The Finance Ministry immediately announced that as a result of the price cut, Mexico would have to increase its international indebtness by US$1.2 billion over and above expected borrowing. Predictions were that the price reduction would result in a US$2 billion drop in earnings.

Following closely upon the heels of the price reduction announcement was the leaking of confidential Pemex production schedules to the Mexico City daily, Unomásuno, which showed that by July of 1982, Pemex's production would reach 2.93 mbd, exceeding the previously announced platform of 2.75 mbd.[152] The suggestion was that production would rise to 3 mbd by the end of 1982. Members of the economic cabinet charged that they had not been consulted about the price cut and began to mount a serious attack upon Díaz himself. Díaz Serrano had come to be viewed as a prospective presidential candidate which of course made him an enticing target for his political competitors, however, the Pemex Director had become vulnerable on a number of other counts. His ties to the U.S. oil community and his positive disposition towards oil sales to the U.S. had been widely criticized. His expansionary development preferences, charges of unparalleled corruption within Pemex, and very simply, the dimensions of Pemex itself had all become targets of criticism, and contributed to Díaz's resignation.

In the wake of the affair, López Portillo quickly named his political intimate Julio Rodolfo Moctezuma Cid to the director-ship of Pemex.[153] In a significant policy shift, Mexico an-nounced that its price cut would be rescinded after 30 days and that thereafter, Pemex would begin reassessing and renegotiating export contracts and would "purge" those customers that balked at paying the higher price. Moreover, as José Andrés de Oteyza warned, "Buyers will have to contemplate the possibility that a barrel of oil lost today may be a barrel of oil lost forever."[154]

Ultimately, the reality of a depressed international oil market would prove to undercut Mexico's effort to hold the line on price. Contract cancellations by France for example, in the wake of Moctezuma Cid's temporary restoration of higher prices, signaled the end of a seller's market for the Mexicans. Mexico would later move toward a closer relationship with OPEC and would grow increasingly concerned about the need to stabilize the international petroleum market.

Petroleum Development Policy and Associated Dependent Development

The oil development project has reflected the constraints imposed by the pattern of associated dependent development. The export of crude petroleum and natural gas were designated the paramount goals of the project. The contradictions that had produced the mid 1970s crisis were of such magnitude and required such immediate attention that instead of delaying exports until such time as refined products (worth considerably more than crude in international markets) could be exported, production and exports were instead speeded up despite the loss in potential value-added earnings. By 1982, the export of crude oil produced 94.1% of Pemex's earnings from sales abroad.[155]

Production and exports still steadily increased even in the face of damaging oil-fueled inflation that dramatically slashed labor's share of national income and threatened jobs in other sectors as exports from those lost their competitiveness in inter-national markets. Export ceilings were imposed in 1980 because of inflation and because of the astounding argument that there was a "shortage" of solid avenues for petroleum revenues invest-ment. Most importantly, however, the condition of the inter-national oil market essentially mandated a conservative policy so as to stabilize price.

While the state has enjoyed complete control over the manage-ment of the project, the project itself proved to be highly finan-cially and technically dependent upon the center states. As a means of attenuating such influence and the potential monopsony position that could be occupied by the U.S. in particular vis-a-vis petroleum exports, Mexico sought to diversify its oil trade relations. But this diversification has really meant the diver-sification of financial and technological dependence as Mexico deliberately sought to obtain access to finance and technology as part and parcel of oil trade agreements. Ultimately, there would appear to be little virtue or advantage to be found in diver-sifying this dependence, all the while expanding upon it.

The oil project constitutes a classic example of associated dependent development strategy in that backward linkages to the capital goods sector were never really factored into the oil development project per se. While linkages could ultimately be expected to develop as the state engaged in oil revenue based industrial investment, construction of the expanded oil industry itself would not create the demand that would foster that development. As a result, the project became highly import intensive as Pemex looked to foreign sources of supply. Because time was of the essence, the state concluded that it could not delay in its push toward expanded exports and thus would have to forego the development of such linkages directly. It is here that we find the key to the reproduction of the development model-- because of the financial and technological impasse created by previous development, the new project produced similar results... the continued disarticulation of particular economic activities from the larger economic setting because of the urgency of confronting problems already in hand. In the continuing sequence, new elements of dependence would emerge from the project.

Contrary to initial expectations concerning the early emancipation of the state from international financial networks, the oil project, however paradoxically, played an important role in the financial collapse of 1982 that was only temporarily resolved by the intervention of the international financial community. At the same time, revenues from the oil industry undeniably provided the state with new opportunities for containing the impact of certain contradictions within the development model. Yet the fact that the oil development project itself had aggravated the problem of the distribution of income and had caused a worsening of labor's condition, at least in relative terms, as we shall see in Chapter IV, would highlight the deficiencies of the general model of development and compel the state to formulate new strategies for adequately interpreting this outcome so as to defuse discontent of for discovering ways of compensating for these outcomes.

109

NOTES

Proceso, n.75 (10 de abril de 1978), p.34.

Ibid.

Richard Fagen, quoted in "Mexico, Crisis of Poverty/ Crisis of Wealth," Los Angeles Times, p.16.

Metz, p.1261.

Sevinc Carlson, Mexico's Oil Trends and Prospects to 1985, Monograph, Georgetown Center for Strategic and Inter- national Studies (Washington, D.C.:May, 1978), p.1.

Roberto Gutiérrez R., "La balanza petrolera de México, 1970-1982," Comercio Exterior, v.29, n.8 (agosto de 1979), p.839.

Lorenzo Meyer, Mexico and the United States in the Oil Controversy, 1917-1942, translated by Muriel Vasconcellos, (Austin: University of Texas Press, 1977), pp.8 & 12. Also see Merrill Rippy, Oil and the Mexican Revolution (Leiden Netherlands: E.J.Brill, 1972) for an excellent history of the period leading up to the nationalization of the industry and immediately thereafter. Also see Richard B. Mancke et. al., Mexican Oil and Natural Gas (New York: Praeger, 1979), pp.17- 58.

Rippy, pp.235-240.

Ibid., p.265.

Jorge Bouton, "Introducción a una problemática: La política económica del petróleo," Problemas del Desarrollo, v.X, n.37 (febrero-abril de 1979), p.47.

George Grayson, The Politics of Mexican Oil (Pittsburgh: University of Pittsburgh Press, 1981), p.22.

Ibid., pp.22-23.

Samuel I. del Villar, "El significado del petróleo para la sociedad mexicana: Perspectiva y síntesis del debate," in Las Perspectivas del Petróleo Mexicano (Mexico City: Centro de Estudios Internacionales, El Colegio de México, 1979), p.4.

110

[14] Grayson, The Politics of Mexican Oil, p.36.

[15] Edward J. Williams, "Mexican Hydrocarbons Export Policy: Ambition and Reality," Paper presented at the Annual Meeting of the Latin American Studies Association, Pittsburgh, PA., April, 1979, p.2.

[16] Edward J. Williams, Jan K. Black, Michael Meyer and Martin C. Needler et. al., The Latin American Oil Exporters and the United States, unpublished manuscript, p.129.

[17] Fox, Table 1, p.521.

[18] Grayson, The Politics of Mexican Oil, p.47.

[19] Edward J. Williams, The Rebirth of the Mexican Petroleum Industry (Lexington, MA: Lexington Books, 1979), p.7.

[20] Williams, Black et al., p.145.

[21] Alan Riding, "Mexico Grapples with its Oil Bonanza," New York Times, (May 7, 1978), p.F3.

[22] Bouton, p.47.

[23] Hugh O'Shaughnessy, Oil in Latin America (London: Financial Times Ltd., 1976), p.110.

[24] GAO, Prospects for a Stronger United States-Mexico Energy Relationship, p.8.

[25] Edward J. Williams, "Oil in Mexican-U.S. Relations: Analysis and Bargaining Scenario," Orbis (Spring, 1978), p.204.

[26] James Schlesinger, quoted in U.S. Congress, Hearings before the Joint Economic Committee, The 1979 Economic Report of the President, 96th Cong., 1st Session, Part 1, Jan. 23, 25, 29, 30, 1979 (Washington, D.C.: 1979), p.30.

[27] Remy Montavon, Miguel Wionczek, Francis Piquerez, The Role of Multinational Companies in Latin America (New York: Praeger, 1979), p.6.

[28] See Martin Needler, Politics and Society in Mexico (Albuquerque: University of New Mexico Press, 1971), pp.46-49.

Also see Roger Hansen, <u>The Politics of Mexican Development</u>
(Baltimore: Johns Hopkins University Press, 1971), p.XIII.

[29]GAO, <u>Prospects for a Stronger United States-Mexico
Energy Relationship</u>, p.36.

[30]1978 estimate: U.S. Embassy staff, Mexico City. Cited
in "Mexican Oil Could Rival Arab Output," <u>Buffalo Evening News</u>,
(December 6, 1978), p.1; 1979 figures: 500: U.S. Congress,
House Committee on Science and Technology, <u>U.S./Mexico Relations
and Potentials Regarding Energy, Immigration and Technology
Transfer</u>, Report prepared by the Subcommittee on Investigations
and Oversight and Subcommittee on Science, Research and Technology, 96th Cong., 1st Sess., 1979, p.3; 700 billion barrel
figure from Metz, p.1263.

[31]U.S. Congress, Senate, Committee on Energy and Natural
Resources, <u>The Western Hemisphere Energy System</u>, 96th Cong.,
1st Session, p.7.

[32]Richard Halloran, "CIA Oil Report Predicts Output Drop,"
<u>New York Times</u>, (August 31, 1979), p.D-3.

[33]Earl T. Hayes, "Energy Resources Available to the United
States, 1985-2000," <u>Science</u>, v.203, n.4377 (19 January, 1979),
p.234.

[34]Robert Stobaugh and Daniel Yergin, "The End of Easy Oil,"
in <u>Energy Future. Report of the Energy Project at the Harvard
Business School</u>, ed. by Robert Stobaugh and Daniel Yergin
(NY: Random House, 1979), p.4.

[35]Morgan Guaranty Trust, <u>World Financial Markets</u>, (Feb.,
1979), pp.8-9.

[36]Grayson, <u>The Politics of Mexican Oil</u>, p.55.

[37]"Política energética nacional," <u>Energéticos</u>, Ano 1, n.1
(agosto de 1977), p.17.

[38]"Mexico, Crisis of Poverty/Crisis of Wealth," <u>Los Angeles
Times</u>, p.8.

[39]<u>Revista de Instituto Mexicano del Petróleo</u>, (abril de
1977), p.9.

[40]José López Portillo, "Tercer Informe," Hispano, (septiembre de 1979), p.14.

[41]Proceso, n.74 (3 de abril de 1978), p.27.

[42]SEPAFIN, "Programa de energía. Metas a 1990 y proyecciones al ano 2000," en "Documento: Objetivos y prioridades del programa de Energía," Comercio Exterior, v.30, n.11 (noviembre de 1980), p.1264.

[43]Ibid.

[44]Secretaría de Hacienda y Crédito Público (SHCP) and Secretaria de Programación y Presupuesto (SPP), "Documento: La política económica para 1980," Comercio Exterior, v.30, n.1 (enero de 1980), p.71.

[45]SEPAFIN Secretary José Andrés de Oteyza, Excelsior (17 de noviembre de 1978), p.21.

[46]Olga Pellicer de Brody, "Segundo comentario" in Las Perspectivas del Petróleo Mexicano, p.60

[47]René Villarreal, "El petróleo como instrumento de desarrollo y de negociación internacional. México en los ochentas," El Trimestre Económico, v.XLVIII (1) n.189 (enero-marzo de 1981), p.11.

[48]SHCP and SPP, La política económica para 1980," p.71.

[49]Eduardo Turrent Díaz, "Petroleo y economía. Costos y beneficios a corto plazo," Foro Internacional, v.XVIII, n.4 (1979), p.625.

[50]Jorge Díaz Serrano, "Economic and Social Conditions in Mexico," Comercio Exterior, (English edition), v.23, n.12 (diciembre de 1977), p.483.

[51]See for example, GAO, Oil and Natural Gas from Alaska, Canada, and Mexico -- Only Limited Help for U.S. (Washington, D.C.: September 11, 1980).

[52]U.S. Congress, House, U.S./Mexico Relations and Potentials Regarding Energy, Immigration and Technology Transfer, p.22.

[53]Fox, pp.528-529; GAO, Prospects for a Stronger United States-Mexico Energy Relationship, p.4; Alvaro Franco, "Gigantescas reservas garantizan brillante futuro petrolero a México," Petróleo Internacional (junio de 1977), p.28.

[54]Jorge Díaz Serrano, "Mexico: El Gigante se Agiganta," Petróleo Internacional, (noviembre de 1977), pp.25-26.

[56]Fox, pp. 528-529.

[57]SEPAFIN and Pemex estimates, Examen de la Situación Económica (agosto de 1977), p.356.

[58]U.S. Congress, Senate, Committee on Energy and Natural Resources, Mexico. The Promise and Problems of Petroleum, 96th Cong., 1st Sess., 1979, p.49; James Flanigan, "Why Won't the Mexicans Sell U.S. More Oil," Forbes (October 29, 1979), pp.41-52.

[59]"La actividad petrolera de México en 1980," p.452; "La actividad de Pemex en 1982," Comercio Exterior, v.33, n.4 (abril de 1983), p.293.

[60]Williams, "Oil in Mexican-U.S. Relations: Analysis and Bargaining Scenario," p.206.

[61]"Oil-fired Wealth and Controversy," Latin America Weekly Report, p.9.

[62]Maria del Rosario Green, "Mexico's Economic Dependence," in Mexico-United States Relations, ed. by Susan Kaufman Purcell (New York: The Academy of Political Science, 1981), p.110.

[63]EUROMONEY, Annual Financing Report, p.4.

[64]Williams, The Rebirth of the Mexican Petroleum Industry, p.146.

[65]"Mexico's Financial Wizards Outmanoeuver U.S. Banks," Latin America Weekly Report (3 April, 1981), p.7, and "Pemex Considers Bigger Financing," New York Times, (May 19, 1981), p.D-11.

[66]Williams, The Rebirth of the Mexican Petroleum Industry, p.36.

114

[67]Miguel S. Wionczek, "Algunas reflexiones sobre la futura política petrolera de México," Comercio Exterior, v.33, n.11, (noviembre de 1982), p.1234. Also see Mario Ramón Beteta, "La necesidad de estabilizar el mercado petrolero," Comercio Exterior, v.33, n.11, (noviembre de 1983), p.1030.

[68]"How Factors Affecting Mexican Peso Movement are Likely to Develop," Business Latin America, (April 1, 1981), p.101.

[69]Ibid.

[70]1975: Carlson, p.16; 1978 and 1979: "Aspectos financieros del sector presupuestario en 1979," Comercio Exterior, v.30, n.9, (septiembre de 1980), p.939; Beteta, "La necesidad de estabilizar..", p.1030.

[71]Beteta, "La necesidad de estabilizar..", p.1030.

[72]David Ronfeldt, Richard Nehring, and Arturo Gandara, "Mexico's Petroleum and U.S. Policy: Implications for the 1980s," Rand Corporation report in U.S. Congress, Senate, Geopolitics of Oil, Hearings before the Committee on Energy and Natural Resources, 96th Cong., 2nd Sess., p.309.

[73]"La actividad petrolera de México en 1980," p.447.

[74]"Informe de Petróleos Mexicanos, 1979," p.391.

[75]Mancke, p.86.

[76]Metz, p.1265.

[77]Ibid.

[78]Grayson, The Politics of Mexican Oil, p.63.

[79]Mancke, pp.88-89.

[80]Williams, The Rebirth of the Mexican Petroleum Industry, p.151.

[81]Leopoldo García-Colín Scherer, "La ciencia y la tecnología del petróleo. Situación actual y perspectivas futuras en México," in Las Perspectivas del Petroleo Mexicano, p.72.

[82]Ibid., p.76.

[83]Ibid.

[84]Ibid., p.78.

[85]"Bienes de capital para la industria petrolera," Comercio Exterior, v.29, n.8, (agosto de 1979), p.855.

[86]Reynolds, p.263.

[87]"Mexico Likely to Limit Growth in Oil Production," Latin America Economic Report, (26 January, 1979), p.28.

[88]"Bienes de capital para la industria petrolera," p.856.

[89]Ibid., p.855.

[90]Ibid., p.856.

[91]Frederick J. Tower, "Mexico. Oil Leads Economic Growth, Promising Big Opportunities," Business America, (July 30, 1979) and Arturo Bonilla Sánchez, "Energéticos y la nueva riqueza petrolera," Problemas del Desarrollo, v.X, n.37 (febrero-abril, 1979).

[92]"Oil-fired Wealth and Controversy," Latin America Weekly Report, (20 June, 1980), p.10.

[93]Excelsior, (1 de enero de 1979), p.21-A

[94]See for example "New Pemex Plan Opens a Wealth of Opportunities for International Firms," Business Latin America, (December 31, 1978), p.395.

[95]"Bienes de capital..", p.851.

[96]Bank of London and South America Review, v.11, 11/77, (November, 1977), p.618.

[97]Williams, The Rebirth of the Mexican Petroleum Industry, p.33.

[98]Latin America Weekly Report, (27 February, 1981), p.7.

116

[99] Excelsior, (4 de noviembre de 1978), p.1.

[100] "Schlesinger Puts Spanner in Mexican Gas Works," Latin America Economic Report, v.VII, n.3,(19 January, 1979), p.18.

[101] Henry Giniger, "Mexico to Sell Oil to Canada," New York Times, (May 28, 1980), p.D-5.

[102] Latin America Economic Report, v.VI, n.44, (2 November, 1978), p.4.

[103] Platt's Oilgram News, v.56, n.211,(November 2, 1978), p.4.

[104] "Iran's Political Troubles Boost Mexican Oil Sales to Japan," Latin America Economic Report, v.VI, n.44,(November 10, 1978), p.346.

[105] Excelsior, (2 de noviembre de 1978), p.1.

[106] "Iran's Political Troubles Boost Mexican Oil Sales to Japan."

[107] Excelsior, (14 de julio de 1978), p.20-A.

[108] Platt's Oilgram News, v.56, n.203, (October 23, 1978), p.3.

[109] Handelsblatt, (April 12, 1978), p.9.

[110] "Mexico Oil Unit Set in Japan," New York Times, (November 20, 1979), p.D-11, and Journal of Commerce, (November 20, 1979) cited in ISLA, v.19, n.5,(November, 1980.)

[111] Wall Street Journal, (May 28, 1980), p.33.

[112] "Mexico Reassesses Policy Towards Central America and Caribbean," Latin America Weekly Report, (13 February, 1981), p.1.

[113] New York Times, (February 10, 1981.)

[114] "Central America a Key Feature of the President's Latest Grand Tour," Latin America Weekly Report, (13 February, 1981), p.6.

[115]Richard Fagen and Henry Nau, "Mexican Gas: The Northern Connection," in Capitalism and the State in U.S.-Latin American Relations, ed. by Richard Fagen.

[116]Interview, U.S. Department of State, Washington, D.C., February 27, 1979; Leonard Greenwood and Frank del Olmo, "The Gas Fiasco: U.S. Hardnoses, Mexican Honor," in "Mexico. Crisis of Poverty/Crisis of Wealth," Los Angeles Times, p.5.

[117]Ibid.

[118]López Portillo quoted in Proceso, n.61, (2 de enero de 1978), pp.34-35.

[119]Beteta, "La necesidad de estabilizar el mercado petrolero," p.1031.

[120]"Economic and Social Conditions in Mexico."

[121]"El petróleo mexicano reserva de EU ante la OPEP," Proceso, n.66 (6 de diciembre de 1978), p.11.

[122]Interview, U.S. Department of Commerce, Washington, D.C., July 26, 1978.

[123]Lorenzo Meyer, "El auge petrolero," Foro Internacional, v.XVIII, n.4 (abril-junio, 1978), p.585.

[124]Washington Post, (January 11, 1979), p.4 and U.S. Congress, Senate, Committee on Foreign Relations and Joint Economic Committee, Mexico's Oil and Gas Policy: An Analysis, Congressional Research Service Report, 95th Cong., 2nd Sess., 1979, pp.45-46.

[125]Ibid.

[126]U.S. Mexican-American leader Frank Shaffer Corona (member of the Washington, D.C. Board of Education) confirmed in a telephone interview that during a visit to Mexico, highly placed officials confirmed that the charges were true. (August 15, 1978). Shaffer Corona testified to this effect as well in Congressional hearings.

[127]Proceso, n.68 (20 de febrero de 1978), p.26.

[128]New York Times, (February 13, 1979), p.D-15; Prensa (27 de febrero de 1979) cited in the Mexican Embassy Press Review published at the Ministry of Foreign Relations, Mexico City.

[129]Business Latin America, (January 31, 1979), p.39 and Business International, (February 17, 1979), p.90.

[130] Excelsior, (13 de enero de 1978), p.10.

[131] "La actividad de Pemex en 1982," Table 3, p.293.

[132] Mexico agreed to start with a price of US$3.625 per thousand cu.ft. while according to the terms of the 1977 agreement that faltered, the starting price by 1980 would have been well over US$5.00 per thousand cu.ft.

[133] Beteta, Graph 1 and Table 2, p.1032.

[134] Ibid., Table 3, p.1035.

[135] Grayson, "Mexico's Opportunity: The Oil Boom," Foreign Policy, n.29 (Winter, 1977-78), p.75.

[136] "Mexico's Long Term Plans Call for Diversification of Its Energy Sources," Business Latin America, (August 6, 1980), pp.250-5.

[137] Bonilla Sánchez, p.11.

[138] Alva Senzek, "Future Energy Sources for Mexico," Mex-American Review, (June, 1977), p.5.

[139] Alan Riding, "The Mixed Blessings of Mexico's Oil," p.59.

[140] Bank of London and South America Review, v.15, n.I/81, (February, 1981), p.33.

[141] "Mexico's Energy Programme Limits Oil Exports to Meet National Needs," Latin America Weekly Report, (28 November, 1980), p.1.

[142] "Mexico's Latest Plan Sets Conservative Course for Energy Development," Business Latin America, p.383.

[143] "Conflict Pressures on Oil Price Policy," Latin America Weekly Report, p.2.

[144] "Focus on Mexico: the Brilliant Outlook is Not Problem Free," Business Latin America, p.113.

[145] Alan Riding, "Mexico at Odds on Oil Output," New York Times (February 7, 1980).

[146] GAO, Prospects for a Stronger United States-Mexico Energy Relationship, p.50.

[147] "Mexico Likely to Limit Growth in Oil Production," Latin America Economic Report, p.28.

[148]José López Portillo, "Cuarto Informe," _Comercio Exterior_, v.30, n.9 (septiembre de 1980), p.1014.

[149]Beltrán del Río, p.558.

[150]"Mexico Cuts Oil Price," _New York Times_, (April 6, 1981.)

[151]"Mexico Slashes Price of its Oil," _Buffalo Evening News_, (April 3, 1981), p.4.

[152]"Energy Programme Under Threat," _Latin America Weekly Report_, pp.2-3.

[153]Alan Riding, "The Political Background of Resignation at Pemex," _New York Times_, (June 8, 1981), pp.D-1 and D-8.

[154]Alan Riding, "Mexico, in Switch Will Lift Oil Price," _New York Times_, (June 17, 1981), p.D-1.

[155]"La actividad de Pemex en 1982," p.293.

Assessing the Impact of Resource
Development upon the State and the Economy
CHAPTER IV

Overcoming the Crisis of the State

Until the financial collapse of 1982, the oil development
project temporarily served to provide the Mexican state with the
resources necessary to achieve a more complete articulation of
its role in Mexican society. The oil provided the state with
both the wherewithal and the impetus to perfect and "rationalize"
the mechanisms employed to perform required functions and in some
cases to create new mechanisms where deficiencies were perceived
in state capabilities. Oil provided the state with new opportunities to manage the ongoing contradictions emergent from the development model and to preserve the degree of system stability previously achieved without resort to what José López Portillo referred to as the "South Americanization" of the society. As we
noted earlier, Mexico had never been forced to resort to bureau-
cratic-military-authoritarianism as its mechanism for social
control and system reproduction as its own cooptative mechanisms
were actually much more efficient and effective than the more
blunt instruments employed by the regimes of the Southern Cone.

But although the oil would momentarily provide the system
with some new breathing space and enable the state, in the late
1970s, to overcome its internal crisis, the inability to finance
its central activities and to continue in its role as the axis of
accumulation, oil would hardly be able to "solve" Mexico's
problems. As Richard Fagen noted, early in the development
project:

> All that oil can do...is soften and perhaps postpone for
> some years the sharpening of the contradictions that are
> inherent in the Mexican development model. It cannot
> solve them.[1]

Oil would allow the state to circumvent the draconian provisions of the IMF imposed stabilization program and would propel
the state into the rationalization of its tools for economic
management so that it would be able to maintain effectively its
pivotal role in the accumulation process. Without oil, the
financial crisis encountered during the Echeverría period could
easily have led to a serious weakening of the cooptative mechanism and an undermining of the stability of the system. With
oil, that particular crisis was converted into an historical
footnote and attention could be paid to the state's internal
financial crisis and the strengthening of the state's management
role based upon the resolution of the crisis. Another dangerous
crisis would ensue shortly, however.

The refinement and further articulation of the state's role
was both caused and facilitated by the oil, caused in the sense
that a development project of such dimensions within the state
sector would require a substantial degree of sophistication and
planning if the structure of social control were not to be undermined. Given the propensity of the development model to produce
serious and potentially destabilizing contradictions (e.g, in-

creasing concentration of income and wealth and unemployment,the
state would have to devise the means by which these contradictions, which could be expected to become intensified as a result
of the oil development project and the revitalization of the
industrialization process, could be managed. Oil would provide
new financial resources to the state which would enable it to
attempt to contend with these contradictions.
    One observer argued that the crisis of the Echeverría period
derived from the state's inability to "obtain the 'relative autonomy' necessary to overcome systemic contradictions."

>   ...it could be argued that the Mexican state was under-
>   taking a programme designed to renew the natural resource
>   base, revive industrial progress and recapture the support
>   of organised labour, but that domestic capital (particular-
>   ly its financial fraction) was not willing to support such
>   a programme despite the fact that the result would be in
>   their own interests in the long run--in other words, the
>   state could not obtain the 'relative autonomy' necessary
>   in order to restructure productive capital and sustain
>   industrialization... The private sector was unwilling to
>   undertake, or incapable of undertaking this (massive
>   capitalisation of agriculture, minerals, and heavy indus-
>   try) (preferring the high profits of light manufacturing,
>   real estate and tourism)...an expansion of state investment
>   became inevitable.[2]

Specifically, by 1976, the state found itself confronted with a
financial impasse, unable to increase state sector prices or to
overhaul the tax structure and thus unable to generate sufficient
public sector savings to pursue its role as the central axis of
accumulation in society without increasing its dependence on
foreign financing and inflationary deficit spending which it
could not continue to do indefinitely. The private sector
decried the alleged poor financial management within the state
sector, yet the bulk of state sector spending incurred resulted
from massive subsidies to the private sector via reduced costs
for public sector goods and services and from heavy investments
in industry and agriculture. Investment in industry was designed
to sustain industrialization in the face of the failure of the
import substitution industrialization strategy to continue to
unfold and investment in agriculture was required by the failure
of the private sector to commit itself to that sector to the
degree necessary. Finally, the state had engaged in spending in
the social sector in order to insure continued social control.
    Oil would enable the state to pursue these ends without con-
fronting the problem of the tax structure and the issue of government subsidies to the private sector and would allow the state to
continue its dependence upon foreign borrowing. In his Third
Report to the nation, López Portillo confirmed the new opportunities open to the state:

    We now have available planning methods which without doubt

> will permit us to advance more rapidly and in a more
> orderly way, perfecting and systematizing the allied
> participation of the social and private sectors in
> harmony with the government. And to the extent that
> the resources that will shore up the finances of the
> state are now available, the state can assume its
> full position of manager of our mixed economy... the
> state will become organized in order to organize
> the country.[3]

The state would embark upon a three-pronged program of reform
including political reform (the legalization of four heretofore
small political parties), an "Alliance for Production," that
would strengthen cooperation between the private and state
sectors, and finally, administrative reform that would rationalize administration and planning. Together, these actions would,
according to López Portillo, qualitatively change the development of the country.
The program was based upon a philosophy of the state that
asserted:

> ...it is the state that puts forth a national project:
> the state creates the unity, creates the necessary
> conditions for the formation of the social classes in
> the country and acts as the motor of development.[4]

While we have argued elsewhere that in fact the state had
always played such a role in the society, the state's open
avowal of its role as the creator and propagator of the class
structure within society marked a departure from more conservative depiction of the state's role that characterized earlier
periods. The significance of this departure from past political
discourse is reflective of the state's ambitious efforts to
strengthen its ability to manage the development project, to
exercise its relative autonomy to the fullest extent, and to
obtain the private sector's cooperation with the development
project. The private sector would be induced to comply with
state development plans and to acquiesce to the use of policy
instruments anathema to the private sector. The state's attitude toward the private sector was outlined by Miguel de la
Madrid Hurtado during his tenure as Secretary of Programming
and Budgeting in the López Portillo administration:

> ... private enterprise, without forgetting its impor-
> tance in the areas of saving, investment and employment,
> has represented to its owners an end in itself, and
> its success has been measured on the basis of its
> management within the context of market developments.
> To be sure, this traditional attitude will have to
> change so that in the face of society's challenges,
> and to guarantee the survival of private enterprise
> as an economic and legal form, it will have to
> harmonize its legitimate interests with greater social

responsibility and greater solidarity with the
great aims of the national development project.[5]

Essentially, what private enterprise would be asked to harmonize
its activities with in order to guarantee the security of its
"legitimate interests" would be the state development plan which
had everything to do with the reproduction of the prevailing
social and economic order and very little to do with popular
solidarity. The survival of private enterprise was not threatened by the state or its activities. Instead, the state was attempting to both warn and convince the private sector of the need
to contend with systemic contradictions in order to preserve the
system.

Rationalizing Development

The first serious planning efforts were conducted by the Mexican state during the 1960s. This activity was discontinued, however, during the administration of Luis Echeverria. In Latin
America, planning, according to one observer, has consisted
primarily of "programs and plans linked to public investment and
to the stimulation and promotion of private enterprise and activities."[6] For the most part, "planning" has resulted in the setting of a list of economic priorities that have found expression
in public sector budgets and the utilization of more sophisticated techniques for promoting development[7] rather than in the
comprehensive, integrated plans characteristic of socialist
states. In the Mexican case, the most recent planning efforts
have achieved greater sophistication in the utilization of such
techniques than had previously been the case, and in fact, some
success has been measured in obtaining private sector compliance
with state plans as we shall see later. Planning has remained
indicative in nature, however, and has continued to be plagued
with a failure to define the specific means for achieving specific ends. In sum, while recent Mexican planning efforts represent
a quantum leap over past state activity in this regard, planning
remains heavily normative in character and uneven in its technical aspect.

Improvement in Mexican planning capabilities was predicated
upon a program of administrative rationalization that was begun
at the outset of the López Portillo term with the promulgation of
the Organic law of Federal Public Administration. This law
grouped 778 federal agencies into 17 departments that would have
programming and budgetary responsibility for these agencies. The
Ministry of Budget was upgraded to a Secretariat of Programming
and Budgeting and was given responsibility for the overall direction and coordination of sectoral planning and budgeting.[8] As a
result, the Secretariat of Finance and Public Credit lost management responsibility for public spending[9] but retained responsibility for oversight and management of the public debt and for generating revenue and determining monetary policy.[10]

In a move designed to institute uniform administrative practices within the growing state sector, the Law of Budget Accounting and Public Expenditure was created. In the wake of programmatic reshuffling, the Secretariat for National Properties and Industrial Promotion (SEPAFIN) was created as was the Secretariat for Commerce.[11] Pemex was placed within SEPAFIN's jurisdiction as it bore responsibility for monitoring and managing non-renewable resources. Commerce took responsibility for what were to be a wide range of key state agencies involved in rural development and basic goods production.

The reorganization and reform of administration and administrative practice facilitated the enhancement of the state's planning capability. An early "Basic Plan for Government"[12] that had been prepared by a PRI think tank in 1975 set the stage for greatly increased planning activity. The plan itself was never implemented, however, as it was superseded by SPP's comprehensive plan for the public sector "Program of Action for the Public Sector, 1978-82." For the most part, however, the bulk of planning activity involved the creation of sectoral plans that bore little if any relation to each other. Counted among the major plans were:

- National Plan for Agriculture and Forestry, annual plans produced in 1978, 1979 and 1980.
- National Plan for the Fishing Industry, 1977-82.
- National Plan for Industrial Development, 1979.
- National Plan for Urban Development.
- National Plan for Employment, 1980-82.
- National Plan for Tourism.
- Urban Development Plan for the Federal District.
- National Plan for Science and Technology.
- National Plan for Commerce.
- Program for the Education Sector.
- National Plan for Communication and Transport.
- National Plan for Agroindustry.
- National Plan for the Mexican Food System (SAM).

While sectoral plans abounded in the early stages, the goal of the planning effort was "to move away from traditional resource based budgeting toward goal-based budgeting grounded in medium-range planning,"[13] and to achieve the integration of sectoral programming. The latter goal was first addressed with the publication of the "Global Plan for 1978-82", subsequently superseded by the "Global Plan for 1979-82", and still later by the "Global Plan for 1980-82". Of all of the plans produced, however, the National Industrial Development Plan and the Global Plan for 1980-82 were most effectively utilized. Some have gone so far as to dismiss altogether the notion that the plans had any measurable effect, labeling planning activity to date a "useful preparatory exercise for a serious 1983-88 plan,"[14] and maintaining that the plans could have had little impact on state or private sector activity because of the short lead time involved.

While the impact of the early planning activity is problematic, we shall see later that in terms of private sector investment in state determined priority areas, some success was

measured. The most important point to be made is that the state
moved aggressively for the first time to develop an effective
planning capability and provided a fairly clear articulation of
the intended outlines of future development. Moreover, the
state's intention to maintain and even guarantee its "relative
autonomy" was made abundantly clear in its plans and a clear
picture was provided of the state's conception of its expanded
role in the development process. For example, the first of
twenty-two points in the state's development strategy outlined in
the Global Plan, 1980-82 was to "strengthen the state".[15] The
following passage from the Plan further elucidates the state's
philosophy:

> ...strengthening the role of the state as the orientor
> and motivator of economic-social development in Mexico
> constitutes a requirement of the highest order in order
> to boost production and employment according to the
> rhythm and orientation set forth by the overall economic
> policy. Seen from this perspective, it is incumbent
> upon the state, within the context of our mixed economy
> to strengthen both private and public enterprises and
> those of a social character, stimulating and supporting
> the former whenever they comply with the priorities
> established in the Plan, and imbuing the parastatals
> with the character of efficient stimulators.
>   The distinctive importance of the public enter-
> prises as an instrument for orienting and aiding the
> development process resides in the fact that through
> them, the participation of the state is not only of a
> normative character or the developer of infrastructure
> but rather that it assumes the form of a direct partici-
> pant in the production of goods and services, that assures
> tha availability of basic inputs and energy, creates
> external economies, facilitates competitiveness in national
> and international markets, technological progress and a
> just distribution of benefits in society....the important
> growth of the participation of the state principally
> through the public enterprise sector has determined to a
> large extent the social-economic evolution of the country
> by stimulating the development process and at the same
> time ensuring that the development achieved is not simply
> economic growth but economic development, transforming
> growth in national product into increased social welfare
> shared by the entire population.[16]

Planning was clearly to be an indispensible component of a
more dynamic state. The role of the parastatals, frequently the
object of criticism by the private sector, was particularly important. State sector enterprises were openly described as important participants in the production arena and by implication,
were such because of the inadequacy of the dependent business
sector.
  The road to the development of a coherent planning capabil-

ity in any context is hardly free of obstacles and such has been the case in Mexico. As early as 1979, it was reported that the major responsibility of the programmatic content of economic planning (although not the technical aspects of the task) had been transferred from SPP to a special team of Presidential economic advisors headed by Julio Moctezuma Cid.[17] Moreover, SEPAFIN head José Andrés de Oteyza complained that by 1979, following two years of successful budgetary control, there had been a "substantial overrun in public spending."[18] Planning had once again become primarily responsive to the narrow demands of specific sectors and to provincial leaders.

As a result, the verdict as to the success of initial planning activity is decidedly mixed. At the same time, if the state's success in planning is in part judged on the basis of its success or failure in achieving private sector compliance with national sectoral investment plans, then Mexican planning must be regarded as having met with some success. While the coherence of the state's plans was challenged by specific interest groups' demands, the commitment of the state to the rationalization of development planning coupled with the state's power in Mexican society contributed to some success in managing such demands.

Beyond the important question of administrative practice, however, of even greater import is the question of substance. If the state has in fact sought to pursue its role more aggressively, what has been its intent in so doing? According to official policy, oil was to have accomplished a number of spectacular feats for the society. It was to have liberated Mexico from its condition of economic dependence, to have served as the instrument for the structural transformation of the economy, to have set the stage for self-sustained industrialization, to have provided Mexico with financial self-sufficiency, and to have obviated the external constraint upon development. What efforts did the state undertake to achieve these goals and what was accomplished?

State Development Policy

From the outset of the sexenio, the state pursued a policy of supportive overtures to the private sector designed to "restore" business confidence and spur private investment. An "Alliance for Production" agreement was reached with 140 private sector enterprises in 1977[19] and was designed to engage the private sector in cooperative developments efforts with the state. Inasmuch as the Echeverría administration had soured the private sector on domestic investment and had induced a capital flight, the López Portillo administration commenced the new era by offering a wide range of incentives to business in order to encourage investment. Within the context of the agreement, the state persuaded the private sector to freeze prices on ninety basic products in exchange for preferential treatment on imports, taxes and credit access.[20] The economic recovery program also included an agreement with the Confederation of Chambers of Industry

(CONCAMIN) that industry would invest P250 billion during 1977-78.[21] The agreement also included the commitment from labor that wage demands would be held down even though the inflation had been pegged at 60% per annum at the end of the Echeverría sexenio. The price freeze on certain basic goods was to offset losses suffered by labor in wage increase deferrals.

According to López Portillo, the program had more of an equity-social justice intent than anything else.

> ...the Alliance Program calls for the joint conscientious, responsible and determined collaboration of every last one of the Mexican people. It means the pooling of aspirations of the different sectors in order to harmonize identical objectives, to fulfill the needs of the majority sectors of the population, to eliminate luxury goods, to encourage the high income classes to invest more and consume less, and to rationalize manufacturing and marketing processes. It is a concerted action that pursues the country's balanced and equitable development.[22]

Contrary to such undeniably admirable objectives, however, the Alliance marked the return to a development policy analogous to that of the Stabilizing Development strategy followed prior to the Echeverría period. At issue this time, however, was the utilization of the oil-generated resources. Fitzgerald has outlined the policy options considered as the oil based development policy took shape.

> The 'planner' view (i.e., that of SPP and SEPAFIN) appears to be that the resources should be channeled through direct public expenditure on welfare infrastructure (such as schools and hospitals) and productive public enterprises (particularly in heavy industry and capital goods) while national income would be distributed away from profits towards wages: in this way it is proposed to push the import-substituting industrialization process into full maturity on the basis of state enterprise, restrictions on multinationals, technological independence, continued tariff protection for the private sector and a wider domestic market derived from the extension of the benefits of development to a wider section of the population than in the past. In other words, it is proposed to continue the desarrollo compartido of the early 1970s without the restriction of foreign exchange or fiscal resources that frustrated the strategy under Echeverría. The 'treasury' view, (i.e., that of SCHP and the Banco de México) seems to be that the revenue should be transferred through indirect public expenditure so as to stimulate consumption and investment by the private sector, particularly through tax incentives (compensated by the Pemex surpluses) and development credits from the state banks. At the same time, wage levels would be held back, tariff barriers lowered and foreign investment encouraged--introducing

thereby a degree of competitive efficiency to Mexican
manufacturing while the peso would be supported by oil
exports... In other words, it is proposed to return once
more to the desarrollo estabilizador of the 1960s.[23]

The state would in fact, for the most part reject the so-
called "planner" view (witness the shift of central programmatic
planning responsibility from SPP to the office of the Presidency
and the succession of planning directors...) and return to a
policy of direct subsidy to the private sector, wage depression,
encouragement of direct foreign investment and the lowering of
tariff barriers. At the same time, owing to the failure of
private sector investment to produce desired results, the state
would as well pursue substantial investment in public enterprises.
In essence, however, the Stabilizing Development model would
prevail with the characteristic feature of profits being distributed toward capital rather than labor. On balance, it is
probably fair to argue that there was a good deal more unanimity
of opinion within the state sector than is suggested by Fitzgerald's dichotomization of the policy options. While SPP and
SEPAFIN planners may in fact have favored the internal market
option, the debate appears to have been exceedingly short-lived,
if it can be called a debate at all. One of the earliest plans
produced during the sexenio and one of the most influential, the
National Industrial Development Plan, produced by SEPAFIN reflected a clear Stabilizing Development orientation.[24] As such, pronouncements from officials such as Finance Secretary (SHCP) David
Ibarra Munoz were clearly misleading in their contention that:

> The present administration...has channelled the economy
> in the direction of far-reaching structural change...
> The country must concentrate on producing basis products
> for mass consumption.[25]

While some attention would in fact be focused upon basic
goods production during the sexenio, the focus of development
policy was upon industrialization and the manufacture of competitive exports with little attention paid to either equity or
employment concerns beyond the rhetorical level. No effort was
made to pursue programs that would expand the internal market as
this would require a serious income redistribution program. In
the absence, then of a potential for an enlarged domestic market,
production would thus be directed at export markets.

Reliance upon an export led industrialization policy would,
however, provoke a "major constraint to growth...the capacity to
make a dollar of net domestic savings out of a dollar of foreign
exchange."[26] Despite this serious problem and its implications
for intensifying Mexico's external dependence, the state maintained early on that the oil boom would enable Mexico to enjoy
10% p.a. growth rates.[27] Essentially, then, the oil revenues
would be used by the state to sustain the prevailing model of
associated dependent development albeit at faster growth rates
and to contend with the contradictions produced by the model.

Projecting Future Development

The National Plan of 1978-82[28] projected a growth rate of
6-7% p.a., however, this plan was quickly eclipsed by the National Industrial Development Plan of 1979 which projected the nearly
fantastic growth rate of 10% through the 1980s. Growth throughout the 1960-76 period, by comparison, had reached a very respectable 6.3% and had registered a 6.1% rate during 1977-79.

Principal areas of concentration in the plan included export
industries, capital goods, agro-industry, infrastructure, basic
goods and the decentralization of investment.[29] State sector
investment was predicated upon estimated oil export earnings of
US$23 billion between 1979 and 1982, a figure that substantially
understated actual earnings. Industrial growth was targeted at
12% p.a.,[30] compared to 7.8% during the period 1960-76 and 8.3%
during 1977-79. Through a system of incentives and priority
regional development areas, the state would attempt to increase
support for small and especially medium-sized industry and would
attempt to force larger enterprises to subcontract to small and
medium-sized firms.[31] On the basis of this strategy, the employment problem would be "solved" by 1990.

Heaviest state investment would occur in the areas of energy,
minerals, metals, fertilizer and capital goods. Planned investment for the 1979-82 period amounted to over $40 billion, three-quarters of which would be channelled through public enterprises.[32] Over one-third of the investment would be committed to
oil and petrochemicals.[33] Excluding oil and petrochemicals,
state investment in manufacturing would rise to 17% of total
investment in manufacturing and would concentrate in the area of
metals, paper, sugar, textiles and cellulose.[34]

The Plan outlined sectoral shifts that were to be accomplished by 1990. Based upon these projections, the state's intention was to increase employment shares in the tertiary sector,
essentially for agriculturally displaced labor. Planners anticipated that the primary sector's share of national income would
fall from 35% in 1971-76 to 19% in 1990. The tertiary sector
would see income rise from 37.4% in 1971-76 to 52.9% in 1990
while the secondary sector would remain stable.[35] Importantly,
while the massive investment in the industrial sector was intended, employment in that sector would experience only modest
growth, especially when compared with the need to employ huge
numbers of the rural unemployed.

Projections for fixed capital investment revealed the dimensions of planned increases in the state's participation in investment. According to the Plan, the state's share of total national
investment was to rise to almost 47% by 1982. On balance, while
the plan reserved an important place for private investment (and
made no specific mention of any intentions to restrict further
direct foreign investment) the state's activities expanded substantially although by 1982, the state's share fell slightly
under the Plan's projections. Plans called for continued private
sector predominance in the area of "productive" investment,
reaching 57.4% of the total by 1990.

Table 4-1

Gross Domestic Product, 1971-1988

(annual growth rate)

	1971-1976	1977-1982	1981	1982	1985-1988
TOTAL	6.2	6.1	7.9	-0.5	5.0-6.0
Primary	2.7	4.0	6.1	-0.6	3.5-4.5
Mining	6.1	14.0	15.3	9.2	3.7-4.7
Manufacturing	6.8	6.0	7.0	-2.4	6.7-7.9
Construction	6.7	6.7	11.8	-4.2	7.0-9.0
Electricity	10.3	7.9	8.4	6.8	6.2-7.2
Commerce, restaurants, hotels	6.0	6.1	8.5	-1.6	4.3-5.4
Transport,retail & communications	11.0	9.5	10.7	-2.3	6.5-7.0
Financial services, insurance	5.4	4.3	4.3	2.9	3.2-4.0
Social Services	6.6	6.4	7.7	4.7	4.1-4.5

(Primary includes livestock, agriculture, forestry & fishing.)
(Mining includes petroleum and natural gas.)

Source: 1971-88: Plan Nacional de Desarrollo, 1983-88, Suplemento de Comercio Exterior, v.33, n.6 (junio de 1983), p.68
1982: "La economía en 1982: cifras definitivas," Comercio Exterior, v.33, n.10 (octubre de 1983), Table 1, p.903.

Table 4-2
Fixed Capital Investment, 1975-1982

(percentage)

	1975	1979	1981	1982
Public Investment	37	39.1	44	45
Private Investment	63	60.9	56	55

Source: 1975-79: Mexico: National Industrial Development Plan, Volume One, Table III, p.113; 1981-82: "La economía en 1982: cifras definitivas," Table 3, p.904.

The plan appeared to promise a worsening of income dispari-
ties in Mexican society and did little to guarantee that substantial strides would be made in the employment area, relying
instead upon a fast growth track to solve the problem. The plan
also ignored the serious problem associated with the oil-fueled
development project, such as bottlenecks and inflation that would
be seriously disruptive in character.

Among the myriad of serious bottlenecks that were in fact
encountered were rail transport, ports, warehousing, shortages of
construction materials such as cement and steel, heavy trucks,
water, electricity, fertilizers, car parts and a shortage of
personnel.[36] As a result, industrial development projections
were undermined by problems that had been underestimated in the
developmental equation.

The Global Plan for Development 1980-82 which superseded the
two earlier global plans and which both integrated and modified
the National Industrial Development Plan, reduced the projected
growth rate in GDP from 10% to 8%. The growth rate achieved
between 1977-81 reached 7.4%.[37] Projected sectoral growth rates
put industrial growth at 10.8%, down from 12% in the Industrial
Plan. Manufacturing was targeted at 10%, capital goods production at 13.5%, oil and petrochemicals at 14% and electricity at
10.7%. In most instances, however, the growth rates achieved, as
is seen in Table 4-1, were less than what had been anticipated
even prior to the collapse of 1982.

The Plan adopted a more self-critical tone and reviewed the
pitfalls associated with the development project. Included were
financial, technological and food dependence, the non-competitiveness of Mexican industry vis-à-vis the international market,
bottlenecks in key sectors, problems in the commercial sector
(specifically the basic goods area and profiteering) and regional,
sectoral and personal concentration of income.[38]

In order to overcome these problem areas, the Plan emphasized investment in agriculture and rural development, social
welfare and education, transport and communications.[39] At the
same time, however, this emphasis did not mean that industry and
capital goods would be neglected. Public investment in those
areas, along with private investment naturally, would remain
strong. Industry would receive 40% of the state's investment
although this figure was down from the 47% registered in 1978.[40]
Regional development policy for industry would continue to be
emphasized as would petroleum development. Interestingly, regional development policy emphasized coastal development in Coatza-
coalcos, Tampico, Salina Cruz and Lazaro-Cárdenas (mainly centers
for oil and steel) as might be expected, but the policy also promoted the development of frontier areas on the U.S. border including Baja California, Chihuahua, Tijuana, Mexicali, Reynosa
and Nogales.[41] This emphasis was highly suggestive of the
external export orientation of the development model as opposed
to a domestic market orientation and was also suggestive of what
would be Mexico's increasing dependence upon the U.S. and a dire
need to obtain clear access to the U.S. market.

For the first time, the disposition of petroleum revenues in sectoral terms was discussed. Oil export receipts for 1980-82 were anticipated at US$40.7 billion. Pemex would receive 32% of the amount remaining after the enterprise had subtracted expenses and development costs, meaning essentially that Pemex was to continue to absorb a huge share of the earnings, leaving the state with less in the way of freely disposable revenues than early optimistic assessments had suggested. Of the remainder, agriculture would receive 24%, transport and communications 20%, industry 16% and states and municipalities would receive 15%.[42]

Despite the enormity of the oil revenues, the state admitted in its Plan that renewed efforts to improve the internal savings picture would have to be mounted, and also acknowledged that external financing "would continue to play an important role...in development."[43] The state projected that by 1982, one-third of its financing would come from the exterior.[44] Thus, early expectations concerning oil's ability to confer financial independence upon Mexico seem to have rather rapidly evaporated.

In order to boost public sector savings, the Plan called for a rise in domestic energy prices. Private consumption, in particular, the consumption of luxury imports, would have to be curtailed. In fact, in March of 1981, the importation of sixty-three luxury items was banned with an estimated savings of US$640 million annually. Luxury items had flowed into Mexico as the oil boom unfolded and reflected the oil project's tendency to exacerbate income inequality. The flood of luxury items had of course worsened the country's balance of payments situation and as a result, the state sought to diminish the influx.[45] Furthermore, the state would take a closer look at subsidies to the private sector via pricing of state sector goods and services aside from energy, including petrochemicals, sugar, and rail transport charges. SEPAFIN Secretary José Andrés de Oteyza had complained in 1979 that a figure equivalent to one-half the expected 1980-82 petroleum earnings would be expended on subsidies to the private sector during that period.[46] Collectively, these changes were designed to reduce the worsening credit squeeze felt by the private sector that was caused primarily by state financing requirements. Naturally, the state hoped to avoid any worsening of the situation as this had been a major complaint of the private sector during the Echeverría period. Despite the oil revenues, the state found its savings capacity to be insufficient particularly in light of its growing investment and spending profile and thus sought to develop new areas of savings. As has traditionally been the case in Mexico, however, no serious effort was undertaken to overhaul the tax structure in order to generate new revenues.

Mexico's planners anticipated a continuation of the import intensive character of the development model and predicted a growth rate in exports of 20.8% p.a. for 1980-82, up from 12% during the 1977-79 period. By contrast, exports were expected to grow at a slower pace than imports and were to achieve a growth rate of 14.4% in the 1980-82 period.[47]

Aside from the growth seen in petroleum exports and natural

gas the boom produced a destabilization of the external sector of the economy. Imports as a percentage of total national product rose from 21% in 1970 to 31% in 1980. The development model pursued evidenced "a greater dependence in terms of overall growth and in terms of industrialization upon imports. This phenomenon of 'desubstitution' was particularly evident in the capital goods and intermediate goods sectors."48

Between 1977 and 1981, imports rose at an average annual rate of 43%. In fact, at the end of the four year period the value of imports quadrupled.49 Imports levels tumbled in 1982 as is seen in Table 4-3 as a result of the extreme contraction of the economy.

Table 4-3

Imports and Exports, 1977-82

(millions of dollars)

	Imports		Exports
1977	5,704	1977	4,650
1978	7,917	1978	6,063
1979	11,980	1979	8,818
1980	18,856	1980	15,109
1981	23,930	1981	19,420
1982	15,076	1982	21,944

Source: 1977-81, Banco de México, "La actividad económica en 1982," Comercio Exterior v.33, n. 5 (mayo de 1983), Table 2, p.463; 1982: "La economía en 1982: cifras definitivas," Comercio Exterior, Table 4, p.904.

Paradoxically, the state harbored the intention to transform the nation into the Latin American equivalent of the Japanese miracle. It would not be an easy task in light of the fact that Mexico's manufactured exports actually fell by 14% between 1978 and 1981.50 Continually frustrated by its small export capacity (blamed amazingly enough on high internal demand... in other contexts, increasing internal demand would be welcomed...) Mexico mounted an ambitious campaign to boost exports from the transport sector and border assembly plants.

In a particularly candid and revealing statement, Nathan Wartman, Subsecretary for Industry at SEPAFIN, outlined Mexico's development objective:

But the main problem that Mexico faces is the size of
its plants. The traditional small plants simply aren't
competitive, because of their very low productivity
levels.

...In some sectors, though not all, we would like
to have Japan as a model. We really have to get over
the internal market mentality of many local industrialists.[51]

Aside from the peculiar notion being advanced by Wartman
that an "internal market" mentality has been at the root of Mexico's industrialization problems (one could argue that Mexican
business suffered from neither an "internal market mentality"
nor an "external market mentality" in the normal sense of the
terms, but instead suffered from its dependent status), Wartman's
statement belied the state's declaratory policy of being first
and foremost interested in promoting small and medium-sized
industry in order to address the national employment problem.
According to Wartman, the state's plan was to transform industry
"from small, low productivity units to large modern plants able
to compete internationally." With an emphasis on external
markets, imported technology, capital intensivity and high "productivity" (usually understood as entailing reduced labor and
high capital factors), the prospects for either equity or employment appeared dim. While Japanese industry utilizes labor substituting robot technology and is known for its productivity, its
policy of redirecting technologically displaced labor into new
avenues of productive employment is a pattern that is at least in
part culturally rooted. It is most unlikely that within the Mexican context, such measures would be employed.

It was evident from the extensive economic ties that were
developed with Japan and from Mexican development priorities,
that a serious attempt would be undertaken to transform Mexican
industry into a world class exporter of manufactures. This particular development is consistent with patterns of development
presently being observed that indicate that industries of low
profitability in the developed countries are now shifting to
peripheral dependent states. This shift in the international
division of labor has been seen in autos, electronics, chemicals,
steel, assembly, shipbuilding and food processing.[52] It was
exactly within these areas (with the exception of shipbuilding)
that Mexico hoped to establish an international presence in
exports. Unlike the developed states, however, the operative
model precludes the normal first step--the development of an
internal market for these products. Instead, the option of the
development of a mass internal market is ignored as we have noted
before, because of the income redistribution that would be
required.

On balance, then, formal Mexican state commitments to the
development of decentralized, labor intensive small and medium-
sized industry as a first priority appeared hollow and the
central thrust of development policy remained quite different.
Thus, while the Global Plan for Development 1980-1982 and the

Table 4-4

Real Growth in Public Sector Budget, 1977-1981

1977	-4.2	1980	14.8
1978	6.3	1981	11.4
1979	6.0		

Source: 1977-81: Villarreal and Villarreal, Table II.4, p.37.

Table 4-5

Distribution of Public Investment by Sector, 1977-1982

(percentages)

	1977	1978	1979	1980-82
Industry	45.18	48.05	49.0	40.0
Agriculture	18.58	18.86	20.3	25.0
Transport & Communications	18.96	14.52	13.0	15.0
Social Welfare	13.80	16.03	13.0	16.0
Administration & Defense	2.80	2.17	n.a.	n.a.
Tourism	0.67	0.37	n.a.	n.a.

Sources: 1977-78: Villarreal and Villarreal, Table 1.1, p.10; Industry, "La política económica para 1980," p.71; 1979 and 1980-82: Plan Global de Desarrollo, 1980-1982, p.97.

National Industrial Development Plan appeared to signal a re-
thinking of development strategy, in fact such was not the case.

State Sector Growth

Until the 1982 collapse, the Mexican state sector substantially expanded its activities during the course of the oil boom
as is indicated by the growth in the public sector budget. As a
result of increased state activity, the state's share of GDP
climbed throughout the period. Contrasted to a share of 18% in
1970, that figure rose to 27.3% in 1979 and to 36% by 1981.[53]
Moreover, considering the understated value of public sector produced goods and services due to subsidy pricing, and to the activity of the state that is systematically underestimated, the real
value of state sector production and activity is actually much
greater than the figures would indicate. One analyst has argued
that the state's true share of GDP is probably closer to 55%.[54]
State spending during the period had far exceeded the IMF's recommended ceiling of a 24.5% share for 1979. Particularly notable
as well was the growth in public enterprise spending as a percentage of GDP.

Table 4-6

Public Enterprises Spending as a Percentages of GDP*

1970-1980

1970	10.9	1976	17.0
1971	11.7	1977	16.7
1972	11.8	1978	18.0
1973	13.1	1979	20.2
1974	15.1	1980	31.0
1975	17.6		

*includes budgetary controlled enterprises constituting the
bulk of state sector enterprises.

Sources: 1970-79: Villarreal and Villarreal, Table II.4, p.37;
1980 calculated from public sector budget data in "New Budget
Goes for Growth Rates Rather than Control of Inflation,"
Latin American Weekly Report ,(5 December ,1980), p.5 and GDP
calculated on basis of data in "Documento: El comportamiento
de la economía mexicana durante 1980," Banco de México,
Comercio Exterior, v.31, n.3 (marzo de 1981), p.325.

Table 4-7

Growth Rate in Investment by Participant, 1965-80

(in real terms)

	Public	Private
1965-76	10.0	8.0
1976	-7.2	4.2
1977	-5.1	-5.6
1978	19.0	12.8
1979	17.0	15.0
1980	12.0	14.9

Sources: 1965-77: "Documento: La evolución económica de México en 1978," CEPAL, Comercio Exterior, v.29, n.7 (julio de 1979), Table 2, p.790; 1978-79: "Documento: La política económica para 1980, SPP and SHCP", Comercio Exterior, v.30 n.1 (enero de 1980), p.71; 1980 public figure from Alan Robinson,"Mexico Draws Investments from Home and Abroad," Journal of Commerce (April 14, 1980), ISLA, v.20, n.4, p.8 and private figure from "Documento: El comportamiento de la economía mexicana durante 1980," Banco de México, Comercio Exterior, v.31, n.3 (marzo de 1981), p.325.

In terms of the rate of growth of private and public sector investment, the outcome was quite positive. The state's policy of encouraging private investment through a system of generous incentives and basic investments had succeeded in spurring private sector investment. Total investment grew by an average annual rate of 15% during the period 1978-1981 although that rate plummeted in 1982 registering a 14.2% rate.[55] The state's share of fixed capital formation rose from a late 1960s level of 28.1% to a 1982 level of 40%.[56]

Investment by the state in rural development proved to be minimal during the boom. Only 10.8% of total spending in the period 1977-82 was directed toward that sector. Investment in transport and communication fell from 22% of capital spending in the period 1971-76 to 15% in the period 1977-82. Spending for social welfare as a share of total spending remained stable during the period.[57] Spending for science and technology remained quite limited and was pegged at only 1% of GDP in 1982, an increase of only 0.4% over previous spending.[58] The bulk of public sector spending was directed to Pemex and CFE and in general targeted industrial development as the nation's chief priority.

Much of the state's expenditure took the form of direct subsidy to the private sector. Martínez and López Tijerina estimated that by the late 1970s, the figure had reached approximately 40% of the value of annual public investment.[59] The policy of direct incentives was called into question by one observer who argued that an increase in investment stimuli would probably fail because most private sector activity had been "self-financed."[60] Yet, the system of incentives appeared to have met with some success both in channeling new private investment into targeted areas and in encouraging greater investment. Counted among the most important incentives provided by the state that were developed during the period of the oil boom are:

Regional incentives--incentives designed to boost investment in specifically targeted coastal and frontier areas:
- 30% discounts on energy and basic petrochemicals[61]
- tax rebates of up to 45% for 10 years[62]
- 20% tax credit on cost of construction and fixed assets on new investment [63]
- 20% rebate on the annual minimum wage of each new employee to be forgiven in the form of tax credits
- export tax rebates--known as CEDIS. Reactivated under the López Portillo administration
- CEPROFIS--tax rebates on investment and labor costs. Used primarily to promote capital goods investment.

Other incentives include:
- CEPROFIS credits to large investors in mutual funds, designed to stimulate the infant Mexican stock market
- tax credits to sellers of "basic goods"
- tax credits to producers on imports where domestic production is insufficient. In the capital goods area and in auto parts, the credits can rise to 100% of import costs.[64]

Despite the oil revenues, heightened public spending unfortunately meant that the public sector deficit would have to be financed. Despite the fact that the IMF stabilization agreement had required that the deficit drop to 2.5% in 1978, state spending had proceeded apace and the public sector deficit rose to 18% of the GNP in 1982, a deficit that was without precedent in Mexico. Initially, oil had reduced the deficit level from 1976 levels but the problem had by no means been eliminated. For a time, the state was able to pursue a pattern of heavy state spending without incurring the wrath of the IMF or the private sector, however, this was an exceedingly short-lived experience.

Despite administrative adjustments and some public sector price increases, public sector enterprises by 1979 still commanded the same share of the public sector deficit as they had in 1976.[65] As a result of continuing budgetary deficits, the public external debt took on unprecedented proportions. Total indebtedness reached a staggering US$83 billion in 1983. Private sector debt rose from US$6.8 billion in 1977 to US$13.8 billion by mid 1982. [66]

Table 4-8

Public Sector Deficit, 1977-1982

	BILLIONS OF PESOS	% of GDP
1977	126	6.8
1978	156	6.7
1979	224	7.3
1980	322	7.5
1981	853	14.5
1982	-	18.0

Source: Banco de México, "La actividad económica en 1982,"
Table 2, p.463; Miguel de la Madrid Hurtado, "Primer Informe
de Gobierno," Comercio Exterior, v.33, n.9, (septiembre de
1983), p.788.

Table 4-9

Mexican External Public Debt, 1977-1983

(billions of dollars)

1977	22.9
1978	26.2
1979	29.7
1980	33.8
1981	53.0
1982	58.9
1983*	60.0

*Mid-year

Source: Rosario Green, "Mexico: crisis financiera y deuda
externa," Comercio Exterior, v.33, n.2, (febrero de 1983),
Table 1, p.105; Miguel de la Madrid Hurtado,"Primer Informe
de Gobierno," p.788.

By 1981 and 1982, Mexico's level of indebtedness had simply become unsustainable and the US$9 billion in payments due in 1983 were rescheduled through a complex series of negotiations organized by the U.S. which held approximately 38% of the total debt.[67] The growth rate of Mexico's debt registered 23.3% per annum during the period 1976-82, outpacing the 18.3% average growth rate in borrowing for the period 1965-76.[68] In 1981 alone, the public sector borrowed US$20 billion and in that year, the country had to rely upon more external resources than it had needed in the entire period 1975-1980.[69]

The phenomenal increase in the nation's level of indebtedness overshadowed the diversification in external financial sources of support achieved during the boom. The shift into the Eurocurrency market meant that by 1980, only 29% of Mexico external financing came from the U.S. contrasted with the 47% figure registered in 1977.[70] The dimensions of foreign borrowing were particularly startling in view of the fact that Mexican policy makers had actually anticipated an end to foreign financing by 1981. Instead, 1981 proved to be a year that saw an extremely rapid increase in external financing.

Despite accelerated exports, Mexico's external financial profile deteriorated especially in the early 1980s for a variety of reasons:
- high interest rates
- poor performance in the export sector
- shortfall in petroleum revenues for 1981 due to diminished demand, price changes and shipment problems.[71]
- import intensivity of the development model. The rate of growth in imports quadrupled during the boom.
- speed with which hydrocarbon development was pursued provoking a massive incursion of external debt.
- overvaluation of the peso, inflation and the massive inflow of imports as a result.[72]
- corruption and inefficiency[73]
- the necessity of continuing to borrow simply to service existing debt. The debt service ratio had risen to 64% even by 1979 and by 1982, the situation had essentially become insupportable.

By 1981, the public sector debt had reached a level of 17.8% of the GNP.[74] The disequilibrium of the external sector generated by the accelerated pace of dependent development and negative factors in the international economic environment proved devastating for Mexico. The financial chaos that had been sparked by the oil development project bore witness to the developmental pitfalls characterizing the model of associated dependent development.

Economic Performance During the Period of the Oil Boom

> We have been capable
> of producing but not
> of distributing.
>
> José López Portillo
> Third Report to the Nation[75]

Although oil had initially produced boom times in Mexico,
even the Mexican president publicly agreed that not everyone
had shared in the fruits of recent development. The National
Plan for 1983-1988 lamented the nation's inability to deal
successfully with the problem of distribution. In aggregate
terms, however, the growth had been impressive prior to 1982.
Compared to the period 1971-1977 when the economy had grown at
an average annual rate of 5.8%, the years of recovery, 1978-
1981 had seen an average annual growth rate of 8.5%.[76] As a
percentage of GDP, total fixed investment had risen from 17.3%
in 1960 to 24.1% in 1980. The public sector's ability, despite
new oil revenues, to finance its activities independently did
not show any improvement, however. Public sector savings plummeted from 3.3% of GDP in 1970 to 0% in 1981-1982. Subsidies
and transfer payments grew in an explosive way during the boom,
with subsidies rising from 7% of the GDP in 1977 to 15% in
1981.[77] This growth rate seriously undermined the potential
for savings in the state sector.
    Gross investment as a percentage of GDP rose, however,
from 23% in 1976 to 29% in 1981.[78] Per capita income rose from
US$1,240.3 in 1970 to US$1,381.5 in 1975 to an estimated figure
of US$1,534.5 in 1980.[79] Given the degree of income concentra-
tion in the society, the benefits flowing from these increases
were felt by relatively few citizens.
    By 1979, the growth rate in manufacturing had reached 8.5%,
consumer durables 13.5%, capital goods 16.6%, and petroleum and
petrochemicals 15% and 13.9% respectively. The automobile
sector was growing at an annual rate of 17% and the growth in
value added in manufacturing had reached a very positive 9.7%.
Growth in employment averaged 4% during the period. Much of
this increase was accounted for by growth in the construction
industry which is an unstable area for employment growth.
    Even before the collapse of the external sector in 1982,
problems had surfaced. Growth in agriculture fell by 3% in 1979.
Manufacturing growth declined in 1980 to a 5.6% growth rate,
still respectable but a decline nonetheless. Essentially, the
boom had run into a series of difficult impasses. By late 1978,
the productive capacity of Mexican industry was being used to
the fullest extent. Saturation of installed capacity and bottlenecks in transport and supply challenged the talents of admin-
istrators to circumvent almost insurmountable problems. The
problems became so severe, however, that blockages indeed throt-

Table 4-10

Mexico's Inflation Rate, 1973-1983

(percent per annum)

1973	15.0	1980	30.0
1977	32.0	1981	35.0
1978	17.3	1982	100.0
1979	18.2	1983*	53.8

* 1st 8 months of 1983

Sources: Villarreal and Villarreal, p.45; Comercio Exterior, v.31, n.1 (enero de 1981), p.14; Rosario Green, "Mexico: crisis financiera y deuda externa," Comercio Exterior, p.103; Comercio Exterior, v.33,n.10,(octubre de 1983), p.905.

tled growth, aggravated the inflation, and boosted the deficit on current account.[80]
    The inflation rate, which had become particularly trouble-some, had been provoked by a number of developments:
    - huge imports of basic grains due to a deterirorating profile in the agricultural sector.
    - capital imports at high prices
    - external financing at high interest rates
    - bottlenecks
    - electricity shortages
    - the new value added tax
    - high money supply
    - increased public and private spending
    - speculation and greed[81]
    Attempts were made to contend with the problem by employing wage and credit restrictions (although wages had never been identified as a source of the problem),and by increasing imports to curtail the inflationary effect of rising   internal demand that could not be met by the already overloaded domestic pro-ductive capability.[82] Steel production, for example, not only failed to increase in 1980 but actually fell by 22%, largely due to sectoral bottlenecks.[83]
    The state continued to espouse the fast growth track, how-ever, and López Portillo blamed inflation on imported "inter-national inflation", unwarranted price hikes and speculative maneuvers, thus placing a significant share of the blame upon the private sector. He did not, however, place any of the blame upon accelerated growth. Claiming that "the only alternative is infla-tion or catastrophe," López Portillo warned the private sector that it had "everything--and I mean everything--to loose if the structure of society explodes or comes crashing down,"[84] and

cautioned moderation in pricing increases.

Private sector enterprise had shown substantial profitability during the period. A survey of fifty-one of Mexico's largest corporations in 1980 showed that profits had risen by 72.1% in 1978 and 71.7% in 1979 despite sales increases of 32.4% in 1978 and 41% in 1979. In the steel industry, profits rose in 1979 by 290.4% while sales increased by only 39.4%.[85] Banks showed strong profitability as well. In 1980, BANCOMER's profits rose 66% and BANAMEX profits were up by 71%[86] Despite the state's public castigation of profiteering, virtually nothing was done to restrain profits and in fact the whole thrust of state policy was to shore up the private sector's potential for profit-taking as a means of encouraging investment. Public warnings without doubt contained at least a kernel of authenticity, as the state was interested in positioning itself politically, in terms of public perceptions, in the corner of the "popular sector". In practice, however, the warnings had no teeth.

While growth proceeded with vigor in certain sectors, other sectors, in particular wage goods, fared less well. In 1980, consumer non-durables (mainly indigenous industry with a high labor factor) grew by only 3.1%, compared to the growth in consumer durables of 12.8%,[87] directed at upper and median income strata. Textile production actually fell by 4.9% in 1980 and production in the clothing industry fell by 1.6%.[88] Further, a decline was experienced in those industries utilizing large quantities of sugar (nearly the staple of the Mexican diet). In sum, these developments mirrored a serious contraction in the buying power of the lower income strata of the population, a phenomenon to which we shall turn later.

Imports of capital goods and intermediate goods were the growth leaders although food imports commanded a large share. By contrast, the value of Mexican manufactured exports actually fell by 8.4% in real terms in 1980 although increased oil exports temporarily saved the trade balance from further deterioration. Capital goods imports as a percentage of the value of internal capital goods production rose to 55.6% in 1980, up from 48.9% in 1979[89] and promised to continue to maintain high percentages as industrialization proceeded. Moreover, capital goods and intermediate goods rose as a share of total imports from 72% in 1940 to over 80% between 1970 and 1980. In the 1970s, 45% of fixed capital formation in machinery and equipment derived from the import of these goods.[90] By the government's own admission, according to the analysis of this tendency found in the 1983-88 National Plan, this particular pattern causes greater external dependence for the country due to the need to finance these costly imports.

The tremendous surge in imports experienced during the sexenio was made possible by the oil development project and the revenues generated thereby, but was also made necessary by the need to import capital equipment and intermediate products for the oil development project and for other industrial development projects. The import intensivity of this process stemmed from the economy's failure to develop sufficiently in these areas both prior to the

146

boom and during the accelerated phase of development. Huge imports were also necessitated by

> ...insufficient coordination between plans for expansion and plans for production of capital goods and industrial inputs, provoking influxes of imports of goods and services...[91]
> The policy of import substitution has been in general, indiscriminate in favoring the domestic production of consumer durables and has failed to spawn the development of intermediate and capital goods, producing disequilibrium and rigidity.[92]
> Industrial production has taken place within the framework of external dependence... This has limited our national technological development in particular by having inhibited further progress in the substitution of imports of capital goods.[93]

Also contributing to the import bill was the need to import large quantities of food grains.

The U.S. continued to command a large share of Mexico's import-export trade and Mexico climbed to third place among U.S. trading partners after Canada and Japan based upon an increasing volume of trade. Despite this growth, trade with Mexico constituted only 5% of all U.S. trade.[94]

As a result of the oil fueled reinvigoration of industrialization in Mexico, the importance of the U.S. market for Mexico remained steady rather than having diminished despite Mexico's avowed intention to diversify its trading relationships. Moreover, as the revitalization of the economy was based upon a policy

Table 4-11

U.S. Share of Mexican Trade, 1976-1981

(percentages)

1976	57	1979	69
1978	66	1980	63
1979	69	1981	60

Source: U.S. Department of Commerce, Overseas Business Reports United States Foreign Trade Annual, 1975-1981 (Washington, D.C.: July, 1983), p.30.

of export growth rather than primarily growth in the internal market, the implicit expectation was that the U.S. market would inevitably play a crucial role in Mexican development.

As we have noted before, foreign exchange earnings are in fact only partially convertible and ultimately serve as stimuli to external economies through purchases abroad. This was made most evident by the intensified program of imports supported by oil exports and the US$2.5 billion trade deficit incurred by Mexico with the U.S. in 1980. Prior to the financial collapse, Laura Randall estimated that Mexican imports of capital equipment and industrial inputs would reach US$21.2 billion by 1990, indicating a sustained reliance upon external economies for the development of domestic industrial processes and a continuance of the tendency for Mexican industrialization to provide stimuli to external economies.[95]

Direct Foreign Investment

In line with the state's pursuit of accelerated growth, foreign investment was encouraged and interested investors met with a "marked reduction in the antagonism towards foreign companies."[96] One leading U.S. business publication, hostile towards the policy of Mexicanization, noted the change:

> The attitude toward foreign investment is almost cordial and recognizes international companies' importance in launching Mexico's economic take-off. The foreign investment law's restrictions on new investments, expansions and new products are balanced against the need to boost exports, create jobs and stimulate industry. If a company presents an attractive enough offer in terms of balance of payments, employment, exports, etc., the law can be bent to accomodate majority foreign equity. ...The Foreign Investment Commission will sometimes even help a firm put together an acceptable package... Another marked change in the investment picture is on the horizon. The FIC will become an active promoter of foreign investment in selected projects, putting together total packages, including incentives in some cases, for initial majority foreign ownership.[97]

Early in the sexenio, López Portillo had made it clear that the state would welcome foreign investment applications that were deemed "beneficial" to the "nation". These would not be rejected because of any "formal prohibition".[98] The policy of Mexicanization would not be rolled back to the extent that 100% foreign ownership would be endorsed, but joint ventures (JV's) with majority foreign equity in crucial sectors would be approved more easily. Deadlines for the Mexicanization of certain companies would be waived and Mexicanization via the stock market, though challenged in several instances by the FIC, was allowed to go through despite the fact that such a policy would enable minority interests to exert majority control. It has been estimated that as little as 25% stock ownership could conceivably guarantee control of a corporation.

Nonetheless, the development of a vigorous stock market in Mexico, it was argued, would be enhanced by permitting "foreign investors" to have "freer access to our own equities market."[99] In fact, one official charged with responsibility for state monitoring of securities exchange acknowledged that foreign investment in the stock market was being vigorously pursued and that toward that end, the 1973 laws governing foreign investment would simply be reinterpreted. "So what we will do is change the interpretation and enforcement of the law to allow foreign investors to buy Mexican shares even where the 49% limitation applies."[100]

At the same time, however, in order to offset the increasing influence of external financial interests in Mexico while still increasing Mexico's reliance upon them, the state developed a new fund, Fondo México, that would be offered on the New York, European and Japanese stock exchanges by NAFINSA.[101] The Fund would invite the purchase of stock in domestic corporations that would in turn be held and managed by NAFINSA with shareholders receiving returns on investment but exercising no control over the management of the corporations involved. On balance, however, foreign investment was viewed as an essential component of the accelerated development program.

As a result of Mexico's brightened oil-based early financial prospects and the advent of a sympathetic "pro-business" administration, direct foreign investment grew substantially during the oil development period. In the view of the Mexican state, DFI would boost domestic supplies, theoretically providing some edge on inflation, would add to the job pool (although López Portillo had himself complained that by the mid-70s, foreign investment accounted for 15% of production while only employing 3% of the population), and would provide access to the latest technologies. Moreover, DFI would support Mexico's ailing non-oil exports, although by all estimates, the activities of the foreign corporations were highly import intensive and thus tended to aggravate the balance of payments situation.

The return on investment rose substantially for foreign investors during the period, rising to 21.3% on all investment and to 21.5% on manufacturing investment,[102] up from an average of 18.3% in the early 1970s. Althought foreign investors were cautious at the outset of the sexenio, by 1979, new investment had risen dramatically as is shown in Table 4-12, and during 1981, the increase in new foreign investment was expected to be nothing short of spectacular. As Rogelio Sada Zambrano, head of the influential Vitro Industrial Group noted, "The Foreign Investment law is no discouragement to a foreign company interested in Mexico."[103] By 1981, total foreign investment in Mexico would reach a figure of between US$8.2 billion and US$10 billion,[104] up from US$5.384 billion in 1975.

The U.S. share of new investment fell slightly during the period, dropping from 81% in 1971,[105] as Japan and the West European nations moved more aggressively into the market, to a large extent motivated by the desire to develop an alternative supply of oil to that of the Middle East. The U.S. share of total direct

Table 4-12

New Direct Foreign Investment, 1975-1981

(billions of dollars)

Year	Amount	% Increase	Year	Amount	% Increase
1975	.609	-	1979	1.339	61
1976	.628	3	1980	1.852	38
1977	.555	-11	1981	3.0*	85
1978	.828	49			

*estimate

Sources: IDB, Economic and Social Change in Latin America, the External Sector, 1982 Report, Table 49, p.382 for 1975-1980 data. 1981 estimate from "Update 1980 Mexico," Nation's Business (January, 1980), p.4m.

foreign investment in Mexico was 62% by the late 1970s.[106] During the 1977-82 period, Japanese investment was expected to have risen by 200-300%.[107] In cases where a potential new oil supply did not constitute the principal lure as with West Germany, the availability of petrochemical feedstocks at subsidy prices included substantial investment. Relying upon German technology, Mexico concluded an agreement with BASF, the German chemicals concern for the construction of two plastics factories to be built by Polioles de México in 57% ALFA-43% BASF JV.[108] Other chemicals concerns that pursued substantial new investment in Mexico as a result of the availability of cheap feedstocks were Celanese, Monsanto, Union Carbide (building three plants at Villahermosa), and B.F. Goodrich among others.[109] In the huge secondary petrochemicals complex, La Cangrejera, ALFA participated with several of these TNCs in its development and construction.[110]

Among the developed states, it was Japan that launched the most aggressive new investment effort, and while its total investment in Mexico amounted to only 2% of the total by 1980, at the end of 1979, Japan declared its intentions to invest over US$1 billion by the end of 1981. Under the auspicies of the "Japanese-Mexico Businessmen's Committee," plans were mapped out for joint ventures in export industries, capital goods, and infrastructure (including seaports, mass transit and shipping.) Mexico sought to facilitate the growth of the Mexico-Japan relationship by establishing an array of missions to Japan in addition to the regular consular offices. These included NAFINSA, the Secretariat of Agriculture and Water Resources, CONACYT (the National Council for Science and Technology), the Secretariat for Marine Affairs, the Mexican Institute of Foreign Trade, the National

Council for Tourism, Pemex, and two private banks.[111]

While Japan was eager to increase its investments in Mexico, it complained bitterly to Mexico about the restrictive character of Mexico's foreign investment laws,[112] and along with the U.S., sought to pressure Mexico into liberalizing trading regulations by insisting that Mexico pursue membership in the General Agreement on Tariffs and Trade (GATT), a subject to which we shall return later. In response to Japanese concerns, José Andrés de Oteyza, SEPAFIN Secretary, promised that a flexible attitude on the subject of DFI would be maintained.[113]

In addition to petrochemicals, the greatest areas for foreign investment during the sexenio included transport equipment, non-electrical machinery and food,[114] with the bulk of investment, as in the past, flowing into the manufacturing sector. Much of the investment that occurred was in the form of joint ventures, for the most part undertaken in conjunction with large Mexican grupos, but also with the state or tri-partite foreign-local-state ventures.

CYDSA and Vitro[115] actively pursued new JVs, with CYDSA building upon its already established network of JVs with B.F. Goodrich, Bayer A.G. and Allied Chemical. ALFA and Visa, the largest of the grupos, also sought to develop new JVs. These would be added to their list of affiliations that already resembled a "Who's Who of international business."[116] In accord with state sectoral development goals and the incentives made available for companies complying with such goals, ALFA emphasized chemicals, petrochemicals, capital goods, electronics and tourism in its investment plans. Visa moved into fisheries, tourism and food processing.

Recent Visa activity include :
- A JV with Spain's Barreiros Hermanos in a 60% Visa - 40% Barreiros Hermanos split in Industrial Maritima, S.A., a fishing venture,
- A JV with two Japanese fishing concerns for a swordfish project,
- A JV with the Hyatt Hotel chain for a chain of luxury hotels and in the Acapulco Hyatt Regency,
- A JV with France's Novo Hotel, S.A. for a chain of first class hotels,
- A JV with United Brands' subsidiary "Clement Jacques" in food processing,

Alfa activities include in addition to earlier JVs:
- A JV with the Netherland's Azko in Fibras Quimicas, S.A.,
- A JV with Hitachi in Megatec, S.A., producer of motors and generators,
- A JV with Mercofina, subsidiary of Hercules (US) and American Petrofina (US) in Petrocel, S.A.,
- Acquisition of Admiral Home Entertainment line from Rockwell International. Alfa will use Admiral trademark.
- JV with BASF in Polioles, S.A.,
- A JV with Club Mediterranée for tourism,
- A JV with Moulinex (France) in Vistar, S.A. to produce electric home appliances,

State co-investment with foreign interests has included a wide
variety of projects of which the following are representative:
- A JV with the state's Altos Hornos (steel) and the Dravo
  Corporation (US) in an iron ore treatment plant in
  Monclova,
- A JV involving Mexicana Airlines, NAFINSA, and Pratt
  Whitney for a turbine maintenance plant,[117]
- A JV in Productora Mexicana de Tubería involving NAFINSA
  Sidermex and Sumitomo Metal Industries to produce pipe
  for gas and oil,[118]
- A JV in heavy foundry and forging equipment involving
  Kobe Steel, NAFINSA and Sidermex in "Grupo NKS",[119]
- A JV "Turborreactores, S.A." involving NAFINSA, Aeromex-
  ico, Mexicana de Aviación (mixed) and the U.S. firm
  International Support Systems.[120]
Other sources of new investment from the U.S. included among
a whole array of investors, Scott Paper, Kimberly Clark and ITT.
Joint ventures with French concerns that were agreed to in 1980
alone included telecommunications, petrochemicals, mining, steel
and port infrastructure. A West German mission to Mexico in
1981 produced a number of agreements and arrangements for JVs
with Sweden now include steel, naval construction, cellulose,
paper, energy generating equipment, chemicals, and petrochemicals.[121] Denmark also concluded plans for over US$300 million
in investment in food production to be completed in the early
1980s.
     Within the tourism sector, the state and banking sectors
have sought foreign investment and have used FONATUR credits to
induce investment. Representative of this trend is the Multi-
banco Comermex-Hilton agreement for JV in the construction and
management of four new Hilton hotels.[122]
     In the banking sector, laws restricting the activity of
foreign banks in Mexico were revamped to allow the conversion of
representative offices into "offshore branches." Essentially,
these branches were to be permitted to take deposits from and
grant loans to nonresidents.[123] While hardly a major alter-
ration of the restrictive banking policy, the new law acknowledged the continuing and expanding presence of foreign business
interests in Mexico.

The Auto Industry as the Industrial Centerpiece

     The Global Plan of 1979-82 called for massive investment in
the automobile industry in order to serve the domestic market
and crucially, brighten Mexico's export profile in manufactures.
As a result of the state's effort to expand and reinvigorate the
industry which had been depressed in the mid 1970s, a series of
financial and administrative incentives were developed to attract
increased investment. These included exemptions on import duties
for some components, income tax forgiveness of up to 25% for
companies producing diesel engines, trucks and buses, outright
grants to parts manufacturers, and of course, discounted energy
prices.[124] Mexico's comparative labor cost advantage (U.S. auto

workers earn on the average US$14.50 per hour while their Mex-
ican counterparts earned only US$1.30 per hour)[125] provided an
additional incentive for investment. Finally, Mexico's local
content regulations governing the domestic content of automobiles manufactured in Mexico, compelled international automakers
to increase investment in Mexico. As a means of placating TNC
automakers, in the Increased Exports Decree of 1977, Mexico provided that insufficient domestic content could be offset by
increased exports and to that end, allocated to each manufacturer a foreign exchange ceiling. By 1981, each company was
directed to achieve a 1:1 ration of import value to export
value.[126] This requirement was designed not only to spur domestic development, but also reflected the continuing proportion of
the deficit in the nation's commercial balance accounted for by
the automobile industry. That share had been measured at 19.9%
and 36.5% in 1976 and 1977 respectively. Unfortunately, however,
the situation only became intensified as investment proceeded.
By 1980, the figure had risen to 47.2% and by 1981, a startling
57.7%.[127]

Mexico became a "magnet for foreign auto giants"[128] during
this period. The advisability of undertaking such a development
effort was addressed in a report by the U.N.'s Economic Comis-
sion for Latin America (CEPAL). The report noted that the
project reflected total adherence to standard development strategy where export growth in the manufacturing sector (in this
case automobiles) is mainly accounted for by TNCs. Normally,
what increase there has been in internal demand justifying the
expansion has been at the upper middle and upper income levels.
Growth in the market for luxury consumer durables reflects a
worsening in the distribution of income within the context of
overall aggregate economic gains. The export drive in this
sector, as in others, is based upon a depressed wage policy, a
policy maintained during the oil boom of sub-inflation wage
guidelines and agreements.[129]

The drive for the establishment of a major auto export component within the Mexican economy implied continued and increased
susceptibility to the fluctuations experienced in external economies and dependence upon decision making for the industry in
Detroit, Tokyo, and Paris.[130]

Overall, at least US$2billion in investment would be poured
into the auto industry during 1980-82 alone.[131] The state also
invested substantial sums in other areas of the motor vehicle
industry. Plans called for the production of one million autos
per year by 1985 and 1.7 by 1990.[132] During the course of the
sexenio, however, the state was forced to ease local content
rules in assembly operations because of the local industry's
inability to meet demands for auto parts.[133]

As a means of overcoming this problem, the state had, by
early 1980 concluded an "Action Agreement" with one hundred-fifty
companies involved in supplying the industry. These companies
pledged investments totalling US$1 billion to be completed during
the 1980-82 period in return for a host of generous incentives.
In so doing, the state hoped to achieve a consolidation and ex-

pansion of production based upon anticipated growth rates of 13% through 1982 and 15% by 1990.[134]

The structure of the industry would remain stable with no challenges to 100% foreign ownership of the basic auto production companies. In the cases of partially state owned manufacturers, shares of the domestic and export market dropped rather substantially since 1976.

During the _sexenio_, TNC investment plans involved the following projects:

General Motors
- 5 new plants including the Saltillo engine plant, assembly, and several border plants. Estimated investment: US$350 million.[135]

Chrysler
- A 4 cylinder engine plant. Estimated investment of US$130 million.[136]

Ford
- US$42 million expansion of assembly plant at Cuautitlán. Extending LTD (one of Mexico's luxury models) production.[137]
- 4 cylinder engine plant for export to Canada and U.S.[138]
- JV with ALFA in lightweight motors.
- JV with ALFA - aluminum cylinder heads plant. Estimated investment of US$65 million.[139]
- JV with Vitro - auto safety glass
- JV with Visa's Valdres Industriales - plastic products for autos. Exports to U.S.

Nissan
- expansion to production level of 120,000 cars per year.

Volkswagen
- major investment planned.

DINA
- Renault plans major expansion estimated at US$50 million.

Cummins Engine
- JV with DINA, US$100 million investment.[140]

Mack Trucks
- JV with mixed state/private _grupo_ SOMEX in trucks.[141]

International Harvester (now Mexicanized)
- Major expansion.[142]

Metallgesellschaft A.G.
- JV with Saltillo Industrial Group in auto supply.[143]

In short, the state had opened the floodgates. Its policy of export-led industrialization was not only import intensive by design (even given local content requirements), but inevitably had the effect of tremendously increasing direct foreign investment, technical dependence, and financial dependence. Probably even more importantly, the policy would cast in iron the development model...one essentially designed to serve a restricted market basket.

Despite an increase in state subsidies to the industry of over 100% between 1977-1981,[144] aspects of the industry's performance proved to be disappointing. While impressive growth was seen in the number of vehicles produced, an increase from

Table 4-13

Ownership and Market Shares in

the Mexican Auto Industry

	Percentage of Foreign Ownership, 1981	Market Share, 1980
Chrysler	99.1	19.9
Ford	100.0	13.5
General Motors	100.0	6.0
Nissan	100.0	12.6
Renault/DINA	n.a.[1]	7.5
VAM (American Motors/ Renault)	100.0[2]	7.3
Volkswagen	100.0	33.2

[1]State divestiture in 1983.

[2]State divestiture in 1983 and Renault takeover.

Sources: Bennett and Sharpe, "Transnational Corporations and the Political Economy of Export Promotion," Table 1, p.83; Euromoney Country Risk Report, Mexico. the Next Ten Years, (London: Euromoney Publications Ltd., 1981), Table 9.2, p.132, and LAWR, various 1983 issues for divestiture data.

Table 4-14

Growth in Employment in Border Industry

1965-1980

	Number	Percentage Increase		Number	Percentage Increase
1965	3,000	–	1978	90,000	15
1975	67,000	210	1979	115,000	28
1977	78,000	16	1980	119,546	4

Sources: McClelland, pp.5-6 and William Chislett, "Waiting for the Giant to Sneeze," Financial Times (May 16, 1980); C. Daniel Dillman, "Assembly Industries in Mexico," Journal of Interamerican Studies and World Affairs, v.25, n.1 (February, 1983), Table 1, p.36.

280,813 autos in 1977 to 597,118, the deficit in the industry's commercial balance skyrocketed. The deficit jumped by 172.3% in 1979 from 1977 and by 457.4% between 1979 and 1981.[145] Between 1977-1981, the industry increased its exports by 46.1% while imports increased by 294.1%.[146] The industry was also beset by the contraction in demand experienced worldwide and saw auto production fall by 21% in 1982 and by 18% in 1983. Nearly 20,000 autoworkers experienced lay-offs as a result.[147]

Other problems plagued the industry and many were of long-standing concern to Mexican planners...the existence of an overly diversified production capacity, problems of product quality, production of luxury vehicles that were regarded as inordinately wasteful, lack of integration within the industry, failure to achieve economies of scale and accelerating prices.[148] The development effort, thus suffered from numerous difficulties. Very troublesome, however, was the fact that the industry had enormously contributed to disequilibria in the external sector, rather than providing relief to the economy. The effort to pursue development in this area became ensnarled in the liabilities created by the prior results of dependent development. Specifically, as the state sought to encourage development in this industry, the need to import and the need to pursue foreign investment in turn aggravated problems the project was intended to remedy.

Border Industry

Another major economic priority of the Mexican state within the context of its export drive was the strengthening of the in-bond industry. A new package of incentives was introduced in 1978 toward this end.[149] In addition, the state established a number of goals for the sexenio in this sector:
1) create 175,000 new jobs in the sector
2) boost exports by US$1 billion
3) increase the value of Mexican components utilized in assembly operations
4) promote the import substitution of products used by twin plants
5) increase foreign and national investment in the sector.[150]

The in-bond industry constituted one of the fastest growing employment sectors during the sexenio although it failed to achieve the growth rate targeted at the outset of the program. By 1980, the number of plants in operation had risen to 620, up from 457 in 1978. According to a BANAMEX report, the hope was that despite earlier measured growth, sales might top US$10 billion by 1990 and that the industry would employ 450-500,000 persons.[151] Given the capital intensity of the petroleum development program and the drive for industrialization, state planners understandably looked imploringly toward the in-bond industry as a relatively cheap and painless means of creating employment and absorbing some of the labor flow that would be seeking entry into the U.S. employment market.

One of the principal concerns regarding the industry's health was the pressure that oil had exerted on the peso and the inflationary cycle resulting from the development project that could well "damage" the wage structure. Wage increases induced by inflation could conceivably boost Mexican labor costs and in an industry built first and foremost upon the premise of cheap labor, the results could be quite serious.[152] At the same time, the industry was completely dependent upon the vagaries of the U.S. and Japanese economies and due to the 1980 recession in the U.S., employment and production growth experienced a downturn. Thus, the state was in fact engaged in promoting the development of a uniquely dependent type of sectoral growth and moved to broaden the "border" area to include areas in the interior where wages are even lower and where IBM, Burroughs Corporation and General Electric had already located.[153]

Mexicanization Policy

Little was done during the period of the oil boom to strengthen the policy of Mexicanization. The state did move to promote joint ventures, however, in the automobile sector, and did issue a document in 1980 which made known the state's intention to pursue Mexicanization within the pharmaceuticals industry.[154] Importantly, the announcemnt of the policy change came in the form of a document rather than a law as would normally be the case, suggesting that the state really intended to float a trial balloon on the issue, at least in part to mollify the CTM which had called for the nationalization of the industry along with banks, insurance companies, textile companies, the food industry and construction.[155]

The document called for a freeze on majority foreign capital already in place and specified that the local capital share be brought up to 51% in four years from the 28% share that had existed. In the case of firms already majority owned domestically, the share of domestic capital was to increase by 30-50%. Not surprisingly, the state proposed state financing for the acquisitions which would mean that the state would at once move into a new productive area and increase its cooperation with foreign capital. The policy intended to increase local content, install Mexican management, and increase exports. It need hardly be reiterated, however, that Mexican pharmaceuticals companies would continue to depend upon TNCs for technology, financing and marketing for exports and internal production despite such changes. Clearly, the state's tentative movement into this area was facilitated by its improved financial status which was based upon oil.

The commitment to the original outline of the policy of Mexicanization seemed to have eroded further as the problems of the development model seemed to outweigh any benefits that oil had been able to confer. The National Plan for 1983-88 appeared to formally reaffirm what had become a more accomodative environment for foreign investment. The plan stated that "Foreign investment is viewed as a complement to national investment..."[156]

The plan called for decentralization of decision-making regarding decisions authorizing new investment and called for the adoption of a more "flexible" policy toward foreign investment. The plan emphasized the importance of aquiring technology through direct foreign investment.[157]

Finally, the plan went a step further when it stated the following regarding the policy of Mexicanization:

> ...the process of Mexicanizing business with foreign participation has proved illusory in many cases and has had undesirable effects on industrial concentration, pricing policy and upon the availability of resources for investment.[158]

Agriculture, Rural Development and Marginal Groups

The rural population saw no immediate benefits from the oil production program. By the late 1970s, over two-thirds of all Mexican un/underemployed workers were still to be found in the agricultural sector.[159] A BANRURAL study showed that by the late 1970s, of 7,252,000 peasants of working age, fully 5 million were un/underemployed.[160] Moreover, the commitment of huge sums of investment capital to the industrial sector, and in particular to Pemex, constrained public sector spending in rural areas through the 1970s. The rationale for this strategy was of course, that future earnings from Pemex would ultimately be used to ameliorate problems in the agricultural sector, but more importantly, would be used to promote economic growth that would in turn foster increased employment in the urban industrial sector. (As we noted earlier, the employment profile projected in the National Industrial Development Plan unfortunately did not mesh with this aspect of declaratory policy).

In fact, the oil development program and related sectoral spending priorities were, not surprisingly, analogous to the very pattern condemned in the Global Plan for Development, 1980-82.[161] The Plan quite openly admitted that agriculture had suffered because it had supported the push for industrialization after 1941 by absorbing the impact of worsening internal terms of trade and by its virtual subsidization of the urban sector. Despite such admissions, the pattern would endure throughout the oil boom.

In this instance, however, the problem of the marginalized character of the rural population, coupled with falling production (on a per capita basis) and the high birth rate, alarmed the state because of widely held fears that the need to import huge amounts of food and to subsidize (however minimally) the marginal population would monopolize energy earnings, leaving Mexico no further ahead than in the pre-oil boom period.[162] Moreover, the need to import tremendous amounts of food could conceivably weaken the "energy bargaining chip" in the international economic arena, the tool upon which Mexico was so desperately counting.

Despite huge food imports, the state admitted that by 1980, 19 million persons were known to have a "very low nutritional

level." Further, the diet of 35 million persons did not meet
minimum daily caloric intake standards. Of the most seriously
malnourished 19 million persons, 13 million were in rural areas
and of those 19 million, fully 14.5 million were children
under the age of 15. Overall, 90% of the rural population was
classified as malnourished.[163]

The state became particularly concerned about the dimensions of the nation's food imports as they produced bottlenecks
in transportation and warehousing. Massive food imports clogged
ports, rail facilities and warehousing and interfered with the
steel and oil industries.[164] Food imports reached 10.4 million
tons in 1980 at a total cost of US$2 billion. In 1981 and
1982, food imports totaled US$2.2 billion and US$.9 billion
respectively,[165] the bulk of which emanated from the U.S.[166]

Early in his sexenio, in a radical departure from the traditional revolutionary symbolism utilized by the PRI, López
Portillo asserted that land ownership was henceforth to be recognized as only a "secondary issue" and complained that "land
distribution is an obsession with us."[167] Mexico, he argued,
needed to strengthen its production system and achieve greater
efficiency and productivity rather than concentrating attention
upon further land distribution. The capitalization of agriculture and concentration of landholding were viewed as appropriate
means to this end. Small cultivators were recognized as being
more productive than their TNC counterparts, producing crops
for domestic consumption, for the most part without benefit
of irrigation and access to credit or new technologies. Yet
the fact that the number of landless persons had remained high
and little headway had been made in agrarian reform or land
redistribution due to the "shortage" of land, an abundance of
applicants and bureaucratic foot-dragging, on top of the poor
performance in the sector pushed the state to abandon once and
for all the rhetoric of the Mexican Revolution and embark upon
a program of converting the peasantry into an organized, union-
ized proletariat. Surplus labor would be employed in new agro-
industrial enterprises of both domestic and foreign origin.[168]
The Echeverría emphasis on the ejido would be abandoned.[169] The
agro-industry that was in place was clearly dominated by TNC
interests, chiefly from the U.S. and was characterized by capital intensivity and land concentration. By 1978, 77 U.S. agro-
industrial companies accounted for 80-90 percent of total
Mexican food production.[170] Counted among the largest were
Campbell Soup, Del Monte, Carnation, Kraft, Gerber, Kellog, CPC
International, Anderson-Clayton and General Foods. The state
would attempt to complement this production by consolidating
minifundios and creating small agro-industrial enterprises that
would be fully integrated from crop production through food
processing.

As a result of this shift in policy, the Secretariat for
Agrarian Reform was quickly eclipsed in budget and responsi-
bility by the Secretariat of Agriculture and Water Resources.
(SARH). SARH was charged with

...coordinating the planning, development and complete

Table 4-15

Growth Rates in Mexican Agriculture, 1950-82

(Percentage per annum)

1950-1959	3.8	1979	-2.1
1960-1965	4.7	1980	7.1
1965-1976	0.85	1981	6.4
1977	6.5	1982	-2.5
1978	4.1		

Sources: 1950-65: Looney, Income Distribution Policies in Semi-Industrialized Countries, p.7; 1965-78, Plan Global de Desarrollo, 1980-82, vol. 2, p.10; 1979-81: IDB, Economic and Social Development in Latin America, The External Sector, 1982 report, p.281; 1982: "La balanza de pagos en 1982," Comercio Exterior, p.399.

Table 4-16

Percentage of Total Bank Credits Given

to Agriculture by the Private Banking Sector, 1954-1975

1945-55	12-17%
1955-60	15%
1969-1975	under 10%

Source: "Foreign Money Seen as Remedy for Mexican Agriculture," Latin America Economic Report, v.VII, n.11 (16 March 1979), p.87.

organization of agricultural and livestock production,
the establishment of production units, the association
of rural producers, the delimitation and operation of
districts without irrigation, cultivation of idle lands
and the optimum use of resources allocated to the rural
sector.[171]

Early plans for the further development of agro-industry
called for the formation of 335 vertically integrated state-
sponsored agro-industrial enterprises that would do everything
from growing to packaging food.[172] Under the program, _ejido_ and
community lands could be rented to agro-industry under "association contracts". Peasants with land would thus rent their land
and sell their labor. The outside investor would provide machinery, technology, marketing and management. Profits would then
be distributed on the basis of the particular contribution made
to the enterprise. The state would provide the new associations
with credit at very favorable rates for "insurance, fertilizers,
seeds, technical assistance, machinery, transport and warehouse
facilities."[173]

The agricultural sector had consistently experienced a
shortage of credit (Table 4-16) and the state would attempt to
circumvent this situation by providing increased credit, and by
seeking increased direct foreign investment in agriculture as
well as foreign financing. By 1979, the state was providing two-
thirds of all agricultural credit.[174]

As a direct result, in 1978, the World Bank granted to Mexico a record US$200 million loan for agriculture which the Bank
at the time labeled the largest single loan ever made to a Latin
American state for a single purpose.[175] In 1980, the Bank
granted Mexico still another huge loan for agriculture totalling
US$325 million which it termed the "largest ever made by the Bank
in its 33 year history."[176] In 1981, Mexico also received
another US$280 million credit from the Bank for agriculture and
a US$165.5 million credit from the Inter-American Development
Bank for irrigation in Sinaloa.[177]

Despite widespread malnutrition and the need for huge grain
imports, the state was committed to maintaining a strong agricultural export sector (which had been running a positive trade
balance for the sector as a whole)[178] rather than attempting to
attain agricultural self-sufficiency for the nation. At the same
time, labor intensive export crops were to be favored in order to
mitigate the unemployment problem. Not only did the state intend
to support existing export enterprises, but as well, it sought to
shift production--where possible--to increased exchange earning
export crop production. López Portillo explained his intentions
in this area in his Third Report to the Nation. He argued that
export crops were more desirable as compared to corn (the national staple food) because strawberries or cotton "provide work and
foreign exchange precisely to purchase corn reserves and to
profit in our international trade."[179] This attitude toward the
purchase of huge amounts of basic grains abroad was to change,
however, as ports, warehouses and rails became choked with these

commodities and as the annual tab for these imports mounted.

Aside from the bottlenecks incurred, the notion that it makes more sense to produce strawberries for the export market rather than corn (or some other products) for the domestic market merits examination. While in theory, Mexico may well enjoy a comparative advantage in the production of labor intensive export crops (because of low wages), in practice, only a very restricted portion of Mexican society "profits" from this type of international trade. When staples must be imported, food simply becomes more expensive for an already malnourished population even though prices are controlled by the state. The population ultimately supports the cost of the expensive imports through the regressive system of taxation. While state monies are utilized to support the prices received by domestic producers of basic grains, the cost of importing exceeds even these costs. Furthermore, the highly valued foreign exchange is used to continue the importation of frequently inappropriate technologies (to say nothing of luxury imports) which intensify the problem of marginalization. The all-important foreign exchange receipts earned by the production of export crops, unfortunately are utilized in ways that do little to benefit those who are paying for the importation of staples. Since 1970, subsidies for basic commodities experienced an average annual increase of 39%,[180] reaching US$3.7 billion in 1980.

To facilitate the financing of the drive for agroindustrial progress, the state established the Fund for the Promotion and Support for Agro-industry in 1979 which would extend credits to the new associations and small agro-industrialists.[181] The state embarked upon a major new initiative in the agricultural sector beginning in 1980, in part because of the attention traditionally paid to "social" issues in the latter stages of Mexican presidential terms and in part because oil project investments had achieved targeted production levels. This freed investment capital for other uses. Most important, however, was the threat that problems of the agricultural sector threatened to cancel the gains achieved during the costly oil development project. Projections for food import bills throughout the 1980s were most troubling.

The sectoral program known as the Mexican Food System (SAM) was announced in March of 1980 although the legislative program, the Law for Agricultural Promotion, was formally submitted in November of 1980. Total funding for the series of projects contained within SAM during 1980 and the first half of 1981 reached nearly US$4.2 billion,[182] and for 1981 alone, the figure would climbed to US$10 billion.[183]

The announcement of the new program was prefaced by a critique of past approaches to the problems of the agricultural sector. These had included:

> ...increases in guaranteed prices, indiscriminate mechanization, the orientation of commercial agriculture toward export, the cultivation of highly profitable crops and the importation of basic grains.[184]

Unfortunately, the critique had something of a hollow ring inasmuch as the state evidently had no intention of dismantling the structure of foreign investment in agriculture (the matter was put under study), or to transfer export land to basic production, or to disavow mechanization. The state did, however, reverse its position on the issue of self-sufficiency, declaring it to be the paramount goal for the sector (citing a 1982 target for corn and beans, for example),[185] and maintained that exports would be permitted only after domestic needs had been met.

That the state saw for itself a greatly expanded role in the sector is indicated by López Portillo's remarks upon the unveiling of the new program:

> The State must be the guide, the fomenter, promoter... with this system (SAM), we want to go further; the Mexican state wants to advance within the context of the Alliance for Production and to share risks with the peasants...(the state would) institute technological changes and support the development of a peasant organization of a superior order.[186]

The state would attempt to promote small and medium-sized agro-industrial enterprises, employing peasants in which labor intensive operations would be harmoniously allied and integrated with capital intensive operations.[187] Larger production units were favored and the state would actively seek the abolition of the minifundio and would encourage peasants to form associations with other farmers in order to consolidate small holdings.[188] The plan thus amounted to a reiteration of development goals that had been articulated earlier. The concept of decentralized agro-industry was nothing new. The formation of SAM meant, however, a renewed commitment in terms of resources and a more clearly articulated intention to organize the peasantry and to convince small producers to cooperate with the scheme.

The overall goal of the project was to stimulate production and increase mechanization. The increased use of tractors (up from 1 per 145 hectares to 1 per 100 hectares)[189] was an important component of the strategy. As such, the plan called for increased state incentives to the agricultural machinery industry. In order to increase production, not only would producers' "cooperatives" have to be organized, but usable land not currently in production would have to be brought into cultivation. Of an estimated usable acreage of 57 million hectares, only 40 million were in production. SAM would expand irrigation and the cultivation of an increased 5 million acres of rain-fed land and would open up an additional 11.6 million acres between 1980-82.[190]

In part, this latter goal would be achieved by enabling farmers (small and large) to insure the cost of their crops for 100% of value rather than the previous 70%. Subsidies of 75% would be offered on improved seeds and 30% subsidies would be offered on insecticides and fertilizers.[191] Guaranteed prices for a number of products would be boosted 50% such as in the case of corn and beans and credit would be made more readily available.

The system of incentives contained within SAM sought to
foster increased local content and increased employment although
production rather than employment remained the principal goal.
Within the food processing sector, companies would be eligible
for incentives only if their products had 100% local content, if
they were able to demonstrate that they had attempted to boost
productivity and if they had a high labor factor (normally, the
latter two features are mutually exclusive and no explanation
was provided as to how this issue would be resolved.) Further,
to qualify for incentives, these producers would have to demonstrate that they had given preference in providing supplies to
CONASUPO, union stores and other state agencies that sell to
consumers.

Among agro-industrial suppliers, qualification for incentives was to be based upon 70% Mexican content, exports equivalent to 50% of raw materials imports and the payment of fees
for transfers of technology in the area of basic engineering
only. Within the non-food agricultural industry, qualification
was to be determined according to the labor factor and to
linkages to local producers.[192]

Small producers would qualify almost automatically but would
be required to demonstrate linkages with local farmers,[193] or
that they were involved in the production of strategic goods.
SAM had also built into it incentives for the simplification of
packaging and the addition of vitamins and nutrients to foods.

As part of the overall strategy of rural development, the
Secretariat of Human Affairs and Public Works (SAHOP) initiated
efforts to grapple with the problem of dispersed rural populations, and efforts complementing plans to establish decentralized
agro-industry and to speed the concentration of land holding.
SAHOP plans called for initial creation of 3,250 new seats of
development in the countryside to be populated by the residents
of 90,000 small communities formerly dispersed throughout the
countryside. Each polo or development site was to be equipped
with adequate infrastructure and employment opportunities to
serve the population.[194]

Another major feature of the program was the improvement of
the food and basic goods distribution system. By providing
reliable and affordable supplies of basic goods, the state would
attempt to change the Mexican diet (e.g., Mexico has the highest
per capita consumption of soft drinks in the world) which, it is
argued, has been distorted by TNCs. Furthemore, the state would
use media campaigns and education to alter dietary patterns.[195]

Under SAM, the distribution network would be based upon a
program of subsidies to all products within the "Recommended
Basic Marketbasket." The state had moved during the sexenio to
assure adequate supplies of basic goods beginning with the
National Program of Basic Products created in January of 1977.
The initial program provided that producers of basic goods, in
voluntary agreements with the Secretary of Commerce, would
accept price ceilings established through negotiations on 90
basic goods, guarantee quantity and supply to specific regions,
and accept Conasupo marketing and distribution assistance

(through its 2,000 urban and 4,000 rural retail outlets) in exchange for a variety of subsidies, and credit at favorable rates.[196]

The program fared badly, however, as was noted earlier in the poor performance of wage goods' growth, chiefly because subsidies were insufficient, in the eyes of the producers, to offset price ceilings and because workers' limited purchasing power, which had declined substantially throughout the sexenio, had shrunk the market. The government's policy of increasing subsidies to somewhat offset losses experienced by workers at or near the minimum wage proved unsuccessful in this regard. The no-frills "Alianza" brand that the state had introduced in 1979 under the Basic Products Program had failed to grow to the extent hoped for due to the reluctance of suppliers to cooperate.

In a reaction to this failure, the state established several programs to remedy the problem. In 1980, it established the Fund to Guarantee and Promote Production, Distribution and Consumption of Basic Products. The SCHP established a Financial Commission for support of Basic Products. The state also upgraded its program of tax credits for basic goods producers to mitigate employment costs, equipment purchases and product distribution costs,[197] all of which were designed to allow the producer to circumvent price ceilings with the state absorbing the cost.

The original Alianza brand agreement of 1979 called for participating companies to reserve 25% of their production for state marketing agencies. In the revised agreement of 1980, CONASUPO, Grupo SOMEX (mixed state-private participation) and Mexican majority owned producers agreed to expand production in exchange for the previously detailed benefits. The state provided new guarantees for the supply of raw materials[198] that were increasingly problematic in the oil-heated economy where production had fallen short of demand and bottlenecks continuously delayed available supplies. Plans called for an 8% per annum growth rate in wage goods during the early 1980s.[199]

The distribution system would rest fundamentally upon Distribuidora CONASUPO (DICONSA), the rural arm of CONASUPO which sold goods at a 35% discount from normal prices. Plans called for DICONSA facilities to reach 60% of the rural population in the early 1980s with 10,000 small stores (tiendas rather than almacenes.)[200] This would mean that approximately 1,361 persons would be served by each tienda, clearly a remarkable feat. Planners maintained that with 14,000 stores, DICONSA could reach all of the rural population in villages of over 500 persons.[201]

The management of the rural development and basic goods projects would be reliant upon a complex and sometimes competitive network of bureaucratic empires. The fishing industry, for example, would be overseen by a new state Commission for the Promotion and Development of Fishing, established in 1980, which would aid in the operation and modernization in the industry and would foster the establishment of fishing cooperatives. This commission would in turn be overseen by the National Bank for

Fishing and Ports.202 Rural development programs would be
managed by COPLAMAR, the General Coordinating Body for the
National Plan for Depressed Zones and Marginal Groups, which had
been established in 1977. COPLAMAR would cooperate with another
coordinating mechanism and revenue sharing program203 designed
to encourage federal-state cooperation, the United Agreement on
Coordination (CUC) that had absorbed PIDER, the Integrated
Program for Rural Development initiated under the Echeverría
administration,204 and the Distritos de Temporal established in
1977 to assist the much neglected rain-fed areas. COPLAMAR, CUC,
SAHOP and CONASUPO would also cooperate with SAHR, the principal
SAM administrator, as well as with other large institutions such
as the Mexican Social Security Institute (IMSS). In fact, however, local management committees within SAM would be totally
within the province of the SAHR. SAHR was charged with setting
production goals, crop mix, price supports, distribution and
marketing needs and for setting goals for agro-industry. In all,
the implementation of the program along with the development of
plans that were sufficiently technicallly specific were certain
to remain problematic.

In its first evaluation of SAM, the state concluded that
efforts had been inadequate during the first stage. Price guarantees would be strengthened, producers of agricultural capital
goods such as tractors and other farm machinery would be required
to guarantee 22% annual growth in production, fertilizer production would be increased, and finally, 31 state subcommittees
would be created in order to coordinate production, processing,
distribution and consumption.205 Further, the system of incentives for SAM and basic goods production was overhauled, increasing subsidies to producers.

The state's intention to abandon the hallowed article of
faith of the Mexican Revolution, that of land redistribution,
(which it announced would be completed by 1981!) and to restructure the ejido system invoked the wrath of the Mexican Labor Confederation (CTM) and the major peasant organization, the CNC.206
However, despite this opposition, the state proceeded with its
plans, arguing that the scheme was intended to revitalize the
relationship of the state with the peasantry.207 In this
instance, "revitalization" meant that as a response to contradictions within the development model, the state had embarked
upon an effort to complete the transformation of the peasantry
into a rural proletariat, to restructure the system of land
holding among smallholders, and to increase production in order,
ultimately, to defend the gains achieved through oil development
in the industrial sector.

In the period 1980-82, agricultural and rural development,
the Global Plan estimated, would receive 17% of oil revenues.
Spending in these areas, compared with the early years of the
sexenio, increased from 8.4% of total public sector spending in
1978 to 12.5% in 1981 and 13.8% in 1982.208 The share of public
investment for this period would climb from 13.5% during 1967-76
to 19.3% in the period 1977-79, and finally to 22.4% during the
early 1980s. The oil revenues thus both facilitated the state's

new initiatives and also in a real sense, pushed the state to confront continuing contradictions. Planning for the rural sector continued to fall short of providing a convincing solution to the problem of rural un/underemployment despite increased spending. As Wayne Cornelius noted:

> While this new emphasis on rain-fed agriculture will certainly help to achieve the government's objective of national self-sufficiency in basic food grains, the investments in this sector are not expected to generate much new permanent employment.[209]

In an abrupt turnabout, the de la Madrid government terminated SAM in early 1983 in a testament to the failure of the program to achieve meaningful results.[210] With food grain imports put a 8.5 million tons in 1983, four times the amount imported in 1982, state enthusiasm for the program had diminished considerably.[211] Plans called for a renewal of commitment to integrated rural development although this was virtually the same goal that had been identified at the time that SAM was put into place. For that matter, the need for integrated rural development was hardly a new idea even in terms of SAM planning. Ultimately, neither oil nor increased state sector activity had contributed to the development of solutions for the agricultural sector.

The State and Labor

Indicative of the degree to which the state had failed to address the problem of unemployment was the fact that by 1981, it could still be said: "There are no official, national-level statistics on unemployment in Mexico."[212] The Third National Congress of Economists concluded that by 1977, under and unemployment had reached 57%,[213] a figure close to the Ministry of Labor's 1978 figure of 57.2%.[214] Yet for the most part, the state continued to discuss unemployment only in terms of the so-called "modern sector" and thus could state that "unemployment" had "dropped" in Mexico from 8.7% in 1977 to 5.8% in 1979 and to 4% in 1981.[215] While some progress had in fact been seen in the urban industrial unemployment picture during the period of the oil boom, with shortages of skilled labor plaguing the sector by 1980, little progress was seen in ameliorating the overall employment problem. The collapse of 1982 in fact brought unemployment back to an 8% level according to the state's statistics.[216]

With an estimated demand for 31-33 million new jobs by the year 2000, if new job seekers and those already un/underempoyed were to be provided with employment opportunities, the economy would have to produce approximately 1.65 million new jobs per year for the next 20 years to keep pace.[217] The state, however,

did little to provide plans during the course of the _sexenio_ that
would in any way address this problem. As in the past, the state
continued to embrace the notion that fast growth _per se_ could
solve the employment problem. Typifying this approach was the
statement by José Andrés de Oteyza that "The challenge we face is
to raise our growth rate to 9% or 10% for a period of 10 years.
Then there will be a reasonable prospect of solving the unemployment problem by the 1990s."[218]

The National Employment Plan of 1978, as well as the 1979
Industrial Development Plan provided for special support for
small and medium-sized industry located in decentralized areas
with a view toward increasing employment opportunities. The NIDP
opted for fairly low growth rates in employment, however, (2.4%
--below the growth rate of the labor force) in the belief that
employment increases to be derived from the fast growth track
would be superior to any that would be achieved through special
programs specifying employment gains as their principal goal.
According to a critique of the NIDP published by _Comercio
Exterior_, the plan:

> ...(did) not guarantee in any mechanical form the massive
> absorption of workers nor (did) it assure the achievment
> of an improved standard of living for the bulk of the
> population... Moreover, the high composition of organic
> capital that in all probability will characterize the
> industrial sector and the determination salary level
> will assure a profit level that will further the gap
> between profits and wages.[219]

Thus, early planning during the _sexenio_ for development in the
most dynamic growth sector included little in the way of guarantees for increased employment and set the stage for growth in
the disparity between returns to labor and capital in the production process.

Employment growth fell far short of the 1.65 million jobs
per year required by the labor force. According to figures presented by López Portillo in his Fourth Report to the Nation, 4
million jobs were created between 1978 and 1981.[220] During this
period, employment in the "modern" sector grew at an average annual rate of 5.4%, dropping to 0.8% in 1982. Hardest hit in 1982
were the construction, manufacturing and agricultural sectors.[221]
The contraction of 1982 was so serious that the state moved to
put an emergency employment program into place for 1983 and 1984.
The state sought to create 500-700,000 jobs in 1983 and 400,000
for 1984.[222]

According to tentative estimates, the private sector accounted for 74% of new employment in 1978 and 60% in 1979,[223]
despite the tremendous growth in state sector spending. Between
1978 and 1982, Pemex employment rose by 79%, reaching a figure of
125,000 which accounted for only a small share of public employment. Of the employment growth in the public sector, much occurred in the construction sector and involved only temporary employment, although these jobs were counted as permanent new

sources of employment. Similarly, much of Pemex's "new" employment was really of a temporary nature involving construction. The fact that employment growth in the petroleum industry was minimal is consistent with the intrinsic capital intensivity of this industry. On balance, despite a temporary improvement in the employment picture, the erosion seen beginning in 1982 suggested that the state had not succeeded in arriving at a permanent solution to the employment problem, particularly in the agricultural sector.

The state's incomes policy continued to place heavy burdens on wage earners during the sexenio. Despite the new oil wealth, income to labor continued its decline in real terms. Following a 25% decline in real wages during the period 1974-76,[224] wages continued their downward spiral. Between 1976 and 1979, the average minimum wage rose by 35% (the minimum wage affects only approximately 48% of the work force) while prices rose by about 60%. By 1979, the labor component of production costs had fallen to its lowest point since the 1960s, reaching only 13.7% of total costs.[225] For these not protected by the minimum wage or unemployed, living conditions had become even more precarious than for salaried workers as a result of the "boom."

Data for the early 1980s showed that the situation had continued to worsen. In 1980, the minimum wage experience a minimum 10.3% drop in real value [226] (with the minimum wage in the industrial sector faring a bit better). In 1981, the minimum wage again fell below the consumer price index.[227] Although the 1982 devaluations were compensated by emergency increases in the minimum wage, there was little certainty as to how many workers had received the mandated compensation.[228]

At the beginning of the sexenio, labor had agreed to curb wage demands, limiting them to 10% in the context of the Alliance for Production.[229] In 1980, with the state still clinging to a minimum wage increase of 21.5% while inflation raged at 30%, the CTM finally broke ranks and its leader Fidel Velázquez announced "the policy of wage moderation is now finished."[230] The CTM quickly reversed its position, however, and approved the state's guidelines,[231] reflecting the near total control exercised by the state over labor leadership.

Workers, however, despite the acquiescence of their leadership, were not swayed by the panaceas offered by the state such as tax breaks and promises regarding control of the prices of basic goods. Instead, they repeatedly resorted to work stoppages and the number of strikes rose during the late 1970s[232] and early 1980s.[233] In one sector where strikes were resorted to, it was estimated that white collar employees had seen real wages drop 64% between 1976-1983 and that the loss was substantially worse for blue collar workers.[234]

The oil development program pursued by the state thus afforded the private sector tremendous profit-taking opportunities but did little in the short term to benefit the mass of the Mexican population either in terms of income or employment opportunities. Even in the longer term prospect, and even before the financial collapse of 1982, it was difficult to discern any major

Table 4-17

Evolution of the Minimum Wage, 1976-1979

	General Minimum Wage Index	Consumer Price Index	Index of Real Wages
1976			
October	100	100	100.0
December	100	107.1	93.4
1977			
January	110	110.5	99.5
July	110	120.5	91.3
December	110	129.3	85.1
1978			
January	125.5	132.1	95.0
July	125.5	142.5	88.1
December	125.5	150.2	83.6
1979			
January	146.6	155.4	94.3
July	146.6	167.3	87.6
December	146.6	181.7	80.7

Source: "Salarios mínimos 1980," Comercio Exterior, v.30, n.1 (enero de 1980), Table 2, p.24.

170

benefits that would accrue to the mass of the population. Certainly, employment was boosted in the industrial sector but then only for skilled workers. Even these relatively better off individuals continued to see real income shrinking at the same time that tremendous new wealth was being accumulated in the society. Even for automobile workers, the return to labor in terms of salaries diminished by 1980 over the share commanded in 1970.[235]

Oil revenues afforded the state the opportunity to apply band-aids to the open wound in the form of tinkering with tax schedules, basic goods programs and investment in small and medium-sized industry, but oil revenues have precipitated only marginally encouraging signs in the area of employment and outright deterioration in income to labor. The state's relationship with labor remained static during the period with the exception of the still to be specified "superior form of labor organization" that would be created in rural areas. With the exception of this innovation, the evidence suggests that the traditional labor-state relationship was maintained during the period of the oil development project.

A Final Note on the State and the Private Sector

The private sector's attitude toward state sector activities was divided although the largest and most politically influential financial grupos appeared to support the thrust of the state's development project and complied with the investment priorities designated by the state. Yet there was criticism.

After an early honeymoon period between the state and the private sector brought about by the pro-business "Alliance for Production,"[236] criticism of the expansion of the state was seen. The employer's organization COPARMEX accused the state of orchestrating a "Marxist inspired attack on private enterprise,"[237] principally through its extension of the state food and basic goods marketing agency CONASUPO (long a favorite whipping boy of conservatives despite its 5% share of national food distribution). At the same time, however, the criticism was far from unanimous with Prudencio López, president of the Businessmen's Coordinating Council (CCE), the preeminent private sector representative, acclaiming the Global Plan, 1980-82 as "the first major effort at the integral rationalization of the economy."[238]

A survey conducted among Mexico's industrial elites demonstrated a high degree of satisfaction with the López Portillo government's policies. 82.2% of the CANACINTRA sample respondents and 92.6% of the CONCAMIN sample respondents regarded state policies as favorable to the industrial sector.[239]

From other quarters, Bernardo Garza Sada of the huge Monterrey Garza-Sada industrial dynasty, maintained that such criticism of the government as that by COPARMEX was unwarranted. Instead, he maintained that he was not concerned about the burgeoning nature of state activities.[240] As one Alfa executive put it:

...the federal government here has tremendous power.

They have a huge machinery of economic forces to determine the tempo, the pace of the economy. It's just a
matter of convenience to move in the direction the
government wants you to.[241]

Such equanimity in the face of state activism, of course, is
spawned by the nature of government-business relationship. The
state's activities are ultimately designed to insure the continuous reproduction of the economic order. The representatives
of what J.K. Galbraith would call the "planning" sector understand the state's efforts to confront systemic contradictions and
applaud this activity as long as it is conducted within accepted
parameters. During the late 1970s, and very early in the
1980s, surely only a fleeting moment historically, oil did
provide the state with some leeway although never approximating
the dimensions envisioned early on. The state was able to pursue
necessary investment without jeopardizing the private sector's
access to capital and while pursuing a policy of massive subsidy
to private business interests. By 1982, however, the picture
would change dramatically.

Conclusion

Oil in fact did lead to a strengthening of the state capitalist form in Mexico, initially through enhanced oil revenues
and later through the nationalization of the banking system in
1982. In the areas of planning, investment and production, the
state expanded its activities and in the area of labor mediation,
the state maintained its earlier preeminent position in the urban
sector and attempted to exert greater control in the primary
sector through the establishment of new forms of labor organization.
Because of the continued weakness and dependence of the
national entrepreneurial class, the state expanded upon its
previous activities and sought to rationalize its activities as a
means of strengthening its position in order to successfully
manage the oil development project and the industrial revitalization project. At the same time, the state moved to address (to
the extent that the internal logic of the model allows) the
problem of stagnation in the primary sector. While it may be
argued that such efforts were hardly novel (witness the series
of collectivization schemes attempted as far back as the Cárdenas
period and as recently as the Echeverría administration)[242] oil
enabled the state to pursue these activities more aggressively
and in a tremendously expanded form.
In the initial period, oil enabled the state to once again
exercise a degree of relative or instrumental autonomy necessary
to initiate a revitalization of the industrial development
project. The new resource did not, however, lead as some would
have predicted, to the emancipation of the state sector from its
relationship with the dominant capitalist class, or the creation
of a new "class fraction" acting independently and pursuing goals
that diverged from previous practice. Instead, the development

model pursued by the newly energized state adhered to the classic
outlines of associated dependent development:
- increasing disparity between income flowing to labor and
  capital,
- continued marginalization of large sectors of the population,
- continued recourse to foreign technology and direct
  foreign investment to serve as the motor of industrialization,
- continued recourse to foreign financing and rising indebtness.

To rephrase Cardoso's litmus test of dependency, the Mexican
elites embarked upon a development project whose essential
dynamic component lay outside of the system. We say this for two
reasons.

First: The project was based upon the earning of foreign
exchange from the export of a primary product used to acquire
capital goods and technology required by the industrial project.

Second: The commitment to an export-led form of industrialization required that:

A) The industrial plant be competitive with other world
   class producers and thus had to rely upon imported technology to guarantee this competitiveness inasmuch as
   domestic technology and capital goods production were
   inadequate.

B) The economy conform to the contemporary international
   division of labor (aside from the export of unrefined
   primary products such as oil) that relegates industrial
   processes no longer profitably operated in the developed
   countries to the semi-industrialized countries. Thus,
   the industries that were logically pursued (based upon
   the availability of technologies and the feasibility of
   market access) were essentially externally determined.

C) Despite the favorable size (approximately 130 million
   persons by the year 2000) of a potential Mexican domestic market--a size that could easily support a substantial internally directed industrial plant, the Mexican
   industrial infrastructure continued to be developed in
   conformity with the consumer profiles and technological
   requirements of external economies.

In sum, then, the oil-based strengthening of the state meant
the strengthening of the commitment by the dominant classes to
the already well established model of development, a commitment
that would provoke financial catastrophe.

NOTES

[1]Fagen, "The Realities of U.S. Mexican Relations," p.698.

[2]E.V.K. Fitzgerald, "Stabilisation Policy in Mexico: The Fiscal Deficit and Macroeconomic Equilibrium 1960-77," in Inflation and Stabilisation in Latin America, ed. by Rosemary Thorp and Laurence Whitehead, (London: Macmillan Press Ltd., 1979), p.58.

[3]José López Portillo, "Tercer Informe," Hispano, pp.12-13.

[4]Secretaría de Programación y Presupuesto, Plan Global de Desarrollo 1980-1982 (Mexico: 1980), Vol. 1, p.35.

[5]Miguel de la Madrid Hurtado, "La regulación de la empresa pública en México," p.216.

[6]Marcos Kaplan, "Aspectos políticos de la planificación en América Latina," Problemas del Desarrollo, n.6 (enero-marzo de 1971), cited in Jose Luis Cecena Cervantes, Introducción a la Economia Política de la Planificación Económica Nacional (Mexico City: Fondo de Cultura Económica, 1975), p.25.

[7]Cecena Cervantes, p.25.

[8]E.V.K. Fitzgerald, "A New Direction in Economic Policy?" Bank of London and South America Review, v.12, n.10/78 (October, 1978), p.532.

[9]Grayson, The Politics of Mexican Oil, p.127.

[10]Ibid.

[11]Fitzgerald, "A New Direction in Economic Policy?" pp.532-533. See also John J. Bailey, "Presidency, Bureaucracy and Administrative Reform in Mexico: The Secretariat of Programming and Budget, Interamerican Economic Affairs, v.34, n.1 (Summer, 1980), pp.27-59.

[12]Humberto S. Tapia, Mexico's Basic Government Plan: History Focus and Future, (Tempe, AZ: State University, Center for Latin American Studies, 1976).

[13]Bailey, p.43.

[14]Chumacero, pp.580-594.

[15]Plan Global de Desarrollo 1980-1982, vol. 1, p.7.

[16]Ibid., pp.102-103.

174

[17] "Social Cuts and Oil Wealth Ease Mexican State Finances," Latin America Economic Report, v.VII, n.27 (13 July, 1979), p.213.

[18] Latin America Weekly Report, (14 December, 1979), p.77.

[19] Bank of London and South America Review, v.II, 10/77, (October, 1977), p.556.

[20] "Fragmento del Discurso Pronunciado por el Licenciado Gustavo Romero Kolbeck, Director-General del Banco de México, S.A.," Boletín de Indicadores Económicos Internacionales, v.IV, n.1, (enero-marzo de 1978), p.33.

[21] Looney, Mexico. A Policy Analysis, p.135.

[22] "Mexico's New Strategy Begins to Take Shape: Slow Recovery Seen," Commerce America, v.III, n.1, (January 2, 1978), p.17.

[23] Fitzgerald, "A New Direction in Economic Policy?" p.23.

[24] Mexico: National Industrial Development Plan, Volumes One and Two, (London: Graham & Trotman Ltd., 1979).

[25] David Ibarra Munoz cited in "Mexico. Crisis of Poverty/ Crisis of Wealth," Los Angeles Times, p.11.

[26] Rocío de Villarreal and René Villarreal, "Public Enterprises in Mexican Development Under the Oil Perspective in the 1980s," Paper presented at the Second BAPEG Conference "Public Enterprise in Mixed Economy LDCs," Austin, Texas, University of Texas, 1980, p.1.

[27] José Andrés de Oteyza, "El petróleo permitira un crecimiento económico del 10%: Oteyza," Excelsior, (17 de noviembre de 1978), p.27.

[28] Bank of London and South America Review, v.12, n.2/78, (February, 1978), pp.95-96.

[29] "Los objetivos del Plan Industrial," Comercio Exterior, v.29, n.5 (mayo de 1979), p.520.

[30] "Mexico Unveils Ten-Year Industrial Development Plan," Latin America Economic Report, v.VII, n.27 (13 July, 1979).

[31] "Mexico's Industrial Plan Plots the Course of a Daring Bid for Growth," Business Latin America, (April 11, 1979), pp. 117-119 and "López Portillo Stresses Aggressive Growth for Mexican Economy," Business Latin America, (September 5, 1979), pp.28-34.

[32] Francisco Javier Alejo, "Las empresas públicas y el

Plan Industrial," El Economista Mexicano, v.XIII, n.6 (noviembre-diciembre de 1979), pp.28-29.

[33]"Mexico: An Amazing Economy that Keeps on Booming,"
Fortune, (June 16, 1980), pp.44-45.

[34]Alejo, p.29.

[35]Mexico: National Industrial Development Plan, Volume
One, Table 1, p.111.

[36]"Mexico Takes New Weapon to Fight Anti-Inflation Battle,"
Latin America Economic Report, v.VII, n.4 (26 January, 1979),
p.30; "Higher Interest Rates Spell Credit Squeeze in Mexico,"
Latin America Economic Report, v.VII, n.33 (24 August, 1979),
p.258; Morgan Guaranty Trust, World Financial Markets, (June,
1979), p.11; "Mexican Cement Plan Trades Lavish Incentives
for Production Gains," Business Latin America, (July 16, 1980),
pp.230-231.

[37]Banco de México, "La actividad económica en 1982,"
Comercio Exterior, v.33, n.5, (mayo de 1983), Table 2, p.463.

[38]"Documento: Plan Global de Desarrollo, 1980-1982," SPP
Comercio Exterior, v.30, n.4, (abril de 1980), p.370.

[39]Ibid.

[40]Plan Global de Desarrollo 1980-1982, Vol.1, p.97.

[41]Ibid., p.173.

[42]Ibid., p.152.

[43]Ibid., p.117.

[44]Ibid.

[45]Riding, "The Mixed Blessings of Mexico's Oil," New York
Times Magazine, p.24.

[46]Comercio Exterior, v.29, n.5, (mayo de 1979), p.526.

[47]Plan Global de Desarrollo, 1980-1982, p.83.

[48]Poder Ejecutivo Federal, Plan Nacional de Desarrollo
1983-1988, Suplemento de Comercio Exterior, v.33, n.6, (junio de
1983), p.137.

[49]"La actividad económica en 1982."

[50]Bela Balassa, "Trade Policy in Mexico," World Development, v.11, n.9 (September, 1983), p.805.

176

[51]"The Rising Sun of the Americas," <u>Latin America Weekly Report</u>, (10 April, 1981), p.9. Also see <u>Plan Global 1980-1982</u>, <u>Vol.2</u>, p.22, for this line of analysis.

[52]"Latin American Investment Outlook Bright," Chase Manhattan Bank, <u>International Finance</u>, v.XV, n.23 (November 24, 1980), p.8.

[53]IDB, <u>Economic and Social Progress in Latin America, The External Sector, 1982 Report</u>, (Washington D.C.: 1982),p.283.

[54]Bueno, p.284.

[55]"La economía en cifras definitivas," <u>Comercio Exterior</u>, v.33, n.10 (octubre de 1983), Table 3, p.904 and "La actividad económica en 1982," p.461.

[56]<u>Plan Nacional de Desarrollo 1983-1988</u>, p.40.

[57]<u>Ibid</u>., p.71.

[58]
<u>Ibid</u>., p.38. A leading economist claimed in 1980, that Mexico was committing only 0.2% of GDP to science and technology and that this figure included the social sciences and humanities. See Victor L. Urquidi, "Planeación de la ciencia y tecnología," <u>Comercio Exterior</u>, v.30, n.11 (noviembre de 1980), p.1242.

[59]Martínez and López Tijerina, p.47.

[60]Fitzgerald, "Capital Accumulation in Mexico," p.411.

[61]"Spending the Cash is Hard too," <u>Economist</u>, (February 1, 1979), p.90.

[62]<u>Ibid</u>.

[63]"Mexico. Crisis of Poverty/Crisis of Wealth," p.12.

[64]"Mexico Takes Action to Revitalize Sluggish Stock Market," <u>Business Latin America</u>, (January 14, 1981), p.11. Also see "Capital Goods Decree Highlights Mexico's Shift to More Liberal Incentives," <u>Business Latin America</u>, (February 21, 1979), p.64.

[65]Villarreal and Villarreal, p.47.

[66]Rosario Green, "Mexico: crisis financiera y deuda externa," <u>Comercio Exterior</u>, v.33, n.2, (febrero de 1983), Table 1, p.105.

[67]Morgan Guaranty, <u>World Financial Markets</u>, "International

Lending: Implications of a Slowdown," (October, 1982), Table 2, p.3.

[68] Ibid., Table 1, p.3.

[69] "La actividad económica en 1982," p.405.

[70] "Mexicans Attend Investment Seminar," Journal of Commerce, (March 28, 1980), ISLA, v.20, n.3 (March, 1980), p.34.

[71] IDB, Economic and Social Progress in Latin America, 1982 Report, p.285.

[72] Green, "Mexico: crisis financiera y deuda externa," p.102.

[73] Ibid., p.103.

[74] "Documento: Política fiscal y financiera para 1982," SHCP y SPP, Comercio Exterior, v.32, n.2, (febrero de 1982), p.187.

[75] José López Portillo, "Tercer Informe," Hispano, p.12.

[76] IDB, Economic and Social Progress in Latin America, 1982 Report, p.284.

[77] Plan Nacional de Desarrollo 1983-1988, pp.40-41.

[78] Ibid.

[79] IDB, Economic and Social Progress in Latin America, 1980-81 Report, TAble 3, p.400.

[80] "Aspectos financieros del sector presupuestario en 1979," p.938.

[81] "La inflación, el cascabel y el gato," p.1067.

[82] "Mexico. Not by Oil Alone," p.16, and Villarreal and Villarreal, p.30.

[83] Wall Street Journal, (May 16, 1980), p.47.

[84] "LP Speech Avows Bold Course but Sidesteps Problems," Business Latin America, (September 10, 1980), p.260.

[85] "Profitability Soars for Firms in Mexico Despite Operating Woes," Business Latin America, (August 20, 1980), p.269.

[86] Riding, "The Mixed Blessings of Mexico's Oil," p.25.

[87] "El comportamiento de la economía mexicana durante

1980," p.326.

[88]Ibid.

[89]Ibid.

[90]Plan Nacional de Desarrollo 1983-1988, p.41.

[91]Ibid., p.136

[92]Ibid., p.39.

[93]Ibid., p.136.

[94]Olga Pellicer de Brody,"Consideraciones acerca de la política comercial de Estados Unidos hacia Mexico," Comercio Exterior, v.30, n.10 (octubre de 1980), pp.1114-1120.

[95]Laura Randall, "Mexican Development and its Effects Upon United States Trade," in Mexico and the United States, ed. by Robert H. McBride (Englewood Cliffs, N.J.: Prentice-Hall, 1981), p.49.

[96]Fitzgerald, "A New Direction in Economic Policy?", p.534.

[97]"Focus on Mexico: Rosy Prospects Don't Obscure Need for Careful Treading," Business Latin America, (April 25, 1979), p.131.

[98]"No somos Suicidas: Inversión externa con soberania, JLP," Excelsior, (1 de noviembre de 1978), p.1.

[99]James L. Srodes, "Mexico: Is It as Good as It Looks?" Financial World, (March 15, 1979), p.54.

[100]Ibid., pp.56 and 98.

[101]"Stock Exchange Set for a Larger Slice of the Capital Market," Latin America Weekly Report, (20 February, 1981), p.6.

[102]"U.S. Investment in Latin America Slows Growth Pace but Boosts Profits," Business Latin America, (November 12, 1980), pp.364-366.

[103]"Mexico: An Amazing Economy that Keeps on Booming," p.47.

[104]8.2 figure from Riding, "The Mixed Blessings of Mexico's Oil," p.25; 10 billion figure from Latin America Weekly Report, (6 March, 1981), p.7.

[105]"Latin American Investment Outlook Bright," p.8.

[106] Eduardo Basualdo, "Tendencia de la transnacionalización en América Latina durante el decenio de los setenta," Comercio Exterior, v.32, n.7, (Julio de 1982), Table 7, p.760.

[107] Latin America Weekly Report, (16 May, 1980).

[108] Roger Boyes, "Mexico Seeks W. German Links," Financial Times, (May 21, 1980), ISLA, v.20, n.5, (1980), p.3.

[109] "Mexico's Reluctant Oil Boom," p.70.

[110] Business Latin America, (August 27, 1980), p.277.

[111] "En Japón, presencia mexicana," Visión, (5 de mayo de 1980), pp.36-38.

[112] Latin America Economic Report, v.VI, n.39, (October 6, 1978), p.311.

[113] "Mexican Businessmen Urge Japanese Firms to Increase Investment," Business Latin America, (November 7, 1979), pp.359-360.

[114] "Plant Equipment Spending by U.S. Affiliates in Region Slated for 11% Rise in 1980," pp.12-13.

[115] "Two Bullish Groups Offer JV Possibilities for Firms in Mexico," Business Latin America, (May 28, 1980), pp.174-176.

[116] "Mexico's ALFA and VISA Beckon the Attention of Expansion Minded Firms," Business Latin America, (March 28, 1979), pp.98-99.

[117] "Mexico. An Amazing Economy that Keeps on Booming."

[118] Comercio Exterior, v.30, n.11, (noviembre de 1980), p.1207.

[119] William Chislett, "Ohira Plans May Visit to Mexico to Boost Oil Supply," Financial Times, (March 31, 1980), ISLA, v.20, n.3, (March, 1980), p.11.

[120] Comercio Exterior, v.30, n.6, (junio de 1980), p.553.

[121] "Mexico Broadens Economic Ties," Business Latin America, (June 4, 1980), p.179.

[122] Latin America Weekly Report, (5 December, 1980), p.6 and Alan Riding, "Mexico Drawing Foreign Hotels," New York Times, (May 6, 1980).

[123] The Banker, (April, 1979), p.89.

180

[124] "Mexico. Automakers Flock to a Surging Market," Business Week, (July 2, 1979), p.32-33.

[125] "Auto Plants Sprout in the Mexican Sun," Industry Week, (May 12, 1980), pp.51-55.

[126] Richard E. Feinberg,"Bureaucratic Organization and United States Policy Toward Mexico," in Mexico-United States Relations, ed. by Susan Kaufman Purcell, p.33.

[127] Héctor Islas, "La industria automovilística: un repaso general," Comercio Exterior, v.33, n.3, (marzo de 1983), Table 10, p.228.

[128] "Mexico. Auto-makers Flock to a Surging Market," p.33. Ramón Martínez Escamilla, "México, Explotación petrolera e ideología dominante," Problemas del Desarrollo, v.X, n.37, (febrero-abril, 1979), p.162.

[129] "Documento: La evolución económica de México en 1978, CEPAL," p.788.

[130] Bennett and Sharpe, "Transnational Corporations and the Political Economy of Export Promotion: The Case of the Mexican Automobile Industry," International Organization, v.33, n.2, (Spring, 1979), p.186.

[131] "Little Detroits Bloom in Mexico," New York Times, (March 3, 1980), p.D-11.

[132] Journal of Commerce, (March 29, 1980), ISLA, v.20, n.3, p.29.

[133] "Mexico Moves to Ease Production Constraints on Automobile Industry," Business Latin America, (October 22, 1980), pp.340-341.

[134] "Mexico's Auto Parts Plan Lays Out Incentives/Goals to Spur Sector's Advances," Business Latin America, (February 6, 1980), p.43.

[135] "Auto Plants Sprout in the Mexican Sun," pp.51-55; American Machinist, (July, 1979), p.35.

[136] "U.S. Business Pumping Huge Sums Into Mexico, " Los Angeles Times, (February 11, 1980).

[137] Ibid. LTD sales (considered the preferred luxury car in the market) jumped 26.4% in 1979 and Mustang (a preferred sport model) sales jumped 74% in the domestic market.

[138] "Ford Finds a Place at Court in Land Where the Gas Guzzler is King," p.6.

[139]"U.S. Business Pumping Huge Sums Into Mexico."

[140]"Mexico. Auto-makers Flock to a Surging Market," pp.32-33.

[141]"Mexico. Not By Oil Alone," p.50.

[142]"Mexico," Business Latin America, (August 27, 1980), pp.276-277.

[143]"Mexico. Not By Oil Alone," p.50.

[144]Héctor Islas, "Una industria en busca de soluciones: la automovilística," Comercio Exterior, v.33, n.11, (noviembre de 1983), Table 1, p.991.

[145]Ibid., p.992.

[146]Ibid., Table 1, p.991.

[147]Ibid., p.998.

[148]Ibid., p.991.

[149]"Mexico Tries to Promote More Vigorous Activity in Border and Free Zones," Business Latin America, (December 6 1978), pp.391-392.

[150]McClelland, p.3.

[151]Chislett, "Waiting for the Giant to Sneeze."

[152]McClelland, p.9.

[153]"Little Detroits Boom in Mexico," p.D-1.

[154]"Mexican Development Plan Raises a Red Flag for Pharmaceutical Firms," Business Latin America,(May 14, 1980), pp.153-154; "Mexico Seeks to Set 51% Domestic Holdings in Drug Firms There," Wall Street Journal, (May 8, 1980).

[155]Latin America Weekly Report, (2 May, 1980), p.5

[156]Plan Nacional de Desarrollo 1983-1988, p.83.

[157]Ibid., p.84.

[158]Ibid., p.81.

[159]Wayne Cornelius, "Immigration, Development Policy, and Future U.S.-Mexican Relations, " in Mexico and the United States, ed. by McBride, p.108.

182

[160] *Latin America Economic Report*, v.VII, n.20, (25 May, 1979), p.157.

[161] *Plan Global de Desarrollo*, 1980-1982, p.34.

[162] "El SAM, principio de una estrategía," *Comercio Exterior*, v.30, n.7 (julio de 1980), p.686. Also see Cassio Luiselli, *The Mexican Food System: Elements of a Program of Accelerated Production of Basic Foodstuffs in Mexico*, Research Report No.22, Center for U.S.-Mexican Studies, University of California, San Diego, 1982.

[163] "El SAM, principio de una estrategía," *Comercio Exterior*, v.30, n.7, (julio de 1980), p.686.

[164] "Agricultural Development Bill to Get Food Programme Under Way," *Latin America Weekly Report*, (28 November, 1980), p.7.

[165] Homer Urias, La balanza de pagos en 1982," *Comercio Exterior*, v.33, n.5, (mayo de 1983), p.686.

[166] *Latin America Weekly Report*, (29 May, 1981), p.6.

[167] "Mexican Reform Questions Principle of Land Reform," *Latin America Economic Report*, v.VI, n.23, (16 June, 1978), pp.180-181; also see "Mexico Puts Pragmatism before Rhetoric on Land," p.276.

[168] *Ibid*.

[169] Merilee S. Grindle, *Official Interpretations of Rural Underdevelopment: Mexico in the 1970s*, Research Report No. 20, Center for U.S.-Mexican Studies, University of California, San Diego, 1981, p.25.

[170] Martin Luis Guzman Ferrer, "Alimentación y política económica," *El Economista Mexicano*, v.XII, n.5, (septiembre-octubre de 1978), p.7.

[171] "New Mexican Policy Opens Door to Agro-Industry," *Latin America Economic Report*, v.VII, n.20, (25 May, 1979), p.156.

[172] "Mexico's Financial Success Masks Structural Problems," p.284.

[173] "New Mexican Policy Opens Door to Agro-Industry."

[174] Economist Intelligence Unit, *Quarterly Economic Review of Mexico, Annual Supplement*, 1979, (London: 1979), p.8.

[175]Press release from the World Bank quoted in Corréo Económico, (6 de julio de 1978), p.4.

[176]"Mexico Gets Record Loan," New York Times, (July 11, 1980), p.D-9.

[177]Latin America Weekly Report, (13 February, 1981), p.7.

[178]"Mexico," Business Latin America, p.404.

[179]José López Portillo, "Tercer Informe," Hispano, p.17.

[180]José López Portillo, "Cuarto Informe," Comercio Exterior, p.1013; William Chislett, Sharing Out the Cake More Evenly," Financial Times, (May 13, 1980.)

[181]Comercio Exterior, v.29, n.4, (abril de 1979), p.396.

[182]"Mexico. Not by Oil Alone," p.33.

[183]Ibid., p.34.

[184]"El SAM, principio de una estrategía," p.684.

[185]Alan Riding, "Mexican President Emphasizes Farming," New York Times, (April 9, 1979), p.A-9.

[186]"18 de marzo, tres decisiones y un plan," Comercio Exterior, v.30, n.3 (marzo de 1980), pp.200-201.

[187]"Mexican Draft Law Firmly Backs Up Effort to Modernize Agriculture," Business Latin America, (November 12, 1980), pp.364-366.

[188]"El SAM, principio de una estrategía," p.686.

[189]"Global Plan Maps Out Social/Economic Path of Mexican Development," pp.137-138.

[190]"Mexico: Blueprint for the Future," Business Week, (November 24, 1980), p.29. Also see "Mexico Takes Major Step Toward Restructuring Its Agro-Industry," Business Latin America, (May 21, 1980), pp.161-162.

[191]"Mexico. Not by Oil Alone," p.34.

[192]"Mexico Gives Push to its Ambitious Plans for Agro-Industry," Business Latin America, (February 18, 1981), p.50.

[193]Ibid.

[194]Comercio Exterior, v.30, n.10, (octubre de 1980), p.1082.

184

[195] "El SAM, principio de una estrategia," p.687.

[196] Latin America Economic Report, Special supplement on Mexico, (March, 1977), p.9.

[197] "La inflación, el cascabel y el gato," pp.1068-1069.

[198] Business Latin America, (July 16, 1980), p.231.

[199] Plan Global de Desarrollo, 1980-1982, p.85.

[200] "El SAM, principio de una estrategia," p.687.

[201] "Utopia o panacea?" Visión, (19 de mayo de 1980), p.40.

[202] Comercio Exterior, v.30, n.11, (noviembre de 1980), p.1207.

[203] Cornelius, p.120.

[204] See Merilee S. Grindle, "Policy Change in an Authoritarian Regime," Journal of Interamerican Studies and World Affairs, v.19, n.4, (November, 1977), pp.523-555 for a discussion of agricultural policy during the Echeverría period.

[205] "Evaluación y segunda etapa del SAM," Comercio Exterior, v.31, n.4, (abril de 1981), p.382; "Mexico's New Incentives Seek to Stimulate Output of Consumer Basics," Business Latin America, (January 21, 1981), pp.22-23.

[206] Latin America Weekly Report, (2 January, 1981.)

[207] "Documento: Plan Global de Desarrollo, 1980-1982," p.376.

[208] 1978: Williams, The Rebirth of the Mexican Petroleum Industry, p.158; 1981: "New Budget Goes for Growth Rather than Control of Inflation," p.5; "El presupuesto de egresos para 1982," Comercio Exterior, v.32, n.2, (febrero de 1982), Table 4, p.122.

[209] Cornelius, p.121.

[210] "SAM Sinks Without a Trace," Latin America Weekly Report, (7 January, 1983), p.10.

[211] "Facts and Hopes Do Not Match," Latin America Weekly Report, (7 October, 1983), p.9.

[212] Cornelius, p.108.

[213] "Mexico Launches Ambitious Programme to Create Jobs," p.200, and Business Latin America, (September 10, 1981),

pp.289-291.

[214]"Conclusiones. Tercer Congreso Nacional de Economistas," Comercio Exterior, v.29, n.4, (abril de 1979), p.472.

[215]Cornelius, p.108; Miguel de la Madrid Hurtado, "Primer Informe de Gobierno," Comercio Exterior, v.33, n.9, (septiembre de 1983), p. 794.

[216]Miguel de la Madrid Hurtado, "Primer Informe", p.794.

[217]Cornelius, p.108.

[218]"Mexico's Reluctant Oil Boom," Business Week, p.67.

[219]"Los Objetivos del Plan Industrial," p.523.

[220]"La actividad económica en 1982,", p.461.

[221]Ibid., p.471.

[222]Plan Nacional de Desarrollo, 1983-1988, p.91.

[223]Based on private sector employment figures of 336,000 in 1978 and 420,000 for 1979 in "Update 1980 Mexico," p.3m.

[224]Montavon et. al., p.7.

[225]Riding, "Amid Oil Riches, Mexico's Poor Fare Badly," New York Times, (November 18, 1979), p.A-2.

[226]"Documento: El comportamiento de la economía mexicana durante 1980," p.327.

[227]Business Latin America, (January 14, 1981), p.12.

[228]"La actividad económica en 1982,", p.471.

[229]Grayson, The Politics of Mexican Oil, p.129.

[230]Whitehead, p.854; see also, "Mexican Labor Outlook Becomes More Uncertain as Discontent Worsens," Business Latin America, (July 9, 1980), p.220.

[231]"Mexico," p.278. See also José Luis Reyna, "El movimiento obrero en una situación de crisis: México, 1976-78," Foro Internacional, 75(enero-marzo de 1979), p.390-401.

[232]Whitehead, p.864.

[233]"Mexican Labor Outlook Becomes More Uncertain as Discontent Worsens," p.220.

[234]"Inside View of a Success Story," Latin America Weekly

Report, (2 December, 1983), p.10.

[235]Islas, "La industria automovilística," p.227.

[236]Gerald F. Seib, "Role of Industrialists of Monterrey Grows as Country Develops," Wall Street Journal, (November 12, 1979).

[237]"Business Places Its Cards on the Table in Presidential Race," Latin America Weekly Report, (31 October, 1980), pp.5-6.

[238]"Update 1980 Mexico," p.13m.

[239]Dale Story, "Industrial Elites in Mexico," Journal of Interamerican Studies and World Affairs, v.25, n.3, (August, 1983), Table 1, p.358.

[240]"Business Places its Cards on the Table in Presidential Race," p.6.

[241]Seib, "Role of Industrialists of Monterrey Grows as Country Develops."

[242]"Harvest of Anger, " NACLA's Latin America and Empire Report, v.X, n.6, (July-August, 1976), p.22.

Oil and Mexico's International Bargaining

Relationship: The Impact of Dependency

CHAPTER V

188

A thesis that found favor among petroleum enthusiasts was that
Mexico's enormous oil resources would enable the state to dimin-
ish its dependence, or at the very least to renegotiate some of
the terms of its dependence with its major partner, the U.S. In
this way, lost economic sovereignty would be restored. As Olga
Pellicer de Brody adroitly observed, however, "There do not
exist in history countries that have been able to overcome structural dependency through the accelerated export of natural resources."[1]
      We shall examine specifically the areas of trade and labor,
the dominant issues on the U.S.-Mexican bargaining table during
the period of Mexico's oil development project in order to
assess the extent to which the bargaining equation and structure
of interests was influenced by oil. Included in our discussion
will be consideration of the concept of the North American
Common Market or Energy Union that emerged during the period.

Undocumented Workers

      Mexico's primary interest was, of course, that of main-
taining its "safety valve," that of a relatively open frontier
with the U.S., affording its citizenry ample access to the U.S.
employment market. It had been stung by the passage of the Immigration and Nationality Act of 1976 in the U.S. which reduced
the flow of legal immigrants from Mexico to the U.S. from 45,000
per year to 20,000. At the time, Mexico had not been in a position to protest the action as it was engaged in delicate financial negotiations with the U.S. Treasury and the International
Monetary Fund that were designed to stave off economic collapse.[2]
The official curtailment of legal Mexican migration to the U.S.
was somewhat offset, however, by the fact that high levels of
non-quota immigration (largely relatives of those having already
obtained American citizenship) were permitted entry, boosting
the number legally entering to 44,446.[3] Between 1924 and 1965,
there had been no quota restrictions limiting entry into the
U.S., but in 1965, Mexico began to be included in a hemispheric
quota of 120,000. Between 1965-1976, the U.S. had accepted an
average of 50,000 legal immigrants per year from Mexico.[4]
      The problem for Mexico--even more than the curtailment of
legal immigration--was the maintenance of a relatively open
border to facilitate the entry of undocumented workers. In this,
we shall argue, Mexico was successful--not because of the power
of the new energy bargaining chip, but instead, because of fears
among U.S. policy elites and economic actors that stability in
Mexico might become unhinged were the safety valve to be shut
off, and because of the desire to maintain access to Mexican
labor.[5]
      Maintenance of the open door was also important to Mexico
because remittances from workers abroad figured substantially in
the balance-of-payments equation. Annual remittances were estimated at US$3 billion, a figure that was higher than total annual
earnings from Mexico's tourist industry.[6] Moreover, Mexico
viewed the emigration of a portion of its citizenry as essential

to its future development as was indicated by López Portillo's
comment early in his administration:

> I believe our country in the long run can solve its
> problems with its own resources. However, part of the
> population may have to migrate in the same way the pop-
> ulation of Europe in its time migrated to the United
> States.[7]

In general, the Mexican state has sought to define the issue
of illegal immigration as essentially a U.S. concern. Cornelius
has summarized the attitude of Mexico's policy elite as follows:

> Recent Mexican administrations have been content with
> ignoring the problem as much as possible, limiting their
> diplomatic petitions to requests for greater protection
> of the rights of workers while in the United States and
> periodic efforts to conclude new temporary workers
> accords...[8]

Worker migrations to the U.S. are explained by Mexican policy makers as a "natural phenomenon associated with the growth
of capitalist market systems."[9] An emphasis is placed upon the
benefits that accrue to the U.S. economy from the presence of a
cheap and exploitable labor force. The argument is frequently
made that the U.S. government receives more from undocumented
workers in the form of tax payments and social security deduc-
tions than is received in services and in fact, Jorge Bustamente,
an advisor to the Mexican government and a sociologist associated
with El Colegio de México has argued that:

> In theory, a case could be made in an international
> court of law by the Mexican government that the Mexican
> undocumented immigrants have an uncollected balance in
> their favor chargeable to the U.S. Treasury.[10]

This position was supported by the testimony of two Rand Corporation analysts during hearings held by the U.S. Congress on the
isssue of undocumented workers:

> ...recent field research indicates that the undocumented
> workers contribute more to the U.S. economy than they
> take out. Accordingly, the undocumented workers often
> take the lowest paying, least-skilled, dirtiest jobs--in
> agriculture, canneries, packing houses, restaurants,
> hospitals, machine shops, garment and construction indus-
> tries--while Americans prefer to collect unemployment or
> welfare. These workers enable some industries to survive
> that otherwise might succumb to rising wages or cheaper
> imports. The undocumented workers pay far more in taxes
> and social security than they consume in social services.
> Extremely few seek welfare or unemployment benefits. And
> the aliens are carefully law-abiding to avoid detection

190

and deportation. The vast majority are temporary
migrants who work in the United States about a half
year befor returning to Mexico; very few stay longer
than a year.11

Mexican Undocumented Workers in the U.S. Economy

One analyst has put the U.S. demand for unskilled migrant
labor in all sectors at 15-30 million persons by the year 2000.12
Predicting a shortfall in the domestic supply of unskilled labor,
Reynolds argues that in lieu of immigration, enterprises dependent upon unskilled labor would either emigrate or mechanize. A
third alternative, of course, would be the "upgrading of pay
and working conditions to attract workers from higher echelons."
In essence, he argues that the U.S. and Mexican economies will
be uniquely complementary by the year 2000.
Conflicts abound concerning the dimensions of illegal Mexican immigration to the U.S. A Census Bureau study conducted for
the Congressional Select Committee on Immigration and Refugee
Policy concluded that there were between 3.5 to 6 million illegal
workers in the U.S., nearly half of whom were reported to be Mex-
ican.13 Other major sending countries included Jamaica, the Dom-
inican Republic, El Salvador, Haiti, several South American
countries and Asia. It has been estimated that 800,000 undocumented workers enter the U.S. each year with under 50% origin-
ating from Mexico.14 Not surprisingly,a long awaited Mexican
government study of migration to the northern border differed
from U.S. studies in terms of estimates of numbers of Mexicans in
the U.S., and reported that only 480,000 to 1.25 million Mexican
undocumented workers were in the U.S. at any one time.15 The
wide variation between the upper and lower Mexican estimate is
explained by fluctuations caused by seasonal labor movements.
Using U.S. estimates of 2.5 million Mexican undocumented
workers in the U.S., nearly 14% of Mexico's economically active
population of approximately 18 million persons, had already
been absorbed by the U.S. Clearly, the U.S. employment market
had served a protective function for Mexico's unemployment
wracked system. In a real sense, the safety valve served U.S.
interests as well because it provided a cheap source of labor
to the competitive sector of the U.S. economy and acted as a
kind of economic assistance program to Mexico that in turn
helped to guarantee stability on the U.S.'s southern flank.
As the number of undocumented workers has risen so, too, has
pressure been placed upon U.S. administrations by labor organizations to restrict the flow. Labor argued that undocumented
workers took away jobs from U.S. workers, depressed wages and
working conditions and also constituted a threat to the power of
organized labor. Despite the fact that the Carter administration
acknowledged that there was no fundamental conflict of interest
between the U.S. and Mexican workers illegally working in the U.S.
because "Mexicans do the jobs the gringos don't want,16 the administration introduced the Illegal Alien Control Bill in August
of 1977, which was designed to arrest the flow of undocumented

workers. In essence, the bill served as a means of paying off
George Meany of the AFL-CIO to whom Carter owed political debts.[17]
The bill was based upon work done by the Domestic Council Committee on Illegal Aliens and its Domestic Council Report of 1976.
The work of this committee had grown out of increased sensitivity
to the issue in some governmental quarters during the mid 1970s
typified by ex-CIA director William Colby's charge that the
influx of illegal aliens from Mexico constituted a greater threat
to U.S. security than did the Soviet Union.[18]
    The key features of the plan included the following points:
1) Those living continuously in the U.S. since 1970 were
    to be granted amnesty.
2) A new procedure would be established for registering
    seasonal workers.
3) A new five year temporary alien status would be intro-
    duced.
4) Fines would be levied against individuals found to be
    consistently hiring illegal aliens.
5) Border security would be strengthened.[19]
The plan was based upon the premise that undocumented
workers caused high rates of unemployment and boosted social
welfare spending.[20] With the introduction of the bill, the administration catapulted the "problem" of undocumented workers
(if only momentarily) to the position of a preeminent policy
concern:

> At present, the problem of undocumented aliens is the
> most important and the most serious we have with Mexico.
> Until we are able to solve this problem amicably and
> cooperatively with Mexico, it will be a festering sore
> which will adversely affect the totality of our bi-
> lateral relations with Mexico.[21]

    In fact, however, from the outset, there was virtually no
support evidenced in the Congress for the proposal, nor did the
administration press the issue. So reluctant was the Congress
to consider the issue that the Attorney General reportedly had
to "arm twist" the Senate Judiciary Committee Chairman Eastland
so that perfunctory hearings would be held. Subsequently, with
little administration opposition evidenced, the proposal was
"deep-sixed" by Senator Eastland and sunk into oblivion to the
apparent consternation only of U.S. labor interests.[22]
    In the aftermath of the bill's introduction, Mexico argued
that it had been ignored during the bill's formulation stage and
one U.S. State Department official argued that a "poisonous"
atmosphere between the two countries had resulted.[23] Beyond the
the lack of consultation to which Mexico felt itself entitled,
there was resistance expressed by Mexico as to the substance of
the plan itself.

> Mexico has made very clear to us its deep concern that
> enactment of the illegal alien proposal might result in
> deportation of a large number of undocumented aliens,

> thus causing a massive disruption of the Mexican economy.
> We agree that this would be seriously disruptive as well
> as inhumane and therefore not in our best interests...
>   We are also sensitive to the Mexican government's
> concerns that in the short run, a substantial reduc-
> tion in the flow of undocumented workers will aggravate
> Mexico's economic and social problems. The elimination
> of remittances from the undocumented workers would have
> an immediate effect on many rural areas of Mexico.[24]

Such testimony indicates that the administration had submitted
the proposal in order to placate domestic labor interests and
had never been serious about shutting off the safety valve.

The bill was, however, conceived of as a warning to Mexico
that some efforts would have to be undertaken in major "sending"
areas to boost employment opportunities. The bill had proposed
U.S. assistance to Mexico in two areas, both designed to stimulate rural employment. First, the U.S. would pressure the World
Bank and the Inter-American Development Bank to grant Mexico generous loans for rural development on the condition that Mexico
would itself boost investment in the industrialization of rural
areas and would take steps to improve the rural standard of
living.[25] Secondly, a bi-lateral assistance program was proposed
that would establish a "United Fund for Development" that would
be jointly operated, although funded by the U.S. at a level of
US$2-3 billion.[26] The new fund would also be complemented by a
reduction in U.S. tariffs on fruits, fibers and vegetables, an
increase in the number of Mexican export goods enjoying Generalized System of Preferences (GSP) status, and an increase in technical assistance.[27]

Mexico rejected the concept of the United Fund, claiming
that Mexico would only be increasing its dependence upon the U.S.,
and maintaining that the Fund would provide the U.S. with an opportunity to meddle in Mexican affairs.[28] At the same time, however, (as has been discussed earlier), Mexico in fact received
unprecedented financial assistance for rural development from the
World Bank and assistance as well from IDB. Moreover, Mexico
launched programs for rural development and agro-industrializa-
tion that were directly in conformity with U.S. proposals.

The entire matter of controlling illegal immigration was
shifted to the Select Committee on Immigration and Refugee Policy
for further study. Much of the impetus for congressional activity came not from a desire to seal the border for economic
reasons, but instead, was based upon social, political and racial
considerations. Interviews with U.S. government officials
revealed a substantial concern for the potential for social transformation, or what was rather crudely termed the "browning" of
the Southwest. The prevalence of this concern accounts for the
seeming contradiction between the plethora of congressional
hearings, specialized committees and legislative initiatives and
the failure to act upon the matter which is explained by the
degree of economic advantage accruing to capital (not to labor,
however) in maintaining the open border. Additionally, the ad-

ministration was concerned with maintaining the appearance, as
was noted earlier, of doing something about the "problem" at the
behest of U.S. labor interests.

In this same vein of "doing something while avoiding really
doing anything," Carter and López Portillo agreed at their February, 1979 summit to initiate a policy of close cooperation, as
it was termed, on the issue (which López Portillo had called the
"most explosive issue between the U.S. and Mexico")[29] in order
"to find a realistic long-term solution..."[30] Essentially, this
meant that the Migration Working Group of the U.S.-Mexico Consultative Mechanism (established in 1977 by the two presidents),
would engage in the following projects:

> ...joint training session for U.S. and Mexican immigra-
> tion officials, exchange of information and research
> including joint review of methodology of a major Mex-
> ican migration study, cooperation against undocumented
> alien smugglers, and improving channels of communication
> to insure high human rights standards in the treatment of
> undocumented workers.[31]

Such cooperative efforts, however, could not disguise the
fact that the U.S. would continue to devise policy in this area
on a unilateral basis despite what former Immigration and Natur-
alization Service director, Leonel Castillo had desribed as Mexico's increasingly "assertive posture" on the issue, which
stemmed from the "oil discoveries (which gave) them more muscle
to flex."[32] The Select Commission on Immigration and Refugee
Policy's 1981 report recommended an increase, although moderate,
in legal immigration, a one-time amnesty for most illegal
workers in the country, enforcement of the law, and civil and
criminal penalties for those hiring undocumented workers. The
panel also recommended the development of an automated system
that would track non-leavers (those overstaying the length of a
visitor's visa, for example).The commission cited as its principal concerns the potential emergence of a subculture of il-
legality which would encourage the spread of a lack of respect
for the law.[33] Significantly, the panel did not recommend the
establishment of a large guest worker program,[34] and it also
recommended that a system of more secure identification be established.

The recommendations of this committee were soon overshadowed,
however, by the announcement of the outlines, in July of 1981, of
the R eagan administration's immigration plan. The plan was the
product of an eleven member committee chaired by the Attorney
General William French Smith. The plan called for a ban on the
employment of undocumented workers with a corresponding fine
upon employers of $5000 to $1000 for each illegal worker hired.
(Enterprises employing three or more workers would be exempt
from the ban). Injunctions would be placed against employers
found to be repeat offenders.

Legal status would be afforded to workers illegally residing
in the U.S. who entered before January 1, 1980. These workers

would be required to reside in the U.S. for ten years before attaining permanent resident status. (Cubans and Haitians would only be required to wait five years, although Cubans had been previously required to wait only one year). During the ten year waiting period or temporary resident period, workers would not be allowed to bring into the U.S. spouses or children under the age of eighteen. Moreover, during the temporary residency period, workers would not be eligible for welfare, subsidized housing, food stamps or unemployment insurance.

The administration proposed as well, an additional expenditure of $40 million for border security, a figure clearly inadequate for the task, and $35 million for detention facilities at the border. Further, the quota for legal migration from Mexico to the U.S. would be doubled, increasing the yearly figure to 40,000 persons.

Importantly, however, no provision was included for a secure form of identification such as a national identity card.[35] The intention was to allow the Congress jurisdiction on this issue although the administration claimed that it would be too costly to institute such a program. (The estimated cost was put at $2 billion). The omission of such a provision remained the clearest signal of U.S. intent to maintain a policy of lax enforcement and rendered toothless the provisions for employer sanctions.

Finally, the plan called for the introduction of an experimental two-year guestwork program that would entail the admission of 50,000 Mexican workers per year. These workers would be directed to locales where "real" labor shortages were being experienced, thus avoiding complaints concerning the displacement of U.S. workers. The Mexican government was reportedly consulted regarding the outline of the proposal and expressed little interest in the establishment of a guestwork program.[36]

Even if the plan were adopted _in toto_, the U.S. had essentially made a decision to maintain an open border. In March of 1981, Reagan had termed the immigration from Mexico a vital "safety valve" for Mexico and for the U.S. "It is to our government's interest also that the safety valve is not shut off" so that there is no "breaking of the stability south of the border."[37] Reagan also noted that he was considering a proposal submitted by U.S. and Mexican border states governors that the border be completely opened to allow free movement of U.S. and Mexican nationals across the border. Although the plan that was finally introduced did not contain this feature, in effect, western political interests that favored the continued accessiblity of Mexican labor had prevailed.

In an early reaction from Mexico, Jorge Bustamente condemned the plan arguing that it would "insure employers the availability of cheap labor."[38] The Bustamente reaction typifies the Mexican tendency to mystify domestic realities, to ignore the Mexican system's desperate reliance on the safety valve (which would in fact make the Reagan plan eminently acceptable to the Mexican state) and to emphasize cynically, as López Portillo had frequently done, the exploitation of Mexican labor in the U.S. While the policy preserved the system of exploitation, the Mexican state

and dominant sectors would clearly profit from the arrangement.
Yet for obvious domestic political reasons, Mexican leaders
postured on the issue, portraying themselves as defenders of the
defenseless. In a rebuke to Carter at the February, 1979 summit,
López Portillo complained:

> This, Mr. President, I believe, is the most serious
> matter of our times--the fact that there are men that
> have to sell themselves. And this is what happens very
> frequently with our poor people that go to the United
> States.[39]

Despite the rhetoric on both sides and despite suggestions
to the effect that oil would allow Mexico to write its own ticket
on the undocumented workers issue, the oil bargaining chip
remained all but irrelevant to the course of policy formulation
on the issue. With 56% of the U.S. population reporting in a
CBS/New York Times Poll conducted in 1979, that they believed
illegal workers hold jobs U.S. citizens don't want,[40] U.S. political leaders could painlessly continue to serve the interests of
U.S. and Mexican economic elites by maintaining a virtually open
border. There appears to be no evidence to suggest that any
linkage with oil was involved in the formulation of the policy.
Neither did we find evidence suggesting that Mexico attempted to
exert pressure on Washington in this area by means of its oil
resource, nor do we find any suggestion that Washington sought to
define its policy in such a way that Mexican oil production would
be boosted or that Mexican export contracts would be more favorably written. Finally, it appears that the oil resource was not
in any way utilized by the Mexican state to alter the dependency
relation with the U.S. in this area.

Trade Relations

As we noted earlier, Mexico's oil boom had translated into a
substantial increase in trade between the U.S. and Mexico. By
the early 1980s, Mexico had become the U.S.'s third largest
trading partner. While the U.S. maintained its dominant position
in Mexican international commerce despite Mexico's declared intentions to substantially diverse its trade relationships, the
trading relationship between Mexico and the U.S. during this
period proved to be an uneasy one.

In 1976, the U.S. had registered its first negative balance
of trade due largely to the growth in payments for petroleum
imports. By 1979, the deficit had grown to US$30 billion,[41] and
by 1980, it had reached US$36.4 billion, and the trend showed no
signs of abating.[42] As a result, the U.S. had become increasingly interested in pressing for further liberalization of the international trading environment to remedy the situation. In
particular, the U.S. began to press Mexico to dismantle its protectionist structure so as to facilitate greater U.S. exports to
that country, in order to offset a portion of its petroleum
import bill. The U.S. objected to what it considered to be high

tariffs erected by the Mexican state, as well as to the import licensing system and other barriers to trade such as domestic content requirements and the system of official valuation of imports.[43] In response to Mexico's charges that the U.S. itself was protectionist in its approach to trade, the U.S. argued that Mexico's non-oil exports to the U.S. lagged more because of their lack of competitiveness than because of U.S. import barriers.[44]

And in fact, Mexican policy makers to a large extent concurred in this analysis despite their protests. As Mexico launched its drive for export-led industrialization, it was keenly aware of the need to overcome the problem of non-competitiveness that had developed from the protectionist policy adopted in order to shield infant import-substituting industry from international competition. An official of Mexico's Secretariat of Commerce noted the negative results that had been incurred:

> Indiscriminate protection, whose fundamental objective was to achieve the import substitution of consumer and intermediate goods through a system of import licenses, considerabley limited the export capacity of Mexican industry, introduced a gravely deformed and oligopolistic system of internal commerce and impeded a more adequate distribution of productive factors throughout Mexican industry.[45]

As a result of its protectionist policy, Mexico had encountered a number of serious problems including:
1) a very small level of participation in international commerce,
2) acute dependency on a single market,
3) an insufficient diversification of the export basket,
4) limited power of negotiation with other countries and international organizations.[46]

In response to these problems, and as a result of continuing pressure from the U.S., Mexico undertook a program of reform at the outset of the López Portillo administration. One analyst has argued that "Working through and with the World Bank and the International Monetary Fund, the United States succeeded in convincing the Mexicans to begin a wholesale revision of their protective barriers."[47] This reform was initiated just as the IMF Stabilization Agreement was concluded in late 1976.

In addition to a number of administrative reforms (such as the creation of the Secretariat of Commerce and the centralization of trade policy within the Secretariat), the administration initiated an overhauling of its import licensing system, substituting tariffs for what was felt to be a more cumbersome, inefficient and "restrictive" system of import licenses. What the change meant, however, was that the state had embarked upon a program which would limit its ability to ban the import of products produced locally or for which substitutes were available.[48] In 1976, 85% of all products imported required an import license. This had resulted from a tremendous increase in protectionism during the Echeverría administration.[49] By early 1980, fully 4,000 items of a total of 7,200 had been removed from the licensing list although two-thirds of the value of all Mexican imports was still covered by the remaining 3200 items.[50] By early 1981, the list of products requiring an import license had dwindled to 1700 items,[51] marking a very substantial reduction in the protection afforded to industry. The more non-competitive elements of Mexican industry were naturally more than a bit skeptical regarding the initiatives.

The dismantling of the protectionist structure proved to be a first step toward Mexican entry into the General Agreement on Tariffs and Trade (GATT). Both the U.S. and Japan had pressured Mexico to liberalize its trading structure through incorporation into the GATT. The U.S. in particular, wanted not only a reduction in tariffs and a reduction in import licensing, but also pushed Mexico to abandon some of its non-tariff barriers such as domestic subsidies to industry.[52] Mexico, like many other non-member developing states, had participated actively at the Tokyo Round of the GATT negotiations which had been in progress since 1973, but were not obliged to conform to the protocols. At the same time, the argument was made to Mexico that membership would strengthen the country's bargaining position in international trade negotiations and generally that the benefits of membership would outweigh any negative effects. Thus, Mexico initiated its application for GATT membership in January of 1979, and commenced negotiations with the GATT for its protocol of adhesion. Publicly, Mexico maintained that it was seeking membership in order to obtain greater acceptance of its manufactured and agricultural exports in world markets. With the stagnation seen in manufactured exports, Mexico's hopes for avoiding the familiar outcome experienced by some oil exporters of total dependence upon oil had dimmed. Moreover, its policy of export-led industrialization made conformity to prevailing international trading arrangements a virtual necessity.

Although trade with the U.S. had grown substantially, Mexico had good reason to be unhappy with the course of the relationship. On December 2, 1977, the U.S. and Mexico had signed a bi-lateral trade accord known as the "Tropical Products Agreement" which was to have gone into effect on March 1, 1978. This was the first reciprocal trade agreement negotiated between the two countries in thirty-five years.[53] The pact had been negotiated during the Multilateral Trade Negotiations (MTN) at the Tokyo Round of the GATT. The agreement reduced import duties on a wide number of products but affected only 2% of Mexico's exports to the U.S. and 1% of U.S. exports to Mexico.[54] The accord did, however, include the important provision that the U.S. would grant Most-Favored-Nation status to Mexico and would confer the same preferential treatment accorded to a GATT member.

The agreement was never ratified by the U.S. Many of the items included in the agreement were subsequently renegotiated between the U.S. and Mexico under the auspicies of the MTN at the Tokyo Round. These items were to become part of the agreement concluded between the U.S. and Mexico under Mexico's Protocol of Adhesion to the GATT. The agreements would thus go into effect when Mexico officially became a signatory. In the interim, Mexico continued to enjoy Most-Favored-Nation status but was not accorded privileges accruing to a GATT member.[55] There was apparently substantial resentment in Mexico over the U.S. Senate's failure to ratify the treaty. The perception was that the Senate had done so to create further pressure upon Mexico to join the GATT,[56] a charge that was never been denied by the U.S.

Another point of contention between the U.S. and Mexico was the program of the Generalized System of Preferences (GSP), first enacted by the U.S. in its Trade Law of 1974. The GSP is a United Nations Conference on Trade and Development (UNCTAD) project designed to aid developing state's exports. Although the GSP project was initiated in 1968, the U.S. did not establish its own GSP program until 1976 and it was scheduled to end on January 4, 1985.[57] Because of the short period of the program's duration, Mexico would have little time to plan for investment in the manufacturing of products granted eligibility by the U.S., its biggest customer. What was even more disturbing for Mexico, however, was the U.S.'s application of the Competitive Need Limitation Clause (CNL) to eliminate items from GSP status when they lose their "need for concessions."[58] Mexican exports to the U.S. under GSP rose from US$245 millon in 1976 to US$368 million in 1977, US$458 million in 1978 and US$545 million in 1979.[59] Despite increases in the absolute value of items eligible for entry under the GSP, only 6% of Mexico's exports enjoyed GSP status during this period. In addition, since the start of the program, the U.S. took action, under the CNL, against US$1 billion of Mexico's exports, cutting 60 products in 1978, 25 in 1979 and 44 items in 1981. While a few items were admittedly added during the period, Mexico felt that the program had been unfairly managed, as for example when the U.S. took action against the importation of kitchen utensils of which Mexican imports amounted to only 5% of total U.S. imports of those items.[60]

U.S.-Mexican skirmishing also erupted over tomatoes, leather goods and tuna. Mexico had long protested what it felt to be a lack of accessibility to the U.S. market for its important winter vegetable exports.[61] In September of 1978, Florida growers filed a suit with the U.S. Treasury Department against Mexico for allegedly "dumping" tomatoes in the U.S. market, thereby jeopardizing the position of Florida growers. With exports of US$200-300 million per year and agricultural export based employment in northwestern Mexico put at 200,000 persons, Mexico viewed the possibility of a negative ruling with alarm.[62] Ultimately, the issue was resolved in Mexico's favor by the Department of the Treasury and later by the U.S. Commerce Department. The U.S. rejected a request for tariff relief on tomatoes made by the U.S. International Trade Commission on behalf of the Florida growers.[63] The U.S. apparently acted to maintain the flow of inexpensive winter produce from Mexico for several reasons. First, the prospect of worsening Mexico's unemployment picture in areas adjacent to the border was unappealing. Secondly, with U.S. inflation creating political problems for the U.S. administration, the prospect of worsening the growth rate in the consumer price index wasalso very unappealing. Third, U.S. food retailing interests lobbied against the imposition of tariff relief and had sought as well a favorable ruling on the dumping issue. Finally, at a time of spiraling oil prices and the continued dependence on OPEC oil, the administration did not want to appear to be engaged in a worsening of U.S.-Mexican relations. Clearly, Mexican oil imports would not have been threatened by unfavorable rulings on tomatoes. Instead, the administration preferred to be perceived in the domestic political arena as doing everything within its power to maintain access to non-OPEC oil. During the course of the affair, winter vegetable exports were never linked by Mexico with petroleum exports in an attempt to force the U.S.'s hand. Rather, the U.S. appears to have acted principally on the basis of its own domestic political interests.

On the issue of leather imports, Mexico fared less well. According to U.S. law, all of Mexico's production incentives programs were considered to be "countervailable." U.S. domestic producers could demand that countervailing duties be erected against imports shown to have benefited from subsidies to production. This provision is particularly troublesome for developing states such as Mexico that provide a wide range of incentives to industry. Such incentives, (including fuel discounts) are theoretically subject to countervailing action as provided for in the U.S.'s 1979 Trade Act.

In the case of leather, a suit was brought by a U.S. producer of leather apparel against Mexico (which was also directed against Argentina, Colombia and Uruguay).[64] At issue in the Mexican case was the CEDI (Certificate of Tax Forgiveness) tax rebate incentive. The Department of Commerce ruled that Mexican leather apparel enjoyed an average CEDI subsidy to production of 5.2%. As a result, a countervailing duty of 5.2% was imposed on Mexican imports in this category. State Department intervention in such cases had been standard practice previously, however, under the tougher terms of the 1979 Trade Act, little leeway was permitted in International Trade Administration rulings.[65] Short of formal membership in GATT, Mexico's only possible escape from future significant penalties would be the formulation of a bilateral agreement between the two countries which would allow the U.S. to require an injury test in such cases. Without such an agreement, injury would not have to be demostrated, only the prohibited practices. GATT members are automatically accorded injury tests in such instances.

In 1980, Mexican imports to the U.S. of tuna were banned by the U.S. following the breakdown of negotiations over tuna fishing rights in the eastern Pacific and the seizure by Mexico of six American tuna boats. Negotiations on the issue of Mexico's claim to a two hundred mile limit on offshore fishing, which had been in progress since 1978, failed to be concluded. The U.S. refused to recognize Mexican claims to tuna fishing rights within the two hundred mile limit because of the migratory nature of the fish.[66] Following the embargo, Mexico cancelled two fishing agreements regarding coastal fishing rights for tuna and shrimp that had been concluded with the U.S. in 1976 and 1977,[67] a decision that would potentially have serious implications for future exports to the U.S. The rupture was to a large extent precipitated by Mexico's intention to become the world's sixth largest producer of fish by 1982. As such, the need to protect territorial waters was most compelling. Yet with little internal demand for fish or fish products and plans for huge increases in fish exports, the jeopardizing of access to the U.S. market for these products could prove to be very injurious to development plans.

Following the negotiation of the protocol of adhesion to GATT, in what constituted a departure from standard practice, in November of 1979, the Mexican government initiated what was termed a period of national consultation over the advisability of finalizing the country's entry into GATT. López Portillo himself had favored Mexico's entry into GATT, arguing that Mexican industry had to achieve a competitive profile in the world market.[68] Due to growing skepticism within leftist, "nationalist" and certain industrial sectors, the decision was made to encourage an open discussion of the relative merits associated with entry.

The protocol had been applauded by the state as having achieved Mexico's entry on very favorable terms. Mexico would be granted twelve years to complete its process of substituting tariffs for import licenses. Tariff reductions on 1,329 export products were negotiated at a total value of US$2.491 billion. Should Mexico refuse entry, the negotiations would yield US$1.835 billion in tariff reductions.[69] Mexico forced to concede tariff reductions on only 21 products, 19 of which would be implemented over a ten to fifteen year period.[70] Mexico would be allowed to pursue its Industrial Development Plan despite the fact that certain features ran directly counter to GATT principles. Its policy of requiring fixed percentages of national content in the automobile industry would be permitted although further requirements of this type would be allowed only after multilateral consultations had been conducted.[71]

Further, according to a Mexican Commerce Secretariat official,

> Mexico would maintain full flexibility to continue using all types of incentives for its exports and industrialization program including subsidies and tax incentives. The only reservation in this regard would be that the GATT would have to be notified when a change was made or contemplated.[72]

Essentially, Mexico would then be required to modify those subsidies were any contracting party to show injury. Without GATT membership, the practice alone (without any demonstration of injury, as was mentioned earlier) would warrant compensatory duties.

Support for entry came from CONCAMIN (Confederación de Camaras Industriales), the representative of big industry and the Monterrey group. CANACINTRA (Camara Nacional de la Industria de la Transformación), the representative of small and medium-sized industry, strongly opposed entry.[73] Entry was also opposed by the National College of Economists which advocated the pursuit of the principles of trade reform embodied in the program for the New International Economic Order (NIEO) on a bi-lateral basis.[74] Arguments were made in other quarters that GATT entry could reinforce a pattern of industrial development oriented towards upper income levels and that small and medium-sized industry would be displaced.[75]

CANACINTRA maintained that the experiences of Argentina and Chile had shown that small and medium-sized industry suffered "massive injury" upon entry.[76] In Chile, the metallurgical industry had practically been all but obliterated and the electronics industry had been converted into an "importer of those products it used to produce."[77] CANACINTRA claimed that entry would severely jeopardize the National Industrial Development Plan, and maintained that while the GATT had accepted the Plan as it existed in 1979, it would be essentially frozen in place. That is, its system of incentives could not be expanded or altered without incurring penalties. The Global Plan 80-82 remained a question mark. CANACINTRA asked "Is the government's ability to legislate national development going to be frozen?"[78] CANACINTRA also expressed skepticism regarding the extent to which the NIDP had in fact been accepted.

> Also, (the Accord) maintains that the members recognize the NIDP but we don't know what this means because during a visit of U.S. officials, it was made clear that all products produced in Zones 1-A and 1-B (priority development zones enjoying exceptionally high subsidies), when exported to the U.S. would automatically be subject to compensatory payments to compensate for the subsidies used in their production.[79]

Another source of concern was the fact that the GATT mandated the discontinuance of preferential treatment for domestic production in public sector purchasing. Imports were to be accorded equal treatment in purchase considerations.[80] Public sector purchases comprised a key element of state development strategy for the capital goods sector, and as a result, this particular GATT article would be particularly injurious.

A final major point of criticism regarding the protocol was the fact that GATT would not recognize a country's right to restrict external sales of non-renewable resources (such as oil) without the imposition of identical restrictions upon consumption in the domestic market.[81] This was viewed as an unacceptable strong-arm tactic devised by the developed states to force oil exporters to maintain export levels.

The decision to reject GATT membership, announced on March 18, 1980, (the national holiday marking the expropriation of the oil industry) undoubtedly stemmed from the recognition that GATT membership struck directly at the heart of the development strategy being pursued by the state...that of oil-based, state-induced

development. At the same time, the state chose not to risk any
damage to productive capacity (that of small and medium-sized
industry) because its production and employment problems were
already sufficiently severe. In the wake of the rejection of
GATT entry, and due to slowed growth in the industrial sector in
1980, Mexico raised its tariff barriers marking a resort to
increased protectionism.[82]
    The U.S. viewed the Mexican decision with displeasure.
Ambassador Krueger, the Coordinator for U.S.-Mexican affairs,
summed up the U.S. position:

> Our trade relations with Mexico are in a state of un-
> certainty, resulting from the recent Mexican decision
> not to join the General Agreement on Tariffs and Trade
> (GATT). This decision nullified the agreement on tariff
> concessions which we concluded with Mexico last December
> under the multilateral trade negotiations (MTN) after 5
> years of tough negotiations. Mexico's nonadherence to
> the code on conduct on subsidies/countervailing duties
> will encourage countervailing duty petitions by U.S.
> industry. The bilateralization of our trade with Mexico
> will doubtless require protracted trade negotiations.[83]

    In the aftermath of the rejection by Mexico of GATT entry,
the U.S. and Mexico established a U.S.-Mexico Trade Board to move
forward on a new bi-lateral accord.[84] The achievement of an
agreement would not be easy, however, given the 1979 Trade Act's
incorporation of codes negotiated by the developed states in the
MTN concerning non-tariff barriers, compensatory rights, public
sector activity, techinical obstacles to trade and import
licenses.[85]

The North American Common Market

    The concept of a North American Common Market or Energy
Union began to emerge in U.S. business and political circles as
the dimensions of Mexico's energy resource unfolded. Much had
been said of the need for the U.S. to afford Mexico "special
status" given the complex network of interrelationships that
linked the two countries and the desire on the part of the U.S.
to guarantee access to Mexican oil. Inasmuch as the conferring
of special status upon any particular nation ran counter to the
globalist, multilateral approach being insisted upon by the U.S.,
particularly in the context of international trade negotiations,
the concept of a regional "community" was devised that would
circumvent the problem of appearing to favor any particular
nation over another.[86]
    Under the rubric of a North American community (variously
conceived of as a union, customs union or common market), Mexico and Canada would be linked with the U.S. Essentially, the
plan was in line with a Carter administration study of U.S.-Mex-
ican relations known as Presidential Review Memo-41 (PRM-41)
which advocated that officials explore "potential U.S. induce-

ments to influence Pemex to expand production capacity" and "possible joint planning for the structural evolution of a U.S.-Mexican refining and petrochemical capacity."[87] According to its proponents in U.S. political circles along with representatives of the business community and the media, the plan would roll in Canadian and Mexican energy supplies to the U.S. with substantial (though unenumerated) benefits accruing to Mexico and Canada.[88] It was argued that the U.S.'s economic clout would be diluted by the tri-lateral arrangement, and that a "semblance of political balance" might emerge,[89] which would then entice the U.S.'s southern and northern neighbors into agreeing to the partnership.

In May of 1979, a resolution was introduced into the U.S. House of Representatives calling for the establishment of a bond of energy cooperation between the U.S., Mexico and Canada.[90] Interest had been sparked in a North American economic community not only because of Mexico's oil riches, but also because of the growing U.S. trade imbalance. Subsequently, legislation was introduced to encourage economic cooperation, particularly in the energy field. Studies were undertaken by the U.S. Congress and the administration which were designed to facilitate the encouragement of "economic interdependence."[91]

The Canadian reaction was less than enthusiastic. Resentment of U.S. control of the Canadian economy was already rife and the concept of affording the U.S. even greater access to the Canadian economy was something other than appealing. With the U.S. controlling forty-five of Canada's largest companies, and 58% of all oil and natural gas companies, and the expectation that the establishment of a common market would spur a shift of production from Canada to the U.S. due to lower U.S. labor costs,[92] the antipathy shown toward the idea was easy to understand.

Mexico also rejected the concept (and the two countries did so formally at the López Portillo-Trudeau summit of January, 1981)[93] claiming that Mexico would be permanently relegated to an inferior position in such an arrangement. López Portillo argued that Mexico: "would remain condemned to extract and export in perpetuity primary materials to the advantage of more advanced societies."[94] Commenting further on the proposition, Andrés Rozental, then Mexico's Deputy Foreign Minister for North-American Affairs, noted Mexico's preference for "bi-lateral" trading arrangements and also explained:

> ...when there is such great disparity in the size of the partners, it is just too difficult to imagine how a fair common-market relationship could be worked out. So let me just agree with President López Portillo that this may be an interesting idea but it won't come in our lifetime.[95]

Although the "Common Market" approach to the management of relations with Mexico failed to come to fruition, the U.S. sought to strengthen bi-lateral relations by expanding upon its network

of cooperative mechanisms. The Mexico-United States Interparliamentary Group continued to engage in exchanges and discussions as in the past. The Mixed Commission, established in 1972
by the "Scientific and Technical Cooperation Agreement between
the United States and Mexico," expanded its energy related activities beginning in 1979 at the instigation of the U.S.
Department of Energy. Included in the list of new cooperative
activities were: 96

   - solar systems research and design
   - geothermal cooperation
   - uranium exploration, (involving technical exchanges only,
     rather than actual U.S. exploration in Mexico)
   - fossil fuels research (involving joint seminars covering
     enhanced oil recovery, the design construction and opera-
     tion of pilot plants, and offshore drilling technology)
   - hydrogen storage
   - industrial energy conservation
   - electrical energy conservation.

In sum, twenty energy related research and development projects
were undertaken by the Commission.97 Following Carter's trip to
Mexico in 1979, the Mixed Commission was expanded to include
seven working groups:

   1) railway research and development
   2) new crops, arid lands and agricultural productivity
   3) energy research and development
   4) industrial measurement and instrumentation
   5) technical information transfer
   6) National Science Foundation - CONACYT cooperation
   7) housing and urban development.98

The major bi-lateral mechanism was, however, the Consultative Mechanism that had been established following the López
Portillo-Carter meetings in 1977. The Mechanism was substantially restructured and strengthened after the 1979 summit
meeting and grew from three working groups to eight. These
include trade, tourism, migration, border cooperation, law
enforcement, energy, finance and industry, and development.99

According to a U.S. General Accounting Office report, the
Consultative Mechanism had, by 1979, not lived up to "original
expectations" essentially because of the absence of "strong
executive support."100 The Mechanism had served as a forum for
expanded discussion rather than policy coordination. In an
effort to improve upon coordination, a U.S. coordinator for
Mexican Affairs was appointed and was to serve as the executive
director for the Consultative Mechanism. At the same time, the
Carter administration established a Senior Interagency Group on
U.S. Policy Towards Mexico.

Importantly, however, the agreements reached between the
two countries through the reorganized Consultative Mechanism
had virtually nothing to do with the major issues affecting
U.S.-Mexican relations. The Coordinator for Mexican affairs
could cite only peripheral issues in his list of achievements:

   ...a major sale to Mexico of U.S. agricultural com-

modities formerly earmarked for the Soviet Union;
agreement on a joint marine pollution contingency
plan and the final capping of the runaway Ixtoc I
oil well; progress on border sanitation agreements;
progress on a revised treaty on the return of stolen
vehicles and aircraft; expanded air routes and
increased tourism as a result of a broad civil
aviation agreement; and continued close cooperation
on narcotics control.[101]

In fact, the major outcome of the activation of the various
bi-lateral cooperative mechanisms was first, the expansion of
the means of transferring technology to Mexico and secondly, the
placating of those within the U.S. domestic political arena who
felt that something must be "done" by the U.S. in order to guarantee for itself continued access to Mexico's oil. While the
administration did adopt what appeared to be an activist posture
vis-à-vis Mexico, the operating principle during the period was
the belief that:

Mexico would ultimately end up selling the bulk of its
oil and gas exports to the United States because of the
low transportation costs involved...[102]

Despite the fact that Mexico had made much of the fact that oil
would allegedly become a new and valued instrument for international negotiation, little if any effort was made to link oil
exports to the issue of trade or migration in its dealings with
the U.S. According to the U.S. GAO:

The Mexican Embassy's Minister of Economic Affairs...
told us that there has been no attempt to link sales
of Mexican oil and gas exports in return for favorable
treatment in other areas.[103]

In sum , one may view the rejection by Mexico of the
"Common Market" proposal (informal as it was) as a "defeat" for
the U.S. or a "victory" for Mexico only if one views the establishment of such a union as having been essential for the U.S.
to maintain access to Mexican oil. The evidence suggests that
this was not the case nor was it believed to be so by U.S.
political elites. Instead, the series of cooperative ventures
devised by the U.S. government may be interpreted as a means of
deflecting criticism, which had been rampant, of incompetence
in foreign policy management and a failure to come to terms
with U.S. energy problems.

Conclusion

At first glance, it might appear that Mexico's rejection
of GATT membership, its rejection of a North American alliance
concept, and the perpetuation of the status quo along with U.S.
policy on immigration together provide evidence that Mexico's

position vis-à-vis the U.S. was in fact enhanced by the oil bar-
gainig chip. Instead, it appears that Mexico's bargaining
leverage was never really enhanced during the period nor was
its dependence significantly altered.

First, there was virtually no evidence to suggest that the
oil was used by Mexico as a bargaining chip in its relationship
with the United States. Oil did have, however, a major impact
upon Mexico's wider international position in terms of affording Mexico greater access to international credits and diversified foreign investment. Mexico deliberately and repeatedly
utilized the oil chip to obtain increased technical and financial assistance from Europe and Japan. Mexico refrained from
attempting to invoke the oil "weapon" in obtaining advantages
with the U.S. and instead, welcomed increased foreign investment from the U.S. and pursued increased U.S. financial assistance. Further, the oil card appears to have had little impact
upon U.S. policy. This was hardly surprising given Mexico's
desperate need to earn foreign exchange in sales to the U.S.
market, its desire to sell a hefty proportion of its petroleum
exports to the U.S., its reliance upon the U.S. employment
safety valve for its unemployed workers, and its continued adhesion to a development model that incorporates substantial U.S.
foreign investment and U.S. absorption of Mexican production.

With regard to the trading relationship, while Mexico rejected GATT membership, it was unable to resist the pressure to
modify its protectionsit structure. Mexico had been placed in
what amounted to a "no-win" situation by the U.S. With GATT
entry, Mexico would have jeopardized the entire thrust of its
development strategy--state induced industrialization. Without
GATT entry, Mexico's plans for export-led industrialization
would have been threatened inasmuch as the Tokyo Round of the
GATT, under U.S. leadership, had established a series of penalties upon state subsidization of development--a policy that
would, of course, fall most heavily upon developing states and
would only partially be mitigated through GATT membership. In
the absence of GATT entry, Mexico would be forced to renegotiate
its bi-lateral trade relationship with the U.S. under the framework of the more punitive 1979 Trade Law. With GATT entry, Mexico would have been forced to concede to the industrial states
control over its major resource--oil. On balance, the oil
"weapon" had apparently had little clout and had not prevented
the U.S. from maneuvering Mexico into a corner.

Nor was Mexico able to substantially diversify its overall
trade relationship, a goal long and loudly touted by the López
Portillo administration. The U.S. maintained its dominance pro-
portionately in Mexico's trading profile even in the face of
Mexico's increased diversification of oil markets, all the while
affording Mexican exports little advantage under the GSP.
Although there was much discussion on both sides of the border
concerning the linkage of issues on the negotiating table
because of the oil, in fact, oil does not appear to have brought
about such linkage.

On the issue of undocumented workers, while it might be

argued that the U.S. had maintained a relatively open border because of a desire to maintain access to Mexican oil, there was no evidence to support this interpretation. While there were some who suggested that the U.S. would engineer a direct one-to-one exchange of barrels of oil for undocumented workers, U.S. immigration policy reflected other U.S. domestic interests. The desire to maintain a safety valve for Mexican elites was apparent. Just as significantly, however, maintaining an open border meant little in the way of sacrifice for U.S. elites and in fact entailed considerable benefit.

The underlying pattern of relations remained stable throughout the period although the state of U.S.-Mexican relations was frequently misperceived by those focusing upon Mexico's "independent" foreign policy line. Mexico's refusal to readmit the Shah of Iran, its failure to support the U.S. inspired boycott of the Moscow Olympic games, support for the Sandinistas in Nicaragua, and skepticism toward the U.S. backed "reform" junta ruling in El Salvador and participation in the Contadora group were positions frequently cited as evidence of Mexico's flexing of its oil muscle and its independence from the U.S. Yet as the Central American region became further destabilized with intensified civil warfare in El Salvador and Guatemala, the increasing influx of Guatemalan refugees into Mexico, the introduction of U.S. advisors into El Salvador and Honduras and the development of insurgent forces mounting a challenge to the Sandinista government, Mexico supported U.S. initiatives in the Central American-Caribbean area. Mexico offered to cooperate with the U.S., Canada, and Venezuela in a Caribbean Development Plan that would seek a solution to the region's problems via increased direct foreign investment and multilateral financial support.[104]

Thus, while Mexico eschewed formalized cooperative arrangements relating to strategic issues such as the United Fund for Development and the North American Common Market, at the same time, more informal patterns of cooperation were maintained with the U.S. It could be argued that cooperation with the U.S. on the Caribbean Development Plan constituted something of a departure from past practice. Clearly, Mexico had felt sufficiently threatened by the unsettled Central American-Caribbean environment that it was willing to adopt a more direct approach to cooperation with the U.S. in regional initiatives. Significantly, however, the arrangement that was proposed was not strictly bi-lateral in nature and thus easier to defend politically. At bedrock, however, the oil proved to be ineffective in altering Mexico's preeminent external relationship with the U.S.

208

NOTES

[1] *Proceso*, n.89, (17 de julio de 1978).

[2] Testimony of Cesar Sereseres, U.S. Congress, Senate, Committee on the Judiciary, <u>Immigration</u> and <u>Nationality</u> <u>Efficiency</u> <u>Act</u> <u>of</u> <u>1979</u>, <u>S.1763</u>, Hearings, 96th Cong., 1st Sess., October 17 and 26, 1979, p.52.

[3] U.S. Congress, Senate, Committee on the Judiciary, <u>Immigration</u> <u>and</u> <u>Nationality</u> <u>Efficiency</u> <u>Act</u> <u>of</u> <u>1979</u>, <u>S.1763</u>, 96th Cong., 1st Sess., p.101.

[4] Testimony of Vernon Briggs, U.S. Congress, House, Committee on International Relations, <u>Undocumented</u> <u>Workers</u>: Implications <u>for</u> <u>U.S.</u> <u>Policy</u> <u>in</u> <u>the</u> <u>Western</u> <u>Hemisphere</u>, 95th Cong., 2nd Sess., 1978, p.88.

[5] Richard Fagen,"Mexican Petroleum and U.S. National Security," <u>International</u> <u>Security</u>, v.4, n.1, (Summer, 1979), pp. 39-53.

[6] Richard Fagen, "An Inescapable Relationship," <u>Wilson</u> <u>Quarterly</u>, v.III, n.3, (Summer, 1979), p.145.

[7] "Time Bomb in Mexico. Why There'll Be No End to the Invasion of Illegals," <u>U.S.</u> <u>News</u> <u>and</u> <u>World</u> <u>Report</u>, (July 4, 1977), cited in Barry W. Poulson, "The Brain Drain from Mexico to the United States," in <u>U.S.</u>-<u>Mexico</u> <u>Economic</u> <u>Relations</u>, ed. by Poulson and Osborn, p.245.

[8] Wayne Cornelius, 'La imigración ilegal mexicana a los Estados Unidos: conclusiones de investigaciones reciente, implicaciones políticas y prioridades de investigación," <u>Foro</u> <u>Internacional</u>, v.XVIII-3, (enero-marzo de 1978), p.417.

[9] Testimony of David Ronfeldt and Cesar Sereseres (Rand Corp.) in U.S. Congress, House, Committee on International Relations, <u>Undocumented</u> <u>Workers</u>: <u>Implications</u> <u>for</u> <u>U.S.</u> <u>Policy</u> <u>in</u> <u>the</u> <u>Western</u> <u>Hemisphere</u>, pp.362-363.

[10] Bustamente cites a U.S. Department of Labor study regarding services utilized and payments made by undocumented workers: See David North and Marion F. Houston, "Illegal Aliens: Their Characteristics and Role in the U.S. Labor Market," (unpublished) Executive Summary, Department of Labor, Washington, D.C., 1976. See Jorge Bustamente, "Facts and Perceptions of Undocumented Immigration," in <u>U.S.</u>-<u>Mexico</u> <u>Economic</u> <u>Relations</u>, ed. by Poulson and Osborn, p.175.

[11] Testimony of Ronfeldt and Sereseres, p.36.

[12]Reynolds, pp.248-250.

[13]"Excerpts from Final Report of the Commission on Immigration and Refugee Policy," New York Times, (February 27, 1981), p.B-5.

[14]U.S. Congress, Committee on the Judiciary, Senate, Immigration and Nationality Efficiency Act of 1979, S.1763, p.40.

[15]Juan M. Vasquez, "U.S. and Mexico Issue Upbeat Report on Ties," Los Angeles Times, (November 30, 1980), p.1.

[16]Interview, U.S. Department of State, February 27, 1979.

[17]Ibid.

[18]Fagen, "The Inescapable Relationship," p.145.

[19]Rosemary Jackson, "United States-Mexican Relations," in U.S. Congress, Joint Economic Committee, The U.S. Role in a Changing World Political Economy: Major Issues for the 96th Congress, 1st Sess., June 25, 1979, p.363.

[20]See Wayne Cornelius, "Undocumented Migrations: A Critique of the Carter Administration's Policy Proposals," Migration Today, v.5, n.4, (October, 1977), cited in Olga Pellicer de Brody, "La política de los Estados Unidos hacia México en la coyuntura actual," p.11.

[21]Deputy Assistant Secretary for Inter-American Affairs Richard G. Arrellano in Department of State Weekly, v.LXXVII, n.2001, (October 31, 1977), p.592.

[22]Interview, U.S. Department of State, February 27, 1979.

[23]Ibid.

[24]Testimony of Sally A. Shelton, Deputy Assistant Secretary, Bureau of Inter-American Affairs, Department of State, in U.S. Congress, House, Committee on International Relations, Undocumented Workers: Implications for U.S. Policy in the Western Hemisphere, p.33.

[25]"The Vice-President: Visit to Canada and Mexico," pp.12-13; and Undocumented Workers, pp.44-46.

[26]Reubens, p.142; Speech by Patrick Lucey, cited in Proceso, n.70, (16 de marzo de 1978), p.29.

[27]Excelsior, (21 de enero de 1978), p.1.

[28]Excelsior, (7 de abril de 1978), pp.1 & 8; Reubens, p.142.

[29]Patricia Nelson, "Emigrant Problem Stressed by López," Journal of Commerce, (June 30, 1978), ISLA, (June, 1978), p.16.

[30]Robert Krueger, U.S. Coordinator for Mexican Affairs, Department of State Bulletin, (September, 1980), p.76.

[31]Ibid., and "Report on the Consultative Mechanism," Office of the White House Press Secretary, September 28, 1979.

[32]Los Angeles Times, (December 16, 1979), p.12.

[33]"Excerpts from Final Report on Commission on Immigration and Refugee Policy," p.B-5.

[34]Robert Pear, "Panel Asks Rise in Immigration with Tighter Enforcement," p.A-11.

[35]Robert Pear, "White House Asks a Law to Bar Jobs for Illegal Aliens," New York Times, (July 31, 1981), p.A-1 & A-2; John M. Crewdson, "Reagan Immigration Plan," New York Times, (July 31, 1981), p.A-12; Robert Pear, "New Policy on Aliens to Omit Worker Identification Card," New York Times, (July 20, 1981), p.A-1, A-18.

[36]Robert Pear, "New Policy on Aliens to Omit Worker Identification Card;" Steven R. Weisman, "Mexico's Leader Ends Visit on Bright Note," New York Times, (June 10, 1981), p. A-3; Lee Lescaze, "López Portillo, Reagan Talk of Friendship, Differences," Washington Post, (June 10, 1981), p.A-3.

[37]Lee Lescaze, "Reagan Eyes Open U.S.-Mexican Border," Washington Post, (March 4, 1981), ISLA, (March, 1981), p.4.

[38]Robert Pear, "Adviser to Mexican Government Assails Reagan Immigration Plan," New York Times, (August 5, 1981), p.A-18.

[39]Weekly Compilation of Presidential Documents, v.15, n.7, (February 19, 1979), p.283.

[40]William K. Stevens, "Millions of Mexicans View Illegal Entry to U.S. as Door to Opportunity," New York Times, (July 12, 1979), p.A-1, B-10.

[41]Pellicer de Brody, "Consideraciones acerca de la política comercial de Estados Unidos hacia México," p.1115.

[42]"Trade Deficit Widens on a 'Payments' Basis," New York

Times, (August 6, 1981), p.D-16.

[43]U.S. Congress, Senate, Finance Committee, Subcommittee on International Trade, North American Economic Interdependence Part I, 96th Cong., 1st Sess., June 6, 1979, pp.6-7.

[44]Ibid.

[45]Roberto Dávila Gómez Palacio, Director general de Cooperacion Económica Internacional de la Secretaría de Comercio, "Comercio exterior y relaciones internacionales," Comercio y Desarrollo, ano 1, vol. 1, n.3, (enero-febrero de 1978), p.5.

[46]Ibid.

[47]Williams, The Rebirth of the Mexican Petroleum Industry, p.76.

[48]GAO, Prospects for a Stronger United States-Mexico Energy Relationship, p.25.

[49]IBRD, Mexico. Manufacturing Sector, pp.16-18.

[50]William Chislett, "Decision Imminent on GATT," Financial Times, (January 11, 1980), ISLA, v.20, n.1, (January, 1980), p.41.

[51]Business Latin America, (April 22, 1981), p.124.

[52]"Swimming Against the Trade Tide," Latin America Weekly Report, (April 4, 1980), p.8.

[53]Organization of American States, CECON Trade News, v.11, n.12, (December 1977); "The Economy in Review," Mexican-American Review, (January, 1978), p.23.

[54]GAO, Prospects for a Stronger United States-Mexico Energy Relationship, p.29; Bagley, pp.19-20; "The Vice-President: Visit to Canada and Mexico," pp.9-13.

[55]GAO, Prospects for a Stronger United States-Mexico Energy Relationship, p.25.

[56]U.S. Congress, Senate, Committee on Foreign Relations, Nineteenth Mexico-United States Interparliamentary Group. Report of the Senate Delegation on the Nineteenth Meeting held at Mexico City, Mexico, 96th Cong., 2nd Sess., 1980, p.18.

[57]See Rodolfo Cruz Miramontes, "El sistema general de preferencias de la Ley de Comercio de 1974 de Estados Unidos," Comercio Exterior, v.28, n.9 (septiembre de 1978), p.1111; Al R. Wichtrich, "Mexican-American Commercial Relations," in

Mexico and the United States, ed. by Robert McBride, p.91.

[58]Wichtrich, p.91.

[59]Ibid.

[60]Hector Hernández Cervantes, "El futuro del comercio entre México y Estados Unidos," Comercio Exterior, v.30, n.10, (octubre de 1980), p.1129; Comercio Exterior, v.31, n.4, (abril de 1981), p.384; Comercio Exterior, v.29, n.4, (abril de 1979), p.398; "Oas Study Pinpoints Major Shortcomings In U.S. GSP Program," Business Latin America, (June 7, 1978), p.177; "Lopez Portillo Prepares to Lock Horns with Reagan," Latin America Weekly Report, (May 15, 1981), p.7

[61]Bagley, p.70.

[62]Latin America Economic Report, v.VI, n.27, (July 14, 1978), p.214.

[63]Leonard Curry, "Probe Finds No Dumping of Tomatoes," Washington Star, (October 31, 1979), p.E-1; Clyde H. Farnsworth, "U.S. Bars Tariff Rise for Leather Apparel and Mexico Tomatoes," New York Times, (March 25, 1980), p.D-1, D-11; Also see Steven Sanderson, "Florida Tomatoes, U.S.-Mexican Relations and the International Division of Labor," Paper presented at the Latin American Studies Association Annual Meetings, Bloomington, Indiana, 1980.

[64]"Mexican-U.S. Clash on Export Subsidies Signals Trouble Ahead," Business Latin America, (February 4, 1981), pp.34-35.

[65]See "Latin America Takes Dim View of MTN Results," Business Latin America, (February 27, 1980), p.71.

[66]G. Hovey, "U.S. Seeks Tuna Pact with Mexico," New York Times, (July 17, 1980).

[67]Pamela G. Hollie, "The 'Tuna War' with Mexico," New York Times, (July 31, 1980), pp.D-1 & D-10.

[68]Wall Street Journal, (March 24, 1980), ISLA, v.20, n.3, (March, 1980), p.19 and Financial Times, (November 7, 1979), ISLA, v.19, n.5 (November, 1980), p.19.

[69]Fernando de Mateo, Asesor del Subsecretario de Comercio Exterior, Secretaría de Comercio, "Contribución a la polémica sobre el GATT," Comercio Exterior, v.30, n.2, (febrero de 1980), p.115; "Negotiations Reveal What Joining GATT Will Mean for Mexico," Business Latin America, (December 5, 1979), pp.385-6.

[70]Ibid.

[71] Ibid.

[72] Ibid., p.113.

[73] "Mexican Industry Splits on GATT," Latin America Weekly Report, (February 29, 1980), pp.5-8; Alan Robinson, "Mexican Private Sector Split on GATT Membership Question," Journal of Commerce, (March 7, 1980), ISLA, v.20, n.3, (March, 1980), p.17; Also see "Mexican Groups Fight GATT Membership," New York Times, (June 9, 1979), p.18.

[74] Christopher Dickey and Marlise Simons, "Mexico Postpones GATT Membership," Washington Post, (March 19, 1980), ISLA, v.20, n.3, (March, 1980), p.18.

[75] Rudy Omar Albertos Camara, "El ingreso de México al GATT," Comercio Exterior, v.29, n.3, (marzo de 1979), pp.275-279.

[76] CANACINTRA, "La industria de transformación y el GATT," Comercio Exterior, v.30, n.2, (febrero de 1980), p.175.

[77] Ibid.

[78] Ibid., pp.176-177,

[79] Ibid., p.177.

[80] Ibid., p.181; Also see Rocío de Villarreal and René Villarreal, "El comercio exterior y la industrialización de México a la luz del Nuevo GATT," Comercio Exterior, v.30, n.2, (febrero de 1980), p.146.

[81] Ibid., p.153.

[82] "An Oil Producer in Troubled Waters," Latin America Weekly Report, (July 17, 1981), pp.9-10.

[83] Update: United States-Canadian/Mexican Relations, p.32.

[84] "U.S.-Mexico Trade Board," New York Times, (June 24, 1981), p.D-7, and "U.S. and Mexico Establish Joint Commission on Trade," New York Times, (June 24, 1981), p.A-4.

[85] Pellicer de Brody, "Consideraciones acerca de la política comercial de Estados Unidos hacia México," p.1116; Tomas Penaloza,"La Ley de Acuerdos Comerciales de 1979 de Estados Unidos," Comercio Exterior, v.30, n.2, (febrero de 1980), pp.123-132.

[86] Viron Vaky, Assistant Secretary of State for Inter-American Affairs, Remarks to Latin American Studies Association

Pittsburgh, PA., April 7, 1979.

[87]Portion of the PRM-41 cited in Metz, p.1261.

[88]See "The Tough Job of Forging a Good Neighbor Energy Policy," Business Week, (August 20, 1979), pp.42-43; "Economic Alliance Urged for U.S., Canada, Mexico,"Buffalo Evening News, (April 5, 1980), p.46; Kenneth E. Hill, "3 Nations Together on Energy," New York Times, (March 23, 1979), p.A-24.

[89]"The Tough Job," p.43.

[90]U.S. Congress, House, Committee on Foreign Affairs, Hearings before the Subcommittee on International Economic Policy and Trade on Inter-American Affairs and on International Organizations, North American Energy Cooperation, 96th Cong., 1st Sess., Part I, September 27, 1979, p.36.

[91]See for example, the following titles: U.S./Mexico Relations and Potentials Regarding Energy, Immigration and Technology Transfer; The Western Hemisphere Energy System, Oil and Natural Gas from Alaska, Canada, and Mexico - Only Limited Help for U.S.; Prospects for a Stronger United States Mexico Energy Relationship; Mexico, The Promise and Problems of Petroleum; North American Energy Cooperation, North American Economic Interdependence, Alternatives to Dealing with OPEC; Mexican Oil and Technology Transfer.

[92]Herbert E. Meyer, "Why a North American Common Market Won't Work Yet," Fortune, (September 10, 1979), p.20; also see Aaron Segal and Wallace C. Koehler, Jr., "Canada-Mexico-USA, Prospects for Energy Cooperation," Paper prepared for the Southern Economic Association Meeting, Atlanta, Georgia, November 7, 1979.

[93]Latin America Weekly Report, (January 30, 1981), p.12.

[94]"Rechaza México el mercomún con Canada y Estados Unidos," Unomasuno, (27 de mayo de 1980), p.1 cited in René Villarreal, "El petróleo como instrumento de desarrollo y de negociación internacional. México en los ochentas," El Trimestre Economico, v.XLVIII, n.189, (enero-marzo de 1981), p. 35.

[95]Millard C. Browne, "Common Market Idea Sounds Fine - But Not for Mexico," Buffalo Evening News, (November 28, 1979), p.8.

[96]GAO, Prospects for a Stronger United States-Mexico Energy Relationship, pp.17-18.

[97]U.S. Congress, House, Committee on Science and Technology, Subcommittee on Investigations and Oversight, Mexican

215

Oil and Technology Transfer, 96th Cong., 1st Sess., p.255,
and U.S. Congress, House, Committee on Foreign Affairs, Sub-
Committee on International Economics, Politics and Trade, Subcommittee on Inter-American Affairs and Subcommittee on International Organizations, North American Energy Cooperation,
Part II, pp.52-53 and 65.

[98]North American Energy Cooperation, Part II, p.69

[99]GAO, Prospects for a Stronger United States-Mexico
Energy Relationship, p.31.

[100]Ibid., p.30.

[101]Robert Krueger, "U.S.-Mexican Relations," U.S. Department of State Bulletin, v.80, n.2042, (September, 1980), p.75.

[102]GAO, Prospects for a Stronger United States-Mexican
Energy Relationship, p.29.

[103]Ibid., p.30.

[104]"Mexico's President Arrives in the U.S. for 2 Days of
Talks," New York Times, (June 8, 1981), p.A-1 & A-10 and
Latin America Weekly Report, (July 17, 1981), p.5.

The Financial Collapse and Prospects

for State Capitalism in Mexico

CHAPTER VI

Mexico's oil development project had brought the nation cle economically. The onset of the oil boom had coin-　　　th Mexico's acceptance of an IMF Stabilization Agreement and regrettably, the boom concluded with the state's acceptance of still another such agreement as the economy teetered on the brink of insolvency. The country had simply lurched from one financial disaster to another despite the black gold. By December of 1982, having been snatched from the brink of collapse by the financial intervention of the United States, Mexico initiated implementation of its "Program for the Immediate Reorganization of the Economy" (PIRE) which was designed to restore the nation's economic health.

According to the National Plan for 1983-88, PIRE's focus could be divided into two parts. The first included

> ...austerity, discipline, honesty and greater productivity for public spending; the strengthening of public revenues, the moderation of profits and wages, encouragement of savings and more modest lifestyles and a new strategy for international exchange and foreign trade.

The second part of the program included:

> ...the restructuring of public administration, the reorganization of priorities for public spending and investment, an effort to pursue tax reform seriously, protection of sources of employment, basic needs and productive capacity, and a restructuring of the financing system.[1]

While the Plan claimed that the accord with the IMF did not really amount to an orthodox Stabilization Agreement, in fact, many of the usual features of such Agreements had been targeted. For 1983, the public sector deficit was to drop from 16.5% of GDP to 8.5%. Taxes were to be increased from 2 to 2.5% of the GDP. Domestic financing of the public deficit would drop from P1.4 billion in 1982 to P787 million in 1983. External borrowing would be limited to US$5 billion. The rate of inflation was to drop from nearly 100% in 1982 to 60-70%. Imports were to be cut by US$6 billion. Subsidies provided by the public sector such as via cut-rate energy prices for the domestic market would be moderated.[2]

The program implied a reduction in economic activity and a general cooling off period with cutbacks in foreign financing and public spending. According to SHCP, in the first trimester of 1983 for example, the number of persons covered by IMSS had dropped by 4.3% from 1982 levels due to layoffs. Employment in the manufacturing sector fell off by a whopping 8.5%. Demand for goods and services in the economy dropped by 29% during this period[3] and the economy was expected to register a negative growth rate in 1983 of -5%.[4] Un/underemployment reached 60% of the economically active population in 1983.[5] For 1984, the growth rate was anticipated at only 1%,

with external borrowing limited to US$4 billion. Inflation
continued to rage throughout 1983 averaging an estimated 78%,
further eroding the population's ability to purchase even the
bare necessities. The abolition of price controls on 4700
products (only 300 products remained with price ceilings) had
already done much to reduce the mass of the population's
effective purchasing power.[6]
Not only had virtual economic disaster befallen the Mexican economy by 1982 in terms of the country's inability to
support its external public debt, the state had also come to
the belief that a major change in the nation's financial
structure was warranted. On September 1, 1982, President
López Portillo announced the state's takeover of the nation's
domestic financial institutions. Compensation would be provided to the expropriated bankers. Bank holdings in the
hundreds of Mexican corporations affected would be sold to
private interests. The state would also absorb the banks'
US$6 billion in liabilities. The reorganization of the domestic
banking sector involved a reduction in the total number of
institutions from 60 to 29. Renamed "National Credit Corporations", fully 70% of the resources in the sector would remain
in BANCOMER, BANAMEX, SERFIN, COMERMEX and SOMEX.[7] Further
steps were taken to strengthen and rationalize the public
sector as the de la Madrid government settled into place.
    Commenting upon the nationalization, billed in some
quarters as the most significant assertion of state power
since the Cárdenas period, President de la Madrid declared:

> The nationalization of the banks is a transcen-
> dental step forward in the strengthening of the
> Mexican state's leadership role in national dev-
> elopment.[8]

    What had happened to cause the economic difficulties
experienced beginning in late 1981 and continuing into 1982 and
1983? What had caused the nation's financial insolvency? Indeed,
how could the world's fourth largest producer of petroleum be
bankrupt?

Background to the Crisis

    There were numerous factors that contributed to the extreme
imbalance that had emerged in the economy and in the external
sector in particular in 1981 and 1982. To begin with, the development project that had been initiated in 1977 was extremely
import intensive as has been previously noted. Unfortunately,
the precipitous increase in costly imports was not adequately
offset by petroleum export earnings. Manufactured exports fell
during the period and agricultural earnings did little to
brighten the export picture. Manufactured exports suffered
from a decline in demand due to international recession as
well as the overvaluation of the peso that had been caused
by petroleum induced inflation. The overvaluation undercut

the competitiveness of Mexico's prices in the international arena. Mexico's exports were hurt by a wave of protectionism in critical developed states' markets and export prices for coffee, cotton, shrimp and silver were also depressed during this period.[9]

Petroleum earnings in the export market also proved disappointing. Revenues for 1982 had been anticipated at US$26-27 billion but petroleum exports generated only US$16.594 billion that year.[10] Pemex's exports for 1981 had been expected to rise to US$20 billion but only reached US$14.585 billion. The world price for oil had begun to drop in mid-1981, causing Mexico to roll back its prices in order to hold contracts. Mexico's initial reluctance to acknowledge the world market situation by reducing its prices had led to some contract cancellations that the state simply could not afford.

The contraction in world demand had caused a major depression in price as an oil glut emerged in the market. Mexican and North Sea production had entered the market just as demand had begun to shrink. By 1982, a 10% reduction had been achieved in consumption over 1979 when the total non-communist world's oil consumption had peaked at 52 mbpd. The major consuming states had cut oil use per unit of output by 30% between 1973-1982. Fully 80% of those savings had been accomplished in the 1980's. Consumers had implemented conservation strategies successfully and had also pursued substitution. Finally, the sluggish state of the industrialized economies had contributed substantially to falling demand.[11] Even the cutback in production deriving from the Iran-Iraq conflict had not outweighed the cumulative impact of those factors that had contributed to the depression of the market.

The economy was also hurt badly by the nation's level of indebtedness and servicing requirements. The debt had exploded during the oil boom as a result of aggressive borrowing and skyrocketing interest rates. The record of economic expansion during rhe period demonstrated the increased importance attached to international loans. Direct foreign investment had certainly registered growth during the period but relatively, borrowing abroad had come to typify the developmental financing strategy.[12] During 1976-1982, the total external debt grew at an average 23.3% per annum and in 1981-1982, the rate of increase jumped to 26.9% per annum.[13] By the late 1970's, the country was borrowing just to try to meet the service obligations on the debt.[14]

The bulk of the external debt had been incurred by the public sector in order to finance development in the petroleum sector and to finance other public sector projects. By early 1982, the government faced the prospect of having to raise US$25-28 billion to meet repayment obligations and to pay for ongoing projects. 60% of the debt was owed to U.S. banks. By August of 1982, Mexico faced the impossible prospect of US$40 billion coming due by August, 1983.[15]

Beginning in 1980, the inflation that been so feared in fact appeared and by 1982, the Mexican economy was being

ravaged by an inflation rate of 100%. A number of factors
contributed to the inflation:
- initial expectations of a 15-20% inflation emerging
  in 1978-1979 due to oil revenues and interest rates
- introduction of the value-added tax in 1980
- rising interest rates
- industry price adjustments due to minor devaluations
the state implemented beginning in 1980.
- jump in inflationary expectations based upon previously
mentioned factors
- workers' wage pressure
- international inflation[16]
The state attempted to regain control of the crisis situation in the external sector by devaluing the peso in February,
1982, and by slashing public sector spending. By August 1982, the
peso had actually experienced three devaluations. In the first
half of 1982, the peso had lost half its value.

In February of 1982, the Mexican Petroleum Institute
recommended the elimination of petroleum export ceilings in
order to salvage Mexico's financial situation.[17] This recom-
mendation was rejected not only because of the depressed international oil market but also because of limitations in the
nation's ability to deliver substantially increased amounts.
Substantial new infrastructural spending would have been
required precisely at the most difficult economic juncture.
Furthermore, Mexico had moved into an observer status with
the now wounded OPEC and was increasingly committed to the
idea of partnership with other producing states in order to
stabilize the market.[18]

Devaluation, the principal instrument for management of
the problem, proved to be less than satisfactory. Indeed,
the devaluations spawned capital flight of over US$20 billion
in 1981-1982, a situation that the government regarded as
disasterous. An estimated US$14 billion had been deposited
in foreign banks and an estimated US$8.5 billion had been
placed as downpayments on US$25 billion worth of real estate.[19]
Following still another devaluation on August 6 and the imposition of a two-tier exchange system, the situation continued
to become more grave. Cutbacks on loans by West Germany and
Canada had dealt still another blow; however, the crisis
appeared to peak when European bankers refused refinancing
requests on obligations that would soon be due. Subsequent
to this blow, the government closed the exchange markets and
imposed exchange controls. By the third week in August, Mexico
had requested a 90 day moratorium on repayment of loans from
major lenders.[20]

With Mexico close to default, the U.S. began to mobilize
a financial "rescue" operation. According to U.S. Treasury
Secretary Donald Regan, Mexico was "very close to default.
That's why the United States acted as quickly as it did. The
United States would have been in a tough situation" if the
substantial American capital involved had been jeopardized.[21]
According to one report, Citibank, Chase Manhattan and the

Bank of America had 40% of their capital tied up in Mexico.[22]
It might also be noted that Mexico had, by August, 1982,
become the U.S.'s leading supplier of imported oil, replacing
Saudi Arabia. In sum, the U.S. had numerous reasons for
wanting to resolve the situation.

Under the tutelage, influence and leadership of the U.S.,
a "rescue" package was arrived at that included the following
features:

- immediate rescheduling of US$23 billion
- US$1.5 billion in short term support from the Bank for
  International Settlements.
- agreement by the U.S. to purchase US$1 billion worth
  of oil for the strategic reserve to be paid in advance.
- US$1 billion in loan guarantees from the Commodity Credit
  Corporation to ensure favorable interest rates on credits
  for agricultural products imported by Mexico from the
  U.S.
- agreement with the IMF to receive US$4.1 billion over
  the next three years in exchange for agreeing to the
  terms of a Stabilization Agreement to include a ceiling
  of US$5 billion on new borrowing for 1983.[23]

As events unfolded, the Mexican system was to receive still
another jolt.

Nationalizing the Banks

President López Portillo announced to a weary nation that
the state would undertake the nationalization of the domestic
banking sector in an effort to restore the integrity of the
nation. In his September 1st announcement, López Portillo
charged the banks with having sacked the nation and with having
undermined national confidence. The action was taken because,
in López Portillo's words:

> ...the critical conditions now require and justify
> it. It is now or never. They have already sacked
> us. Mexico is not finished. They will not sack us
> again.[24]

The measure involved the seizure of billions of dollars of
banking assets with shareholders receiving compensation over
a ten year period. Depositors with dollar accounts were hurt
badly by the compensation scheme as the multi-tiered exchange
system was applied in a most disadvantageous manner.

Reaction to the move was predictably mixed. Some of course
regarded the takeover as definitive proof of the continued
dynamism of the Mexican Revolution. The PRI organized demonstrations proclaiming the heroic nature of the measure. Support
from labor was strong although there was objection to the
state's intention to sell off bank holdings in corporations to
the private sector. From the business side, reaction was
considerably less enthusiastic. While CONCAMIN supported
the measure, the Business Coordination Council (CCE) as well

as the Federation of National Chambers of Commerce voiced
their disapproval. Business charged that 35% of the nation',
private industry would be in the state sector as a result
of the takeover.[25] References were made to an emerging government empire. The National Bankers Association argued that

> State ownership of the banks is a definite blow
> to private enterprise and a clear signal the country
> is entering socialism, a measure that is unaccept-
> able because it concentrates all political and
> economic power in the government, turning it
> totalitarian.

> The flight of dollars originated in the government's
> economic policy; Mexicans lost their confidence in
> their rulers and tried to protect their savings.[26]

In essence, business interests argued that the nationalization
amounted to the state's having scapegoated the banks, refusing
to acknowledge its own incompetence. According to Carlos Tello,
the architect of the nationalization and subsequent state
director of the Bank of Mexico, the bank nationalization did
not constitute socialism and signified something quite different: "It simply involves placing (private banks) at the
service of the people."[27]
      A showdown over the seizure was planned by Monterrey
interests. The intention was simply to shut down operations
locking out workers. The state apparently threatened labor
union seizure of the plants in this event and as a result,
the planned closings were cancelled.[28] VITRO proceeded with
a suit against the government to stop nationalization of VITRO's
BANPAIS. The U.S. was none too pleased about the development.
At the outset, the U.S. suggested, apparently unconvincingly,
that the IMF credits might not be forthcoming unless the
nationalization were reversed.[29] The measure was not reversed,
however, and the financial "rescue" operation remained unimpeded.

Corruption

      It was evident that the nation had been "sacked" by more
than one set of actors. While López Portillo had denounced
the greed of the "sacadolares" as having played a major role
in plunging the nation into crisis, President de la Madrid
cast the net a bit more widely. According to the government's
own admission, the oil boom had whetted unsavory appetites in
the nation and had spawned a substantial increase in the level
of corruption throughout Mexican society. De la Madrid called
corruption "a profound cultural problem that permeates to the
very root of Mexican culture." The problem was common to the
private sector, to the labor movement, to the educational
system, to news organizations and to the government in the
President's view. For de la Madrid, a critical goal was for

"public immorality" to cease. He declared his intention
to close administrative and legal loopholes in the bureaucracy
that made corruption all but inevitable.[30]
    This was not a new theme for Mexican politics. In fact,
in his 1976 campaign for the Presidency, López Portillo had
declared: "Corruption is the cancer of this country. Mexico
runs the risk of devouring itself if we do not control corruption."[31] Yet during his tenure, allegations of massive corruption swirled around the center of government itself. López
Portillo's close ally and former Pemex Director Jorge Díaz
Serrano found himself languishing in jail charged with fraud.
Díaz was regarded in some quarters as a lightening rod for
charges of corruption at the pinnacle of government. The construction of palatial homes by and for members of the López
Portillo family overlooking Mexico City failed to squelch such
allegations. Apparently, the practices indulged in during the
1976-1982 sexenio went beyond the society's normal expectations
regarding Presidential self-enrichment while in office. De la
Madrid asserted that "Now as never before the people demand a
moral renewal..."[32] He might well have added "economic renewal"
to the list of popular demands.

A Nation in Crisis

    According to President de la Madrid's first report to the
nation in September, 1983, his administration had encountered
an
        economy characterized by collapse and a contraction
        of production, hyperinflation, growing unemploy-
        ment, explosive growth of the public sector deficit...
        reduction in savings in the domestic financial
        system, severe devaluation of the peso and loss of
        monetary sovereignty, depletion of international
        reserves, an external debt of unprecedneted mag-
        nitude and the virtual suspension of payments to
        international creditors...

A more devastating portrait of the state of the nation could
have hardly been painted.
    The economic crisis jeopardized further the ability of
most Mexicans to sustain a reasonable level of existence. The
1982 crisis and the ensuing austerity program only intensified
the shift in the distribution of income that had been noted
during the boom. The distributional impact of the oil boom
had clearly favored profits over wages.[33] The crisis brought
massive layoffs and the devaluations meant an erosion of purchasing power that affected citizens equally across all income
levels. The state boosted the cost of basic commodities in an
effort to curtail its own spending. It was estimated that
the crisis had doubled the number of illegal immigrants
entering the U.S.[34] According to World Bank statistics, the
poorest 40% of the population commanded 10% of total income
while the richest 10% commanded 40% of the nation's income.
These figures signaled a decline in the position of the bottom

40% of the population since 1977.[35]
According to Finance Minister Jesús Silva-Herzog, the nation's problem stemmed from the fact that "we grew too quickly."[36] As a systematic explanation of the problem, the analysis left much to be desired. The state had posited a number of goals at the outset of the oil boom that the state anticipated would be reached easily:

- liberation from economic dependence
- self-sustained industrialization implying the successful structural transformation of the economy
- financial self-sufficiency
- the end of external constraints upon development
- a solution to the problem of unemployment by 1990

When assessed from the perspective of the achievement of these goals, the project was an unmitigated failure. It is to an analysis of the sources of failure that we now turn.

Assessing the Development Project

This study of the development of Mexico's petroleum resource within the context of the model of associated dependent development began with the hypothesis that the development would both strengthen the state capitalist form in Mexico and deepen Mexico's dependence. Some theorists of state capitalism argued that the strengthening of that form would provide the dependent state with new bargaining leverage, enabling it successfully to redefine some of the terms of the nation's dependence. Others argued that the strengthening of the state capitalist form and the achievement of financial autonomy would spawn the emergence of a new state bourgeoisie that would either act in the "common interest" or in its "own interest", but would in either case no longer serve the interests of the dominant capitalist class. We argued that this was an improper conceptualization of the thrust of state capitalism and suggested instead that its development was primarily accounted for by the contradictions emergent from the development of capitalism within the context of dependency.

With a weak and dependent bourgeoisie, the state would serve as the central axis of accumulation, directing the economy's development (albeit within the context of dependency) and would attempt to confront obstacles to that development. In so doing, the state apparatus did not develop a class of its own, somehow separate from that of the capitalist class, but remained a leading element of that class. Its central function remained the safeguarding of the economic order. We suggested that the present Mexican oil development project and the burgeoning of the state sector would provide evidence supporting our theoretical understanding of the functions of state capitalism.

The financial crisis in Mexico during the mid 1970s brought about what we termed the crisis of the Mexican state because the state had lost the financial ability to exercise instrumental autonomy in the management of the development

226

project. The state viewed the development of the oil resource
as its only hope for re-establishing its ability to exercise
this instrumental autonomy. It sought, as well, to liberate
itself from the external financial constraints that were seen
to be inhibiting its pivotal role in society. The state's
principal objective was the setting in motion of the next
phase of Mexico's industrialization project which the dependent
business sector was incapable of initiating or managing.
Without such action, the task, were it to be undertaken at all,
would have fallen exclusively to TNC interests.

During the Echeverría period, the state had been heavily
engaged in infrastructural and productive sector investments
in order to provide a platform for the launching of a new stage
of industrialization but had reached a financial impasse in its
efforts. Unable to mobilize sufficient domestic savings to
finance its activities and with the door closing upon access to
international credit, the situation would have become exceedingly difficult had there been no recourse to the additional
resources provided by the oil. Without oil, the IMF Stabilization Agreement would in all probability have had to have been
implemented in its totality, creating serious political problems
in the society. With oil, the state was able to momentarily
regain a substantial degree of its instrumental autonomy which
enabled it to pursue major new planning activities, to further
its participation in the production arena, and to continue to
fulfill its labor mediation function, expanding its activities
in that area within the agricultural sector.

The state's activity was substantially expanded as indicated by the accelerated growth in the state sector budget.
State spending as a percentage of the Gross Domestic Product
rose to unprecedented levels. State sector planning and investment grew as well, with the state achieving remarkable success
in spurring private sector (both local and foreign) investment
and facilitating increased profitability for the private sector.

While the state did pursue new investment, the sum of its
increased expenditures was geared toward supporting the private
sector and spurring production in that area, where possible,
rather than attempting to compete with or displace the private
sector. The growth of state sector activities did not signal
the emergence of an independent, self-serving state bourgeoisie,
but instead reflected the state's effort to facilitate the
economy's entry into a new phase of industrialization in which
the private sector was to have the leading role. While revenues from the petroleum developemnt project enhanced the state's
position, this was never designed and in fact was never intended to be at the expense of the private sector.

The Development of a Major Resource Within the Context of
Dependency

The petroleum development project itself was conditioned
by the context of dependency in which it was immersed. Because
of the absence of a capital and intermediate goods sector, the

project produced devastating imbalances in the external sec
The project was import intensive and dependent upon external
financing. To complement external borrowing, the state shif
Pemex's central activity from the provision of internal subsidies to industry, to the earning of foreign exchange in
export markets. This in turn introduced a major development
dilemma: how to convert "a dollar of net domestic savings out
of a dollar of foreign exchange"?[37] In effect, the state had
opted for a strategy of petroleum development in which the real
value of the resource would be realized primarily in the international arena. Oil and gas were exported in order to earn
foreign exchange to support the accelerated import of capital
goods and technology and to service the growing external debt.
Thus, major stimuli were provided to foreign economies through
the purchases of enormous amounts of supplies and equipment.
Moreover, because Mexico was financially unable to defer petroleum exports until such time as the domestic refining capacity
could be enlarged, unrefined oil was sold, thereby denying the
country huge potential additional earnings from sales of refined
products.

Even more critically Mexico embarked upon its petroleum
development project with such speed that no provisions were made
for backward linkages to other sectors of the economy, especially to the capital and intermediate goods sectors which were
already sorely underdeveloped, even when compared to Brazil and
Argentina. As a result, Mexican industry was not provided with
sufficient lead time to establish a supply capability sufficient
to meet Pemex's demands and in so doing, the Mexican economy
was denied a crucial opportunity to begin to overcome its technical and capital goods dependence. Instead, the enterprise
resorted to foreign suppliers as it had done in the past for
much of its capital goods needs. Dependency theorists have long
pointed to just such a pattern of development activity, wherein
imports and resultant technological and financial dependence are
opted for rather than vertical integration of domestic economic
sectors, as a principal means by which the condition of dependency is reproduced. Crucially, it was the condition of dependence itself that mandated (in the absence of any intention to
reform the system) that the state adopt such a policy. With an
import and capital intensive model of industrialization operative (although in dire need of revitalization in capital and
intermediate goods), with international creditors increasingly
soured on Mexico's financial outlook, with restrictive IMF
policies to contend with, and with a commitment to attracting
increased levels of direct foreign investment that would require
several years lead time, the state could not wait for the development of indigenous capital and intermediate goods capabilities.
It argued that new investments financed with revenues from oil
would incorporate plans for backward linkages but that the
petroleum sector itself had to be developed immediately.

The state's plan for developing a world-class petrochemical
sector was also severely influenced by the country's dependence.
In the absence of an indigenous scientific and technological

capability in some basic and most secondary petrochemical areas, the industry would develop a highly technologically dependent character. Further, this dependence, coupled with the state's deliberate policy of maintaining subsidy prices on petrochemical feedstocks, served to attract substantial TNC investment in secondary petrochemicals. In effect, this major new area of industrial development, managed and guided by the state, reinforced the position of TNC investment in the economy and spawned considerable new investment.

The state argued that it would use the oil to minimize its dependence by diversifying its oil export markets. While it did in fact manage to diversify, Mexico became the U.S.'s major supplier of imported oil. More importantly, however, there appeared to be no evidence to warrant the conclusion that Mexico's dependence was significantly diminished by the strategy of diversification. Instead, the strategy was actually used by the state to solicit direct foreign investment, transfers of technology, technical assistance and financial assistance, hardly the hallmarks of a move toward independence. In fact, we would suggest that all of this marked a greater internationalization of the Mexican economy than ever before.

Another manifestation of external imbalance surfaced in Mexico's export profile. Contrary to what the state had hoped to achieve, the dominant position that oil came to occupy in the export profile increased Mexico's financial vulnerability. This became painfully apparent as the world oil market deteriorated in 1981 and 1982. Furthermore, the state had come to rely upon oil earnings for fully a third of its revenues as the upheaval in the market had devastating consequences for the nation. In sum, the external imbalance provoked by oil development within the context of dependence ultimately provoked new efforts by the state to remedy the financial problem.

In 1976, the state had encountered problems in adequately mobilizing domestic savings and a shortfall in the availability of foreign capital. The convenient remedy proved to be oil - at least for a time - but the structural external imbalance imbedded in the development model led the state in 1982 once again to confront the problem of a shortfall in domestic savings and an erosion of international financial support. This time, the instrument of salvation would prove to be neither as convenient nor as politically neutral. In an attempt to manage these enduring contradictions, the state moved to nationalize the banking system and to breathe life once again into the model of development as it had done in 1977-78. By 1982, however, the problems could arguably be described as having become more profound in terms of the deepening of the dependency.

Oil and the Internationalization of the Economy

We may recall that Cardoso and Faletto argued that dependent states "have their main features determined by the phases and trends of the expansion of capitalism on a world scale."[38] Importantly, we found that Mexico's oil fueled, state induced industrial revitalization program contained as its centerpiece what amounted to complete conformity to the contemporary shift in the international division of labor. Mexico's program of export-led industrialization emphasized just those areas of production being exported by the developed states to the semi-industrialized countries: autos, electronics, chemicals, steel, assembly and food processing.

To support this endeavor, the state constructed a system of incentives designed to stimulate local investment, but which also benefited foreign investors. The state actively solicited new foreign investment, calling it essential for the new industrialization project and for agricultural development, and as a result, new direct foreign investment flowed into the country at a rapid clip. According to one report, U.S. direct foreign investment in Mexico had risen to 68% of the total value of industrial investment in the nation by 1980.[39]

From the outset of the petroleum boom, the López Portillo government provided clear signals to the international community regarding the key role new direct foreign investment was expected to play in launching Mexico's program of industrial revitalization. The Foreign Investment Commission became an active promoter of new investment from abroad and sought to facilitate such investment even to the point of selectively permitting foreign majority ownership. Both the state and the local private sector vigorously pursued broadened international linkages and as a result, both the state and private grupos initiated numerous joint ventures. Mexicanization was increasingly discredited as an arbitrary and counter-productive measure.

Lured by the prospect of petroleum wealth, cheap labor and subsidized energy prices along with a host of other incentives, TNCs invested heavily in the pivotal petrochemicals sector and in the transport sector. Mexico was in fact transformed into a magnet for foreign auto giants. Such activity conformed with the state's professed interest in transforming its small labor intensive industry into large modern plants able to compete internationally. This transformation was grounded upon a primary focus upon external markets, imported technology, and capital intensivity. Direct foreign investment thus constituted an essential component of the accelerated development program.

These developments ran directly counter to several of the goals announced by the Mexican state at the outset of the oil development project. Oil was to have provided the means by which the country would overcome its dependence and was seen as the instrument to be employed by the state in the structural transformation of the economy. Mexico, it was argued, would be able to achieve self-sustained industrialization and would experience the end of external constraints upon its development.

The evidence suggests, however, that none of the goals set by the state were accomplished. Despite enormous oil revenues, the state and private sector continued to adhere to standard development patterns. The process of industrial development continued to be dependent upon imports of technology and capital

goods, and reliant upon external financing. The external imbalance inherent in the model was actually intensified by the
oil boom, resulting in the choking of development.

The Structure of Internal Relations and the Internal Imbalance

The process of industrial development continued to be
targeted toward consumption patterns characteristic of foreign
economies. Virtually no effort was made to provide for the
development of a larger internal market. Instead, the relative
position of the poor deteriorated while income continued to be
concentrated at the upper reaches of the socio-economic ladder.
The already exceptionally skewed income distribution pattern
(registering a Gini coefficient of 0.6 at the mid-point of the
1970s, indicating that Mexico was already one of the world's
most unequal societies)40 continued to worsen.

While a certain degree of progress was seen in employment
in the "modern sector" until 1981, the crisis of 1982-83 greatly
undermined the growth that had been achieved. Further, the capital intensivity of the project and the market skew of the
project limited employment creation opportunities even during
the boom years of 1978-81. While growth in employment surpas-
sed 4% during those years, much of the employment was in the
unstable construction sector. In sum, the state had not moved
any closer to resolving the enduring employment problem.

In fact, the state failed to directly address the two major
internal contradictions arising out of the development model,
unemployment and income mal-distribution. We had expected that
some efforts in this direction would have been undertaken as the
state regained some degree of instrumental autonomy. While the
introduction of the Mexican Food System (SAM) may be interpreted
by some as evidence of the state's having attempted at least to
address the problem of rural unemployment, it became apparent
that the program's target was production, the achievement of
food self-sufficiency, and the protection of the "oil bargaining
chip" rather than employment. Similarly, while some might argue
that the state's emphasis on small and medium-sized decentralized
industry constituted evidence of an attempt to deal with the unemployment problem, we would argue that while the NIDP did
contain some provisions in this regard, the major focus of industrial policy emphasized the development of an internationally
competitive export oriented capacity that was necessarily
characterized by concentration, capital intensity and technological dependence.

With regard to income distribution policies, we found that
the state's punitive wage policy prior to the crisis exacted a
high price from labor while income to capital soared. Subsequent
devaluation coupled with soaring inflation, the lifting of most
price controls, serious unemployment and uneven application of
compen ating minimum wage increases for those few covered,
served to increase the pressure on the population. Even with
the black gold, beans and tortillas became more difficult for
the average Mexican to acquire, surely a benchmark of the oil

project's failure.

Negotiating Some of the Terms of Dependence

We had anticipated that the state would attempt to renegotiate some of the terms of Mexico's dependence based upon its
new petroleum bargaining chip. What we discovered was that
prior to the crisis, the Mexican state had in fact attempted to
do so chiefly by diversifying its relations with the industrialized countries rather than by modifying the character of
the relations of dependence per se. Specifically, Mexico did
not reject the idea of increased DFI but instead sought to
diversify the national sources of that investment. Similarly,
it did not in practice reject its de facto policy of extensive
dependence upon petroleum exports but rather sought to alter
the near monopsony position occupied by the U.S. in terms of
Mexico's oil exports. The policy of diversification tied to oil
exports was used to encourage unprecedented levels of direct
foreign investment, transfers of technology and external financing.

The U.S. continued in its position as Mexico's dominant
trading partner, preeminent source of external financing and
lone recipient of a substantial portion of Mexico's un and
underemployed population. While Mexico did succeed in diversifying its oil exports, the U.S. remained Mexico's principal
source of direct foreign investment. Ultimately, what we have
observed is that the oil proved, within the operative model of
dependent development, to be a facilitator of even greater
dependence rather than a liberating mechanism.

Conclusion

Unfortunately, the past always constitutes a preface to the
future, and in Mexico's case, it does not make for pleasant
reading. On the basis of the oil boom experience, one is hard
pressed to conclude anything other than that dependence, inequality, and marginalization will characterize that country's
development for the foreseeable future. As a model, associated
dependent development appears to offer a more limited prospect
for growth than has previously been envisioned. The external
and internal imbalances generated by the model in the Mexican
case appear to have a crippling effect when aggressive development is pursued. Triggered are a series of processes that
appear to contribute to financial insolvency.

It is not often that a poor nation finds itself blessed
with major new resources and thus it is particularly lamentable
that such an opportunity as oil presented for the Mexican population may have been lost. Ironically, Mexico's leaders recognized that the oil constituted what may have been the nation's
only chance to escape the condition of underdevelopment.

Rather than constituting a harbinger of a new level of
material well being for the mass of the population, the development of Mexico's petroleum resource signaled the opening of a

new era of dependence for the nation. Significant policy
choices have been made that will not be undone easily. The
opening of the floodgates for a new period of direct foreign
investment fashioned from the demand profiles of foreign
economies will mean the further elaboration in Mexico of a productive structure that neither provides a satisfactory level of
employment nor produces goods that are compatible with the needs
of the mass of population.

NOTES

[1] Plan Nacional de Desarrollo 1983-1988, p.49.

[2] Homer Urias, "Algunos aspectos de la coyuntura," Comercio Exterior, v.33, n.7, (julio de 1983), p.598 and "Documento: México y el FMI: la carta de Intención,"SHCP, Banco de México Comercio Exterior, v.32, n.11, (noviembre de 1982), pp.1247-1251; "De la Madrid Must Formulate Fiscal Recovery," Buffalo Courier Express, (July 6, 1983.)

[3] Urias, p.599.

[4] "Silva-Herzog Talks About Realism," Latin America Weekly Report, (16 September, 1983), p.6.

[5] "Mexico. Another Lean Year Looms Ahead," Latin America Weekly Report, (9 December, 1983), p.8

[6] "The People Feel the Pinch," Latin America Weekly Report, (21 January, 1983), p.9.

[7] "Banks to be Divested of Holdings," Latin America Weekly Report, (16 September, 1983), p.10. Also see "Documento: La nacionalización de la banca privada. Reglas para fijar la indemnización," SHCP, Comercio Exterior, v.33, n.7, (julio de 1983), pp.654-655.

[8] "Smoothing the Transition," Latin America Weekly Report, (10 October, 1982), p.5.

[9] Bela Balassa, "Trade Policy in Mexico," World Development, v.11, n.9, (September, 1983), pp.759-812, and Julio López C., "The Mexican Economy: Present Situation, Perspectives and Alternatives," World Development, v.11, n.5, (May, 1983), pp.455-465; Alan Riding, "Mexico Devalues Peso 30%," New York Times, (February 19, 1982.)

[10] "Mexico to Turn Inward Under New President," Washington Report, v.2, n.21, (July 13, 1982), pp.1 & 7; Douglas Martin "Mexico's Elusive Oil Boom," New York Times, (May 13, 1982.)

[11] "The Implications of Falling Oil Prices," Morgan Guaranty, World Financial Markets, (March, 1982), pp.1-8; "Lower Oil Prices and World Recovery," Morgan Guaranty, World Financial Markets, (April, 1983), p.10.

[12] Gary Gereffi and Peter Evans, "Transnational Corporations, Dependent Development and State Policy in the Semiperiphery: A Comparison of Brazil and Mexico," Latin American Research Review, v.XVI, n.3, (1981), p.33.

234

[13]"Global Debt: Assessment and Prescriptions," Morgan Guaranty, World Financial Markets, (February, 1983), pp.1-14; "International Lending: Implications of a Slowdown," Morgan Guaranty, World Financial Markets, (October, 1982), Table 5, p.3.

[15]"Mexico's Economic Woes Are Tied to Its Huge Debt," Buffalo Courier Express, (August 19, 1982.) Robert A. Bennett, "Mexico Seeking Postponement of Part of Debt," New York Times, (August 20, 1982.)

[16]López G., pp.458-459.

[17]"Mexican Oil Plan Reported," New York Times, (February 4, 1982), "Exchange Rate Policy in Latin America: Mexico," Morgan Guaranty, World Financial Markets, (February, 1982), pp.8-9.

[18]"Role for Mexico in OPEC is Reported," New York Times, (May 30, 1982.)

[19]Washington Report, v.3, n.3, (November 2, 1982.)

[20]"Mexico Asks Postponement of Debt," and Alan Riding, "Mexico Reopens Exchanges with High Rate for the Dollar," New York Times, (August 20, 1982.)

[21]"Plans for Reagan Trip to Mexico End Schultz Mission on High Note," Buffalo Evening News, (April 20, 1983.)

[22]James D. Cockcroft, Mexico: Class Formation, Capital Accumulation and the State, (New York: Monthly Review Press, 1983), p.309.

[23]"Aid Package Scheduled for Mexico," Buffalo Evening News, (August 21, 1982); "Mexico Claims Agreement on Loan Payments," Buffalo Courier Express, (August 21, 1982). "Silva-Herzog Order Shock Treatment for Mexico's Ailments," Latin America Weekly Report, (20 August, 1983), p.1; "Hat Dance on Mexican Border," Washington Report, v.3, n.3, (November 2, 1982), p.3.

[24]"Mexican President Orders Controls on Currency, Nationalizes Banks," Buffalo Courier Express, (September 2, 1982.)

[25]"Mexican Seek Strategy," Buffalo Courier Express, (September 8, 1982); "López Portillo Tightens His Grip," Washington Report, v.3, n.1, (October 5, 1982), p.1. Mexicans Applaud Bank Nationalization at Workers' Rally," Buffalo Evening News, (September 4, 1982.)

[26]" 1 Million Mexicans Rally to Support Nationalization," Buffalo Courier Express, (September 4, 1982.)

[27] Ibid.

[28] Monte Hayes, "Mexico Aims to Curb Purchases at Border," _Buffalo Evening News_, (September 8, 1982), "Mexican Businesses Vow Mass Lockout," _Buffalo Evening News_, (September 7, 1982.)

[29] Reported by U.S. Treasury Undersecretary Beryl Sprinkel in "Takeover of Banks Spurs Suit," _Buffalo Evening News_, (September 4, 1982,) and "Mexico Firm Prepares to Fight Bank Takeover," _Buffalo Evening News_, (September 5, 1982.)

[30] Alan Riding, "Once Again a Mexican Leader Tilts at Corruption," _New York Times_, (May 28, 1982); Alan Riding, "Mexican Faulted Over Leadership," _New York Times_, (April 9, 1983.)

[31] William D. Montalbano, "Corruption a Cancer in Mexico," _Buffalo Evening News_, (September 19, 1982.)

[32] Ibid.

[33] López G., p.464.

[34] Marlese Simons, "Washington Drops in on 'the Last Domino'," _New York Times_, (April 17, 1983.)

[35] 1977: Saul Trejo Reyes, "Distribución del ingreso, empleo y precios relativos," _Comercio Exterior_, v.32, n.10, (octubre de 1982), Table 1, p.1104; World Bank data: Richard Boudreaux, "De la Madrid Must Formulate Fiscal Recovery," _Buffalo Courier Express_, (July 6, 1983.)

[36] "Zero Mexican Growth Seen," _New York Times_, (May 19, 1982.)

[37] Villarreal and Villarreal, p.1.

[38] Cardoso and Faletto, p.XXIII.

[39] Robert Looney, _Development Alternatives of Mexico Beyond the 1980s_, (New York: Praeger, 1982), p.11.

[40] This figure was offered by Bernardo Sepulveda Amor, cited in Michael R. Redclift, _Development Policymaking in Mexico: The Sistema Alimentario Mexicano(SAM)_. Research Report No. 24, Center for U.S.-Mexican Studies, University of California, San Diego, 1981.

Bibliography

Selected Bibliography

Books, Chapters in Books and Monographs

Aguilar, M., Alonso et. al. Politica Mexicana Sobre Inversiones
Extranjeras. Mexico City: UNAM, 1977

Angotti, Thomas. "The Political Implications of Dependency
Theory." In Dependency and Marxism. Toward a Resolution of
the Debate. Edited by Ronald H. Chilcote. Boulder, CO.:
Westview Press, 1982.

Baerresen, Donald, W. The Border Industrialization Program of
Mexico. Lexington, MA.: Lexington Books, 1971.

Barkin, David. "Internationalization of Capital. An Alternative
Approach." In Dependency and Marxism. Toward a Resolution
of the Debate. Edited by Ronald H. Chilcote. Boulder, CO.:
Westview Press, 1982.

_____. "Summary Notes." In Latin America in the International
Economy. Edited by Victor L. Urquidi and Rosemary Thorp.
N.Y.: John Wiley and Sons, 1973.

Botero, Rodrigo. "Relations with the United States: a Latin
American View." In Latin America in the International
Economy. Edited by Victor L. Urquidi and Rosemary Thorp.
N.Y.: John Wiley and Sons, 1973.

Brothers, Dwight, S. "Mexico-U.S. Economic Relations in Histor-
ical Perspective." In U.S.-Mexican Economic Relations.
Edited by Barry Poulson and T. Noel Osborn. Boulder, CO.:
Westview Press, 1979.

Bustamente, Jorge. "Facts and Perceptions of Undocumented
Workers." In U.S.-Mexican Economic Relations. Edited by
Barry Poulson and T. Noel Osborn. Boulder, CO.: Westview
Press, 1979.

Carlson, Sevinc. Mexico's Oil Trends and Prospects to 1985.
Monograph. Georgetown Center for Strategic and International Studies. Washington, D.C.: May, 1978.

C ecena Cervantes,José Luis. Introducción a la Economía Política
de la Planificación Economica Nacional. Mexico City:
Fondo de Cultura Económica, 1975.

Cardoso, Fernando, H. "Associated-Dependent Development: Theoretical and Practical Implications." In Authoritarian
Brazil. Edited by Alfred Stepan. New Haven, CT.: Yale

University Press, 1977.

_____. "Imperialism and Dependency in Latin America." In Structures of Dependency. Edited by Frank Bonilla and Robert Girling. Stanford, CA.: Institute of Political Studies, 1973.

_____. "On the Characterization of Authoritarian Regimes in Latin America." In The New Authoritarianism in Latin America. Edited by David Collier. Princeton, NJ.: Princeton University Press, 1979.

Cardoso, Fernando, H. and Faletto, Enzo. Dependency and Development in Latin America. Translated by Marjory M. Urquidi. Berkeley, CA.: University of California Press, 1979

Cockcroft, James. "Mexico." In Latin America: The Struggle with Dependency and Beyond. Edited by Ronald H. Chilcote and Joel Edelstein. N.Y.: Halstead Press, 1974.

_____. Mexico: Class Formation, Capital Accumulation and the State. N.Y.: Monthly Review Press, 1983.

Consumer Markets in Latin America. London: Euromonitor Publications Limited, 1978.

Cornelius, Wayne. "Immigration, Development Policy and Future U.S.-Mexican Relations." In Mexico and the United States. Edited by Robert H. McBride. Englewood Cliffs, N.J.: Prentice-Hall, 1981.

del Rosario Green, María. "Mexico's Economic Dependence." Mexico-United States Relations. Edited by Susan Kaufman Purcell. N.Y.: The Academy of Political Science, 1981.

del Villar, Samuel, I. "El significado del petróleo para la sociedad mexicana: Perspectiva y sintesis del debate." In Las Perspectivas del Petróleo Mexicano. Mexico City: Centro de Estudios Internacionales, El Colegio de Mexico, 1979.

Delli Sante, Angela. "The Private Sector, Business Organizations and International Influence: A Case Study of Mexico." In Capitalism and the State in U.S.-Latin American Relations. Edited by Richard Fagen. Stanford, CA.: Stanford University Press, 1980.

Durandeau Palma, Leoncio. "The Sources of Recent Mexican Inflation." In U.S.-Mexican Economic Relations. Edited by Barry Poulson and T. Noel Osborn. Boulder, CO.: Westview Press, 1979.

Eckstein, Susan. The Poverty of Revolution. The State and the
    Urban Poor in Mexico. Princeton: Princeton University
    Press, 1977.

Evans, Peter. Dependent Development: The Alliance of Multi-
    national, State and Local Capital in Brazil. Princeton:
    Princeton University Press, 1979.

Fagen, Richard and Nau, Henry. "Mexican Gas: The Northern Con-
    nection." In Capitalism and the State in U.S. Latin
    American Relations. Edited by Richard Fagen. Stanford,
    CA.: Stanford University Press, 1980.

Fajnzylber, F.; Martínez, A. Las Empresas Transnacionales.
    Mexico City: Fondo de Cultura Económica, 1976.

Feinberg, Richard, E. "Bureaucratic Organization and United
    States Policy Toward Mexico." In Mexico-United States
    Relations. Edited by Susan Kaufman Purcell. N.Y.: The
    Academy of Political Science, 1981.

Fernandez, Raul. The United States-Mexico Border. Notre Dame
    Indiana: Notre Dame University Press, 1977.

Ffrench Davis, Ricardo. "Foreign Investment in Latin America:
    Recent Trends and Prospects." In Latin America in the
    International Economy. Edited by Victor L. Urquidi and
    Rosemary Thorp. N.Y.: John Wiley and Sons, 1973.

Fitzgerald, E.V.K. The Limitations of State Capitalism as a
    Model of Economic Development: Peru 1968-1978. No.27
    Working Papers, Latin American Program. The Wilson Center,
    Washington, D.C.

_____. The Political Economy of Peru, 1956-78. Cambridge:
    Cambridge University Press, 1979.

_____. "Stabilisation Policy in Mexico: The Fiscal Deficit
    and Macroeconomic Equilibrium 1960-77." In Inflation and
    Stabilisation in Latin America. Edited by Rosemary Thorp
    and Laurence Whitehead. London: Macmillan Press Ltd.,
    1979.

Frenkel, Roberto and O'Donnell, Guillermo. "The 'Stabilization
    Programs' of the International Monetary Fund and their
    Internal Impacts." In Capitalism and the State in U.S.
    Latin American Relations. Edited by Richard Fagen.
    Stanford, CA.: Stanford University Press, 1980.

The Future of Central America. Policy Choices for the U.S. and
    Mexico. Edited by Richard Fagen and Olga Pellicer.
    Stanford, CA.: Stanford University Press, 1983.

García-Colín Scherer, Leopoldo. "La ciencia y la tecnología del petróleo. Situación actual y perspectivas futuras en México." In Las Perspectivas del Petróleo Mexicano. Mexico City: Centro de Estudios Internacionales, El Colegio de México, 1979.

González Casanova, Pablo. Democracy in Mexico. New York: Oxford University Press, 1970.

Grayson, George. The Politics of Mexican Oil. Pittsburgh, P.A.: University of Pittsburgh Press, 1981.

Grindle, Merilee, S. Bureaucrats, Politicians, and Peasants in Mexico. Berkeley: University of California Press, 1977.

_____. Official Interpretations of Rural Underdevelopment: Mexico in the 1970s. Research Report No. 20, Center for U.S.-Mexican Studies, University of California, San Diego, 1981.

Hansen, Roger, D. The Politics of Mexican Development. Baltimore: Johns Hopkins University Press, 1974.

Interamerican Development Bank. Economic and Social Progress in Latin America, 1979 Report. Washington, D.C., 1980.

_____. Economic and Social Progress in Latin America. 1980-81 Report. Washington, D.C., 1981.

_____. Economic and Social Progress in Latin America. The External Sector. 1982 Report. Washington D.C., 1982.

International Bank for Reconstruction and Development. Mexico. Manufacturing Sector: Situation Prospects Policies: A Country Study. Washington, D.C., 1979.

International Monetary Fund. Government Finance Statistics Yearbook, v.IV, 1980. Washington, D.C., 1979.

Hellman, Judith Adler. Crisis in Mexico. N.Y.: Holmes and Meier Publishers, 1978.

Johnson, Kenneth, F. Mexican Democracy: A Critical View. N.Y.: Praeger Publishers, 1978.

Kalecki, Michal. "Observations on Social and Economic Aspects of Intermediate Regimes." In Essays on Developing Countries. NJ: Humanities Press, 1976.

_____. Problems of Financing Economic Development in a Mixed Economy. Cambridge: Cambridge University Press, 1972.

242

King, Timothy. Mexico: Industrialization and Trade Policies
    Since 1940. London: Oxford University Press, 1970.

Latin American Perspectives. Mexico in the Eighties. Issue 32,
    V. IX (Winter, 1982.)

Looney, Robert. Development Alternatives of Mexico Beyond the
    1980s. N.Y.: Praeger, 1982.

_____. Income Distribution Policies and Economic Growth in
    Semi-Industrialized Countries. A Comparative Study of
    Iran, Mexico, Brazil and South Korea. N.Y.: Praeger
    Publishers, 1975.

_____. Mexico. A Policy Analysis with Forecasts to 1990.
    Boulder, Colo.: Westview Press, 1978.

Levy, Daniel and Szekely, Gabriel. Mexico. Paradoxes of
    Stability and Change. Boulder, Colo.: Westview Press, 1983.

Magdoff, Harry. The Age of Imperialism. N.Y.: Monthly Review
    Press, 1969.

Mancke, Richard, B. Mexican Oil and Natural Gas. N.Y.: Praeger
    Publishers, 1979.

Meyer, Lorenzo. "Historical Roots of the Authoritarian State in
    Mexico." In Authoritarianism in Mexico. Edited by José
    Luis Reyna and Richard Weinert. Philadelphia: Institute
    for the Study of Human Issues, 1977.

_____. Mexico and the United States in the Oil Controversy,
    1917-1942. Translated by Muriel Vasconcellos. Austin, TX:
    University of Texas Press, 1977.

Mexico's Political Economy. Edited by Jorge Domínguez. Beverly
    Hills, CA.: Sage Publications, 1982.

Mexico: Business Opportunities. London: Metra Consulting and
    International Joint Ventures, 1977.

Mexico: National Industrial Development Plan, Volumes One and
    London: Graham and Trotman, Ltd., 1979.

Montavon, Remy; Wionczek, Miguel; Piquerez, Francis. The Role
    of Multinational Companies in Latin America. N.Y.: Praeger
    Publishers, 1979.

Moran, Theodore. Multinational Corporations and the Politics of
    Dependence. Princeton: Princeton University Press, 1974.

Munck, Ronaldo. "Imperialism and Dependency: Recent Debates and
    Old Dead-Ends." In Dependency and Marxism. Toward a

Resolution of the Debate. Edited by Ronald H. Chilcote.
Boulder, Co.: Westview Press, 1982.

Needler, Martin. Politics and Society in Mexico. Albuquerque:
University of New Mexico Press, 1971.

O'Connor, James. "The Meaning of Economic Imperialism." In
Readings in U.S. Imperialism. Edited by K.T. Fann and
Donald Hodges. Boston: Porter Sargent, 1971.

O'Donnell, Guillermo. Modernization and Bureaucratic-
Authoritarianism. Institute of International Studies.
Politics of Modernization Series, No.9. Berkeley:
University of California, 1973.

O'Shaugnessy, Hugh. Oil in Latin America. London: Financial
Times Ltd., 1976.

Pellicer de Brody, Olga. "Segundo Commentario." In Las
Perspectivas del Petróleo Mexicano. Mexico City: Centro de
Estudios Internacionales, El Colegio de México, 1979.

Petras, James; Morley, Morris; Smith, Steven. The Nationalization of Venezuelan Oil. N.Y.: Praeger Publishers, 1977.

Purcell, John, F.H. and Purcell, Susan Kaufman. "Mexican
Business and Public Policy." In Authoritarianism and
Corporatism in Latin America. Edited by James M. Malloy.
Pittsburgh, PA.: University of Pittsburgh Press, 1977.

Purcell, Susan Kaufman. "The Future of the Mexican System."
In Authoritarianism in Mexico. Edited by José Luis Reyna
and Richard Weinert. Philadelphia: Institute for the Study
Human Issues, 1977.

_____. The Mexican Profit-Sharing Decision. Berkeley:
University of California Press, 1975.

Randall, Laura. "Mexican Development and Its Effect Upon United
States Trade." In Mexico and the United States. Edited by
Robert H. McBride. Englewood Cliffs, NJ.: Prentice-Hall,
1981.

Redclift, Michael R. Development Policymaking in Mexico: The
Sistema Alimentario Mexicano (SAM.) Research Report No. 24.
Center for U.S.-Mexican Studies, University of California,
San Diego, 1981.

Reubens, Edwin, P. "Surplus Labor, Emigration and Public
Policies: Requirements for Labor Absorption in Mexico."
In U.S.-Mexico Economic Relations. Edited by Barry
Poulson and T. Noel Osborn. Boulder, Colo.: Westview Press,
1979.

244

Reyna, José Luis. "Redefining the Authoritarian Regime." In
    Authoritarianism in Mexico. Edited by José Luis Reyna and
    Richard Weinert. Philadelphia: Institute for the Study of
    Human Issues, 1977.

Rippy, Merrill. Oil and the Mexican Revolution. Leiden,
    Netherlands: E.J. Brill, 1972.

Ross, John, B. The Economic System of Mexico. Stanford, CA.:
    Stanford University Press, 1971.

Rozo, Carlos, A.; Livas, Raul, A. "The Internationalization of
    U.S. Capital in Mexico." In U.S.-Mexico Economic Relations.
    Edited by Barry Poulson and T. Noel Osborn. Boulder, CO.:
    Westview Press, 1979.

Scott, Robert, E. Mexican Government in Transition. Urbana,
    Ill.: University of Illinois Press, 1964.

Serra, José. "Three Mistaken Theses Regarding the Connection
    between Industrialization and Authoritarian Regimes." In
    The New Authoritarianism in Latin America. Edited by David
    Collier. Princeton: Princeton University Press, 1979.

Smith, Peter. Labirynths of Power. Political Recruitment in
    Twentieth Century Mexico. Princeton: Princeton University
    Press, 1979.

_____. Mexico. The Quest for a U.S. Policy. N.Y.: Foreign
    Policy Association, 1980.

Stevens, Evelyn. "Mexico's PRI: The Institutionalization of
    Corporatism." In Authoritarianism and Corporatism in Latin
    America. Edited by James M. Malloy. Pittsburgh: University
    of Pittsburgh Press, 1977.

Stobaugh, Robert; Yergin, Daniel, eds. Energy Future. Report
    of the Energy Project at the Harvard Business School. N.Y.:
    Random House, 1979.

Tapia, Humberto, S. Mexico's Basic Government Plan: History
    Focus and Future. Tempe, AZ.: State University Center for
    Latin American Studies, 1976.

Tello, Carlos. La Política Económica en México, 1970-1976.
    Mexico City: Siglo XXI Editores, 1979.

Turner, Frederick, C. The Dynamic of Mexican Nationalism. Chapel
    Hill, NC.: University of North Carolina Press, 1968.

U.S.-Mexico Relations: Economic and Social Aspects. Edited by
    Clark W. Reynolds and Carlos Tello. Stanford, CA.:
    Stanford University Press, 1983.

Vernon, Raymond. The Dilemma of Mexican Development.
Cambridge, MA.: Harvard University Press, 1964.

_____. Sovereignty at Bay: The Multinational Spread of U.S.
Enterprise. NY: Basic Books, 1971.

Villarreal, René. "Import Substituting Industrialization."
In Authoritarianism in Mexico. Edited by José Luis Reyna
and Richard Weinert. Philadelphia: Institute for the
Study of Human Issues, 1977.

Volk, Steven. "The International Competitiveness of the U.S.
Economy: A Study of Steel and Electronics." In Capitalism
and the State in U.S.-Latin American Relations. Edited
by Richard Fagen. Stanford, CA.: Stanford University
Press, 1980.

Wallerstein, Immanuel. The Capitalist World-Economy. London:
Cambridge University Press, 1979.

Weinert, Richard. "The State and Foreign Capital." In Author-
itarianism in Mexico. Edited by José Luis Reyna and
Richard Weinert. Philadelphia: Institute for the Study of
Human Issues, 1977.

Wichtrich, Al, R. "Mexican-American Commercial Relations." In
Mexico and the United States. Edited by Robert H. McBride.
Englewood Cliffs, NJ.: Prentice-Hall, 1981.

Williams, Edward. The Rebirth of the Mexican Petroleum
Industry. Lexington, MA.: Lexington Books, 1979.

Articles

Aguilar Monteverde, M. "La fase actual del capitalismo en
México." Economía y Desarrollo (enero-febrero de 1978),
85-109.

Alejo, Francisco Javier. "Las empresas públicas y el Plan
Industrial." El Economista Mexicano v. XIII, n.6
(noviembre-diciembre de 1979), 26-33.

Asuad Sanén, Normand, E. "La intervención del estado en la
economía mexicana de 1917 a 1974 y sus antecedentes." El
Economista Mexicano v.XI, n.5 (marzo de 1977), 111-128.

Baerresen, Donald. "Unemployment and Mexico's Border Industrialization Program." Inter-American Economic Affairs
v.29, n.2 (Autumn, 1975), 79-90.

246

Bailey, John, J. "Presidency, Bureaucracy and Administrative Reform in Mexico: The Secretariat of Programming and Budget." _Inter-American Economic Affairs_, v.34, n.1 (Summer, 1980), 27-59.

Baird, Peter; McCaughan, Ed. "The Electrical Industry. What Price Power?" _NACLA North America and Empire Report_ v.XI, n.6 (September-October, 1977), 4-9.

Bamat, Thomas. "Relative State Autonomy and Capitalism in Brazil and Peru." _Insurgent Sociologist_ v.VII, n.2 (Spring, 1977), 74-84.

Barkin, David. "Mexico's Albatross: The U.S. Economy." _Latin American Perspectives. Mexico: The Limits of State Capitalism_ v.II, n.2 (Summer, 1975), 64-80.

Balassa, Bela. "Trade Policy in Mexico." _World Development_. v.II, n.9 (September, 1983), 795-812.

Bennett, Douglas; Sharpe, Kenneth. "Agenda Setting and Bargaining Power: The Mexican State versus Transnational Automobile Corporations." _World Politics_ v.XXXXII, n.1 (October, 1979), 57-89.

_____. "The State as Banker and Entrepreneur. The Last Resort Character of the Mexican State's Economic Intervention, 1917-1976." _Comparative Politics_ (January, 1980), 165-189.

_____. "Transnational Corporations and the Political Economy of Export Promotion: The Case of the Mexican Automobile Industry." _International Organization_ v.33, n.2 (Spring, 1979), 177-201.

Berberoglu, Berch. "State Capitalism and National Industrialization in Turkey," _Development and Change_ v.II, n.1 (January, 1980), 97-122.

Biersteker, Thomas, J. "The Illusion of State Power: Transnational Corporations and the Neutralization of Host Country Legislation." _Journal of Peace Research_ v.XVII, n.3 (1980), 207-221.

Bonilla Sánchez, Arturo. "Energéticos y la nueva riqueza petrolera." _Problemas del Desarrollo_,v.X. n.37 (febrero-abril de 1979), 11-25.

Bouton, Jorge. "Introducción a una problemática: La política económica del petróleo." _Problemas del Desarrollo_ v.X, n.37 (febrero-abril de 1979), 43-56.

Caporaso, James. "Dependence, Dependency, and Power in the Global System: A Structural and Behavioral Analysis."

International Organization v.34, n.1 (Winter, 1978), 13-43.

_____. "Dependency Theory: Continuities and Discontinuities in Development Studies." International Organization v.34, n.4 (Autumn, 1980), 605-628.

Cardoso, F.H. "Consumption of Dependency Theory in the United States." Latin American Research Review v.12, n.3 (1977), 7-23.

_____. "Current Theses on Latin American Development and Dependency: A Critique." New York University, Ibero-American Language and Area Center, Occasional Papers, n.20, May, 1976.

_____. "The Originality of a Copy: CEPAL and the Idea of Development." CEPAL Review (1977, Second Half), 7-40.

Chilcote, Ronald. "A Question of Dependency." Latin American Research Review v.XIII, n.2 (1978), 55-86.

Chumacero, Antonio. "Consideraciones sobre la política mexicana en materia de inversiones extranjeras." El Economista Mexicano v.XIII, n.6 (noviembre-diciembre de 1977), 34-51.

_____. "Los planes del sector público mexicano: metas y magnitudes macroeconómicas." El Trimestre Economica v.XLVII (3) n.187 (julio-septiembre de 1980), 579-609.

Cornelius, Wayne. "La migración ilegal mexicana a los Estados Unidos: conclusiones de investigaciones reciente, implicaciones políticas y prioridades de investigación." Foro Internacional v.XVIII, 3 (enero-marzo de 1978), 399-429.

Cueva, Augustin. "A Summary of 'Problems and Perspectives of Dependency Theory.'" Latin American Perspectives v.III, n.4 (Fall, 1976), 12-16.

Dillman, C. Daniel. "Assembly Industries in Mexico." Journal of Interamerican Studies and World Affairs. v.25, n.1 (February, 1983), 31-58.

Dore, Elizabeth; Weeks, John. "International Exchange and the Causes of Backwardness." Latin American Perspectives Issue 21, v.VI, n.2 (Spring, 1979), 62-87.

Dunn, C. Chase. "The Effects of International Economic Dependence on Development and Inequality: A Cross National Study." American Sociological Review v.40 n.6 (1975), 720-738.

Dupuy, Alex; Truchil, Barry. "Problems in the Theories of State

Capitalism." Theory and Society v.8, n.1 (July, 1979), 1-38.

Fagen, Richard. "A Funny Thing Happened on the Way to the Market: Thoughts on Extending Dependency Ideas." International Organization v.32, n.1 (Winter, 1978), 287-300.

_____. "An Inescapable Relationship." Wilson Quarterly v.III, n.3 (Summer, 1979), 142-150.

_____. "The Realities of U.S.-Mexican Relations." Foreign Affairs v.55, n.4 (July, 1977), 685-700.

_____. "Mexican Petroleum and U.S. National Security." International Security v.4, n.1 (Summer, 1979), 39-53.

_____. "Studying Latin American Politics." Latin American Research Review v.XII, n.2 (1977), 3-26.

Fitzgerald, E.V.K. "A New Direction in Economic Policy?" Bank of London and South American Review v.12, n.10/78 (October, 1978), 528-538.

_____. "Some Aspects of the Political Economy of the Latin American State." Development and Change v.7, n.2 (April, 1976), 119-133.

_____. "The State and Capital Accumulation in Mexico." Journal of Latin American Studies v.10, n.2 (1978), 263-282.

Flanigan, James. "Why Won't the Mexicans Sell US More Oil?" Forbes, (October 29, 1979), 41-52.

Flores, Edmundo. "Mexico's Program for Science and Technology, 1978-1982." Science v.204 (22 June 1979), 1279-1282.

Fox, David. "Mexico. The Development of the Oil Industry." Bank of London and South America Review v.11, n.10/77 (October, 1977), 520-532.

"Fragmento del Discurso Pronunciado por el Licenciado Gustavo Romero Kolbeck, Director-General del Banco de México, S.A." Boletín de Indicadores Económicos Internacionales v.IV, n.1 (enero-marzo de 1978), 30-35.

Franco, Alvaro. "Gigantescas reservas garantizan brillante futuro petrolero a México." Petróleo Internacional. (Junio de 1977),25-46.

García-Torres, Arturo; Serdán Alvarez, Manuel. "Apoyo crediticio del gobierno federal a la industria nacional." El Economista Mexicano v.XIII, n.5 (septiembre-octubre de 1979) 87-110.

Gereffi, Gary and Evans, Peter. "Transnational Corporations, Dependent Development and State Policy in the Semiperiphery: A Comparison of Brazil and Mexico," Latin American Research Review, v.XVI, n.3 (1981), 31-64.

Goldfrank, Walter. "World System, State Structure, and the Onset of the Mexican Revolution." Politics and Society v.5, n.4 (1975), 417-439.

González Casanova, Pablo. "Sistema y clase en los estudios de América Latina." Revista Mexicana de Sociología v.XL, n.3 (1978), 867-879.

Gordon, T.S. Stewart. "Mexico's Oil. Myth, Fact and Future." World Oil. (February 1, 1979), 35-41.

Grayson, George. "Mexico's Opportunity: The Oil Boom." Foreign Policy n.29 (Winter, 1977-78), 65-89.

Grindle, Merilee, S. "Policy Change in an Authoritarian Regime." Journal of Interamerican Studies and World Affairs v.19, n.4 (November, 1977), 523-555.

Guzmán Ferrer, Martin Luis. "Alimentación y política económica." El Economista Mexicano v.XII, n.5 (septiembre-octubre de 1978), 5-10.

Hamilton, Nora. "The Limits of State Autonomy." Latin American Perspectives. Mexico: The Limits of State Capitalism v.II, n.2 (Summer, 1975), 81-108.

Harding, Timothy, F. "Dependency, Nationalism and the State in Latin America." Latin American Perspectives, Issue 11, v.III, n.4 (Fall, 1976), 3-11.

"Harvest of Anger." NACLA Latin America and Empire Report v.X, n.6 (July-August, 1976.)

Hayes, Earl, T. "Energy Resources Available to the United States, 1985-2000." Science v.203, n.4377 (19 January 1979), 233-239.

Ibarra Munoz, David. "Reflexiones sobre la empresa pública en México." Foro Internacional v.17, n.2 (1976), 141-151.

International Monetary Fund, "World Oil Situation," World Economic Outlook, May, 1980, 67-80.

Jackson, Steven. "Capitalist Penetration: Concept and Measurement." Journal of Peace Research v.XVI, n.1 (1979), 41-55.

James, Dilmus; Evans, John. "Conditions of Employment and Income Distribution in Mexico as Incentives for Mexican

Migration to the United States: Prospects to the End of the Century." *International Migration Review* v.13, n.1 (1979), 4-24.

Jameson, Kenneth. "An Intermediate Regime in Historical Context: The Case of Guyana." *Development and Change* v.11, n.1 (January, 1980), 77-95.

Kalecki, Michal; Kula, M. "Bolivia - An 'Intermediate Regime' in Latin America." *Economía y Administración* 16 (1970), 75-78.

Kaplan, Marcos. "Aspectos políticos de la planificación en América Latina." *Problemas del Desarrollo* n.6 (enero-marzo, 1971), 73-92.

_____. "El leviathan criollo: Estatismo y sociedad en la América Latina contemporanea." *Revista Mexicana de Sociología* v.XL, n.3 (1978), 793-829.

López G., Julio. "The Mexican Economy: Present Situation, Perspectives and Alternatives." *World Development* v.11, n.5 (May, 1983), 455-465.

Martínez Escamilla, Ramón. "México, explotación petrolera e ideología dominante." *Problemas del Desarrollo* v.X, n.37 (febrero-abril, 1979), 149-168.

Martínez Hernández, Ifigenia; López Tijerina, Gilardo. "El sector público federal en México, su importancia y control." *El Economista Mexicano* v.XIII, n.6 (noviembre-diciembre de 1979), 46-65.

Metz, William. "Mexico: The Premier Oil Discovery in the Western Hemisphere." *Science* v.202 (22 December, 1978), 1261-1265.

Meyer, Lorenzo. "El auge petrolero." *Foro Internacional* v.XVIII, n.4 (abril-junio de 1978), 581-587.

Miliband, Ralph. "The Capitalist State: Reply to Nicos Poulantzas." *New Left Review* 59 (January-February, 1970), 53-60.

_____. "Poulantzas and the Capitalist State." *New Left Review* 82 (November-December, 1973), 83-92.

Moran, Theodore. "Multinational Corporations and Dependency: a Dialogue for Dependentistas and Non-Dependentistas." *International Organization* v.32, n.1 (Winter, 1978), 79-100.

Mueller, Ronald. "Poverty Is the Product." *Foreign Policy* 13 (Winter, 1973-74), 71-103.

Munck, Ronaldo. "State Capital and Crisis in Brazil: 1929-1979." *Insurgent Sociologist* v.IX, n.4 (Spring, 1980), 39-58.

Niblo, Stephen, P. "Progress and the Standard of Living in Contemporary Mexico." *Latin American Perspectives*. *Mexico: The Limits of State Capitalism* v.II, n.2 (Summer, 1975), 109-124.

O'Donnell, Guillermo. "Apuntes para una teoría del estado." *Revista Mexicana de Sociología* v.XL, n.4 (1978), 3-38.

Ojeda, Mario. "México ante los estados unidos en la coyunctura actual." *Foro Internacional* v.XVIII, n.1 (julio-septiembre de 1977), 32-53.

Ortiz Wadgymar, Arturo. "Impacto del petróleo en el comercio exterior de México." *Problemas del Desarollo* v.X, n.37 (febrero-abril de 1979), 109-122.

Oszlak, Oscar. "Notas criticas para una teoría de la burocracia estatal." *Revista Mexicana de Sociología* v.XL, n.3 (1978), 881-926.

Pellicer de Brody, Olga. "La crisis mexicana: hacia una nueva dependencia." *Cuadernos Políticos* v.14 (octubre-diciembre de 1977), 45-55.

Pérez-Sáinz, Juan Pablo. "Towards a Conceptualization of State Capitalism in the Periphery." *Insurgent Sociologist* v.IX, n.4 (Spring, 1980), 59-67.

Pérez-Sáinz, Juan Pablo; Zarembka, Paul. "Accumulation and the State in Venezuelan Industrialization." *Latin American Perspectives* Issue 22, v.VI, n.3 (Summer, 1979), 5-27.

Petras, James. "Class and Politics in the Periphery and the Transition to Socialism." *Review of Radical Political Economy* (Summer, 1976), 20-35.

_____. "State Capitalism and the Third World." *Journal of Contemporary Asia* v.6, n.4 (1976), 432-443.

Petras, James; Morley, Morris. "Petrodollars and the State: the Failure of State Capitalist Development in Venezuela." *Third World Quarterly* v.5, n.1 (January, 1983), 7-27.

"El petróleo mexicano reserva de EU ante la OPEP." *Proceso* n.66,(6 de diciembre de 1978),10-11.

"Política energética nacional." *Energéticos* ano 1, n.1 (agosto de 1977), 16-19.

Portes, Alejandro. "Towards a Structural Analysis of Illegal (Undocumented) Immigration." International Migration Review v.13, n.1 (1979), 469-484.

Prebisch, Raul. "A Historical Turning Point for the Latin American Periphery." CEPAL Review No.18 (December, 1982), 7-24.

Purcell, Susan Kaufman. "Business Government Relations in Mexico. The Case of the Sugar Industry." Comparative Politics v.13, n.2 (January, 1981), 211-230.

_____. "Decision-making in an Authoritarian Regime: Theoretical Implications from a Mexican Case Study." World Politics 26 (October, 1973), 28-54.

Purcell, Susan Kaufman; Purcell, John F.H. "State and Society in Mexico: Must a Stable Polity be Institutionalized?" World Politics v.XXXII, n.2 (January, 1980), 194-227.

"Registro de la administración pública paraestatal." El Mercado de Valores ano XXXVIII, n.41 (9 de octubre de 1978), 833-844.

Reyna, José Luis. "El movimiento obrero en una situación de crisis: México 1976-78." Foro Internacional 75 (enero-marzo de 1979), 390-401.

Riding, Alan. "The Mixed Blessings of Mexico's Oil." New York Times Magazine, (January 11, 1981).

Rodriguez Castaneda, Rafael. "Aplica el gobierno las directrices del Banco Mundial." Proceso n.29 (17 de julio de 1978), 6-9.

Saxe-Fernández, John. "Importancia estratégica del petróleo mexicano." Problemas del Desarrollo,v.X, n.37 (febrero-abril de 1979), 77-105.

Selowsky, Marcelo. "Income Distribution, Basic Needs and Trade-Offs with Growth: The Case of Semi-Industrialized Latin American Countries." World Development v.9 (1981), 631-648.

Skouras, Thanos. "The 'Intermediate Regime' and Industrialization Prospects." Development and Change v.9, n.4 (October, 1978), 631-648.

Smith, Tony. "The Underdevelopment of Development Literature." World Politics v.XXXI, n.2 (January, 1979), 247-288.

Story, Dale. "Industrial Elites in Mexico." Journal of Interamerican Studies and World Affairs v.25, n.3 (August, 1983), 351-376.

Turok, Ben. "Zambia's System of State Capitalism." Development and Change v.II, n.3 (July, 1980), 455-477.

Turrent Díaz, Eduardo. "Petróleo y economía. Costos y beneficios a corto plazo." Foro Internacional v.XVIII, n.4 (1979), 623-654.

van Ginneken, Wouter. "Socioeconomic Groups and Income Distribution in Mexico." International Labor Review v.118, n.3 (May-June, 1979), 331-342.

Villarreal, René. "El petróleo como instrumento de desarrollo y de negociación internacional. México en los ochentas." El Trimestre Economico v.XLVIII (1) n.189 (enero-marzo de 1981), 3-44.

Whitehead, Laurence. "Mexico from Bust to Boom: A Political Evaluation of the 1976-1979 Stabilization Programme." World Development v.8, n.11 (November, 1980), 843-864.

Williams, Edward, J. "Oil in Mexican-U.S. Relations: Analysis and Bargaining Scenario." Orbis (Spring, 1978), 201-217.

Yunez Naude, Antonio. "Politica petrolera y perspectivas de beneficios de la economía mexicana. Un ensayo explorativo." Forò Internacional v.XVIII, n.4 (1979), 597-622.

Government Documents

"La actividad petrolera de México en 1980." Comercio Exterior v.31, n.4 (abril de 1978), 446-454.

"La actividad de Pemex en 1982." Comercio Exterior v.33, n.4 (abril de 1983), 292-298.

Albertos Camara, Rudy Omar. "El ingreso de Mexico al GATT." Comercio Exterior v.30, n.9 (marzo de 1979), 275-279.

"Aspectos financieros del sector presupuestario en 1979." Comercio Exterior v.30, n.9 (septiembre de 1980), 937-944.

Banco de México. "El comportamiento de la economía mexicana durante 1980." Comercio Exterior v.31, n.3 (marzo de 1981), 323-332.

Banco de México. "La actividad económica en 1982." Comercio Exterior v.33, n.5 (mayo de 1983), 460-474.

Basualdo, Eduardo. "Tendencia de la transnacionalización en América Latina durante el decenio de los setenta." Comercio

Exterior v.32, n.7 (julio de 1982), 754-263.

Beltrán del Río, Abel. "El sindrome del petróleo mexicano." Comercio Exterior v.30, n.6 (junio de 1980), 556-569.

Beteta, Mario Ramón. "La necesidad de estabilizar el mercado petróleo." Comercio Exterior v.33, n.11 (noviembre de 1983), 1030-1035.

"Bienes de capital para la industria petrolera." Comercio Exterior v.29, n.8 (agosto de 1979), 851-856.

Bueno, Gerardo, M. "Hacia una evaluación de la política económica de México." Comercio Exterior v.33, n.4 (abril de 1983), 283-291.

CANACINTRA. "La industrial de transformación y el GATT." Comercio Exterior v.30, n.2 (febrero de 1980), 174-185.

"Características del crédito otorgado a México por el FMI." Comercio Exterior v.30, n.2 (febrero de 1980), 352-356.

Cardoso, F.H. "El desarollo en el banquillo." Comercio Exterior v.30, n.8 (agosto de 1980), 846-860.

Cordera Campos, Rolando. "Estado y economía, Apuntes para un marco de referencia." Comercio Exterior v.29, n.4 (abril de 1979), 411-418.

"Cronología de la exportación de gas natural." Comercio Exterior v.30, n.5 (mayo de 1980), 433-442.

de la Madrid H., Miguel. "Primer Informe de Gobierno." Comercio Exterior v.33, n.9 (Septiembre de 1983), 783-799.

_____. "La regulación de la empresa pública en Mexico." Comercio Exterior v.30, n.3 (marzo de 1980), 215-219.

de Mateo, Fernando. "Contribución a la polémica sobre el GATT." Comercio Exterior v.30, n.2 (febrero de 1980), 111-117.

de Villarreal, Rocío; Villarreal, René. "El comercio exterior y la industalización de México a la luz del nuevo GATT." Comercio Exterior v.30, n.2 (febrero de 1980), 142-155.

Díaz Serrano, Jorge. "Economic and Social Conditions in Mexico." Comercio Exterior (English edition) v.23, n.12 (diciembre de 1977), 475-485.

_____. "Informe de Petróleos Mexicanos, 1979." Comercio Exterior v.30, n.4 (abril de 1980), 386-394.

"Documento: La actividad de Pemex en 1978." Comercio Exterior v.29, n.5 (mayo de 1979), 554-561.

"Documento: La evolución económica de México en 1978." CEPAL. Comercio Exterior v.29, n.7 (julio de 1979), 786-798.

"Documento: México y el FMI: la carta de Intención." SHCP, Banco de México. Comercio Exterior v.32, n.11 (noviembre de 1982), 1247-1251.

"Documento: La nacionalización de la banca privada. Reglas para fijar la indemnización." SHCP. Comercio Exterior v.33, n.7 (julio de 1983), 654-655.

"Documento: Política fiscal y financiera para 1982." SHCP y SPP. Comercio Exterior v.32, n.2 (febrero de 1982), 186-197.

Green, Rosario. "Mexico: crisis financiera y deuda externa." Comercio Exterior v.33, n.2 (febrero de 1983), 99-107.

Gutiérrez R., Roberto. "La balanza petrolera de México, 1970-1982." Comercio Exterior v.29, n.8 (agosto de 1979), 839-850.

Hernández Cervantes, Hector. "El futuro del comercio entre México y Estados Unidos." Comercio Exterior v.30, n.10 (octubre de 1980), 1128-1130.

Hernández Laos, Enrique; Córdova Chávez, Jorge. "Estructura de la distribución del ingreso en México." Comercio Exterior v.29, n.5 (mayo de 1979), 505-520.

Islas, Hector. "La industria automovilística: un repaso general." Comercio Exterior v.33, n.3 (marzo de 1983), 223-230.

_____. "Una industria en busca de soluciones: la automovilística." Comercio Exterior v.33, n.11 (noviembre de 1983), 991-999.

López Portillo, José. "Documento: Cuarto informe presidencial." Comercio Exterior v.30, n.9 (septiembre de 1980), 1007-1026.

"Medición del comercio intraindustrial entre México y Estados Unidos." Comercio Exterior v.28, n.10 (octubre de 1978), 1243-1262.

Pellicer de Brody, Olga. "Consideraciones acerca de la política comercial de Estados unidos hacia México." Comercio Exterior v.30, n.10 (octubre de 1980), 1114-1120.

Penaloza, Tomas. "La Ley de Acuerdos Comerciales de 1979 de Estados Unidos." Comercio Exterior v.30, n.2 (febrero de 1980), 123-132.

Poder Ejecutivo Federal. Plan Nacional de Desarrollo 1983-1988. Suplemento de Comercio Exterior v.33, n.6 (junio de 1983).

Ramírez de la O., Rogelio. "Industrialización y sustitución de importaciones en Mexico." Comercio Exterior v.30, n.1 (enero de 1980), 31-37.

"Salarios mínimos 1980." Comercio Exterior v.30, n.1 (enero de 1980), 21-24.

Secretaria de Hacienda y Crédito Público (SHCP) and Secretaría de Programación y Presupuesto (SPP). "Documento: La política económica para 1980." Comercio Exterior v.30, n.1 (enero de 1980), 59-75.

Secretaría de Patrimonio Nacional y Fomento Industrial (SEPAFIN). "Documento: Los objetivos y prioridades del programa de energía." Comercio Exterior v.30, n.11 (noviembre de 1980), 1262-1266.

Secretaria de Programación y Presupuesto (SPP). "Documento: Plan Global de Desarrollo, 1980-1982." Comercio Exterior v.30, n.4 (abril de 1980), 367-379.

Secretaría de Programación y Presupuesto (SPP). Plan Global de Desarrollo 1980-1982. Vol.I and Vol.II.

Trejo Reyes, Saúl. "Distribución del ingreso, empleo y precios relativos." Comercio Exterior v.32, n.10 (octubre de 1982), 1103-1111.

United Nations. Economic Commission for Latin America. Statistical Yearbook for Latin America, 1978.

Urias, Homer. "La balanzade pagos en 1982." Comercio Exterior v.33, n.5 (mayo de 1983), 399-405.

U.S. Central Intelligence Agency. National Basic Intelligence Factbook. January, 1980.

U.S. Central Intelligence Agency. National Foreign Assessment Center. International Energy Statistical Review, 1981.

U.S. Congress. House. Committee on Foreign Affairs. North American Energy Cooperation, Parts I and II. Hearings before the Subcommittee on Inter-American Affairs and on International Organizations. 96th Cong., 1st sess., 1979.

U.S. Congress. House. Committee on Foreign Affairs. Update: United States-Canadian/Mexican Relations. Hearings before the Subcommittee on Inter-American Affairs. 96th Cong., 2nd sess., 1980.

U.S. Congress. House. Committee on International Relations. Undocumented Workers: Implications for U.S. Policy in the Western Hemisphere. Hearings before the Subcommittee on Inter-American Affairs. 95th Cong., 2nd sess., 1978.

U.S. Congress. House. Committee on Science and Technology. Subcommittee on Investigations and Oversight. Mexican Oil and Technology Transfer. H. Report. 96th Cong., 1st sess., 1979.

U.S. Congress. House. Committee on Science and Technology. Sucommittee on Investigations and Oversight and Subcommittee on Science, Research and Technology. U.S./Mexico Relations and Potentials Regarding Energy Immigration and Technology Transfer. H. Report. 96th Cong., 1st sess., 1979.

U.S. Congress. House. Select Committee on Population. Legal and Illegal Immigration to the U.S. H. Report. 95th Cong., 2nd sess., December, 1978.

U.S. Congress. Joint Economic Committee. The 1979 Economic Report of the President, Part I. 96th Cong., 1st sess., 1979.

U.S. Congress. Joint Economic Committee. Recent Developments in Mexico and their Economic Implications for the U.S. Hearings before the Subcommittee on Inter-American Economic Relationships, 95th Cong., 1st sess., 1977.

U.S. Congress. Joint Economic Committee. The U.S. Role in a Changing World Political Economy: Major Issues for the 96th Congress. "United States-Mexican Relations." By Rosemary Jackson. 96th Cong., 1st sess., 1979.

U.S. Congress. Senate. Committee on Energy and Natural Resources. Geopolitics of Oil. Hearings. "Mexico's Petroleum and U.S. Policy: Implications for the 1980s." Rand Corporation Report by David Ronfeldt, Richard Nehring and A. Gandara. 96th Cong., 2nd sess., 1980.

U.S. Congress. Senate. Committee on Energy and Natural Resources. Mexico. The Promise and Problems of Petroleum. S. Report. 96th Cong., 1st sess., 1979.

U.S. Congress. Senate. Committee on Energy and Natural Resources. The Western Hemisphere Energy System. S. Report. 96th Cong., 1st sess., 1979.

U.S. Congress. Senate. Finance Committee. Subcommittee on International Trade. North American Economic Interdependence. Part I. S. Report. 96th Cong., 1st sess., 1979.

U.S. Congress. Senate. Committee on Foreign Relations. Market Power and Profitability of Multinational Corporations in Brazil and Mexico. A Report to the Subcommittee on Foreign Economic Policy by John M. Connor and Willard F. Mueller. 95th Cong., 2nd sess., 1977.

U.S. Congress. Senate. Committee on Foreign Relations. Multinational Corporations in Brazil and Mexico: Structural Sources of Economic and Non-Economic Power. Report to the Subcommittee on Multinational Corporations by Richard S. Newfarmer and Willard F. Mueller. 94th Cong., 1st sess., August, 1975.

U.S. Congress. Senate. Committee on Foreign Relations and Joint Economic Committee. Mexico's Oil and Gas Policy: An Analysis. Congressional Research Service Report. 95th Cong., 2nd sess., 1979.

U.S. Congress. Senate. Immigration and Nationality Efficiency Act of 1979. S. 1763. Hearings. 96th Cong., 1st sess., 1979.

U.S. Department of Commerce. Overseas Business Reports. United States Foreign Trade Annual 1975-1981. Washington, DC., 1983.

U.S. Department of Labor. Mexico. Profile of Labor Conditions. 1979.

U.S. Government Accounting Office. Oil and Natural Gas from Alska, Canada, and Mexico - Only Limited Help for U.S. September 11, 1980.

U.S. Government Accounting Office. Prospects for a Stronger United States-Mexico Energy Relationship. 1980.

U.S. International Communications Agency. "U.S. Investment in Mexico: Attitudes of Key Mexican Elite Groups." Research Report r-29-78. October 18, 1978.

Warman, Arturo. "Desarrollo capitalista o campesino en el campo mexicano." Comercio Exterior v.29, n.4 (abril de 1978), 399-403.

Wionzek, Miguel S. "Algunas reflexiones sobre la futura política de México." Comercio Exterior v.32, n.11 (noviembre de 1982), p.1229-1237.

Unpublished Manuscripts, Conference Papers

Bagley, Bruce. "Mexico: The Promise of Oil." In U.S.-Latin

American Relations in the 1980s. Edited by Riordan Roett and Margaret Daley Hayes. Boulder, Colo.: Westview Press, pre-publication manuscript.

Bennett, Douglas; Blachman, Morris; Sharpe, Kenneth. "National and Integrational Constraints on the Exercise of Power by the State: The Echeverría Sexenio in Mexico." Paper presented at the Latin American Studies Association Annual Meeting, Pittsburgh, PA., April, 1979.

Bennett, Douglas; Sharpe, Kenneth. "Controlling the Multi-nationals: The Ill Logic of Mexicanization." February, 1977. Prepared for publication in Global Dominance and Dependence: Readings in Theory and Research. Edited by Lawrence V. Gould, Jr. and Harry Torg. Brunswick, Ohio: King's Court Communication, forthcoming.

de Villarreal, Rocío; Villarreal, René. "Public Enterprises in Mexican Development Under the Oil Perspective in the 1980s." Paper presented at the Second BAPEG Conference "Public Enterprise in Mixed Economy LDCs." Austin, TX: University of Texas.

Dore, Elizabeth. "The State and Dependency Analysis: A Critique." Paper presented at the 8th National Meeting of the Latin American Studies Association, Pittsburgh, PA., April 5-7, 1979.

_____. "The State and Class Formation in Post-Revolutionary Mexico." Paper prepared for presentation at the Join National Meetings of the Latin American Studies Association and the African Studies Association, November 2-5, 1977, Houston, Texas.

Oveisi, Hadad Fardovie. Entrepreneurial Activities of the Public Sector in the Economic Development Process. Un-published Ph.D. dissertation. University of Texas at Austin, 1979.

Segal, Aaron; Koehler, Wallace C., Jr. "Canada-Mexico-USA. Prospects for Energy Cooperation." Paper prepared for pre-sentation for the Southern Economic Association Meeting, Atlanta, Georgia, November 7, 1979.

Williams, Edward, J.; Black, Jan, K.; Meyer, Michael; Needler, Martin, C. et al. The Latin American Oil Exporters and the United States. Unpublished manuscript.

Williams, Edward, J. "Mexican Hydrocarbons Export Policy: Ambition and Reality." Paper presented at the Annual Meeting of the Latin American Studies Association, Pittsburgh, PA., April, 1979.

Other Sources Consulted

American Machinist
Bank of London and South America Review
The Banker
Buffalo Evening News
Business Latin America
Business Week
CECON Trade News
Commerce America
Comercio Exterior
Comercio y Desarrollo
Correo Economico
Economist
El Sol
Economist Intelligence Unit, Quarterly Economic Review of Mexico
    and Annual Supplement.
Energético
Euromoney
Examen de la Situación Económica
Excelsior
Financial Times
Financial World
Foreign Economic Trends
Fortune
Handelsblatt
Hispano
Indicadores Económicos
Industry Week
International Finance (Chase Manhattan Bank)
Journal of Commerce
Latin America Economic Report
Latin America Weekly Report
Los Angeles Times
Mexican Newsletter (Office of the Mexican Presidency)
Miami Herald
Morgan Guaranty. World Financial Markets.
Nation's Business
New Republic
New York Times
Overseas Business Reports
Petróleo Internacional
Petroleum Economist
Pipeline Industry
Platt's Oilgram News
Proceso
Revista de Instituto de Petróleo
Vision
Wall Street Journal
Washington Post
Washington Report
Weekly Compilation of Presidential Documents

Voytek Zubek

Soviet Industrial Theory

American University Studies X (Political Science), vol. 3
319 pages   paperback $ 30.00

The study identifies the principal theoretical features of the various periods in the development of Soviet industrial theory and then proceeds to explore the reasons for the dramatic changes and shifts seen in the development of the theory. Following this close examination and analysis of the dynamics determining the development of Soviet industrial theory, the study then addresses the probable future development of the theory.

Peter Kien-hong Yu

A Strategic Model of Chinese Checkers

Power and Exchange in Beijing's Interactions with Washington and Moscow

American University Studies X (Political Science), vol. 4
233 pages   hardcover $ 28.50

This is a study of the attempt by the People's Republic of China to remove perceived nuclear threat and to maximize its foreign policy interests, the issue of Taiwan in particular. The study is analogized from the playing of the board-game of Chinese Checkers, because the dynamics of the Chinese–US–Soviet interactions at both the strategic and tactical levels can be described, explicated, and interpreted from its rules, principles, and structures (including the game-board itself and overall power capabilities of each player). Thus, for example, power, exchange, and the factor of distance are involved, when and where appropriate.

PETER LANG PUBLISHING, INC.
34 East 39th Street

USA-New York, NY 10016

Issam Suleiman Mousa

The Arab Image in the US Press

American University Studies XV (Communications), vol. 1
203 pages   paperback $ 19.20

Contemporary research on the Arab image in the US press has invariably shown Arabs linked to Israel and Middle East conflict. These studies, thus, have ignored the development of the Arab image prior to 1948.

The present work content-analyzed Arab image in a major US newspaper since the beginning of modern Arab history, starting with the downfall of the Ottoman control. Beginning in 1917, every third year was represented by the *New York Times* coverage during the even numbered days of March, until 1948, when Israel was created.

The analysis examined conflict and cooperation as underlying themes of the Arab image (across nine major categories). The findings allowed to present a comprehensive view for the development of the Arab image in the American mind from a pre-1916 romantic image to a more realistic one at present.

PETER LANG PUBLISHING, INC.
34 East 39th Street

USA-New York, NY 10016